T0368902

THE LUSITANIAN WAR

Roman conquest of Lusitania 155 BCE - 139 BCE

Luis M. Silva

authorHOUSE®

AuthorHouse™
1663 Liberty Drive
Bloomington, IN 47403
www.authorhouse.com
Phone: 1 (800) 839-8640

Published by AuthorHouse 08/12/2019

ISBN: 978-1-5049-7793-7 (sc)
ISBN: 978-1-5049-7792-0 (hc)
ISBN: 978-1-5049-7791-3 (e)

Library of Congress Control Number: 2016901956

Print information available on the last page.

This book is printed on acid-free paper.

CONTENTS

Introduction 1

Chapter 1 HISPANIA AT THE END OF THE SECOND PUNIC WAR 5
Chapter 2 FIRST CELTIBERIAN WAR 65
Chapter 3 THE LUSITANIANS 96
Chapter 4 LUSITANIAN WARFARE & WEAPONS 210
Chapter 5 VIRIATHUS THE MAN 261
Chapter 6 THE LUSITANIAN WAR WITH ROME BEGINS ... 292
Chapter 7 THE VIRIATHAN WAR (The Second Lusitanian War) 321
Chapter 8 THE END OF THE VIRIATHAN WAR 361
Chapter 9 CAMPAIGNS OF LUSITANIAN PACIFICATION ... 380
Chapter 10 THE ROMANIZATION OF LUSITANIA 407
Chapter 11 VIRIATHUS THE KING AND THE LEGEND 454

About the Author 493

THE LUSITANIAN WAR (155 TO 139 BC) VIRIATHUS THE IBERIAN AGIANST ROME

INTRODUCTION

The Roman conquest of the Iberian Peninsula lasted for 200 years (218 BC – 19 BC) beginning when the Scipio brothers landing at Ampurias, on the Catalonian coast in the southeast of Spain at the start of the Second Punic War and ending with the final Roman military campaign against the Cantabrians in northern Spain.

During this long period of conquest, classical historians recorded the names, places and actions associated with the indigenous resistance to Roman control. Iberian commanders of autochthonous groups fighting against Rome are mentioned, and the most prominent among these were the Celtiberians and Lusitanians. The story begins with an early Lusitanian leader, Punicus, who incited another native group, the Vettones, to joined him to fight against Rome in 155 BCE and together they drove the conflict deep into Baetica where they attacked the Blastofenicios, Roman subjects that occupied the Spanish Mediterranean coast. Upon Punicus's death in battle, he was succeeded by another Lusitanian, Cesaro, who went on to incite the Celtiberians to continue the war against the Romans. The next major Lusitanian warrior mentioned in the classical text was Cauceno. Elected as tribal leader, his troops traveled the whole region south of the Tagus River, attacking the Conii who were allies of Rome and their city of Conistorgis.

Other Iberian warrior chiefs continued to be mentioned in Roman historiography, such as Curius, Apuleius and Connoba, Retogenes, Megaravico, Tautalus and Corocota, but there was no other warrior chief and military commander more celebrated and more dangerous to the Romans, during the entire period of Rome's conquest of Hispania than a Lusitanian by the name of Viriathus. Viriathus relied on guerrilla tactic, possessing an enormous mobility that bewildered the Romans. His actions and military victories embraced a very wide area of the peninsula's territory that his successes incited other tribes to either join his cause or start their own rebellious actions against Rome. Viriathus became a great leader and tactician because he knew his people and the Romans very well. With this knowledge, he was able to transform a disordered group of individual warriors into a disciplined army. Although guerilla warfare in the ancient world is occasionally mentioned in texts about Alexander the Great's campaigns and during the Jugurthine War (112-150 BCE), it was the Lusitanian War driven by Viriathus that is said to have made such an impact that it was passed down throughout the centuries as the model on which to conduct a guerrilla campaign.

Justinus, summarizing the account of the Lusitanian War by Gnaeus Trogus Pompeius, the Gallic historian during Augustus's reign, declared that the Lusitanians did not have a better general than Viriathus. All of the Greco-Roman authors that wrote about the Lusitanian War, they agree that Viriathus was of a humble origin, shepherd and bandit, and that in time he became a great leader of men; he was also unanimously praised for his virtue and austerity.

Iberian historian, the late professor Adolf Schulten, as well as other twentieth-century historians and scholars rank Viriathus among the great barbarian leaders similar to Armínius, Vercingetorix, Boudica, Tacfarinas and Decebalus. But the difference between these barbarian kings and others was that Viriathus was the first barbarian on record to united and integrate warriors from different tribes to fight against Rome for their liberty.

As for the death of Viriathus, due to betrayal, it marked the end of the organized resistance movement against Rome's power in Hispania, with the result that it ended up with Rome imposing its imperialistic policies all across the Iberian Peninsula.

Maurico Pastor Muñoz, professor of history at the University of Granada, Spain, has written two important books on Viriathus that document both the historical facts as they are known, as well as those stories about Viriathus that may be fictitious or mythical. As it happens with many great persons of the past, many aspects of Viriathus's life were transformed into legend. Writing about the life and exploits of a person like Viriathus, whose life was half history and half legend, is not an easy task to put together for it requires meticulous analysis of the classical sources and of the modern interpretations in order to fully understand who this man was and what he represented in the historical record. In this work I will attempt to separate the historical facts from legend and fiction but at times it may not be possible.

Portugal and Spain did not exist in Viriathus's time; the land that encompasses much of those modern countries was known as Lusitania. Therefore, he was neither Portuguese nor Spaniard, but Lusitanian. Along the lines of his personality, the classical authors present him as an intelligent strong leader who rose up to defend a particular political and military unification (an entity we might call a state today) against Rome and perhaps even create the idea of a 'monarchy' in Lusitania.

Roman historiography presents Viriathus as having a strong personality similar to other military commander of the time, such as Hannibal, Sertorius, Julius Ceasar and many others. Thanks to this personality, during the ten years that his war lasted he led the Lusitanians not just as a military commander, but as their 'king'; even the Roman Senate recognized him as such in the year 140 BCE.

Viriathus was part of a society that was fundamentally made up of warriors, of which we know very little apart from small amount of information from ancient Roman texts and archaeological data. Although we know something about the Lusitanian family system, the ownership of land, the position of women had within this society, and the tribe's class structure, it is hard to distinguish whether the classes intertwined with one another or not. We also know that these people had iron weapons, gold and jewelry that were works of art. The data that exists about the Lusitanians though small gives up a glimpse into the social political and economic life of the Lusitanians.

The Lusitanians were an aristocratic society. This aristocratic society dedicated itself mainly to war. Like many other ancient Celtic societies, war was the road for social promotion, but a hard and risky road, in which only few succeeded. And this was, precisely, the case of Viriathus.

Because of his personality and fighting prowess, Viriathus became the leader of just not his Lusitanian clan, but of all Lusitanians that lived between the Douro and Tagus Rivers. The consolidation of his power was recognized by the Roman Senate who named him *amicus poplui romani.* With this declaration, Rome put Viriathus at the same level as other detached allied kings. With this recognition, Lusitanian society transformed, evolved and integrated itself into becoming Roman. It also began to form into a political entity that changed from a motely group of clans into the beginning of a monarchy, headed by Viriathus, something that was unheard of within Iberian-Celtic societies. Though there were others before and after him that were nominated as leaders of the Lusitanians, there was no other that gained the fame he had done for his actions.

In conclusion for everything that Viriathus did within the realm of Iberian Peninsula's history, it is important to remember that his life and times played and still plays an important part of Portugal's and even Spain's early history and society. But if nothing is learned from this book about this individual, one should at least remember Viriathus, the Lusitanian, who lead the first tentative organized resistance to oppose Rome's imperialistic policies at the point of Rome's early endeavors to grow beyond the borders of Italy.

CHAPTER I

HISPANIA AT THE END OF THE SECOND PUNIC WAR

End of the Punic War in Hispania

With the Carthaginian defeat at the battle of Illipa and the naval defeat of Hannibal's youngest brother, Mago Barca, off the southern coast of Spain near Gades, (modern day Cadiz) in 206 BC, the Romans had successfully driven out the Carthaginians from Hispania.[1] With Hispania now under their control, the Romans began to consolidate and stabilize their newly acquired territory. Rome had inherited this region' s wealth, as well as its problems, most notably rebellious Iberian tribes.

Prior to the Second Punic War in 218 BC, Rome had no interest in Hispania except to maintain a watch over the growth of Barcas family power and its influence in the Mediterranean.[2] But when the Romans became involved in a war with Carthage, the status quo had changed. With the expulsion of the Carthaginians, Rome decided to stay on, fearing that if they withdrew from Hispania, the Carthaginians would quickly return. Thus, to maintain a long-term presence, it became clear to Rome that it needed to replace the military consular *imperium* (power) given to military commanders with some form of an organized

[1] Polybius 11.20.1; Livy 28.12.4; R. Corzo Sanchez, 'La secunda Guerra punica en la Betica', Habis 6, 1975, p 234-40

[2] Richardson, J.S, Hispaniae, Spain and the development of Roman imperialism, 218-82 BC, Cambridge Univ. Press, London, 1986, p. 54-55

government.[3] But for this to happen, Hispania had first to be labeled as a *'provincia'* by the Senate. Although labeled as a province, it would but become officially ratified until 197 BC making Hispania an official state of the empire, enabling Rome to quickly gain some control over this new addition to its growing empire by allowing Roman settlements and soldiers to be stationed within its borders in order to combat any future Carthaginian or indigenous threat. As all powerful nations and empires have discovered, breaking off from an involvement of this magnitude is not so simple, even if they had wanted to. The Romans had realized that their presence in the Iberian Peninsula during the last twelve years had altered the status quo in the Mediterranean. Rome, which had formed alliances with the Iberians were now obligated to support its allies on the peninsula and disregarding those obligations might weakened Rome's ability to control what had become an important area, both strategically and economically. Their so-called Iberian "allies" were disobedient, unruly and unpredictable; thus, they could not be trusted to keep out the Carthaginians. Therefore, it was important for the Romans to maintain some sort of governance and a military presence within Hispania because the distance from Italy to Hispania would prevent Rome from quickly responding to any crisis.[4] Thus direct control from within Hispania by Senate elected officials was the only practical solution. Furthermore, Roman presence had resulted in the creation of commercial avenues of interests, such as trading and mining, which brought considerable additional wealth into Rome.

With the war over, military commanders now became administrators and began developing a structure that would determine the life of the province. Besides caring and training their army, these commanders also began to collect taxes and tributes, set up and maintain friendly relations with local tribes, institute laws and practices, and establish new settlements. As Roman influence grew within Hispania's coastal areas, the appearance of more Roman settlers led to the exploitation of

---

[3] For a detail look at the type of *imperium* that Roman commanders were given in Hispania see Richardson, J.S., op. cit., p. 55-57, 75-77, 104-112

[4] Richardson, J.S., op. cit., p. 51; Curchin, Leonard, A., Roman Spain, Barnes & Noble Inc, NY, 1995, p. 28-29.

the peninsula's mineral and agricultural resources and peoples. This would cause the indigenous population to rebel against the new occupier within a year after the Punic War.

Rome and the Indigenous People of Hispania

The decision to get involved in Hispania in 218 BCE came primarily from the Senate after the fall of the city of Saguntum,[5] an Iberian city that had become a Rome ally at the start of the 2nd Punic War. While the Senate provided a command-structure, supply and manpower and sent elected commanders onto the shores of Hispania, all decisions were made by the commanders in the field, especially the Scipio family, which was in charged of the entire military operation.[6] The reasons why a military commander was delegated senatorial power once he was assigned to Hispania was basically due to the Senate's war against Hannibal in Italy and that the Spanish campaign was in a remote area, therefore, distant from any type of senatorial supervision and control.[7] Because of distance and the need to make rapid and immediate decisions, an ad hoc mechanism of a military government had been set up in 217 BC.[8] Despite the Senate's interest in the war, its advice and decisions appear to have had no effect on the conduct of military operations. In the end, it was the commander's decision that counted, for he was the one who was there fighting the Carthaginians not politicians in Rome.

After the war, according to Professor J.S. Richardson the governmental/ military command structure in Spain remained the same, but on how

---

[5] Today Sagunto is the capital of the district of *Camp de Morvedre*, which is located in the northern part of the province of Valencia. For a better understanding of the siege of Saguntum see http://en.wikipedia.org/wiki/Siege_of_Saguntum; Astin, A.E., "Saguntum and the Origins of the Second Punic War, Latomus #26, 1967, pp. 577-596 and Richardson, J.S., op. cit., p. 20-30

[6] Richardson, J.S., op. cit., p. 42-43

[7] Ibid. p.43

[8] For a more detailed look at the patterns of command during the war in Hispania see Richardson, J.S., 'The Romans in Spain', Blackwell Publishers Ltd, Oxford, 1996, p.35-43 and "Hispaniae, Spain and the development of Roman imperialism, 218-82 BC", Cambridge Univ. Press, London, 1986, p.42-43 and 55-57

governors were elected changed. In his study on the history of the Roman campaign and occupation of Hispania, from the year 206 BC onwards these military governors were elected by a popular assembly, either by the *comitia centuriata* or by the *comitia tributa*.[9] With the war over, the Senate wanted decision making to be shared by the senators and the military governors, but it proved impractical for the same reasons as mentioned before and it was decided that the military governors would continue to be the deciding governing body on Roman policies in Hispania, but they would have to inform the Senate on what they had instituted.

At the time of the Roman invasion of Hispania, manpower, supplies, and money for the army came from Rome. By 215 BC, there were signs that the Romans began rooting themselves in Hispania, making them a self-sufficient force.[10] By the end of the war, not only was P. Scipio Africanus able to meet his demand for supply, troops and money from Rome, he was also able to levy fresh troops from his allies and requisitioning land and money from defeated tribes allied to the Carthaginians.[11] It was from these exactions of money and provisions from the Iberian tribes that Scipio Africanus was able to pay a *stipendium* for his army.[12]

Maintaining good relations with the indigenous people proved to be the hardest job for Roman commanders in Hispania. Although it is difficult to assess the type of relations that existed because reports and histories were susceptible to being reworked by Romans to either favor or disfavor a people, several accounts state that when the Romans

---

[9] The *comitia centuriata* was the democratic assembly of the Roman soldiers, while the *comitia tributa* was the democratic assembly of Roman citizens. For a better understanding of these two assemblies see http://en.wikipedia.org/wiki/Comitia_centuriata and http://en.wikipedia.org/wiki/Comitia_Tributa as well as G.W. Botsford, Roman Assemblies, New York, 1909. As for the subject of the election process for service in Hispania see, Richardson, J.S, op. cit., p. 64-70 and 75

[10] Livy 21.61.6-11; 23.48.5

[11] Livy 28.25.9; 29.12; 34.11; for more details see Richardson, J.S., op. cit, p. 57-58.

[12] Livy, 21.61.6 – 11; 23.48.5; Richardson, J.S., op. cit., p.57.

arrived in Hispania, they were determined to win over local backing.[13] It was in the Romans' best interest to persuade the Iberians to support them and during the war they won over as many allies as they could.[14] One of the main reasons Scipio was successful in gaining tribal support was the harsh rule the Carthaginians imposed on the Iberians.[15] In addition, the Romans commissioned Iberian soldiers, who were mostly Carthaginian defectors, to fight as mercenaries, rather than conscripting them, as the Carthaginians did.[16] In some case, these mercenaries were at times better paid than they were by the Carthaginians.[17]

Although Scipio rewarded his allies he also punished. In the aftermath of the Roman victory at Illipa (modern-day Alcalá del Río, near Seville), Scipio decided to make an example of those tribes or towns that had sided with Carthage. The two Iberian towns that were selected to be the first to feel Rome's power was Castulo and Ilurco.[18] The reason why these two cities were chosen was because their citizens had participated, respectively, in Scipio's father's death at the Battle of the Upper Baetis and his uncle's at Ilorco in 211 and 210 BC.[19]

---

13 Livy 21.60.3; 22.20.10-12; 21.1-8; 22.22.4-21; 23.49.14; 24.49.7-9 Polybius 3.76.2; 3.97.2; Sanctis, G. de., Storia dei romani, 4 vols. Turin/Florence 1907-1964, vol. III.2, 236, n.73.

14 Livy, 26.47.1-26.50.7, 28.15.14; Polybius, 10.17.6-8, 18.3-15, 19.3-7

15 Polybius, 10.6.3, 10.7.3 and 10.10.9; Livy, 26.41.20; Diodorus, 25.12

16 Livy, 21.11.13, 23.46.6, 24.47.8, 24.49.5, 24.49.7-8, 26.41.20

17 Ibid.; Polybius 10.6.3; 10.7.3

18 According to Professor J.S. Richardson there seems to be some confusion in which city his father and uncle were killed. Many scholars claim that these two men were killed at Castax (Scipio's father) and Ilyrgia (Scipio's uncle). But in his research on the subject he writes that the Scipio in fact attacked the town of Castulo (the city was entirely destroyed in 1227 during the Reconquista) and Ilurco (today it is an ancient ruin near Pinos Puente) and not Castax and Ilyrgia for in Pliny's work *Natural History* (3.13) he cites that Ilurco was where his uncle funeral pyre took place. As for Castulo, Livy (28.19-20) makes references to this city, while Appian calls it Castax for some unknown reason.

19 Livy 28.19 -20 Castulo and Iliturgi were names used by Appian, while the names of Castulo and Iliturgi where the names for the same city used by Livy 32.127 and 32.128; as for Scipio's father and uncle's death see Appian 16.61 and Livy 25.32-36 The details of these campaigns are not completely known, but

A Legion under M. Junius Silanus, Scipio's deputy, was sent from Tarraco (modern-day Tarragona) to Castulo to make sure its inhabitants accepted Roman rule.[20] They refused to swear allegiance to Rome, and soon became hostile. When this was communicated to Scipio, he immediately set out from Carthago Nova (modern-day Cartagena) to assist Silanus's attack on the city of Castulo. On his way to Castulo, he decided to changed direction and attacked the town of Ilurco, which was 19 miles (30 km) away from Castulo.[21] In Livy's account, Scipio marched from Carthago Nova to the outskirts of Ilurco in five days, covering about 124 miles (200 km) through mountainous terrain. The reason for his change of plan was because during his father's time in Hispania, Ilurco had been friendly to Rome, but after his father was killed in battle, this city welcomed his father's surviving Legion into its city, only to be handed over to the Carthaginians.[22] At the same time, he may have also changed his battle plan because perhaps he thought Castulo may warn Ilurco of his coming or when Castulo was taken by Silanus, Ilurco would perhaps rally it forces against the Romans having received survivor stories from Castulo. Livy, as well as Appian, goes on to say that Ilurco was taken in four hours, and that although he was wounded in the neck, Scipio did not desist from fighting until the city was in his hands. In their fury to take the city as quickly as possible, his legionnaires killed everyone, including women and children. Even though they had not received orders to destroy the town, they razed the entire town in search of plunder.[23] After Scipio had captured Ilurco, he seemed to have been in a rush that according to Appian, his soldiers did not get the chance to plunder the town for booty for he quickly reorganized and redirected his troops toward Castulo.[24] We can only

---

it seems that the ultimate defeat and death of the two Scipiones was due to the desertion of the Celtiberians, who were bribed by Hasdrubal Barca, Hannibal's brother.

[20] Appian, Ib, 32.127; 11 Livy 28.19.1-20.12; Appian Ib 32.127-31; Polybius 11.24.10.

[21] Schulten, Adolf, "Iliturgi", Hermes #28, 1928, pp. 288-301

[22] Appian, 32.128; Livy 28.19 and 20 also describes the attack on both towns.

[23] Appian 32.129

[24] Ibid., 32.129

assume perhaps he did this was so that he reach Castulo before any survivors of Ilurco did.

Arriving at Castulo to support Silanus's siege of the city, Scipio divided his army into three sections and set up camp around the city. At first, he did not press the siege, but instead watched the town to see if they would surrender to him, for he had received intelligence that the Castacians had intended to give in to Scipio's demands. But after hearing about of what had happened at Ilurco from several of its survivors, the Castacians quickly and quietly gave up. Scipio then stationed a garrison there and placed the town under a pro-Roman government made up of Castacian citizens under the leadership of a man named Cerdubelus.[25] Scipio then returned to Carthago Nova and sent Silanus, and L. Marcius Septimius into Hispania's unconquered northern central regions to devastate, plunder, and take control of as much territory as they could.[26]

Moving west into the Baetis Valley (now Guadalquivir River Valley) these two commanders took several Iberian cities and continue to move in a south-westerly direction to deal with Gades (today Cadiz), the last pro-Carthaginian stronghold. The best recorded siege of this campaign concerns the town of Astapa, another pro-Carthaginian town (today it is an ancient town ruin on the Guadalquivir River, north of Astigi, modern Écija)). Appian writes:

Marcius Septimius on arriving at Astapa quickly laid siege to the city, and the inhabitants foreseeing that when the city was taken by the Romans, they would be reduced to slavery. To deny the Romans that victory, they brought all their valuables into the marketplace, piled wood around it, the men then placed the elderly, their wives and their children on the heap while calling out to their gods for what they had done. Fifty of their best men took an oath that whenever they should see that the

[25] Appian, 32.130-131; as for who was put in charge of the town Appian just writes a Castacian with a good reputation while Livy, 28.20.11-12 gives his name.

[26] Appian, 32.131

city was about to fall, they would kill everyone, set fire to the pile, and slay themselves.[27]

From Livy's account of the battle, which is more detailed than Appian's, he writes:

…committed to their word, the Astapians warriors flung open the town gates and burst out in a tumultuous charge, which Marcius Septimius, did not anticipate anything of the kind. On seeing the human wave coming, he quickly deployed the entire cavalry and light infantry against them. Fierce fighting ensued in which the legionnaires, who had been first to come into contact with the enemy were soon routed; this created a panic amongst the light infantry. The Iberian attack would have been pushed to the foot of the Roman camp's defense perimeter if it had not been for Marcius' leadership in getting his men back on line.[28]

He goes on to write:

… at first there was some wavering amongst the Roman front ranks, for the enemy, blinded by rage, fury and desperation rushed with mad recklessness upon wounds and death, allotting the Romans a few minutes to get into a line formation. On seeing the human wave, many of the inexperienced Roman soldiers at the front rank began to waver. Unshaken by the frantic onset, the veterans came up in support and cut down the enemy's front ranks. When the Roman line began to waver due to the Astapians' ferocity, Marcius extended his lines and outflanked the enemy. With sheer numbers, the Iberians fighting in a compact body and the Roman's tactical maneuvering, the Romans wipe them all out.[29]

When all had fallen, the fifty who remained behind killed the women and children, kindled the fire, and flung the bodies of the dead, as well as themselves. From Livy's account, he continues on that by the time

---

[27] Appian, 33.132-134

[28] Livy, 28.22.18 - 26

[29] Ibid.

the Romans arrived on the scene, all had perished and wrote of the aftermath:

At first the Romans stood horror-stricken at such a fearful sight, then, seeing the melted gold and silver flowing amongst the other articles which made up the heap, the greediness common to human nature impelled them to try and snatch what they could out of the fire. Some were caught by the flames, others were scorched by the heated air, and those in front could not retreat owing to the crowd pressing on behind to get a look.[30]

Appian writes that although Astapa was taken and practically destroyed, the Legionnaires left without any plunder and Maricus received a barren victory. In admiration of the Astapians' bravery, Maricus spared the town's structures.[31]

After taking Astapa and accepting the surrender of the remaining pro-Carthaginian cities in the area, Marcius led his victorious army back to Carthago Nova. At the same time some Carthaginian deserters came from Gades and promised to deliver the city with its Carthaginian garrison and its commandant, who had anchored his ships in the city's harbor.[32] The commandant of Gades was Mago Barca Hannibal's brother. After the battle of Illipa, Mago decided he would continue to take up arms against the Romans and took up quarters in the fortified city of Gades. With the help of the ships that he had assembled, along with a mixed army of Carthaginian soldiers and Iberian allies, he had a considerable force to face the Romans. After guarantees of good faith had been given between the Carthaginians and Romans, Scipio sent Marcius Septimius with a cohort of light infantry and Laelius with seven triremes and one quinquereme to conduct joint operations against

30 Livy, 28.23.1-6

31 Appian 33.136

32 Livy, 28.23.9

Gades.[33] But this operation was delayed when Scipio became sick and a munity took place.[34]

During Marcius very short generalship two incidents took place. Soon after Marcius took charge of the army many of the Legionnaires had spent all their money and had not been paid; a large number of men stationed at Surco mutinied by saying that Scipio had taken from them what they had worked for and the glory that came with it.[35] Some of them went on to join Hannibal's brother, Mago Barca at Gades.[36] These Roman deserters, who had joined up with Mago soon returned to their appropriate garrisons with money and attempted to urged the rest of the army to desert and join Mago's army at Gades, who by the way was planning on making a move against the Romans. Many of the Roman soldiers took the money, but instead of joining Mago, they took it upon themselves to swear an oath of allegiance to one another and elect their own officers.[37]

Soon rumors ran amok that Scipio illness had killed him. The whole of Spain, especially the Roman controlled parts, were joyous of the news for he was known to command with an iron fist. At Surco, these rumors had a dangerous effect on the Legionnaires. This camp, according to Livy, held a force of 8,000 men, stationed there to protect the peaceful tribes on the south side of the Ebro River.[38] Although there were rumors

---

[33] Livy 28.23.7-8

[34] Appian, 43.137; Appian writes that Marcius was elected by Scipio but in Livy's and Polybius' work it is Silanus who was put in charge. According to Professor Richardson he believes that the text is defective in that Μάρκος should be read as Μάρκιος, but Appian always writes Silanus as Σιλανός elsewhere. Richardson, J.S., Appian: Wars of the Romans in Iberia, Warminster, UK, 2000, p. 132

[35] Appian, 34.138; Livy 28.24.5 Livy is the only person who states the location of the mutiny.

[36] Gades was the last Carthaginian stronghold in Hispania after the 2nd Punic War in which had not yet been taken.

[37] Appian, 34.137 - 138

[38] Livy, 28.24.5 Surco is the Roman name for the Júcar River. According to J.S. Richardson, the location of the camp could not have been the purpose of controlling the tribes that lived on the north side of the Ebro and instead they were

about their commander's death, it was not the primary cause of the mutiny. Accustomed to living on captured enemy plunder, and long periods of inactivity, chafed against the restraints of peace and horrors of war, many of the Legionnaires were becoming demoralized. At first their discontent was confined to simply murmurs.[39] But as time passed, they began to demand to be paid with insolence quite inconsistent with military discipline that at some point soldiers became rouge and went out on their own to steal from the peaceful surrounding inhabitants. Although these soldiers committed crimes and fought to get paid, Livy writes that they still continued to do their military duties such as guard duty.[40] Livy goes on the say that the mutiny occurred when they found that the tribunes in Rome had censured and reprobated their pay with an endeavor to repress them, which the Legionnaires openly declared that they would have nothing to do with the Senate's insensate folly, braking out into open mutiny. They drove out the tribunes from the camp, and amidst universal acclamation placed as commander of the camp the mutiny's ringleaders, two common soldiers, named C. Albius of Cales and C. Atrius, an Umbrian.[41] Livy states that the false belief that Scipio had died without paying his army would spread and kindle the flames of war throughout Hispania. Thus, the Romans levied contributions on its Iberian allies, while plundering its enemies round them.[42]

---

stationed at the mouth of the Júcar River. I also agree with Richardson for if the Romans were based at the Surco River it would be impossible for 8,000 men to patrol such as vast area for the distance from the Júcar River to the nearest point of the Ebro River is about 140 miles (225 km). If the military was place on the Ebro River it would have made command and control very difficult in an area that was not completely pacified. It was also would have made it difficult for military orders to arrive from Carthago Nova which is some 248 miles away (400 km), so it is more like that Richardson is correct in his statement thus this military base was then only 124 miles away (200 km) from Carthago Nova making it a bit easier to control 8,000 soldiers.

39 Livy, 28.24.9

40 Livy, 28.24.14; This is somewhat different from what Appian writes.

41 Livy, 28.24.16-17 He is the only one that names the mutiny's ringleaders

42 Livy, 28.24.19-20

When the sick Scipio heard this, he wrote to the rebellious soldiers that he was alive and getting better and because of his illness he was not able to pay them, but if they came to Carthago Nova he would reward them properly and all would be forgiven. But Scipio had other plans for these men. Scipio ordered several of his officers to head on out to Surco and befriend the mutiny's ringleaders so as to gain their confidence. Once that was accomplished, they would be brought to Carthago Nova where a trap would be sprung and the men arrested before they realized what was going on.[43] The news was brought by a party of seven military tribunes, who read the letters and dictated Scipio's terms.[44] Some were suspicious, while others trusted Scipio's word and decided to proceed to Carthago Nova.

Arriving at Carthago Nova, the trap was sprung.[45] With all the mutineers assembled, waiting for their fearless and sick leader to compensate them, they were arrested. Scipio then appeared, spoke to and released the men back to their units, while the ringleaders were shackled in chains and later executed, announcing amnesty to the rest who did not show up at his camp, thus ending the mutiny, restoring order to his army.[46]

With the mutiny ongoing, along with the rumors of Scipio's "death", former Iberian allies to the Romans, decided not to preserve their fidelity. This was the case of Scipio former allies, Mandonius and Indibilis. After the expulsion of the Carthaginians from Hispania, these two brothers believed that Hispania's sovereignty would be passed on to them. As ruler of Hispania they would continue to maintain an alliance with Rome. But when they realized this was not going to happen for the Romans were establishing permanent bases and settlements, implying

---

[43] Appian, 35.141-142

[44] Livy is the one who state the number of tribunes that were sent (28.25.5) and what the terms were and what went on during the meeting 28.25.6-15

[45] For the entire episode see Appian verse 35 and 36; Livy, 28.26, 28.27, 28.28, 28.29; Polybius, 11.29

[46] Appian, 36.146; Livy, 28.26.6 For Scipio's speech see Bryan, W.J.," To His Mutinous Troops", The World's Famous Orations. Rome (218 B.C.–84 A.D.), Rome, 1906; Livy is the one who mentions that there were five other involved in the mutiny.

that Hispania was in the process of becoming a Roman province and that Scipio had not delivered on his promises, they became somewhat disgruntled. When rumors of Scipio's death spread, they came to the decision that this was their chance to shake off Rome's imperial yoke just as they had done to Carthage.

Believing that Scipio's 'death' would cause disorganization among the Roman Army for they now had no leader to lead them. They encouraged a general revolt not only among their own subjects, as well as several neighboring Iberian tribes such as the Lacetani and Celtiberians. Once aroused, Mandonius and Indibilis's army began to ravage Suessitanians and Sedetanians territory, both of which were Roman allies.[47] When the two brothers heard that Scipio was still alive, they gave up their enterprise and retired within their frontiers.[48] Over the years there have been suggestions as to why they did this, but it could have been that it was either fear or respect of Scipio fighting prowess, although the actual reasoning for their withdrawal is lost forever to history.

Although Mandonius and Indibilis had returned to their lands, Scipio, recovered from his illness, was not inclined to leave their disloyalty unpunished. According to Livy and Appia, soon after the mutiny had been quelled, Scipio marched against the two brothers. On hearing that Scipio was coming, they summoned their tribesmen to arms, and gathered an army of 20,000 infantry and 2,500 cavalrymen and crossed their frontiers into Sedetania to meet Scipio.[49]

From his camp at Carthago Nova, Scipio marched for several weeks until he reached the Ebro River where he met the rebel army head on. A battle was fought, but unfortunately the classical records did not leave behind many battle details, only the results. It was a costly Roman victory. According to Livy, the Roman suffered over 5,000 casualties,

---

[47] Livy, 28.24

[48] Livy, 28.25.9

[49] Livy, 28.31.6-8

while taking 3,000 prisoners and booty.[50] Along with the high casualty rate, Livy states, the victory would not have been so costly to the Romans had the battlefield been fought in a wider plain to allow room for the Iberians to retreat, which would have been their better choice if they saw themselves in trouble. But it seems that the Roman battle plan had worked for the Iberian were surrounded and strategically outmaneuvered, thus the Iberians fought harder in an enclosed area allotting to the high number of casualties between both armies. In Appian's work, he claims that the Romans suffered 1,200 causalities and killed as many as 20,000 Iberians, which seem somewhat exaggerated when the Iberian army according to Livy was 22,500 of which 3,000 Iberians were taken prinsoner.[51] If one believes these numbers, then not one Iberian warrior survived.

Facing defeat, both brothers decided it would be better for them if they laid aside all ideas of continuing their campaign against Scipio, and that the safest course to take, considering their hopeless position was to throw themselves on Scipio's clemency. Indibilis sent his brother Mandonius to speak about making peace with Scipio. Having trusted that their strength and cause would lead them to victory they were now hopeless and decided to put all their trust in their conqueror's mercy.

Throwing himself before Scipio, Mandonius declared that he and his brother and the rest of their countrymen were in such a bad state, that if Scipio spared them a second time, they would devote the whole of their lives to the one man to whom they owed their lives to.[52] Scipio, after sternly reprimanding Mandonius and the absent of Indibilis at considerable length, said that their lives were justly forfeited by their crime, but through his own kindness and that of the Roman people, they would be spared.[53] With that said, he did not demand hostages nor take away their arms; instead he would take an indemnity or preferred the

---

[50] Livy, 28.34; As many as 2000 Romans and allies fell in the battle; the wounded amounted to more than 3000.

[51] Appian, 37.148

[52] Livy, 28.34.5

[53] Livy, 28.34.7

wrath of Rome.[54] Dismissed, Mandonius returned to his brother with Scipio's terms and conditions. As I mentioned before, the only condition imposed upon the two brothers was the indemnity that according to Livy, "was sufficient enough to furnish the pay which was owed to the troops."[55]

It is essential to understand the importance of why Scipio had to punish his former allies, for a hostile enemy force in this position could easily disrupt the communication and supply lines along the coastal strip and Ebro River. In addition, had he not made an example of these two men, there would perhaps be more native insurrections, so it was imperative to make them an example. Lastly, this action produced a statement which made it clear to the Iberians that the Romans "were here to stay", a claim that was to show the Iberian tribes the type of power Rome had. In the end, these actions against the Iberian population, suggests that Scipio had intentions of controlling the indigenous people of the peninsula.

Once Scipio had quieted down the rebellious Iberians, he sent Marcius on ahead into southern Spain to capture Gades (Cadiz) from Mago Barca, while Scipio, with a light-armed force, stayed behind a few days until the Ilergetes paid their indemnity in full, which he then set out to meet Marcius, who was already nearing Gades.[56]

Unaware of what the Romans had in store for him, Mago decided to take advantage of the following events: an Iberian insurrection under Indibilis and Mandonius, and the mutiny of the Roman troops

---

[54] Livy, 28,34.10 This is somewhat surprising for it was the traditional practice of the Romans, in the case of a conquered nation with whom no friendly relations had previously existed either through treaty or community of rights and laws, not to accept their submission or allow any terms of peace until all their possessions sacred and profane had been surrendered, hostages given, their arms taken away and garrisons placed in their cities.

[55] Livy, 28.34.12

[56] See above: this was the restart of the previous military operation against Gades just prior to Scipio's illness.

along the Sucro River.[57] Believing that these events might help restore Carthaginian power on the peninsula, he decided to lead a raid against Carthago Nova, which was thought to be lightly defended. Having received erroneous intelligence about the city's defense, his forces were repulsed with severe losses.[58] While Mago was at Carthago Nova, Marcius took Gades without a fight. Upon his return, Mago found the gates of Gades barred, and sailed away to the Balearic Islands.[59]

The Romans had finally ousted the Carthaginians of a vital land base filled with mineral resources and agricultural wealth. They now were able to lay down their own foundation for a continuous Roman presence on the Iberian Peninsula with the establishment of Roman military bases at Tarraco (modern-day Tarragona), Carthage Nova, and Gades along with the newly established settlement at Italica (modern-day Santiponce), which provided an outline for the colonization of the entire peninsula. Moreover, the way the Scipio family had set about the tasks of supplying themselves with provision and money for the troops and determining their relations with the various Iberian tribes, was to shape Roman policy and begin the emergence of Roman institutions in the peninsula.[60]

To the indigenous people of the peninsula, Scipio's actions such as the founding of Italica, the establishment of a Roman *praefectus*, and the placement of Roman troops in former Carthaginian strongholds,[61]

---

[57] Livy, 28.36.1

[58] Livy, 28.36.3-16

[59] Livy, 28.37

[60] Richardson, J.S., "Hispaniae, p. 61

[61] Appian, 38.153; Livy 28.24, 28.37 and 32.2; Badian, E., "The prefect at Gades", Classical Philolgy #49, 1954, p. 250-252; Richardson, J.S., op. cit., p. 61; Pellicer, M., Hurtado, V. and La Bandera, M.L. 'Corte estratigrafico de la Casa de Venus', in Italica: actasde las primeras journadas sobre excavciones en Italica', Excavaciones arqueologicas in España 121, 1982, p. 29-73; Richardson, J.S.,'The Romans in Spain', Blackwell Publishers Ltd, Oxford, 1996, p. 39 and 222. As for the founding of Italica, the town would become the forerunner of towns and cities that would eventually "Romanized" the peninsula, but this would not happen until the reign of Julius Caesar, a century –and-a-half after its founding.

brought a feeling that perhaps confirmed that the Romans had intentions of staying. It seems logical that Scipio's intentions of establishing a permanent Roman presence on the Iberian Peninsula, in the name of Rome, had been hard fought, thus it became important to hold on to what the Romans had gained during twelve years of war against Carthage. These events foreshadowed future developments in the peninsula, but before this could happen Rome would have to first conquer and pacify the entire peninsula.

Roman Conquest of Hispania Begins

Before Scipio Africanius left in 206 BC, to be elected consular for his success in defeating the Carthaginians, he had shown the Iberians that the end of the fight against Carthage in Hispania did not mean the end of Roman interests in the peninsula. The Roman occupation of Hispania during the war had substantial cultural and technological influences over the tribes under Roman control. The practices and ideas employed by the three Scipios established a foundation that subsequent governors would continue to employ or modify. To solidify Hispania as part of the Roman Empire, he presented to the Senate several reasons why it was important to remain in Hispania. To further his idea, he brought with him an Iberian delegation from the city of Saguntum to thank the Romans for the benefits of their alliance with Rome and for relieving them from the Carthaginian menace.[62] Scipio's petition was answered, for the Senate had decided to send two military commanders, L. Cornelius Lentulus and L. Manlius Acidinus to Hispania instead of one to govern to country.[63] With the election of two men to run the government in Hispania, it was clear that Rome's presence was permanent.

During this new phase of Roman occupation, Hispania in the eyes of the Romans was quite primitive, requiring time to pacify its indigenous tribes. It became important to Rome that their elected official to Hispania undertake certain obligations and policies to 'Romanize' the Iberian

[62] Richardson, J.S. "Hispaniae, p.63

[63] Livy 28.38.2

tribes, which in the minds of the Romans could not be disregarded, for if these commitments were ignored it could weakened Rome's ability to control an important area in the known world, as well as leave the Peninsula open for Carthaginian reoccupation, which was still a threat. Furthermore, Rome's 12-year presence in Hispania resulted in the emergence of further Roman imperial interests, such as an increased in trading connections within the peninsula which introduced Iberian products and a new variety of food products to Rome, thus magnifying Roman quality of life. But for this to happen, Rome would have to find a way to pacification and control the Iberian tribes.

With this in mind, the Romans launched on an imperialistic endeavor to take advantage of the enormous wealth that Hispania had to offer. In antiquity, the Iberian Peninsula was famous for its richness in metal ores, such as silver, gold, tin, and copper. The resources of the metal – rich western area of Iberia was in high demand since the Bronze Age.[64] Besides Hispania's abundance in mineral deposits, its soil, in certain parts of the peninsula was rich and fertile to grow plenty of crops to feed Rome's growing population. After the Roman victory over Carthage, the Senate and its Roman patrician oligarchy began to reorganize the land that they had conquered. One such example was Scipio's establishment of Italica, far away from any significant strategic areas of the eastern route to the Pyrenees. This shows that he was aware of the benefits that might be accrued to the state from the control of the fertile area of the Baetis Valley in southern Spain and the silver mines of the Sierra Morena.[65] Hence, the Romans developed the greatest economic diversification and subsistence strategy based on the exploitation of all

[64] Gamito, Teresa Júdice, "The Celts in Portugal", Journal of Interdisciplinary Celtic Studies, 6 vols., University of Algarve, vol. 6, p. 571-604.

[65] Strabo 3.2.1-8; Polybius 34.9.8-11; Schulten, A., Iberische Landeskunde, II vols., Strasbourg, 1955-1957, vol. I, p. 195-197. *The Sierra Morena is a mountain range which stretches for 400 km East-West across southern Spain, forming the border of the central plateau (*Meseta Central*) of Iberia, and providing the watershed between the valleys of the Guadiana River to the north and the Guadalquivir River to the south. It has valuable deposits of lead, silver, mercury, and other metals, some of which have been exploited since prehistoric times.

the resources available: agriculture, livestock breeding, hunting, mining as well as handicrafts.

By the early part of the 2nd century BC, Rome controlled the eastern fertile plains of the Baetic River Valley and the Ebro and began to produce crops in these areas. As for mineral deposits that were in the areas controlled by the Romans, they were exploited to their full capacity, while the rest of the peninsula was still far away from being under Roman controlled. To reach further deep into the peninsula, the Romans needed to launch military/exploratory expeditions to contact the other Iberian tribes to begin some type of relation. This relation, in the eyes of the Romans would hopefully later form into a social system that would determine the future life of the province. While the Romans attempted to pacify Hispania's remote area, they began to collect taxes and tribute, and build political and social system with local Iberian communities with their realm, while establishing new Roman settlements in these areas.

By the latter part of the 2nd century BC, some actions and decisions made by several Roman governors gave way to abuses, exploitation, spoliation and violations that harmed, harassed and intimidated the Iberian population[66]. All this, together with the obligation of paying heavy annual taxes, ended up waking the rebellious spirit of the natives. Greed and the inexperience of many governors and government officials, the annuity of the position and the scarce knowledge of the autochthonous Iberian world provoked serious disorders among the population. In Rome, the Senate tried to end these abuses, but at times it failed.[67]

Though Roman governmental representatives caused dissension among the Iberian population, it was the Roman soldiers and their allies that had the most significant effect on the local populace's actions, particularly in

---

[66] Munoz, Mauricio P., "Viriato, O Herói Lusitano que lutou pela liberdade do seu povo" Esfera dos Livros, Lisbon, 2006, p. 39

[67] Ibid. p. 39

place where troops were stationed such as Tarraco, Carthago Nova and Emporion. During the lieu in fighting, Roman influence spread across the country for Roman soldiers intensified Roman habits and culture among the Iberian population. While merchants brought to the Iberians, new wares and products and technological advances that they had never seen before. With troops being stationed in Hispania and traders lurking at every port across the eastern and southern Spanish coastline, many opportunities arose for those Iberians who were skilled craftsmen, artists and entrepreneurs. For entrepreneurial Romans and freedmen and aspiring politicians, Hispania presented itself as a golden opportunity to get ahead and become wealthy. Because of Roman presence, its culture gradually spread across the eastern and southern coastal lands of the Iberian Peninsula that it began to influence the Iberians to take the patterns of Roman life. As for the rest of the country, this wave of Roman influence was still years away.

A year after the Carthaginian expulsion from the Peninsula, the Roman provincial government under L. Cornelius Lentulus and L. Manlius Acidinus, faced its second major rebellion. According to Livy, Indibilis and Mandonius, continuing to witness Rome's takeover of their land. Once again, they rallied up their tribes, along with the Ausetani and other neighboring tribes to take up arms against the Romans. They brought together an army of 34,000 warriors and marched into Sedetani territory north of the Ebro River.[68]

Livy goes on to say that Lentulus and Acidinus were determined not to let the rebellion spread. So, they united their forces and marched through Ausetanian territory, without inflicting any hostility upon the peaceable districts, until they came to where the enemy was encamped. Pitching camp three miles from the enemy's camp, the Romans sent envoys to persuade the brothers to surrender. Indibilis asked the envoys to give him time to discuss the surrender terms with his captains. A few days later, the Romans got their answer; a group of Iberian cavalry

[68] Livy 29.1.19-20; cf. Appian, 38.156-7 and Diodorus, 26.22

attacked a Roman foraging party. In support, a Roman cavalry squadron was quickly dispatched, and a skirmish took place.[69]

The following day, Indibilis and Mandonius' Iberian army marched within a mile of the Roman camp. According to Livy, the enemy formed up into a battle formation consisting of the Ausetani in the center, the Ilergetes on the right flank, with the left flank made up of various indigenous tribes. Meanwhile, between the wings and the center of the formation, open spaces were left wide open enough to allow cavalry through when the signal was given for the cavalry to attack.[70]

The Romans formed up in their usual battle formation, except that they copied the enemy's formation by also leaving spaces between the legions so that their cavalry could pass through.[71] Both sides moved in to attack. Seeing that his infantry was making no progress and his left wing was beginning to give ground to the Ilergetes, Lentulus decided to bring up his reserves. At the same time, Lentulus realized that whomever was the first to use their cavalry through the wide gaps against the opposing line would probably have a chance in defeating the enemy. As soon as the left wing was restored, Lentulus gave one of his military tribunes, Servius Cornelius, orders to send the cavalry at full speed through the openings. Lentulus then rode up to Acidinus, who was at the front encouraging his men, informed him on the situation. Livy writes that he had hardly finished his commands, when the Roman cavalry slammed into the middle of the enemy formation throwing the enemy infantry into confusion, barring the passage for the Iberian cavalry to counter-attack.[72]

Finding themselves unable to conduct mounted cavalry tactics, the Romans dismounted in mid – battle and fought on foot. When the Roman commanders saw the enemy's ranks in disorder, they instructed their

[69] Livy, 29.2.1-4

[70] Livy, 29.2.6-7

[71] Livy, 29.2.8

[72] Livy 29.2.9- 11

men to break up the enemy into segments so as not to let them re-form their lines. Confusion and panic began to spread among the Iberians. Not being able to withstand the furious Roman attack much longer, Indibilis and his cavalry also dismounted and placed themselves in front of his brother to protect his infantry, so that his brother, Mandonius could regroup his battle formation.[73] The fighting lasted for some time, neither side giving way. Indibilis, wounded and fatigued, kept his ground till he was killed by a javelin. After seeing one of their great leaders killed, many of the Iberians lost hope and began to withdraw. With many of the Iberians withdrawing from the battle, the battle turned into a rout. The Iberian quickly dispersed and stealthy returned to their respective communities. At the end of the battle, 13,000 Iberians were killed and about 1,800 prisoners were taken. Of the Romans and allies a little more than 200 fell, mainly on the left wing.[74] Although Indibilis was killed, his brother, Mandonius escaped with the remnants of the army.

On his return to his village, Mandonius summoned a tribal meeting. During the tribal summit, complaints were uttered about the disaster they had incurred, and all the blame was thrown upon Mandonius and Indibilis for starting the rebellion. After the tribal council, envoys were sent to the Romans to make a formal surrender and plea to not have their arms taken away.[75] The reply they received from the Romans was that their surrender would only be accepted on condition that they give up Mandonius and the other instigators of the rebellion; failing to do so, the Roman army would march into Ilergetes and Ausetani country and wreck havoc upon their kingdoms.[76] When this reply was reported to the tribal council, Mandonius and several other chiefs were arrested and handed over for punishment. Peace was re-established amongst the Iberian tribes. Under the peace agreement, the Iberians were required to furnish double tribute to pay the Roman troops for that year, a six month supply of corn, and cloaks and togas for the army. The Romans also took

[73] Livy, 29.2.12-14

[74] Livy 29.2.15- 20; As for the casualties it is questionable if that is an exact number to be used for propaganda purposes or if it actually happened.

[75] Livy, 29.3.1 and 29.3.3

[76] Livy, 29.3.2 and 29.3.4

away their weapons and demanded hostages from the noble families of about thirty tribes, so as to keep the tribes in line.[77] To make matters worse a strong Roman garrison was installed in the territory to watch over them, according to Appian. Roman Spain's second major revolt had been crushed without any further serious disturbance.[78] As for Mandonius, according to Appian, he was brought to trial, found guilty for instigating the rebellion and put to death along with the others.[79]

Apart from their participation in putting down the rebellion and of their extension as military governors in Hispania, nothing more is heard of Lentulus and Acidinus until 201 BC. After six years in Hispania, Lentulus was finally recalled back to Rome[80] and replaced by C. Cornelius Cethegus, who only served two years.[81] Cethegus having been elected *curule aedile*[82] in 199 BC was replaced by Cn. Cornelius Blasio (Hispania Citerior) until 196 BC. As for Acidinus, he remained in Hispania until 199 BC, and was replaced by L Sertinius (Hispania Ulterior), who served in Hispania until 196 BC.[83] In between all these governors, Livy mentions C. Sergius, who had taken command of the province in the year 200 BC when Cethegus and Acidinus left for Rome. According to Livy, he stayed behind to award land to those veteran soldiers that had served for many years in Hispania.[84] Not much is known of these other proconsul's exploits in Hispania except of their *ovatio* in Rome, which indicates that they had conducted some type of military campaign against the Iberians.[85] Although much is not

---

[77] Livy, 29.3.5-6; Appian 38.157

[78] Livy 29.3.5 – 9

[79] Appian, Ib, 38.157

[80] Livy 31.20.1-6

[81] Livy 31.49.7 Livy does not mention about Cethegus' elections but writes that a large Iberian army was routed in the Sedetan district in 200 BC that resulted in 15,000 Iberians being killed in that battle and seventy-eight standards taken.

[82] An elected official of ancient Rome who was responsible for public works and games and who supervised markets, the grain supply, and water supply.

[83] Livy 33.27.1-4; Richardson, "Hispaniae, p.69

[84] Livy, 32.1.6

[85] ovatio was a less-honored form of the Roman triumph. Ovatio were granted, when war was not declared on the state level, when an enemy was considered basely

said about these men, we can see changes happening within Hispania's occupied areas such as the formation of two provinces for administrative purposes instead of one huge and uncontrolled province[86].

Peace settled after the rebellion and the benefits of Roman civilization quickly began to exhibit results upon on those so-called "barbarians". Tribal villages became towns and cities, and roads were beginning to be built along with aqueducts and bridges. Hispania would provide hardy soldiers and cavalry, as well as poets, rhetoricians, geographers, historians and a series of successful emperors such as Trajan, Hadrian and Marcus Aurelius. Due to large food demands, the Romans initiated improvements in irrigation and agriculture, imported new crops, and introduced animal husbandry. Lastly, advanced mining techniques were brought in to extract the peninsula's mineral wealth. The newly forming province of Hispania had much to offer and Rome would benefit greatly in the years to come.

With the Carthaginian threat diminished after the Battle of Zama[87], peace settled throughout Hispania, bring into question the necessity of a Roman military presence in Hispania. Prior to Hispania becoming a permanent chess piece in Rome's growing empire, it was important to have two military commanders with a large army within each command structure of their area of operation for Rome's Spanish allies were new and unreliable, thus leaving essential strategic points such as certain coastal routes and cities open to enemy attacks and raids. But with the subsequent changes that were occurring within Hispania after the Punic

---

inferior, and when the general conflict was resolved with little to no bloodshed or danger to the army; Lentulus ovation see Livy 31.20; Sertinius ovation see Livy 33.17.1-4; about Blasio ovation see Sumner, G.V., 'A New Reading in the Fasti Capitolini', Phoenix #19, 1965, p. 95-101; on Stertinius' arches see Coarelli, F., 'La Porta Trionfale e la Via dei Trionfi', Dialoghi de Archeologia #2, 1968, p. 55-103

[86] Livy begins to make references about Hispania as two Spains starting in Book 33

[87] The **Battle of Zama** was fought in North Africa around October 19 of 202 BC, it marked the final and decisive end of the Second Punic War. A Roman army led by Publius Cornelius Scipio defeated a Carthaginian force led by Hannibal Barca. For more information see http://en.wikipedia.org/wiki/Battle_of_Zama

War and having allocated the country into a Roman province, the Senate believed that its vast army in Hispania needed to be downsized from two armies to two Legion and 15 cohorts of Latin allies with the remaining veterans brought back to Italy with the returning proconsul.[88]

This change in policy at the very least, given the size of the territory controlled by the Romans in 201 BC, suggests that the Senate's concerned about reducing their commitment in Hispania was, "Why have such a large army to protect Hispania against disorganized and undisciplined bands of barbarians?" The reasoning is perhaps derived from Lentulus and Acidinus amazing victory over the Iberians, enforcing the Senate's belief that a small force of professional Roman soldiers could control the area with no problem. With this in mind, the Senate released a decree to decrease the size of its military presence and reduce its military governor to one.[89] But we shall never know exactly what the Senate's intentions were for Livy is silent on the matter, but in the end, it seems that this reduction in force was never carried out. Perhaps one of the reasons why it did not happen was because Rome's newly established "allies" were still unreliable; therefore, there was a need for flexibility in the deployment of troops throughout strategic points within their realm which was beginning to expand further inland. Thus, it would become difficult for a small army to cover or fight against indigenous tribes over such as vast area.

The other reason for this force reduction was political. Professor Richardson states that the Senate's force reduction proposal was linked with the cutback on the number of military governors there were in Hispania with *imperium pro consule* that controlled large armies.[90] The change of *imperium* power was perhaps a way for the Senate to control such men who with such a large army may have hungered for absolute power so as to establish their own independent state or pose a threat to

---

[88] Livy 30.41.4-5; Richardson, J.S.,"Hispaniae, p.68

[89] Livy 30.41.4-5; Brunt, P.A., Italian Manpower, 225 BC – AD 14, Oxford, 1971, p. 661; Richardson, J.S., 'The Romans in Spain', p. 45-46; Richardson, J.S."Hispaniae, p.68

[90] Richardson, J.S., "Hispaniae, p.69

Rome in a bid to become emperor. Unfortunately, with the absence of details on the matter makes interpretation difficult and it shows that this policy change may have not been important enough to be addressed. On the other hand, though it has not been documented, it is possible that the Senate had changed its mind about the force reduction and decided to keep things as they were because they perhaps realized that with Rome's imperialistic attitude these men would be kept busy enough with an unruly populace, while at the same time gaining Rome's favor for expanding the empire. In the end, whatever intentions the Senate had about withdrawing troops and a governor, it never occurred.

During the Punic War, Scipio had laid out the foundations of how Hispania would be governed, which would continue on until the end of the Republic era in 27 BC, when Augustus became emperor. The militaristic-governmental structure that was emplaced by Scipio was based on the need to pay, feed and supply the army.[91] The command structure during the war came under a single commander with *consular imperium*, who had to send back reports to keep the senate informed of the war's progress and of their needs.[92] During the war, it was better to have one man in control instead of two or more, so as to conduct successful military operations against an enemy, for if there were two commanding generals there would always be one who would try to either outdo the other or counter the other's orders causing chaos within the command structure. As mentioned before, the major decisions that shaped the progress of the war in Hispania were taken by the commanders on the spot and not by Rome. The only thing the Senate could do from such a long distance was express its approval, disapproval or grief.

But after the war, it seems that the pattern set by Scipio continued for there is little information of Hispania's early administrative developments with the exception of a few changes as we shall soon see. Scipio established policies and a governmental structure in Hispania to administer a huge piece of land and its people. With such a vast area

---

[91] Richarson, J.S., Hispaniae, p. 57-58

[92] Richardson, J.S., Hispaniae, p. 20-30, 55-56

to control for one man, the Senate allowed two men to act as governor and establish Roman policies and institution within the two different regions of the province making Romanization of the area much easier.

The next change came in the form of paying taxes. During the war, Rome sent money, food and supplies to support and maintain the army in Hispania. But after the war, to be self-sufficient, the Romans began to collect a tax[93], which was more of a *stipendium* that was used to pay the army. This seems to have been the beginning of a more systematic taxation that would later be used in Hispania, as well as the rest of the empire, but at this stage it was an ad hoc levy to pay soldiers.[94] But to obtain this *stipendium,* the Romans collected it from Iberian tribes that had revolted against them as in the Ilergetes and Ausetani did in 205 BC in the manner of food, clothes, and at times gold and silver. The penalties suffered by the Iberians were beneficial to Rome such as the price of corn, which was reduced because of the large quantity that was being sent from Spain. Also, Rome did not have to send as much money as they had done during the Second Punic War because by 203 BC the army was self-sustaining from the constant collection of clothing, corn, weapons and various supplies.[95]

With governmental administrative policy somewhat installed, the next step was to instill Senate policy within the realm. At first, we see one proconsul being elected by the Senate, empowered with *consular imperium* upon reaching Hispania's shores, he governed as he saw fit, which continued until 201 BCE, but this was somewhat modified after that point. We being to see two men rule with *imperium* after the Punic War for Rome had captured so much Spanish territory that two men were needed to run the country. But around 201 BC,E the Senate,

---

[93] The word tax in this context does not mean here at this point in time as it did later when the Romans actually began to levy taxes on an annual fixed sum drawn from across the province.

[94] For further information see Richardson, J.S., Hispaniae, p. 72 and 115-117, Richardson, J.S., 'The Spanish Mines and the Development of Provincial Taxation in the Second Century BC', Journal of Roman Studies 66, 1976, pp. 139-152, for on the subject of the stipendium see p. 147-149

[95] Livy, 30.3.2 31.4.6-7

thinking about downsizing it forces in Hispania, throws in the idea of just having one man governing the entire province and emplacing actual Senatorial policies made in Rome rather than by men who conduct the day-to-day governmental business in Hispania. But that policy, just as in the reduction in force, also never materialized for it would be difficult for the Senate, itself, to keep control and manage policies from so far away, compared to what a praetor did or did not do while stationed in Spain. So, the final outcome was left to the governors to instill Senatorial policies on their arrival in Hispania.

It is difficult to know when the Senate made its decision about having one instead of two governors, but it probably happened after Cethegus and Acidinus were reassigned back to Rome.[96] If the Senate was going to replace both men, the Senate would have sent two other men to replace them, but it did not. With this in mind, C. Sergius[97] who was *praetor urbanus* during 200 BCE comes into play for Livy states that his term as praetor was extended, thus providing him with just not the power as *praetor urbanus*, for the purpose of allotting land to the veterans that had served in Hispania, but also giving him *imperium* to run the country. Thus this was perhaps the Senate's attempt at setting up one governor for one province, but it seems that it failed for the following year, 199 BCE, we see two new governors in the written record, Cornelius Blasio and L. Stertinius.[98] Perhaps after consultation with Lentulus, Cethegus and Acidinus about what was happening in Hispania, the Senate changed its mind and reversed back to two praetors instead of one. The sending out of two praetors in 199 BCE and the fact that their tenure lasted only two years suggests that a regular pattern was beginning to evolve on how Hispania would be administered.[99]

---

[96] Richardson, J.S., Hispaniae, p. 70

[97] Livy, 31.1.6

[98] Livy, 33.27

[99] For more details about one praetor see Ibid., p. 68-74 and Richardson, J.S., 'The Romans in Spain', p. 46-49

Another interesting change that was occurring around this time can be seen in Livy's 'History of Rome', book 32 and 33 that describes Hispania as two different provinces. The influence of geography on political and municipal organizations was too great for one man to govern, as mention before. At the same time without provincial boundaries for administrative purposes the entire region that would be governor as one enormous province would become an administrative abyss. So, in 198 BC the *comitia centuriata* elected two men for the praetorship of Hispania with the decreed that the newly elected praetors should determine the boundaries of their *provinciae* to better administer Hispania.[100] The titles given to these new provinces were Hispania Ulterior ("Farther Hispania") and Hispania Citerior ("Nearer Hispania"). The use of farther and nearer is in reference to how close these provinces were near to Rome.

The newly formed Roman province consisted of:

Hispania Ulterior, a region of Baetica roughly located in the Guadalquivir valley of modern Spain and extending to all of Lusitania (present day Portugal south of the Minho River) and Gallaecia and Asturias (presently Northern Portugal and Galicia (Spain)) Cantabria and Basque Country.

Hispania Citerior, a region encompassing of southeastern and northeastern coast of Hispania including the Ebro valley of modern Spain.

The division, which occurred in 197 BCE, was not only created to conduct administrative business, but also to have an area of operation so praetors would be able to control the constant fighting against the Iberians along the Ebro River Valley, as well as the Iberians to the south which seems to have attacked or raided Roman settlements in spurts

[100] Livy 32.28.11; Pliny the Elder, Naturalis Historia, 3.5.56 Beside these two men four other were elected as praetors; one each was sent to Sicily and Sardinia the other two were positioned as *praetor urbanus* of the city of Roman and *praetor peregrine* to deal with issues about foreigners.

throughout this period. Though little is known about how much fighting went on, we can only assume the reason for this split was that it would be easier for the praetors to control their respective areas to conduct military operations to quell native rebellions, instead of chasing Iberians all over the countryside.

According to J.S. Richardson's research on the subject of Rome's early administrative development much is still unknown, so it must be assumed that the governing patterns set by the Scipios continued.[101] What can be stated for sure is that the basic administrative arrangement that had been installed was to pay, feed and supply the army, but once the coastal Iberian population had been somewhat pacified other administrative institutions were established and later modified. The difference between the pre- and post- 197 BCE regime in Spain was that at first it was an ad hoc government due to the war begin fought against Carthage and the uncertainty of duration of Rome's occupation of the Iberian Peninsula. But after the defeat of the Carthaginians and the discovery of the vast wealth in fertile land and minerals, and upon realizing how long Rome had committed itself to the region, Rome decided it would alter its commitment in Hispania from temporary to permanent. [102] Thus, the two Hispanias were created.

ROMAN OCCUPTION OF HISPANIA

After Scipio's departure from Hispania in 206 BCE, the decade that followed was a period in which the developments of the previous years finally began to blossom. The crucial decision during those early years was whether or not to remain in Spain. But once the decision was made to stay, it simply remained that those who were entrusted with the task of governing the Spanish province should continue to maintain law and order, ensure the upkeep of military forces under their command and extend Roman control throughout the entire peninsula. At first this was achieved by the continuation of the ad hoc methods of governing,

---

[101] for details see Richardson, J.S., Hispaniae, p. 54-60.

[102] For a more detailed account see: Richardson, J.S., The Romans in Spain, p.2-6, 41-50.

employed by the three Scipios, but as time went on, modifications were added on until a permanent system of government was in place.

Within this newly established province and the beginnings of a stable government, the Romans managed to emplace the *ager publicus.*[103] With this law they could found colonies and set the status quo of conquered cities and towns. The Romans also continued to integrate the *stipendium.* Also implemented obligations to provide local products and provisions in the event Roman legionnaires went on military campaigns, including supplies for auxiliary troops. Mining towns were allowed to mint coinage of bronze and silver to facilitate payments of tribute, for the acquisition of food, and salaries for the military. [104] Concerning the Iberian tribes, the Romans found it impossible to deal with the leaders of each tribe, even though the tribes had a highly personal system of allegiances among themselves. To deal with them, the Romans developed a loose non-formal series of arrangements and alliances that would serve the Romans adequately during this time period.

In 198 BCE, two new governors were elected. These newly elected praetors were given senatorial power to govern the province, but overall management of the provinces was supervised by the Senate.[105] The two men that were elected to Hispania were C. Sempronius Tuditanus for Hispania Citerior and M. Helvius in Hispania Ulterior.[106] Arriving in Hispania in 197 BCE, each praetor brought with them 8,000 infantry

---

[103] Stephenson, Andrew, PH.D., Public Lands and Agrarian Laws of the Roman Republic, Baltimore, John Hopkins Press, July-August 1891, Sec. 3. Ager publicus is the Latin for the acquiring of public land for the Roman Republic via expropriation from Rome's enemies.

[104] Hill, G.F., Notes on the ancient coinage of Hispania Citerior, New York, 1931; Gundan y Lascaris, A.M. de, La Moneda Iberica, Madrid, 1980; Crawford, M.H., 'The Financial Organization of Republican Spain', Numismatic Chronicle #9, 1969, p. 79-93; id, 'Money and Exchange in the Roman World', Journal of Roman Studies #60, 1970, 40-48; Knapp, R.C., 'The Date and Purpose of the Iberian Denarii', Numismatic Chronicle # 17, 1977, p. 1-18

[105] Mackie, Nicola, 'Local Administration in Roman Spain', British Archaeological Report International Series #172, 1983. This would later be reverted back to the praetors.

[106] Livy, 32.28.3

and 400 cavalry, to replace the army that had been serving in Hispania prior to their arrival.[107] With orders from the Senate, these two men had the task of demarcating the borders between the two provinces, which according to A. Schulten, the division was established between Carthago-Nova and Baria (modern Villaricos) and would move north-east towards the Gaul (modern France) and north west to the far reaches of the Ebro River and south-west along the Spanish coast toward Gibraltar.[108]

Though these men had senatorial arrangements, the ability of the praetors to pursue their own policies to get the Iberians to produce more grain, clothing and money began to enrage many of the tribes. Though not connected, the indigenous peoples of both provinces simultaneously rebelled against the Roman government. The heads of these rebellions were two tribal kings, Culchas, a former Roman ally from the Punic Wars from Baetica (today Andalusia) and Luxinus, a ruler of two kingdoms in the north-western sector of the Guadalquivir Valley in the south.[109]

Late in the year 197 BCE, a letter arrived in Rome from praetor M. Helvius in Ulterior, reporting that large-scale fighting between Roman forces and the two tribal kings, Culchas and Luxinius, had broken out. According to the dispatch, fifteen to seventeen fortified towns had taking sides with Culchas.[110] While Luxinius had strong support from the cities of *Carmo* (modern-day Carmona) and *Bardo* (location unknown). To make matters worse the Malacini and Sexetani tribes from the southeast coast of Hispania and several other southern tribes within Baetica decided to join Culchas and Luxinus's cause.The rebellion overtook the entire eastern and southern region.[111] It seemed

---

[107] Livy 32.28.14

[108] For details see Schulten, A., Fontes Hispaniae Antiquae Vol.III, XI Vols., Barcelona, 1935-1987, p.174

[109] Livy 33.21.6-9

[110] Livy, 33.21.8

[111] Livy 33.21.6-9; Tsirkin, J.B.. Romanization of Spain; socio-political aspect, Gerion #10, Universidad Complutense de Madrid, 1992, p. 205-242, p. 214-217 is about Culchas and Luxinius.

that the rebellion would spread further inland that even the Phoenicians on central southern coast of Hispania and the inhabitants of the region between the Guadalquivir and Guadiana rivers were going to join in.[112]

Although fighting had been going on for some time, the rebellion was not considered by the Senate as full-scale war, because in their eyes the rebellion was small-scale for up there had been little fighting. The praetors went on campaign and both earned a *ovatio* when they returned to Rome after their governship.[113] This was also reaffirmed when Helvius, who had a successful campaign against the Iberians, returned to Rome with a considerable amount of loot: 12,675 pounds of silver and 17,023 Spanish denarii,[114] while L. Stertinius brought with him 50,000 pounds of silver.[115]

Soon things would change. At the end of 197 BCE, another letter arrived in Rome stating that the governor of Citerior, C. Sempronius Tuditanus's forces had been defeated and that the proconsul had been mortally wounded.[116] With the news of the Roman defeat against the Iberians and the death of a praetor which may have been due to the small reduction of troops that was forced upon them by the Senate due to military operational needs elsewhere;[117] the situation changed.

In 196 BCE two new praetors were elected, Q. Fabius Buteo (Ulterior) and Q. Minucius Thermus[118]. Arriving in Hispania, they quickly

---

[112] Tsirkin,J.B., The Phoenician Civilization in Roman Spain, Gerion #3, Universidad Complutense de Madrid, 1985, p. 245-270

[113] Richardson, J.S., Hispaniae, p. 79.

[114] Livy 34.10.3

[115] 33.27.3

[116] Livy 33.25.5, thought the letter stated he was mortally wounded he ended up dying from his wounds.

[117] For these soldiers were probably needed in the east to fight in the **Second Macedonian War** (200–196 BC) which was fought between Macedonia, led by Philip V of Macedon vs Rome.

[118] Livy, 33.26.2; Sumner, G.V., 'Proconsuls and provinciae in Spain, 218 – 195 BC', *Arethusa* 3 (1970) 85-108; Develin, R, 'The Roman command structure in Spain', Kilo 62 (1980) 355-367

recognized the difficult plight that the army faced, and requested the Senate to deploy an additional Roman legion to each province. The consuls were ordered to furnish the two praetors with one legion each from the four new legions that were recently raised and also 4,000 allied infantry and 300 cavalry.[119] When these two men arrived in Hispania, Minucius quickly went into action against two Iberian chief, Budar and Baesadines of the Turboletae tribe.[120] Despite some success by Minucius, the Romans did not meet with rapid success. With the arrival of Roman reinforcements, the two Iberian chiefs were defeated at Turda, which resulted in 12,000 Iberian warriors killed and Budar being captured.[121]

---

119 Livy 33.26.3

120 Livy, Ab Urbe Condita, 24.44.4; Appian 10.36 The Turboletae were a warlike people whose tribal name later became a byword for unruly behavior (trouble), the Turboletae were a constant source of trouble to most of its neighbors. Not only did they harass the Belli and Titti, but also raided Iberian tribes in southeastern Hispania particularly the Edetani city-state of Saguntum. As former allies of the Carthaginians the Turboletae actively participated in the incident that triggered the Second Punic War, the siege of Saguntum in 219 – 218 BC. The Turboletae assisted the Carthaginian troops in the final assault and looting of the city, slaughtering a great deal of its inhabitants. After the Second Punic War the exhausted Turboletae sued for peace, on which the Roman Senate forced them to pay a huge compensation to the surviving citizens of Saguntum. However, the resentment fuelled by the heavy tribute imposed, coupled with the destruction of their capital city in 212 BC, (212 BC when the Romans and their Edetani allies invaded Turboletania, seized the capital Turba and razed it to the ground, selling his residents to slavery Livy, Ab Urbe Condita, 24.42.11) may account for the Tuboletae revolt of 196 BC.

121 Livy 33.44.4-5; Turda sometimes pronounced Turta or as some may believe that this city was the ancient legendary city of Tartessos. This harbor city is believed to have been located at the mouth of the Guadalquivir River. Other scholars claim that Turta was not a city but the name of a ancient region in Andalucía. The remaining Turboletae population appears to have been either obliterated or simple assimilated into the neighboring tribe for their devastated lands were divided among the Bastetani and Edetani, resulting in their total disappearance from the historical record. Montenegro, Angel, Historia de España 2 – colonizaciones y formaciŏn de los pueblos prerromanos 1200 – 218 a.C., Editorial Gredos, Madrid 1989; Motoza Francisco Burillo, Los Celtìberos – Etnias y Estados, Crìtica, Grijalbo Mondadori, S.A. Barcelona 1998

However, before the year drew to a close, the Celtiberians began mustering a new army. This army was so massive that it became apparent that it would take more than the two Roman legions to deal with them. So, at the beginning of 195 BCE, when the annual allocations for the provinces came before the Senate, it decided that because the rebellion in Spain seemed to have escalated into a full-scale war, it was necessary to send reinforcements commandeered by an experienced consular general. [122] The consul who was elected and given *consular imperium* to "govern" Spain took with him two legions, 15,000 allied infantry, 800 cavalry and 20 warships to assist in ending this war. The entire operation, as well as command over the two praetors, would fall onto M. Porcius Cato to resolve the Iberian problem. [123]

Along with Cato, the newly elected praetors P. Manlius (Citerior) and Ap. Claudius Nero (Ulterior) arrived in Hispania. The Senate still worried that Cato's army was not large enough to subdue the Iberians, sent another addition force of 2,000 infantry and 200 cavalry to reinforce Cato's army.[124] Having sailed with a fleet of 20 warships from Portus Lunae, north of Pisa,[125] Cato moved south by sea towards Emporion (modern-day Ampurias), eliminating an Iberian stronghold that dominated the Massiliote port of Rhoda (modern-day Rosas).[126] From Rhoda, he sailed onto Emporion.

He disembarked and quickly set-up several camps outside Emporion, with the intention of ending the insurrection as quickly as possible.[127] From Livy's work, he seems to suggest the reason why Cato chose Emporion was because the city comprised of Greek and Roman settlers and pro-Roman Iberians and a seaport. The city welcomed the Romans.

---

[122] Livy, 33.44.5

[123] Livy 33.43.1-5

[124] Livy 33.43.7-8

[125] Portus Lunae later became Luni but 1059 its population abandon the city due to constant attacks by Muslim pirates and a pitch battle that was fought there against the Muslims and forces from the of Pisa and Genoa.

[126] Livy 34.8.4-7; Dennis, George, The Cities and Cemeteries of Etruria, John Murray, London, 1848.

[127] Appian, 40.161

Within Emporion's population there was an element of Roman colonists that help in the matter of influencing the locals into accepting the Romans.[128] Once his army had made camp, Cato occupied his time gathering intelligence on the enemy's strength and position, as well as conducting a number of forced marches and tactical training exercises around his base at Emporion. Trained, Cato was able to conduct several raids into the countryside to provide the necessary food and supply for his troops. So successful were the raids into enemy territory that he was able to dismiss the *redemptores* (Roman merchants who followed the army), and sent them back to Rome with the remark, "War feeds itself."[129]

During his short stay at Emporion, Cato was approached by three envoys from Bilistages, the chief of the Ilergetes, one being the chief's son.[130] They reported that they were under heavy hostile pressure from a neighboring tribe who had recently attacked one of their settlements. Without Roman assistance they could not hold out much longer and with the help of 3,000 Roman legionnaires they could dislodge the enemy.[131] Unwilling to divide his army and having information that an enemy force was close by, Cato devised an elaborate ruse. He announced to the ambassadors, despite his own difficulties, that he would help them and issued the order to prepare the ships so that a force of 3,000 men would deploy. Satisfied on seeing the Roman soldiers boarding the ship, the ambassadors left to report to their king that the Romans were coming to their rescue. But as soon as the Ilergetes were gone, Cato ordered his men to disembark and marched them into winter quarters 3 miles (5 km) from Emporion.[132] The intention of this ruse, according to Frontinus, was to discourage Ilergetes's enemies from further conducting their operations once they received news that the Romans were moving

[128] Livy 34.9.1-10; Almagro, M, Las Fuentes escritas refrentes a Ampurias, Barcelona, 1951, 47-60

[129] Livy 34.9.11-13

[130] Livy 34.11.2

[131] Livy, 34.11.3

[132] Livy, 34.11, 34.12 and 34.13

troops into the area. At the same time, it boosted the morale of the Ilergetes to hold out a little longer.[133]

This deception was quickly followed by a military encounter soon after setting up a *castra hiberna* (winter quarters). Cato marched his army from Emporion and began to lay the enemy's fields and towns to waste with fire and sword, spreading terror, while his army plundered the towns scattering the local inhabitants in all directions.[134] According to Livy, compared to other Roman generals, Cato generally marched at night in order to cover as much ground as they could between their camp and the enemy. These night marches were perhaps done this way, so as not to give away their location, in addition these night movements were conducted to take the enemy by surprise when contact was made. This kind of maneuver was at first a training exercise for the new soldiers, but during one of these training exercises an enemy force was encounter, which led to the capture of numerous prisoners causing the enemy to no longer venture outside their fort's defenses at night.[135]

On another such night march, Livy writes that Cato brought his army upon an enemy camp. After positioning his troops, he waited to make his move at daybreak, at which time he launched one legion against the Iberians. Alerted, the Iberians drew up men to fight the Romans. The Roman cavalry, which held the flanks, was the first into action. Charging head on into the enemy's ranks, the cavalry immediately ran into trouble. The cavalrymen that held the right wing of the charge were quickly repulsed that their hasty retirement created alarm and panic amongst the Roman infantry, who were moving towards the enemy's battle formation. Seeing this, Cato resorted to psychological warfare by ordering two cohorts to be taken around the enemy's right, to show themselves in their rear before the infantry became engaged. This menacing Roman presence to the enemy's rear made the battle even for

---

133 Frontinus, *Strategemata*, 4.7.31, Frontinus states that the trick actually worked. See Richardson, J.S., Hispaniae, p. 53-54; 67-68 about the Ilergetes frequent alliances and defections.

134 Livy, 34.13.2

135 Livy, 34.13.3-9

the enemy had to now worry about being attacked from the rear. Still, the Roman right wing had become so demoralized that many of the men panicked and took flight, making it difficult for the Romans to hold the line. The left wing, on the other hand, was pressing back the barbarian's frontline. The Roman cohorts to the barbarian's rear were creating panic amongst them. After hard hand-to-hand fighting, the Iberians were forced back into their camp, at which point Cato sent in his reserve legion to storm the fortifications. Surveying the enemy's position for a weak point, Cato discovered that the defenders were vulnerable at the left gate of their camp; at this point he directed the *hastati* and *principes* of his second legion to concentrate their attack on that position. The defenders who were holding the gate could not withstand the attack any longer and abandoned it, leaving an opening for the Romans. All further attempts to retain their camp were discarded and after some fighting, the Iberians flung away their arms and standards and surrendered.[136] Livy states that many were killed, especially the Iberians for on seeing that they were facing defeat, the Iberians crowded together at the narrow space of the gates in an attempt to enter their camp, while Roman soldiers cut the enemy from behind.

After the battle, the Romans plundered the camp and harried the local fields in search of supply until the signal was given for his men to stop. Allowed several hours to rest, Cato then decided to move his victorious army to Tarraco. Advancing uninterrupted along the coast due south, Cato's plunderous march through enemy territory scattered many tribesmen over a wide extent of the country causing many inhabitants in the area to submit to his rule. Being that they did not fight Cato's army, he addressed them in kind terms and dismissed them to their homes. As he continued his advance, delegates from various communities met with him, only to surrender. By the time he reached Tarraco, the whole north side the Ebro River had been subjugated and the Roman soldiers who had been made prisoners through various mishaps were brought by the natives as a gift to the consul.[137]

---

[136] Battle details comes from Livy 34.14, 34.15

[137] Livy, 34.16.4-5-9; Appian 41.167-170

This was seen as an amazing victory. Livy, goes on to say the reason for the victory was because Cato had led his army into hostile territory, placing his army in a dangerous position far from his ships, supplies and his own camp, where the only thing his men could trust was each other, their courage and skills to survive such a perilous campaign. The second reason was his strategic maneuver against the Iberian encampment, at which point he decided to throw his reserve cohorts to the enemy's rear. And thirdly, was his order for a second legion to advance in battle formation right up to the camp's gate, while the rest of his troops were scattered in pursuit of the retreating enemy.[138] Overall this seems to have been a successful campaign for by the end of it, according to Plutarch, Cato claimed he had subdued over 300 Iberian towns.[139]

While encamped at Tarraco, rumors soon spread among the Iberians that Cato intended to invade Turdetania in the south and march against the Bergistani.[140] From these false rumors, seven fortified cities belonging to the Bergistani decided to revolt. But as quickly as it started, the Bergistani rebellion was suppressed without any serious fighting. But no soon after Cato had returned to his base at Tarraco and before he made any further plan to advance south into Turdetani, these same people for some unknown reason (not mentioned in the ancient texts) again revolted and again they were subdued, but this time they were not treated so leniently as before, for Cato had sold a large portion of them into slavery, to discourage any repetition of revolt.[141]

Cato's campaign in and around Emporion and the Ebro River Valley has received several different evaluations from scholars. Some scholars, those favorable to Cato, assume that he was in the right in conducting military operation in the area to quell the troublesome Iberians for the area was supposedly the heartland of rebellion, which had beset the

[138] Livy, 34.16.2-4

[139] Plutarch, Cato maior, 10.3

[140] Livy 34.16.15; Astin, A.E., Cato the Censor, Oxford, 1978, p. 304-05; Turdetania was a region covering the Guadalquivir River Valley which coincided with the former territories of ancient Tartessos. Bergistani was a tribe that live around foothills of the Pyrenees

[141] Livy, 34.16.16-17

province for two years prior to Cato's arrival. But there is little reason to believe this. If these people had been in open conflict with the Romans before Cato's arrival, it is extraordinary that they took no action against him when he first arrived in Emporion.[142] According to Professor J.S. Richardson's research, he claims that although the first signs of hostility came from the local tribes, the Romans were at fault, due to their repeated plundering expeditions and raids on friendly Iberian villages mounted by Cato, for the purpose of training and provisioning his army. If Cato had not inflamed the local tribes, rebellions in the areas under Roman control would have not occurred. But it seems that the self-appraising Cato wanted a magnificent victory, so he chose where to fight and against who to win against even if they were Rome's allies. Not only was it important to be a successful commander and consul in the provinces, but his success had to be recognized by Rome if he was to advance his military and political career.

While Cato was putting down the Bergistani rebellion, he ordered praetor P. Manlius to gather an army and march inland towards Turdetania to take control and resolve the rebellious Turdetani.[143] With this in mind, the question arises what was Manlius doing in Ulterior if he was praetor of Citerior? Although the answer, according to the ancient texts is not so clear, it seems that part of the answer is based on location of Turdentani. Turdentani in Roman geography was in the Valley of the Baetis, and although most of the region was in Ulterior, a part of its northern lands was situated in southern part of Citerior. With this said, it seems to indicate that Manlius pushed the war across the provincial boundary.

The second part of the answer is perhaps that Praetor Appius Claudius Nero may have requested Manlius's assistance to crush the rebellion. But according to Livy, Nero is mentioned only three times in connection with the events in Spain during 195 BCE.[144] One must assume that Nero

---

[142] Richardson, J.S., Hispaniae, p. 84

[143] Livy, 34.17.1 This army consisted of not only his but also a part of praetor Appius Claudius Nero; Livy, 33.25 and 33,44 The Turdetani rebellion had been going on for at least a year when Minucius Thermus was praetor of Citerior.

[144] Livy 33.43.7; 34.10.1-6; 34.17.1

had left the province to fulfill another assignment for the absence of any mention of Nero in the report of the fighting against the Turdentani confirms this. If Manlius was campaigning in Ulterior, it is difficult to imagine that Nero would allow someone else to command his troops and conduct a campaign within the province assigned to him.[145] Perhaps it can be said that Nero left the province a few months after he arrived, giving command to Manlius, taking another position elsewhere in the Empire.[146]

Initially Manlius had no difficulty with the Turdentani for they were considered the least warlike of all the Iberian tribes.[147] Nevertheless, trusting to their numbers, the Turdentani ventured to oppose the Romans. When both armies met, the Romans began the battle with a cavalry charge that threw the Turdetani into disorder. This was followed by an infantry attack against the Turdentani line. The Romans decimated them for the Turdentani warriors were hardly a contest for seasoned Roman troops, who were familiar with the enemy's tactics.[148] Still, that battle did not end the rebellion for the Turdetani hired a force of 10,000 Celtiberian mercenaries prepared to carry on hostilities.[149]

Cato, perturbed by the Bergistani uprisings and receiving news of what Manlius was up against, began to be convinced that all Iberian tribes would do the same whenever they had the chance. So, he decided to disarm the entire Iberian population north of the Ebro River. This step aroused such bitter feeling that many Iberians, according to Livy, supposedly committed suicide because they believed that life was not worth living without the right to possess arms.[150] On hearing this news, Cato summoned all the tribal chiefs to meet him and informed them that it was not in the interest of Rome to see the Iberians suffer, and that it

145 Briscoe, John, A Commentary on Livy, books XXXIV-XXXVII, Oxford Univ. Press, Oxford 1981, p.80

146 Livy and Polybius mentions an Appius Claudius Nero who was stationed as a legate in Greece.

147 Livy 34.17.2; Strabo, 3.2.15

148 Livy 34.17.3

149 Livy, 34.17.4

150 Livy 34.17.5-6

would be in their best interest to abstain from hostilities. After giving them a few days for deliberation, they were summoned to a second conference, which produced no answer. Angered by their response, Cato announced that he would level their city walls in a single day. Suddenly, some tribal chiefs gave in, while other did not. Those who were noncompliant suffered the consequences; their walls were torn down at which point they soon surrendered with the exception of the wealthy Iberian city of Segestica (ruined city near Zaragoza), which was taken by storm.[151]

The Celtiberian mercenaries, employed by the Turdetani, further added difficulties to praetor Manlius' campaign. Manlius wrote to Cato for assistance. The consul immediately marched his legions into the region and found on arrival that the Celtiberians and the Turdetani were occupying separate camps. Encountering Turdetanian patrols, skirmishes broke out; resulting in Romans victories, however desultory the fighting was.[152] During the campaign, the Celtiberians were treated differently and respected for their fighting skills:[153] To stop the Celtiberians, Cato sent a military tribune to them with three choice: join the Romans, receive double the pay that they were getting from the Turdetanians; go home under a guarantee from the Roman government that they would not suffer for having joined the enemy, or, if they were in any case bent on war, fix a time and place where they could decide the matter by arms. The Celtiberian leader asked for a day's grace for consultation. When the Celtiberian war council met, no decision was made because of indecisiveness. While the question of war or peace was still in suspense at the council meeting, the Romans brought up provisions from the fields and Turdentani from fortified villages to their own encampment. Being that Cato could not induce the enemy to fight during this lull, for he had made a bargain with them, he secretly sent some lightly-armed cohorts on a plundering expedition into Celtiberian country, which had not yet suffered from Roman encroachment. At the

---

[151] Livy, 34.17.10-14

[152] Livy, 34.19.1-3

[153] During the second Punic War Romans and Carthaginians had employed many Celtiberians and Lusitanian mercenaries.

same time, he clandestinely marched to Segontia (modern day Sigüenza, Spain) with plans of attacking it, after receiving information that a large amount of supplies belonging to the Celtiberians mercenaries had been left there for safekeeping.[154] On Cato's return from his secret raid, he discovered that the situation with the Celtiberians had not changed. Being that winter was coming, he left the situation as it was and ended the campaign season by paying the army with the captured plunder. The following spring, he set out with seven cohorts for another expedition north of the Ebro River, leaving four legions under Manlius' command as a show of force in Celtiberian country.[155]

The next venture consisted of a small army of the seven cohorts which he marched north into the Ebro River Valley to conduct separate campaigns against the Sedetani, Ausetani, Lacetani and the Suessetani.[156] After fighting, the Sedetani, Ausetani, and the Suessetani near the Ebro River, a number of Iberian towns surrendered to Cato. Of the four tribes that Cato went up against the Lacetani, a remote forest tribe remained in arms, partly through their love of fighting and their fear of retribution from the tribes friendly to Rome, amongst whom they had raided while Cato was occupied with the Turdetani.[157] It was for this reason – their raiding – that he attacked them. Cato halted his men a little less than half a mile from an unnamed Lacetani town. Leaving a cohort to guard his camp with strict orders not to move until he returned, he led the rest of his force around to the other side of the town. His auxiliaries, mostly Suessetani (now allies), were ordered to advance up to the city's walls for the assault. As soon as the Lacetani recognized the Suessetani arms and standards and remembering how they often raided their fields with impunity, they flung open the city gates and rushed out to attack them.

Cato expecting this and seeing what was happening, quickly galloped to the enemy's city walls to see if he would be seen by the enemy.

---

154 Livy, 34.19.12

155 Livy 34.19.12; Astin, A.E., Cato the Censor, Oxford Univ. Press, Oxford, 1978, p. 43-46

156 Livy, 34.20.1

157 Livy, 34.20.2

Successful, he signaled to his men to come forward. Along the city's wall and through the open gate they went, as the defenders had forgotten to close the gate, when they rushed out in a mad rage in pursuit of the Suessetani. Before the Lacetani realized what was happening the town had passed quietly into Cato's hands. On seeing this diabolical ruse, the Romans had inflicted upon them, they had nothing left but surrender.[158]

These accounts show Cato's ability in deceiving friend and foe by gaining maximum effect with minimum effort. Through these reports, his actions could be seen as propaganda for career advancement for it shows that his tactical skills were not merely to suppress rebellions, but to make resurgence impossible, and to save manpower for it would be easier to deceive an enemy than to spill blood. As for reading these accounts, one might think of Cato as an ambitious militaristic politician, but there are some accounts on how he also acted with compassion, such as when he rescued the town of Vergium from an army of brigands.

According to Livy, Cato led his army against Vergium (modern-day Berga, Spain), a fortified town which served as a haunt and shelter for brigands who were in the habit of raiding the peaceable districts of the province. Vergestanus, the town's chief, came to Cato and ask for his help. Once Cato had come up with a plan, he directed Vergestanus to return home. When the bandits returned from a raiding expedition and settled down, Cato made his move. On seeing the Romans approaching the town walls, they went into a frenzy and readied themselves for battle. When the Romans reached the city's walls, Vergestanus carried out his instructions to seize the citadel with his sympathizers and open the main gate. By the time the brigands realized what was happening, they found themselves caught in the middle. On the one side, the brigands faced the Romans who were scaling the walls, and on the other side the townspeople began to arm themselves and joined the fighting, while several townsmen opened the main gate to allow the Romans in. When the consul had gained possession of the town, he gave orders for those who had held the citadel to be set free and to retain their property; the

[158] Livy 34.20.3-9

rest of the townsfolk who had sided with the brigand were sold into slavery and the surviving bandits were summarily executed.[159]

The subjugation of the Iberian people was a bit more difficult for Cato than it had been for those generals who had served in Spain before him. The reason is that prior to the Second Punic War, the Carthaginian treated the Iberians as second-class citizens, but when the Romans came over to the Iberian Peninsula many tribes saw the Romans as liberators and allies; thus, many tribes sided with the Romans. But after the war, Iberian attitudes changed for the Romans were now exploiting them. So, by the time Cato arrived in Hispania, the Iberians had had enough. On his arrival in Hispania, some 40,000 tribesmen were up in arms.[160] Had it not been for Cato's arrival, their powers of resistance would have perhaps exhausted Rome's involvement in Hispania. But Cato was a man of such force, energy and ambition that he took up and executed single-handedly the greatest and smallest tasks alike, changing the outcome of what might have happened in Hispania.

Cato's time in Hispania is of importance in examining why the native populace came to detested Rome's presence on their beloved land. The reason for this statement is because of the abundance of information in Livy's, Appian's and Cato's own writing. On analyzing the historical accounts, it suggests that the people Cato fought were not actively opposed to the Romans, until he arrived and savagely plundered and ravaged their territory in order to supply his coffers and equip, feed and pay the army. There is no doubt that Cato was a successful commander, but whether his campaigns were necessary and to what extent it helped pacify Hispania is questionable, but invaluable information.

The ampleness of sources makes it possible to see how Cato governed the provinces.

The sources show that his style of government was harsh on the locals, making this one of the reasons why the Iberians disliked the Romans.

---

[159] Livy 34.21.1-8

[160] Appian, 40.161

As with everything else in the administration of Hispania at this time, relations with the Iberian tribes lacked any formal legal structure that would later become a feature in the life of the province. What made matters worse for the following praetors and even those before Cato, is that their rule shows the apparent disregard for the alliances previously made by former commanders. But in some cases, instead of making a *foedus* (treaty) to solidify a treaty as official, the Romans at first built a *societas* (a partnership/alliance) with the tribes, even though they could not be fully trusted when the Romans needed them to come to their aid. Although there were several existing treaties such as with Saguntum and Gades the use of the full-scale *foedus* was not implemented.[161] Although there had been new alliances, which in reality were shaky; it still signaled to the Iberians that Rome's word was not to be trusted. The results of these unsteady treaties, which were satisfactory for Cato, however, were unlikely to gratify Rome's allies or awe her enemies. Though Cato claimed that Hispania was pacified by the time he left in 194 BCE, the province over the next 50 years was more rebellious than before. [162]

On the other hand, Cato's presence saw the establishment of some new basic financial arrangements that would improve Rome's and Hispania's future.[163] The coastal territory along with the Ebro River Valley had been finally subdued, and a systematic policy of economic exploration, especially in mining had been emplaced by Cato.[164] As for the administrative functions of the provinces, Cato made few or no alterations except the regularizing of tribute (*stipendium)* and the institution of income from the silver and iron mines.[165] Also throughout

---

[161] A *foederatus* did not identify a tribe that was bound by a treaty (***foedus***), who were neither Roman colonies nor had they been granted Roman citizenship (*civitas*), but were expected to provide a contingent of warriors when trouble arose. For more information see: Richardson, J.S., Hispaniae, p. 58- 61, 73-74

[162] Livy 34.21.7

[163] Nostrand, J.J. van, Roman Spain, An Economic Survey of Ancient Rome #3, Baltimore, MD, 1937, p.126-137

[164] Livy 34.21.7

[165] Bernhardt, R., 'Die Entwicklung römischer Amici et Socii zu Civitates Liberae in Spainien', Historia 24 (1975), p. 411-424; Richardson, J.S, 'The Spanish Mines",

the ancient accounts, we see Cato's desire to carefully not overspending his budget by demonstrating his refusal to buy food and supplies for the army; instead he seized it from the locals.[166] According to Livy, in his speech for consulship, Cato proclaimed how he was able to cut on his expense via to the quantity of booty he had taken.[167] This evidence also shows that he introduced measures which brought large sums of money from the iron and silver mines throughout the provinces.[168] Although Hispania was governed by an ad hoc government, it was economically successful, even though at times it was blended with violence and opportunism; after all Cato did not come to Hispania to reorganize the administration of the province, but came to fight a 'war' and win victories to further advance his career and expand the Roman realm.[169]

By the end of his tenure in Hispania, Cato claimed that the province was at peace. On his return to Rome, the Senate, in recognition of this, voted him a three-day *supplicatio* and a triumph.[170] The Senate also decided to withdraw two of the four legions so as to celebrate Cato's triumph and to show the Roman population that Hispania had been pacified.[171] However, as the following years demonstrated, the Senate was wrong in believing Cato proclamation.

In 194, in the aftermath of Cato's campaigns and Manlius praetorship, two new praetors were sent to Hispania. P. Cornelius Scipio Nasica (son of Cn. Scipio who had been killed while on campaign in Hispania in 211

Journal of Roman Studies 66 (1976) p. 139-152.

166 Livy, 34.9.12-13

167 Cato, 51-59

168 Livy. 34.21.7; Schulten, A., 'Fontes Hispaniae antiquae, Vol 3' 4 vols., Barcelona, 1934-37, p.185, R.Way and M. Simmons, 'A Geography of Spain and Portugal', London, 1962, p. 155-158.

169 Livy, 34.9.12-13; Richardson, J.S., 'Hispaniae, p. 93

170 Livy 34.21.7-8, 42.1; 46.2-3; A thanksgiving to the gods decreed by the Senate. For more information see http://en.wikipedia.org/wiki/Supplicatio

171 Livy 34.43.3, 43.8 and 35.1; Astin, A.E., Cato the Censor, Oxford Univ. Press, Oxford, 1978, p. 47-48; Richardson, J.S., 'The triumph, the praetor and the Senate in the early second century BC', Journal of Roman Studies #65, 1975, p. 60-62; Richardson, J.S., 'Hispaniae, p. 95

BC) was sent to Ulterior and Sextus Digitius (who had fought alongside Scipio Africanius during the 2nd Punic War) was assigned to govern Citerior.[172] In the aftermath of Cato's controversial 'victories', the newly elected governors had to face the enemy with forces less than half of their predecessor. Because of Cato's ruthless campaign these men had to deal with several rebellions that began to erupt all over the country, especially against the Celtiberians, Lusitanians, and several other tribes whose main objective was to defend their rich and productive lands.[173]

During the first few months of Digitius governorship a large-scale rebellion quickly broke out. So large was the rebellion that Digitius could not contain it and was defeated. Digitius's defeat took him somewhere north of the Ebro River to lick his wounds and better prepare his army for another campaign against the skilled warriors of the Celtiberians. Utterly demoralized, the remnants of Digitius's army stayed within the compounds of their camp until more reinforcements could arrive; the Celtiberians had won this rebellion.[174]

Digitius's governorship was saved only by the assistance of Nasica. Livy writes that had it not been for Nasica's victory against the Lusitanians, all of Hispania may have been lost.[175] Nascia's campaign against the Lusitanians, a tribe that was feared among all Iberian tribes, seems to have ended the thought or continuation of the general uprising that was occurring throughout Hispania. According to Livy's account, Nasica's small army attacked a large Lusitanian army of bandits who had completely devastated Roman southern Spain and were on their way home with an immense quantity of plunder. As the story goes, it seems that the Lusitanians had been marching back to Lusitania when the Romans ran into them. At first the spirited Lusitanians threw the Romans into disorder, but soon the fighting evened out as the Romans were able to organize themselves into close and serried ranks. Though they were outnumbered, they fought for several long hours until the

172 Livy, 34.43.11

173 Livy, 35.1

174 Livy 35.1.1-3

175 Livy, 35.1.3

Lusitanian battle line became hampered by the herds of cattle they had with them, and that the Lusitanian warriors began tiring out for they were weary from their long march across the country. During the struggle, the praetor vowed to his staff that he would celebrate Games to Jupiter if he should rout and destroy the enemy. At length, the Roman attack became more insistent and the Lusitanians began to give ground. Finally, they broke and fled, and in hot pursuit which followed, 12,000 enemy warriors were supposedly killed, 540 prisoners taken, and 134 standards captured.[176] Roman losses amounted to 73. Enriched with the spoil of war, which was taken from the enemy, Nasica led his victorious army to the city of Ilipa, which was one of the cities that had been ransacked by the Lusitanians. Upon arriving within the city's walls, he laid out his captured booty in front of the city's folk and allowed them to reclaim their property. The rest of the booty that was unclaimed was handed over to the quaestor for it to be sold and the proceeds distributed among the soldiers.[177] With this large-scale defeat of the most feared tribe in Hispania, the Iberian tribes stopped rebelling and fifty Iberian towns, according to Livy, surrendered to the Romans.[178] Though this battle had stopped the Lusitanians and Celtiberians from further rebelling, it showed that Cato's statement revealed an instability which he had left behind.

Cato's departure from Hispania, transformed many tribal groups that lived within the Roman realm from a nomadic and pastoral lifestyle to a sedentary and agricultural one. On the other hand, Roman occupation harmed many of the tribes' way of life and social classes, especially among the young men who were the future of the tribes. Without a warrior's lifestyle, many youths reverted into becoming mercenaries,

---

[176] Livy 35.1.1-12 For the number of casualties that Livy claims that the Romans inflicted on the Lustiani seem a bit much, for upon further reading into his work every time the Romans encountered another army in battle, according to Livy inflicted thousands of casualties upon the enemy. If this were the case I perhaps would not be here today. The high number of casualties was perhaps used for propaganda purposes. It is likely that during this battle 1,200 were killed instead of 12,000

[177] Livy, 35.1.1-16

[178] Livy, 35.1.4

Roman auxiliaries, bandits or rebels in order to follow their forefather's way of life. Outside Roman occupied territory, fear and rumors of Rome's hand reaching further inland incited other tribes to rebel against the oncoming Roman occupation, such as the Celtiberians and Lusitanians, who lived in the interior and western coast of the Peninsula. The continuation of warfare in areas allegedly pacified by Cato, demonstrated again the effects of how misinformed Rome was due to the distance between Hispania and Rome. The information which had reached the Senate through Cato about the true state of affairs was very different of the reality of what was happening to Roman control in the provinces.[179] This can be seen more clearly during the years of 193 and 192 BCE.

After the battle near Ilipa, there were no further problems with any other tribes for Nasica astonished the tribes that lived in the southern and central part of Hispania by a series of victories due to his generalship and veteran soldiers. The only tribe that constantly caused problems for Nasica during his governship was the Lusitani, who although had just been defeated, continued to cause devastation in the south-western part of Hispania.

It is also interesting to see that during Nasica and Ditigius praetorship we find Nasica, governor of Ulterior, fighting in the northern Meseta while his colleague from Citerior was campaigning in the south. From Livy's writings on the locations where the campaigns took place, it seems that interprovincial boundaries were confined to the coast, and the interior of the country. It seems a commander was free to engage any tribe when opportunity or provocation presented itself.[180] Given the uncoordinated nature of these campaigns, it shows that there was no grand design for the eventual conquest of the Iberian Peninsula.

With the onset of the year 193 BC two new praetors were elected to take over Hispania; Gaius Flaminius went to Hispania Citerior and M.

---

179 Richardson, J.S., 'Hispaniae, p. 96

180 Curchin, Leonard, A., op. cit., p. 31; Richardson, J.S., 'Hispaniae, p. 96

Fulvius Nobilior was allotted Hispania Ulterior.[181] On hearing talk of the poor state of affairs in Hispania, before leaving Rome, Flaminius tried to induce the Senate to assign him one of the City's legions. However, they refused for senior members of the Senate said that their decisions must not depend upon rumors stated by private individuals in the interest of particular magistrates, and that no importance should be attached to anything, but to the dispatches from the praetors and the reports which their officers brought home.[182] If there was a sudden uprising in Spain that needed more men, the praetor had the power from the Senate to raise emergency troops outside Italy. What is not clear in the Senate's statement is where these soldiers would come from. What the Senate had probably in mind when they set up this policy was for these troops to be raised in Spain. But that was improbable because the Roman population in Spain around that time could not have been very large and many of the Iberians, whom were once friendly to Rome were now enemies.

Livy goes on to say that just before Flaminius left Rome, Senator Valerius Antias asserted that he should going to Sicily to enlist men.[183] With this say, the Senate gave him the power to enlist men into his army. As a consequence of this statement, on his way to Spain, he was suddenly carried by a storm to Africa, where he immediately decided to administer the military oath to veteran soldiers who had once belonged to Scipio Africanus's African Army that settled had in North Africa after the Second Punic War. From Africa he was able to conscript an army of 6,200 infantry and 300 cavalrymen, and with that legion - for there was not much to be expected from Digitius' army - Livy said he manage very well.[184]

Seeing the remoteness of Hispania and the limitation which the Senate had with their source of information, one can clearly see the difficulties

---

[181] Livy, 34.55.6 Flaminius was a veteran who fought in Spain during the 2nd Punic War

[182] Livy, 35.2.3

[183] Livy, 35.2.5

[184] Livy, 35.2.2

that the Senate experienced in keeping a close watch on events that occurred within the province and on the activities of the proconsuls.

Arriving in Hispania, the rumors of war that Flaminius so proclaimed turned out to be less of a threat than he had feared. But believing that it would come, he initiated a pre-emptive campaign. His first target was the Oretani tribe, who lived on the southern side of the Sierra Morena, which bordered his province.[185] Though the Oretani lived in the province of Ulterior, Flaminius ignored provincial boundaries and crossed over. Within a few months of setting out onto the Sierra Monena, Flaminius captured the Oretani's main city of Inlucia.[186] While Flaminius was busy campaigning against the Oretani, Nobilior became engaged in a campaign against a confederation of tribes made up of Vaccaei, Vettones and Celtiberians, who came from the northern part of the peninsula near the border of Citerior. In hot pursuit of these Iberians, Nobilior climbed out of the Guadalquivir River Valley and marched to the Sierra Morena, just passing Flaminius and fought the confederation near the city of Toletum.[187] By the time Nobilior took the city of Toletum (modern-day Toledo), he had marched his men some 125 miles (200 km).[188]

The following year, these two praetors again faced the same tribes. Flaminius laid siege to and captured the wealthy and well-fortified Vaccaei city of Licabrum (today it is part of modern-day Córdoba) and defeated their leader Corribilo.[189] Meanwhile, Nobilior fought two successful actions against the Oretani and captured their fortified towns of Vescelia (modern-day Vilches) and Helo (location unknown); while several other towns surrendered voluntarily. While campaigning against the Oretani, he seized two major Carpetani towns; Noliba and Cusibis (locations unknown), and then advanced east as far as the source of the

185 Livy 35.7.5-6

186 Livy 35.7.8; Inlucia or sometimes pronounced Ilucia is an ancient town in central Spain which was situated on the bank of the Guadiana River.

187 Livy 35.7.7

188 Livy 35.7.6-8

189 Livy, 35.22.9

Tagus River.[190] There was a small, but strongly fortified city ofToletum, and whilst he was attacking it, the Vettones sent a large army to relieve it.[191] Like Flaminius, he defeated them in a pitched battle, and after routing them he took their city. But unlike Flaminius, Nobilior invested time to "Romanize" the city, further extending the Roman provincial border. 192 BCE was a successful year for the Romans in both provinces. Because of Nobilior accomplishments in Hispania, he entered Rome in *ovatio* bring with him over 10,000 pounds of silver, 13,000 silver denarii and 127 pounds of gold.[192]

Although provincial borders existed, there was disregard of provincial borders between the two administrative zones because of the enemy's constant movement across borders forcing praetors to conduct many cross-border raids onto each other's territory. Though these men crossed each other's borders, there was no clear pattern of set strategies on how these men and future praetor were to conduct solo military operations or combined operations. The strategy that these men employed was that if a warring tribe was within his province, he would try to contain it, but if the tribe withdrew across the border back to its territory or into the neighboring province the praetor transferred his attention there by pursuing his enemy. It was in the best interest of the Romans to take out the enemy as quickly as possible and not wait for permission from the other praetor because of the difficulty and the length of time communications would take to reach the other praetor. Though these provinces were created for administrative purposes, militarily it was a different story for the land in which the Romans occupied was regarded by the Romans as hostile.

In 191 it was decreed that L. Aemilius Paulus was to take over the governorship. Along with taking command of Nobilior's army, he was also allowed to raise 3,000 fresh infantry soldiers and 300 cavalrymen

---

190 Livy, 35.22.10-11; There is debate whether the town of Helo sometimes pronounced Halon is the modern city of Ayllon. Both these cities have an abundance of ancient ruin to see.

191 Livy, 35.22.11

192 Livy 36.39.1

for service in Hispania Ulterior; the end result was that his new legion was made up of two-thirds of allied troops, the remainder being Roman.[193] A force of reinforcements of the same strength was sent with C. Flaminius, who was to govern Citerior.[194] These two men were stationed in Hispania for two years instead of one year, because of the war against Antiochus in Greece had begun.[195] Nothing more is heard of Flaminius after 192/191 BCE until 187 BCE.[196]

As soon as Paullus set foot in Hispania, he began campaigning against the Bastetani and Lusitanians, two tribes that lived in the eastern part of the newly extended province.[197] These two campaigns were marred by gloom; 6,000 Roman soldiers had fallen. His worse defeat was against the Lusitanians near the town of Lyco (modern-day Pinos Puente); the survivors fled to their camp, which they had difficulty defending. Unable to defend their camp, they abandoned the camp and retreated from the enemy into friendly territory.[198] Once he had reorganized his legions, Paullus immediately set out again and besieged the Bastetani city of Hasta (an ancient town near Jerez de la Frontera). Facing stiff resistance, Paullus was compelled to issue an edict that freed the slaves belonging to the inhabitants of Hasta, and that these newly freed people would hold and possess the land which at that moment they toiled over. News of the edict spread across the city like wildfire that within a few days the city's slave population revolted, and the city surrendered and Paullus kept his promise.[199] Once he had pacified the Bastetani, he set

---

193 Livy 36.2.3

194 Livy, 36.2.3

195 Livy 37.2.11 Because of the war in Greece praetors now had to serve two years in Hispania instead of one. At the end of the war in 188/187 BC it reverted back to one year.

196 Next time we read about Flaminius is when he was elected to the Senate and when he is given the task to fight the Ligurians who had been raiding in Northern Italy.

197 Polybius, 32.8

198 Livy 37.46.8

199 Mommsen, Theodore, Bemerkungen zum Decret des Paullus, Hermes 3, 1869, p. 261-271; Mishulin, A.V., On Interpretation of Aemilius Paullus' Inscription, in Izvestia AN SSSR, 1946, p 166-169, 178-184; *Corpus Inscriptionum Latinarum,*

eyes on the stubborn Lusitanians, which he managed to defeat before his governorship ended in 189. According to Livy, this campaign had a demoralized effect on the Iberian tribes that continued to rebel, as the Romans had inflicted on the Lusitanians 18,000 casualties and had captured 2,300 men, who were later sold into slavery.[200] This report of Paullus' victory was heard across the peninsula and Rome which in turn made matters quieter in Spain, but only temporary.

According to Livy, P. Iunius Brutus quickly replaced L. Baebius Dives, for he had died at Massilia (modern-day Marseille, France) on his way to Hispania.[201] Ready for action, Brutus was surprised that Ulterior was peaceful on his arrival. In Rome, the Senate sent 1,000 Roman infantry and 500 cavalrymen, as well as 6,000 allied infantry and 200 cavalrymen.[202] The same can be said for Flaminius' replacement, L. Plautius Hypsaeus who witness the same situation as Brutus, upon his arrival in Hispania. It seems that Paullus's victory over the Lusitanians had caused a quieting of the Iberian tribes will to fight.[203] On his return to Rome, he received a triumph.[204]

CIL II, 5041; CIL I(2), 614; A. Degrassi, *Inscriptiones Latinae Liberae rei publicae.* Firenze, 1957-1963, no. 514, n. 3; Hasta also pronounced Asta was later changed to Asta Regia during Rome's occupation. Today it is the city of Jerez la Frontera. Guerrero, E.M., Excavaciones de Asta Regia (Mesas de Asta, Jerez). Campaña 1942-43. Acta Arqueológica Hispánica III. Madrid. 1945; Excavaciones de Asta Regia (Mesas de Asta, Jerez). Campaña 1945-46. Informes y Memorias de la Comisaría General de Excavaciones Arqueológicas, nº 22. Madrid. 1950; Excavaciones de Asta Regia (Mesas de Asta, Jerez). Campañas 1949-50 y 1955-56. Centro de Estudios Históricos Jerezanos, no. 19. Jerez. 1962. This information comes from a bronze tablet found near the town of Alcala de los Gazules, 50 miles east of Cadiz

[200] Livy, 37.57.5

[201] Livy 37.57.1 L. Baebius Diveswas elected to take over Paulus' praetorship in Hispania but on his way there he was mortally wounded in an ambushed by the Ligurians

[202] Livy 37.50.11-12

[203] Livy 37.57.6

[204] Livy, 37.5.6

In 188 BCE, L. Manlius Acidinus (Citerior) and C. Atinius (Ulterior) were elected as praetors. With these two newly elected governors, the senate allotted more troops, this time 3,000 soldiers and 200 cavalry were added to each provincial legion stationed in Hispania.[205] Their arrival in Hispania was peaceful, but by 187 BCE, the Celtiberians and Lusitanians were up in arms again and ravaging the lands of the tribes friendly to Rome. The Senate left the new magistrates to deal with the situation.

In late 187, C. Atinius, who was into his second year as praetor, fought a pitched battle with the Lusitanians near Hasta. As many as 6,000 (supposedly) of the enemy were killed; the rest were routed and driven out of their camp. He then led the legions to attack the fortified town of Hasta, which he captured with little difficulty. But while he was approaching the walls somewhat incautiously, he was struck by an arrow and in a few days died of his wound.[206] When Atinius's death was announced in Rome, the Senate quickly elected C. Calpurnius Piso for the job as praetor of Ulterior.[207] With the Senate's advice to hasten his departure, he rapidly sailed out from the port of Luna in northern Italy, so that the province might not be left without an administrator for long.[208]

In Citerior, rebellion broke out; L. Manlius Acidinus end up fighting and indecisive battle with the Celtiberians. A few days later, the Celtiberians, having collected a larger force, attacked the Romans near the town of Calagurris (modern-day Calahorra). There is no explanation as to why, though their numbers were increased, they proved to be the weaker side, for Livy records that 12,000 were killed, 2,000 made prisoners, and the Romans gained possession of their camp and booty.[209]

---

205 Livy 38.35.10

206 Livy, 39.21.1-5

207 Livy, 39.21.6

208 Livy 39.21.7

209 Livy 39.21.8-10; Once again these casualties numbers seem to be exaggerated.

With Piso already in Hispania and the arrival of Acidinus's successor L Quinctius Crispinus, both men decided that at the outset of the new year (186 BC) to combine forces and lead a campaign against the Celtiberians and Lusitanians. The praetors took both their armies into winter quarters.[210] Together they commanded the largest army in Hispania since Cato. Along with the two legions that were permanently based there, an additional 3,000 Roman Legionnaires and 20,000 allied infantry, and 200 Roman and 1,300 allied cavalrymen were sent to Hispania to bring up Roman military presence in Hispania from two to four legions.[211] As amazing as on how this army was, unfortunately Livy does not give details for the levying and distribution of armies of that year.

Once spring arrived, each army left their winter quarters and the two praetors, C. Calpurnius Piso and L. Quinctius Crispinus, marched into Baeturia towards Carpetania. Both men joined forces in preparation to carry out their operations in mutual concert against an enemy encampment in Carpentania. According to Livy, the first battle began at an unknown spot not far from the cities of Dipo (modern-day Elvas, north-east part of Portugal) and Toletum (Toledo) between foraging parties, who were soon reinforced from both camps, and gradually the whole of the two armies were drawn out into battle.[212] Because of the enemy's knowledge of the countryside and the nature of tactics, the Romans were routed and driven back to their base camp. Luckily for the Romans the enemy did not press their demoralized adversaries. Roman losses amounted to 5,000 casualties, while the enemy's were light.[213] Fearing that the camp might be attacked, both commanders withdrew their legions during the night. At dawn, the Iberians attacked the camp's rampart; surprised to find that the camp was empty; they entered it and appropriated what had been left behind in the confusion of the

---

[210] Livy 39.21.10

[211] Livy 39.20.3-4; Brunt, P.A., 'Italian Manpower, 225 BC – 14 AD', Oxford Univ. Press, Oxford, 1971, p.166.

[212] Livy, 39.30.1-2

[213] Livy, 39.30.6

night's withdrawal.[214] After this incident according to Livy, the Iberian remained inactive for several days and return back to their villages.

To recuperate their troop losses, the two praetors spent time drawing Iberian mercenaries and auxiliary troops from friendly cities and restoring the courage of their shaken men. When they were strong enough, the soldiers began to petition to their leaders to meet the enemy and wipe out their disgrace.[215] On seeing their motivation, the two praetors decided to move forward with a new campaign. Marching onto the Meseta, the Romans fixed camp at a spot twelve miles away from the Tagus River. Then, taking up their standards, they formed into a closed square and marched at night to the banks of the Tagus River. At daybreak, they saw an enemy hilltop fort on the other side of the river. Finding two places where the river was fordable, the army split in two and crossed - Piso on the right and Crispinus on the left. Spotted, the Lusitanians and Celtiberians stirred for action. The Romans, meanwhile, transported their baggage across and began to set up a new camp. But seeing the enemy in motion from the hilltop fort, the Romans deployed into battle formation.[216]

The Iberians, full of spirit after their recent victories against the Romans at Dipo and Toletum, fought fiercely. While the Romans, still smarting under their previous embarrassing humiliating defeat, fought like wild men. During the battle, the Roman center, made up of two of the bravest cohorts fought so gallantly that the Iberians found themselves unable to dislodge them at first. But they soon formed themselves into a wedge formation and began to cut through the Roman center. When he saw that his line was in trouble, Piso sent two of his staff officers, T. Quinctilius Varus and L. Juventius Thalna, to the center to stimulate their men's courage, and to warn them that all hopes of victory and of keeping their hold on Spain rested with them; if they gave way, not a man would ever see the other side of the Tagus, let alone return to Italy.[217] Piso, along

[214] Livy, 39.30.3-9

[215] Livy, 39.30.11-12

[216] Livy 39.30.13-15

[217] Livy,39.30.16 and 39.31.1-4

with the cavalry, made a short detour and charged into the flank of the enemy's wedge as it was pressing back the center. Crispinus delivered a similar charge on the other flank. The cavalry under Piso, fought with great tenacity. Livy goes onto claim that Piso was the first to strike down an enemy and rode so far into the hostile ranks that it was difficult to recognize which side he belonged.[218] The praetor's conspicuous courage had fired up the cavalry so much that the cavalry's charge ignited the infantry to fight harder. Motivated, the Romans bore down and began to sweep away their foe.

The cavalry pursued the fugitives up to their camp and plowed through the crowded enemy as they tried to escape to Roman onslaught. Here a fresh battle began with those left behind to guard the Iberian camp. The Roman cavalry was obliged to dismount and fight on foot, according to Livy, while the reserve infantrymen were called up to help the cavalry take the camp.[219] The Iberians were cut down; it is said that not more than 4,000 men escaped into the countryside from an enemy that had numbered more than 35,000.[220] Of the Romans and their allies, little more than 600 fell, and of the native auxiliaries about 150.[221] Exhausted from fighting, Piso and Crispinus order the men to remain in the enemy's camp. The next day, both praetors addressed the men and awarded the soldiers.[222] It is remarkable to see these two independent commanders, who had been assigned separate provinces, working together as they did. Perhaps their success can be contributed to these two men ignoring egos, attitudes, ambition, and protocols.

The following year, this experiment of cooperation was not repeated by the next two praetors, A. Terentius Varro (Citerior) and P. Sempronius Longus (Ulterior). During Longus's tenure (184 BCE and 183 BCE) it is said that Ulterior was quiet because of the successful campaign conducted by Piso and Crispinius the year before. Unfortunately, during

[218] Livy, 39.31.5-6
[219] Livy, 39.31.13-15
[220] Livy, 39.31.16-17
[221] Livy, 39.31.18
[222] Livy 39.31.19-22

his second year as praetor, Longus was incapacitated by illness of which he died before returning home.[223]

In Citerior, Varro arrived and immediately took his army on campaign against the Suessetani, who lived north of the Ebro River. After winning several victories, he took the Suessetani's main city of Corbio, from this point on Varro's province was quiet.[224] The following year, 183 BCE, he campaigned against the Ausetani, who lived in the coastal areas south of the Pyrenees and against the Celtiberians. Unfortunately, this is the only information Livy gives us until book 40 where Varro enters to Rome in an *ovatio,* bring with him 9,320 pounds of silver, 82 pounds of gold and seven golden crowns weighing 60 pounds each.[225]

---

[223] Livy 39.42.1, 39.56.2; 40.2.6

[224] Livy, 39.42.2; The ancient Iberian town of Corbio sometimes pronounced Corbion is situated near Sangüesa (Navarre). It is also assumed in the mountainous area of Cataluña

[225] Livy 40.16.18

CHAPTER II

FIRST CELTIBERIAN WAR

During the early part of 182 BCE, two new praetors were elected and were quickly sent to Hispania for the Senate had received news from Varro that the Iberians, especially the Celtiberians, were up in arms in Hispania Citerior and Hispania Ulterior, owing to the long-continued illness and death of the previous praetor, which led to the lapse of military discipline, as well as the Romans impeding on Celtiberian lands. [226] The praetors who took up their respective commands were P. Manlius (Ulterior), which he had administered before, and Q. Fulvius Flaccus (Citerior).[227] When Flaccus arrived in Citerior, he immediately went on the offensive and attacked the town of Urbicua.[228] During the

[226] Livy, 40.1.5

[227] Livy, 40.1.2

[228] It ruins lie between Cesaraugusta (Zaragoza) and Libisosa (Lezuza) according to the Antonine Itinerary*. Some scholars put it in the heights of Turia, while others in the Oretania country, in the area of Montiel (Ciudad Real). Others say it is on the banks of the Douro River and south of Ocellodurum (Zamora).

*The **Antonine Itinerary** (in Latin: **Antonini Itinerarium**) is a register of the stations and distances along the various roads of the Roman empire, containing directions how to get from one Roman settlement to another. 'Antonini Itinerarium' is seemingly based on official documents, probably of the survey organized by Julius Caesar, and carried out under Augustus. Due to the scarcity of other extant sources of this information, it is a very valuable source. Nothing is known with certainty as to the date or author. It is consideredprobable that the date of the original edition was the beginning of the 3rd century, while that which we possess is to be assigned to the time of Diocletian. Although traditionally ascribed to the

siege of Urbicua, the Celtiberians counter-attacked Flaccus's rear. A fierce battle took place with the Romans suffering heavy losses. But no display of force could draw Flaccus away from the siege, and his perseverance finally won out. The Celtiberians, exhausted by so many minor battles, withdrew and left the city a few days later. This enabled the Romans to take the city and sack it. As for the large amount of booty that was captured, Flaccus gave it to his soldiers.[229] Beyond this event, Flaccus, according to Livy did nothing worth recording.

Although Livy writes that after the taking of Urbicua, Flaccus did nothing worth writing about, Appian does. In Appian's work, Flaccus, besides combating the Celtiberians, he had an encounter with a small nomadic tribe called the Lusones that supposedly lived on the Ebro River along with several other small Iberian tribes who had very little land.[230] According to Appian, it seems that Flaccus fought and defeated the Lusones. With this defeat, the Iberians dispersed to their towns. But those who were lacking in land and lived out a nomadic existence, fled to Complega.[231] Basing themselves within the city's walls, they made demands on Flaccus that he should compensate them with a *sagos* (Celtic word for cloak), a horse and sword for each man's family that had been killed by a Roman during the battle and that the Romans should leave Hispania before things got worse for them. As an act of intimidation, Flaccus set up camp in front of the city's gate and promised that he would bring them their demands. But despite the Iberian threats and demands and not trusting the Romans, they abandoned the city.[232]

---

patronage of Antoninus Augustus, if the author or promoter of the work is one of the emperors, it is most likely to be Antoninus Caracalla.

229 Livy 40.16.12-15

230 Appian, 42.171; Unfortunately, Appian does not mention the other tribes except the Lusones, who, being that he makes mention of them, may mean that they perhaps instigated the revolt. But according to Strabo, the Lusones lived along the eastern part of the Tagus River (3.4.13) and not the Ebro River as Appian claims. So the question arises who did Flaccus actual fight against?.

231 Appian, 42.172; There is a similar story in Diodorus 29.28 As for Complega,there has been debate in identifying it, it has been suggested that it is close to Caravis while other scholars claim it identifies with the site Complutum near Madrid

232 Appian, 42.173 and 174

As for P. Manlius, who had been Cato's second-in-command in 195 BCE, arrived in Ulterior and quickly organized the province's affairs and reassemble the army which had scattered after Longus's death. During his first year, his province was quiet. But the following year, a large-scale rebellion broke out in Citerior. The Celtiberians were able to around up as many as 35,000 men.[233] Flaccus on hearing that the Celtiberians were arming themselves, began to draw auxiliary troops from friendly tribes, but was only able to gather a small number. At the onset of spring 181, he led his army into Carpetania and set up his camp near the town of Aebura (modern-day Talavera de la Reina), while a small detachment was sent to occupy the town.[234] A few days later, the Celtiberi encamped at the foot of a hill about two miles away from the Romans. When the Roman praetor became aware of their proximity, he sent his brother Marcus Flaccus with two squadrons of native cavalry to reconnoiter the enemy's camp. His instructions were to approach as closely as possible to the camp's rampart to get some idea of the size of the camp, but if the enemy's cavalry was spotted on the move, he was to pull back without fighting.[235]

For several days the cavalry squadrons probed around the enemy's camp. Each time the Celtiberians saw them, their cavalry emerged from their camp in an attack formation. But the Romans would not fight, instead they withdrew into the countryside. At last, the Celtiberian leader ordered his entire army to form a battle line midway between the two camps, but not to attack the Romans. Each morning for the next four days the Celtiberian army formed up to antagonize the Romans into coming out and fight, but the Roman general kept his men within the ramparts of his fort. Seeing that the Romans were not moving, the Celtiberians gave up antagonizing the Romans and returned to their camp.[236]

---

233 Livy, 40.30.2

234 Livy, 40.30.3-4

235 Livy 40.30.5-7

236 Livy, 40.30.7-14

For the next several days both armies sent out cavalry units on patrol in case of any movement on the part of their enemy. While each army watched their fronts, both sides went out to collect supplies and wood at the rear of their camps, with neither side interfering with the other. After many days of inactivity, Flaccus decide to initiate an attack and ordered L. Acilius to take a cohort of allied troops and 6,000 native auxiliaries to make a circuit around the mountain which was behind the enemy's camp. When he heard the sounds of battle he was to charge down on the enemy's camp.[237]

The Romans started their march in the middle of the night to escape observation. At daybreak, Acilius sent C. Scribonius, the commander of the allied troops, with his cavalry up to the enemy's camp rampart. When the Celtiberians saw the Romans approaching, their cavalry streamed out to intercept. The signal was given for the Roman infantry to ready themselves. No sooner had Scribonius heard the clatter of the advancing enemy cavalry followed by several infantry units, he turned to his men and made for their camp. As soon as Flaccus considered that the Celtiberians were sufficiently drawn off from guarding their camp, he sallied his army forth from his camp in three separate groups. Without delay the Romans charged down the hill and into the enemy's camp. When the camp was captured, Acilius set a signal fire to show Flaccus that the Romans had taken the fort.[238]

The Celtiberians, who were in the rear of the fort were the first to catch sight of the flames; this was followed by a rumor through the entire Celtiberian battle line that the fort had fallen. Dismayed about the news, the Celtiberians uncertain what to do, for there was no shelter for them, decided to keep on fighting.[239] As the battle raged for several hours, the Celtiberian center began to weaken, while its right flank pressed hard against the Roman left flank. The Roman left flank would have been repulsed had it not been for the arrival of reinforcements. The Romans who had been left to hold the Celtiberian town of Aebura appeared in the

[237] Livy 40.31.1-2

[238] Livy 40. 31.3-11

[239] Livy, 40.32.1-4

middle of the battle. Between Acilius and these soldiers from Aebura, the Celtiberi were cut to pieces; the survivors fled in all directions. The Roman cavalry was sent after them, either killing or capturing as many of those who tried to escape. According to Livy, as many as 23,000 men were killed that day and 4,700 were made prisoners; 500 horses and 88 military standards were captured.[240] Of the two legions that fought more than 200 Roman soldiers, 830 Latin allies, and 2,400 native auxiliaries were killed.[241] The praetor led his victorious army back to camp, while ordering his second in command, L. Acilius to remain at the enemy's camp, which had just been taken. The following day the spoils were collected, and those who had shown conspicuous bravery were rewarded in the presence of the entire army.[242]

Aebura was turned into a military outpost and hospital for the wounded to be attended to. Once the town was modified into a Roman outpost, Flaccus marched his legions through Carpetania to Contrebia (modern day Albarracin).[243] When Contrebia was about to be besieged, the townspeople sent an envoy to the Celtiberian for assistance. After several weeks, despairing that any help from their countrymen would arrive, the inhabitants surrendered. This delay was not through any reluctance on the part of the Celtiberian, but because of the harsh winter weather which rendered roads impassable and river crossing difficult because of flooding due to incessant rain.[244] Flaccus, found himself compelled by the terrible storms to move his entire army into the city. When spring arrived, the Celtiberians moved against the Romans, ignorant of the city's surrender. After they succeeded in crossing the rivers and marching through the countryside, they arrived before Contrebia. To their bewilderment, they saw no Roman camp outside the walls, and concluded that it had been transferred elsewhere, or the enemy

[240] Livy, 40.32.5-10

[241] Livy, 40.32.12

[242] Livy 40.32. 13-14

[243] Livy, 40.33.1; About the site of Contrebia see: A. Beltran and A. Tovar, Contrebia Belaisca I: el bronce de Botorrita, Zaragoza, 1982, 9-33; Fatas, G., Contrebia Belaisca I: Tabula Contrebiensis, Zaragoza, 1980, p. 46-57

[244] Livy, 40.33.2-4

had withdrawn. So, they decided to approach the town without taking precautions or keeping proper formation. Suddenly, the Romans made a sortie from its two gates, attacking and routing them. This surprise attack amounted to 12,000 killed and more than 5,000 captured along with 400 horses and 62 standards. According to Livy, this second major defeat prompted the locals to dispense any further planned attacks against the Romans, but rather bolster the defense of their forts and villages.[245]

Leaving Contrebia, Flaccus led his legions through the Celtiberian countryside, ravaging the land as he marched. He stormed many of their city forts until the greater part of the Celtiberian nation surrendered, increasing the Roman Empire further west. In Ulterior, praetor Manlius fought several successful actions against the Lusitanians.[246] After these campaigns, both provinces remained quiet.

Shaping the Province

In 180 BCE, two new praetors T. Sempronius Gracchus (Citeriror) and L. Postumius Albinus (Ulterior) were elected to take over Hispania. During the election, L. Minucius, a staff officer, and two military tribunes, T. Maenius and L. Terentius Massiliota, who had come from Flaccus's command arrived in Rome and reported to the Senate their great news about Flaccus's victorious campaign, the Celtiberian surrender, and the establishment of order throughout the province. In addition, they told the Senate that there was no need of the subsidy which was usually sent to supply the army for the following year because the province was now able to sustain itself.[247] They then requested that homage be paid to the gods for these successes and that Flaccus be allowed to bring back on his departure from Spain the army whose courage served him well.[248] According to Livy, this was a must, for the soldiers were in such a determined mood that it appeared impossible to keep them any

245 Livy 40.33.5-10; Appian 42.171.4; Diodorus Siculus, 29.28

246 Livy 40.33.11-12

247 Livy, 40.35.5-6

248 Livy, 40.35.7

longer in the province, and they were prepared to leave without orders, so this decision was necessary to avoid mutiny.[249] Gracchus who was to succeed Flaccus, strongly objected to this proposal arguing that he would be robbed of a veteran army and be forced to control an unsettled and rebellious province with raw recruits.[250]

The question of the army for Gracchus was settled and in defense of the veterans, the debate ended with a compromise. Gracchus was ordered to enlist a fresh Legion of 6,200 infantry and 450 cavalry along with 7,000 allied infantry and 300 allied cavalry.[251] As for the veterans who had been stationed in Hispania for several years or close to retirement, these men were tired and wanted to come home. Thus Flaccus received permission to bring away with him, as he saw fit, those soldiers whether Roman citizens or allies, who had been transferred to Hispania prior to 186 BCE would return home, while those who arrived after 186 BCE would stay on and honor their contract with Gracchus.[252] Flaccus was also at liberty to bring all those whose bravery had served well during Flaccus's two successful campaigns against the Celtiberians.[253]

While Gracchus debate went on in Rome, Flaccus led his army out from winter quarters and initiated a third campaign against the Celtiberians whom had not surrendered. Irritated more than intimidated, the Celtiberians had been secretly building an army and planning a strategy to strike at the Romans at Manlian Pass, which they were certain the Romans would march through.[254]

In the meantime, while Gracchus was building his army, he instructed his colleague, L. Postumius Albinus, who was on his way to Ulterior, to inform Flaccus that he was to bring his army to Tarraco (modern-day Tarragona), where Gracchus intended to disband the old Legion, and incorporate a new Legion with some of the veterans into various

249 Livy 40.35.8
250 Livy, 40.35.12-16
251 Livy, 40.36.9-10
252 Livy, 40.36.12
253 Livy 40.36.14
254 Livy, 40.39.1-2

corps and reorganize the entire army.[255] This information compelled Flaccus to abandon his operation and withdraw his army hastily from Celtiberia.[256]

The barbarians, ignorant of Flaccus's real reason for his withdrawal, believe he had become aware of their uprising and turned yellow and fled. With this thinking, the natives continued to invest time in setting up their trap at Manlian Pass in case the Romans decided to make a move. When the Romans made their move, so did the Iberians. The Flaccus's column entered the pass, the enemy ambushed them from both sides. As soon as Flaccus saw this, he gave the order for every man to stand, fight and hold their ground. The Roman packs and baggage animals were piled up in the middle. Readying his men for battle, Flaccus reminded his men that they were dealing with uncivilized barbarians who had twice submitted to Rome's power, but who are compelled to fight by treachery and not by true courage. He continued to tell his soldiers that they would not return home without distinguishing themselves for at this moment the enemy has given them the chance of a glorious and memorable triumphal homecoming, where they would march through Rome with their swords reddened and dripping in blood with the slaughter of their foes and every man would be a rich from the spoils of war. Time did not allow him to say more for the enemy had reached the formation.[257]

The battle was fierce and desperate, the Legionnaires and their allied troops fought splendidly at first, but then the native auxiliaries could not hold their ground as the Celtiberians realized they were no match compared to the Romans and concentrated their attack on them. With the auxiliaries faltering, the Celtiberians fought harder that they began throwing the Legion's ranks into disorder.[258]

---

[255] Livy 40.39.4-5

[256] Livy, 40.39.6

[257] Livy 40.39.6-15

[258] Livy, 40.40.1-5

Seeing this, Flaccus galloped up to the cavalry and shouted: "Unless you can come to the rescue, it will be all over for this army!" Its commander shouted in reply, "What would you have us do? For we shall not slack in carrying out your orders." He replied: "Close up your cavalry squadrons and let your horses go where the enemy wedge is pressing our men. Your charge will have all the greater force if you make it on unbitten horses." [259] They removed the horses' bits and charged into the wedge from two directions, inflicting great slaughter upon the enemy. With the wedge broken, the Celtiberians completely lost heart and began to look for a means of escape. When the auxiliary cavalry saw the Roman cavalry's notable feat, they too spurred their horses against the enemy, who were now thoroughly shaken and began to flee in all directions. This proved a decisive move.[260]

As Flaccus watched them run, he vowed to build a temple to Fortuna Equestris and celebrate in solemn Games to Jupiter Optimus Maximus.[261] As the Celtiberians scattered, the Romans regrouped and began cutting them to pieces all throughout the pass. It is asserted that 17,000 enemy were killed on that day, and more than 4,000 were taken alive, together with 277 military standards and nearly 600 horses. The victory was not without loss for the Romans lost 472 Roman soldiers, 1,019 allied soldiers and 3,000 native auxiliaries.[262]

For the rest of the day the victorious Roman army remained encamped just outside of the pass. With its former glory renewed, the victorious army marched to Tarraco the next day. Tiberius Sempronius Gracchus, who had landed two days before, went to meet Flaccus and congratulated him upon his successful conduct. The next day, these two men went among soldiers to decide which should be release from military service in Hispania and which were to be retained. After releasing the

[259] Livy 40.40.6-11; There are accounts that the Roman cavalry had often done that maneuver and covered themselves with glory.

[260] Livy, 40.40.12-14

[261] Livy 40.40.14

[262] Livy 40.40. 15-17

time – expired men from their military service, Flaccus returned to Italy with his veterans, while Gracchus led his legions back into Celtiberia.[263]

Once in command, Gracchus immediately went into action. Appian tells us that the city of Caravis (Magallón), which was in allegiance with Rome, was being besieged by 20,000 Celtiberians.[264] Receiving news that the city would fall in the next few days if not rescued, Gracchus hastened his march all the more to relieve it. Stopping a few miles away, he assessed the situation. Having no means of secretly communicating to the town to alert them of his presence, Cominius, a commander of a cavalry squadron, came up with an idea and presented his plan to Gracchus. That night, Cominius donned a Spanish *sagum* (a military type cloak) and mingled with the enemy. Once he gained entrance to their camp as an Iberian, he attempted to make his way into Caravis. Finding an entrance through the city's wall, he told the people that Gracchus was at the city's outskirts, so they should hold out a bit longer. Three days later, Gracchus attacked the besiegers who fled into the countryside.[265]

Around the same time, some 20,000 "inhabitants" of the Celtiberian city of Complega (site unknown) came to Gracchus's camp in the guise of petitioners for peace by bearing olive branches. When they had entered the camp, the signal went out for the Iberians to attack. The attack threw the Romans into disarray. Gracchus quickly and cleverly abandoned his camp to the enemy and simulated a false retreat; he then suddenly turned around and fell upon the unsuspecting Iberians that were plundering the camp, killing most of them. He then went on to capture Complega and the surrounding countryside and towns.[266] Once everything had settled, he divided the land among the poor of Caravis

---

[263] Livy 40.40. 18-21

[264] The Celtic city of Caravis is said to have been situated around Mount Moncayo and between the Queiles and Huecha River, tributaries of the Ebro River. Mozota, F.B., Sobre el Territorio de los Lusones, Belos y Titos en el Siglo II a. de C., Madrid, n.d., p. 9.

[265] Appian, Ib, 43.175-177

[266] Appian 43.178; at the present time the spot were the city of Complega was is not known except that in was in the Ebro River Valley but close to Caravis.

and Complega and settled them on it and made carefully defined treaties with all the surrounding tribes, binding them to be friends of Rome.[267]

After the winter of 180-179 BCE, both praetors (Gracchus and Albinius) agreed upon a joint plan of operation; Albinus, whose province had been quite since his arrival, was to march through Lusitania against the Vaccaei, and if he encountered stiff resistance, he was to return to his base camp; Gracchus was to penetrate further into Celtiberia. But for some unknown reason he decided to change his plan and march south toward Turdetania, bypassing Carpetania and Oretania, and instead concentrating his troops on the high Guadalquivir Plateau, which borders both Oretania and Turdetania.

Making his way south, Gracchus began conquering the region of Munda, by first conducting a nocturnal attack on the city, taking it in one assault.[268] After taking hostages and placing a garrison to hold the place, he marched on through the Genil River and Seirra Nevada until he reached the southern coast, pillaging several fortified towns and villages and burning their crops until he came to another city of exceptional strength called by the natives, Cértima (modern-day Cartama), north-east of Munda.[269] While Gracchus prepared to bring up siege engines against the city's walls, a delegation arrived from the town. Their words betrayed a primitive simplicity; they made no concealment of their intention to continue the struggle against Rome for they requested permission to visit other Celtiberian towns and ask for help; if it were refused, they would then take counsel among themselves to either fight or surrender. Gracchus gave them permission. A few days later they returned, bringing with them ten more envoys.[270]

Mozota, F.B., Sobre el Territorio de los Lusones, Belos y Titos en el Siglo II a. de C., Madrid, n.d., p.9

[267] Appian, 40.179

[268] Livy, 40.47; Munda today is called Montilla but other scholars and archeologists believe that the city of Monda is the site of the ancient Iberian city

[269] Munoz, M.A., Viriato: o herói lusitano que lutou pela liberdade do seu povo, Lisbon, 2006, p. 41

[270] Livy 40.47.7

According to Livy:

....the delegates ate and drank. Then the oldest amongst them spoke by asking Gracchus on how and with what army he would combat against the Celtiberian nation. Gracchus told them that he relied upon his splendid army, and if they wanted to see it for themselves so that they might carry back an account of it, he would give them the opportunity of doing so.[271]

He goes to write:

So Gracchus then sent word to the military tribunes to order the entire army to equip themselves and practice their maneuvers under arms. After this exhibition the envoys were sent home, and they dissuaded their countrymen from sending any succor to the besieged city.[272] At Certima, on hearing about the Roman army's strength and that their only hope of assistance had failed, they surrendered. At day's end a war indemnity of 2,400,000 sesterces was levied upon the Celtiberians and they had to give up forty noble youths to serve in the Roman army, as a pledge of the loyalty to the Romans.[273]

Gracchus then marched into the Carpetania region to take the city of Alce (modern Ciudad Real). For several days, he confined himself to annoying the enemy by sending skirmishers against their advanced posts in an attempt to draw the full strength of the enemy outside its walls. When he saw that he had gained their attention, Gracchus ordered the commanders of the native auxiliary units to offer slight resistance and then turn back to camp in hasty retreat, as though they had been overwhelmed by the enemy's numbers. In the meantime, he positioned his men behind every gate of his fortified camp. Gracchus soon saw his men running back towards the camp with the enemy following in disorderly pursuit. As the Celtiberians came within close range of the Roman camp's wall, a battle-shout was raised, and the Romans burst

[271] Livy, 40.47.8-11

[272] Livy, 40.47.12-13

[273] Livy 40.47.14-16

forth simultaneously from all the camp's gates. The enemy could not stand against this unexpected formation and were routed. Nine thousand Iberians were killed that day, 320 taken prisoners, 112 horses and 37 military standards were captured. Out of the Roman army 109 fell.[274]

Gracchus then led his legions away from the city and deep into Celtiberian territory, which he ravaged and plundered. When the natives saw him carrying off their property and driving away their cattle, some of the tribes voluntarily bowed their heads to the Roman yoke, and within a few days Gracchus accepted the surrender of 103 towns, while securing an enormous amount of booty.[275] He then marched back towards Alce and besieged the city. At first the townsmen withstood the assaults, but when they found themselves attacked by siege-engines, they lost confidence in the protection of their walls and retired to their citadel. Finally, they sent envoys to place their people and all their property at the disposal of the Romans. The Romans agreed and received a large amount of booty and the children of the noble were taken as hostages, amongst them were the two sons and the daughter of Thurru, the chief of the Celtiberian tribes. On hearing of the Alce's surrender, Thurru ask for safe-conduct to visited Gracchus at his camp. When he arrived his first question was whether he and his family would be allowed to live. The praetor replied that his life and family would be spared. Thurru then asked if he would be allowed to fight on the side of the Romans. Gracchus granted his request and released his family; from that time on he followed the Romans, in which his gallantry and faithful service had been helpful to the Romans on many occasions.[276]

Ergavica, another powerful and influential Celtiberian city, became alarmed by the defeats which had befallen her neighbors.[277] When it

---

[274] Livy 40.48.1-4 to 5-10

[275] Livy, 40.49.1-2

[276] Livy 40.49.3 to 7-11

[277] For many years now there has been debate on the exact location of Ergavica, one thing is for sure that it is situated somewhere in the province of Navarre. Some scholar and archaeologists say the location of the Iberian city is in Arguedas while other claim it is Berbençana. Others say it is an old Celtiberian/Roman city north of the Ebro River, where its ruins lie near the city of Fitero.Etayo, J, Vestigos de

was reported that the Romans were on their way, they opened the city's gates to them. Livy goes on to say that although many cities had surrendered, it was not made in good faith by the Celtiberian, for whenever Gracchus withdrew his legions from these areas, hostilities were renewed. [278] It seems that the reason for this statement from Livy is because soon after Ergavica surrendered, Gracchus fought a major battle with the Celtiberians near Mons Chaunus (probably referring to Mount Moncayo). It was a battle that lasted from dawn until mid-day.[279] Three days later, a bigger battle was fought, which the Celtiberians suffered a striking defeat that supposedly cost them 22,000 casualties, more than 300 taken prisoners, along with the same number of horses and 72 military standards.[280] The defeat was so decisive that it ended the First Celtiberian War.[281] According to Livy, it seems that this battle finally made the Celtiberians assess their situation and instead of being insincere about making peace as before, they committed themselves to having real peace. Gracchus had now become a celebrated hero both in Spain and Rome and was awarded a splendid triumph.[282]

Once the First Celtiberian War was over and treaties signed, he founded the city of Gracchurris (modern-day Alfaro), in the upper Ebro valley. Although the majority of Iberian town had full Roman rights by the time of Caesar Augustus, at their establishment these towns were no more than outposts with no legal right or status of any kind.[283] The

---

poblaciòn ibero-romana cabr Arguedas, Boletin de la Comisiòn Provincial de Monumentos de Navarre #17, 1926, p. 84-90; Taracena, B. and Vazquez de Parga, L Excavaciones en Navarre: Exploracion del Castejòn de Arguedas, Principe de Viana #10, p.129-159; Corona Baratech, C.E., Toponimia Navarre en la Edad Media, Huesca, 1947; Moret, J de, Anales del Reino de Navarre 1665; 1766, Pamplona, 1987.

[278] Livy, 40.50.2

[279] Livy, 40.50.2; The Moncayo or San Miguel is a small mountain system situated between the province of Zaragoza, Aragón (Spain) and the province of Soria, Castilla León.

[280] Livy, 40.50.4

[281] Livy 40.50.5

[282] Appian, 43.179

[283] A. Garcia y Bellido, Las colonias romanas de Hispania, Anuario de Historia del Derecho Espaol 29 (1959) 448ff

establishment of this city marked the beginning of Roman influence in the central northern part of Hispania. For many years it was believed that Gracchus had founded only one city, but during the late 1950s an inscription was discovered near Mengibar on the banks of the Guadalquivir (ancient Baetica) showing that he had founded another. This stone marker records a dedication to Gracchus: '*Ti. Sempronio Graccho deductori populus Iliturgitanus*'.[284] The town was Iliturgi, was a mining town and a frontier military outpost.[285] If Gracchus was active in this region, he was establishing communities not only in his province but outside of it. With the further annexation of Celtiberian lands, the Romans began to consolidate this territory to effectively exploit the land more intensely for economic gains. To accomplish this, Gracchus first had to establish an extension of the provincial border by stationing frontier garrisons and persuading a major portion of the tribes within his realm to sue for peace and build an alliance with Rome.

In view of the time available for Gracchus to campaign and for his reorganization and settlement of the province, it is unlikely that the First Celtiberian War was a full-scale war. According to Polybius and other ancient historians, Gracchus had become renowned for the large number of villages, town and cities that he had captured; in which many of these had actually surrendered to him instead of suffering his wrath.[286] There is further evidence in which Gracchus's arrangements were accepted by the Celtiberians.[287] It was according to Appian that Gracchus made some progress towards peace in the peninsula after years of fighting by having many of the Iberian tribes sign treaties, thus making them 'friends' of the Romans.[288] Compared to most praetors in Hispania, Gracchus spent time negotiating with the Celtiberians leaders and building personal relations with these tribal leaders, reminiscent of the

---

[284] A. Blanco and G. La Chica, *Arch. Español de Arqueologia* 33, 1960, 193-95; Knapp, R.C., Aspects of the Roman Experience in Iberia 206 – 100 BC, Vallodolid, 1977, p. 110, n. 18

[285] Munoz, M.A., Viriato: o herói lusitano que lutou pela liberdade do seu povo, Lisbon, 2006, p. 42

[286] Polybuis 25.1.1; Strabo 3.4.13; Florus 1.33.9

[287] Polybuis 35.2.15; Appian, *Iberika*, 43.179 - 44.183; Plutarch, *Ti. Gracchus*, 5.2

[288] Appian, *Iberika,* 43.179

friendly relationships established by Scipio Africanus during the Second Punic War.[289] His alliances with the Celtiberi and Vascones would facilitate Roman domination of Celtiberia. Along with these treaties, Gracchus interjected the following stipulations among the tribes: pay taxes and render men for military service as auxiliary troops. Along with these stipulations, the *vicensima*, a requisition for five per cent of the grain harvest was established.[290] This annual quota represented a more efficient system of provisioning Roman and allied soldiers than hiring contractors from Italy or Cato's 'live off the land' policy. A final provision to *pax Gracchana* was that the Celtiberians could fortify existing cities, but not establish new ones.[291] There is also some evidence of the introduction of civilian administrative organizations (i.e. issuing rights for mining to minting currency) and public works (i.e. roads). Besides being a war hero, Gracchus is also remembered for his administrative arrangements, which ensured peace within the conquered territory for the next quarter century.[292]

During the First Celtiberian War, Albinus conducted a successful campaign against the Vaccaei in the wilds of central southern Spain, which he supposedly killing 35,000 enemy warriors and collected a large amount of booty.[293] Unfortunately of Albinus's activities, there is practically no information to support Livy's statement. Although he campaigned against the Vaccaei, it may have not been a long campaign for him to cause such high losses for he arrived in his province too late in the summer to undertake a large-scale campaign as Gracchus did. Also Livy seems confused about the time of his arrival in Hispania, for he stated that he was in Hispania before Gracchus, but the following year he denies that he could have won victories against the Vaccaei, because he arrived too late in the province to launch any type of campaign.[294]

---

[289] Livy 40.47.3-10, 40.49.4-7

[290] Curchin, Leonard, A, op. cit., p. 32

[291] Ibid., p.33

[292] For more information on Gracchus contributions in Hispania see, J.S. Richardson,, Hispaniae,, p. 112-123

[293] Livy 40.50.7

[294] J.S. Richardson also states this claim in his book, Hispaniae, p 102

We can only assume that perhaps Livy was right in saying that Albinus had arrived on time in Hispania to take control of his province, but being he was sent as a messenger to contact Flaccus, Albinus lost time in reaching his province and by the time he arrived, it was too late in the campaign season to conduct a full-scale campaign. Perhaps he conducted small-scale raids and attacks to keep the populace in check and plunder booty, food and supplies for his army and probably fought one pitch battle against an anger mob of barbarians.

At the end of their governorship in 178 BCE, these two praetors celebrated their triumph; first, Sempronius Gracchus for his victory over the Celtiberians and their allies, and on the following day L. Postumius Albinius over the Vacccaei and Lusitanians. Unfortunately, there is no account about the campaign against the Lusitanian or further details about the event of the year 178. The account of the Lusitanian campaign seems to have been lost and is only mentioned in Livy's epitome.

Pacification of Hispania Continues

The general picture that emerges from Appian and Livy's writings is one of continuous and unsystematic fighting. In terms of Roman territorial gains or treaties established between the Romans and Iberians, little stability was achieved between these two groups that fully secured some sort of peace in the Peninsula because of the constant breaking of treaties and raiding each other lands. Prior to Gracchus and Albinus, there was no grand design for the conquest of the peninsula for the Romans and the Iberians were in constant state of war. But after Gracchus and Albinus's victories, a period of peace existed. Unfortunately though, Livy and Appian, our two main sources about the Hispania, wrote less about this backwater province during this time and focused their attention elsewhere.

History shows us that during the scarce periods of peace in Hispania, immigration from other provinces and Italy helped the province increase its status through the introduction of Roman culture that contributed to the economic and social transformation of the eastern and southern areas of the peninsula. Immigrants that brought Roman culture to Hispania began with administrators, educators, soldiers, merchants, technicians and craftsmen. Sons of upper class Iberians were assimilated by being sent to Rome for their education.[295] But with new immigrants appearing at this time, many unscrupulous and shady businessmen, tax collectors and even government administrators also arrived, and in times this behavior gave the Iberians a reason to renew rebellions with consequent interventions by the Senate or praetors thus making pacification more difficult to achieve.

Of all the praetors who went to Hispania during the 170s, little to nothing except their names is known. In Livy's book 41, it begins at the end of 178 BCE; unfortunately there is no mention of what went on in the province except that the praetors of 178 BCE were M. Titinius Curvus (Citerior) and T. Fonteius Capito (Ulterior) who were both proconsuls that took governorship of Hispania from 178 - 176 BCE.[296] As praetors, they received a *supplementa* of troops---3,000 Roman citizens and 200 cavalry, with 5,000 infantry and 300 cavalry from their allies.[297] Besides knowing the names of these praetors, it seems that Curvus was the only one involved in some sort of fighting and that the size of his army was reduced from two to one legion during his governorship.[298] Perhaps the reason that these men are not mentioned is because after the Celtiberian defeat and their submission to Gracchus, the province remained quiet during their administration. After the return of Gracchus and Albinus to Rome in 178 BCE, warfare in the two provinces became less intense. Apart from the names and several minor events shown in Livy's work that occurred between 178 – 171 BCE, very little is known.

---

[295] Payne, Stanley G., A History of Spain and Portugal Volume 1, Antiquity to the Seventeenth Century (Print Edition: University of Wisconsin Press, 1973) The chapter on Ancient Hispania can be read online, The Library of Iberian Resources Online, http://libro.uca.edu/payne1/payne1.htm

[296] Livy 41.9.3, 41.15.11

[297] Livy 41.15.9-10

[298] Brunt, P.A., Italian Manpower, 225 BC – 14 AD, Oxford, 1971, pp. 661-63

The *sortitio* (casting of ballots) of 175 BCE has also been lost from Livy's text, but at least the praetor of Citerior is known to have been Appius Claudius Cento. On his arrival to Citerior, the Celtiberians broke Gracchus's treaty and resumed hostilities by attacking a Roman fort. The day had hardly started when Roman sentries on the ramparts and at the gates caught sight of an enemy advance in the distance. After the alarm was sounded, Appius Claudius quickly addressed the men with a few words, after which the soldiers then made a simultaneous exit from the fort's three gates.[299] The Celtiberians met them as they emerged from the gates and for a short time the fighting was equal on both sides because of the tight space of the gates, the Romans were having a hard time getting out and forming up for action. But once they got clear of the gates, the men formed up and deployed their line formation. They then made a sudden charge which the Celtiberians could not withstand. In less than two hours, the Celtiberians were defeated; 15,000 were either killed or taken prisoners and 32 standards were captured. The Celtiberian camp was stormed later the same day and the survivors from the battle dispersed into the countryside; ending the uprising on the same day.[300] After that they submitted quietly to the authority of Rome. This is the only information that Livy's gives about Claudius's praetorship of 175 - 174 BCE, except that at the end of book 41, Claudius is mentioned again. On his return to Rome, he celebrated a *ovatio* of his victory over the Celtiberians, bring with him 10,000 pounds of silver and 5000 pounds of gold.[301]

As for the person who took over for Fonteius, according to Professor Richardson, he believes that a man using the cognomen Centho, found in the *Fasti Triumphales,*[302] may have served as praetor of Ulterior.

---

299 Livy, 41.26.1-4

300 Livy, 41.26.5-11

301 Livy 41.28.5

302 The Fasti Triumphales were published in about 12 B.C. They contain a list of triumphs from the foundation of Rome down to the reign of Augustus. They are preserved as part of a larger inscription, the Fasti Capitolini, which is now displayed at the Palazzo dei Conservatori, Capitoline Museum in Rome. This translation is based on the edition by A.Degrassi ("Fasti Capitolini", 1954.

Though there is a slight mention of this name, there is no surviving record of his activity in Hispania.

In 174 BCE, P. Furius Philus went to Citerior, while Cn. Servilius Caepio went on to govern Ulterior. Each man brought with him 3,000 Roman infantry and 150 cavalry and 5,000 allied infantry and 300 cavalry.[303] In 173, two new praetors were elected and were allowed to take 3,000 Roman infantry and 200 cavalry to reinforce the army in Hispania.[304] Of the two praetors elected to Hispania only M. Matienus arrived and took control of his assigned province, Ulterior; while his colleague, N. Fabius Buteo died at Massilia (today Marseilles, France). On receiving the information of his death, the Senate decreed that one of the two returning praetors, P. Furius and Cn. Servilius, would have to decide which of them should have his governorship extended for another year. It fell to P. Furius Philus.[305] The following year, 172, M. Iunius Pennus (Citerior) and Sp. Lucretius (Ulterior) were chosen to go to Hispania.[306] During their first few months in office, these two men asked for a *supplementa* of soldiers, but were refused. But when it was reported that hostilities would soon break out, the Senate provided the praetors with the standard number of required soldiers to keep the legions up to strength.[307] The *supplementa* consisted of 3,000 Roman infantry and 150 cavalry and 5,000 allied infantry and 300 cavalry.[308]

We see from the texts that these praetors' terms after 175 BCE were only one year instead of the usual two. It seems, according to some scholars, that the changes in policy came about with the creation of the law, *lex Baebia de praetoribus* in 179 BCE in conjunction with *lex Baebia de ambitu* of 180 BCE.[309] The creation of *lex Baebia*, according to Mommsen originated from the need for praetors in Hispania to spend

303 Livy 41.21.3

304 Livy 42.1.3

305 Livy 42.1.3, 4.1-3

306 42.9.8

307 Brunt, P.A., Italian Manpower, 225 BC – AD 14, Oxford, 1971, p. 662

308 Livy, 42.18.3

309 lex Baebia de praetoribus prescribed that praetors would be elected in alternate years; Lex Baebia de Ambitu, involved combating electoral bribery.

two years there before returning to Rome to become a candidate for a consulship.[310] But as for the reason why a praetorship in Hispania was reduced from two to one year in unknown, but it has been suggested that the senatorial class preferred to have a larger number of magistracies to compete for office rather than a smaller group when it came for consulship candidacy.[311]

In 171 BCE, in the midst of the war against Perseus, King of Macedon[312], the two provinces were combined into one and L. Canuleius Dives was sent to Hispania for two years.[313] During Dives govenorship two incidents occurred, according to Livy's writings.[314] The first occur before he left for Hispania. A delegation of natives from both provinces were admitted a Senate audience in Rome. They complained of the rapacity and oppression that several Roman magistrates had committed. Falling on their knees, they begged the Senate not to oppress Rome's allies any longer. Though there were other indignities that they complained of, the evidence bore chiefly upon the illegal seizure of money. Dives was instructed by the Senate to appoint four senatorial counsels *(recuperators)* that had previously served in Hispania, and to try each of the individuals from whom the Spaniards demanded redress; also, the emissaries were allowed to pick counselors who had also served in Hispania to represent their case. Several days later, the delegation was called into the senate-house and the decree was read to them, and they

310 Mommsen, Theodore, Römisches Staatsrecht, vol. 2, Leipzig, 3 vols., 1887-1889, p.194

311 For more information on the subject see J.S. Richardson, Hispaniae, p. 109-112; Scullard, H.H., Roman Politics 220-150 BC, (2nd ed.) Oxford, 1973

312 Upon Philip's death in Macedon (179 BC), his son, Perseus of Macedon, attempted to restore Macedon's international influence, and moved aggressively against his neighbors. When Perseus was implicated in an assassination plot against an ally of Rome, the Senate declared the third Macedonian War. Initially, Rome did not fare well against the Macedonian forces, but in 168 BC, Roman legions smashed the Macedonian phalanx at the Battle of Pydna. Perseus was later captured, and the kingdom of Macedon divided into four puppet rupublics that Rome controlled.

313 Livy, 42.28.5-6; Broughton, T.R.S., The Magistrates of the Roman Republic, 2 vols. and supplement, NY, 1951, 1952, 1960, vol 1, p. 421.

314 Livy 42.2; 42.3

were told to nominate their counsel. They named four - M. Porcius Cato, P. Cornelius Scipio, L. Aemilius Paulus, and C. Sulpicius Gallus. The *recuperatores* then commenced with the cases of M. Titinius Curvus, P. Furius Philus, M. Matienus. These former praetors of Hispania had been charged with very serious offences.[315]

It is unclear what satisfaction the Iberians gained from the court proceeding, but according to Livy, there was a rumor that although the Iberians had complaints against these men, their counsels were prevented from summoning members of the Roman nobility and men of influence who had served in Hispania, which perhaps shows that the counselors had been prevented by powerful forces within the Senate from making the accused suffer the punishment they actually deserved.[316] These courtroom events have attracted some scholarly attention, for this is the first occasion on which complaints from provincials were dealt with by a quasi-judicial procedure of its kind.[317] The use of *recuperatores* and the reference to '*pecuniae captae*' (charge of extortion) suggests that these trials were the precursor of those later conducted by the '*quaestio de repetundis*' under the law developed by C. Gracchus.[318] Richardson writes that Gracchus's law and the Senate decree stated that no Roman magistrate should be permitted to impose their own price value on corn which Iberian farmers were required to supply, thereby increasing the amount of money which he would receive from the local communities

---

[315] Livy 43.2.1-5; 43.2.6-9 The first case involved the legations from both provinces against M. Titinius, who was acquitted after two adjournments. After the trial, a disagreement arose between the emissaries and as a result the *patroni* (patrons) split, those from Citerior Hispania chose M. Cato and P. Scipio as their counsel, those from Ulterior Hispania, L. Paullus and Sulpicius Gallus. Livy, 42.2.10-11 The second trial began soon after with each party having its own trial. The representatives from Citerior brought their case against P. Furius Philus, while those from Ulterior brought their case against M. Matienius. After the first adjournment, both accused men went into voluntary exile. Philus went Praeneste (modern Palestrina, Italy), while Matienius went to Tibur (modern Tivoli, Italy).

[316] Livy, 43.2.12-13

[317] Richardson, J.S., *Hispaniae,* p.114; Strachan-Davidson, J.L., *Problems with the Roman Criminal Law II,* 2 vols. Oxford, 1912, vol II, p. 1-4; Gruen, E.S., *Roman Politics and the Criminal Courts*, Harvard, 1968, p. 10.

[318] Richardson, J.S., *Hispaniae,* p. 114.

should he permit them to pay cash rather than handing over the grain.[319] The same decree forbade a Roman magistrate to force the Iberians to sell off the half-tithe of one-twentieth of the crop which was apparently due to the Romans and to impose his own officers on the communities in order to extract money from them by force.[320] These decrees would stabilize the market from magistrate attempting to make a profit from the sell of corn to Rome. Also, Iberian farmer would receive cash payment from the magistrate instead of handing over the grain or corn on credit. The decree also forbade a magistrate to force the Iberians to sell off supply and crops that were due to the Romans and that those officers should not use force upon their towns for the collection of taxes and tribute.[321] It is clear that by 171 BCE, the Senate was dealing with abuses of the taxation system which were causing problems for local populations all across the Roman Empire. Though the Senate and praetors tried to fix these problems of abuse by emplacing a fixed tax, known as a stipendium, tax problems still continued.

With the trails complete, Dives levied troops and went off to Hispania to prevent more Iberians from complain or accusing Roman citizens of crimes. But prior to arriving in Hispania, a second incident occurred. A delegation arrived in Rome representing a new "race" of men (more like a new generation). They declared themselves to be born of Roman soldiers and Iberian women who were not legally married.[322] There were over 4,000 of them, and they hoped that the Senate would give them their own town and Roman citizenship. The Senate decreed that they should send all the names of these individuals and that they would be settled on the coast at Carteia (San Roque, Spain), and as a bonus, they would receive an allotment of land. But as for citizenship, Livy makes

---

[319] Ibid., p. 114

[320] Ibid., p. 115

[321] Livy, 43.2.16; Mackie, Nicola, Aspects of the Roman Experience in Iberia 206 – 100 BC, Journal of Roman Studies # 71, 1981, p. 187

[322] Livy, 43.3.1-2

no mention of it. This place became a Latin colony called the "Colony of the Libertini."[323]

The third and final event can be found in Publius Annius Florus's writing. During Dives second year in Hispania trouble brewed when a messianic figure named Olonicus ran around the province brandishing a silver spear he claimed was sent from heaven. It was said that it was a sign from the gods and that the gods would give the Iberians the power to defeat the Romans, if they followed him. But the revolt soon burned out following his untimely death.[324]

In 169 BCE, M. Claudius Marcellus took over the praetorship of the entire province and brought with him a *supplementa* of 3,300 men to reinforce the existing legions in the province.[325] On his arrival to Hispania, he had orders to draft 4,000 Iberian infantry and 300 cavalry. During his governorship, Livy writes that he captured one town called Marcolica (modern-day Marjaliza). The following year, 168 BCE, he was replaced by P. Fonteius Balbas, of whom nothing is known about.[326]

The lack of information about the 170s was that the affairs of Hispania were less in the forefront because much of the news was the same and important events were happening elsewhere such as the war in Macedonia. Also, during this period, many career-minded Roman military officers and consuls began to believe that serving in Hispania was disadvantageous to their career. This negative outlook can be seen

---

323 Livy 43.3. 1-4; Below the common people were the freedmen or libertini. These were individuals who had formerly been slaves but who were freed by their masters for one reason or another. Although now technically free, the libertini had serious restrictions on their rights and they always maintained close relationship with their former masters. Nevertheless, especially in the first century, many of these freedmen were talented and highly educated individuals and many of them found their way into high places of power and influence, often to the disgust of traditionalists in Roman society

324 Florus, An Epitome of the Histories of Titus Livy, 1.33.13

325 Livy 43.12.10-11; 45.4.1 According the Livy each province held a legion of 5,200 infantry and 300 cavalry.

326 Livy 44.17.5, 10

in 176 BCE, when two praetors of the six that where elected to serve in various provinces, claimed that for religious reasons they were unable to leave Rome and proceed to their designated overseas province. The two as it so happens were the two men that were assigned to take over Hispania.[327]

The sudden decline in the popularity of serving in Hispania is noted on several occasions, such as the account by Livy that occurred in 173 BCE, when praetor N. Fabius Buteo died on his way to Hispania Citerior. With his death, the Senate requiring a new praetor, so it asked the two returning governors to cast lots to see who would stay for another term. This was an odd procedure, since it was obvious the man that had previously governor Citerior should have been the one to stay behind and rule in Buteo's place. But perhaps, not to stir any hard feelings or sentiment, the Senate though it would be much safer to leave the decision for governorship to chance.

Prior to 177 BCE, warfare in Hispania made or broke men's military and political careers, but after the Gracchan settlements and treaties, the likelihood of such success lessened. After 166 BCE, it even further declined. The *Fasti Triumphales*, the triumphal arch in Rome, which records all the triumphs and ovations awarded since the earliest times, are extant for the period from 166 155 BCE and does not record a single celebration by a magistrate returning from Hispania.[328]

With the Roman victory ending the Third Macedonia War in 167 BCE, the Senate decided to revert the Spanish province back to its former

---

[327] M. Cornelius Scipio Maluginensis was expelled from the senate at the next *lustrum* in 174BC (Livy 41.27.2). P Licinius Crassus wished to go to Macedonia as consul in 171 BC to participate in the 3rd Macedonian War, it was argued in the senate that he could not, because of the oath he had sworn in 176 BC. (Livy 42.32.1-5)

[328] Degrassi, A., *Fasti consulars et triumphales*, Insriptiones Italiae, vol. 13.1, Rome 1947, p. 80-83, 556-557; Richardson, J.S., "The Triumph, the Praetors and the Senate in the Early Second Century BC" Journal of Roman Studies No. 65, 1975, p. 50-63; Develin, R., "Tradition and development of triumphal regulations of Rome", Klio No. 60, 1978, p. 429-438

provincial pattern of having two provinces instead of just one.[329] Also during this same year, Cn. Fulvius was sent to Citerior, while C. Licinius Nerva went to Ulterior.[330] The following year, 166, two new praetors were elected, A. Licinius Nerva and P. Rutilius Calvus. Livy mentions the names of the praetors but does not say to which provinces these men were assigned.[331]

Despite the long gaps and fragmented documentation in Livy's work, Appian continues to describe what went on in the Iberian Peninsula after 155 BCE but there is little content between the years after the First Celtiberian War in 179 BCE and onset of the Lusitanian War in 155 BCE. The little information that exists, are vague accounts of skirmishes between Romans and Celtiberians in 170 and 174 BCE [332] and Lusitanians in 163 BC.[333] Though minor revolts broke out, the military successes of Albinus and Gracchus and the peace treaties that came about from these campaigns ushered in a period of relative calm in Hispania that lasted until 155 BCE. This semi-peaceful period was marked by a reduction in military strength in the province and an absence of triumphs and ovations for returning governors.[334] But the days of Gracchan peace were numbered in the tumultuous period that followed.

The Senate's Involvement in Hispania from 205 to 160 BC

Although much of this chapter has concentrated on the governorship of the province and covered many military campaigns and battles, one cannot ignore the Senate's involvement in Hispania. During the Second Punic War and after, the Senate played an important part in forming the province by placing policies, arrangements for sending men to govern

[329] Livy 45.16.1-3

[330] Livy 45.16.1-3

[331] Livy 45.44.1-2

[332] Curchin, Leonard, A., op cit., p. 33

[333] Schulten, A., Fontes Hispaniae Antiquae III, Barcelona, 1935, p.230

[334] Brunt, P.A., Italian Manpower, 225 BC – AD 14, Oxford, 1971, p. 661-63; Richardson, J.S., *Hispaniae,* p. 105.

the provinces, sending provisions to the troops and allowing praetors to enlist new recruits into the army.

Once the Carthaginians had been vanquished from Hispania in 205 BCE, the Roman Senate began electing and sending praetors to Hispania on yearly bases as governors. During Rome's occupation of the peninsula, the Senate installed the practice of sending two praetors to rule over a large piece of territory, which they divided into two sub-provinces in 197 BCE. But there where times, during a national emergency such as war, that the Senate would abandon this method and have one ruler govern the entire province or extend each praetors' tenure from to two to three years. The governors that had served in Hispania during a time of national crisis served three years except C. Flaminius (Citerior), who was the only one on record to have served four years.[335]

The Senate at times would also combine the two *provinciae* into one to make it more economical to the praetor who was sent there. This Senatorial move would free up one praetor to serve elsewhere and allow the army to have extra manpower to fight in the warzone. One example occurred in 171 BCE, during the 3rd Macedonian War (172-168 BCE). War had broken out in earnest and in order to leave one commander free to be deployed to a combat zone, the Senate saw it fit to reduce the number of praetors sent to Hispania to one.[336]

Though Hispania was under military rule due to continuous fighting, senatorial power from Rome came into being between 178 - 167 BCE. At first there was a lack of interest by the Senate in the internal management of the area or on how the praetors conducted their military operations and campaigns. The only time the Senate was involved was over the debate about the application for celebrating a triumph for returning praetors from Hispania.[337] For the praetors to be rewarded with a Senate approved triumph, the governors would have to have led a successful

---

[335] Livy 32.28.2 (197 BC); 33.26.1-3 (196 BC); 33.43.5 (195 BC); 34.43.6-7 (194 BC); 34.55.6 (193 BC)

[336] Livy 42.28.5-6

[337] Livy, 39.29.4-7;39.38.4-12;40.35.3-36.12

military campaign and not just the expansion or stabilization of a territory. In short, the Senate's attitude towards a triumph shows that it was aggression and not imperialist expansion that they encouraged.[338]

But after 178, the Senate became more involved in the affairs of Hispania such as dealing with lawful acts. One such example is recorded by Livy on the hearings of several former praetors that were charged with extortion.[339] After the trial the Senate decreed that the Senate would have a bit more control over Hispania's affairs and its officials.[340]

As for establishing settlements, it was usually done on a praetor's own initiative, even though there was no sign of prior approval by the Senate in the founding of cities. Though the Senate had the power to override the praetor's decision later on, but they never use it veto power for the basic reason that distance made it difficult. By the time the Senate's veto arrived in the praetor's hand, it would have been months too late, at which point the town by that time would have grown roots.

Though there is no record of the Senate using its veto power over the establishment of Roman towns, there is historical evidence and much scholarly research confirming that there was a difference between towns founded by local commanders and those that the Senate had established. Such towns as Gracchurris (est. by Gracchus), Corduba (est. by Marcellus) and several others were not recognized by the Senate. So, these towns did not receive the status of '*colonia civium Romanorum*' until the time of Julius Caesar and Augustus. [341] As mentioned earlier in the chapter, there is one settlement, the town of Carteia which is document of having been established by direct appeal to the Senate from the offspring of Roman soldiers and Iberian women who had no right of

---

[338] For detailed examples of this see Richardson, J.S., *Hispaniae,* p. 108-09.

[339] Livy 43.2.1-11

[340] Richardson, J.S., *Hispaniae,*p. 114

[341] Griffin, M., "The Elder Seneca and Spain", Journal of Roman Studies 62, 1972, p.17-19; Knapp, R.C., Aspects of the Roman Experience in Iberia 206 – 100 BC, Vallodolid, 1977, p. 120-124; Wilson, A.J.N., Emigration from Italy in the Republican Age of Rome, Manchester, 1966, p.16-17

conubium.[342] Although these people had a moral claim on the Roman state for assistance, they were still seen as foreigners (*peregrini*), but being that they directly appealed to the Senate, they acquired a status within the Roman system.[343]

Another recorded incident involved an alteration to the tribute payments and troop levies laid down by Gracchus in 179 BCE, which at first were imposed on only the Celtiberian tribes, but later on it became more widely done with other Iberian tribes. But in 154 BCE, in the course of negotiations with the Senate, the Celtiberian tribes of the Belli and Titthi argued that they had been released from their obligations to Rome, according to the treaty they had signed with Gracchus. Through Appian's writing, the Belli and Titthi's argument was brought forth to the Senate, which granted both tribes an exemption, but added that they should continue to serve Rome for the betterment of their people."[344] It seem that when the Senate was directly approached by provincial delegates, who presented their case to the Senate, the Senate showed no reluctance to act on their requests or demands. But when it came time to put forth the effort of the provincial delegates' appeals, there is little indication that they took any initiative in the internal affairs of the provinces, which was in the hands of the praetors. Even though the Senate may have granted the tribes an exemption, it was only temporary.

---

342 see above p. 31; Humbert, M., "Libertas id est civitas", Mélanges de l'école française de Rome Antiquité 88, 1976, p. 221-142; ***Conubium** –Latin Law (Latin *ius Latii* or *Latinitas* or *Latium*) was a civic status given by the Romans, intermediate between full Roman citizenship and non-citizen status (*peregrines*). The most important tenets of the Latin right were *commercium*, *conubium*, and *ius migrationis*. *Commercium* allowed Latins to own land in any of the Latin cities and to make legally enforceable contracts with their citizens. *Conubium* permitted them to make a lawful marriage with a resident of any other Latin city. *Ius migrationis* gave people with Latin status the capacity to acquire citizenship of another Latin state simply by taking up permanent residence there. People with the Latin right were protected under Roman law.

343 Sherwin-White, A.N., The Roman Citizenship, 2nd ed. Oxford, 1973, p. 110; Knapp, R.C., Aspects of the Roman Experience in Iberia 206 – 100 BC, Vallodolid, 1977, p. 116-120

344 Appian, Ib, 44.183

With all this in mind, it perhaps can be safe to say that the attitude taken by both Roman praetors and the Iberian people, to the conclusion of treaties and other relations and the establishment of settlements, indicates that the power of decision making was mainly in the hands of the praetors whether or not the Senate attempted to enforce its policy. Such independence of action is not surprising, considering that the power of '*imperium*' entrusted to a praetor, was ongoing at the time and would need rapid decision-making being that these individuals were constantly or sporadically in a state of war. Also, because of distance and poor communications from Hispania to Rome, it was vital for the survival of the Roman Empire that these men make on the spot decision. But on the praetor's return to Rome, the Senate was bound to scrutinize the praetor's activities or military failures as well as successes. The Senate also acted if a provincial delegate complained about a praetor's misdeeds by reprimanding or correcting the praetor's mistake.[345] Thus the debate among the Senate about Hispania focused mainly on the praetor's military record and which area or how much more land had been added to the empire and whether he should receive a triumph or not.

Though Rome played a part in the affairs of Hispania, it was the praetors who – in reality – brought Hispania to Rome or vice-a-versa regarding its policies. Though the Iberian Peninsula was constantly at war, from the end of the Second Punic War to the middle of Gracchus's governorship, various civil institutions were beginning to develop. These "civilian" arrangements grew out of military functions, such as taxation of the locals began as a levy of grain and corn to feed the troops. But the most notable changes occurred during T. Sempronius Gracchus and L. Postumius Albinus's praetorship between 180 - 178 BCE. After much fighting, these two men, especially Gracchus, were able to set up peace agreements between the Romans and various tribes, dictating the policies that the Senate had been trying to carry out since the end of the Second Punic War. Although we have a very vague record of the negotiations between Gracchus and the Celtiberians that had transpired, we do not have the details of the treaties for the last chapters

345 Richardson, J.S., *Hispaniae,*p. 125.

of Book 40 and the beginning of Book 41 may have been lost. As for Appian, he is the only source to describe these arrangements, but in minor details.[346] Unfortunately, his brief description is not much help when attempting to determine the extent of Gracchus's arrangements. In other works, Gracchus's endeavors make it clear that these peace arrangements were the basis for relations between the Romans and those tribes that would later be involved in the Third Celtiberian War, also known as the Numantine War. [347] In the end, the emergence of the practices, institution, polices, and cultural influences which were to shape the area into provinces of the Roman Empire resulted from those Roman military commanders/praetors and not by the Senate.

[346] Appian 43.179

[347] Polybius 35.2.15; Plutarch, *Ti. Gracchus*, 5.2; Appian, *Iberika*, 44.182-183. Numantine War was a twenty year long conflict between the Celtiberian tribes of Hispania Citerior and the Roman government which began in 154 BC.

CHAPTER III

THE LUSITANIANS

In the early part of the first millennium BCE, several waves of Celts invaded the Iberian Peninsula from Central Europe and had either intermarried with the local populace or conquered them, eventually becoming the Celtiberians. From then on the "Iberians" lived in isolated groups and formed tribal settlements and their own cultures. Today these 'Iberians' have been categorized into four major groups: Celtiberians, Iberians, and Lusitani (or Lusitanian) and the Conii. Of these groups of people, I will only concentrate on the Lusitanians, which was a tribe that inhabited Lusitania (modern-day Portugal and a large section of central Spain). They have an interesting history because of their fierce resistance against the Romans, which was well documented by ancient chroniclers such as Livy, Diodorous, Strabo and Appian. Presently, there have been several books written about the first two groups in English, but not of the third and fourth group.

Ethnic Origins of the Lusitanians

The ethnic origin of the Lusitani has been hotly debated since the 1950s: one theory is that they were indigenous influenced by the Celtic culture. Other scholars state that they may have been of Celtic origins. In any event, it is known that they were established in the area between the Douro and Tagus River between 1000 and 900 BCE.

The theory that the Lusitani are considered to be of a pre-Celtic Indo-European decent comes from the belief that these migrants came from the Urnfield culture, which was of a German descent.[348] Most scholars adhere to this theory, because of the abundance of archaeological, anthropological and genetic evidences of this group. This early migration was followed by several other migrants such as the Hallstatt Culture that later settled in the Iberian Peninsula.[349] This was then followed by Celtic tribes, especially the Helvetii Celts, who are said to be the ancestors of the Lusitani that settled in the north-west of the Iberian Peninsula (what is now north of Portugal and the Spanish province of Galicia).[350] Along with the Celtic culture, Celtic languages spread from southern France

[348] The **Urnfield culture** (c. 1300 BC - 750 BC) was a late Bronze Age culture of central Europe. The name comes from the custom of cremating the dead and placing their ashes in urns which were then buried in fields. Gimpera, Pedro Bosch, "Two Celtic Waves in Spain" (Sir John Rhs Memorial Lecture of November 8, 1939), *Proceedings of the British Academy*, XXVI, 1940, p.29; Júlio Martínez Santa-Olalla, *Esquema paletnológico de la Península Hispánica* (2nd ed.), Madrid, 1946, pp. 62-68, 78-79; Savory, H.N., Spain and Portugal: The Prehistory of the Iberian Peninsula, Ancient People and Place Seires, Praeger, New York, 1968, Chapter 10, pp. 239-259; J. Briand and M. Le Goffic, *Avant les Celtes. L'Europe a l'age du Bronze,* Association Abbaye de Daoulas, Daoulas, 1988; Briard J., *Âge du* Bronze en Europe 2000-800 avant J.-C., Errance, Paris, 1985.

[349] For an overview of Hallstatt culture in the Iberian Peninsula see Alberto J. Lorrio and Gonzalo Ruiz Zapatero, "The Celts in Iberia: An Overview", E-Keltoi: Journal of Interdisciplinary Celtic Studies, Vol. 6 "The Celts in the Iberian Peninsula", University of Wisconsin, Milwaukee, pp. 167-255. For the other migrants see Martín Almagro, "La Invasión Céltica en España," Historia de España, Tomo I, Vol. II, (Historia de Espana, ed. R. Menéndez Pidal) Espasa Calpe, S.A., Madrid, 1952, p. 262-272; Luis P. García, Las Raices de España, Consejo Superior de Investigaciones Científicas, Madrid, 1952.

[350] The **Helvetii** were a Celtic tribe and the main occupants of the Swiss plateau; Andres Furger-Gunti, *Die Helvetier: Kulturgeschichte eines Keltenvolkes.* Neue Zürcher Zeitung, Zürich, 1984; Alexander Held, *Die Helvetier*, Verlag Neue Zürcher Zeitung, Zürich 1984; Felix Müller / Geneviève Lüscher, *Die Kelten in der Schweiz*, Theiss, Stuttgart, 2004; Munoz, Mauricio P., *Viriato, A luta pela Liberdade*, Esquilo, Lisbon, 2006, p. 21

throughout most of northern Iberia extending southward to include central Portugal.[351]

The Celts had a cultural background not dissimilar to that of some of the inhabitants encountered upon their entry into the peninsula. In certain areas of the peninsula similar background and tastes may have allowed them to easily settle among the indigenous groups.[352] It is also believed that the Celts may have conquered local indigenous tribes forcing them to accept their culture. But in view of the disparity between Celtic tribes it is probable that the situation varied according to time, place, and tribe. As for the Helvetii Celts, which came to be known as "Lusitanians," it seems that they may have had a similar culture to the groups already in Lusitania, which allowed them to settle in the area between of the Tagus River and the Douro River Valley, totally occupying the center of modern-day Portugal. Of all the people rooted in the Atlantic strip of the Iberian Peninsula, the Lusitani were to become the most numerous.

Another modern theory derives from Rufus Avienus Festus' poem '*Ora Maritima*' (sea coasts), written in the 4th century BCE, which is based on the Massaliote Periplus of the 6th century BCE.[353] These works state

---

351 Baroja, Caro, *Los Pueblos del Norte de la Peninsula Ibérica*, Consejo Superior de Investigaciones Cieritificas, Madrid, 1943, pp. 82-84; Schulten, Adolfo, *Historia de Numancia*, Barcelona, 1945, p. 21.

352 Maluquer, de Motes, Juan, "Los Pueblos de la España céltica," *Historia de España*, Tomo I, Vol. III, Pt. 1, p.11, *(Historia de Espana,* ed. R. Menéndez Pidal). Madrid, Espasa Calpe, S.A., 1954

353 The ***Massaliote Periplus*** or ***Massaliot Periplus*** is the name of a now-lost merchants' handbook possibly dating to as early as the sixth century BC describing the searoutes used by traders from Phoenicia and Tartessus in their journeys around Iron Age Europe. Massalia (Marseille, France), however, was a Greek colony. It was preserved by the Roman poet Avienus in his work *Ora Maritima* (The Maritime Shores) who wrote down parts of it much later; during the fourth century AD. It describes seaways running northwards from Cadiz in Spain along the coast of Atlantic Europe to Brittany, Ireland and Britain. The Periplus is the earliest work to describe the trade links between northern and southern Europe and that such a manual existed indicates the importance of these trade links. The trade in tin and other raw materials from the British Isles

that western Iberia was called Oestriminis, named after its original people, which are believed to have been expelled from southern England and arrived on Portuguese shores because they were invaded by the Ligurians.[354] Legend has it that these people were later replaced by invaders called the *Saephe* or *Ophis* (meaning Serpent).[355] It is believed that these invaders were the Indo-European migrations (Celtic) in the sixth and seventh century BCE, which most Iberian historians today relate these people as the Celtiberians. The poem also describes the various ethnic groups present at that time:[356]

---

southwards is attested by archaeological evidence from this period and earlier and the riches to be won probably attracted numerous adventurers to explore and exploit the Atlantic coasts.

354 .**Ligurians/Ligures** were an ancient people who gave their name to Liguria, which once stretched from northern Italy into southern Gaul (France). The Ligures inhabited what now corresponds to Liguria, northern Tuscany, Piedmont, part of Emilia-Romagna, part of Lombardy, and parts of southeastern France. Classical references and toponomastics suggest that the Ligurian sphere once extended further into central Italy: according to Hesiod's *Catalogues* (early 6th century BC) they were one of the three main "barbarian" peoples ruling over the Western border of the known world (the others being Aethiopians and Scythians). Avienus, in a translation of a voyage account probably from Marseille (4th century BC) speaks of the Ligurian hegemony extending up to the North Sea, before they were pushed back by the Celts. Ligurian toponyms have been found in Sicily, the Rhône valley, Corsica and Sardinia. Sarmento, Francisco Martins, "Os Lusitanos—Questões de Etnologia", Despersos Porto, 1880, pp. 41-60 and Ora Maritima: Estudo deste poema na parte respectiva as costas ocidentais da Europa, Antonio Jose da Silva Texeira, Porto, 1896, p. 77-78; Sarmento, Francisco Martins, "A Arte Micenica no noroeste da Espana", *Portugalia*, Porto, vol. 1, 1899, 431-442

355 Avienus, *Ora Marítima*, 154-157, 171-172; Vazquez Hoys, Dr. Ana Maria, "Culto a la Serpiente en la Mundo Antiguo", El Boletín de la Asociación de Amigos de la Arqueología nº14, Madrid, Diciembre 1981, pp.33-39; Gómez Tabanera,J. M.: *Las raíces de España*, Madrid 1967, pp. 330, 337, 340, 341; López-Cuevillas, F. - Bouza-Brey, F.: "Os oestriminios, os Saefes e a Ofiolatria en Galicia", en *Arquivo do Seminario de Estudos Galegos*, II, 1920, p. 119-164; López-Cuevillas, F.: *La civilización céltica en Galicia,* Santiago de Compostela, 1958; Alarcão, Jorge de, "Novas perspectivas sobre os Lusitanos (e outros mundos)", Revista Portuguesa de Arqueologia .vol. 4, no. 2, 2001, p. 321-322

356 For a brief but detailed look at the people see Avienus, 182-223; Alarcão, Jorge de, "*Etnogeografia de Fachada Atlântica Ocidental da Peninsula Ibérica*", Complutum, Madrid, 1992, pp. 339-345; Mendes, Correia, *Os povos primitivos*

- The *Saephe or Ophis* also known as the *Sefes*, were Celts that settled in western Iberia (modern Portugal) between the Douro and Sado rivers.
- The *Cempsi*, were Celts that established themselves in the Tagus estuary and south up to the border of modern-day Algarve.
- The *Cynetes* later known as the *Conii* lived in the extreme south of Portugal and some cities along the Atlantic coast
- The *Dragani*, inhabited the mountainous areas of Galicia, northern Portugal, Asturias and Cantabria.
- The *Lusis*, probably a first reference to the Lusitanians were similar to the Dragani culture.

From then on western Iberia became known by the Phoenicians and Greeks as Ophiussa (Land of the Serpents).[357]

Although the theory is possible, it is questionable. For according to Avienus, the Oestriminis were a people that had been living in Lusitania long before they fled their homeland after the invasion of the "serpent people". These serpent people are believed to be the *Sefes* ("People of the Serpents"), who colonized the territorial entity the Greeks termed *Ophiussa*. According to several historians, the reason early Greek explorers named the region "Ophiussa" (Greek for "land of serpents") was because the natives worshipped serpents (όφις = Greek for snake).[358]

---

da Lusitania, Porto, 1924; Lambrino, Scarlat, Les Celtes dans la péninsula Ibérique selon Avienus", Bulletin des Estudes Portugaises et de l'Institut Français au Portugal, issue #19, 1955-56, pp. 5-33. Sarmento, Francisco Martins, Ora Maritima: Estudo deste poema na parte respectiva as costas ocidentais da Europa, Antonio Jose da Silva Texeira, Porto, 1896; Gómez Tabaner J. M.: *Las raíces de España*, pp. 337, 330, 340, 341, López-Cuevillas, F. - Bouza-Brey, F., "Os oestriminios, os Saefes e a Ofiolatria en Galicia", en *Arquivo do Seminario de Estudos Galegos*, II, 1920, p. 119-164; López-Cuevillas, F.: *La civilización céltica en Galicia.* Santiago de Compostela, 1958.

[357] Avienus, 144-151, 165-167; Gamito, Teresa Júdice, "*The Celts in Portugal*", Journal of Interdisciplinary Celtic Studies, 6 vols., University of Algarve, vol. 6, p. 571-604.

[358] **Ophiussa**, also spelled **Ophiusa**, is the ancient name given by the ancient Greeks to what is now Portuguese territory. Avienus, 170-175; Alarcão, Jorge de, "*Etnogeografia de Fachada Atlântica Ocidental da Peninsula Ibérica*",

According to Avienus' work Ophiussa extended from Cape Carvoeiro near Peniche to the Sado River in the south.

But as for the word "Oestreminis", in Latin poetry it means "Extreme West" which was a name given to the furthermost territory of the known world which of course was what is today modern Portugal, this is comparable to *Finis terrae*, the "end of the earth" from a Medieval and Renaissance perspective. Though there are several hypotheses on Avienus' fanciful account, there is no concrete archeological or historical application, but the poetical name has sometimes been ambitiously applied to popularized accounts of the original Paleolithic inhabitants of Portugal.

But according to the late Professor Adolf Schulten, he partial disagrees with this theory and proposed that the Lusitanians were actually Ligurans, who had come from North Africa instead of England onto the Iberian Peninsula prior to 1000 BCE.[359] He believes that the Ligurians had entered Europe via the Strait of Gibraltar and the toe of Italy and headed north.

An alternative theory to the latter is that the Lusitanians came west with the first Celtic wave. Of all the tribes that arrived in Portugal in the first wave of Proto-Celts, the *Lusis* tribe stands out, who are believed to be the Lusitani. The Lusis, according to this hypothesis, settled down in Ophiussa near the pre-existing tribes of the Dragani, Sefes, Cempsi and

---

pp. 339-345; Schulten, A., Fontes Hispaniae Antiquae Vol.I, 1955, XI Vols., Barcelona, 1935-1987, p.100; Bellido, Antonio Garcia y, "O mais primitivos nomes da Peninsula Hispanica", Revista de Guimarães #56, 1946, 227-250; Hoys, Ana María Vázquez, *Culto a la Serpiente en el Mundo Antiguo*, Boletín de la Asociación de Amigos de la Arqueología nº14, Madrid, December 1981, pp.33-39.

359 Schulten, Adolf, Fontes Hispaniae Antiquae I: Avieno, Ora Maritima, Barcelona, 1955, p. 105, Tartessos, Madrid, 1971, p. 52, 185, Numantia I: Die Keltiberer und ihre Kriege mit Rom, Munich, 1914, p.60; Vilatela, Luciano Perez, Lusitania: Historia y Etnología, Real Academia de la Historia, Madrid, 2000, p. 91; Menédez-Pidal, R., "Sobre el substrato mediterráneo occidental", Ampurias #II, 1940, p.8; Mendes Correia, A.A., Os povos primitivos da Lusitanos, p.86; see p. 57

several other tribes. In time this tribe grew in numbers, engulfing into their culture the Sefes, Cempsi, Drangani and several other tribes.[360]

But there are scholars that disagree with this theory, implying that the Lusis came on the second Celtic wave and not on the first wave. They along with the Celtici, Bardili, Bastuli, Turduli, Turduli Veteres, Tapoli and several other tribes established themselves in the area between the Douro and Tagus, except the Celtici, who settled in southern Portugal's Alentejo region in small groups, assimilating themselves into the people that were already there, become what was later known as the Lusitanians.[361]

A third theory dates back to the late 19th century, when Portuguese historian, the late professor Alexandre Herculano, regarded the Lusitanian as part of the Celtic culture who settled in eastern Spain, but some of its members continued to migrate west along the Douro River until reaching the Atlantic Ocean. But this is probably false for João

---

360 Almagro Basch, Martin, " Ligures en España", Rivista di studi Liguri #15, 1949, p. 201 and, "Las estelas decoradas del Suroeste peninsular, Bibliotheca Preahistorica Hispana VIII, Madrid, 1966, p. 214; Lambrino, Scarlet, "Les Celtes dans la Péninsule Ibérique selon Avienus", pp. 22-25; Mendes de Almeida, Justino, "A Orla Maritima portugesa num texto do séc. IV antes de Cristo", *Boletim do Centro de Estudos do Museu Arqueológico de Sesimbra* #4, 1967, 62; Vilatela, Luciano Perez, op. cit., Chapter 2.

361 This information comes from the original texts: Pliny the Elder, 3.1;3.8; 4.35; Strabo, 3.3.5; 3.1.6; Pomponius Mela, De Situ Orbis, 3.3; The arguments are discussed in: Mendes Correa, A.A., op. cit., pp. 84-88; Mattoso, José (dir.), História de Portugal, Primeiro Volume: Antes de Portugal, Lisboa, Círculo de Leitores, 1992; Berrocal-Rangel, Luis, "The Celts of the Southwestern Iberian Peninsula". *e-Keltoi: Journal of Interdisciplinary Celtic Studies* 6, University of Wisconsin-Milwaukee, 2005, pp. 481-496; James, Simon, *The Atlantic Celts,* London: British Museum Press, 1999; Fagan, Brian M., *People of the Earth: An Introduction to World Prehistory*, HarperCollins Publishing, NY, 1992; Vilatela, Luciano Perez, op. cit. Chapter 2 and Lusitania: Historia y Etnologia, Real Academia de la Madrid, Madrid, 2000, Chapter 2; Silva, Armando Coelho Ferreira da, A cultura castreja no Noroeste de Portugal, Paços de Ferreira, 1986, p.37; Caro Baroja, J., Los pueblos de España, 2 vols., Madrid, 1976, vol.1, p. 184-185;. Octávio da Veiga Ferreira e Seomara Bastos da Veiga Ferreira, *A Vida dos Lusitanos no Tempo de Viriato,* Polis, Lisboa, 1969, p. 27.

Lupi claims that the classic texts tell us that the Lusitanian nation was clearly distinct from that of the Celts, claiming that they had assimilated into the native group.[362]

An alternative theory to the Lusis and Herculano's hypothesis comes from the late Professor Scarlat Lambrino, of the University of Lisbon. She proposed a theory that the Lusitani constituted from a tribal group the Lusoni from Switzerland that penetrated the Peninsula during the second Celtic migration settling in the high Tajuña River, northeast of Guadalajara, Spain, with the remnants travelling further east, settling in modern – day Portugal.[363] Though the Lusoni were well established on the northeastern coast of Spain it seems that the tribe may have split and moved west establishing a settlement somewhere on the banks of the eastern part of the Tagus River, while the future "Portuguese" Lusoni continued west along the river towards the Atlantic Ocean, in search of better lands. It is this branch of the Lusoni that became the Lusitanians. Since her theory, many scholars have suggested that the Lusis and the Lusoni are one and the same.

Some historian/scholars such as the Professor Mendes Correia see the Lusitanians as a native Iberian tribe that became celtizied through domination or intermarriage between Celts and native Iberians.[364] His hypothesis is of an autochthonous nature. He believes that the indigenous

---

[362] Lupi, João, Os Lusitanos e a construção do ideal nacionalista português, Brathair 1 (1), 2001, pp. 16.Os textos clássicos dizem-nos que este povo era claramente distinto dos povos célticos que habitavam mais a sul.

[363] Lambrino, Scarlet, Les lusitaniens Centro de Estudos Classicos, Faculdade de Letras de Lisboa, Lisboa, 1957, p.124 and "Les Celtes dans la Peninsula Ibérique selon Avienus", p. 22; Munoz, Mauricio P., op. cit., p.21; Vilatela, Luciano Perez, op. cit., Chapter 2

[364] This theory can be found in the following books and articles written by Mendes Correia, A.A., op. cit., p.86; see p. 57; "Celtas na Beira," *Boletim de Casa das Beiras,* X, No. 6 (Lisboa, 1943), 5-11; *A Geografia da pré-história.* Porto, 1929; "A Lusitânia pré-romana" *(História de Portugal),* Barcelos, Portucalense Editora, 1928. Vol. I.; *Os Povos Primitivos da Lusitânia.* Porto, 1924; *Raízes de Portugal* (2nd ed.). Lisboa, Revista "Occidente," 1944. Roche, J., "Le Paléolithique supérieur portugais: Bilan se nis connaissance et problèmes"' Bulletin de la Société Préhistorique Français, 1965, p.11-27; Munoz, Mauricio P., *op. cit.,* p. 79

"Lusitanians" had crossed the strait of Gibraltar from North Africa and rooted themselves in Portugal during the Neolithic or Chalcolithic periods. After the first Celtic migration, they were initially dominated by the Celts. In time they either gained full independence from them or one tribe or the other assimilated their culture to the other. His theory is reinforced by Strabo, who distinguishes the difference between the 'Celtic' people from the south of the Tagus River from those to the north, the Lusitanians. For Avienus, Strabo and Diodorus, the Lusitanians were "non-Celtic"; this is also consistent with the linguistics-derived interpretation of the Lusitanian language, which will be looked into at the end of the chapter.[365]

An alternative theory to Correia's comes from the late professor Pere Bosch Gimpera who states that the Lusitanians were part of the original Iberian inhabitants that originated from non-Celtic people in Europe and later immigrated into the Iberian Peninsula prior to the 6th century BC.[366] He claims the people that become Iberians came from the Eastern Mediterranean. This megalithic culture settled on the southeastern coast of Spain and branched out moving west into the Tagus estuary in Portugal.

Though many historians, scholars, historical anthropologist, archaeologist have sought to identify the origin of the ancient Lusitani, and have claimed for them a separate or continuous existence dating back from Paleolithic times, the problem these individuals face is

---

365 Avienus, *Ora Maritima*, 195-204; Diodorus V.34; Strabo 3.1.6; Gamito, Teresa Júdice, "The Celts in Portugal", p. 571-604. Tovar, A, Les ecritures de l'anciénne Hispania. *Proceedings of XXIX Cong. Int. Orientalistes*, Paris: L'Asiatheque, 1975, pp. 15-22. *Lenguas y pueblos de la Antigua Hispania: lo que sabemos de nuestros antepassados protohistoricos*. Vitória: University of Vitória 1985; K.H. Schmidt, R. Ködderitzsch and A. Tovar, The Celts in the Iberian Peninsula: Archaeology, history, language, *Geschichte und Kultur der Kelten*, Heidelberg: Winter 1986, pp. 68-101; Alarcão, Jorge de, "Novas perspectivas sobre os Lusitanos (e outros mundos)", Revista Portuguesa de Arqueologia .vol. 4, no. 2, 2001, p. 320-322

366 Bosch Gimpera, P., "El pobalmiento y la formación de los pueblos de España", Revue de l'institut Français por l'Amérique Latine, Mexico, 1945, p. 150, Etnologia de la Peninsula Ibèirca, Barcelona, 1932

pinpointing the exact ethic origins of the Lusitani for it is a complex one which continues to be debated. Even though many theories are sound, there is still no hard evidence to justify that these theories are true, so their ethnic origin is still presently being discussed by historians and archeologists.

Geographical Location

A total of twenty-four tribes lived in what is now modern Portugal prior to the Roman conquest. But of all the tribes that inhabited Lusitania, the best-known, most numerous and culturally dominant of the pre-Roman peoples were the **Lusitani**, who had at some point in history, colonized the Douro River Valley and the region of Beira Alta. It has been assumed that they stayed in Beira Alta until they were either pushed off or defeated by a Celtic group known as the Vettones. In time, the Lusitani had regained power and expand further west and south – west, covering the territory that reached the entire Tagus River and Spain's province of Estremadura.

Though we have an idea of what the Lusitanian frontier was like, it is very difficult for modern historians to exactly define the frontier limits and the exact location of the Lusitani in the western part of the Iberian Peninsula, because several Roman authors contradict themselves when mentioning the Lusitanian homeland such as Mela, who places them in the western part of the Guadiana, while Pliny at Cape of Saint Vicente and the Douro River and Diodorus in the mountains of Serra da Estrela and the hills of Sintra near the Atlantic coast. While Ptolemy and Strabo, places the Lusitani between the entire area of the Tagus and Douro Rivers and mentions some of their populations and cities, which coincide with Pliny's work. The best description about the boundaries of the Lusitanian homeland that most historians agree upon comes from Starbo. Unfortunately, this problem of location is still reinforced by the scarcity of Lusitanian archeological finds.

Though difficult to pinpoint the exact location of the Lusitanian territory, there is an agreement between historians that their territory was between the Douro and Tagus Rivers and east to the slope of the Central Plateau that penetrates into the province of Estremadura, Spain. From ancient texts, modern historians place the Lusitanian central nucleus in the area between Serra da Estrela and Serra da Gata. The Lusitanian territory was comprised of two very different geographical zones: its interior and the north were mountainous and some what pastoral, while the southern part was plain and excellent for agriculture. Based on this simple geography, it shows us how difficult life was for the Luistanians. Because of the harsh landscape, the Lusitanians to survive had to constantly conduct raids on people that lived in the Meseta Central and Andaluisa. We can also get an idea of the land through several ancient literary sources who speak about the enormous difficulties the Roman soldiers had in surviving in the wilds of Iberia.

Though the Lusitani controlled a vast area, there were several tribes that lived among them, which Pliny points out. Of all the tribes that either surrounded their territory or lived in it, they were surrounded by four large tribes; north of the Douro was the Gallaecian, to the northeast, the Vettones, to the south, the Celtici and Conii. Three smaller tribes lived adjacent to the Lusitani; the Turduli Veteres, Turduli and the Paesuri, while the Tapori, Elbocori and Igaeditani lived among the Lusitani. The Turduli Veteres lived around the estuary of the Douro River in northern Portugal. The Paesuri were a dependent tribe that resided in the northwest between the Douro and Vouga Rivers. The Turduli resided in modern Estremadura while the Tapori, Elbocori and Igaeditani had settled in the south and southeast along the banks of the Tagus River. These tribes would later on rally around Virithus cause. In recent years, some Portuguese archeologists believe that the Lusitanian border went further south into Portugal due to several archeological discoveries in Portuguese Alentejo, which was traditional land of the Celtici.[367]

Lusitanian Society

Of the ancient historians, Strabo, Pliny, Ploybius and Diodorus wrote the largest amount of information on the Lusitanian culture. In Strabo's

[367] Munoz, Mauricio, op. cit., p. 24

book "Geography" he states that the Lusitanians were "the most powerful of the Iberian nations and that they were the one able to stop the Romans."[368] Though Strabo has great respect for the Lusitani, for centuries they have been misunderstood and even have been slandered. For a long time, they were looked as a miserable group of people, given to robbing and banditry, as well as war-mongering barbarians who dressed in animal skins and eaters of raw meat and vegetables who lived in the hills like troglodytes with low cultural and artistic intuition.

But since then through much research and archaeological excavations throughout Portugal and Spain, it has revealed that the Lusitanians were not just a tribe of warlike backward barbarians who survived by hunting and gathering, but an agrarian and pastoral people with an advance culture of their own. Along with their own advanced culture, they had their own language. Theirs was a developed culture, although not as developed as the Romans and Greeks. In order to have a better picture of the mode of life and their physical appearance we must resort to sculptural and pictorial records and the descriptions of the classical texts. This hardy slender race with their fine feature was energetic and a colorful people with a zest for life. With the information that exists through ancient authors and archeological artifacts, we have an idea how they lived, but it is still difficult to define a common way of life or speak of the habits of these people.

Socio-political Structure

Little is known about the political structure of Lusitanian society, but nevertheless, it had a type of politico-administrative structure that elected leaders during peace and war and representative of the tribe when it was necessary to conduct a large – scale tribal meeting, and exercised control of the group's conduct. But the theory that forms the bases that the Lusitanian had some kind of government, comes from the classical texts of Appian, Strabo, Diodorus and several others. From analyzing these sources, there is an agreement that there was a

[368] Strabo, 3.3.3

system of social-political organization that instituted small monarchies or tyrannies whose aristocracy was of a war-like character.

According to geographical areas, each tribe of the Iberian Peninsula was organized in different ways, but the basic cell of society was the extended family (the clan) linked by kinship. From the information that we know from Luso-Roman inscriptions, they show that the clan organization was still effective into the 2nd and 3rd centuries AD. However, these inscriptions are rare and pertain to a later date in Lusitania's history (i.e. Roman occupation). As for the Lusitani, there have been only two documented mentions of the Lustani *gentilitates* in the whole territory and both come from Conimbriga.[369] These inscriptions show that the Roman social structures by the time of the occupation had already begun to be imposed on the indigenous system, which would inevitable be the beginnings of the disappearance of the Lusitani social *gentílica.*

Lusitanian society was broken into three classes: the aristocracy, warriors and populous. The aristocratic society held the socio-political will and the majority of wealth that constituted as the nobility. These aristocrats showed their social status by the ownership of a large herd of livestock and complete panoply of a warrior. Their system, like all political systems, was based on controlling their territory, but the difference between the Lusitanian and other tribes was that the hierarchy was simply marked for the prestige of the tribe/clan, so tribal leaders were elected by the nobles for their capabilities - physical strength, agility, courage, merit, use of weapons, sagacity, orator capabilities and so on and not of bloodline. To unify the clans or build alliances, the chieftains would seek the support of other nobles/warriors by intermingling their blood ties through marriages, such as in the example of Viriathus marriage.[370]

---

[369] Alarcão, Jorge de, "Arquitectura romana", in Alarcão, Jorge de (coord.) História da Arte em Portugal, Vol 1, "Do Paleolítico à arte visigótica "(Lisboa, Pub Alfa, 1986). p. 75-110; O Domínio Romano em Portugal, 1988 Lisboa, Pub. Eur-América, 1988, Forum da História 1; Roman Portugal, 1988 (2 vols.), Warminster, Aris & Philips. 345-351; Munoz, Mauricio P., op. cit., p. 93

[370] Diodorus Siculus, Universal History, III.33.1-5

According to the classical texts, the governing body during war time was the military. These individuals would have complete control of the clans with the nobles assisting these generals in their endeavors. These military commanders (Latin = *dux ducis*) were chosen by popular assembly. And just like the tribal chiefs, these men were elected by an assembly based on their qualification. An example of this comes from Appian, who mentions that at the time the 1st Lusitanian War began Punicus was in command of Lusitanian and Vettonian troops.[371] After his death, a new man was elected by popular assembly among the nobles. This action can be seen in Appian's work which states after Punicus had been killed in battle, a man named Ceasaros/Kaisaros was elected to continue the fight.[372] This also includes Viriathus who later became overall commander and leader of the tribe.

The warrior class was made up of individuals from the gentry class who, as in all military branches throughout the world, formed a group governed on the principals of equality and honor. And according to various archeologically excavations in which a few Lusitanian mortuaries have been found, these military leaders formed an important group within Lusitanian society.[373] The warrior class, at first developed into fighting units so as to consolidate the aristocrats hold on power, but by the time the Romans invaded Lusitania, the warrior class had rallied the nation to become an army under one leader. These men were now in the forefront or equal to the aristocrats. However, though loyal to the nobles, the warrior spirit and honor at times would disappear or fold causing a shameful mark on the class when implicated in an act of betrayal of their leader. As in the example that refers to the murder of Viriathus by three of his lieutenants.

371 Appian, 56.234-235

372 Appian, 56.236

373 There are only a few for the Lusitanian custom was cremation. Munoz, Mauricio P., op. cit., p. 92.

The socio-political characteristic that held the Lusitanians as a people was the practice of *hospitium.*[374] Lusitanian *hospitium* was a much broader concept than the Latin equivalent to *patronatus romanus*. The concept of devotion fell into two elements: one of a religious nature, whereby certain deities would be satisfied with the death of devotees in exchange for his spirit and loyalty to its leader. The second element was purely social for this was an intimate relationship within a brotherhood of warriors. The *hospitium* was a pact between clans or gentiliates under which each member of one clan was considered to enjoy full rights and obligation as a member of the other.[375] During war time, these intra-clan obligations were more pronounced. Compared to other tribes like the Germanic and Gallic tribes, the Iberian tribes had the capacity of receiving and welcoming foreigners and adopting and integrating foreign mannerisms into their own culture. In other words, the Lusitanians followed a sense of hospitality and loyalty towards others if they were peaceful or friendly. This habit was known throughout the Iberian

[374] Mangas Manjarrés, J., "*Hospitium* y *patrocinium* sobre colectividades públicas: ¿términos sinónimos?", *Dialogues d'Histoire Ancienne*, 9, 1983, pp.165-184; Dopico Cainzos, Maria D., *La Tabula Lougeiorum. Estudios sobre la implantación romana en Hispania*, Vitoria, 1988, pp.17-46; *EAD.*, "El *hospitium* celtibérico. Un mito que se desvanece", *Latomus,* 48, 1989, pp.19-35; *EAD.*, "Las Tabulae Hospitalis. Un instrumento de la dominación romana", *Revista de Arqueología*, 196, 1997, pp.30-39

[375] Ramos Loscertales, J.M., "Hospicio y clientela en la España céltica", *Emerita*, 10, 1942, pp.308-337; Salinas de Frias, M., "La función del *hospitium* y la clientela en la conquista y romanización de Celtiberia", *Studia Historica. Historia Antigua*, 1, 1983, pp.21-41; Etienne, R., Le Roux, P. and Tranoy, A., "La *tessera hospitalis*, instrument de sociabilité et de romanisation dans la Péninsule Ibérique", en Thelamon, F., (Ed.), *Sociabilité, pouvoirs et société. Actes du colloque de Rouen (Noviembre, 1983)*, Rouen, 1987, pp.323-336; Sastre Prats, I., Ruiz del Árbolmoro, M. and Plácido Suárez, D., "La integración de las comunidades indígenas del noroeste peninsular en el marco romano: el papel de los pactos de hospitalidad y patronato", en de Balbín Behrman, R. y Bueno Ramírez, P., (eds.), *II Congreso de arqueología peninsular. Tomo IV: Arqueología romana y medieval (Zamora, del 24 al 27 de septiembre de 1996)*, Zamora, 1999, pp.39-50.

Península as *devotio iberica.*[376] The form of devotion had an important influence within public and military life, as well as in private life.[377]

From *hospitium* comes *devotio*, according to Latin writers it was known as *devotio iberica.* Under this oath sealed with religious invocations to the god Tvgoti/Tugotus a man and his family devoted themselves to the service of another individual to defend him to the death, in return for certain obligations were given and taken on by that individual.[378] In this sense, loyal private armies were created. This loyalty had such an effect on the Romans that they put the local custom to good use and formed many unit and even loyal personal bodyguards of Iberian warriors.[379] One such example comes from Appian in that Viriathus had an entourage of 1,000 men under this oath.[380] These men were selected for having proved their valor and dedication to their chieftains in the heat of battle. While their background may vary, they all had in common a religious oath of fidelity sealed by this sacred rite (*devotio ibérica*). If the leader died in combat or was assassinated, the devotee was dishonored, and morally he would sacrifice his life in a ritual

---

376 Caro Baroja, J., "Regimenes Sociales y Económicos de la España Pre-romana", Revista Internacional de Sociologia #1, 1943, pp.149-152; Ramos Loscertales, J.M., "Hospicio y clientela en la España céltica", pp.308-337; Rodriguez Adrados, F., "La *fides* ibérica", *Emerita,* 14, 1946, pp.128-209; Prieto Arciniega, A., "La *devotio* ibérica como forma de dependencia en la Hispania prerromana", *Memorias de Historia Antigua,* 2, 1978, pp.131-135; Dopico Cainzos, Maria D., "La *devotio* ibérica: una revisión crítica", en Mangas, J. y Alvar, J., (Eds.), *Homenaje a José Mª Blázquez,* II, Madrid, 1994, pp.181-193.

377 Martinez, Rafael T., Rome's Enemies (4): Spanish Armies, Osprey Publishing, Men-at-Arms Series #180, Oxford, UK, 1986, p.6

378 Strabo, 3.4.18; Plutarch, *Sertorius,* 14.4; Valerius Maximus, 2.6.11-14 and 5.6.6; Appian 71.301; Livy, 25.17.4 and 38.21; Aulus Gellus, *Attics Nights,* 15. 22; Dio Cassius, LII, 20, 2; Paulus Orosius. *Historiarum Adversum Paganos Libri VII,* 5.23; Julius Cesar, De bello civili, 3.22; Cicero, De /inibus bonorum et malorum, 2.19.21 and Tusculanae disputationes, 1.37.89 and Corpus luris civilis, 7.64.9; Código Teodosiano, 1.2.9; 11.1.20; 29.35; Cassius Dio, 53.20.22; 59.8; Macrobius, Saturnalia, 3.19.10-12; Servius Maurus, Ad Georgicas, 4.218; Suetonius, Vitae Caesarum. Caligula, 14.27; Vegetius, Epitoma rea militaras, 1.28,2.8-9; 3.4;

379 Ibid.

380 Appian, 62.260-262

suicide, delivering his soul to the god to which they had delivered in a ritual for failing to fulfill his oath to his leader.[381]

Though the complete liturgical religious ritual that was used is not known, there are some details that have reached us, that makes it possibly to imagine how the ritual ceremony was conducted. Outside a cave, temple or shrine of stone or wood the ceremony was celebrated under the presence of high ranking warriors and Tugotus, the god of oaths which was represented by a grotesque effigy carved out of stone or wood. In this ritual, the warrior would be naked as a sign of purity and with their arms down as a sign of submissive loyalty to the chief. He would then swear an oath of allegiance to defend the clan and warlord with his life.[382] Also among the Lusitanians there was a special powerful institution that the Romans called *ambacti*, according to Julius Ceasar, it was held among soldiers to express their fidelity to their leaders in thanks for the bond of personal dependence.[383]

Daily Life

The Lusitani, were not a single nation with a concept of nationality, but rather a collection of peoples living under an egalitarian tribal family with ties and alliances to clans that lived isolated from each other, usually behind protected town or village walls set on top of mountains and hilltops. Though these clans were united by either blood or marriage, at times they fought each other or united against another tribe for various reasons. But on several occasion throughout their history, they unite (even during time of bad blood) to fight against the oppression from foreign opponents such as the Carthaginians and Romans. Up until the arrival of the Romans, these tribes had their own

---

381 Ramos Loscertales, op. cit.; Martinez, Rafael T., op. cit., p.6

382 Ramos Loscertales, J.Mª., op. cit.; Rodriguez Adrados, F., "La fides ibérica", pp.128-209; Prieto Arcinega, A., "La devotio ibérica como forma de dependencia en la Hispania prerromana", pp.131-135; Cipres Torres, P., Guerra y sociedad en la Hispania indoeuropea, Vitoria, 1993, pp.126-129; Dopico Ccaozos, Mª.D., "La devotio ibérica: una revisión crítica", en Mangas, J. y Alvar, J., (Eds.), Homenaje a José Mª Blázquez, pp.181-193.

383 Munoz, Mauricio P., op. cit., p. 92

social, economic and religious independence. Testimonies that were left by ancient authors describe Lusitania as a region of dense vegetation, forests, mountains, rivers and natural resources. There is however a serious discrepancy between those who lived on the coast and those who lived in the mountains. The tribes that lived along the coastal zone had access to fertile lands, mild climate, navigable rivers, therefore, making life a bit easier. These people were dedicated to agriculture, fishing, farming and livestock. Those who lived within arid lands and harsh mountain climate had a difficult life. These people became pastoral, but because of the poor living conditions would at times come together as gangs of bandits and raid their neighbors.

With this in mind, life in everyday Lusitania does not leave much to the imagination for it was a simple, but a harsh life. Everyday consisted of hard work, taking care of the family and home, watching out for raiding parties, raiding other tribes, hunting, fishing and gathering food. Though life was hard they enjoyed what they had, and they manifested an intense love for the earth, cooperation and common work. The base of their social organization was the family. Like most early cultures in the western world, the family organization represented the basic characteristic of the tribe and it should be also noted that the concept of a developing civilization was the practice of monogamy. The family member had each a role to play in keeping the family and tribe together. According to Strabo, the Lusitanians married in the same way as the Greeks. Meaning the men could only married one woman and it was she who became the lady of the house and mother to his legitimate children. Besides dining and dancing together, the Romans found it bizarre that a Lusitanian couple slept together on batches of straw and animal skins spread on the ground.[384]

[384] Strabo, 3.3.7; for details see Bonnard, André. *Greek Civilization From The Iliad To The Parthenon Vol. 1.* New York: Macmillan, 1962 and Flacelière, Robert. *Daily Life In Greece At The Time Of Pericles.* New York: Harper and Row, 1970; Octávio da Veiga Ferreira e Seomara Bastos da Veiga Ferreira, *A Vida dos Lusitanos no Tempo de Viriato*, p. 61

The social ranking of the Lusitani, as well as the rest of the Iberians, was based on age and sex, as Strabo says: "They eat sitting on banks constructed around the walls, aligning themselves according to ages and dignities..."[385] Like all ancient and modern cultures, the elders were respected within the group for they were the bearers of wisdom and in a society of oral tradition. It was they who passed on the oral tradition to the next generation by have the young adults and children learn the intricacies of their culture and history. In addition, the elderly member of the family always presided at the forefront of the family and tribal hierarchy for they had the first say when it came to tribal or clan gatherings. Finally, they were the first to sit down at the head of the circular seating arrangement and the first to eat.

When the men were not off fighting, raiding, hunting or fishing, they were farming and herding animals. Marital tells us that the men left home at dawn to work in the fields only to return at dusk.[386] Those who were not farmers conducted trade and busied themselves with their craftsmanship such as blacksmithing. When not farming, raiding or dealing with the political agenda of the tribe, they entertained themselves with games of physical ability and dexterity.[387] Through vase paintings we see how men enjoyed various sports such as gymnastic exercises, boxing, racing and friendly gladiatorial games. At the end of the day, having tended to their daily chores, there would presumably - hopefully - have been time to rest. This may have been a matter of sitting by the fire, eating and drinking freshly brewed beer from a drinking horn made of antler and talking to the other members of the house about past victories, battles and exploits of past heroes. Another leisure activity for both the young and old was a type of board game in which the game pieces were made of either metal, rock or glass, in which such samples have been found in some late Iron Age sites.[388] The same trait appears to an even greater

[385] Strabo, 3.3.7

[386] Arribas, Antonio, The Iberians, Frederick A. Praeger Publishing, NY, 1964, p. 67

[387] Strabo, 3.3.7

[388] Bell, R. C., *Board and Table Games from Many Civilizations*, New York: Dover Publications, Inc., 1979

degree in festive and religious scene where music, dancing, dining and drinking are depicted.

As for the women, when the men were out either raiding or conducting military campaigns against other tribes, they took over the men's roles as farmer and defenders of the castro (village). Besides these two major roles, they still worked at home doing such chores as cooking, cleaning, breeding and raising small livestock, sewing and mending clothes, spinning, weaving wool and linen and teaching and looking after their children. Those who were married to craftsmen continued to run the family business of trading goods, if the husband was not present. Although they were the busiest of the partnership, women according to vase paintings and sculptures seem to have found the time to spend on their personal appearance. Though a patriarchal people, as being that men had ultimate power in politics, war and the everyday running of the tribe, the women were queens of the home. But in some Iberian tribes, they participated in tribal assemblies, and their decision was considered important and, in some cases, they were allowed to be priestesses.

Life for Lusitanian children was not easy; girls helped their mothers; boys helped their fathers. During these times, children of lower and merchant classes were educated to attend to their appropriate gender roles within Lusitanian society, while the children of the very small upper class would learned to be leaders/warriors and good aristocratic wives. All Lusitanian children from all social classes were trained to fight with swords and other weapons. Around age 15, both boys and girls began to think of marriage. Most would marry someone they met at either a festival, grown up with or arranged marriages as it was the case of the upper class. The tallest and strongest of boys might be selected to train as warriors, while other learned an artisan skill, but most would be farmers/warriors. During the day, female children would have helped with the household chores, while the males tended to the livestock, and when working out in the fields both sexes would help raise crops. As for their free time, one can only guess and assume that they played outdoor games just as modern children do with the addition of occupying most of their free time by practicing their skill with a slingshot, spear and sword- a common and accessible weapon of the Iron Age.

Diet

The Lusitanian population subsisted on agriculture, in which the population lived mainly on cereals such as wheat, rye and barley and a variety of vegetables as cabbage, peas and broad beans and roots like turnips.[389] Of the information that is available, barley was cultivated to produce a type of beer that would be nicknamed by classical writers as *zythos*.[390] The beer was disrespected by Greeks and Romans who considered it the "drink of barbarians", given that they were habituated to the refinement of wine. Besides growing vegetables and cereals, the Lusitanian gathered wild plants, fruits, seeds, nuts and wild roots from their surrounding area, while those that lived near the coast collected sea algae and seaweed. One popular nut used by the Lusitanians was the acorn, which was made into bread.[391] Bread was also made out of rye, barley and wheat.

Besides being argicultural, they also lived a pastoral life, as classic documents and archeological registries confirm. Among the Lusitanians there existed a system of animal husbandry of horses, pigs, cows, goats and sheep. Besides raising livestock, they hunted all sorts of wild animals and birds, except the doe for some unknown reason it was considered sacred.[392] The doe was perhaps seen as the incarnation of the

---

[389] Octávio da Veiga Ferreira e Seomara Bastos da Veiga Ferreira, op. cit., pp.91-108; Inês Vaz, João L., Lusitanos no Tempo de Viriato: Quotidiano e Mito, Esquilo Ida, Lisboa, 2009, p. 47-49

[390] The reason why classical writers called barley beer, zythos, was because it referred to the beer's propensity of the foam. The word has the same Greek derivations as the words as leaven and yeast. Hornsey, Ian, A History of Beer and Brewing, Royal Society of Chemistry, Cambridge, 2003, p.36

[391] Strabo 3.3. 7; Alberto Sampaio, "As Vilas do Norte de Portugal," *Estudos históricos e económicos*, Paris-Lisboa, Livraria Chardron, 2 vols. 1923, vol.1, Pt. 1. Octávio da Veiga Ferreira, op. cit., pp.91-108; Inês Vaz, João L., Lusitanos no Tempo de Viriato: Quotidiano e Mito, p. 47-49

[392] Octávio da Veiga Ferreira, op. cit., p. 102-103

hunter-goddess. Just like the doe, certain other animals were not harmed as the horse, cats and dogs. However useful these three animals were in performing their domestic tasks, at times when necessary, they were ritually sacrificed during special religious ceremonies.[393]

A variety of fish was included in the Lusitanian diet, but only for those who lived on or near river banks, streams and coastal salt waters. From archeological evidence the discovery of fishhooks and net weights reveal that they already fished a considerable amount of fish and shellfish which was later cooked or eaten raw.[394] According to Strabo, Lusitanian fishermen used tanned leather boats to fish in flood-tides and shoal-waters, but sometimes they utilized dug-out canoes for fishing trips that were further downriver or deeper waters.[395] Along with fishing, these wooden canoes were also used to transport good to other Lusitanian towns that were situated along river banks.

Compared to today's Portuguese cuisine, Lusitanian cooking according to several ancient writers did not use or have excess to spices or other ingredients except butter, salt and fermented blood which is still used in Portuguese cooking.[396] Salt was another means of preserving meat for the cold winter months, but this was a commodity that could not be made at a typical settlement and was therefore traded. Olive oil was rare for the Lusitanian because they did not have the technology to drain the oil from the olive, so they either used it or not. But if they used it, it came from Roman trading or raiding in southern Spain. So, to supplement olive oil, the Lusitanians used butter. During the Roman invasion and occupation of the Iberian Peninsula, the use of butter was seen as a disgusting culinary act.[397] In time, the Lusitanians began to use olive oil and wine, introduced by the Romans, in their cuisine. Today they still continued use these two ingredients for cooking.

---

[393] Ibid., p.102-103

[394] Figueiredo, A.M. de, "Contribuição para a História de pesca em Portugal na época Luso-romana", Archeologia Portuguesa, vol. IV, no. 1, Lisboa, 1892, p.8

[395] Strabo, 3.3.7

[396] Octávio da Veiga Ferreira, op. cit., pp.91-108

[397] Strabo, 3.3.7; James M. Anderson & M. Sheridan Lea, Portugal: 1001 Archaeological and Historical Guide, Univ. of Calgary, Canada, 1995, p. 25

Dining

Strabo writes that the Lusitanians were sober and frugal people, who ate one meal a day and usually drank water, barley beer or goat milk, while sitting on the ground or on stone seats. The consumption of wine was only used during festivities, but that was not until the Roman conquest.[398] When a feast or banquets was celebrated, it was usually held in the home of the nobles. It was through these banquets that tribal unity was strengthened. During the banquet relatives and guests sat down on stationary seats built into the walls around the room.[399] According to Strabo's texts,

...they sat according to age and social status within the tribe. Once seated the men began to converse and drink, while the women prepared the meal. Once the meal was ready to be served a libation and a small animal sacrifice was performed. Dinner was then passed round or carried around, and amid their metal cups and wooden or clay plates, they danced to the sound of flutes and trumpets, singing and dancing in chorus by springing up and sinking upon the knees. When dinner had been served the women would dance promiscuously with men, taking hold of their hands. The meal at these tribal banquets usually consisted of meat, bread, cheese and beans cooked in salt water, for dessert, fruits and sweet bread made with honey was served. The drinks were mostly beer, water, and goat's milk with honey and at times wine was served.[400]

---

[398] Strabo. 3.3.7; Athenaeus, 4.36 gives a rather full description of the Celtic banquet; Lupi, João, Os Lusitanos e a construção do ideal nacionalista português, p. 21; Octávio da Veiga Ferreira, op. cit., p. 91, 97

[399] Diodorus Siculus, 5.33; Athenaeus, Deipnosophists, or, Banquet of the learned of Athenæus, 2.21 and 4.36 quotes Phylarchus as saying that "the Iberians always eat only one meal a day." Xenophon, *Cyropaedia* 8.8.9. See the translator's note in *Classical Quarterly,* London, July 1917, pp132-134

[400] The cheese that the Lusitanians used was either goat cheese or a type of cheese manufactured using the fermented flower of the thistle. This cheese is still made today in the Beira region of Portugal. Sampaoi, Albero de, As Vilas do Norte de Portugal, Portugália, Vol. 1, Porto, 1923, p.35; Octávio da Veiga Ferreira, op. cit., p. Octávio da Veiga Ferreira, op. cit., p. 97 and 195 from Strabo work, 3.3.7.

The reason why wine was rare during the pre-Roman era was because the Lusitanians had little knowledge of how to cultivate grapes, in addition, much of the land that they inhabited was not very fertile for grape production, so many of the Lusitanians resorted to raiding Baetica and stealing not only wine but olive oil and whatever else they could laid their hands on.

Hygiene

Among the Lusitanians, Strabo records that the Lusitanians had for serious concern over their corporal and dental care.[401] The Lusitanians had a great reverence for natural beauty, including that of the human body. Therefore, the Lusitanians were very hygienic for they always washed and disinfected themselves and prescribed natural medicines to the sick and wounded. Those who dwelt next to the rivers and streams created special spas for bathing. The spa was a building with three rooms built in a triangle shape; the first room dubbed the cold room (i.e. locker room) was where one would prepare himself before crawling through a man size mouse hole into the second room (warm room). This warm room, also called the anointing - room or soap room was the sauna where they took baths in vapors from which heat rose up from an oven at the end of the room. It was in this room that the individual would lather their body of mixture of oil, sweat and heat producing a type of oleaginous cleaning solution which would then be scraped and washed off with cold water or luke warm water on entered the third room (wash room).[402] As for how the hot room was heated, it is not exactly known, but there are a few logical theories on how they did it, such as heated rocks. Once washed, the individual returned to the start point and poured cold water over himself, from one of several basins that were

[401] Strabo, 3.3.6 and 3.3.7

[402] Octávio da Veiga Ferreira, op. cit., pp. 71; Cardozo, M., A última descoberta arqueológica na Citânia de Briteiros e a interpretação da 'Pedra Formosa', *Revista de Guimarães,* 1931, pp. 41(1-2) and (3): 55-60, 201-260, A última descoberta arqueológica na Citânia de Briteiros e a interpretação da '*Pedra Formosa*' (cont.), *Revista de Guimarães,* 1932, pp. 42(1-2) and (3-4): 7-25, 127-139, and Nova estela funerária do tipo da '*Pedra Formosa*', *Revista de Guimarães*, 1949, p. 59(3-4): 487-498.

against the wall, to wash away the leftover dirt and grime[403]. Those who did not have very good access to water are said to have washed their teeth and bodies with urine and rain water which was kept in stone reservoirs.[404] This manner of washing is still used by African Bushmen and Berbers of northwest Africa. For those who were obese, unsightly, dirty and unfit for war, were either fined or ostracize.[405]

Fashion

Our understanding of how people dressed and cared for their appearance has come from classical writers such as Strabo and Diodorus Siculus, who were amazed at the difference from the plain colored togas to the stunning clothing articles of shirts and tunics that were dyed in various colors. Along with these descriptions, Lusitanians fashion has been preserved through sculptures and vase fragments for no textile fragments have been found and little leather items exist. With this information, it shows us that they certainly had their own fashion and style of dressing.

Like the Iberians, Lusitanians' love for clothes and rich adornment were well known. Polybius notes that the difference between Hannibal's Iberian mercenaries to the rest of his army was that they worn purple-dyed linen tunics.[406] The tunic was worn by both sexes and it was made of linen and wool. The tunics worn by men were short, tight fitting sleeved garment; but they also had a long full robe with pleats that was usually worn for ceremonial purposes and winter dressing. According to Professor Antonio Arribas linen and wool was used by the nobility, while wool was used by everyone else.[407] Other archeologists/historians believe that all classes worn the same thing, the only difference would be the type of weaving and coloring.

---

403 Strabo, 3.3.6 and 3.3.7

404 Strabo, 3.4.16

405 Griffin, Nick, The Celts Part II: Celtic Folkways and the Clash with Romans and Germans, National Vanguard Magazine -- Number 116 (August-September 1996)

406 Polybius, 2.29

407 Arribas, Antonio, op. cit., p. 67

For practical purposes the linen tunic must have been worn during the spring and summer months so as to stay cool, while wool was used to stay warm during the chilly winter months. Besides the cloth tunic there are a few ceramic fragments where warriors are seen to be wearing a tunic that appears to be rigid, as if made of leather; this perhaps was a leather armored tunic.

Lusitanian men not only wore tunics, but also accessories. Along with the tunic, men wore large leather belts that were either plain or decorated with gold or silver panels of motifs of animals, abstract shapes or of men doing amazing deeds such as fighting animals. Besides wearing the wool tunic during the winter, they wore some sort of leggings or close - fitting trousers called *braccae.*[408] It is also known that the men wore breeches or a type of undergarment. This can be seen in a rare depiction of undressed men known as the "Cazurro vase" which shows either two young men or boys dressed in undergarments chasing a stag.[409] The mantle (sagulus) or Spanish cape as it is called was worn by men, it was probably made out of wool or goat skin and it was used as a cloak or a poncho that was fastened at the shoulder with a brooch. Fortunately, there is archaeological evidence of brooches, pins and other dress accessories that played both a functional and decorative role on their clothing. For many years, archeologists/historians believed that the Lusitanians walked around barefooted or with rags on their feet, but that changed in the early 1960s, when a Portuguese archeologist discovered leather shoes in a Roman mine near Vila Pouca de Aguiar, proving that they knew how to make leather shoes.[410]

Like Roman and Greek women, Lusitanian women spent a great deal of time on their personal appearance, but had a way of dressing unlike

---

[408] Collis, John, *The Celts: Origins, Myths, Inventions*, Tempus Publishing, Stroud, UK, 2003; Wells, Peter S., *Beyond Celts, Germans and Scythians*, Duckworth Debates in Archaeology, Duckworth Academic and Bristol Classical Press, 2001

[409] Arribas, Antonio, op. cit., p. 67

[410] Cardozo, Mario, A propósito da Lavra do ouro na Província de Tràs-os-Montes, durante a época romana, Guimarães, 1954, p. 12; Octávio da Veiga Ferreira, op. cit., p. 81.

Roman women, by wearing long mantles and gay-colored gowns that were woven by looms.[411] They wore long tunic robes of various colors such as red, blue, white or black. At times textiles were dyed bright colors and were interwoven with striped of thread to make checked patterns. Around the tunic a strip of cloth or a leather belt sweetly wrapped around the waist that girded it to the hips leaving the fabric to fall in pleats to their feet. The winter tunic had sleeves while the summer one was either sleeveless or short-sleeved. Along with the long tunic, they sometimes wore an ornated mantle. Through sculptures, there seems to have been two types; the knee-length shawl and a long one which folded from one armpit to the opposite shoulder, falling over the coiled plaits and fastened from beneath. These cloaks were either used for ceremonial purposes or in winter in which they then used a plain mantle. The best view of a woman's style of dress can be seen from the magnificent statue of Dama del Cerro de los Santos. It is by this statue that one can see how Lusitanian, as well as Iberian women dressed.

Like the men, women also wore accessories. Their undergarments were perhaps made out of linen which looks like a chiton secured at the neck by a ring-fibula. An example of the undergarment is visible on the famous Dama de Elche statue at Museo Arqueológico Nacional de España (Madrid).[412] Lusitanian and Iberian women are portrayed wearing various types of headgear from veils, hoods to hats. Figurines and vase paintings show that women's headgear was usually conical, diadem or plaited fillet while the lower classes worn a turban. Besides the plain everyday headgear there was decorated, ornamental headgear was used during festival and religious ceremonies. Another type of headdress was the ornamental use of two decorated drum-shaped

---

[411] Strabo., 3.37; James M. Anderson & M. Sheridan Lea, Portugal: 1001 Archaeological and Historical Guide, p. 25; Octávio da Veiga Ferreira, op. cit., pp. 71

[412] Eydoux, Henri-Paul, "La Dame d'Elche" Historia #202, Tome XXXIV, Sept. 1963, p. 410

disks called a *tympanium.*[413] This perfectly made round drum was attached to the ears and secured by an adorned leather strap across the top of the head which was either exposed or hidden behind a hood or veil. The most excellent depiction of this headdress can be seen on Dame de Elche. As for footwear, according to archeological artifacts of decorative vases, leather sandals and shoes made of either leather or esparto were worn.

Jewelry to the Lusitanian was extremely ornamental.[414] They used everything from the simplest to intricate necklaces, bracelets, armlets, brooches, rings and earring. Their hunger for jewelry made the Lusitanians make jewelry from any raw material they thought was precious such as gold, silver, copper, bronze, precious rocks such as quartz, turquoise and opals, amber and even bones. Jewelry varied so much in the man, as it did in women. From archeological artifacts found near Monte de São Félix, Portugal in 1904, it seems that men enjoyed wearing torque or smooth rounded necklaces and armlets and round or flat bracelets, while the women wore a much larger variety, but it seems that they had a desire for the more intricate type of jewelry.[415] Lusitanian jewelry reveals a developed technique, very similar to what was done throughout the Mediterranean, namely with the use of plates and solders, filigree and granulated techniques. Though everyone wore jewelry it played a part in class distinction such as in the more one had and the more complex the jewelry was

---

413 Strabo 3.4.17; Eydoux, Henri-Paul, "La Dame d'Elche" Historia #202, Tome XXXIV, Sept. 1963, p. 410

414 For a detailed history about Lusitanian jewelry see Cardozo, Mario, Joalharia Lusitana, Universidade de Coimbra, 1959; Ferreira de Silva, Armando Coelho, "Ourivesaria proto-histórica em território português", in De Ulisses a Viriato: O primeiro milénio a.C., Jorge de Alarcão (ed.), Museu Nacional de Arqueologia, Lisboa, 1996, p. 139-146

415 In 1904, a bricklayer while it built a mill in the top of São Félix's Monte, close to small Castro of Laundos, he/she finds a púcaro there inside with jewels, these jewels were bought by Rocha Peixoto that took them to the Museum of Porto. Silva, Armando Coelho Ferreira da, "*A Cultura Castreja no Noroeste de Portugal*".

the richer one was.[416] As for the torque type necklace worn by the men it did not signify one's social class, but one's power and authority within the tribe.[417]

Classical texts mention that both women and men grew their hair long as the Celts did. Along with the extraordinary headdresses and jewelry, come the hair styles, in which Lusitanian women, as well as Iberian women, had the tendency to elevate their hair to ornament the head by producing eccentric hairdos. One such style was that women fixed a small rod on a pedestal to their skull and fold their hair around it enveloping the entire rod in a black veil of hair.[418] As for the men, their hair was as long as the women and would at times be tied with a leather cord to keep their hair off their face.[419] Men were generally clean-shaven, but there were individuals that sported either beards or long drooping moustaches. According to Diodorus, 'When they ate the moustache would become entangled with food, and when they drank the drink passed through, as if it were a sort of strainer'.[420] Though he makes this reference to the Gauls, it can also be referred to the Lusitanian for they were largely influenced by Celtic culture.

As for Lusitanian women using cosmetics much is not known, but from artifacts of painted vases suggest that Iberian women used cosmetics. One such scene is from a vase painting at Liria, Spain, which shows a woman with dark paint around her eyes checking her appearance in a delicately decorated bronze mirror. Being that the Lusitanian and Iberians had Celtic influences, these women did not only use to make themselves beautiful, but also to say that perfume was used in religious purposes such as to combat malicious spirits such as violet perfume helped the person to frighten their personal ghosts.[421]

---

[416] Octávio da Veiga Ferreira, op. cit., p.86.

[417] Ibid.

[418] Strabo 3.4.17

[419] Strabo, 3.3.7

[420] Diodorus, *Historical Library*, 5.28

[421] Richard Allen and Iona Miller, The Magical and Ritual Use of Perfumes, Inner Traditions/Bear & Co., VT, 1990, p.111

Lusitanian Women[422]

Women played an important role in Iberian society, unlike in other societies. Compared to their counterparts such as Greek, Roman, and other ancient societies, Iberian women were distinct in the ancient world for the liberty and rights they enjoyed and the position they held in their society. Women's personal rights and their rights within marriage further testify to the high regard in which they were held in Celtic-influenced societies. Compared to Roman women, who were property of the husband, these women were allowed much freedom and protection under the law. But such rights varied from clan to clan. In some Iberian tribes, they participated in tribal assemblies, and their decision was considered in important issues.

As for marriage, it seems to have been viewed by the Lusitani as a partnership between men and women. Young women from ever class were allowed to choose a husband that suited them, even though they may have been allowed to choose their husbands, the families were undoubtedly involved in marriage decisions.[423] But in most cases women from the aristocratic class had arranged due to the tribal politics of forming alliances with other tribes. But at times noblewomen may have had the chance to choose a husband as seen in Viriathus' marriage.[424] Besides choosing a husband, they were allowed to choose a wife for their

---

422 Octávio da Veiga Ferreira, op. cit., Ch. 3, p.51-64; James, D. (Ed.), *Celtic connections: the ancient Celts, their tradition and living legacy.* London: Blandford Press, 1996; James, S., *The world of the Celts.* London: Thames and Hudson, 1993; King, J., *Kingdoms of the Celts: a history and guide.* London: Blandford Press, 1998; Markale, J. *Women of the Celts.* (A. Mygind, C. Hauch, & P. Henry, Trans.). Rochester, Vermont:
Inner Traditions International, Ltd., 1972; Walkley, V., *Celtic daily life.* London: Robinson Publishing, 1997; Wilde, L. W., *Celtic women in legend, myth and history.* New York: Sterling Publishing Co., Inc, 1997.

423 Markale, J., *Women of the Celts.* (A. Mygind, C. Hauch, & P. Henry, Trans.). Rochester, Vermont: Inner Traditions International, Ltd., 1972. This can also be read from an online article written by Markale titled "The Lives of Ancient Celtic Women" at http://www.celtlearn.org/pdfs/women.pdf

424 Octávio da Veiga Ferreira, op. cit., p.55-56

brothers. This can be seen were Strabo writes "Daughters are the ones who inherit and choose wives for their brothers."[425] Compared to their Roman or Greek counterpart, they could own and inherit property, as well as pursue legal court cases without the consent of their husbands. They were also allowed to conduct business without the consent or involvement of their husbands or even run the husband's business in his absence. Even married, these women were allowed to be priestesses, and in some cases even become warriors, though few chose to do so. But the majority just ran the household and raised children. Unfortunately, there is a lack of information on the subject. But overall, historian Jean Markale puts it best when he wrote about Celtic marriages, "Celtic marriage was essentially contractual and social, not at all religious, that was based on the freedom of the husband and wife."[426]

With marriage came a dowry. The dowry systems varied among the different groups, but one custom was certain was that each party had to bring an equal sum to the marriage and would be left to accrue some type of profit.[427] However, though the couple brought in an equal sum, the husband or his family usually had to pay her family extra, in other words, the price of her virginity.[428] Upon the death of a partner, the surviving partner would receive his or her original share of the dowry, along with the profits that both dowries made. If the couple divorced, each partner got his and her original contribution and split the profits. This system of a dowry gave women economic independence that afforded them protection in the event of divorce or husband's death: a very different situation from that of other classical women.[429]

Just like the wedding and dowry consummated the marriage; the act of divorce was of a simple matter in that either party could request

---

[425] Strabo, 3.3.7

[426] Markale, J., op. cit.

[427] Markale, J., (2002) "The Lives of Ancient Celtic Women" at http://www.celtlearn.org/pdfs/women.pdf; Volpatto, Rosane, (July 2007) "A Posição da Mulher na Sociedade Celta", Lealdade Sacra, http://s2.excoboard.com/exco/thread.php?forumid=64670&threadid=1660625

[428] Volpatto, Rosane, "A Posição da Mulher na Sociedade Celta"

[429] Markale, J., "The Lives of Ancient Celtic Women"; Volpatto, Rosane, op. cit.

one.[430] According to Markale, compared to other societies, divorced women were not looked down upon and were always free to remarry.[431] If compared to other ancient societies, the Lusitanian, Iberians and Celts were far beyond their time when it came to rights and freedom for women, and though these practices may have been fundamentally the same, there were perhaps different versions of these basic practices throughout the peninsula's tribes.

Medicine

Sickness and health has been man's concerned since pre-history and when men or women felt ill, they would try to find ways to cure themselves by using bad and good medical practices, formulas and cures, gods of health and welfare, hydrotherapy and pharmacopoeia. As for the Lusitanians as most ancient people, they had a substantial amount of medical knowledge of sickness and disease, along with what had 'curative properties.

Lusitanian, Iberian and Celtic medicine was mostly based on herbalism, but there was also a general belief in the healing power of the supernatural world. Although classical texts say little of Lusitanian medicine, we do know, however, that at that time, and in societies of this type, medicine, magic and religion were interconnected.[432] Religious and magical beliefs were complemented by a deep knowledge of the therapeutic properties of plants, animals, minerals and even water.

The ancient people of Hispania had an oral tradition that had been passed down from generation to generation indicating the value they had placed on curative herbs and medicinal plants. With this vast knowledge, a great variety of plants and certain animal byproducts such as the ink of

---

430 Volpatto, Rosane, op. cit.

431 Markale, J., "The Lives of Ancient Celtic Women"

432 Whittet, M.M., "*Historical Aspects of Celtic Medicine*", Proceedings of the Royal Society of Medicine, May 1964, no. 57: 429-36; Paine, Angela, The Healing Power of Celtic Plants: Healing Herbs of the Ancient Celts and their Druid Medicine Men, Ropley O Books, 2006, p.77. Amigos de Ribeiro Sanches. "Estudos de História da Medicina Peninsular", Porto, Typ. Enciclopédia Portuguesa, 1916

mollusks[433] were used in Lusitanian/Celtic medicine. With this general familiarity of these ingredients they made teas, tinctures, fomentations, syrups, and salves in which their therapeutic properties treated fractures, broken bones, cuts, earaches, fevers, rheumatism, certain diseases, stomach aches, rickets, nose bleeds, snake bits, drunkenness, poisoning, and the list goes on. Some of these cures were undoubtedly of real value, though many were probably ineffective and did not achieve any perceived result. Along with these medicinal substances, wise medicine women and men would combine these natural elements with charms and incantations to treat the sick.

Collected by ethnographers, folklorists and family members, many popular remedies of traditional medicine have been conserved over the millennia. One such remedy still used today in Portugal is for the treatment of colds; treated with a concoction of pennyroyal leaves (not the stem for it oil is poisonous), rye and rosemary boiled with wine or water, mixed with honey to sweeten the brew.[434] Another is for diarrhea which is cured with a doughy mush made out of clover mixed with rye flour, egg yolk, and a piece of old goat cheese;[435] as a kid, honey was added to make it more appetizing. For menstrual disorders a flaxseed tea was used.[436] Bleeding wounds were dealt with crushed nettles mixed with vinegar.[437] Skin irritations or infections were treated with urine which was considered as a disinfectant. Urine was also used as a mouthwash to treat teeth.[438] For headache relief was through vapors. This remedy was/is made with rosemary, lavender

---

433 Pliny, NH, 32.6

434 This very tart brew was given to me by my great-grandmother (who died at the age 101) when I was growing up in Portugal as a boy. She use to say drink this up for if it was good in Viriato's day it is good for you today. Now if this tea worked on curing the common cold I don't think so. I also found this remedy and several others on this website: Ancient Spiritual Order of the Lusitanian Paganism, 2006 chapter 3, http://tantraleukuir.home.sapo.pt/ervanaria.html

435 Paine, Angela, The Healing Power of Celtic Plants. This doughy mush actually works.

436 Ibid.

437 Ibid.

438 Strabo, 3.14.16 The Romans would later find this remedy useful.

and garlic mix in a blow of steaming hot water, then the person head is cover with a cloth.[439] To care for jaundice a broth was made out of head lice, animal liver and the loin of a snake.[440] Even blood and certain oils that animals produced were used. One such oil comes from the castor sacs of the European beaver which was considered during this time to be an important product, for not only was it used in making perfume it was also used as an aphrodisiac as well as for medicinal purposes.[441] It seems that these glands were worth they weight in gold for it was believed to an excellent remedy for a number of aliments such as vertigo, fevers, tremor, headaches, nervous disorders, sciatica, stomach pains, paralysis and so on.[442] The down side of castoreum was that though it was considered excellent for some patients, it was poisonous for others, so the right dosage was important.[443] However, with all the ancient remedies that existed and survived into the 21st century some ancient Celtic remedies have been compatible with scientific facts forming the basis of modern pharmacology, while many other folk remedies have been relegated to the realm of folklore.

Besides just using plants and animals, they believed that magic mixed with herbs had stronger curative powers than just using plants and animals alone.[444] There is no doubt that the Lusitanians used plant and

---

439 Ancient Spiritual Order of the Lusitanian Paganism, 2006 chapter 3, http://tantraleukuir.home.sapo.pt/ervanaria.html

440 Ibid.,To use snake loin in the cure, the snake was cut two palm lengths from the head and two palms from the tail end

441 **Castoreum** is the name given to the exudates from the castor sacs of the mature North American Beaver (*Castor canadensis)* and the European Beaver (*Castor fiber)*. Within the zoological realm, castoreum is the yellowish secretion of the castor sac in combination with the beaver's urine, used during scent marking of territory. Both male and female beavers possess a pair of castor sacs and a pair of anal glands located in two cavities under the skin between the pelvis and the base of the tail.

442 Pliny, 32.3; Octávio da Veiga Ferreira, op. cit., pp.151-152

443 Ibid.

444 Rodrigues, Adriano Vasco, A medicina e a herbanária entre os lusitanos, Lucerna, Porto, 1984, p. 6; Leite de Vasconcelos, José, "Medicina dos Lusitanos", OPÚSCULOS, Volume V – Etnologia (Parte I) Lisboa, Imprensa Nacional, 1938, p.266-267

animal products in good faith by believing in their efficacy. But where the natural medicine was not sufficient, men and women would pray and give sacrifices to the gods of health such as Endovelicus. These magical charms, invocations, and spells along with sacrifices were used on all aliments to achieve some kind of immunity or cure. The Lusitanians also believed that certain animals had magical power such as the snake. One example of the 'therapeutic' properties of a serpent was its liver, when cooked the liver was rubbed on the body so as to ward off evil spirits.[445] Skin and other 'magical' animal parts were used in applied medicine as infusions, broths and elixirs.[446] Unfortunately, information about which body parts were used has been lost, but of the little data that is available, it is probable that nothing went to waste. These magical recipes were usually mixed with honey, hydromel, wine, oil, milk, blood and water. It is amazing that many of these magical superstitious practices, remedies and knowledge as primitive as it may be, survived into the Middle Ages and some have even survived into the 21st century.

The earliest surgical instruments used in medical procedures in the Iberian Peninsula were made out of flint or obsidian (shiny volcanic stone) and bone. With the coming of the Bronze and Iron Age, these primitive instruments were converted from stone and bone to bronze and iron. Like today's society, Lusitanians were prone to injuries related to war, hunting, work and other incidents that were involved in everyday life. So care for these injured individuals was needed. Unfortunately because of the Lusitanian funerary rite of cremation, there is very little evidence and information about their operations and treatments. But of the few fragments found throughout Spain and Portugal, it seem that many tribes practice surgical techniques for the treatment of different type of fractures, laceration, and trauma. Of all the surgical practices, trepanation was one of them, thanks to the discovery of several skulls. According to the late Professor Leite de Vasconcelos, ancient people used this technique on individual who suffered from eplisey and hysteria, in the mind of the people who performed this technique they

---

445 Octávio da Veiga Ferreira, op. cit., p. 122

446 Seomara da Veiga Ferreira, Maria da Graça Amaral da Costa, Etnografia de Idanha-a-Velha: Egitânia, Castelo Branco, Junta Distrital, 1970, p. 92

were releasing spirits who had possessed the individual.[447] From the evidence that exists, this type of operation used coarse stone, bronze or metal instruments and many of these surgeries were driven by precepts of magic: rid the weakened and pained body of the patient by an extreme act so as to get rid of evil spirits, in the case of the deceased, it was done post mortem.[448] For many years it was believed that some cultures had no concept of surgical and dental practices or medical knowledge, but it has been proven that these types of operation and other procedures had been performed throughout the ancient world since prehistoric times.[449]

With surgery one must have anesthesia! Though it is not known if the Lusitanian used some sort of potion on a patient before operating, one can only guess they did. Pain has been a physically, mentally and emotionally torment on men and women since the beginning of time, so one would have to find and devise ways to ease it. While taking into account that during man's evolution his nerves became a bit more sensitive, he was now more subject to physical suffering than before, so to sooth one's pain, early man had to come up with ways to alleviate his pain. This brings me to believe that anesthesia was used. Like most ancient cultures, the Lusitanian, had a vast knowledge of the medicinal properties of plants, herbs and vegetables. We know from Strabo, that the Lusitanian manufactured a poison from a celery type plant that killed without pain.[450] So the truth of the matter is that if they could manufacture poison, they could definitely produce some type of anesthesia. As for a type of anesthesia, we can cite opium poppy, fennel, purslane, mandrake, stinking nightshade, rosewood and several others.

---

[447] Vasconcelos, J.L de, *Religiões da Lusitânia*, vol. I, 1897, Imprensa Nacional---Casa da Moeda, Lisboa, 1897-1905, p 171-193

[448] Octávio da Veiga Ferreira, op. cit., p. 145; Leite de Vasconcelos, José, "Medicina dos Lusitanos" Faculdade de Medicina de Lisboa, Lisboa, 1925, p. 12. An example of this surgical technique can be seen at the National Museum of Archaeology in Lisbon. The cranium is of an adult man, presenting an ellipse hole on the sagittal suture which connects the parietal bone of the skull. This specimen was found in a cave at Galinha, near Alcanena

[449] Octávio da Veiga Ferreira, op. cit., p. 149

[450] Strabo, 3.3.18

Therefore, with the knowledge of local plant life, they not only produced cures, but narcotics as well as anesthesia.[451]

According to Lusitanian rudimentary medicine, medicinal water was the basis of all their plant, animal and magical cures and remedies. The medicinal qualities of water were highly regarded, especially if it came from a particular river or a natural well. Throughout the Iberian Peninsula there are a large number of mineralized water sources and springs that are saturated with sodium bicarbonate, calcium bicarbonate, sodium sulfite, calcium sulfite, aluminum potassium sulfate which were used in hydrotherapy.[452] These water wells were used for the treatment of rheumatism, skin aliments, catarrh, gout, respiratory and gynecological issues and other aliments. These Iberian wells became so well known that they became famous throughout the Roman Empire. Since those ancient times many of these wells are still in use today as spas. Along with these natural spring water, the Lusitanian for example had over a hundred herbal infusions/drinks/teas made of aromatic herbs and grasses in which many of these are still used today.[453]

On the superstitious side these wells were often identified with local water gods and the healing properties were attributed to these deities. The reason these water gods were special was because of their associated with mineral and hot water springs which were known to have curative power, thus it was important to deliver offering and sacrifices to these water gods.[454]

---

[451] Soares, Dr. Jose Maria, Memórias para História da Medicina Lusitana, Lisboa, 1821, pp. 25-28

[452] Octávio da Veiga Ferreira, op. cit., p. 145

[453] Rodrigues, Adriano Vasco, A medicina e a herbanária entre os lusitanos, Lucerna, Porto, 1984, p. 14 No passado, certamente que só os enfermos demales crónicos, incuráveis ou de difícil diagnóstico, seriam expostos à beira dos caminhos ou à porta das suas casas, não se pode generalizar.

[454] Vasconcelos, J. Leite de, Religiões da Lusitânia, vol II, p. 94, 224 - 280; Leite de Vasconcelos, José, "Medicina dos Lusitanos", **OPÚSCULOS,** Volume V – Etnologia (Parte I), p. 263-265; Octávio da Veiga Ferreira, op. cit., p.146-147. Of

Like in modern times, epidemics also emerged in these primitive times such as typhus. Strabo writes how Iberia as well as other regions had suffered invasions of rats and the epidemics that often followed them.[455] Strabo wrote that epidemics were a common occurrence in many areas, and that epidemics occurred due to the lack of personal tidiness within social poverty.[456] To the Romans, many of these cultures were very unhygienic; the main cause of epidemics in these areas. But this misconception may be wrong for Strabo writes about the Iberian practice of preventive measures, when someone was sick, the individual was placed at the door of someone's home or on a well traveled road, so that those who had already suffered the same evil (i.e. sickness) could explain the cure or give the remedy.[457] According to Strabo, this was done in the same way as the Egyptians did in ancient times.[458] It is through Strabo and recent archeological excavations that we see that the Lusitanians and Iberians were not dirty savages that history has portrayed them to be. As it may, it was important to have in each castro some type of medical practitioner, whether it was a medicine man or a priest or everyone practiced medicine or a traveling medicine man to help fight sickness and disease.

From this vast knowledge of herbalism and practices it is possible to say that during the Roman occupation Iberian medicine and remedies were highly sought, and once the Romans began to pacify the Peninsula they assimilated Iberian medical practices into Roman medicine.[459] In conclusion all pre-Roman Iberians practiced surgery to pharmacology

---

all the Luso-Roman inscriptions that have been found Nabia, Tongoenabiagus and Bormanicus were the most popular of the water gods.

455 Strabo, 3.3.18

456 Strabo, 3.3.18

457 Leite de Vasconcelos, José, "Medicina dos Lusitanos", OPÚSCULOS, Volume V – Etnologia (Parte I), p.263

458 Strabo, 3.3.7; Since this custom was followed by the Assyrians (Herodotus 1.197_and Strabo 16.1.20), and since there is no other account of such a practice among the Egyptians, some archaeologists/historians presume that the text is right.Usavam manteiga em vez de azeite, e alimentavam-se de pão, da carne dos seus rebanhos, e do que pescavam.

459 Leite de Vasconcelos, José, "Medicina dos Lusitanos", p. 268-277

even though certain tribes were less advanced than others; there was a deep relationship between man and the healing powers of nature. Finally, one of the aspects to one's health that should be taken into account is that from the ancient texts, the Lustianian diet was quite health. In antiquity, everything that related to wealth not only translated into gold and silver, but also of the abundance of health food.

Law and Order

Of all the texts that were written by the classical authors there is a lack of information on Lusitanian law. The only information we have on the subject comes from Strabo. According to Strabo, clan justice was harsh and primitive because crimes that sought the destruction or disrupt the peace between clans and murder were punished by death. The punishment for these crimes was that the convicted were hurled from precipices or stoned to death.[460]

For lesser crimes and the degree in which they were committed, the punitive outcome varied. Here are two examples that I have found on Lusitanian justice. Adultery is typical of any society, but each society has its own method of punishment, to the Iberians, it seems that when the act was committed and the adulterous couple was caught, they would be sentence to a stone throwing and banished from the tribe for they had corrupted the matrimonial and family vow.[461] As for stealing of neighbor's goods, it resulted in stoning and banishment and the sentenced man's belongings would go to the victim.[462]

The reason for this harsh punishment was to instill order and control over the collective group so that individuals could not exact revenge on to other individuals for it would cause anarchy, disorder and lawlessness among the clan or tribe. So, to keep the tribe in check, harsh laws were implemented.

---

460 Strabo, 3.3.7

461 Octávio da Veiga Ferreira, op. cit., p. 66

462 Ibid.

Land Rights and Banditry

According to modern historians, the right to owe property was communal, but such a statement cannot be made categorically. It is probable that in certain areas such as in the plains and steppes, a larger divisions of property existed, while, in the mountainous areas, the individual had little or no property rights due to the terrain.[463] Although the land was communal, in theory, the individual that raised livestock which in turn feed off the land and what was grown on the land was not communal. So in the end, it was the owners of flocks, who came to be seen as aristocratic proprietors of the land, for livestock were worth more than land.[464] This was the case of Astolpas, Viriathus's father-in-law or brother-in-law, who was considered the wealthiest man in the region. This goes without saying, that the person who owed livestock, owned the land. The rest of the population did not own land, but just used it. As within all societies everything comes with a price; this became a serious problem for according to modern historians such as A. Garcia y Bellido, who believes due to the lack of land ownership, the placement of the castros in high places and the enormous population density claimed by the classical texts increased the Lusitanians to resort to brigandage.[465] But this theory is not entirely true, for though the Lusitanians were disseminated within a vast territory and mixed with several small tribes it is believed that they did not participate in barbarism among themselves and their allies in the north and south.[466]

---

[463] Sayas, J.J., "El bandolerismo lusitano y la falta de tierras", Homenaje al Prof. Antonio de Bethencourt y Massieu, Espacio, Tiempo y Forma #4, 1989, pp. 708-710

[464] Munoz, Mauricio P., op. cit., p. 40-41

[465] Diodorus Siculus, Universal History, III. 34.6-7; Garcia y Bellido, A., "Bandas y Guerrillas en las Luchas con Roma" Hispania, Vol. V, # 21, 1945, p.26-50; Sayas, J.J., "El bandolerismo lusitano y la falta de tierras", Homenaje al Prof. Antonio de Bethencourt y Massieu, Espacio, Tiempo y Forma #4, 1989, pp. 708-710; Munoz, Mauricio P, op. cit., p. 111.

[466] Cuevillas, Florentino L., "Estudios sobre a Edad do Ferro no Noroeste peninsular", Fontes Historicas, Seminar de Estudos Galegos VI, 1934, p.14

In the eyes of modern historians and anthropologists, banditry was a problem among Lusitanian society because of social inequality within the tribe. Class evolution of Lusitanian society was basically a military aristocracy that accumulated lands by any means, while forcing the lower class individual to dedicate themselves to a life of banditry.[467] With this basis, modern historians defend that during the 2nd and 1st century BC, there existed a serious socio-political and economic problem within Lusitanian society which originated by the unequal share of lands, forcing needy individuals to turn themselves into mercenaries or form large gangs dedicated to plundering rich or better – well off tribes outside their area.

But in my opinion, I believe that this was not the case, for the ancient texts mention that due to the lack of fertile lands for everyone, Lusitanians became bandits and mercenaries.[468] But at the same time, it can be said because many young men came from a war – like society, many just sought adventure and to make a name for themselves for there are several mentions in the classical texts of how the Lusitanians were mercenaries under Punic and Roman generals and how they loved to fight and plunder the territories subdued by whichever power they fought for. It seems that these Lusitanian raiding expeditions were conducted

---

[467] Garcia y Bellido, A., "Bandas y guerrillas en las luchas con Roma", p. 540-550; Salinas de Frias, M., "Problemática social y económica del mundo indígena lusitano", en El proceso histórico de la Lusitania oriental en época prerromana y romana. Cuadernos Emeritenses, 7, 1993, Mérida, pp.22-29; Munoz, Mauricio P., op. cit., p. 40-41; C. Bernaldo de Quiros and L. Ardila, El Bandolerismo Andaluz, Turner, Madrid, 1988; Chic Garcia, G., "Consideraciones sobre las incursiones lusitanas en Andalucía", Gades, 5, 1980, pp.15-25; Santos Yanguas, N., "Las incursiones de lusitanos en Hispania Ulterior durante el s.II antes de nuestra era", Bracara Augusta, 35, 1981, pp.364-365; Sayas, J.J., "El bandolerismo lusitano y la falta de tierras", Homenaje al Prof. Antonio de Bethencourt y Massieu, Espacio, Tiempo y Forma #4, 1989, pp. 701-714

[468] See these texts and you can formulate your own opinion: Diodorus, 5.34.6-7; 33.1.2; Cicero, Ad Fam. 10.31.1; Anon. Bell. Hisp. 40; Livy 28.22; 28.32; 34.21; 35.7; Strabo 3.3.5-8; cf. 3.4.5, 15; Plutarch, Marius 6.1; Sert. 14.1; 18.1; Appian, Iber. 100; Isid. Etym. 9.2.113; cf. Varro RR 1.16.1-2; Sallust, Hist. 2.88, 92, 96 (ed Maurenbrecher); Vell. Pat. 2.90.4; Herod. 1.10.2; Dig. 3.5.20 (21)

with something more than just a ragtag group of undisciplined bandits; in fact, it was more like a small army. Besides plundering entire town, these armies were capable of beating either Punic army formations and Roman consular troops and even besieging and taking cities.

With so many raiding expeditions, historians have concluded from the classical texts that the Lusitanian search for booty and cattle was attributed from poverty beginning with a social unbalance to aristocratic monopoly. Though historians have placed many reasons why the Lusitanians resorted to banditry, which according to them and the ancient texts are all true, they have forgotten three basic elements that cause this issue: 1) there are individuals who commit themselves to the thrill of adventure or greed, 2) individuals that do what they do because of necessity for survival in a harsh world 3) to be an equal or reach a higher social status. So, for the Lusitanians plundering other Iberian tribes and returning to Lusitania they would become possessors of land and cattle. With these stolen cattle, they perhaps brought land from the aristocracy or they sold them for other material goods, which brought Lusitanian living standards to a new level. The main reason why many classical writers wrote that these people lived in poverty and gave a negative spin on the acts they committed was because the Romans compared Lusitanian living standards to their own. The only difference is that it was not the living standard of the Romans but the Lusitanian way of life.

But Lusitanian brigandage would soon come to an end. In the beginning, the Romans did not bother with Lusitania as much, even though they conducted raids into Roman occupied lands, because they were busy consolidating the territory they had won against Carthage. But as soon as the Roman had somewhat organized its new province and the Lusitanians began to constantly put Roman territories in danger and threatened its economical exploitation of Ulterior, it forced Rome to take action against the Lusitanians and so, the conquest of all Lusitania was in order.

During the Lusitanian War, classical texts frequently mention Lusitanian requests for land shares made to the Roman governors. Here are some examples: in the year 152 BCE, the Lusitanians and the Vetones made a pact with M. Atilius, but it does not state weather it was for peace or land.[469] But one must assume it was for land for Appian writes that in 150 BCE Servius Sulpicius Galba falsely accepted the renewal of Atilius' treaty with the Luistanians in exchange for new land concessions for peace (he later went back on his word and massacred 9,000 Lusitanian in one day);[470] in 147-146 BCE, Gaius Vetilius promised the Lusitanians lands, if they sued for peace, but the Lusitani were discouraged by Viriato for he invoked his people not to trust the Romans and fight on;[471] in 140 BCE after Viriato's victory over Q. Fabius Maximus Servilianus, Viriato accepted a peace treaty from Rome, and was recognized *amicus populi Romani* (friend of the Roman people), in this treaty Viriathus was to rule all the land which he held.[472] In this way the Lusitanian War, which had been problematic for the Romans was resolved over this act. But it was short lived, two years after the peace treaty the Romans broke it and the war began again. With the death of Viriathus in 139 BCE, the surviving Lusitanian army was given land near the *oppidum* of Valentia by Decimus Junius Brutus.[473] Though they were granted land, the problem of brigandage would not finish until Julius Ceasar

---

[469] Appian, *Iberika*, 58.243

[470] Appian, *Iber*., 59.249-250, Suetonius, *Galba*, 3; Valerius Maximus, Factorum et Dictorum Memorabilium Libri Novem, 9.6.2; Orosius, 4.21.10. More info will come in chapter 5 which started the Lusitanian War.

[471] Appian, 61.258-59

[472] Ibid., 69.294; Schulten, A., Fontes Hispaniae Antiquae Vol.IV, XI Vols., Barcelona, 1935-1987, p.117-122

[473] Livy, *Periochae* 55.138.4; Diodorus, 33.1.3. Valentia today is Valencia which is on the south-eastern coast of Spain. It is said that after the war Brutus relocated many of Viriato's followers to this area so as to subdue their warrior spirit. But many critics do not accept this that they were moved from the west to the extreme east of the Iberian Peninsula. They suggest that they were perhaps settled somewhere to the northeast or southeast of the Alentejo region in a newly created oppidum which is now lost. Le Roux, Patrick, L'armée romaine et l'organisation des provinces ibériques d'Auguste á l'invasion de 409, Paris, 1982, p. 36-37; Ventura Canejero, Augustin, "qui sub Viriatho militaverunt" Archivo de Prehistoria Levantina #16, 1981, pp. 539-551; Alarcão, Jorge de,

governorship in 60 BCE, eradicating all of the Lusitanians that had taken refuge in Monte Aeminius or Herminius.[474]

From these situations that have been recorded by ancient authors, one would think that Lusitanian banditry would have died out due to land being allotted to them, but that is not the case. Perhaps the reason for the continuation of Lusitanian brigandage was because there existed an unequal distribution of property within Lusitanian society in that the aristocracy wanted more land for themselves. But at the same time this theory could be wrong for there may have not been a land right issue among the Lusitani for not all Lusitanian care for land ownership such as the merchants or craftsman, while others did what they did for the thrill and adventure and at the same time much of the land were they lived was not best for agriculture.

On a political level, the only thing that Viriathus and those before and after him wanted was for the Lusitanians to have their own autonomy so that they could live in peace and be free. So, with the peace treaty between Maximus Servilianus and Viriathus the consolidation of power and land happened when the Senate named Viriathus '*amicus populi Romani*' which recognized his power on all of the lands that he possessed. With this act, this treaty was necessary for Rome to stop the war, end banditry and have some control over the Lusitani. In this manner, Lusitanian society would develop complex political and cultural ties to Rome and assume a form of a single independent monarchy over a people than just tribal fiefdoms ruled by various chiefs. The economic situation of the Lusitanians hereon would only get better with the arrival of Rome and of the division of lands.

But that was not the case, for after Viriathus' assassination and Rome's double-cross, its armies stormed into Lusitania in an all-out campaign

---

"Sobre a romanização do Alentejo e do Algarve: propósito de uma obra de José d'Encarnação", Arqueologia #11, 1985, pp. 184-194.

[474] Dio Cassius 37.52-53 Schulten, A., Fontes Hispaniae Antiquae Vol.V, XI Vols., Barcelona, 1935-1987, p.12-13

of oppression. Perhaps the reason for Rome's all out attack on Lusitania was because Roman pride and honored had been stained by constantly being robbed and their armies being defeated, so from a Roman point of view these barbarians needed to be either annihilated or controlled. So these Roman writers to save face would have to instill in the reader stereotypes of the day, but in all actuality Rome's greed for more land and an imperialistic policy of expansion created constant campaigns against the Lusitani, enhancing Lusitanian banditry and a war for several more year until the reign of emperor Augustus.

The Castro Culture (Housing/Fortified Villages)

Castro culture (*cultura castreja* in Portuguese, *cultura castrexa* in Galician and *cultura castreña* in Spanish and Asturian) is the archaeologists' descriptor for the culture of fortified villages in central and northwestern part of the Iberian Peninsula (roughly present-day Portugal, Galicia and Asturias). The word "Castro" comes from Latin, *castrum,* which literarily translates into castle suggesting that these establishments were military fortification. The Castro culture was a proto-historical culture that began near the end of the Bronze Age and lasted until the 1st century AD.[475] The most notable and permanent characteristic of this culture is their walled villages and hilltop forts of which information has been vastly provided by archaeology, epigraphy, written textual sources and ethnography.

Prior to the Bronze Age, human settlement in western Iberian Peninsula consisted of small open villages with huts made of perishable materials. The village showed its demarcation line by a relatively shallow perimeter ditch or moat around the village, signifying its border and protective barrier. According to archaeological data of excavated sites, most of these early villages have been discovered on prominent landforms

---

[475] Felipe Arias Vilas and Maria Consuelo Durán Fuentes, Castrexa (HILLFORT) Culture, (Translation Maria Isabel Rubinos Fernández), e-Castrexo, Museo do Castro de VIladonga, 1996, pp. 31-37; p.16 *The Late Bronze Age arrived on the Atlantic Coast between 900 and 1000 BC and it has been known as the Atlantic Bronze Age.

signifying that these villages were naturally built on protected sites (heights, riots of rivers, small peninsulas), near water sources, farmland and higher areas of safely grazing livestock.

During the middle and final stages of the late Bronze Age as a result of strong Celtic cultural influences on the indigenous people, a further advanced culture began to develop. During this formative period which lasted until the 5th century BCE, the *Castro* culture extended from north to south and from the coast of Portugal to the interior of the Iberian Peninsula. In time, these villages began building walls due to their access to stone that eventually walled villages became widespread and remained the dominant settlement type structure.[476] In the first millennium BCE Iberian Peninsula, these new fortified settlements represent a new and novel form of habitation.This culture continued to expand and develop for another three centuries, until it began to be influenced by the Roman Republic around the end of 2nd century BCE. As a result of Romanization within Gallaecia and Lusitania, the heart of the Castro culture began to die out in the 4th century AD.[477]

As for the origin of the castro culture there are two theories. The first states that prior to the castro culture the early "Iberians" people lived in

---

476 Xurxo M. Ayán Vila, "A Round Iron Age: The Circular House in the Hillforts of the Northwestern Iberian Peninsula", E-Keltoi: Journal of Interdisciplinary Celtic Studies, Vol. 6"The Celts in the Iberian Peninsula", University of Wisconsin, Milwaukee, pp. 903-1004; Carballo Arceo, X. and A. González Ruibal A cultura castrexa do NW da Península Ibérica en Galicia. *Boletín Auriense* 33: 2003, Ourense, p. 40; Parcero Oubiña, C., X.M. Ayán Vila, P. Fábrega Álvarez and A. Teira Brión, *Los pueblos de la Galicia Céltica,* Arqueología, Paisaje y Sociedad, Madrid: Akal, 2007, p. 144.

477 Felipe Arias Vilas and Maria Consuelo Durán Fuentes, Castrexa (HILLFORT) Culture, (Translation Maria Isabel Rubinos Fernández), e-Castrexo, Museo do Castro de VIladonga, 1996, pp. 31-37 Cardosa, João Luis, 'O povoamento no Bronze Final e na Idade de Ferro na região de Lisboa", De Ulisses a Viriato: o primeiro milénio a.C., Jorge de Alarcão (ed.), Museu Nacional de Arqueologia, Lisboa, 1996, p. 73-81 Although they ended in the 4th century some castros endured up until the Middle Ages.

unfortified settlements on the plains and lowlands along the rivers.[478] But when the Sefes invaded the west coast of the peninsula, the native tribes moved their homes to sites that were more inexpugnable and easy to defend. The obvious reason why the people went on the defensive makes us think in a society that was very unstable and weak during a time in which war was a daily element against a more powerful group. The other theory deals with climate change. It is believed that hilltop forts were established was because the changes in the subatlantic climatic period which is characterized by an increase in temperature and humidity. These changes in the weather seems to have led to the expansion of the wooded wetland areas, that to some extent would have forced the inhabitants of certain areas to settle in villages situated in high cool areas and seek better protection in higher areas overlooking forests.

The villages and towns were often placed on hills or mountains of medium height, taking advantage of the surrounding natural ground as a defensive position with good visibility (for example, rocky embankments). By the emplacement of these castros, it shows us that defensive needs were paramount. It can be safe to say that height made it difficult for besiegers to climb the hills escarpments. The abundance of hill-forts also leads us to the idea of a society that was small in numbers that lived on large doses of insecurity. Beside security, many castros were placed near water and areas natural of resources, which was important for the well being of the tribe.

The forts in Portugal presented different particularities relative to those in central and southern Spain. In central and southern Spain, the castros formed a quadrangular shape, while the castros in Portugal were round or oval that even the houses were circular. With the passing of time,

---

[478] Paços de Ferreira - As origens do povoamento: do megalitismo à romanização - Estudos Monográficos, *Armando Coelho Ferreira da Silva*, Lisboa, 1986; Felipe Arias Vilas and Maria Consuelo Durán Fuentes, Castrexa (HILLFORT) Culture, pp. 31-37; Cardosa, João Luis, 'O povoamento no Bronze Final e na Idade de Ferro na região de Lisboa", p. 73-81.**Não se conhece ao certo a estrutura da sociedade lusitana mas não teriam contudo uma organização político-administrativa estruturada, elegendo certamente chefes que exerciam um controle da conduta do grupo e que representavam a tribo quando necessário.**

the castros in Spain compared to Portugal reached the status of towns and cities, which became categorized as *oppida, citânias* or *cividades* by the Romans.[479] In Portugal, this was not seen until Augustus began to Romanize Lusitania, so prior to the Romans, the castros were small villages. It is believed the reason why the castro in Spain grew so large was mainly because of the far distances between Spanish castros, while in Portugal the castros were at a closer distance to one another.[480] This short distance between castros was important to the Lusitanians because of the use of a complicated network of signal fires that was established not only for defensive purposes, but for general communication as well.[481] These great bonfires were set up in high places or on watch towers within the castros. These signal fires were usually used to signal that imminent

---

[479] **Oppidum** (plural ***oppida***) is a Latin word meaning the main settlement in any administrative area of ancient Rome. The word is derived from the earlier Latin *ob-pedum*, "enclosed space," possibly from the Proto-Indo-European **pedóm-*, "occupied space" or "footprint." Many oppida grew from hill forts although by no means did all of them have significant defensive functions. The main features of the oppida are the architectural construction of the walls and gates, the spacious layout and commanding view of the surrounding area. The development of oppida was a milestone in the urbanization of the continent as they were the first large settlements north of the Mediterranean that could genuinely be described as towns. In conquered lands, the Romans used the infrastructure of the oppida to administer the empire and many became full Roman towns. This often involved a change of location from the hilltop into the plain. Garcia, Dominique, *La Celtique Méditeranée: habitats et sociétés en Languedoc et en Provence, VIIIe - IIe siècles av. J.-C.* Chapter 4 *La « civilisation des oppida » : dynamique et chronologie.* Paris, Editions Errance, 2004; Cardosa, João Luis, ibid.; Gamito, Teresa Júdice, "O castro de Segóvia e a componente céltica em território português", in De Ulisses a Viriato: o primeiro milénio a.C., Jorge de Alarcão (ed.), p. 107-111**Não se conhece ao certo a estrutura da sociedade lusitana mas não teriam contudo uma organização político-administrativa estruturada, elegendo certamente chefes que exerciam um controle da conduta do grupo e que representavam a tribo quando necessári**

[480] Gamito, Teresa Júdice, "O castro de Segóvia e a componente céltica em território português", p. 107-111**Não se conhece ao certo a estrutura da sociedade lusitana mas não teriam contudo uma organização político-administrativa estruturada, elegendo certamente chefes que exerciam um controle da conduta do grupo e que representavam a tribo quando necessári**

[481] Octávio da Veiga Ferreira, op. cit., p. 48

danger was near or a castro was under siege. The best example we have comes from Livy, who wrote that when Certima was being besieged by the Romans, the townspeople kindled fires from their watch towers signaling for help.[482] Livy's statement clearly shows that the creation of a communications network system between castros was essential.

Using horn-like instruments was another means of communications.[483] We do not know if that type of instruments was used to communicate with other towns and cities or not, but if they did it would have been a Swiss horn like instrument or a large size tuba made of wood or clay instead of metal, but unfortunately archaeological excavation have not yet discovered any objects of that type. What has been found are smaller versions which were used by Lusitanian leaders to signal orders to their men from a distance or to signal the castro's inhabitants.[484]

As for the interior of the castro, the housing was maintained on a very conservative scale. Though there were many castros scattered throughout the Iberian Peninsula, archeologist have divided the castro into three types:

-Hilltop Forts (like the one in Coaña in Asturias and Viladonga, Portugal). As mentioned before these castros are situated on hilltops or some type of high ground within the confines of the country and near a water source. In general, they are either circular or oval shaped, with one or several high walled circuits. They constitute the most frequent and characteristic type of all castros in the western part of the peninsula.

-Mountaintop Forts though rare are situated on higher mountainous areas (such as those in Vilar, Courel and Fonsagrada), generally oval shaped with artificial moats at the top and high walls on the slopes. They were developed especially during the Roman invasion of eastern Galicia.

---

[482] Livy, 40.47

[483] The use of the horn suggests that being that it is still used today in Portugal by shepherds of the Beira region of Portugal Serra da Estrela and Serra de Sintra, it is possible that the Lusitanians may have also used a horn type instrument.

[484] Octávio da Veiga Ferreira, op. cit., p. 190

-Coastal Hilltop Forts (such as Baroña and Fazouro), of which there are many on the Galician and Portuguese coast. They are usually simple and well-defined circle or oval shaped although some variations exist according to the geological and geographical position of each area, like in the case of Santa Trega at the mouth of the river Miño. They have various designs adapted to the land and its most characteristic type is the natural defense barrier; the sea which is complemented by walls and moats inland.

Though castros have been classified into three categories, they all have the same structural formations. Generally, the hill-forts consisted of a small oval or circular fortress wall made out of stone that had a gate at opposite ends. The stone wall was about 5 meters high (16 ft), thickness varied from .31 to .61 meters (1 to 2 feet) and the village stretched out along a circuit that ran for about 1 km (.6 miles).[485] The construction of these walls usually followed the contours of the land and natural features. The thickness of its walls started at the ends where a large wooden gate was placed and would thin out as the wall stretched out, but at other sites two parallel walls of stones were built and then stuffed with stones and dirty.[486] Within the interior of the castros, wooden stairways or stone ramps were constructed along the wall to be used as defensive fighting positions in case the castro was attacked. These ramparts can be compared to the U.S. Army forts of the Old West and the European castles of the Middle Ages. In the larger castros defensive towers existed next to the two main gates. As the wall stretched along, the wall thinned out forming a narrow – covered corridor between the wall and houses which was used as a street corridor.

---

485 Lourido, Francisco Calo, A cultura castrexa, Promocións Culturais Galegas / A Nosa Terra, Vigo, 1997; Carballo Arceo, X., Os castros galegos: Espacio e Arquitectura. *Gallaecia* 14-15, Sada, Ediciós do Castro, 1996, 52; Octávio da Veiga Ferreira, op. cit., p. 39

486 Xurxo M. Ayán Vila, "A Round Iron Age: The Circular House in the Hillforts of the Northwestern Iberian Peninsula", E-Keltoi: Journal of Interdisciplinary Celtic Studies, Vol. 6"The Celts in the Iberian Peninsula", University of Wisconsin, Milwaukee, pp. 903-1004

The sheltered interior was a set of huts that had various layouts. Housing arrangements varied from castro to castro; some were organized into sections; others were setup in a disorganized fashion.[487] In well organized castros, housing was arranged into four sections, divided by two paved stone streets that crisscrossed one another forming either a cross or an X. Each one of those sections held four to six houses. In the middle of each housing section, the doors from each house converged on to a small square. These central squares played an important role, for it was where each family's daily activities would take place and residents would interact with one another. While most of these structures were residences, there were a few that were workshops. But this is a typical small to medium size castro, but even then, not all were as organized as this example. There were other castros that did not have this type of lay out, especially the larger ones which were pretty much setup in a disorderly way. These castros are reminiscent of a medieval walled European town with densely packed edifices and complex network of streets and alleyway. Instead of just have circular home throughout the castro, the large castros had mixed homes; rounded and rectangular houses and courtyard houses which varied in structures and sizes, which can be seen in the Spanish examples. The courtyard houses were usually three circular houses and a large rectangular structure facing a central courtyard. While others either had one to three circular houses or just one large rectangular house divided into sections. Each building or section of the house had a different function, such as a kitchen, bedroom, granary or storage and perhaps even a workshop.

The typical building on a settlement would have been the roundhouse. These homes, at the start of castro development, were huts usually made of straw and mud that resemble an American Indian's tepee or an upside - down bowl, with a central hearth in each home.[488] But with time

---

[487] Vilas, Felipe Arias, La Evolución de la Cultura Castrexa: Cambio y Continuidad, Extracto Unidad Informativa BUP-Bachillerato-FP, Programa de Acción Didáctica, Museo del Castro de Viladonga, 1998.

[488] González Ruibal, A., Galaicos: poder y comunidad en el Noroeste de la Península Ibérica: (1200 a. C.-50 d. C.). *Brigantium* 18-19. A Coruña: Museo de San Antón, 2006-7, p.100, and Fig. 2.14.

construction techniques and technology changed, as well as the materials that were used. By the Late Bronze Age, Lusitanian homes were made with stone foundations and strong walls to keep out the elements, but they still used roofs made of wood and straw. These circular homes had become the main architectural structure for the centuries to come.

The construction of these homes was characteristically circular with diameters between 4 and 6 meters (19 feet) and with walls with 30 to 40 cm (11 to 15 inches) of thickness.[489] The main frame of the roundhouse was made out of hazel, oak, ash or pollarded willow timbers. As for the walls of the house, they were at first made out of wood covered with clay, soil, rye and barley straw and animal manure, which weatherproof the house.[490] By the Late Bronze Age, the walls were made out of granite stones that were chipped into various shapes and positioned in two rows, with the flattest surface faced the interior and exterior of the house. The space among the two stones was filled out with small stones and gravel mortar giving the house a robust structure. In later stages of castro development, houses from around the 7th and 6th century BCE were built out of adobe.[491] During the Iron Age, homes were being built out of stone and cement that was made out of saprolite mortar and quartzite pebbles.[492]

The roof was constructed from large timbers and dense thatch. The roofs were conical or bowl shaped. The thatched roof was constructed out of rye, wheat and barley straw, plant and small tree branches, scrubs such as broom, gorse and leguminous plants like bean stalks.[493] During

---

489 Xurxo M. Ayán Vila, "A Round Iron Age: The Circular House in the Hillforts of the Northwestern Iberian Peninsula", pp. 903-1004; Octávio da Veiga Ferreira, op. cit., p. 43

490 Pereira, Alves, Estudos do Alto-Minho. Habitações Castrejas no Norte de Portugal, Viana do Castelo, 1914, fasc. XIV, p.17.

491 Xurxo M. Ayán Vila, "A Round Iron Age: The Circular House in the Hillforts of the Northwestern Iberian Peninsula", E-Keltoi: Journal of Interdisciplinary Celtic Studies, Vol. 6"The Celts in the Iberian Peninsula", University of Wisconsin, Milwaukee, Jan. 2008, pp. 903-1004

492 Ibid.

493 Ibid.

the Roman occupation (around the 1st century AD) there were two architectural changes to the castro house. The first change was carefully worked masonry walls with square corners, the second innovation was the use of *tegula* (clay tiles) as roofing material and a new spatial pattern defined by very large rectangular houses. These Roman innovations are still used today. As for the door, it was made out of slabs of wood and was usually low, surely to prevent the passage of water into the interior of the house. Attached to the houses were small square buildings which could have been used as a storage room or barn or both. In some of the larger castros, there are square plots which could have been used as vegetable gardens. Unfortunately, none of these original homes have remained intact due to the fragility of the construction. But thanks, to modern technology and archaeology some of these castro have been rebuilt to afford a glimpse into the past.

All domestic life occurred within the roundhouse. The main focus within the house was the open-hearth fire or a fireplace built into the wall, also common within the roundhouse was a type of barbecue grill, using spits for grilling food.[494] But most Lusitanian homes had a hearth in the center of the house. Next to these hearths there may have stood a bronze cauldron held up by a tripod. If there was no cauldron, there was a variety of ordinary hand – made basic cooking pots made from local clay deposits. This area was the heart of the home. This indispensable feature provided cooked food, warmth and the only light in the house for the walls were windowless. Because of its importance within the domestic sphere, a fire would have been maintained 24 hours a day. The fire place along with the interior of the house, was an ideal place for drying and preservation of food. Smoke and heat from the constant fire would have smoked meat and fish and dry herbs and other plants perfectly.

Spread throughout the house was the presence of furniture, rudimentary beds, masonry benches built into the walls and vaulted niches and shelves within the walls that served as cupboards.[495] Unfortunately, no furniture has survived, and the walls have since crumbled. But what

[494] Octávio da Veiga Ferreira, op. cit., p. 45

[495] Ibid., p. 45; Arribas, Antonio, op. cit., p. 63

has been discovered in archeological sites are remnants of everyday life such as parts of upright weaving looms. The looms were used to spin and weave thread so as to make clothes. Spindle-whorls (round clay/stone weights used to make the spindle rotate evenly), carved bone weaving combs, and loom weights of stone or clay - which held down the warp threads on the loom – have been found in many Iron Age domestic sites. Among these sites thousands richly decorated pieces of indigenous ceramics have been found as well as many Roman ceramics of local production, amphoras, glass, coins, tools, weapons, utensils and ornaments like brooches and several types of clasps for clothing, as well as fibulas (buckles) and hair pins (actus) have also been found.[496]

The sleeping quarters within the roundhouse would have been raised from the ground on a wooden base with a hay or feather mattress, strewn with animal skins and wool blankets.[497] The thick thatched roof and the constant heat from the fireplace would have made the interior of the roundhouse quite a snug and comfortable place to live and sleep in.

The floor of early castro homes were just hard dirt floors. But that changed just prior to the Roman occupation when gravel and clay were added in and smoothed out.[498] During the Roman period of influence, some of these floors were laid with Roman mosaic designs, but the Lusitanians were more simplistically decorated with impression of wavy drawings, shapes and smooth rocks pressed into the 'cement' to make shapes the symbolized something.[499]

---

[496] Bubner, Thomas, "A cerâmica de ornatos brunidos em Portugal", in De Ulisses a Viriato: o primeiro milénio a.C., Jorge de Alarcão (ed.), p. 66-72

[497] Octávio da Veiga Ferreira, op. cit., p. 48

[498] Bettencourt, A.M.S., *Estações da Idade do Bronze e inicios da Idade do Ferro da Bacia do Cávado (Norte de Portugal)*, Braga: Universidade do Minho, Instituto de Ciencias Sociais, 2000.

[499] de la Peña, Antonio, Prehistoria, castrexo e primeira romanización, Promocións Culturais Galegas / A Nosa Terra, Vigo, 2003 It is very rare to see a Roman mosaic floor in a Lusitanian home.

Around the 1st century AD, homes began to take a square or rectangular shape form.[500] The wall in this new phase of home construction were square; like earlier Lusitanian homes, two rows of walls were built with space in between them which were then filled with gravel, mud and stones of various sizes. With the introduction of Roman cement, a Roman innovation, masonry techniques changed in that instead of building two separate walls then filling them in, the cement saved time for only one large wall was constructed. The end result was a thick wall 45 to 60 cm (17 to 23 inches) and large square room with space. The roofing stop being of vegetable origin and became *tegula* (clay tiles), another Roman invention. Indoors, the house was divided into rooms; this is evident from excavations that show internal post-holes that were once not only part of the house's frame, but also part of a room's wall. In addition to the new homes, as well as the older round houses, a second story was added. But there were many others that were not remodeled as seen through archaeological excavations. The use of the square house plan appears to have been a way to maximize the internal space available, since a circular construction plan does not make the most efficient use of housing space. Straight lines allow a more organized distribution of the houses, which are attached to one another by means of dividing walls. Along with the square type homes, some of these models in larger castro had a Roman heating and sewer system.[501]

Outside against the walls, square buildings were at time constructed to house livestock, while empty square plots were used as vegetable gardens. During a siege livestock was brought into the walled castro and these building were at times used to help deter besiegers from scaling the town walls, but at the same time it could have been a disadvantage to the besieged for the enemy could have easy access into the fort. In other castros, those that did not build these small barns around their towns, placed moats, pits, and large parapets to stop incoming siege weapons.

---

[500] de la Peña, Antonio, Prehistoria, castrexo e primeira romanización, Promocións Culturais Galegas / A Nosa Terra, Vigo, 2003; Xurxo M. Ayán Vila, "A Round Iron Age: The Circular House in the Hillforts of the Northwestern Iberian Peninsula", pp. 903-1004

[501] Octávio da Veiga Ferreira, op. cit., p. 50

Castros that had little access to rock formations or lowland forts built their small stone walls usually on the edge of a dirt parapet with a deep trench around it.[502]

Unfortunately, knowledge concerning hilltop forts is still limited. The main cause of this is lack of information due to insufficient funding that is need for systematic excavation campaigns. The lack of funding is based upon the lack of governmental and private funding for Portugal is still somewhat poor and needs every dime to support its social benefits. Another problem these sites suffer from is the 'erosion' of these ancient sites due to that many castro are being robbed of their stone masonry by farmers who steal the rocks to make boundary walls to separate their land from their neighbor. So where once these sites had some type of protection from the elements they are now slowly disappearing via the ravages of time and weather conditions. As a result of these two factors, archaeological excavations have not been large scale.

Art

The art styles developed in the Iberian Peninsula is usually distinguished with the name of *Iberian art.* This Iberian artistic period lasted from the Bronze Age to the complete dominion of the area by the Romans. Though pre-Roman Iberian art has its own character, there are foreign influences from the Greek, Phoenician, Egyptian and Assyrian. Iberian art has been classified into groups of different Iberian regions: Levantine, Andalusian, Catalonian, Albacete, Ebro, Lusitanian and Central Iberian. From these styles of art, I will only deal with Lusitanian.

Compared to the rest of the Iberian Peninsula, Lusitanian art was primarily based on simple painting of concentric circles, spirals, swastikas, corrugated lines, etc. It is hard to believe that this culture created some of most beautiful jewelry pieces of the ancient world but were not able to sculpt out of stone no more that crudely shaped figures of men and animals.

---

[502] Ibid., p. 38

Thus, this lack of artistic talent within the Lusitanian culture has come into question. Three hypotheses have come about. The first is due to the harsh lifestyles these people lived, so there is a belief that these people had little time to participate in artistic endeavors. The other reason for the lack of ornamentation within the culture is due to the type of housing the castro system was. Because of its circular shape, early Lusitanian homes lacked space for decorations and elaborate furniture. So that being said, they mostly toiled the soil, hunted and gathered food during day light hour, the Lusitanian house in the evenings was mostly used as a place to sleep, eat, and for protection from the elements such as rain. The third is directly related to the occultist's theory. This third hypothesis is a complicated case. Within the Lusitanian culture the existence of circles and other artistic symbols had mysterious symbolic meaning, which are now lost to us. But these symbolic shapes since antiquity have been interpreted as occult symbols of power such as the protection against the forces of evil.[503] Therefore, certain shapes from concentric circles, corrugated lines, spheres and other shapes that are present in ceramic pieces are identical to the 'mystical stones' that have been discovered at Sabroso and Citânia, not only did it serve individuals, but it was also designed into the architecture of homes and temples and other objects that were used by the Lusitanians, thus they were not only seen as religious, but artistic.

It is believed by a number of Portuguese historians, scholar and archaeologist that Lusitanian art began in the Paleolitic era. This theory is backed-up by archaeological evidence of cave paintings found in the Gruta do Escoural between Évora and Montemor-o-Novo and at Vandoma near Oporto.[504] From prehistoric cave paintings, early people that inhabited Lusitanian began a type of intermediate art (art based

---

[503] A. Viana, L. de Albuquerque e Castro and O. da Veiga Ferreira, "O dólmen pintado de Antelas, Com. Serv. Geol. De Portugal, XXXVIII, 1957; Tondriau, Julien, L'Occultisme: Panorama critique et historique, Dictionnaire des personnages, des mots-clés et des symbols, Verviers, Gérard & Co, 1964, p. 235-236

[504] de Vasconcelos, Flórido, A Arte em Portugal, 2nd ed., Lisboa, Verbo Juvenil, 1975, p. 15.

on stone engravings and simple sculptures) which is relatively plentiful within megalithic sites and ancient villages in northern Portugal. The discovery of these rare simple human and animal figurines was accompanied by numerous etched pictures in stone. These etchings are predominantly of geometrics shapes, which some archaeologists believe that these stone were manifested for idolatry worship.[505] By the time the castro era had further developed, Lusitanian art had advanced a bit more artistically.

Of the many statuettes and some statues of men and animals that have been recovered in archaeological excavations throughout northern Portugal mainly at Briteiros and Sanfins, one can not help notice that these works of art have their own artistic style. One such example of this advance art form was found in Sanfins in the early 1970s. It is a granite head of an indigenous warrior. This statue is noteworthy because one can see the definition of the clothes of that epoch, the warrior's face, helmet and the torque that he wears around his neck which constitute the most perfect representation of these types of pieces. Besides finding human heads, ophidian heads were also uncovered at Sanfins. Finally, at the Museu de Sociedade Martins Sarmento in Guimarães there is a stunning collection of Lusitanian sculptures that are highlighted by some funerary steles and a beautifully designed Pedra Formosa, which will be touched upon later.

There are some scholars that have attempted to hypothesize that Lusitanian art is not indigenous but of a foreign influence. One such person was Martins Sarmento who proposed to explain that Lusitanian art was of Mycenaean influences but this theory was counter by L. Siret, saying that Sarmento was wrong and the basis for their artistic style was Punic.[506] The relation between the Minoan and Mycenaean cultures and 2nd Iron Age people of northwestern Iberian Peninsula was perhaps not factual for evidence show a more Punic influence. Hence Henri Martin defended Siret theory along with his theory that the origin

505 Ibid.

506 Siret, Luis, "Apropos de poteries pseudo-mycéniennes", L'Antrhopologie, XVIII, Paris, 1907, p. 277

of Lusitanian art was pelagic and that it was then influenced by Nordic cultures that landed in Lusitanian around the 5th century BCE.[507] While Joseph Dechelette was of the opinion that Lusitanian art reflected the beginning of Romanization.[508] However, it is the general view of various archaeologists that there is a lack of information to reach any definitive conclusion about the interpretations of Lusitanian art.

Of all the artistic endeavors that have survived, stonework is the most prominent. Stonework played an important part not only in construction, but in art. Overall, sculpturing was practiced more in the east than in the west of the Iberian Peninsula, but that changed under Roman rule when the entire region sculpted. The archaic quality of Lusitanian sculptures is very pronounced by its schematic and geometric volume. All figures are shown in their frontal aspects and are very rigid and lack animation. A large part of their best pieces can be attributed to the transition period between the onset of the hill - top fort world and the Galicia-Luso-Roman period, that is to say, between the 1st century BCE and 1st century AD. These surviving several hundred cravings and sculptures have been classified as follows:[509]

Warriors: Warrior statues are among the most outstanding artistic achievements of pre-Roman Lusitania and Gallaecia. They represent outsized males with a sword or dagger, a small round shield (*caetra*), helmet, torc, bracelets (*viriae*), decorated belt and decorated dress. In some cases, they have a beard. Though these Lusitanian warriors appear to us grotesque, it makes one feel safe and strong. There have been more than two dozen statues found throughout Portugal such as in Montalegre,

---

507 Octávio da Veiga Ferreira, op. cit., p. 137-138; Correspondência Epistolar entre Emílio Hubner e Martins Sarmento, Guimarães, 1947, p. 87-88 and 90.

508 Dechelette, Joseph – *Manuel d'Archéologie Préhistorique Celtique et Gallo-Romaine.* Paris: Auguste
Picard, Éditeur, 1924, *Manuel d'Archéologie,* IV editon, Paris, 1924

509 González-Ruibal, Alfredo, Artistic Expression and Material Culture in Celtic Gallaecia, *e-Keltoi: Journal of Interdisciplinary Celtic Studies vol.* 6, *The Celts in the Iberian Peninsula,* University of Wisconsin-Milwaukee, December 2004 pp. 113-166

São Paio de Meixedo, Santo Ovid of Fafe, Jorge de Odivelas, Capeludos, Cendufe and Mósinho. This art form is believed to have originated when foreign navigators and merchants first came into contact with the simple people of the Peninsula and left in them the canon that served as base for the creation of this Herculean figurative type art. The Herculean style figures probably represent idealized aristocratic warriors. These large statues symbolically protected the entrance to the settlements, while at the same time making explicit the power of the ruling elite. The emphasis on warrior representations fits well with the situation of instability and endemic warfare that characterized the Iberian Peninsula in the second and first centuries BCE. Another assumption about these statues is that they were treated as honorary funerary statues to heroes or deified heroes. Therefore, the funerals of Lusitanian leaders and warriors were illustrated as Herculean warrior in their eccentric protocols with a symbolic purpose, that when these men were put in their grave, these stone figures represented them as if they had been reborn from the ashes.

These statues were made out of granite, and from afar it looks as if they were sculpted from a huge block of stone, but on a closer examination these figures are not craved out from just one block, but from two. One was used for the body and another for the head. The statue of the warriors discovered by Martins Sarmento in Santo Ovid de Fafe (Portugal) presents a square cavity open between the shoulders, evidence that a head was sculpted from a different block of rock making these statues interchangeable. Perhaps the reason why so few statues have been discovered, while many heads have been found is because instead of sculpting another entire statue from a huge piece of solid rock it was much easier to just fashion a head out of a small piece and replace the old honored hero with the new hero.

Female statues: The number of female representations in Lusitanian art as well as in Iberian art in general, is scant. These are less than life-sized representations of women, with their sexual attributes conspicuously marked. The presence of sexual attributes suggests fertility and reproduction. Statues of women are commonly associated with female deities. These statues were at times were not of female gods, but women who had status. The sculptural work appears less skillful when compared to the warrior statues.

Human heads (busts): These head busts can be found throughout the Douro River area to northern Galicia. They are characterized by very simple and crude representations of human heads, often in bas-relief with "owl faces". Two functions can be proposed: an apostrophic one, in which they were placed on statues at the entrances to hilltop forts and oppida or on wall around the castro such as gargoyles were used on cathedrals, and a ritual one, to which specific areas inside the settlements were probably devoted to. Ancient writers wrote about the Gaulish custom of putting human heads in house doors and the practice of severing the enemy's head in war among barbarians (Strabo, 5, 29, 5; Polybius, *Hist.* 2, 28; Livy, *Hist.* 10, 26 and 23, 24; Diodorus Siculus *Hist.* 5, 29, 4-5). The severed head, or its representation, could simultaneously attract the power of the vanquished enemy; serving as a protection against bad spirits and as an image of the power of the community.

Although it has been traditionally linked with Celtic peoples, the magical and social use of heads was very widespread, both in space and time. The spread of head hunting or its representation must be linked to the increased violence that was provoked by the growing hierarchization and territorialization of the Late Iron Age tribal wars and the stress brought on by the Romans. On the other hand, not all heads can be related to severed human heads, some of them probably represent gods, perhaps a local genius (*Genius Castelli*), a protector of the village. Divinities of this kind, such as *Bandua* and perhaps *Coso*, are well attested in Lusitania and Gallaecia. Among the heads of gods, they perhaps represented leaders or warriors. Whether they are related to gods or humans, heads seem to play a central role in the beliefs of Celtic peoples from all over Europe.

Zoomorphic statues: They are found throughout the country. There is no doubt that during these primitive times as the evolution of traditions took root in pre-history; men began to represent animals in art. Compare to other ancient people, Luistanian animal statues are more poignant and ungraceful examples. All the statues are quadrupedal and are sculpted in a rugged and churlish manner of one block of rock. The animal features are basic outlines which show what type of animal these statues represent. Though they lack details, all statues were carved with thick bodies and their legs are united as one which seems to represent stoutness and portliness signifying perhaps that they treated their animals well. The statues that have survived have been of pigs, snakes, goats, horses, bulls and sheep. It is believed that these statues were protectors of livestock or of a fecundity cult. But the meaning of these representations of animals have been unfortunately lost, so one is not exactly sure what are the true meaning of these statues or why they were made.

Seated statues: Only four pieces have been found in Braga, Xinzo de Limia and Lanhoso. These statuettes are either of a divinity, royalty or a warrior. These statuettes clearly resemble that of the warrior styled statues, but instead of standing they are sitting on thrones, an unambiguous symbol of power. The style used is of a masculine representation and seem to have a mortuary function of which is traditional Mediterranean and Egyptian.

Figurines: Throughout the entire territory icons, feminine and masculine figurines and statuettes that have been found and conserved in great quantities. These figurines vary in shapes and sizes and are not as large and are transformed into small votive statuettes made of clay or bronze.

Architectural Decorations: The origin of architectural art is intrinsically linked to the conditions that fostered the development of the *oppida* and a particular type of composite homestead from the time of Romanization. These items served as an arena for social competition in which different households exhibited their power and wealth. It also reflected symbolic concerns such as the use of these items as protective devices against spirits. What remains of these architectural decorations are a large number of decorative stones belonging to friezes, door posts, door and window frames, lintels, jambs, hinges, circular caps, etc. Though these decorations are many, they range from corded-shape, string-work-shaped and herring-bone shape decorations, stylized palm-tree decorations, spirals, triskele, swastika, rosettes, crosses, concentrated "SSSs" design, corrugated lines, crisscrosses, figure eights.

"Pedras formosas" ("Beautiful Stones"): Are special types of architectural decorated stones from ritual saunas. The general consensus is that the huge stones were used in buildings baths (saunas) and that the *pedras formosas* were the monumental façades for those bath houses. These stones were profusely decorated with complex cravings of cosmological symbols. These "beautiful stone" separated the outer chamber (the warm room) from the antechamber (the hot room). These façades were beautifully decorated with a small enterance in which a person would crawl through to enter the hot room.

Omphaloi: There is a small group of stone carvings that cannot be clearly associated with any of the groups previously discussed. They are prismatic pillars with their circular shape divided in the four sides. These four faces were decorated with different motifs. It is believed that they had a ritual purpose roughly comparable to other carved stones and natural rocks in the "Celtic" world, traditionally linked with political power.

The artistic expression of the Lusitanians is archaic, stating an infancy of conceptions and composition. Theories attempting to explain the art of this culture are difficult, but one thing is certain, it is a rough and rugged art form which does not lack beauty. As Mario Cardozo writes, "...these creations are of a native artistic design and implementation of what these people produced naturally where they get their inspiration by direct suggestion of nature and free from any other influences."[510]

The Lusitanian Language

Sometime before 5000 BCE, the people in the area of southwest Asia and the subcontinent of India spoke a common language, now known as

---

[510] Cardozo, Mario, Citânia e Sabroso, 3rd ed., Guimarães, 1948, p.33

the **Indo-European proto-language**, This language, through diffusion, migration, or some other means, gradually split off into a number of different dialects and by the beginning of the third millennium BCE it had spread to most areas of Europe and much of South-West Asia, forming into daughter languages in the process.

After 1000 BCE, the Iberian Peninsula was completely colonized by successive waves of Celtic people who originated in Central Europe along with Greek and Phoenicians. From this influx of people, the languages of pre-Roman Iberian Peninsula formed and have been classified in three groups according to their external cultural relations: 1) **Celtic** 2) **Tartessian,** which is believed to be a mixture of Phoenician and Greco-Iberian the languages of the historically documented colonization: Phoenician, Punic and Greek; and 3) the "native" languages (i.e. Lusitanian)

Of the languages that took root, Proto-Celtic or "Common Celtic", a branch of the greater Indo-European language family was spoken throughout the entire Peninsula. In turn, this language has been classified into three groups: 1) **Celtiberian:** related to Celtic, as its name suggests, but a hybrid Celtic language. 2) **Iberian:** a clearly distinguishable and easily identifiable language, but very poorly known, it is probably related to Basque and ancient Aquitanian, which is still spoken (in a modified way) in some parts of eastern Spain and southwestern France. 3) **Lusitanian:** Lusitani itself would be a dialect with its own personality. It was supposedly spoken between the Douro and Tagus Rivers and would be an archaic Indo-European language different from the other peninsular languages such as Celtiberian or Ibero-Turdetanian. Spite the fact that its origins are unknown; it is assumed that it may have been directly descended from Indo-European, but some scholars regard it as Celtic. With this said, it brings into debate on the filiations of the Lusitanian language in which there are three theories on the origin of the Lusitanian language.

Lusitanian was a paleo-Hispanic language that clearly has Indo-European linguistic roots. There are those who endorse that it is a Celtic language with an obvious "celticity" to most of the lexicon, over its many anthroponyms and toponyms. This Celtic theory is largely based upon the historical fact that the only Indo-European tribes that are known to have existed in Portugal at that time were Celtic tribes.[511] A second theory, defended by Francisco Villar and Rosa Pedrero, relates Lusitanian with Italic languages.[512] Finally, there is the proposed new theory which is called "Galician-Lusitanian".[513] There is a fundamental suspicion that the area of Portugal, Galicia and Asturian which makes up the northwestern area of the Iberian Peninsula, spoke Lusitanian, which was a language on to itself that was not Celtic, but a subgroup of the Indo-European mother tongue. It is very unfortunate that ancient writers did not preserve this now extinct language in the verses of their war hymns or their liturgical songs to the gods, for this would have aided in the knowledge of that people's spirit and culture. Of what is left of the Lusitanian language, there are only five inscriptions and numerous names of places (toponyms) and of gods (theonyms).

With the Latinization of Lusitania, the Lusitanian language, like all other Paleo-Hispanic languages, except for the Basque language, succumbed to the pressure and prestige of Latin. Portuguese, which is considered a Romance language, is a descendant of the vulgar form of Latin along with Spanish and Catalan. Every authority on the subject agrees that the existence of a separate and definable Portuguese language dates back to

---

[511] García Quintela, Marco V., "Celtic Elements in Northwestern Spain in Pre-Roman times", *e-Keltoi: Journal of Interdisciplinary Celtic Studies vol.* 6, *The Celts in the Iberian Peninsula,* University of Wisconsin-Milwaukee, August 2005, pp. 497-569 ; A. Tovar, Lenguas y Pueblos de la Antigua Hispania: Lo que Sabemos de Nuestros Antepasados Protohistóricos, *Veleia* 2-3,1985-1986, pp.15-34; Gorrochategui, Joaquín, "En torno a la clasificación del lusitano", *Studia palaeohispanica, Actas del IV coloquio sobre lenguas y culturas paleohispánicas*, Vitoria, 1994, pp 77-91; Untermann, Jürgen, Lusitanisch, Keltiberisch, Keltisch, *Veleia* 2-3, 1985-1986, pp. 57-76

[512] Villar, Francisco, *Los indoeuropeos y los orígenes de Europa*, Madrid, 1996 and Villar, Francisco & Pedrero Rosa, "La nueva inscripción lusitana: Arroyo de la Luz III", *Religión, Lengua y Cultura Prerromanas de Hispania*, 2001, pp. 663-698

[513] García Quintela, Marco V., "Celtic Elements in Northwestern Spain in Pre-Roman times", pp. 513-516.

the twelfth century.[514] Today not much remains of the Celtic or other pre-Roman influence on the Portuguese language itself, although it is a truism that Portugal has a more "Celtic" culture than other Romance people in its customs, way of life and festivals.

Writing system

The **Paleohispanic scripts** are the writing systems created in the Iberian Peninsula before the Latin alphabet became the dominant script. Most of them are typologically very unusual in that they are semi-syllabic rather than purely alphabetic, despite having been developed from the Phoenician alphabet. Paleohispanic scripts are known to have been used around the 5th century BCE or possibly even early as the 7th century BCE, in the opinion of some researchers, and it was used until the end of the 1st century BCE or the beginning of the 1st century AD. Some researchers conclude that their origin lies solely with the Phoenician alphabet, while others believe the Greek alphabet also had a role.

Paleohispanic writing systems can be classified into two groups: native and non-native. The native systems were made up of three basic kinds that are clearly derived from the same ancestral system of the Indo-European mother tongue. As mentioned in the last section, these native written languages can be classified according to their 'genetical' family relations into three groups: Celtiberian, Iberian and Lusitanian. With these three written languages there is a fourth; the unclassified languages. But among the unclassified languages there is a theory that Lusitanian writing may have derived from Tartessian, more correctly called Sudlusitanian. But there is debate among some scholar that say that Sudlusitanian is not related to Lusitanian. In all likelihood, Tartessian is neither an Iberian language nor an Indo-European one, although it is usually considered as an ascription to Celtic or to Anatolian family tree.

---

[514] Oliveira Marques, A.H. de, History of Portugal: From Lusitania to Empire, Vol. I, Columbia University Press, NY, 1972, p. 91

The Celtic writing system is documented to have existed in Portugal since the early part of the 1st Iron Age.[515] According to C. M. Beirão and M.V. Gomes, who discovered rock inscriptions and graffiti in southern and central Portugal, believe that these early writings come from a writing system known as **Tartessian language**, also known as **southwestern** or **Southern Lusitanian.** Unfortunately, there are only a few samples, so it is difficult to tell whether they are of that language or not. According to the artifacts that have been excavated around this discovery, this script has been assumed that it may be linked to religious conception and funerary rites.[516] Furthermore, it is believed that this writing has a foreign origin not indigenous to the Iberian Peninsula as advocated by some scholars.[517] The belief of its foreign origin is that Luistanian script was created from Phoenician writing (ca. 800 BCE).[518] This hypothesis begins during the sixth century BCE, where there was a cultural shift in the southern Portuguese territory after the fall of Tartessos, with a strong Mediterranean character, it modified

---

[515] Munoz, Mauricio P., *op. cit.,* p. 88

[516] Beirão, C.M. and, *A Idade do Ferro no Sul de Portugal, epigrafia e cultura.* Exhibition Catalogue, Lisboa, Museu Nacional de Arqueologia 1981. A necrópole da Idade do Ferro do Galeado (Vila Nova de Milfontes*), O Arqueólogo Português* 4(1), 1983, pp. 207-266.

[517] De Hoz, J., "Las sociedades paleohispánicas del área no indoeuropea y la escritura" AEspA 66, 1993, 3-29; Rodríguez Ramos, J., *Breve manual de epigrafía ibérica*, 'Dossiers de la Societat Catalana d'Arqueologia' XVI, Barcelona 1995

[518] The "foreign" systems are Phoenician/Punic, Greek and Latin. Greek writing was used also for Iberian language and Latin for Lusitanian, sometimes for Celtiberian, and exceptionally for Iberian. Iberians adopted the elements of the Greek Alphabet into their writing system. Correa, José Antonio (1996): «La epigrafía del sudoeste: estado de la cuestión», *La Hispania prerromana*, pp. 65-75. Correia, Virgílio-Hipólito (1996): «A escrita pré-romana do Sudoeste peninsular», *De Ulisses a Viriato: o primeiro milenio a.c.*, pp.88-94 Guerra, Amilcar (2002): "Novos monumentos epigrafados com escrita do Sudoeste da vertente setentrional da Serra do Caldeirao", *Revista portuguesa de arqueologia* 5-2, pp. 219-231. Hoz, Javier de (1985): «El origen de la escritura del S.O.», *Actas del III coloquio sobre lenguas y culturas paleohispánicas*, pp. 423-464. Rodríguez Ramos, Jesús (2000): «La lectura de las inscripciones sudlusitano-tartesias», *Faventia* 22/1, pp. 21-48

the Tartessian culture.[519] This first form of writing in western Iberia, the Southwest script (still to be translated), denotes a strong Tartessian influence in its use of a modified Phoenician alphabet.[520] This change occurred mainly in Baxio Alentejo and the Algarve, but had littoral extensions up to the mouth of the Tagus River (namely the important city of *Bevipo*, modern Alcácer do Sal) and further north.

The existence of the Lusitanian language is known only by several inscriptions and numerous names of places (toponyms) and of gods (theonyms) which have been found in Arroyo de la Luz (in Cáceres), Spain, Cabeço das Fragas (in Guarda), Portugal and in Moledo (Viseu), Portugal.[521] Taking into account these Lusitanian theonyms, anthroponyms and toponyms, the Lusitanian sphere of influence, including northern Portugal and adjacent areas in Spain, make Serra da Estrela its center. The inscriptions in this language used the southwestern script. Like all the paleohispanic scripts, with the exception of the Greco-Iberian alphabet, this script includes signs with syllabic value for the occlusive and signs with monophonematic value for the rest of consonants and vowels. In the classification of writing systems, these are neither alphabets nor syllabifies; instead, they are mixed scripts that normally are identified as

[519] For information on the Tartessian culture see M. A. Blazquez, *Tartessos y Los Origines de la Colonizacion Fenicia en Occidente* (University of Salamanca) 1968; Jaime Alvar and José María Blázquez, *Los enigmas de Tartessos,* Catedra, Madrid, 1993. Javier G. Chamorro, "Survey of Archaeological Research on Tartessos" *American Journal of Archaeology* **91**.2 (April 1987), pp. 197-232.

[520] Correa, José Antonio, op. cit., pp. 65-75. Correia, Virgílio-Hipólito, «A escrita pré-romana do Sudoeste peninsular»., pp.88-94; Guerra, Amilcar, "Novos monumentos epigrafados com escrita do Sudoeste da vertente setentrional da Serra do Caldeirao", pp. 219-231. Hoz, Javier de, «El origen de la escritura del S.O.», pp. 423-464. Rodríguez Ramos, Jesús (2000): «La lectura de las inscripciones sudlusitano-tartesias», *Faventia* 22/1, pp. 21-48

[521] Gorrochategui, Joaquín, «En torno a la clasificación del lusitano», *Actas del IV coloquio sobre lenguas y culturas paleohispanicas*, 1987, pp. 2-3. Villar, Francisco, *Los indoeuropeos y los orígenes de Europa*, Madrid, 1996; Villar, Francisco and Pedrero Rosa, «La nueva inscripción lusitana: Arroyo de la Luz III», *Religión, 'Lengua y Cultura Preromanas de Hispania*, 2001, pp. 663-698.

semi-syllabifies.[522] About the common origin of the paleohispanic semi-syllabifies, there is no agreement among researchers; some consider them as descended solely from Phoenician alphabet, while others believe the Greek alphabet had an influence as well.[523]

Though southwestern script is very similar to the southeastern Iberian script, by the shape of the signs and their values, the main difference is that southeastern Iberian script does not show the vocalic redundancy of the syllabic signs. This characteristic allows the classification of a great part of the southwestern signs in vowels, consonants and syllabic signs. Unlike the northeastern Iberian script, the decipherment of the southeastern Iberian script and the southwestern script is still not complete, because there is significant group of signs whose meaning remains in dispute.

Southwestern Script

		G/K	B/P	D/T				
A	A	[illegible]	[illegible]	[illegible]	S	[illegible]	M	
E	O	[illegible]	[illegible]	[illegible]	Ś	M	N	[illegible]
I	[illegible]	[illegible]	[illegible]	[illegible]	R	[illegible]	[illegible]	
O	[illegible]	[illegible]	[illegible]	[illegible]	Ŕ	[illegible]	[illegible]	
U	[illegible]	[illegible]	[illegible]	[illegible]	L	1	[illegible]	

[522] Correa, José Antonio, «Los semisilabarios ibéricos: algunas cuestiones», *ELEA* 4, 2004, pp. 75-98. Hoz, Javier de, «El desarrollo de la escritura y las lenguas de la zona meridional», *Tartessos*, 1989, pp.523-587; Rodríguez Ramos, Jesús, «La escritura ibérica meridional», *Zephyrus* 55, 2002, pp. 231-245; Velaza, Javier, *Epigrafía y lengua ibéricas*, Barcelona, 1996; http://en.wikipedia.org/wiki/Southeastern_Iberian_script.

[523] Correa, José Antonio, op. cit., pp. 65-75; Correia, Virgílio-Hipólito, op. cit., pp.88-94; Guerra, Amilcar, op. cit., pp. 219-231; Hoz, Javier de, op. cit., pp. 423-464; Rodríguez Ramos, Jesús, op. cit., pp. 21-48.

Southeastern Script

		G/K	B	D/T				
A					S		M	
E					Ś		N	
I					R		Ḿ	
O					Ŕ			
U					L			

Northern Iberian Script

Southern Iberian Script

Though this language, along with other ancient Iberian languages still remain undeciphered, perhaps someone someday will study and decipher the secrets of Iberian/Lusitanian/Turdetanian writing, whose immense inscriptions have become obscured in museums. With those new discoveries about their life a new chapter in their history will open, but for now much remains to be seen about this vast and heterogeneous group of humans.

Lusitanian Economy and Religion

Money[524]

With the rise of the Phoenicians, their vessels began to sail in the in the Mediterranean Sea around the 12th century BCE. In time, these seafarers began building trading posts all along the Mediterranean coast and barter with the local inhabitants. By the 11th century BCE, these early merchant wayfarers sailed up the west coast of the Peninsula to trade directly with Lusitania and Galicia. Though little trading occurred, the Phoenicians founded a trading post at Keition/Abul (Alcácer do Sal) in the province of Alentejo around 1000 BCE.[525] From this trading post, the Phoenician sailed to Lisbon and Setúbal, and barter with the Lusitanians for salt, salty fish, horses for export and foods for the boats that traded tin with Cornualha. When the Greeks became the dominate power around the 7th century BCE, they too sailed westward past the Straits of Gibraltar and up the Atlantic coast of Portugal. Landing near

---

[524] Faria, António José Marques de, The Celts and Their Coinage, Hispania - Hans Rauch, Vol. I, No. 2, 1969 and The Celts and Their Coinage, Hispania and Gaul - Hans Rauch Society for Ancient Numismatics, Vol. I, No. 3, 1969; As moedas da Lusitânia portuguesa. Sua recente abordagem em duas obras espanholas da especialidade. *Moeda*. Lisboa. 8, 1983, p. 215-217.

[525] Joao Luís Cardoso Manuela Barthelemy and María Eugenia Aubet Semmler, Fenícios e indígenas em Rocha Branca, Abul, Alcácer do Sal, Almaraz e Santarém estudo comparada dos mamíferos Actas del IV Congreso Internacional de Estudios Fenicios y Púnicos: Cádiz, 2 al 6 de octubre de 1995/Vol. 1, 2000, pags. 319-327; L. Barros, J.L. Cardoso and A. Sabrosa, Fenicios na margen sul de Tejo: economica e interação cultural da povoado do Almaraz, Estudos Orientais IV, Os Fenicios no territorio Portuguese, Lisboa, 1993, p. 143-181; Arruda, Ana M., Los Fenicios em Portugal, Publicaciones del Laboratoria de Arqueologia de Universidade Pompeu Fabra de Barcelona, 2000; Arruda, Ana Margarida, "Os Fenícios no Ocidente", De Ulisses a Viriato: O primeiro milénio a.C., Museu Nacional Arqueologia, Lisboa, 1996, p. 19, 35-45 and 52-59 (deals with Abul) There has been some debate on whether Alcácer do Sal was called either Keition or Abul

Lisbon, they began calling the area Ophioussa.[526] Like the Phoenicians, they also began bartering with the locals at first, but near the end of the 4th century BCE and the start of the 3rd century BCE they began to circulate among the Lusitanians, Greek coinage. Compared to the Iberians along the southern seacoast who had been using Greek coinage for some times, the Lusitanians used bars or cut pieces of beaten silver and gold as currency, but direct exchange of goods was still common.[527] It would not be until the Roman conquest of Lusitanian that a monetary system became a permanent part of Lusitanian everyday life. But in the highlands, the populace used direct exchange or barter. In time, coins began to appear via those who had traveled outside the area or traveling merchants that slowly made their way deeper into Lusitanian territory and began introducing coins into the area.

Economy

Given the lack of archeological excavations in Lusitania, it is necessary to appeal to classical texts to illuminate us about Lusitanian economy. From a geographical point of view, the regional areas that the Lusitanians inhabited present a relevant contrast between the interior and the coast. Compared to the rest of the Iberian Peninsula, according to Strabo, Lusitania was ripe with plants and animals. The reason for this richness in fruits, plants, livestock and wildlife was due to the country's climate.

From Strabo's comment and other classical texts, Lusitanian economy was fundamentally pastoral and agricultural, as it was in many other societies that were pre-Roman or pre-industrial. The main economy of the *castros* was based on crops (cereals, vegetables, and fruits) and animal husbandry (cattle, horses, pigs, goats and sheep). They also carried out some relatively important mining and metal work, which led to important finds in metal craftsmanship. The castro

[526] António García y Bellido, *La Península Ibérica en los comienzos de su historia,* Madrid Consejo Superior de Investigaciones Científicas, 1953, p. 183; Octávio da Veiga Ferreira, op. cit., p. 213

[527] Strabo, 3.3.7; Octávio da Veiga Ferreira, op. cit., p. 213

economy was a self-sufficient system. Even though the Lusitanians were self-sufficient it is believed that they traded with Turdetanians, Phoenicians, Greeks, Carthaginians and later the Romans. As for industrialization, it did not occur until the Romans began to Romanize Lusitania, prior to that it was either done on a small scale or non-existent. During the Romanization of the Iberian Peninsula, it had become known as Rome's bread basket for Iberian grain had caused prices on the Roman market to be reduced.[528] Another industry that was later made profitable by the Romans and Lusitanians was the making of wine and olive oil. In general, all these activities that stimulated Lusitanian economy were more of a necessity of everyday life than it was economically prosperous.

Besides being Rome's bread basket, they practiced animal husbandry at an industrial scale. The type of livestock that was raised in Lusitania was the horse, bovine, swine, goat and sheep. According to the classical writers, they proclaimed that the entire Iberian Peninsula was full of livestock. According to Aveinus, of all the livestock that roamed the land, the goat was what stood out for its fur was of high quality.[529] The areas of Alentejo and Ribatejo possessed a lot of cattle inferred by Strabo.[530] While Pliny refers to the magnificent sheep wools of Salacia (Alcácer do Sal, Portugal).[531] With this information it demonstrates that the Lusitanians were not in state of barbarism as some authors believe, but had the beginnings of a primitive civilization.

Of all the domesticated animals raised by the Lusitanians there was a major industry in breeding horses and pigs.[532] The area of Lisbon and the future province of Estremadura were rich in horses. The equus of Lusitania is said to have been ungraceful and small, but resistant, agile and fast. According to legend it was believed that the speed of

---

[528] Arribas, Antonio, op. cit., p. 120; Munoz, Mauricio P., op. cit., p.109

[529] Octávio da Veiga Ferreira, op. cit.,, p. 210.

[530] Strabo 3.3.5

[531] Pliny NH, 8.48; Strabo 3.2.6; Gilroy, Clinton G., The History of Silk, Cotton, Linen, Wool, and Other Fibrous Harper & Brothers, NY, 1845, p. 289. Salacia today is said to be modern Alcacer do Sal, Portugal.

[532] Arribas, Antonio, op. cit., p. 121; Munoz, Mauricio, p. cit., p.109.

the Lusitano came from when Lusitano mares were fecundated by the wind.[533] The Carthaginians and Romans had recognized the superiority of the Iberian horses and horsemanship to the point that the Romans adopted the Iberian equestrian style of warfare. Trained for war, these horses showed their efficiency in the scaling mountainous and hilly areas. So impressed with the Iberian horses, especially the Lusitano, that once the Iberian territory was conquered, the Romans set up stud farms for their cavalry to help accomplish the expansion of the Roman Empire.[534] As for breeding the domestic pig, they provided hams of outstanding quality, in which they still do to this day.[535] In Alentejo the pig was a source of wealth, for Polybius writes that a healthy pig cost more than all other animals besides the horse.[536] The sea around the Iberian Peninsula, as well as its rivers, proved to yield a varied assortment of fish which was exploited by the locals to feed their families.[537] But by the time of the Roman occupation, Lusitania produced four of the largest fishing cities on the Peninsula: Lisbon, Setúbal, Oporto and Alcácer do Sal. It was in these cities that gave rise to a prosperous salt, garum and preserving fish industry.

Mining

For many years it was thought that the mining wealth of Lusitania was inferior compared to the rest of the Peninsula. But the importance of mining within Lusitanian economics has been validated recently, thanks to new archeological discoveries that help prove the data from classical

---

533 Resende, André de, *De Antiquitatibus Lusitaniae*, Evora, 1593

534 Valera-Lema, Juan, Ph.D.,"The Lusitano Horse: Horse of the Wind and Pride of Portugal", *Conquistador Magazine: The World of Spanish Horses,* Amigo Publications, Vol. 4, No. 5, 1997; Munoz, Mauricio, op cit., p.110; Madariaga de la Campa, B. *Origen y características de las primitivas razas caballares de la Península Ibérica.* Inst. Estudios Agropecuarios, Santander, 1975

535 Pliny, Natural History, XV.103; Varro, De Re Rustica, 2. 4.11

536 Polybius, Histories, 34.4.4

537 Polybius, Histories, 34.8

sources.[538] One such example is from Strabo, who wrote that Lusitania was rich in mineral ores,[539] which in turn shows that mining was an integral part of the Lusitanian culture. Gold, iron, copper, tin, and lead were the most common ores mined. With this information Lusitania had a mineral wealth which would later be exploited by the Romans. Unfortunately, there is very little information on how the Lusitanians extracted these metals from the ground.

Of all the metals that the Lusitanians dug up, gold and silver in their eyes had little use in everyday life except that it was beautiful to look at and considered them sacred for they saw these metals as a gift from the gods. According to ancient authors, they speak profusely of the River Tagus and of its gold, calling it aurifer Tagus.[540] This bit of information is backed – up by the discovery of several small religious inscription found at these sites giving us an idea that many gold and silver mines were regard as sacred sites.[541] Within these sacred places, the extraction of gold was related with precepts of a religious order. These sacred noble metals would only be employed in the making of jewelry and religious artifacts. But to extract these metals, it was tedious work. Naturally these nuggets were dragged downstream by currents and landed onto calm river banks in which the Lusitanians would then dredge them out close to the shore with shovels.[542] Women were handed sieves and commenced panning the sand in search of the

---

[538] Vilaça, R., *Aspectos do Povoamento da Beira Interior (Centro e Sul) nos Finais da Idade do Bronze,* "Trabalhos de Arqueologia", 9, IPPAR, Lisboa, 1995, 2 vols.; Muñoz, Mauricio P. op. cit., p. 41

[539] Strabo, 3.3.5

[540] Mela, De situs orbis 3.1 (Hispania); Pliny, NH, 33.4; See Chap. 2, section on Natural Resourses; Strabo, 3.2.8; Schulten, Adolf, Geografia y Etnografia antiguas de la Peninsula Ibérica, 2 vols., Madrid, Vol. II, p. 245-46

[541] Vasconcelos, J. Leite de, Religiões da Lusitânia, 3 vols., Impresa Nacional, Lisboa, 1897-1913, vol II, 1905, p. 105.

[542] Strabo, 3.2.9; Allan, John C., "A mineração em Portugal na Antiguidade", Boletim de Minas 2, vol. 3, 1965, p. 137-173

precious metal.[543] As for mining in the hills, it was done by basically digging into the hillside.

Besides mining for precious metals, lead and tin mines also existed.[544] Near Vipasca, in the municipality of Aljustrel in the Lower Alentejo and Castelo Velho de Safara (near Moura) much ore was mined by the Lusitanian, as well as the Romans.[545] These two mines demonstrate their importance in Lusitanian culture in tool and utensil making use in everyday living.[546] Compared to Vipasca one cannot think about mining in great scale, for in some areas small scales mining was conducted to satisfy the local needs of the population. It would not be until the Roman occupation that Lusitania became an important mining center, particularly for gold, copper, lead, tin and iron. During Rome's occupation of Lusitania, they greatly exploit Iberia's mineral wealth that they were obligated to pass laws regulating work and regarding ownership.[547]

From mining the economic activity of metal work appears, which there has been many archaeological discoveries throughout the hill-fort culture. Metal work with its local and regional production, were signs of a certain commercialization amongst the different areas. Though Lusitanian metal work has its own roots, it was born during the Bronze Age and was gradually influenced by Celts from Central European and Eastern Mediterranean societies.[548] With this knowledge, castro metallurgy refined the metals and cast them to make various tools and

---

543 Strabo, 3.2.8; Schulten, Adolf, Geografia y Etnografia antiguas de la Peninsula Ibérica, Vol. II, p. 245-46

544 Pliny, NH, 34.47, 48; Strabo, 3.3.10; Cardozo, Mario, A metalurgia na Proto-história da Peninsula Ibéria, Dédalo #2, São Paulo, 1965

545 Domergue, C., La mine antique d'Aljustrel (Portugal) et les tables de bronze de Vipasca, Paris 1983; Lazzarini, S. Lex metallis dicta: studi sulla seconda tavola di Vipasca, Rome 2001.

546 Monge Soares, Antonio M., Valerio, Pedro, Araujo, M.F., "Um novo vestígio da prática da metalurgia no Castelo Velho de Safara (Moura)", Arqueologia. volume 8.número 2.2005, p.215-224

547 Alarcão, J. de, Roman Portugal, Vol. I, Aris & Phillips Ltd., Warminster, UK, 1988, p.73-75

548 Octávio da Veiga Ferreira, op. cit., p. 19

jewelry. The result of this union produced for example jewelry like torques (rigid necklaces which are curved but not closed and of which there is a great variety of types), bracelets, rings, earrings, pendants and charms, spirals and rings and other objects.

Within each castro existed specialists in metal works, especially bronze, which mostly dealt with the manufacturing weapons and armor for warriors. But in time, as the Lusitanians became more technological evolved, this metal work industry of warlike character changed and increased with the manufacturing of agricultural instruments and craftworks destined for different uses for everyday life such as buckets, pitchers, mirrors, cups, axes, shovels, picks, sickles, fibulae, brooches, buckles, bronze jewelry, and so on. Besides metal work that dealt with luxury and religious items there seems to have been an increase in military productivity for a large amount of spear heads and swords have been found in much of the region south of the Douro River like in Alcàcer do Sal.[549]. Unfortunately, the archeological track north of the Douro is very scarce. Also, there is some evidence of early iron tools which were made near the end of the Bronze Age.[550]

Of all the industrial metal work activities that the Lusitani carried on, the business of jewelry stands out. Besides using bronze, the Lusitanian used all ores from tin to gold, along with precious stones. The Lusitanians did not constitute any expectation to the rules of how and what type of jewelry they created, representing a continuity in different styles of jewelry that still exists today. The creation of new designs and ways of making jewelry was endless. Jewelry was habitually attributed to the representatives of a high social class, but that was not the case with the Lusitanians for rich or for poor all wore some type of jewelry.

Because of the metal's ductility and beautiful color that gold and silver reflected, Lusitanian metallurgists came to know how to work these

---

549 Muñoz, Mauricio Pastor, op. cit., p. 41

550 Savory, H.N., Spain and Portugal: The Prehistory of the Iberian Peninsula, p. 238

metals well, for their work can be seen in the rich collection of jewelry at the National Museum of Archeology of Lisbon and other museums around Portugal. The Lusitanians used two processes when they created these works of art: cold hammering and lamination and fusion/rolled jewelry.[551] At that time of Lusitania's proto-historic era, goldsmiths had learned to weld the gold creating magnificent pieces of filigree (lacy decorative work).[552] By the beginning of the Iron Age, Lusitanian metallurgists had become masters specialized in the technique of working gold and silver.[553]

By the beginning of the Roman occupation of Lusitania, goldsmiths had learned how to purge impurities from gold and silver. Unfortunately, Lusitanian gold jewelry stopped existing after the Romans completely dominated the area, but they continued making silver jewelry. The reason for the lack of gold jewelry during this time period was simply because of the drainage of gold from the area.[554] From the artifacts and tools that have been excavated, it is safe to say that these ancient technicians were distinguished, with well-equipped workshops showing that there was a large valuable amount of peninsular jewelry within the Iberian and Roman culture.[555]

Before the metals were made into works of art, tools and weapons, they first had to be smelted down. It has been propounded by archaeologists and ethnologists that the Lusitanians used smelting techniques from the

---

551 **Cold hammering** is the process of hardening metal by hammering it when cold. **Lamination** is to beat or compress into a thin plate or sheet. **Rolled gold** is a very thin sheet of gold that is laminated to a lesser metal. The two layers of metal are heated under pressure to fuse them together. Octávio da Veiga Ferreira, op. cit., p. 207

552 Cardozo, Mario, Jóias áureas proto-históricas da Citânia de Briteiros – contribuição para a indústria de filigranas no Norte de Portugal, Petrus Nonius, Lisboa, 1938, vol. I, p. 254-260

553 Cardozo, Mario, Das origins e técnicas do trabalho do ouro e sua relação com a joalharia arcaica peninsular, Guimarães, 1957, p. 18

554 Ibid., p. 20

555 Cardozo, Mario, "*Joalharia Lusitana*", Conimbriga, Coimbra, Faculdade de Letras, Instituto de Arqueologia, vol. I, 1959, p.16

Hallstatt culture.[556] To extract the precious metal from its impurities smelting ovens were built. These furnaces were small isolated thick clay ovens made out of a mixture of clay, straw, flint wand and other materials fashioned into small ovens that were designed to use high temperatures to help the metals become ductile or malleable. These furnaces were first dug into a hillside or man-made dirt mounds so as to prevent heat loss, but with experimentation many of these ovens were later installed in the walls of what has been considered metal workshops (this has been identified at several excavation sites) and used three types of smelting furnaces for different ores.[557]

---

[556] Octávio da Veiga Ferreira, op. cit., p.207

[557] Ibid., p.207; The inner surface of the furnace was lined with a mixture of clay and charcoal dust (lute), which consolidated heat and protected the smelting process from being disrupted by a cave or collapse of the oven due to cracking of the inner wall as the temperature increased. Some ovens were divided into two chambers by clay grills, the lower one has been assumed that it was use to stoke the fire with bellows, while the upper level used for the ore's smelting process. Above the oven was a chimney with a small outlet, to allow some heat to escape and circulate the heated air to feed the fire. As for the smelting process, the same technique that was used for smelting copper and tin was also utilized on iron. Compared to today's smelting process the end result was that these metals did not come out in liquid form but as a pasty lump called 'bloom' which was then worked on. Strabo, 3.2.8 Srabo mentions the uses of charcoal in smelting gold; Ramos, Pablo Gómez, Obtención de metales en la Prehistoria de la Península Ibérica BAR internacional Series, n. 753, Archaeopress, Oxford 1999; Salvador Rovira and Paul Ambert, Pottery vessels for smelting copper minerals in the Iberian Peninsula and the Southern France Departamento de Historia de la Ciencia. Instituto de Historia, Trabajos de Prehistoria, 59 (1), 2002, pp. 89-105; The first type of furnace was a clay-lined hearth, made out of clay, straw, crushed flint grit, and sheep dung, with an air intake provided by homemade leather bellow and pipes, called tuyeres. The second unit was similar, only it was not lined with clay, but it was dug into the side of a nearby hill or they made their own dirt mounds. The third furnace was the crudest of all. Smelters simply put a rough clay dish at the bottom of a small narrow hole in the ground with a tuyere inserted into one side. As with the other furnaces, air intake was controlled by a homemade bellows, which this time was stuck into a tuyere. The smelting of copper and tin was done by preheating the furnace with burnable materials to dry it out and warm it, which then the ore was added onto the top of the burning material. The ore was then covered up with a pile of fresh fuel. The speed of combustion and the sealing of

Pottery

Pottery is the most abundant archaeological element amongst Lusitanian artifacts found on hilltop-fort sites. Ceramic production played a large role in Lusitanian culture, for pottery was used in domestic chores and ritual ceremonies. Iberian ceramics have been found in great numbers among the castro of Portugal and northwestern Spain, showing that ceramic pottery was cheap to produce. Unfortunately, there is scarce documentation about the production of ceramics. But the discovery of artifacts such as at Cárcoda Castro near São Pedro do Sul, Portugal clearly demonstrates how ceramic pottery was manufactured by hand. This hand technique dominated Lusitanian culture until the arrival of the potter's wheel in the 1st century BCE.[558] Though the latter system became more generalized it never completely substituted the former. As for firing 'Iberian wares' it seems that they may have used three types of rudimentary kilns.[559]

---

furnace gases were expedited by the addition of a pile of unburnt charcoal or a piece of cut turf known as "black hat"

[558] The artifact was used in the Near East 4,000 years BC. It must have been brought to the Iberian Peninsula by the Phoenicians and Greeks, but it was the Romans who spread its use to the north and east of the region. Other scholars believe that through their contact with the Tartessians or the Iberians, the Celts that were migrating west took with them the technology of the potter's wheel. Alberto J. Lorrio and Gonzalo Ruiz Zapatero, "The Celts in Iberia: An Overview", pp. 167-255; Harrison, R.J., *Spain at the dawn of history. Iberians, Phoenicians and Greeks.* London, Thames & Hudson, 1988; Quesada, Fernando, From Quality to Quantity: Wealth, Status and Prestige in the Iberian Iron Age, (Ph.D. thesis) Universidad Autónoma de Madrid, n.d., chapter 1; González Wagner, C., "Tartessos en la historiografía: una revisión crítica". *La colonización fenicia en el sur de la Península Ibérica. 100 años de investigación,* Almería, Instituto de Estudios Almerienses 1992, pp. 81-115.

[559] The first was of oval or circular shaped chimney oven in which the pottery was placed on top of the material that was being used as the kiln's fuel source. The second type was square with a grating, supported by a central pillar, separating the baking chamber from the fire below. These two types of kiln are found in the larger castros for in the smaller ones the kiln was constructed by digging a small simple earthen trench in which the trench was filled with the pots and fuel. For fuel, the kilns used burnable materials such as wood shavings, pieces of wood, leaves, metal oxides, salts, sawdust and dried manure. In the trench type kiln the

Lusitanians ceramics have been divided into two categories: ceramics for domestic use and funerary use.[560] The ceramics that were used in daily life constituted small canisters, containers, bowls, basins, vessel and drums (smooth and floridly ornated), while large vessels known as *dolia* were used as reservoirs for oils, wine, honey, water, beer, etc. For funerary rituals, clay urns were made to place to deceased's ashes.

Compared to Iberian ceramics, Lusitanian ceramics were not as sophisticated in their designs and decorative themes. The ornamentation of these small vessels were incise with a matrix of concentric circles, triangles, squares, rosettes, representations of SSSs or having a stylized base that was web-footed. The wings or handles were in the style of gemma, bud, burgeon, sprout; knob, button, stud or nipple shape.

Among the multitude of ceramic objects that have been excavated, they consist of the smooth type ceramics which is typical of the Iron Age. Though not very decorative they were well made. They were made by using the smoothing and flattening technique and the pottery designs were predominantly globe-like and spherical with decorative themes that were fairly uniform. Lusitanian pottery is generally smooth, though there are some examples of coiled rope form. The bottom usually remained unfinished, though there are some exceptions of finished bases with decorative works. Another common characteristic is that the designs often include one or more wings or handles. If there were any decorations, it was usually on the edges, necks and rounded parts of the vessels, with geometric and schematic patterns. The designs that were commonly used were parallel, vertical and horizontal lines, stripes, triangles, stars, zig-zag, concentric semicircles, S-shaped patterns and curves, and fish-spine designs. All these designs were painted in red, black or purplish-blue tones by using iron oxides or manganese on a background of white

---

unfired pots were nestled together in the pit and then they were covered with the burnable materials that were just mentioned. The top of the pit may have been protected with moist clay, shards, and large pieces of wood or metal baffles. The filled pit was then set on fire and carefully tended until most of the inner fuel had been consumed.

[560] Octávio da Veiga Ferreira, op. cit., p. 228

paint. It is also common to see interlacing designs, impressions using ropes or "mamelóns", as well as other varied ornamental designs. But a major part of the Lusitanian ceramics was plain and undersigned. The undersigned pot shaped ceramics were used for cooking and while the smaller designed ones were used for food and drink and the larger bowls were mainly used to store food (such as grains) or liquids. However, the amphorae and the use of the glass only started to be common with the Romanization of Lusitania. These amphorae served essentially for the transport and storage of cereals, wine and olive oil.

Glass

The Lusitanians did not have a glass industry. The glass which has appeared during the excavation of Lusitanian homes were not works of the Lusitanian castro industry but of Punic or Egyptian pieces and possibly products from Betica.[561] It was not until the Romans that Portugal had a small glass industry. The glass found in Portugal was discovered in Braga and Conimbriga suggesting that there were glass workshops for making green glass for bottles, ointment jars and several other products.[562]

Textile

Textile work is also archaeologically documented. It is believed that the Minoans, who had commercial dealing with the Turdetanians since 18th century BCE, introduced the technique of dying fabric to the Iberian people around 1600 BCE.[563] In exchange for this knowledge, the Minoan merchants demanded from the Iberians gold, copper and silver. By 2500-2200 BCE, the Lusitanians dressed in dyed linen cloths signifying that they too had been introduced to the dying technique.[564] This goes

---

561 Ibid., p. 227-228

562 Alarcão, J. de, Roman Portugal, Vol. II, p. 87; J.J. Rigaud de Sousa and Eduardo A. Pires dee Oliveira, "Subsidios para o estudo das olarias de Bracara Augusta", Trabalhos de Antropologia e Etnologia 24 1982, pp. 360-370.

563 Octávio da Veiga Ferreira, op. cit., p. 201.

564 Ibid.

to show that dying cloth had become an established technique that had gained a footing on the Iberian Peninsula.

In most of the hilltop-forts there have been discoveries of *fusayolas* (loom) with its spindle, spinning wheel weights that were made out of polished granite, calcedonia and other rocks and bronze needles. These looms seem to have belonged to either a family or used in textile production for exportation. The loom that was used at that time was the warped vertical loom.[565] In time, weaving became so widespread that Strabo praises the Iberians in their specialized knowledge of weaving linen.[566]

The end result of the Lusitanian textile industry was a comfortable fabric. According to some classical texts, linen was abundant in Iberia, followed by wool.[567] Strabo speaks about the abundance of the material used in the fabrication of clothes throughout Iberia.[568] To the Romans, Iberian linen was popular amongst men and women, especially for the men for when women wore this garments of linen cloth it was so sheer that they were reproached for wearing "woven wind."[569]

In the area of the Beiras in western Portugal, linen is still made and treated as in the old days, constituting a successful local industry of a home-made character. The making of linen was a long process. When linen sheets are completed by the flax being woven together on a loom,

---

565 It was made from large wooden poles tied together in a rectangular shape. The poles would then be mounted on a wall or dug into the ground to make a freestanding loom. Threads were tied to the top pole and at the bottom of the frame the threads were tied together in groups and secured to free hanging clay or stone weights. The weaver would then place the weft threads through the hanging thread by hand while standing in front of the loom.

566 Strabo, 3.4.9

567 Mela De situ orbis, 2.4, Pliny, NH, 8.191 and 19.10; Strabo 3.2.6; Silva, Armando Coelho da, A Idade do Ferro em Portugal, in *Nova História de Portugal*, 1990, vol.I, p.310; Alarcão, Jorge, O Domínio Romano em Portugal, Publicações Europa-América, LDA, Sintra, 1988, 147; Cuevillas, Florentino L., "Estudios sobre a Edad do Ferro no Noroeste peninsular", Fontes Historicas, Seminar de Estudos Galegos VI, 1934, p.30

568 Strabo, 3.4.16

569 Gaius Petronius Arbiter, The Satyricon of Petronius Arbiter, Chapter 55

it is then beaten, soaked in water and beating again, until only the fibers remain. It takes about a week of constant treatment until the linen is white and ready for drying. It is then kneaded so as to soften the material. Then washed and dried to make it ready for the dying process.

Once dried, the fabric would be dyed. Strabo writes about the abundance of plants used in this industry, unfortunately he does not refer them by name.[570] Besides using plants, the Lusitanians also used other natural products for making colors, such as oxides and hematites, but the most popular was royal purple that comes from the mollusk Purpura haemastoma. The linen that was dyed in this color was the most expensive in all of classical and oriental antiquity. The Purpura haemastoma is found along the Portuguese coast from Minho to Algarve. Another popular color used by the Lusitanians was red which was obtained the Kermes insect *Kermes ilicis* that lived off by eating the leaves of the Quercus coccifera L. (Kermes oak) shrub.[571]

Besides growing flax to make linen, some Lusitanians became wealthy from herding sheep which was cheaper than cattle, but they made their money by selling the animal's wool.[572] This comes with the discovery of sheep shears at Cividade de Terroso located near Póvoa de Varzim, Portugal. The discovery of these shears strengthens the idea of systematic breeding of sheep for its wool.[573] Being that Lusitania's weather was usually warm throughout the year; wool was used to making warm clothing and capes for the chilly Iberian winters.

Leather

Though the Lusitanians worn linen and wool, they also wore leather from several well-preserved leather objects that have been found.[574]

---

[570] Strabo 3.4.16

[571] Octávio da Veiga Ferreira, op. cit., p. 202

[572] Cardozo, Mario, "A fiação e tecelagem na antiguidade peninsular" Congresso Internacional de Etnografia, Vol. II, Lisboa, 1963, p.29

[573] Flores Gomes, José Manuel & Carneiro, Deolinda: *Subtus Montis Terroso.* CMPV (2005), "Economia e ergologia", pp.133-187

[574] Octávio da Veiga Ferreira, op. cit., pp. 217-218

Despite the fact that they wore leather there is no archeological proof of the existence of a major industry of tanning leather within the castro culture because no large tanks used in the tanning process have been discovered. Compare to the tanning industry among other ancient civilizations, the Lusitanian business of making leather goods was minute. The business of leather making was either done at a family level as in making leather apparel for individual family members or done by a local tanner who sold his leather goods to the surrounding castros.

The treatment of such material was extensive that there are four techniques historian believe that were used to cured leather. These ancient techniques of tanning[575] was, and still is, considered a noxious or

---

[575] This first technique comes from the idea of how Paleolithic man tanned leather. Skins during that time period rapidly putrefied and became useless, so a method of preservation was needed. The earliest method known was to stretch the hides and skins on the ground to dry, rubbing them with fats and animal brains while they dried. This had a limited preserving and softening action. This is represented as the first rudimentary tanning process and is also documented in Homer's Illiad and Odyssey and various Roman and Assyrian writings. The second is that smoke from wood fires could preserve hides and skins which was discovered by primitive man accidently or out of curiosity. The third technique is most likely that early man had discovered how to make leather when he found that animal skins left lying on a wet forest floor became tanned naturally. This is done by chemicals being released naturally by decaying leaves and vegetation. With this knowledge he may have begun treating skins by an infusion of tannin-containing barks, leaves, twigs and fruits of certain trees and plants. Later on salt was used in the drying of skins. The fourth technique was a bit more odiferous, gory and unhygienic. It is believed that the Lusitanians may have learned tanning from either the Iberians who were taught by either the Phoenicians or Greek or directly from the Greek or Phoenicians, no one knows exactly who taught them or how. But as for the technique, which is still used today in Morocco, skins typically arrived at the tannery dried stiff and dirty with soil and gore. The ancient tanners would first soak the skins in water to clean and soften them. Then they would pound and scour the skin to remove any remaining flesh, fat, dried blood and dirt. Next, the tanner needed to remove the hair fibers from the skin. This was done by either soaking the skin in urine or simply letting the skin putrefy for several weeks in a salt solution. After the hair fibers were loosened, the tanners scraped them off. Once the hair was removed, the tanners would bate the material by pounding dung into the skin or soaking the skin in a solution of animal brains. Among the kinds

"odiferous trade" that was/is relegated to the outskirts of town. Tanning by ancient methods was so foul smelling that some tanneries are still isolated from those towns that still use these ancient methods.

Trade and Commerce

The Atlantic coast of Lusitania since the beginning of the Bronze Age has had active commercial relations and interests with many other Mediterranean civilizations. The discoveries of amphorae and Greek coins along coastal excavation sites prove that the Lusitanians had conducted trade since the 4th century BCE.[576]

Lusitania's coastal shores possessed excellent developmental conditions, which made it possible for the Lusitanians to reach a higher standard of living than that of those in the interior. But to arrive at that point,

---

of dung commonly used were those of dogs or pigeons. Sometimes the dung was mixed with water in a vat, and the prepared skins were kneaded in the dung water until they became supple, but not too soft. The ancient tanner might have use his bare feet to knead the skins in the dung water, and the kneading could last two or three hours. The dung was washed from the hide after bating and placed in a clay-lined pit or vat with a log or pole laying across it. The hide was then hung over the pole and soaked in a mixture of water and crushed oak bark (this is what produces the tannin). The hide would soak for a couple of days, then removed and spread out to dry. Two of the best places to see this ancient technique would be in Fez and Marrakech, Morocco. Faber, G.A., Dyeing and Tanning in Classical Antiquity, New York / Basle, Switzerland, The Society of Chemical Industry Represented By Ciba Company Inc., Ciba Review #9, May 1938; In Homer's day tanning was partly a domestic occupation carried on by the peasantry, and partly a craft, which was, however, not yet independent, but practiced by the leatherworking trades. The first Greek leather-worker of whom we have evidence was one Tychios of Boeotia, a native of Hyle, described by Homer as the maker of the famous shield of Ajax, and by Pliny as the inventor of tanning. Polybos, who supplied balls of red leather to the Phaeacians, is mentioned in the Odyssey, and Homer is familiar with many kinds of leather goods; only the beggar is content to have an untanned hide for a couch. Homer's heroes have beds made of the skins of sheep, oxen, or bisons, Aeneas slept on a bear-skin. Sheep-skins served as blankets, and Pliny mentions a rug made of moleskins, which he saw on a journey to Greece.

[576] Ibid., p. 114; Cartailhac, Emile, Les âge pré-historiques de L'Espagne et du Portugal, Paris, 1886, p.21

they had to externalize trading. With the arrival of the Phoenicians, Carthaginians, Greeks and later the Romans on their shores, the Lusitanian that inhabited the coast began to change from an internal to an external market. Internal trading was the main stream within the Iberian Peninsula in which different tribal markets exchanged goods such as textiles, metals (gold, silver, copper, tin and lead), animal skins, salt, ceramics and other objects among the different cities and villages of the castro culture. With the arrival of the Phoenicians and Greeks, the Lusitani traded precious metals for glass, exotic ceramic, wine, and oil, as well as coming into contact with different people from the Mediterranean or from other areas of the Peninsula which also played a part in technological, cultural and agricultural advances.[577] Compared to the Phoenician, the Greeks seem to have been more influential, for they had either set up or taken over trading posts belong to the Phoenician. According to Florentino Cuevillas, this competition/takeover of commercial market was in retaliation to the North Atlantic Sea routes and the geographical knowledge about Cassiterides or Land of Tin that the Phoenician kept secret from their competitors: the Greeks.[578] Finally there is a belief among some Portuguese historian that the inhabitants of the British Isles also negotiated trade amongst the Lusitani.[579]

In the interior and mountains of central Lusitania information is lacking. We can only theorize that these towns allowed themselves to establish relations or influences between the castro world of the Hispanic northwest and the Lusitanians of coastal Portugal. Unfortunately, we are not able to determine what type of relations they had with each

---

[577] Cuevillas, Florentino L., "Estudios sobre a Edad do Ferro no Noroeste peninsular", Fontes Historicas, Seminar de Estudos Galegos VI, 1934, p.15; Octávio da Veiga Ferreira, op. cit., pp. 209; One such example is the vineyards and olive groves of Tagus. According to legend, it was the Greeks that brought the grapevine and the olive tree to Lusitania and placed them in Lisbon and the surrounding area.

[578] Herodotus, *Histories* 3.115;Diodorus Siculus, *Historical Library* V. 21, 22, 38; Strabo, *Geography* 2.5.15, 3.2.9, 3.5.11; Pliny the Elder, *Natural History,* iv.119, vii.197, xxxiv.156-158; Cuevillas, Florentino L., "Estudios sobre a Edad do Ferro no Noroeste peninsular", p.7

[579] Octávio da Veiga Ferreira, op. cit., pp. 211

other; also there is a lack of ancient data about continental as well as Mediterranean contacts with the Iberians.

In spite of the shortage of terrestrial roads, there existed an extensive mercantile trade along the Atlantic coastline and fluvial roads. The reason for this type of transportation was because it was safe from bandits and many of Lusitania's major towns were strategically located close to the sea and rivers. It would not be until the Roman occupation that stone roads became a way of travel. The reason that many Portuguese historians believe that river travel was the most common way of importing/exporting goods is because until the mid-20th century this type of commercial transportation was still common. But today, instead of dealing with commercial transports, the rivers of Portugal see many river boat tours or local fisherman. During the Roman occupation the regions of the Algarve and Baixo Alentejo played a part in the Mediterranean trade routes that were used by the Greeks and Phoenicians.

As for terrestrial roads, the first roads were built in the south of the Iberian Peninsula by the Phoenicians, which are used today as Portugal and Spain main coast highways.[580] The Romans would continue where the Phoenicians and Greeks left off and build long stretches of highway throughout the peninsula by building stone paved road on top of pre-existing trails, thus improving the Iberian trade routes.[581] A route, which is said to have been built during the Tartessian culture, is the Via de Prata (in Latin: Via di Argentum, Road of Silver). Though its historical origin is uncertain, it is believed, based on diverse archaeological findings, that the route was used for commercial purposes involving tin, gold and silver. Originally, tin was present in many of the places that this road ran through. Therefore, it would be more appropriate to call it Via de Estanho (in Latin: Via di Plumbum, Road of Tin). The location of this old commercial road crossed the western part of the Peninsula where the modern - day border of Spain and Portugal resides. Though we know

---

580 Octávio da Veiga Ferreira, op. cit., pp. 188-189

581 Martins, Sarmento, "Acerca das escavações de Sabroso, Dispersos, Coimbra, 1933, p. 22-35; Octávio da Veiga Ferreira, op. cit., p. 189

of this commercial highway, there is no information on how frequent it was use by the Phoenicians, Carthaginians, Greeks and later Romans. The only sources we have comes from the Romans in which according to the Itinerary of Antonino, it describes the course of the road from its start point in the north at Santiago de Compostela crossing through several towns, like Norba Caesarina (Cáceres); Salmantica (Salamanca), Brigaecium (Benavente), August Emerita (Mérida, capital of Lusitânia), August Asturica (Astorga, capital of the conventus Asturum) ending at Hispalis (Seville).[582] With the annexation of the area into the Roman Empire, trade passing via this highway becomes one of the main means of regional economic development for Lusitania. By the 1st century AD roads facilitated a larger relationship among the Iberian provinces and Rome.

Religion

From the time man set foot on the Peninsula to the arrival of the Phoenicians, Greeks and Celts, to the time this region was incorporated into the Roman Empire, Iberian religions underwent various transformations.[583] But instead of writing about the entire Peninsula which is a work in itself, I will only touch upon Lusitania.

Portugal has some of the oldest megaliths in Europe, in which some of them are quite remarkable. Along with these megaliths, there is much evidence of various Pagan cults and places of worship. As such,

---

[582] Associación de los Amigos del Camino de Santiago Vía de la Plata de Sevilla, Vía de la Plata. Guía del Camino Mozárabe de Santiago, Ed. Diputación de Sevilla, 2001; La Ruta de la Plata a pie y en bicicleta, Ed. El País-Aguilar (insuficiente, sólo describe el Camino entre Mérida y Astorga) 2000; La Ruta de la Plata por Extremadura, Ed. Junta de Extremadura, 2001; ***El Camino Mozárabe,*** Ed. Ayuntamiento de Orense, 1999; de Castro, Alfonso Ramos, Caminos Jacobeos de Zamora: Pueblos y Valores, 2000; Camino Portugués de la Vía de la Plata, Ed. A.D.A.T. Proyecto de Cooperación Transfronterizo, 2002. Currently, the road is a part of Spanish highway N-630 and Spanish highway A-66/AP-66.

[583] Rodrigues, Dulce, Les Religions de la Lusitanie, *Archéologia* #408, Feb. 2004, p.10; Blazquez, J.M., Historia de las religions de la España Antigua, Madrid, 1994, "Aportaciones al estodio de la religions primitvos de España", *AEspA* #30, 1957, p. 15-85, and "El legado fenicio en la formacion de la religion Ibera", Roma #35, March 1994, p. 107-117

Lusitania has had deep religious roots since man has walked the earth. As for the people of the Iberian Peninsula, as like other primitive people, they followed a primitive naturistic and animistic belief system. Though there is no written record and very little archaeological data of these pre-existing Iberian religious beliefs or practices; we can assume that it was perhaps a very elementary belief system. However, as rudimentary as it was, archeologists have recognized that they also worshipped the dead, employed spells, used amulets, and worshipped the stars, sun and moon.

The main facet of Lusitanian religion was naturistic and animistic that was based on natural phenomena. These unexplainable natural occurrences were deified by the Lusitanians. To them these occurrences did not have any explanation, so to make sense of what they saw, they deified these occurrences with human-like characteristics. Deification of the land, sun, moon, water, plants, animals, rivers, forests, and hills had special influences on the Lusitanians. The deification of nature played an important part in Luistanian religious life that in time these beliefs formed into an organized religion.

Lusitanian religion though barbaric and primitive, incorporated into their beliefs Turdetian influences, whose religion was inspired by the Greeks and Phoenicians and naturistic and animistic beliefs.[584] This new Lusitanian belief system was based only based on Turdetian religion, but added in their superstition, polytheists, magic, omens, dreams and prophecy. By the time of the Roman occupation, Roman cults and religious beliefs continued to enlarge the Luistanian pantheon.

With the deification of nature, Lusitanian religion became an objective way to harmonize peace and tranquility between humanity and the forces of the nature. Within these cults, as well as in all religions,

---

[584] Tartessian culture had its core in lower Andalusia and seems to have developed from the cultural contact between the indigenous late Bronze Age population and Semitic colonizers who arrived from the eastern Mediterranean. Arribas, Antonio, op. cit., p. 131-132; Vasconcelos, J.L de, Religiões da Lusitânia, vol. 1, p. 62

ceremonies and sacrifices were created with the intention of praising, appeasing and capturing the thanks or goodwill of the gods.

These religious ceremonies according to archaeological artifacts and historical data followed the character of each tribe or social grouping, for example; warrior tribes would sacrifice with more frenzy to the gods of war, while people dedicated to agriculture, or fishing would make libations or sacrifices to the gods of harvest and of the oceans and rivers. While some divinities 'demanded' blood from either human or animal; others 'wanted' hydromel, wine, flour, fruits, milk, or whatever else that the earth granted to these people.

Along with their belief system and ceremonies, they employed the use of talismans and amulets. These religious items came from nature or where manufactured out of teeth, bones, shells, colorful and precious rocks, animal feet and other objects.[585]

One aspect that we do not know is if the Lusitanians practiced astronomy or not, but it is possible that they had a pure primitive intuition to the changing of the seasons and the movements of the stars, sun and moon, comets, eclipses, lightning, shooting stars, etc.[586] These men who worshipped the sun and the moon believed that the destiny of human beings was related with the properties of the heavenly bodies. Given the tentative study of heavenly bodies, they had some knowledge on forecasting the weather and the changing of seasons and if they did practice astronomy, it is possible they practiced astrology to predict their future. The Lusitanians were quite culturally late to have had conceive astrology for it is believed that if they had gain this knowledge from abroad or from their advanced neighbors, the Turdetians.[587] It is also

---

[585] Carlos Consiglieri and Marilia Abel, Os Lusitanos no contexto peninsular, Lisboa, Editorial Caminho, 1989, p. 68-69; Vasconcelos, J.L de, *Religiões da Lusitânia*, vol. I, Chapter 2(b), p136-166

[586] Vasconcelos, J.L de, *Religiões da Lusitânia*, vol. I, p. 103-104; Inês Vaz, João Luis, Lusitanos no Tempo de Viriato, Esquilo Ida., Lisboa, 2009, p. 67

[587] Octávio da Veiga Ferreira, op. cit., p. 115-117

suggested that they also believed in omens, which the gods showed the Lusitanians signs from flights and songs of the birds to comets.

The Lusitanians worshipped a pantheon of gods in a very chaotic polytheistic way. From rudimentary sculptures, epigraphs and inscriptions, nearly 200 gods have been recognized but we do not know if they are all different or if they correspond with the same deity due to geographical area or tribe in which they used a different name.[588] So it is possible that instead of 200 gods, there might be less than what has been believed. Though the Lusitanians had many gods, I am not going to write about all of them because that would be a work in itself, becoming a book on Luistanian religion instead. The one thing I will do is touch upon is the grouping of gods to give you, the reader, an idea of what kind of gods the Luistanians had.

The Lusitanian pantheon can be divided into two groups; gods of nature and animals. The Lusitanians were animists to the extent that they believed that all aspects of the natural world contained spirits, divine entities with which humans could establish a rapport with the gods. Though they believed in divine entities, it has been projected that the peoples of Hispania did not seem to have worshipped natural powers directly; as a matter of fact, the invisible divinities manifested themselves through visible signs like trees, springs, mountains or specific animals. The numinous presence of deities undoubtedly formed the background to everyday life. Both archaeology and the literary records indicate that ritual practice in Lusitanian society lacked a clear distinction between the sacred and profane in which rituals, offerings, and correct behavior maintained a balance between gods and man that harnessed supernatural forces for the benefit of the group. The pagan Lusitanians perceived the presence of the supernatural as an integral part of their world. The sky, the sun, the moon, a mountain, a river, a spring, a marsh, a tree and so on had their own individual divine spirits, life-forces and personalities. Sanctuaries were sacred spaces separated from the ordinary world, often in natural locations such as springs,

---

[588] Vasconcelos, J.L de, Religiões da Lusitânia, vol. 1, Albertos, Maria L., Organizaciones Suprafamiliares en la Hispania Antigua, Valladolid, 1975.

sacred groves or lakes. Many topographical features were deified as gods: many divine names refer to specific locations or geographical features, a clear indication of how closely Lusitanian/Iberian societies identified themselves with the place.

The second group dealt with zoolatry (animal worship). The character and vitality of certain animal species seems to have been considered numinous. Certain spirits were associated with animals such as, Iccona, the equine goddess.[589] Though animals were perceived as similar to humans there were still very different from humans.[590] The reason behind this association was because certain creatures were observed to have particular human physical and mental qualities and characteristics, and distinctive patterns of behavior. An animal like a stag or horse could be admired for its beauty, speed or virility. Dogs were seen to be keen-scented, good at hunting, guarding and healing themselves. Snakes were seen to be destructive, fertile and having a curious habit of regenerating themselves by sloughing their skin. Birds were keen-sighted, and by flight, able to leave behind the confines of the earth. Thus, admiration and acknowledgment for a beast's essential nature easily led to the reverence of those qualities and abilities, which humans did not possess at all or possessed only partially.

In ancient Indo-European mythologies and polytheistic religions, various gods, goddesses or demi-gods appear as a triad, either as three separate beings who always appear as a group (the Greek Moirae, Charites, Erinnyes and the Norse Norns) or as a single deity who is commonly depicted in three aspects (Greek Hecate and the cult image of Latin Diana Nemorensis, of whom Hecate is one part). Of all the gods and demi-gods that the Lusitanian worshiped there were three

---

[589] Maggi, D. 1983. «Sui teonimi *Trebopala* e *Iccona* nell'iscrizione lusitana del Cabeço das Frá
guas», in: E. Campanile (ed.), *Problemi di lingua e di cultura nel campo indoeuropeo.* Pisa, 1983, pp. 58-59; Witczak, Krzysztof T., On the Indo-European Origin of Two Lusitanian Theonyms (*LAEBO & REVE*), Lódz, EMERITA (*EM*) LXVII 1, 1999, p. 66

[590] Green, Miranda, *Animals in Celtic life and myth*, London, Routledge, 1992, p. 196

main characters in their massive pantheon. As with all religions there also existed a sort of a trinity concept within the Lusitanian religion. According to Professor Inês Vaz, he believes that this trinity functioned to assure the tribes sovereignty, strength, and fecundity as well as a type of hierarchy of the divinities.[591]

This loose Lusitanian Trinity that supposedly existed consisted of ***Endovelicus, Ataegina,*** and ***Runesocesius***. Endovelicus, is undoubtedly the best known of the Lusitanian gods that was worshipped in pre-Roman and Roman Lusitania.[592] He was a divinity of earth and creation, vegetation and animals, god of heaven and hell and of medicine.[593] After the Roman invasion, his cult spread across the Iberian Peninsula and beyond to the rest of the Roman Empire in which his cult existed until the 5th century AD.[594] The next god in the Lusitanian trinity was **Ataegina**. She was the goddess of rebirth (spring), fertility, agrarian, nature, and healing.[595] She also had a dark side for she represented the moon, the underworld and death. Being that she was the goddess of life it is only logical that she be the goddess of death.[596] By the Roman era,

---

591 Inês Vaz, João Luis, Lusitanos no Tempo de Viriato, Esquilo Ida., Lisboa, 2009, p. 69

592 Bouché-Leclerq,A, Histoire de la divination dans L'antiquité, vol 3, 4 vols., Paris, 1879-1882, p. 275; Lambrino, Scarlat, "Le Dieu Lusitanien Endovellius", Bulletin de l'etudes portuguaise, Combria, 1952, vol 15, #58, pp. 93-147.

593 Vasconcelos, J.L de, *Religiões da Lusitânia*, vol. II, 1905, Imprensa Nacional---Casa da Moeda, Lisboa., 1897-1905, pp. 124-125, 127-128; 245; Amilcar Guerra, Thomas Schattner, Carlos Fabião and Rui Almeida, Novas investigações no santuário de Endovélico (S.Miguel da Mota, Alandroal): a campanha de 2002 Revista Portuguesa de Arqueologia, volume 6, no.2, 2003, p.415-479; Octávio da Veiga Ferreira, op. cit., p. 124

594 Vasconcelos, J.L de, *Religiões da Lusitânia*, vol. II, 1897-1905, pp. 122-124, 145-146

595 Vasconcelos, J.L de, *Religiões da Lusitânia*, vol. II, p.163

596 Espírito Santo suggests that Ataegina is a composite deity arising from other foreign religious syncretic tendencies. For more details on Ataegina's religious syncretism see Espírito Santo, Moisés. *Origens Orientais da Religião Popular Portuguesa*. Lisbon: Assírio & Alvim, 1988; Melero, Raquel López Melero, "Nueva evidencia sobre el culto de Ategina: el epígrafe de bienvenida", Primeras

the goddess was renamed by the Luso-Romans as Proserpina.[597] The third was Runesocesius, the god of war.[598] There are few references of this Lusitanian divinity from classical authors, but there are several Latin inscriptions on Luso-Roman altars. Much is not known of this god expect that Portuguese historians like Leite Vasconcelos go on the say that it was a "mysterious god armed with a javelin", and that he is attributed to Celtic origins.[599]

Many other indigenous divinities existed whose names are documented on Luso-Roman epigraphs. These gods dealt with medicine, home, cosmic, aquatic, naturalistic and telluric characteristics. These epigraphs mostly found around the Douro and Tagus areas, conserved testimonies of indigenous gods whose epithet invokes an organized gentilicia. To the local populace, these gods were highly regarded as protectors of a sacred places, towns or villages. On the other hand, during the pre-Roman era, there were many ethnic divinities of unknown names that later became associated with Roman demi-gods in which these would at times accompany the Lusitanian gods. Though it seems that the Iberian Peninsula suffered from a fragmented and disorganized pre-Roman pantheon due to the abundance of gods, we can now discard that notion, for in actuality the number of deities was much smaller than recently thought. The reason being that there seem to have been many gods was because of the various tribes from different regions gave different names to the same god for either they used a different dialect, or they view these gods with different characteristics than what another tribes might have viewed the god.

It is in the Lusitanian-Galician regions that the largest number of indigenous deities in the whole of the Iberian Peninsula is found, due

---

Jornadas sobre manifestaciones religiosas de la Lusitania / coord. por César Chaparro Gómez, 1986, pp. 93-122

597 Vasconcelos, J.L de, *Religiões da Lusitânia*, vol. II, 1905, Imprensa Nacional---Casa da Moeda, Lisboa, 1897-1905, pp. 159, 163-165

598 Blázquez Martínez, José M., Las religiones indígenas del área noroeste de la Península Ibérica en relación con Roma, *Imagen y mito,* Madrid 1977, pp. 369-384 and in his book *Legio VII Gemina*, León 1970, pp. 63-77

599 Vasconcelos, J.L de, *Religiões da Lusitânia*, vol. II, p. 303-303

to the considerable amount of epigraphic material found in this area. Therefore, due to the large amount of information I will just touch upon a few important gods and goddesses with the Lusitanian pantheon.

The first group of Lusitanian gods is made up of deities who have a wide geographical distribution. Though the Lusitanian trinity was widespread throughout the region, these three gods were not the only ones that were popular. According to research of inscriptions found in Portugal and northwestern Spain, 80% of the inscriptions mention *Bandua*, *Arentius*, *Quangeius*, *Reue*, *Crouga*, *Salamati*, *Lugus*, *Aernus*, *Cariociecus* and *Cohue* and some female deities such as *Nabia*, *Trebaruna*, *Munidis*, *Arentia*, *Erbina*, *Toga*, *Laneana*, *Ataecina* and *Lacipaea*.[600] The widespread worship of these very ancient Celtic gods must have been worshipped in many different places before the Roman occupation. Indo-European in origin, these gods were introduced onto the Iberian Peninsula by immigrants who had settled in the western part of the Peninsula sometime before the 6th century BCE.

The Lusitanians for the most part, having been a tribe of warriors, prayed and made human sacrifices not only to Runesocesius, but also to the following regional god of war: **Cariociecus**. We know of the name of Cariociecus, for he was a regional divinity of Galicia and Lusitania. Cariociecus had the meaning of Corpus, because this was the god to whom warriors would pray to for personal glory and courage before the battle.[601] Before setting out on a raid or battle they would pray, sacrifice, dance and chant to the war god for success.[602] With the Roman occupation of Lusitania, this god became to be associated with Mars and after some time, Cariociecus became known as Mars-Cariociecus as most gods of war did when they became Romanized.

---

600 Olivares Pedreño, Juan Carlos., *Los Dioses de la Hispania Céltica.* Madrid: Real Academia de la Historia, Universidad de Alicante, 2002, p. 27-66

601 Menéndez Pidal R, "Mars Cariociecus y la etimología de Quiroga", Toponimia prerrománica hispana, Madrid, Gredos, 1952, p. 263-6

602 Strabo, 3.3.6, 7; Silio Italico, Punica, 3.345-349, Vasconcelos, J.L de, *Religiões da Lusitânia*, vol. II, p. 306-307

Though the gods of war were held in high respect and honor due to the Lusitanian's nature for war, they also held nature gods in high regards. Throughout the entire region, Celtic magic was rooted strongly in the four natural elements: earth, air, fire and water. But of all the elements, water was held in high esteem. Being that there was a good number of gods associated to these four elements, the most popular of these gods within the Lusitanian pantheon were the water gods. Of all the water gods, **Bormanicus,** god of thermal waters[603] and **Tongoenabiagus**[604] were very popular.

The gods that I have mentioned have all been male gods, except Ataegina. But besides Ataegina, the Lusitanian pantheon did not only worship this female god, but other regional feminine divinities; *Trebaruna, Nabia and Reva.* The importance of goddesses within the Lusitanian religion was that they on only signified female fertility, but also for crops and domesticated and wild animals which were all paramount to the tribe's survival. In addition, the female life-giving principle was considered divine and of a great mystery. Sacrifices to these regional female goddesses were usually conducted during the celestial equinox in which an animal and crops were sacrificed. During a wedding ceremony, the

---

[603] Bormanicus is believed to have its Celtic origins in Gaul or of a Liguria origin His name means "do to boil", that is, the water that sprouts from hot springs. In the area of Vizella this god was quite revered for its thermal waters' which are known for it curative power. This spring was known to relieve patients that suffered from rheumatism and various skin diseases. Sarmento, Francisco Martins, "O Deus Bormanico, Subsídios para o estudo da Mitologia dos Lusitanos" Dispersos, Coimbra, 1933, p. 191; Vasconcelos, J.L de, *Religiões da Lusitânia*, vol. II, p. 266-276; Octávio da Veiga Ferreira, op. cit., p. 146-147; F. Adolfo Coelho; "Nomes de Deuses Lusitanicos", in Revista Lusitana I, 1887, pp. 351-378, p.358 (Celtic origin); d'Arbois de Jubainville, Marie Henri, *Les Premiers habitants de l'Europe*, Vol. II, 1894, p. 119-120, (Ligurian origin)

[604] They also rendered high praises to the river gods, which the Lusitanians believed was the source of life giving energy. Of all the river gods that were venerated, their main water guardian was Tongoenabiagus which meant 'god for the riverside (or source). It seems, according to the translation that Tongoenabiagus played a dual part in Lusitanian society as not only a water god of natural springs, but also as a god of oaths and promises. Vasconcelos, J.L de, *Religiões da Lusitânia*, vol. II, p. 239-261

couple sacrificed an animal to their appropriate goddess at the height of the ceremony ensuring that the couple produces children.

As the Lusitanians had male water gods, they also had female one such as Nabia and Reva who seem to have been popular within the Galician and Lusitanian pantheon. These goddesses were so popular that they had cults throughout the entire region. As for Nabia, she was also associated with valleys, plains and slopes other than on mountains, while *Reva* has been interpreted as the personification of flowing water and water streams.[605] Because of Reva significance with running water, she is the goddess of the source of rivers, making her the mother of all water gods and goddesses and making her husband to the mountain god, Reve.[606] This makes the association that river sources usually begin in the mountains.

Lusitanians families had a protector gods and goddesses that protected the household, according to Professor Leite Vasconcelos.[607] The most popular one was Trebaruna. But according to Scarlat Lambrino, she tells us that Trebaruna was not just a simple family goddess, but a protective goddess of a tribe, region or town, according to Celtic interpretation.[608]

---

605 Melena, José Luis, 'Un ara votiva romana en Elk Gaitán (Cáceres)', *Veleia* 1, 1984, p. 233-259; Rodríguez Colmenero, Antonio, Montanhas Sagradas no Noroeste Hispánico: Larouco, Marâo e Teleno. In Luis Raposo (ed.), *Religiôes da Lusitânia. Loquuntur saxa*, Lisboa, Museu Nacional de Arqueología, 2002, pp. 33-38; Marco Simón, Francisco, "El paisaje sagrado en la Hispania indoeuropea", In José María Blázquez Martínez and R. Ramos Fernández (eds)*Religión y Magia en la Antigüedad. Valencia del 16 al 18 de abril de 1997*, Valencia: Generalitat Valenciana, pp. 47-165

606 Olivares Pedreño, Juan Carlos, Los dioses de la Hispania Céltica. Madrid: Real Academia de la Historia, 2002, p. 169; Rodríguez Colmenero, Antonio, Montanhas Sagradas no Noroeste Hispánico:, pp. 33-38. Untermann, Jürgen, "A Epigrafia em Língua Lusitana e sua Vertente Religiosa", In Luis Raposo (ed.), *Religiôes da Lusitânia. Loquuntur saxa*, Lisboa: Museu Nacional de Arqueología 2002, pp.67-70

607 Vasconcelos, J.L de, *Religiões da Lusitânia*, vol. II, p.300

608 Lambrino, Scarlat, "La déesse celtique Trebaruna", Lisboa, Livraria Bertrand, 1957, pp.87-109.- Sep. de Bulletin des Études Portugaises, Tomo 20/Inscrições - Coria (Espanha)

Besides being a protector she also became a war goddess, which would be natural, being that the Lusitanians were a nation of warriors.[609] With the coming of the Romans, Trebaruna would become known as Victoria, Roman goddess of victory. The reason why the Romans transformed Trebaruna to Victoria is not completely known.[610] These are just a few examples of the types of gods the Lusitanians had within their vast pantheon.

Along with the gods, the Lusitanian also believed in spirits and demigods, which have been classified into three categories: Lares Genius and Nymphs. 1)Lares - There are a number of Luso-Roman inscriptions found throughout Portugal that are dedicated to these gods/spirits. Along with these inscriptions many small statues have been found in individual castro houses. These **tutelary spirit** or **patron deity** served as the guardian to watch over and protect a person, particular site, city, town, culture or nation.[611] Being that these demigods existed in different forms and types. 2) Genii - Originally, the genius were ancestors who guarded over their descendants. Over time, they turned into personal guardian angels follow each man from the hour of his birth until the day he died. On and individual's birthday a sacrifice was made. In the end, these two demigods were used to either ward off evil or used for good luck. Lusitanian religion had dozens of tutelary spirits in which some of the deities were attributed with strong powers, while others had less. But overall, the lares compared to the Genius had inferior powers, but over time, their power was extended, they became conflated with other Genii and protective spirits.[612] The last group of demigods and spirits were the Nymphs. These spirits were feminine nature spirits, who populated, inhabited and protected woods and forests, mountains and hills, river, streams well and so on.[613] Unlike the lares and genius, who were individual protectors, the nymphs protected natural areas.

---

609 Vasconcelos, J.L de, *Religiões da Lusitânia*, vol. II, p. 301

610 Ibid., 301-302

611 Ibid., p.179-184, 191-192

612 Ibid.

613 Ibid.

With the decline of the castro's political power and the centralization of power in Romanized *oppida*, the significance of Lusitanian deities began lose to Roman gods. With the introduction of Roman gods, Lusitanian gods only maintained their function as protector gods for the individual person or home. In summary, it is in the castro communities that the native inhabitants continued to entrust their protection to the deities of their ancestors, while in the new *municipia* or in the capital cities of the *ciuitates,* the Roman guardian deities were becoming progressively more established through the patronage of the native elite.[614]

Through the process of religious acceptance and tolerance, the great gods of the Lusitanian pantheon had been assimilated with Roman gods by the late 1st century AD. The main reason for this merger was that Lusitanian gods had similar characteristics and attributes to the Romans ones, but were considered more powerful, which is due to the equivalence to Rome power as a state.[615] Several examples of this divinity association can be seen in Luso-Roman epigraphs. At the same time, many Romans began to worship several Lusitanian gods, such as Endovllico. From this large number of indigenous divinities, many Lusitanian gods were assimilated into the Roman religion.

---

614 Olivares Pedreño, Juan Carlos, "Celtic Gods of the Iberian Peninsula", *e-Keltoi: Journal of Interdisciplinary Celtic Studies* 6 University of Wisconsin-Milwaukee, Nov. 2005, pp. 607-650Quanto aos Lares, são várias as inscrições encontradas em Portugal dedicadas a estas divindades, os Lares eram na crença romana, divindades que protegiam não apenas as casas, os campos e as cidades mas também os seus habitanSendo os lusitanos um povo de guerreiros é natural que tivessem no seu panteão várias divindades de carácter guerreiro que os protegessem aquando das suas emboscadas e batalhas. A norte do Tejo, os lusitanos segundo Tito Lívio e Estrabão, adoravam Ares Lusitano, a quem sacrificavam um bode e um cavalo de guerra. Segundo Leite de Vasconcelos, existiam diversos lares conforme a situação, Lares viales para os viajantes, Lares vicorum para os bairros, Lares compitales para as encruzilhadas.

615 Rodrigues, Adriano Vasco, Os Lusitanos (mito ou realidades), Academia Inernacional da Cultural Portuguesa, 1998, p. 190

Cults

Archeology has elucidated us with the theory that these gods played an important part in Lusitanian life, for there is information about the characteristic and attributes of the gods and sacrificial rites. Being that they all had a role in Lusitanian society, it appears that all these gods had cult status, for each god rendered a cult following with votive offerings and prayers.

According to several Iberian historians, they believed that the source of god cults in Lusitania began in several place. One of these sites is in the sierra around *Promunturium Sacrum* (Cabo de São Vicente) and in Tavira in southern Portugal's region of the Algarve. [616] The creation of shrines in this area were erected by the Phoenicians to honor their god Baal Saphon, the god of thunder and sea, during the time when they sailed up and down the Iberian Peninsula's Atlantic coastline. Being that the Phoenicians were connected to the sea, it is therefore very likely that they had cultivated moon, stars and sun cults in this region, because these celestial objects had always accompanied seafarers to help them navigate across the open seas.[617] With the coming of the Greeks, a temple was erected on the same spot and dedicated to Hercules. Another well-known site is in the hills around Sintra which was known by as the sierra of the sun and moon, better known to the ancients as *Lunae Mons.*

These two promontories (which are among several others along the Portuguese coastline) were sacred sites that were placed on high cliffs and mountains for it was the highest point that allowed man to touch the gods. The presence of Semitic and Greek populations along the Iberian

---

[616] Mário Varela Gomes and Carlos Tavares da Silva - Levantamento arqueológico do Algarve. Concelho de Vila do Bispo, Delegação Regional do Sul, Secretaria de Estado da Cultura, Lisboa, 1987; Quintela, M. V. García - Mitología y Mitos de la Hispania Preromana, vol. III, Madrid, 1999; Vasconcelos, J.L de, *Religiões da Lusitânia,* vol. II, pp.199-206; Maria G. Pereira Maia and Luis F. de Silva, "Culto de Baal en Tavira", Campo Arqueologico de Tavira, Huelva Arqueologica, 2004, pp. 171-194.

[617] le Fay, Morgana, "Serra da Lua", Religiões da Lusitânia, n.d. http://morganalefay.br.tripod.com/morganalefay/id3.html

coast seems to have left a deep mark on the origins of Iberian cults and indigenous religion. These marks also resulted from the repatriation and installation of large contingents of Carthaginian and the adoption of eastern deities, represented in objects of Iberian worship and shrines.[618]

Information on the organization of Lusitanian cults is either non-existent or it has not been researched or discovered. But as for the religious ceremonies and venerations to the gods, there is some information, thanks to the classical writers. According to these texts along with modern-day research and archeological artifacts, it seems that the community would gather together to generally pray, make sacrifices and libations, eat and dance to show their faith so as to be granted good will from the divinities that were being venerated at that time. During these cult celebrations and ceremonies, small votive offerings that were made up of food, animals, small statues and many other different items (which have been recovery by archeologists) were placed in small ritually dug storage pits. Larger and more elaborate deposits were left in specially dug ritual shafts or holes. At times, these items were ritually tossed into lakes, rivers and streams. These offerings linked the donor to the god in a concrete way, since complex and varied rituals involved the individual's personal contact with the sacred sites devoted to their respective god.

But for these ceremonies to take place, not anyone person could conduct the rituals that were significant to each ceremony. To execute these rituals, priests called Druids were used. What is known of the Celts, the Druids carried out combined duties of priest, judge, scholar, and teacher.[619] Little evidence about them exists, and thus little can be said

---

[618] José María Blázquez Martínez e María Paz García-Gelabert, "El impacto fenicio en la religiosidad indígena de Hispania", *Actas del IV Congreso Internacional de Estudios Fenicios y Púnicos. Cádiz, 2-6 de octubre de 1995*, Madrid 2001, pp. 551-560

[619] A **druid** was a member of the priestly and learned class in the ancient Celtic societies of Western Europe. The Druids were polytheistic. The earliest record of the name *druidae* (*Δρυΐδαι*) is reported from a lost work of the Greek doxographer Sotion of Alexandria (early second century BCE), who was cited by Diogenes Laertius in the third century CE. They were suppressed by the Roman government

of them with assurance. Though we have some information about Lusitanian ritual sacrifices, we do not have data about the priestly class that conducted these and other religious ceremonies. Although there is no specific mention of Druids among the Lusitanians, there is a possibility that Druids were present among them. This hypothesis is supported by texts whose Celtic tone would be difficult to explain without the presence of a common caste of priests, responsible for the tribe's religious maintenance and diffusion. But with the lack of references to these men, it is perhaps that the Lusitanians did not have a priestly breed as an organized class, but someone with the right character and prestige that was specialized to conduct religious rituals. Perhaps the reason for the absence may be explained if we consider that the dominant Classical ethnographies and historiographies avoided the topic of religious issues. But for now, we can only deal with the little information that exists.

These priestly men not only showed signs of animism, in their reverence to various aspects of the natural world, such as the land, sea and sky, but also practiced the ancient knowledge of fortune-teller, sorcery and magic. It also believed that these individuals were healers that used nature's ingredients along with formulated magic or 'enchantment' spells against diseases and sickness. Sacrifices were also done as part of the religious ceremony. Of all the sacrifices that were performed by these holy men, purported ritual killing and human sacrifice were aspects of this druidic culture that shocked classical writers.[620] Finally, within the temple grounds no 'impure' human could enter sacred ground for it was intensely taboo to enter the mysterious realm of the gods without being properly cleansed of evil.[621]

---

and disappeared from the written record by the second century CE. Diogenes Laertius, *Lives and Opinions of Eminent Philosophers* Introduction, Chapters 1 and 5 (Book A 1 and 6 in the Greek text). Hutton, Ronald, *The Druids,* London, Hambledon Continuum, 2007, p.2

[620] Gruesome rites were noted by Lucan, *Pharsalia* 1.450-58; Caesar *Gallic Wars*, 6.16, 17.3-5; Suetonius *Life of Claudius* 25; Pomponius Mela 3.2.18-19; Cicero, *Pro Fonteio.* 31 and *De Repubblica* 9.15.

[621] Octávio da Veiga Ferreira, op. cit., p. 115

The origins of animal worship has been the subject of many theories, but overall, when a god was respected or worshipped by means of a representative animal, an animal cult was formed.[622] The origin of such cults developed from the lack of distinction that primitive man had between animals and humanity.[623] This lack of discernment caused humans to look upon animals as equals. Therefore, it was just as simple for them to represent their gods in animal form as opposed to human form because in primitive man's judgment animals and human were equal.[624] Hence the animal cults! As for the animals that roamed Lusitania, a large number of them had a sacred place in Lusitanian culture such as the bee, tuna, dove and bear, but only a handful had cult status.

Of the animal cults that existed within Lusitanian culture, the best known is the serpent cult. Many serpent cult relics have been found at Santuario de Baldoeiro and at Moncorvo which has been considered their main place of worship.[625] The importance of ophiolatry (worship of serpents) played a large part in Lusitanian culture for its properties were not only religious, but also used in medicine and magical application.[626] Its application in medicine was used as cooked meat in broths, elixirs and potions, while the skin and 'magical' parts of the body (i.e. organs) were used in infusions.[627] Ophiolatry seems to have had such an impact in Lusitania that it is still practiced today by modern-day pagans in areas of the Beira (around the area of Idanha-a-Velha e Monsanto) attesting to the cults influence.[628]

---

[622] Teeter, Emily, "A History of the Animal World in the Ancient Near East", ed. Collins, Billie Jean, Vol. 64, Brill, Boston, 2002, p. 355.

[623] FitzRoy Richard Somerset, 4th Baron Raglan, "The Cult of Animals ", Folklore # 46(4), 1935, p. 331.

[624] Ibid.

[625] Junior, A.S., "As Serpentes gravadas do Baldoeiro" Actos do Congresso Internacional de Antropologia, Lisboa, 1930

[626] Octávio da Veiga Ferreira, op. cit., p. 121

[627] Pliny, Natural Histories, 30.10

[628] Carlos Consiglieri and Marilia Abel, Os Lusitanos no contexto peninsular, Lisboa, Editorial Caminho, 1989, p. 70-71; Octávio da Veiga Ferreira, op. cit., p. 122.

Another important cult among the several known animal cults was the cult of Verrasco (cult of the pig). In references to Luso-Roman epigraphs, the wild and domesticated pigs were associated to Endovellico and Mars.[629] The cult since ancient times has had an enormous influence on the Portuguese, mainly because it has been a primary source of food. So important was this animal in Lusitanian cuisine and economy that it was worship as a god.[630] This ancient link to the pig was so strong that it was carried on into present times. The pig is so highly praised in Portugal that it has a patron saint, Santo Andre Avelino, Christian protector of pigs.[631] The importance of the pig/hog can be seen from the abundance of statues such as the famed Porca de Murça (Sow of Murça) which is the most well-known of about 400 known monuments. Its mystic function has generally been assumed from their high visibility in their original surroundings that these sculptures had some protective religious significance as a reproductive function, guarding the security of livestock or as funerary monuments (there are some statues that bear Latin funerary inscriptions).

The most revered animal among the Lusitanians was the horse. Though highly praised, the horse did not have its own cult for the ancient texts do not mention one, but not all is entirely lost, for being that the horse was man's best friend, they had a protector goddess, known by three names: Epona/Epane/Iccona. Though well known throughout the peninsula, it seems she may not have been venerated much by the Lusitanians for only one inscription has been discovered at Cabeço das Fraguas near Guarda, Portugal. Being that the horse had a protector goddess and the Lusitanians did not have a horse cult, they did worship a horse god. According to Strabo, this god's name was Ares Lusitani and the Lusitanians sacrifices horses to this god.[632]

---

629 Vasconcelos, J.L de, *Religiões da Lusitânia*, vol. III, 127-128; Azevedo, Rogério, 'O porco na Etnografia Ibéica, Trabalho de Antropologia e Etnologia, vol. XIX, fasc. 1, Porto 1963, p.80; Octávio da Veiga Ferreira, op. cit., p. 140

630 Octávio da Veiga Ferreira, op. cit., p. 141

631 Silva, Pedro, Historia dos Lusitanos, Lisboa, Prefacio, 2006, p. 53

632 Strabo, 3.3.7

An animal that was revered by the warrior was the wolf. Appian states in his account about Nertobriga that its men pranced around wearing wolf skins,[633] indicating that perhaps 'wolf-men' cults may have existed among the Iberians. This was enforced by archaeological finds proving this cult's existence through vase painting from Numantia showing warrior wearing wolf furs.[634] Besides the European lion,[635] the wolf was one the most feared of all the beasts because of its associations with the underworld, night, war and death, making it an ideal symbol for Indo-European warrior fraternities.[636] According to Peralta Labardor, man's spiritual connection to the characteristics of the wolf and the wearing of wolf skin as a disguise may symbolized the mystic union with the animal and the transformation of the warrior into a wild beast, like the Germanic *berserkir* who made up Odin's *comitatus.*[637]

There is also some evidence of bull cults among the Iberian tribes under Roman occupation for there is some evidence due to large sculptures of bulls found in sanctuaries and sacred places signifying that even though they did not worship the bull they practiced killing the sacred bull (tauromachy).[638] The origin of this practice is said to have begun

---

[633] Appian, 48.204

[634] Romero, F., *Las cerámicas polícromas de Numancia.* Valladolid: CSIC-Centro de Estudios Sorianos, 1976, lám. 11, nº 20.

[635] Panthera leo europaea - European lion. Extinct around 100 AD? due to persecution and over-exploitation, though may have been Panthera leo persica. It Inhabited the Balkans, the Italian Peninsula, southern France and the Iberian Peninsula. It was a very popular object of hunting among Romans, Greeks and Macedonians.

[636] Martín Almagro-Gorbea and Alberto J. Lorrio, "*War and Society in the Celtiberian World*"' *e-Keltoi: Journal of Interdisciplinary Celtic Studies* 6, University of Wisconsin-Milwaukee, Oct. 2004, 73-112; Georges Dumézil, *La religione romana arcaica*, Milano, 1977, p. 180, 192

[637] Peralta Labrador, Eduardo, *Los cántabros antes de Roma.* Madrid: Real Academia de la Historia, 2000; Marco Simón, Francisco, Religion and Religious Practices of the Ancient Celts of the Iberian Peninsula", *e-Keltoi: Journal of Interdisciplinary Celtic Studies* 6, University of Wisconsin-Milwaukee, Mar. 2005, p. 290-291.

[638] Vasconcelos, J.L de, *Religiões da Lusitânia*, vol. III, pp. 514-515; Maria Cruz Fernandez Castro, *Iberia in Prehistory, the Shrines of the Iberians*, United

during prehistoric times, but in Iberia it is believed that bull worshipping began with the Romans for it was an essential part of the iconic act of Mithras, which was commemorated in the *mithraeum* wherever Roman soldiers were stationed.[639] These are just few of the known cults that existed in Lusitania.

Sacrifices

The act of sacrifices and offerings has been constituted as the maximum expression of giving thanks in order to appease the gods or/and to build a connective relationship between men and gods to achieve health, peace and harmony and well-being amongst the tribe and individuals. As with all ancient civilizations, they all practiced some type of sacrificial offerings of animal, plant and even human. The performance of sacrificial offerings as part of religious rituals was common among various peoples of Europe in ancient times, and therefore among the Iberians. The slaughtering of animals was a significant contribution from nature to the economy and feeding of the community, but the act of sacrificing was done in exceptional cases especially in times linked to either a crisis or tribal successes, which was necessary to search for divine support and cohesion through this social ritual. As for human sacrifices and their divinatory dimensions, it played its part in religious rituals in time of a particular crisis such as war, disaster or an epidemic.

Of all the classical texts that have survived, it seems that the Iberians practiced four different types of sacrificial rites: the divinatory human sacrifice, the sacrificing of male goat-man-horse to the god of war, the animal 'victims' of the "hecatombs" and agrarian and fertility worship.

Human sacrifices have been relatively well documented among Phoenicians, Carthaginians, Gauls, Bretons, and Germanic tribes, unfortunately within the Iberians there is sparse documentation, however, there is some information among the Lusitanians. Human

---

Kingdom, 1995, p. 278.

639 Ulansey, David, "The Mithraic Mysteries" Scientific American, December 1989 (vol. 261, #6), pp. 130-135

sacrifices were a reality during Rome's conquest of Lusitania, as inferred in classical writings. Livy, Strabo and Plutrach provide testimonies of those sacrifices where hundreds of Romans soldiers were taken prisoner to die on Lusitanian sacrificial altars with their viscera overstepped by the knife of the auspice.

We also know from Appian, that one of the most frequent rites the Lusitanians practiced during the Lusitanian War was to amputation of the prisoner/victims' right arm or hand that seized a sword against Lusitania, in which the body part was then offered to the god of war for their good fortune in battle.[640] Besides the ritual of amputating, the Lusitanians practiced a peculiar rite of human sacrifice, that was recorded by Strabo; the examination of viscera of sacrificed prisoners of war to predict the future then offered to the gods of war for god fortune.[641] The practice of vivisection has been much discussed by modern historian/ archeologist and ancient cultural anthropologists. After analyzing the classical texts in relation with Celtic divinatory sacrificial rites of human sacrifices, it has been verify that many of these practices and rituals are of Celtic nature (of Indo-European origin), while other practices such as child sacrifices originated from the Carthaginians.[642] The ritual we have the best testimony is from Strabo, which is the most complete account of all classical writings about the Lusitanians. In the sequence of a passage almost entirely dedicated to this description, Strabo writes that "The Lusitanians are frequent in the performance of sacrifice; they draw their first auguries from the fall of the body and then examine the entrails, but without cutting them out of the body; they also examine

[640] Appian, 68.291; Herodotus, IV, 62, 2, Strabo, 3.3.6

[641] Strabo, 3.3.6

[642] Blázquez, J.M., Diccionario de las religions prerromanas de Hispania, Ediciones Istmo, Madrid, 1975, p. 145-146; Curchin, Leonard, A., Roman Spain, p. 170; Marco Simón, Francisco, "Religion and Religious Practices of the Ancient Celts of the Iberian Peninsula, ", *e-Keltoi: Journal of Interdisciplinary Celtic Studies* 6, University of Wisconsin-Milwaukee, Mar. 2005, p. 317; García Quintela, M.V., "El sacrificio humano adivinatorio celtico y la religion de los Lusitanos", Polis, revista de ideas y formas políticas de la Antiguedad Clásica, 3, 1991, p.32

the veins from the inside, and practice augury by the touch whom they first cover the body with a military cloak" (sago).[643]

The one ritual sacrifice that seems to mark any type of importance, which is particularity a Lusitanian rite, has been the sacrificing of goat-man-horse, which is evident with warlike connotation for Livy reports it as a ceremony in preparation for war .[644] The religious theme is taken from the ancient texts, "…and to Ares they sacrifice a he-goat and the prisoners and horses; and they offer hecatombs of each kind, after the Greek fashion of sacrificing a hundred of every kind."[645] This passage unfortunately, is not found in any of the odes of Pindar surviving working. However, as Strabo reports, the ritual of sacrificing a male goat-man-horse is of Lusitanian origin, but it is believed to have been of an Indo-European origin, but a ritual that was also practiced by the Greeks.[646] Though these human sacrificial rites were practiced, it was not the norm, for it seems to have been utilized as a last resort used in extreme ceremonial situations (a practice that is well documented in Rome itself).[647]

They also practiced horse sacrifices to Ares Lusitani. Between the Lusitanians and Galaicians, it has been pointed out that they practiced two types of sacrifices: the propitiatory sacrifice in the context of warlike rituals involving human and horse immolation and propitiatory sacrifice of purification in the agrarian ritual context, involving a specific group of

---

643 Strabo, 3.3.6

644 Livy, *periochae*, 49

645 Strabo, 3.3.7; Silius Italicus 3.361; Horace, Carmen III, 4.34

646 Marco Simón, Francisco, Religion and Religious Practices of the Ancient Celts of the Iberian Peninsula", *e-Keltoi: Journal of Interdisciplinary Celtic Studies* 6, University of Wisconsin-Milwaukee, Mar. 2005, p. 290-291.

647 Marco Simón, Francisco, Deis Equeunu(bo). In Francisco Villar and F. Beltrán (eds), *Pueblos, lenguas y escrituras de la Hispania prerromana*, pp. 481-490. Zaragoza-Salamanca: Ediciones Universidad de Salamanca, 1999, pp. 481-490 and "Religion and Religious Practices of the Ancient Celts of the Iberian Peninsula", p. 317.

animal and plants.[648] As for animal sacrifices, they were more frequent, which attests to by remarkable epigraphic evidence and sanctuaries like the one at Picote (Tras-os-Montes, Portugal).[649] Though literary sources allude to sacrifices without specifying whether the victims were human beings or animals, the lack of details suggests that the killings referred to animals. Here are some examples of animal sacrifices; from Frontinus - he says that during the Lusitanian War, the people from Segobriga were surprised that Viriathus, during his attack on the city had time to perform a sacrifice to his war god.[650] Other references of this practice was performed at weddings or at funerals, such as that of the Lusitanian chieftain Viriathus, in which a multitude of 'victims' were immolated.[651] According to Horace and Silius Italicus, the Cantabri Concani drank the blood of sacrificed horses during a ritual that is described belonging to the Scythians and Masagetes religion.[652]

Of all the sacrifices that were practiced, the Iberians, in general, practiced animal sacrifices which they basically sacrificed up to ten animal species: goat, sheep, rams, pig, boar, bull, cows, deer, bear, horse. But only the Lusitanians performed sacrifices that dealt with the last two including human. Through archeological data and artifacts, it shows that these rituals sacrifices were performed on platforms or altars that date back to the seventh century BCE. From the dozens of animal bones that have been found, the rituals seem to have used young animals. Of the ritual itself, the animals were killed; then either burned or cooked to be consumed in a ritual banquet.[653]

---

648 Blazquez, José M., *La religión celta en Hispania*, Biblioteca de Gonzalo de Berceo, 2001, "http://es.wikipedia.org/wiki/Sacrificios_humanos_en_la_Europa_Antigua"

649 Marco Simón, Francisco, Religion and Religious Practices of the Ancient Celts of the Iberian Peninsula" p. 317

650 Frontinus, *Stratagemata,* 3, 2, 4

651 Diodorus: 33, 7, 2; Appian, 72.317 only mentions the funeral rite but is detailed in Diodorus 33.22

652 Horace, *Carm.* 3.4.34; Silius Italicus, 3.361

653 Renero Arribas, V.M., Diccionario del mundo Celta, Alderabán, Madrid, 1999, 170-172; This assumption also comes from the recorded information about these well-known practices documented in the biblical texts of *Exodus* (29:15–18) and

By the time of Roman occupation of Lusitania, religious bloody acts of human sacrifices were forbidden, although they did not disappear completely, as the old American saying goes "Old habits die hard". But in 97 BCE this would change; according to Plutarch and Strabo, when proconsul P. Licinius Crassus took command of the area, he introduced laws that outlawed human sacrifice and being that these religious act were still being conducted he decided to make an example of some tribes to show all the other Iberian tribes that he meant what he said. The day came to past when he received information that the Bletonenses were still performing human sacrifices. So he called on their tribal chiefs to meet with him to desist from these acts, and if not they would punish them.[654] Unfortunately, there is no information about the details of the meeting or if he punished them. But one can imagine what the outcome was for after that event it seems that human sacrifices disappeared from the written record.

Lusitanian Funerary Rites

When dealing with mortuary rituals, the Lusitanian cremated the body and placed the ashes in urns, which were then placed in dug – out holes inside the house or in a sacred place. Unfortunately, in Lusitania, none have been found to date. As for cremating the body, it was part of their culture since the Bronze Age.[655]

The best source of Lusitanian funeral rites comes from Viriathus' death and funeral. Classical sources inform us that the cremation of the corpse proceeded around the funeral pyre, soldiers paraded and sung in honor of the deceased. This continued until the fire extinguished itself. Soon

---

Leviticus (7:32–33), thus assuming that the Iberians, like most ancient cultures followed this practice.

654 Strabo 3.5.11; Plutarch, Quaestions Romanae, 83; García Quintela, M.V., "El Sacrificio Lusitano", Latomus, Revue d'Études Latines, sep., Paris, 1992, 342-343; (Cuestión Romana 83; Arez, João Santos, O Sacrifício entre os Lusitanos, june 2007 http://www.naya.org.ar/congreso2002/ponencias/maria_joao_santos_arez.htm Bletonenses were from Bletisa in the northern half of Ulterior, near today's Salamanca.

655 Octávio da Veiga Ferreira, op. cit., p. 136

afterwards, mock gladiatorial games of combat were celebrated on the grave site. The ritual mortuary rite common to the pre-Roman people of Lusitania was the rite of incineration, in which the bodies of the deceased were burned and the ashes of the dead were then deposited in an urn and placed in a small circular hole with masonry ornaments inside the house.[656] Except for the practice of cremation, funerary rites are mostly unknown.

There is no doubt the Lusitanian practiced the funerary rite of cremation within the confines or in the proximities of their castros. The proof of this comes from several castro sites such as the one near Castelo de Paiva. In a certain section of the castro which is away from the homes, the earth in this one spot was darker for it was blackened by debris and ash, demonstrating the use of cremation.[657] From this archaeological data along with a written record from Appian and Diodorus describing Lusitanian funerary rites, it has been deduced that these rituals were perhaps common.[658]

As we can see from Viriathus' funeral, great warriors and rich "nobles" received special funeral honors that were usually bestowed upon Iberian upper class. During these funerals, the deceased's body was dressed in the finest clothing. We do not know if the body was washed or rubbed with aromatic oils, but the texts are unanimous in speaking of the rich dress that was put on the corpse. The next sequence of events was that some men surrounded the corpse to take special care of it, while others raised a funeral pyre and prepared to make sacrifices.

Dressed in splendid garment and with his weapons at his side, because even in death, an Iberian men were not supposed to leave his weapon behind, the pyre was lit with odoriferous plants.[659] During the cremation ceremony

---

656 Hübner, Emílio, "Citânia", Translated by Joaquim de Vasconcelos. "Archeologia Artística", Vol. I, Fasc. V, Imprensa Literario-Commercial, Porto, 1879; Belo, a. Ricardo, Símbolos astrais das lápides luso-romanas: Sua origem e significacão, Lisboa, 1957, pp. 143-168.

657 Octávio da Veiga Ferreira, op. cit., p. 130-145

658 Appian, 75.317-318; Diodorus, 33.22

659 The destruction of his beloved weapons was done so that no other person could use them for the weapon, especially the sword, was a living part of the warrior or

warriors paraded around the funeral pyre, singing and beating their weapons on their shields, while, relatives, women and children looked on. This would continue until the burning pyre burned out. This can be seen in Appian's description of the event.[660] As is the habit in several modern-day cultures, it is also suggested that these primitive people mourned the dead with high pitched shouts and moans along with pulling their hair and giving punches in the face, with great cries that finished in hysteria scenes.[661] When the fire died out and the funeral rites were over, the ceremony was concluded with friendly gladiatorial games on the sepulcher.[662] In the case of Viriathus, there were 200 warriors that participated in mock combat.[663] But before the games commenced, there was usually a moment of silence with the participants seating themselves in and around the deceased's ashes.[664] As for the gladiatorial games and mock combat it was very symptomatic of warrior type societies during prehistory.

After the cremation and the games had ceased, the ashes were gathered up and deposited in a clay urn. The container was then placed either in a dug-out pit or an especially made necropolis, such as the one in Citânia de Briteiros. Ancient necropolises in Portugal are rarely discovered for these monuments were usually reserved for tribal chiefs and heroes such as Viriathus. Unfortunately, his had not been found as of yet. As for the lower social classes, they were treated with the same ceremonial rites, but not as exuberant and lavish. Their remains were also gathered in clay urns and placed in an ancestral pit within the home or surrounding area.

Along with the remains of the deceased, small items such as pins, fibulas, earrings, bracelets, belt buckles, neck torques and other personal belongings were stored in the urn, while slightly larger items that could not be stowed inside the urn was usually place in a larger one close to the remains.[665]

---

tribal chief. Octávio da Veiga Ferreira, op. cit., p. 136

[660] Appian, 75.317; Diodorus, 33.21-22

[661] Octávio da Veiga Ferreira, op. cit., p. 135

[662] Appian, 75.317

[663] Diodorus, 33.21a

[664] Octávio da Veiga Ferreira, op. cit., p. 136

[665] Ibid., p. 137-138

The funerary and burial rites in Lusitania lasted until the end of the third century AD or the onset of the fourth century AD for that is the time when Christianity had reached the Iberian Peninsula.[666] With the newly established Roman Catholic Church's discouragement of cremation, it soon became an abandoned practice.

From these types of monuments and few graves, we know that the Lusitanians possessed a strong faith in the existence of life after death. Apart from helping the living, Endovelicus also helped assure his faithful followers a happy eternal life after death. In one of the best known altars dedicated to this god, we see additional representation dedicated to the pig or wild boar, along with a crown of laurels symbolizing immortality (the laurel of the plants that remain green in winter).[667] As for the burning of the body, it is seem from a spiritual level that fire was a way of purifying the body and spirit before releasing one's spirit into the next world, while saving the ashes was so that the dead would still be part of the family and to watch over the living.[668]

Conclusion

Though the Lusitanians have been classified as having been influenced by the Celtic culture, ancient writers have written that the Lusitanians were very different from their Celtic counterpart. Diodorus not only tells us explicitly that the Lusitani were of Celtic origin, but that their nature and character was entirely different from the Celts and Iberians.[669] This perhaps means that the Lusitanians at first and for some time did not mix with Celtic blood or culture. Fortunately, archaeology has allowed the rebuilding of this interesting warrior culture that seems that they denominated all the "Iberians", as if they were the only people that inhabited the entire peninsula.

---

666 Ibid., p.133

667 Miguel Sanchez de Baêna and Paulo Alexandre Louçao, "Grandes Enigmas da História de Portugal, Vol. I, Esquilo, Lisboa, 2008, p. 34.

668 Carlos Consiglieri and Marilia Abel, Os Lusitanos no contexto peninsular, Lisboa, Editorial Caminho, 1989, p. 70.

669 Diodorus, 5.34

CHAPTER IV

LUSITANIAN WARFARE & WEAPONS

If we study with close attention the history of the Iberian Peninsula, especially the Western part of the peninsula between the years 155-138 BC (the campaigns of Viriathus), we cannot help but be amazed on how an area composed of several dispersed tribes without cohesion, discipline, espirit de corps, and military training were able to humiliate and defeat in battle after battle the most fantastic war machine ever: the Roman Army. It is estimated that during this period the Lusitanians killed over 25,000 Roman Legionnaires, and seriously injured so many others that they were unable to return to the Roman rank and file.

In order to understand the dimension of the conflict and the reasons for the success of the Lusitanian army, we must examine the socio-clannish military formations and weapons of the people living in the territory the Romans called Lusitania. Though each tribe operated independently, these disorganized tribes were obliged at times to ally themselves to combat a common enemy. Through my research, I have been able to layer the dimension and reality of the conflict that pitted these people in a 10-year war against an organized, disciplined and experienced Roman army.

Before we begin the study of the war, we must look at the life of a Lusitanian warrior, their ideals and combat techniques, their character, armament, influences and contacts for us to understand the aspects of Lusitanian military tactics.

The Warrior

In order to understand the behavior of the Lusitanian in the field of battle and the measure of their weapons, we must try to assume the shape of the combatant. Though the Lusitanian Army had men from the warrior class, the majority of the army was non-professional soldiers. The army was made up of citizen-soldiers that came from all professions such as craftsman, farmers and shepherds. Although most Lusitanian men were not from the warrior or nobility class, they were used to constant tribal warfare and, as such, became skilled and resolute citizen-soldiers. In addition, many of these men had also been mercenaries and bandits at one time or another.

Despite the fact that these men were citizen soldiers, their soldiering skills were top notch that according to the classical texts, the Lusitanian warrior was agile, cunning, ferocious, versatile, indefatigable, and brave – but still somewhat inferior to the Roman Legionnaire for Lusitanians lacked unit cohesion and professionalism. The “Iberian” fighting skills and their system of warfare were far more apparent than what they did on an everyday basis. The aggressive nature of all Iberians, especially the Lusitanians, was due not only to an innate warlike disposition, but of the poverty of the land to grow and the unequal distribution of wealth which turned those without material property into outlaws.[670]

The Lusitanian had a basic attitude about life, and so, they regarded warfare as a part of it, as did many societies of this type throughout the ancient world. War was considered part of their background and it was a rite that all young men had to participate in to pass from adolescence to manhood. Diodorus reports that there was a habitual characteristic of the Iberian people, particularly with the Lusitanians, that when a boy reached adulthood, in order to show his courage and newly gained skills with weapons, the young man would be sent into the mountains and left there for some time.[671] This process would show which youths

[670] Arribas, Antonio, The Iberians, Frederick A. Praeger Publishing, NY, 1964, p.73.
[671] Diodorus, 5.34.7

were the fittest and strongest, thereby enabling them to progress into mature warriors. The weaker youths and the physically uncoordinated did not survive and would often be cast out of the tribe and perish when left to fend for themselves. This brutal method occurred among various peoples such as with the Spartans for it ensured that the tribe remained strong and healthy.

The style of training and the constant practice these young men were put through was intended to build a formidable fighting man capable of facing and evading all types of situations, no matter how tough. To the Romans, linked to the old methods of fighting as a unit, these barbaric guerrilla tactics used by Iberian tribes constituted a huge surprise. Life for these people was hard, living in a hostile environment of harsh mountain living and everyday hazards. One can say that the mountains, hills and plains were their home and the wars against other tribes were a form of ultimate survival.

But to the Lusitanians, this did not mean that the weaker youths were outcasts. Those youths that showed a high degree of intelligence would be placed under the care of the priests, who would nurture and encourage their talents for the good of the tribe, while other would become apprentices under the tutelage of a craftsman. It was through these people that new techniques and advances would come. Others, who did not possess the physical build to be a warrior, would become farmers and food gathers. There was at least some way each member could contribute to the tribe.

With the young man's baptism into adulthood, many would perhaps receive a tattoo. This idea is suggested because the Romans recorded how tattooing was practiced in cultures, they considered barbaric (the practice of tattooing in Roman eyes was considered a barbarian trait). Consequently, it was deemed unseemly for a Roman to get a tattoo. Therefore, the Romans primarily used tattoos to mark slaves and condemned criminals. But this does not mean that ordinary Romans did not tattoo themselves. Many often did, especially during their military service.[672] However once certain individuals, such as noblemen, began to move up in the social ranks of Roman society, they often found it wise to consult the services of a physician to have their tattoos removed. By virtue of Roman records, it appears that there was a booming business in tattoo removal, which conversely, attests to the fact that Roman citizens did indeed get tattoos - no matter how 'barbarian' the practice was considered.[673] Unfortunately, for the Iberian cultures there is no proof of tattoos except the assumption that Pre-Christian Germanic, Celtic and other central and northern European tribes were often heavily tattooed, according to surviving Roman accounts.[674] With this said, many scholars speculate that with all the Celtic cultural influences that were instill on the Iberian people, they assimilated the desire to have tattoos in their culture.[675]

The dance in prehistory, initially was the ceremonies of the hunt for food was covered in a halo of magic. In time, the hunting dances were transferred to the hunt of humans (i.e. the war dance). The war dance involved mock combat performed as a ritual connection with endemic warfare. The warriors preceded the war dances and songs with magical rites; the Lusitanian culture always sacrificed a male goat, horse or human to *Cariocecus,* the god of war. The hypothesis is that such dances and songs formulated magical spell that perhaps was used to recall their ancestors' warlike audacities to ask them for their blessing and success in either battle or raid.[676]

---

[672] Jones, C.P. "Stigma: Tattooing and Branding in Graeco-Roman Antiquity." Journal of Roman Studies 77 (1987) 139-155; W. M. Gustafson, "Inscripta in fronte: Penal Tattooing in Late Antiquity", Classical Antiquity 16 (1997) 79-105

[673] Ibid.

[674] One such example comes the the Picts for they were famously tattooed (or scarified) with elaborate dark blue woad (or possibly copper for the blue tone) designs as described by Julius Caesar in Book V of his *Gallic Wars* (54 BC).

[675] Octávio da Veiga Ferreira e Seomara Bastos da Veiga Ferreira, *A Vida dos Lusitanos no Tempo de Viriato,* Polis, Lisboa, 1969, p. 175; Leite de Vasconcelos, José, "Medicina dos Lusitanos", **OPÚSCULOS,** Volume V – Etnologia (Parte I) Lisboa, Imprensa Nacional, 1938, p. 291-293; Fontes, Joaqium, "Contribuição ao estudo da tatuagem", Arquivo de Antropologia, vol. II & III, 1914-1915

[676] Octávio da Veiga Ferreira e Seomara Bastos da Veiga Ferreira, op. cit, p. 180

Upon the death of a warrior, funerary rites were preformed. Several ancient texts mention various funerary practices among the Iberian peoples, especially those of the Lusitanians. The best example of Lusitanian funeral rites is that of Viriathus' own.[677] On his death, the corpse attired in his best raiment with his weapon at his side and was burnt on a tall pyre. While his cremation took place, warriors began a frenzied dance around the pyre, while a squadron of horsemen executed funerary marches and bards sang about the glorious deeds of the dead hero. Once the flames died down, there were funerary games comprising of 200 contestants above his remains. This text was written based on funerary rite that only took place for great warriors or tribal chiefs, while funeral ceremonies for lesser men were probably of a simpler nature.

After the funeral pyre had cooled down, the warrior's ashes were placed in an urn and buried in a small grave with his falcata (a Lusitanian curved sword) and all of his other weapons and personal belongings, while funerary games were celebrated.[678] The celebration of these games was perhaps a reminder of the famous "*devotio iberica*", practiced by the Lusitanians. Even in death the oath of loyalty that had been taken between warriors and their leaders, still held until the death of the warriors.

The Horse

To understand properly the importance of the horse in Lusitanian culture, we must look back to the 6th century BC when the Celtic tribes of Central Europe emigrated west in direction of the Iberian Peninsula. These tribes despite minority status were technically more advanced than the local inhabitants, such as in the use of iron compared to the majority of the Iberian tribes that still used bronze. Along with these technical advances, the Celts also had magnificent horse.

---

[677] Ibid., pp. 130 – 144 (entire section on Lusitanian funerary rites); Diodorus, 5.33.21

[678] Ibid., pp. 134 – 137

The Celts had a type of horse from Central Europe that was a scale above the horse from Western Europe. Though very robust, its mobility and speed were reduced, and its handling was somewhat difficult. But when Celts arrived in the Iberian Peninsula, they quickly noticed the equine population that roamed the land. In the mountainous buttresses of the Northwest, the Garranos dominated the landscape. Despite the fact that these horses were small and rustic, they had great mobility, with an incredible capacity of surviving a harsh land, no matter how inhospitable. In the area around the rivers of Mondego, Tagus, and Sado, the region was dominated by the Sorraias, a race considerably larger and heavier than the Garranos, but also rustic with great mobility. In time these people created a gene pool that became known as the current Lusitano horse.

The crossbreeding of the Central Europe horse with peninsular horses gave birth to a breed that became celebrated by Pliny, Possidonius and Silio Italicus. So respected and esteemed were these horses that many of them went on to be honored as heroes and deities by the Lusitanians. This passion for the Iberian horse, well expressed the almost divine character they gave the horse.

The horse enjoyed such great importance in the social and military activities of the Iberian people that they were honored and considered as a divinity, as well as a warrior and that in some places such as at Mula (modern-day Murcia) sanctuaries and temples praising *Ares Lusitani* (God of horses) were built to honor these magnificent animals. Another source that provides information that the horse played a part in a warrior's life is evident by the numerous action poses painted on vases, statues and votary figurines found throughout the peninsula. Finally, there are the horse burial sites that contributed to our knowledge about the horse in Lusitanian culture.[679] On worshipping *Ares Lusitani,* the Lusitanians sacrificed a goat and a horse, which perhaps portrayed a very strong symbolic significance that the horse would be the very representation of the warrior's spirit who rises to the heavens in hope for their sacrifice and triumph.

679 Arribas, Antonio, op. cit., p. 141

By the time of the Lusitanian War began, the horse and not the infantry was the backbone of the Lusitanian Army. In order to understand properly the impact that the horse had in the victorious campaigns of Viriathus, we must take a look at its training and equipment.

The robust Central European horse the Celts utilized was somewhat difficult to handle. This meant that there had to be a harness and irons to have total control of the mount. The Celts, who had become skillfully with iron, had managed to create devices for the horse's mouth and harness to handle horses better. These Celtic inventions (halter, bridle bit and reins in which a vast number of horse bits have been discovered in Iberian site) made it very easy for the rider to control the new Iberian breed. On further looking at the bits, they are more like snaffles acting on the flesh by pressure from front to rear. But these snaffles were simple wings that prevented sideways movement and did not put pressure on the palate.[680]

The Iberian wild horses as described in many Roman texts were very fast and of great beauty, while being a moderate size. They were also praised for their stamina and strength, as they were usually ridden by two men over long distances.[681] With this information, plus recent discovered fragments of vases and painted stucco, shows that it was true that two horsemen often rode a single horse. Even though the horseman's effectiveness depended on his riding ability, a large part depended on the use of saddles. At this time, actual saddles were not used, but saddle pads made out of wool, linen, weaved vegetable material, animal pelts or leather hides secured by a broad leather girth.[682] Sometimes the padding was extended to cover the horse's neck in order to protect it from the reins and trappings. Usually the rider had to manage the reins with one hand and hold his weapon with the other. Nevertheless, some cases exist where the neck-guard became a rein-control to enable the horseman to

---

[680] Ibid., p. 85

[681] Strabo, 3.4.18; Martinez, Rafael T., Rome's Enemies (4): Spanish Armies, Osprey Publishing, Men-at-Arms Series #180, Oxford, UK, 1986, p. 40

[682] Arribas, Antonio, op. cit., p. 84; Martinez, Rafael T., op. cit., p. 40

use both hands to handle weapons.[683] They undoubtedly rode astride and yet there are vases that depict a rider mounted side-saddle. Though a possibility, this effect however, is probably due to the artist's inability to apply true perspective to his artistic rendering. With the makeshift saddle and bridles, spur can be seen being used throughout many Iberian vase paintings and statues. Although spurs can be seen, stirrups cannot, thus implying that they were not used in Iberia.

Today among Celtic scholars there is some controversy as to who invented the horseshoe, which became an important contribution to the art of cavalry warfare. It is alleged that the Celtiberians may have introduced it in the 4th century BCE.[684] This statement is boldly asserted by author Rafael Martinez from his discovery of some of the oldest known examples found in burials sites in central Spain.[685] But the theory is questionable because early Asian horsemen used horse booties made from leather and plants and in time introduced them to the eastern European tribes, who then emigrated west.[686] Another hypothesis claims that the Celts had invented the horseshoe.[687] But no matter who invented the horseshoe, this invention greatly increased the military potential of the Iberian/Lusitanian cavalry and influenced the reorganization of their enemy's forces and for them to used Celtic technology.

With the type of 'superhorse' the Celts had bred and the equipment they used, increased the mobility of the Lusitanian cavalry, becoming the very essence of their army. It is estimated that the Lusitanian cavalry

683 Arribas, Antonio, op. cit., p. 84

684 Pidal, Ramon Menendez, História de España vol. I, Espaca-Calpe S.A., Madrid, 1947, p. 36 Martinez, Rafael T., op.cit., p. 40; Octávio da Veiga Ferreira e Seomara Bastos da Veiga Ferreira, op.cit, p. 176

685 Martinez, Rafael T., op. cit., p. 41

686 Weber, S.E. (translated from German), "Historical Development of the Horseshoe". Scientific American Supplement No. 819, Volume XXXII, September 12, 1891 (originally written by district Veterinrian named Zippelius of Wurtzburg)

687 Fleming, George, Horseshoes and horseshoeing: their origin, history, uses and abuses, London, Chapman & Hall Gasner, 1869; Mgnin, J. P, De l'origine de Ia ferrure du cheval, Paris, P Asselin, 1865.

made up 20 – 25% of the total force compared the Romans 14% of their total force.[688] Also with these horses, they developed a tactic of speed and surprise in which each horse carried two men: the horseman and auxiliary.[689] On the battlefield, the auxiliary dismounted and would go into battle on foot, while the rider stayed on horseback. After the battle or if they needed to quickly withdraw, the auxiliary would mount the steed and rapidly move out beyond the battle line or field.

The training of Lusitanian horses and horsemen was intense, but careful to not injury the horse. The horse was trained to kneel and wait in silence for his master until a signal was given by the rider to stand up and walk towards him. It was also taught to climb and run on rough terrain, and how to stand still during combat.[690] In open combat on the battlefield, when the cavalrymen fought on foot, they would leave their horse behind the battle line and the horse would not move until its master returned (if the horsemen did not return the auxiliary would take it).[691]

Lusitanian horses were held in great esteem. To demonstrate the affection and respect that the warriors had for their beloved horses, horsemen extravagantly decorated them with lavish headdress, decorated parasols, a wide variety of prominent frontal ornaments attached to the brow, decorative chest plates, colorful wool caparisons, and bells hanging from a throat-lash and some horses even wore chainmail.[692] Even the wings of bridle bits were decorated with metal rings, crescents and other shaped metal decorations. Today within the Iberian Peninsula the custom of dressing up horses still exists; many anthropologists have traced this tradition of dressing the horse to the ancient Iberians.

---

[688] Miguel Sanchez de Baêna and Paulo Alexandre Louçao, "Grandes Enigmas da História de Portugal, Vol. I, Esquilo, Lisboa, 2008, p. 57. Martinez, Rafael T., op. cit., p. 41

[689] Strabo, 3.4.18; Martinez, Rafael T., op. cit., p. 40; Miguel Sanchez de Baêna and Paulo Alexandre Louçao, op. cit., p. 56.

[690] Strabo, 3.4.15

[691] Miguel Sanchez de Baêna and Paulo Alexandre Louçao, op. cit., p. 57

[692] Arribas, Antonio, op. cit., p. 84-86; Martinez, Rafael T., op. cit., p. 41-42

But in war, all decorations were withdrawn being limited to essential items. Beside essential equipment, each horse had on its neck, fixed on its halter, a rattle or a headpiece that permitted the rider in the middle of all the chaos of battle to recognize his horse by the sound of the rattle's tinkle or headpiece design.[693] These small decorations must have played an important part in combat for there are representations of these items on paintings of Iberian horses in which I had the opportunity to see. Along with the bell, there have been some archaeological finds of a picket pin. This picket pin which was attached to the reins was perhaps use during battle. When caught in the melee of battle, the horsemen would dismount and tether the horse, and being the horse was relished by these warriors, they perhaps form a circle around them to protect them, while fighting off the enemy at the same time.[694]

Compared to the Lusitanian cavalry, the Romans were by nature, poor horsemen. From archeological data about saddles, it seems the Roman cavalrymen straddled the horse on its kidneys instead of closer to the front. The reason for this was because the horse's reins were longer thus limiting the animal's mobility.[695] At the same time, equitation was restricted to the aristocracy who trained in the many schools through Roman Italy; thus, the horse was not taken seriously as a weapon of war.[696]

---

693 Miguel Sanchez de Baêna and Paulo Alexandre Louçao, op. cit., p. 57

694 Martinez, Rafael T., op. cit., p. 42

695 Miguel Sanchez de Baêna and Paulo Alexandre Louçao, op.cit.,p. 55

696 It is strange on how the Romans were the first to create specialized horses for different purposes such as hunting horses, delivery service horse, horses for long and short journeys, show and race horses but ignored the war horse. All these types of horses especially racing horses, were carefully created and selected from the best stud of Rome and the empire. But the war horse was relegated to a secondary position when it should have been a priority. Overall perhaps the two major reason why the Romans did not concentrate on the cavalry was because the Roman interest in horses were in other ways more based on profitable business ventures than in war, this is perhaps why they did not have a strong cavalry tradition compared to the Lusitanians. With this said this may the reason why the Roman generals incorporate little cavalry and relied mostly on heavy and light infantry. In other words the cavalry was the weakest link of the Roman Army.

The Lusitanian Army

The Lusitani warrior, in Roman literary works was usually described as a mercenary incorporated into Hannibal's army during the 2nd Punic War.[697] These men under Hannibal became skillful in the art of war. During their time with the Carthaginians, the Lusitanians had learned much about war, that they would later apply this knowledge for generations to come, especially in their fight against Rome. According to Livy, these shepherds, as well as other Iberian tribes, were incited to fight Rome by Hannibal's blistering speeches.[698] From this incitement, the Iberian tribes sustained 200 years of fighting without truces for their independence (218 -18 BCE).

At the onset of Rome's conquest of the Iberian Peninsula, it was relatively easy for the Romans to occupy Iberian lands for they had encountered friendly or submissive tribes throughout the Peninsula. However, the further they marched deep into the peninsula, the more resistance they met. Of all the tribes that they encountered the Lusitanians were the most challenging, due to their warlike mentality. According to Livy, the Lusitani were warlike because of their appearance and their love for raiding and fighting, but when not raiding they were quite peaceful.[699] However, being that the way of life was being threatened by the Romans, they went on the warpath.

With this said, one has to look at why the Lusitani were warlike and why the Romans attempted to pacify them. For starters, the Romans had a belief that if one was not Roman, then one was a barbarian, and so there was a cause for Roman imperialism to extend their power by bringing

697 Diodorus 15; Livy 21.43.8-9, 24.12 (Italian Campaign); Silius Italius, *Punica*, 3.354-356; Polybius, 3.56, 72; Hanno, Los Mercenarios Hispanos durante la Segunda Guerra Puncia, Celtiberia.net, Oct. 4, 2006 http://www.celtiberia.net/articulo.asp?id=846; García-Gelabert Pérez, M. P. and Blázquez Martínez, José María, " Mercenarios hispanos en las fuentes literarias y en la Arqueología"; Habis 18-19.; Sevilla, Publicaciones de la Universidad de Sevilla, 1987-1988, págs. 257- 270.

698 Livy, 21.43

699 Livy 39.56

their culture to the Peninsula and have under their domination. At the same time, the Lusitanian way of life was considered by the Romans to be disgraceful (mercenary and banditry).[700] Thirdly, the Lusitanians were a proud and independent tribe, something the Romans disliked for if this tribe was independent from the Roman yoke of power, then all those other tribes that were under Roman control would also want to be free and independent. Thus, it became important that Rome control the western part of the peninsula.

With Roman encroachment on their territory, along with the threatening of Lusitanian way of life, the Lusitanians began causing trouble for the Romans after the First Celtiberian War. The Lusitanians at first launched border incursions, later followed by systematic raids into Hispania's rich southern cities of Rome's newly established ally, the Turdetanians. Between 193 and 180 BCE there were a number of military dispatches and reports from Roman governors about the Lusitanians.[701] With this in mind, the Romans, classified the Lusitanian as uncivilized because they devoted themselves to theft, fighting, raiding and plundering. So from a Roman point of view, they had to be put in their place to prevent the Lusitanian way of becoming infectious to the other Iberian tribes.

With part of the Iberian Peninsula under the yoke of Roman imperialism and the violence that the Romans committed against the Iberian tribes caused many tribes to rebel. Rome had made enemies of the Iberians due to its policies and ploys of hypocritical political tactics such as making the Iberians believe that they had declared war on Carthaginian oppression and tyranny, by boasting that Rome fought under the flag of pacifism and peace, which in reality was false. Because of this, the Lusitanians remained in a state of war with the Romans from 193 BCE up to 138 BCE. Based on these Roman falsehoods and lies, the Lusitanians launched a guerrilla war that successfully held off the Romans for

---

[700] Diodorus, 5.34.6; Martinez, Rafael T., op. cit., p.7; Garcia y Bellido, A., "Bandas y guerrillas en las luchas con Roma", *Hispania*, 21, 1945, p. 19; Abengochea, Juan Jose Sayas, El bandolerismo lusitano y la falta de tierras, Revista de la Facultad de Geografia e Historia #4, Univsidade de Santiago de Compostla, 1989, 704-714.

[701] See Chapter 1

several decades. Overall, one should not overlook the existence of the state of affairs of the Lusitanians, although the lived-in areas that were poor in rich soil for growth, this incited men to become armed robbers and mercenaries, later proving to be an important practice that development into guerrilla tactics against the Romans and their allies during the Lusitanian War. With this said, we must assume that when the Lusitanian War began, the campaign against the Romans was not about raiding or robbing Roman territories, but rather a military operation for freedom.

Among the able and skilled warriors within the newly formed army, some of the veterans were dedicated to Virathus' cause and were able to assume positions in his army as captains, which were seen as a more permanent role similar to chieftain. As in similar armies, these men who had shown exemplary conduct or heroism were perhaps granted land or cattle as reward for their services. But in battle, the ultimate prize for a Celt was not the victory, but the taking of a human head from the enemy. If a warrior took a head from an enemy, he believed that he took on the heroic qualities of his victim.[702] Heads were kept as trophies and the slaying of an opponent and if a youth removed a head, it was seen as an automatic qualification for manhood. With this said, it is believed that the Lusitanians and Iberian may have participated in the practice of head hunting.

To built and organize his army, it was important for Viriathus to garner the fidelity of his soldiers. Viriathus' army was not just composed of Lusitanians, but of men from others Iberian tribes that were integrated

---

[702] Gunn, Robert M., The Ancient Celtic Warrior of Europe, Edinburgh, 2004, Part 8: Celtic headhunters; Rodrigues, Adriano Vasco, Os Lusitanos: Mito e realidade, Lisboa, Academia Internacional da Cultura Portuguesa, 1998**Tal como a arqueologia mais tarde comprovou, em combate usavam um pequeno escudo redondo que seguravam com correias e que tinha como finalidade interceptar os dados e setas lançados pelos inimigos, utilizavam punhais, espadas, lanças de arremesso empregavam a metalurgia do ferro e bronze para fabricarem as suas armas.**

into a multi – ethnic army made up of Callaeci, Celts, Vettones, Turdetanians, Bastetanians, Conii, and Vacceus.[703]

In spite of ethnic diversity, Viriathus seem to have given excellent military training and logistical preparation for his upcoming guerrilla operations. Showing great leadership skills, he was able to build a base with strong discipline and appropriate training. According to several classical texts and the research conducted by Professor Muñoz and the late Professor Schulten, Viriathus gained his combat experience by leading bandit incursions and raids into central and southern Spain and from tribal warfare as a young man.[704] With this said, he probably had some organizational skills that led to the formation of his army into combat units instead of a ragtag army of marauding barbarians. In time, the Lusitanians expanded their campaign across central and southern Hispania, recruiting other allies, thus improving his numbers.

As for training his army, Viriathus had them continue doing what any tribal warrior would do when they were not out fighting. As a pastime, warriors were continuously fine tuning their skills by conducting 'gladiatorial' combat (this ranged from friendly contests to fights to the death to settle serious difference between warriors), weapons training, boxing, combat simulations for his troops and hunting and raiding expeditions on neighboring tribes allied to Rome, which served as preparation and training for the soldiers that would become his army.[705]

---

703 Diodorus 33.1.1; Pérez Vilatela, Luciano, "Procedencia Geográfia de los Lusitanos de las Guerras de siglo II a.C. en los Autores Clásicos (159 – 139)", *Actas del VII Congreso Español de Estudios Clásico,* Madrid, 1989, pp. 257-262, "Notas Sobre la Jefatura de Viriato en Relación con la Ulterior", *Archivo de prehistoria Levantina,* XIX, Valência, 1989, pp. 191-204, Lusitania: Historia y Etnología, Madrid, 2000, pp. 203-204 (from pages 204 – 238 deal with Viriathus allies)

704 Diodorus, 2.33.1,7,19,21; Cassius Dio, Historae, 73,77, 78; Munoz, Mauricio op. cit., p. 51-52; Schulten, A., "Viriato" Boletin de la Biblioteca Menéndez y Pelayo, vol. II, (4part series) #3, pp. 126-149; #4,5,6, pp. 272-281. Santander, 1920, In Portuguese it is a book entitled "Viriato" Porto, 1940.

705 Strabo, 3.3.7

The Lusitanian Army was composed of two bodies: infantry and cavalry. These military branches were prefect for Lusitanian hit-and-run tactics for these warriors carried light armor and weapons. In comparison to the Roman army, the Lusitanians lacked engineers (i.e. Siege warfare) and artillery (catapults and ballistas) as well as elephants, for it seems that the Romans had used elephants against the Celtiberian and Vacceus, but we have no specific information that indicates that these animals were ever utilized against the Lusitanians.[706]

The Lusitanian army relied heavily on ambushes, so it was important to have mobile infantry. Most of the infantry units wore light armor and carried javelins, shields and swords. These war bands were the lightest armed and among the most 'annoying' at harassing Roman troops. They would cause many Roman casualties throughout the day before withdrawing back into the night. They would hideout in the surrounding hills or forests, only to attack again the following day. Besides using guerrilla tactics, the Lusitanians at times, copied Roman military formations and tactics to defeat a Roman legion at their own game.

Through Iberian vase paintings and sketchy information from classical authors, several historians have come up with theories on how the Lusitanians may have conducted themselves while on campaign.[707] The

[706] Appian, 46. 188-193, Valerius Maximus, 2.4.10 and 5.2-4; Garcia y Bellido, A., "Elefantes antes Numancia" Veinticinco estampas de la España Antigua, Madrid, 1968, p. 58 and in the book La Peninsula Ibérica en los comienzos de su Historia, Madrid, 1952, p 335.

[707] Quesada Sanz, Fernando, "Not so different : Individual Fighting Techniques and Small Unit Tactics of Roman and Iberian Armies, in P.François, P. Moret, S. Péré-Noguès (eds), L'Hellénisation en Mediterranée Occidentale au temps des guerres puniques, Actes du Colloque International de Toulouse Mars-Avril 2005; Quesada Sanz, F., "Innovaciones de raíz helenística en el armamento y táticas de los pueblos ibéricos desde el siglo IIIa.C", in M.Bendala, P.Moret, F. Quesada Sanz (eds.), Formas e imágenes del poder en los siglos III y II a.C: Modelos helenísticos y respuestas indígenas, in Cuadernos de Prehistoria y Arqueología de la Universidad Autónoma de Madrid no.28-29, Madrid, 2002-2003,pp.96-94; Quesada Sanz, F., Military Developments in the Late Iberian Culture (c.237-45 BC): Helenistic influences via the Carthaginian Military,

infantryman is believed to have carried several javelins with bronze or iron metal tips or "*sude*", which is a wooden javelin, sharpened and fire-hardened on both ends, along with a s*cutati* (a long oval shield) for protection and a sword for close-quarter fighting. Along with these weapons, some Lusitanians were experts with a sling, carried an assortment of different size slings used for various distances. Each soldier took three javelins, in which two would be used as offensive weapons and the third as a defensive one if needed. In an open pitched battle, they would form a loose shield wall and from a distance they would throw two javelins towards their objective, while the third javelin served as a defensive weapon for an oncoming attack from the enemy's light infantry and skirmishers or regular cavalry charges. This did put them at a disadvantage against trained heavy assault infantry. While this would seem ineffective against heavy armored Roman soldiers, they played havoc on lightly armored or unarmored men and horses.

To incite the Romans to attack, the Lusitanians would prematurely organize themselves on the battlefield into an unorganized battle formation in front of the Roman's main battle line. They would then release volleys of slingshots and javelins until the Romans gave the order to attack. When the Romans began to move, the Lusitanians would retreat behind their main battle line which was waiting in ambush. The aim of this type of skirmishing was to disrupt enemy formations by causing casualties before the main battle, and to tempt the opposing infantry into attacking prematurely, throwing their organization into disarray. Once the preliminary skirmishing was done, the skirmishers would participate in the main battle by being used as a reserve that

---

N. Sekunda (ed.) First International Conference on Helenistic Warfare, Torun, Poland, 2003; Garcia Alonso, F., La Guerra en la Protohistorica: Héroes, nobles, mercenarios y campesinos, Barcelona, Ariel, 2003; Hernandez Cardona, F.J., La batalla de Ampurias, Historia #16, 1991, pp.101-112; Martinez Gazquer, J., La Campaña de Catón en Hispania, Barcelona, 1992; P. Moret and F. Quesada (eds), La Guerra en el mundo ibérico y celtibérico (ss.VI-II a.C. de C), Collection de la Casa de Velázquez, Madrid, 2002; Quesada Sanz, Fernando, La Guerra en las comunidades ibéricas (c. 237-195 a.C.): Un modelo interpretativo, in A. Morilo, F. Cadiou, D. Hourcade (eds.), Defensa y territorio en Hispania de los Escipinoes a Augusto, Casa de Velázquez Madrid, 2004, pp. 101-156.

would participate in the melée. Due to their mobility, skirmishers were valuable for they would instigated an ambush after having harassed a Roman unit, hoping that the Romans would give chase and follow them into the ambush's kill zone.

The Iberians were skilled riders, who made widespread use of cavalry in all their campaigns, not only on Spanish soil but overseas during mercenary service with the Carthaginians and later on with the Romans. From these experiences, especially under Hannibal, they not only fulfilled the tradition of light cavalry as a force to distract the enemy, but also proved capable of defeating cavalry formations in battle.[708] The Lusitanian were skillful horsemen who rode surefooted, agile and resilient Iberian horses that were excellent for a country with rough terrain. Altogether they had the ability to fight on the battlefield, they could only battle for a limited duration due to the lack of armor, thus they were used as shock troopers against infantry.

During Viriathus generalship he used the cavalry as a stealthy, mobile guerrilla force to harass and cut down unwary enemy formations before disappearing back into the hills instead of wasting his cavalry in costly pitched battles. This was possible due to one of the surprising characteristics within Iberian armies: their peculiar training of horses.[709] As such, many of the deceptive ambushes performed by the Lusitanians were surprising to an incautious enemy. This skillful training of Iberian horses combined well with hit-and-run surprise tactics caused Romans to wonder why they could not beat an uncivilized rag-tag band of warriors.

Though the cavalry was not often used in pitched battles, there were times when they were called upon to inflict a decisive blow to the Romans. These horsemen were used to great effect against Roman infantry. But most of the time, the cavalry played the role of dragoons, dismounting to fight on foot alongside the hard-pressed infantryman.[710]

---

708 Martinez, Rafael T., op. cit., p.40.

709 Strabo, 3.4.15; See section on horses in this chapter

710 Martinez, Rafael T.,op. cit., p.42

As dragoons, these men would charge into the battle and formed a protective ring around their beloved animals to keep them from harm's way or leave them behind several yards away.[711] Though they wore light armor and were armed with several small javelins, labeled by the Romans as *veruti*, the Iberian sword, the "*falcata*", and a small rounded shield, the "*caetrati",* this could be a disadvantage to less hardy horsemen, but their ferocity, martial arts skills and thirst for freedom took precedence.

Still the cavalry was excellent for skirmishing tactics as they were able to carry many short light throwing spears and hurl them at enemy formations, while staying out of the enemy's reach. Once the spears were thrown, they would enter the melee, if they were needed. They were armed and fast enough to stand up to most light and medium cavalry and medium infantry but would get cut to pieces by heavier infantry or cavalry, if they fought them in a pitch battle. So, at all cost these types of battles were avoided.

From the ancient texts, it has been presumed that Viriathus may have had an elite cavalry troop that was made up of men who had proved their worth and dedication to their chieftain in the heat of battle.[712] While their backgrounds might vary, they all had in common a religious oath of fealty. Being that these men were considered elite, they perhaps protect themselves with light armor made up of quilted linen under a composite of leather and "esparto" fibers attached to another layer of quilted linen and thin metal plates that absorbed cutting blows. Although not numerous, these cavalrymen were fundamental used as scouts and bodyguards. Being an experience combat veteran and leader, he probably utilized these men as reconnaissance due to their mobility.[713]

---

[711] See section on horses in this chapter

[712] Appian, 64.262-263

[713] Quesada Sanz, Fernando, "Aristócratas a caballo y la existencia de una verdadera 'caballería' en la cultura ibérica:dos ámbitos conceptuales diferentes", in C.Aranegui (ed.), Los Iberos, principes de Occidente, Actas del Congreso Internacional, Barcelona, 1998, pp. 169-183

As for the warriors under Viriathus's banner, these fierce men were in a constant state of warfare, having served on countless raids and attacks on neighboring tribes, probably having even served as mercenaries at some point, which afforded them their equipment and battlefield experience. Lusitanian warriors, according to Livy, seem to have been the most feared soldiers the Romans faced.[714] Their camouflage abilities and to seemingly appear out of nowhere, attack quickly and suddenly disappear, worried and demoralized their opponent time and time again. When properly organized, these men were able to cut off retreats, harass supply lines and lower the enemy's morale to the point of making the enemy take winter quarters before the campaigning season was over. What contributed to Viriathus's success in conducting guerrilla warfare against the Romans were the following four things: his army's agility and flexibility on the battlefield, the use of the javelin, Iberian ferociousness and superb swordsmanship and horsemanship.

Strategy and Tactics

To set the stage for this war, we must take a look at the Lusitanian military strategy. The strategic process in which Viriathus's Army won their victories over Rome's legions was due to its intelligence network, deception, surprise attacks and ambushes, the black spirit of revenge and the thirst to remain free. This shepherd-soldier's guerrilla strategy derived from his experience in robbery and raiding neighboring people.[715] These men exercising their skills as outlaws and the knowledge on how to use the surrounding terrain to their own advantage turned these bandits into guerrilla fighters for they began using their skills as highwaymen into a military tactics of surprise, forecast, ambush, and false escape. This style of warfare was used at first as a defensive strategy, but under Viriathus, it became a terrible offensive strategy that put fear into the Romans.[716]

---

[714] Livy 37.57.6

[715] Octávio da Veiga Ferreira e Seomara Bastos da Veiga Ferreira, op. cit., p 167

[716] Schulten, A., "Las guerras de 154 – 72 AC", Fontes Hispaniae Antiquae IV, Barcelona, 1937; Munoz, Mauricio P., op. cit., p.93

Viriathus' political-military objective was for his homeland to remain independent in relation to Rome's imperial expansion into the rich southern (Beturia, Carpetania and Betica) regions, which threatened Lusitania. So instead of waiting for the Roman war machine to come onto his land, he went on the offensive to keep out the Romans from his homeland. But as a consequence of his action, he became deeper involved in attempting to liberate the territories under the Romans or causing his rebellion to expand to other territories. Though Viriathus and his army fought and defeated the Romans outside their territory, he never turned the conquered territories into Lusitanian possessions, having preferred to heighten his victory by increasing his men's booty through raids and attacks on the Romans and their allies and allowing the tribes to live out their lives as they saw fit. For an occupation to take place, the Lusitanians would need man and material means, as well as above all else, an organized and administrative capacity that they did not have at their disposal. When speaking of Viriathus' strategy and of the wear and tear strategy against the Romans, this dilatory strategy had on occasions led to mortal tactical blows onto the Roman army.

A dilatory strategy of skirmishes, instead of battling on open fields was preferred because the Lusitanians were not able to maintain the necessary perseverance for a lingering campaign. So, the tactics used by Viriathus varied according to the situation he found himself. At times, the Lusitanians attempted to tire the opponent by disturbing and impeding the Roman Army of their provisions; other times they sought to eliminate them through surprise ambushes and attacks, or raids. Along with the employment of guerrilla tactics, the Lusitanians used the land's natural terrain and any other land formations that offered abundant natural defenses. But for these tactics to work, speed and surprise were the essential ingredients for this type of warfare.

Viriathus's mobile strategy required that his army be constantly on the move so as not to give the Romans any chance or reason to capture or destroy it. Thus, Lusitanian tactics greatly relied on mobility, which the use of the horse was highlighted as a determining factor. But when operating far outside the borders of Lusitania, his soldiers would need to rest and resupply themselves. It was on these few occasions that his men occupied a friendly fortress, city or stayed in the hills of nearby towns as a temporary base of operations. Two such places have been recorded: Tucci (modern-day Martos, Spain) and Mons Veneris (Sierra of San Vicente in the province of Toledo, Spain.).[717]

Besides on just relying on mobility and outside 'allies', one of the tactics that was constantly used by Viriathus, was the hit-and-run ambush, according to the ancient texts. This guerrilla tactic was usually employed with speed and surprise within a mountain pass, a valley, in a narrow passage of a heavily forested area or anywhere enemy soldiers were obligated to march in long and narrow columns or tight formations. In an open or wooded area, Viriathus would try to annihilate the Roman legions through an ambush by attempting to disperse the Romans by simultaneously conducting a surprise attack using infantry soldiers and cavalrymen. He would then concentrate his forces on Roman formations, which had broken off from the main body. Once the Roman unit was devastated the Lusitanians would quickly disappear. Their 'inhuman' ability to hide in the grass and thick hard terrain, allowed them to ambush enemy columns quickly and then disappear into thin air.

When Viriathus wanted to completely withdraw from battle and mislead the enemy, he used the following tactic: he would first choose a group of soldiers and launch an unexpected attack at a different place along the Roman line, while the Romans reacted to this new attack, the main Lusitanian formation had time to flee and hide. He would also at times withdraw his troops from battle by simultaneously dispersing his army into small groups and reuniting it at a pre-determined spot.[718]

---

[717] Schulten, A. op. cit., p.110, Gonzalez-Conde Puente, Pilar, Romanidad e indigenism em Carpetania, Unversidad de Alicante, 1987, p. 32; Arce, J., "Las guerras Celtibero-Lusitanas", Historia de España: Histoira Romana, Tome II, Madrid, 1988, pp. 79-99; Bonilla Martos, Antonio Luis, "Poblamiento y Territorio en el suroeste de la provincial de Jaén en época romana", Arqueologia y Territorio #1, Universidad de Granada, 2004, pp.119-133

[718] Munoz, Mauricio P., op. cit., p. 68

The one tactic that the Lusitanians rarely used was an open battlefield formation. When the Lusitanians did fight the Romans on open ground they usually used deception. The reasons for not fighting the Romans in the open was due to their shortage of warriors, weapons, provisions and the lack of disciplined warriors to fight in organized military formations as the Romans did. Like the samurai of Japan, the Lusitanian warrior had their own sense of the warrior spirit and individual glory for these elements played an important part in the Lusitanian warrior's ethos. Knowing the negatives characteristics of his army, Virithus took advantage of the negatives and transformed them into a ponderous weapon. The Lusitanian/Celtiberian warriors went to war not for the glory, but for the thrill of the assault, the robbery and the raid.[719]

But when the Romans and the Lusitanians did meet on the battlefield, mobility, deception and the assault were crucial for victory. Therefore, throwing weapons were more important than the sword when it came to mobility. While the fundamental line of Viriathus's battle plan was the assault, deception played an important role in disorienting the Romans into making mistakes which cost them dearly. It is precisely this new modality of guerrilla war, along with a daring person who had an offensive spirit that distinguishes of Lusitanian War from the other wars that took place on the Peninsula (i.e. Numancia War was defensive war).

The deceitful tactic that was used by Viriathus was the attacking retreat. On the battlefield, Lusitanian formations perhaps impressed and instilled fear among the well-disciplined Roman legions, for the Lusitanians, as did most Celtic warriors, wore face paint of a blue dye made from a substance called *'pastel de tintureios'*. But before the fighting commenced, the Iberian warriors would use loud tremendous war cries the Roman soldiers called *barritus*.[720] Issued by thousands

---

[719] Schulten, A., Historia da Numantia, Barcelona, 1945, p. 171

[720] Diodorus 5.34.6, Miguel Sanchez de Baêna and Paulo Alexandre Louçao, op. cit., p. 73; Frye, David, G., "Rome's Barbarian Mercenaries", Military History Quarterly, Spring 2007 Vol. 19, No. 3, pp. 68-81 Estes símbolos esculpidos nesta ara aqui presente, são já um sinal do culto romano a este deus.

of warriors, this tremendous war cry perhaps froze the blood of many bold Legionnaires.

After a great deal of preparatory chanting and ritual dancing on an open battle field, trumpets blared out giving the signal to attack. Viriathus's warriors would attack in a disorganized mass formation. At a pre-arranged signal given by the trumpets, the fighting was halted, and the warriors would retreat giving the appearance of a defeat.[721] Once the Lusitanians began to retreat the Romans chased them. With each 'withdrawal' the Romans most of the time mounted a pursuit, while maintaining their formation. After several attacks of this kind, the Romans would sometimes lose their discipline and break formation to pursue the retreating warriors. At this point a pre-arranged signal was given and the warriors would quickly regroup and mount a counterattack, which would frequently decimate the disorderly and heavily armored Roman legion ranks, making them less agile in individual combat.[722]

At times, this Lusitanian maneuver would continue for several days forcing the Romans to pursue the Lusitanians. But it was difficult to maintain such a pursuit for occasionally Roman military discipline would turn into bloodlust; turning their military formation into a chaotic state, which would later cost the Romans dearly. Fighting against masters of guerrilla warfare in this manner would cost Roman lives and materiel. After several day of pursuing the Lusitanians, the Romans would perhaps begin to lose their nerve and patience and withdraw from the pursuit. At this time, the Lusitanians signaled their pre-determined signals, regrouped and counter-attacked the Romans, massacring and dispersing the demoralized Roman formations, who were exhausted and slow due to their heavy equipment.

---

[721] It is perhaps noteworthy to mention that on many archaeological excavations throughout Spain and Portugal hollowed animal or ceramic horns are believed to have been used to transmit signal during battle or on a hunt. Martinez, Rafael T., op. cit., p.8; Arribas, Antonio, op. cit. p.74; Miguel Sanchez de Baêna and Paulo Alexandre Louçao, op. cit., p. 73

[722] Martinez, Rafael T., op. cit., p.7-8

This sort of military maneuvering was known by Romans as *concursare,* described by historians as a simple absence of tactics.[723] However, this belief has been misconstrued; for the Lusitanians to have held off the Romans for ten years, there had to be some kind of coordination that allowed these ambushes, advances and retreats to occur simultaneously in the heat of battle without leaving a group of warriors outnumbered or isolated. Therefore, it is clearly seen that this model of combat was not developed at random, but masterfully well designed and magisterially implemented.

In judging Viriathus's strategy, which has received many complimentary remarks from classical Latin authors, as well as modern-day historians, it is necessary to point out that Viriathus drove the Lusitanians to war because of circumstance and not of personal decision, ambition or for glory.

Weapons

Throughout museums of Portugal and Spain there are various Iberiaic statues in which we can see clearly the similarity of the clothes and armaments which the warriors wore throughout the Peninsula.[724] These

---

[723] Martinez, Rafael T, op. cit. p.8; Arribas, Antonio, op. cit., p.74.

[724] For more information see: Connolly, P., "Pilum, Gladius and Pugio in the Late Republic", in M. Feugère (ed.), L'équipement militaire et l'armement de la République, JRMES #8, 1997, pp.41-57; I. Filloy and E. Gil, Las armas de las necrópolis celtibéricas de Carasta y La Hoya (Alava, España). Tipologia de sus puñales y prototipos del pugio, 137-150;Garcia-Gelalbert, M.P., "Estudios del armamento prerromano em la peninsula Ibérica a través de los textos clásicos", Espacio, Tiempo y Forma Serie II, Historia Antigua, 2, 1989, pp.69-80; Quesada Sanz, Fernando, El armamento ibérico, Estudio tipológico, geográfico, functional, social y simbólico de las armas en la Cultura Ibérica (siglos VI-I a.C.), Monique Mergoil, Montagnac, 1997; Quesada Sanz, Fernando, Gladius hispaniensis: an archaeological view from Iberia, in M. Feugère (ed.), L'équipement militaire et l'armement de la République, JRMES #8, 1997, pp. 251-270; Quesada Sanz, F., "Armamento indigena y romano republicano en Iberia seculos III – I a.C., compatibilidad y abastecimient de las legiones republicanas en campaña", A. Morillo (ed.), II Congreso de Arqueologia Militar Romana en Hispania. Producción y abastecimiento en el ámbito military, Unversidad de León, 20-22 Octobro 2004;

statues give us an idea of the type of tunics they wore and the various types of shields, daggers, axes, spears and slings and swords they used. Many warriors in Hispania used the combination of javelin, spear and sword to fight. Although lightly equipped they were badly armored if one compares them to the Romans, their only protection was either a bare quilted tunic, or a quilted tunic with thin metal plates, a breastplate or chain mail along with either a helmet or leather cap.

As with most warriors throughout history, weapons were a matter of individual preference and fighting style. Therefore, Lusitanian warriors had their preferences of using different combinations such as the "*falcata*" and "*caetrati*" (small shield), or the spear and "*gladius*" with a large oval shield, or the spear and the '*falcata*" with a small shield or long shield, while some others preferred carrying axes instead of a sword. Though axes were mentioned in some classical texts, they do not appear to have been favored much in Hispania.[725] With their martial arts skills of sword and buckler, allied to the unpredictability and ferociousness, the Lusitanians were excellent in single combat and were often able to surprise and kill Roman soldiers in this manner.

Swords

Of all the weapons the Lusitanians bore, the sword is the one that stands out the most. Within their hodgepodge of weaponry, the swords used by all Iberians tribes fell into two simple classifications: the straight (*gladius hispaniensis* and atrophied-hilted antennae sword) and the curved (falcata).

Quesada Sanz, F., Las armas del legionario romano en época de las Guerras Punicas: influencias hispanas y formas de combate, in P. Fernández Uriel (ed.), Armas, legiones, y limes: el ejército romano. Espacio, Tiempo y Forma (Historia Antigua); Sandars, H, The Weapons of the Iberians, Archeaologia #64, Oxford, 1913; Fernando Quesada Sanz "¿Qué hay en un nombre?. La cuestión del gladius hispaniensis."Boletín de la Asociación Española de Amigos de la Arqueología 37, 1997, pp. 41-58; Fernando Quesada Sanz, "Armamento romano e ibérico en Urso (Osuna): testimonio de una época", Cuadernos de los Amigos de los Museos de Osuna, 10, Diciembre 2008, pp. 13-19.

[725] Martinez, Rafael T., op. cit., p. 37.

In the last few decades, it has been possible to identify the prototype of the Iberian straight sword. The original influence can be found in the Greek *Xiphos, Makhaira* and *Kopis* swords introduced to the Peninsula from Greek commercial endeavors or when the Iberians took up mercenary service with the Greeks.[726] This sword design was then imitated by the natives. But the actual Greek sword was short-lived for the Celtic sword was quickly adopted by the Iberians.

With the arrival of the Celts in Spain around the 10th to the 6th century BC, the Celtic long sword began to be locally adopted.[727] It has been suggested that the first model of Iberian swords was not of a Greek design, but derived from the Celtic sword in which the blades were straight and long .[728] Perhaps by the 4th century BC, it had been adapted by the entire region, giving origin to the Iberian styled atrophied-hilted antennae sword. These swords had a flat iron double-edged blade and were shorter, topped by two small horizontal balls or discs. Compared to the early Roman sword that was a little longer and thinner but shorter than the standard Greek *xiphos*, the Iberian sword was sharpened on both edges with a sharp stabbing point making the 'gladius hispaniensis' ideal for encounters with foes with longer weapons enabling the swordsman to swing, cut and slice from side to side.[729] Using a buckler or small shield to block or parry his enemy's spear or sword, the wielders

---

[726] Sanz, F. Quesada, "*Gladius hispaniensis: an archaeological view from Iberia*", Journal of Roman Military Equipment Studies, vol. 8, Armatura Press, UK, 1997, p. 251-270; "Máchaira, kopís, falcata", *Homenaje a Francisco Torrent*, Madrid, 1994, pp. 75-94; I. Filloy Nieva & E.Gil Zubillaga, *Las armas de las necropolis celtibéricas de Carasta y La Hoya (Alava, España). Tipologia de su puñales y prototipos del pugio,* Journal of Roman Military Equipment Studies, vol. 8, Armatura Press, UK, 1997, pp.137-150; A. García y Bellido, Arte Ibérico, *Historia de España. España Prerromana* I.3, Madrid, 1954, 422-428. Arribas, Antonio, op. cit., p. 82 (in Arribas book the useage of the word 'falchion to describe the Iberian straight sword known as an espada is incorrect. The falchion was not invented until the 11th century AD.)

[727] Martinez, Rafael T.,op. cit., p.38

[728] Miguel Sanchez de Baêna and Paulo Alexandre Louçao, op. cit., p. 67

[729] Being that the Romans were pragmatic people they had taken Greek technology as their own. The Roman legionnaires at the time were equipped with a sword identically used by the Greek infantry. The Greek sword of that time, mainly used

of the double-edged gladius would then step inside the swing of the longer weapon and use their short sword to slash side to side and pierce their opponent at close range with staggeringly brutal efficiency and force.[730] The transformation of the Celtic model into an Iberian version made the sword effective and fatal.

References to this Iberian sword, known to the Romans as the ***gladius hispaniensis***, are abundant within classical texts. During Rome's Iberian campaign, the Roman's experienced firsthand the effectiveness of the ***gladius hispaniensis***.[731] In the beginning of Roman presence on the Peninsula during the Second Punic War, Roman legions came into contact with Iberian mercenaries, impressed with the technical and operational level of their swords; they quickly adopted and began using Iberian swords.[732]

Being very pragmatic people, the Romans never hesitated to adopt for their own benefit the technology and practices of other cultures that they brought within the Empire. The adaptation of the short sword was one such example that the Romans took from Hispania. But there has been some controversy over this subject. Several scholars believe that the Romans did not get their idea for their famous short sword from the Iberians but from the Greek *xiphos* sword.[733]

---

by the cavalry was longer and heavier and its technology was Bronze Age design. Miguel Sanchez de Baêna and Paulo Alexandre Louçao, op. cit., p. 67

[730] For more information on this sword see, Quesada, F., El Armamento Ibérico. I-II. Madrid, 1996; Viana, Abel, "Uma espada de antennas, Portucale vol. II, Porto, 1924; Aguilo, Cabre, "La espad de antennas tipo Alcácer do Sal y su evolución en la necropolis de la Osera, Chamartin de la Sierra", Homenagem a Martins Sarmento, Guimarães, 1933, p.85

[731] This episode dealt with the falcata in which the Romans also considered it as a gladius hispaniensis Seneca, De Beneficiis, V.24; Polybius, Histories, 3.144.3-4

[732] Miguel Sanchez de Baêna and Paulo Alexandre Louçao, op. cit., p. 64; Ethridge, Charles E., Reinventing the Sword: A Cultural Comparison of the Development of the Sword in Response to the Advent of Firearms in Spain and Japan, Louisana State University, 1999, p.10-11

[733] The **xiphos** is a double-edged, single-hand sword used by the ancient Greeks. It was a secondary battlefield weapon for the Greek armies after the spear or javelin. The blade was around 65 cm long. The xiphos was good for both cutting

It has also been the general thought that the later *Mainz* type swords were similar to the Iberian *gladius*, but to some scholar this is not the case, while to others, the Iberian *gladius* is the mother sword of all other Roman sword designs.[734] But in my opinion and others it seems that these early blades follow the same Celtic pattern, with the difference being in a longer and narrower blade. I believe that in time the *gladius* changed to a blade that was thicker and shorter, which can be seen in the later *gladii* that are now known as the *Mainz, Fulham* and *Pompei* types.[735] But as mentioned before, there are many reference within the

---

and stabbing attacks due to its leaf-shaped blade. It was generally used only when the spear was discarded. The straight, double-edged design of the xiphos lends it the same overall martial versatility found in the swords used by infantry until the firearm supplanted the sword on the battlefield. Its design lent itself to cutting and thrusting. Sandars, Horace, "*The weapons of the Iberians*", Archeologia #25, Oxford, 1913, p.58-62 Sekunda, Nick, *The Ancient Greeks*, Elite Series #7, Osprey Publishing, Oxford, 1986; *The Spartan Army,* Elite Series #66, Osprey Publishing, Oxford, 1998; *Greek Hoplite 480-323 BC,* Warrior Series #27, Osprey Publishing, Oxford, 2000; *Greek swords and swordsmanship,* Osprey Publishing Online, 2004 http://www.ospreypublishing.com/content2.php/cid=217

[734] There is much debate over the origin of the Roman gladius and there are quite a few theories (in which a book could be written about it) but in the end they are seen to end up complementing the Spanish sword. The Mainz pattern is thought to have developed from the leaf-bladed short swords used on the Celt-Iberian peninsula (what is now Spain) and adopted for use in the Republican Legions. Rather than fighting as individual warriors (like their competition, the Continental Celts) the Roman legions eventually developed a new way of fighting -- massing together with overlapping shields, using their short stabbing'cutting swords to strike from behind this shield wall. As these battle tactics for the Legions changed, a shorter, broader stabbing/cutting sword had to be developed to use in combination with these newer types of shield and new styles of fighting. The Mainz pattern is deeply waisted and has a long point section like the earlier gladius Hispaniensis, but is shorter and broader than its predecessor. Unlike the later Pompeii style, the Mainz pattern was still capable of delivering strong cutting blows, though its primary purpose was for thrusting. There are many articles and even several books written on the subject.

[735] **Mainz** was founded as the Roman permanent camp of Moguntiacum probably in 13 BC. This large camp provided a population base for the growing city around it. Sword manufacture probably began in the camp and was continued in the city; for example, Gaius Gentilius Victor, a veteran of Legio XXII, used his discharge bonus on retirement to set up a business as a **negotiator gladiarius**, a

classical texts that mention the "Spanish sword" and not the Greek sword.[736] But a majority of scholars believe that the *gladius hispaniensis* derived from an early Iberian sword commonly known as atrophied-hilted antennae sword. If we look closely at this weapon, we quickly realize that there are two separate types:[737]

---

manufacturer and dealer of arms. Swords made at Mainz were sold extensively to the north. They are characterized by a slight waist running the length of the blade and a long point. Blade width 7-8 cm. Blade length 66 cm - 70 cm. Sword mass: 1.2 kg - 1.6 kg. **Fulham** or **Mainz-Fulham** sword was given the name to the type that was dredged from the Thames near Fulham and must therefore date to a time after the Roman occupation of Britain began. That would have been after the invasion of Aulus Plautius in 43 AD. It was used until the end of the same century. It is considered the conjunction point between *Mainz* and *Pompei*. Some consider it an evolution or the same as the *Mainz* type. Blade length 70 cm blade width: 6 cm at the base, 4 cm in the middle, 7 cm in the end. **Pompei** (or **Pompeianus** or **Pompeii**): Named by moderns after the Roman town of Pompeii, which was destroyed by volcanic eruption, 79 AD, with great loss of life, despite efforts of the Roman navy to get them out. Four instances of the sword type were found there, with others turning up elsewhere. The sword has parallel cutting edges and a triangular tip. Blade length of 60 cm, blade length from circa 75 A.D. of 68 cm - 71 cm. From circa 100 A.D. of 83 cm (semi-spatha). From now on the Roman Gladius will be of middle-length. Verboven, Koenraad S., Good for Business: The Roman Army and the Emergence of a Business Class in the Northwestern Provinces in the 1st Century BC - 3 AD, in Lukas, De Blois & Elio, Lo Cascio, *The Impact of the Roman Army (200 BC - AD 476). Economic, Social, Political, Religious and Cultural Aspects*, Leiden & Boston: Brill, 2007, pp. pages 295-314; Lang, Janet, Study of the Metallography of Some Roman Swords, Britannia # 19, 1988, 199-216; Burton, Sir Richard F., "The Sword amongst the Babarians (Early Roman Empire), Book of the Sword, Chapter 13, Kessinger Publishing, Whitefish, MT, 2006, p. 265-266. these are just sample of the many book on the subject.

736 Polybius 2.30.8; 3.144.3-4; 6.23.6; 6.25.8-11; Gellus, 9.13.14; Livy, 22.46.5; 31.34; Aguilera y Gamboa, E., Las necrópolis ibéricas. Madrid, 1916, p. 13, 29; Walbank, F.W., A Historical commentary on Polybius, Oxford, 1957-79.

737 Miguel Sanchez de Baêna and Paulo Alexandre Louçao, op. cit., p. 67; Fernando Quesada Sanz; E. Kavanagh de Prado "Roman Republican weapons, camps and battlefields in Spain: an overview of recent and ongoing research" In A. Morillo, J. Aurrecoechea (Eds.) The Roman Army in Hispania. University of LEon, 2006, pp. 65-84

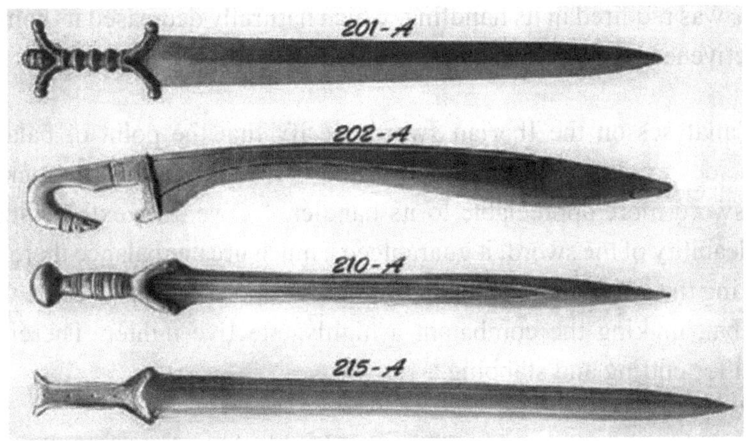

Type I – Antenna swords that originated from Central European models during the La Tene period I and II.

Type II – Atrophied-hilted antennae sword from the Iberian Peninsula

Aside of all the controversy and speculation about what sword the Romans adopted, the fact of the matter is that the design of the Iberian sword at that time was considered ideal for the people the Romans referred to as barbarians.

Prior to the *gladius hispaniensis*, the Romans used the Greek design, a sword that had been unaltered since the Bronze Age. During the epoch of the Greek sword, it was designed to stab and gorge an opponent with its thick and heavy blade. As a weapon made for stabbing rather than slicing or cutting, the point of balance and center of percussion was not important in the manufacturing of Greek swords, so it was naturally an unbalanced weapon.[738] As an unbalanced weapon, much

[738] As for the Iberian swords, it had two neuralgic points: point of balance (POB) and center of percussion (COP). The point of balance on a sword is simply the sword's center of gravity. This can easily be found by balancing the sword, lengthwise, upon one's hand making the blade balanced for there is an equal mass on each side. The **point of balance** will vary widely from type to type. An early medieval sword will not balance the same as an 18th century sword. Statements to the effect of "my sword has to have a POB four inches from the guard" will often be heard, but if the aforementioned medieval sword has a POB of two inches below

force was required in its handling, which naturally decreased its combat effectiveness and tired soldiers quickly.

But analyses on the Iberian swords verify that the point of balance coincides exactly with the union of the blade and the handle making the sword more appreciable to its handler.[739] Given the extraordinary malleability of the sword, it guaranteed a much greater balance therefore making the sword more efficient. Being a weapon that was used in close combat, making the combatant a highly effective fighter. Therefore, ideal for cutting and stabbing.

To make such amazing swords, Lusitanian blacksmiths were extremely skillful and zealously hid their specifications which were transmitted in great secrecy from generation to generation. Therefore, the degree of perfection in the manufacturing of weapons throughout the peninsula was enormous. Diodorus reports that preparing the sword for manufacturing,

---

the guard, it probably was not an efficient performer regardless of how "alive" it felt to the owner. In terms of comparing a early Roman/Greek sword to a Iberian sword, the Greek sword's point of balance is located 1/3 below the blade's handle, which in real terms turned the weapon into an unbalanced sword. A sword's point of balance is only one small piece of the complex puzzle that makes up a sword. The next part of the blade's success was the center of percussion. The **center of percussion**, or sweet spot, of a sword is the point on the blade where cutting is most effective. It is also the division between the *weak* and *middle* sections of the blade. Like any solid object, a sword vibrates when impacted (such as during cutting). In a sword, such vibrational waves are typically almost imperceptible. Every wave expressed by a solid object has rotational nodes where the wave reverses at either end of the object. On a properly-balanced sword, one node is in the tang of the sword (inside the hilt), ideally directly under the primary hand. On such a "harmonically balanced" sword, this means that a solid blow can be delivered without causing discomfort in the hands, therefore, ensures greater target penetration. The center of percussion of a sword is related to its center of balance, and both can be moved by employing a heavier pommel or changing the mass distribution of the blade. The more regressive or greater the zone of COP is the better the quality of the blade. Miguel Sanchez de Baêna and Paulo Alexandre Louçao, op. cit., p. 66; Turner, George Sword Motions and Impacts An Investigation and Analysis, *The Association for Renaissance Martial Arts*, 2001, http://www.thearma.org/spotlight/GTA/motions_and_impacts.htm

739 Miguel Sanchez de Baêna and Paulo Alexandre Louçao, op. cit., p. 66

the Iberians practice a peculiar method before fashioning their swords.[740] Uncertain of the quality of the steel, the Iberians had a habit of burying their iron because soft iron rusts more quickly than steel.[741] Left in the ground over a period of time, the rust would have eaten the weak iron and what was left was forged into excellent swords. The weapons that were fashioned were so magnificent that Polybius writes that these swords were considered good for both cutting and thrusting and would cut through anything which got in its way.[742]

The sword was manufactured by a process called pattern welding,[743] a process that was popular and widely used until the 8th century AD. The blade was composed of three parts: two tempered and highly resistant lateral metal strips and one metal strip that was the central nucleus of the blade. It was done by a process of composing several thin strips of steel that was less tempered to guarantee flexibility to the blade. When these three metal plates were put into the hearth, it was kept there until the outside of the metal had a slight glow. The reason for this was while the outside of the blade was hot, the central nucleus remained "soft" to preserve the sword's flexibility upon completion. When the sword blade was taken out of the hearth, it was slightly cooled down and hammered on both sides while continuing to cool off. This process would be repeated two to three times.

The sword was then polished by a wooden wheel with fat pig and fine sand and immediately afterwards with talcum powder, leaving the sword brilliant as a mirror. To demonstrate the quality of the product

---

740 Diodorous 5.33.3-4

741 Davies, Oliver, Roman Mines in Europe, Oxford, 1935, p. 59

742 Polybius, Histories, 3.144.3-4

743 **Pattern welding** is the practice in sword and knife making of forming a blade of several metal pieces of differing composition that are forge-welded together and twisted and manipulated to form a pattern. Blades forged in this manner often display bands of slightly different coloration along their entire length. These bands can be brought out for cosmetic purposes by proper polishing or acid etching. Originally, pattern welding was used to combine steels of different carbon contents, providing the desired mix of hardness and toughness needed for highly demanding tasks such as cutting through armor.

and the purity of the steel, Philon tells us that the sword-maker would pick up the sword horizontally over his head and with one hand on the sword hilt and the other at the tip of blade, he would bend the sword. The sword bowed with both ends of the sword touching his shoulders. He would then let go of the sword blade and if it straightened itself out without any distortion on the blade it was ready for use.[744]

It was from this technical superiority of this Celt-Iberian weapon that the Romans after the Second Punic War abandoned their old sword modeled on Greek design and adopted the Iberian sword. But though the Romans adopted the Iberian sword, they only took the design but not the manufacturing technology and techniques of the sword's secrets. Without a doubt Lusitanians swords were technically much better constructed and much more balanced, therefore making them more effective than any sword that was around that time.

With the type of sword that was created for the Lusitanian warrior's way of life and later to fight a lightning war against Rome, a special scabbard was developed to deal with how the sword was transported. The *gladius* was placed inside a leather sleeve that was reinforced with two metal bars on each side attached to three to four rings. At the end of the scabbard the two metal bars were welded together forming a stud. As for the metal rings, the front rings protruded outward forming a bulge in the center of the scabbard to be used to place a small knife and spear heads. When traveling throughout the countryside, the scabbard was suspended on a leather belt on the right or left side of the waist, while others might have carried the sword by a leather strap suspended from either shoulder.

Falcata

The third Iberian sword which has not been mentioned yet was the famed curved saber or *falcata*. The *falcata* was the most emblematic and effective weapon in the Lusitanian arsenal that brought terror to

[744] Philo, *mechaniké syntaxis*, IV-V

the toughest Roman legionnaire.[745] This weapon without a doubt was the favored weapon of choice among all Iberian warriors over several centuries. This can be said due to the large amounts of these swords found on excavation sites throughout Spain and Portugal.

Its origin is unknown, but there are three schools of thought on the subject. The first is based on the theory that the sword evolved from the curved "Halstatt" knife of Central Europe, which had spread to Italy, Greece and later Spain.[746] The second, claims that the *falcata* was a direct copy from the Greek *Makhaira* or *Kopis* sword that were introduced by Greek merchants or by Iberian mercenaries recruited by the Greeks around the fifth or sixth century BC.[747] There is also a third theory, which holds that the *falcata* was of an indigenous creation, but many historians give little credence to this idea for Greek influence was rampart throughout the Mediterranean.[748]

The term f*alcata* is not ancient. The Romans had a habit calling all Iberian swords, *gladius hispaniensis* except the *falcata* which they

---

[745] Diodorus reports that the falcatas were of superior quality that no helmet, shield or bone could resist its devastating effect. Seneca, De Beneficiis, V.24, Seneca regard an episode which demonstrates the terror that Roman legionnaires felt from falcata.

[746] Martinez, Rafael T., op. cit., p. 38; Allen, Stephen, Lords of Battle: The World of the Celtic Warrior, Osprey Publishing, Oxford, UK, 2007, p.117 Miguel Sanchez de Baêna and Paulo Alexandre Louçao, op. cit., p. 69

[747] Quesada Sanz, F., "*Gladius hispaniensis: an archaeological view from Iberia*", Journal of Roman Military Equipment Studies, vol. 8, Armatura Press, UK, 1997, p. 251-270; "Máchaira, kopís, falcata", *Homenaje a Francisco Torrent*, Madrid, 1994, pp. 75-94; "En torno al origen y procedencia de la falcata ibérica", Archivo Español de Arqueología #63, 1990, pp. 63-95; El armamento ibérico. Estudio tipológico, geográfico, funcional, social y simbólico de las armas en la Cultura Ibérica (siglos VI-I a.C.), 2 vols., Monographies Instrumentum, 3rd ed., Monique Mergoil, Montagnac, 1997; Miguel Sanchez de Baêna and Paulo Alexandre Louçao, op. cit., p. 69 The oldest examples were found in Villaricos dating from the V or IV century BC, it probably copies of the Greek models.

[748] Martinez, Rafael T., op. cit., p. 38; Miguel Sanchez de Baêna and Paulo Alexandre Louçao, op. cit., p. 69

named it, *machaera hispaniensis*.[749] Unfortunately, we do not know what the Lusitanians called it. But the name *falcata* seems to have been coined by Fernando Fulgosio in 1872, on the model of the Latin expression *ensis falcatus* "sickle-shaped sword".[750] He presumably went with *falcata* rather than *falcatus* because the Spanish word for sword, *espada* is feminine. Although there are other presumable theories, this one seems to be the most popular and logical following grammatical rules of the language. The name caught on very quickly and is now firmly entrenched in scholarly literature.

The *falcata* has a peculiar shape for it is a one edged blade that pitches forward towards the pointed end of the blade with the sword edge being concave on the lower part of the sword, but convex on top.[751] The sword's design characteristic is an unnatural large curved blade of which its point of balance was near the tip of the blade, making the weapon basically unbalanced and therefore delivering a very lethal blow because its weight is near the tip of the blade.[752] The *falcata's* blade shape distributed the weight in such a way that it was capable of delivering a blow with the momentum of an axe, while maintaining the cutting edge of a sword. So, while the Roman legionnaires used the *gladius* to stab, the *falcata* was used to stab, slice and cut. The Lusitanians being a warlike tribe constantly fought in agglomerated formations; therefore, a short weapon brought enormous advantages

---

[749] Seneca, De Beneficiis, V.24

[750] Fulgosio, Fernando, "Armas y utensilios del hombre primitivo en el Museo Arqueológico Nacional", José Dorregaray (ed.), Museo Español de Antigüedades, Madrid, 1872, Vol. I, pp. 75-89.

[751] Many falcata have been found in Portugal and in Spain which have been Low into two groups based on the blade size:

A – Long bladed falcatas

B – Short bladed falcatas

From these two groups they have been placed into three subgroups bases on their hilts:

I – Falcatas with a hilt ending with a head of a bird

II - Falcatas with a hilt ending with head of a horse

III - Falcatas with a hilt ending with head of a wolf

[752] Miguel Sanchez de Baêna and Paulo Alexandre Louçao, op. cit., p. 69

in malleability and effectiveness. So, the length of the sword was very important. The usual length of the Iberian *falcata* was 60 to 70 cm, (23 to 27 inches) but the length of Luistanian *falcata* was much smaller from 40 to 50 cm long (15 to 20 inches) and although it was a single-edged weapon, double-edged *falcatas* have been found.

Though mostly used for combat, the section of the sword that was adorned was the hilt. The handle of the hilt was usually ornamented with a frieze of plaited and interlaced scrolls inlaid with granules of animal heads and or in the shape of an animal body. The end of the hilt usually ended with a head of an animal such as a horse, wolf, bird or feline, and sometimes they were inlaid with precious stones for eyes. Besides using these swords in combat, they had ritual swords that were highly decorated.[753]

On seeing many statues of armed warriors; the *falcata* was encased in the same type of metal frame leather scabbard that the Iberian *gladius* used, mention in the pervious section. The manner in which these men carried their weapon was that the *falcata* was hung from a leather strap from the shoulder across the body to the opposite hip in which the strap was attached by metal rings on the scabbard or stung across either shoulder by a leather strap across the back. What is known for certain is that the *falcata* was manufacture to perfection and used throughout the Iberian Peninsula according to the classical texts.[754] Like the samurai of Japan, the Lusitanian warriors maintained a spiritual connection to their swords that when he died his sword would be buried with him.

---

[753] Sopeña, G., Dioes, ética y ritos, Zaragoza, p. 94; Quesada, F., Arma y símbolo: la Falcata Ibérica, Alicante, 1992, p. 38

[754] Filon, *Mechaniké syntaxis*, IV-V, Siudas, s.v. machaira, Diodorus, 5.33.3-4; José M. Blázquez Martínez – M. Paz García-Gelabert, "Estudio del armamento prerromano en la Península Ibérica a través de las fuentes y de las representaciones plásticas" *Hispania Antiqua* 14, 1990, 91-115; Garcia-Gelabert, M.P., "Estudio del armamento prerromano en la península ibérica a través de los textos clásicos", *Espacio, Tiempo y Forma Serie II. Historia Antigua,* 2, 1989, pp. 69-80; Martinez, Rafael T., op. cit., p. 38-39

Shields

The Lusitanians were master swordsmen, using a fast-moving style that required light equipment and quick handling weapons. With this in mind, one wonders what type of shields they used to protect themselves. The Lusitanians used two types of shields: the *caetra*, a small circular shield used by *caetrati* or light infantry and the *scutum*, modeled after the long shield of Celtic origin used by *scutati* or heavy infantry.[755] The *scutum*, despite its popularity in the south and central Hispania, was never much appreciated among the Lusitanians because it impeded the warrior's sword fighting movements and mobility.

Of both shields used by the Lusitanians, it seems, according to many statues and vase drawings, that the *caetra* was the preferred shield. Known as the buckler, this 30 - 60cm diameter (1ft -2ft) light round shield was constructed from wood sections attached together by two metal bars made out of as bronze, copper or iron, covered with leather. Although the buckler was commonly rounded, it took on many shapes and sizes. The size of these pieces varied from two feet (60 cm) across to perhaps a foot (30cm) in diameter. All shields had metal fittings and ornaments on the face with an iron boss in the middle which was added on to deflect sword blows as well as arrows and spears.

In combat, the shield was not only effective at blocking, but as a secondary weapon; Iberians used the boss to punch opponents. When on the move, these compact bucklers could be hung on a belt or across the back by a strap, not to be burdensome to the soldier on the march or forging for food, but still handy for when the enemy was close.[756] It was such a convenient and handy piece of equipment that it survived into the Renaissance.

---

[755] The Caetrati, light infantry and the scutati or heavy infantry* were Iberian soldiers who had been formed into these perspective unit serving under Hannibal during the 2nd Punic War.

[756] Melinda, Jose, Arquelogia Española, Madrid, 1942, p. 244; Arribas, Antonio, op. cit., pp. 78-80; Martinez, Rafael, op. cit., p. 36

The other shield, the *scutum,* though used, it was not as popular. This shield was the classical long flat shield of Celtic origin, not the Roman curved version. As with the Roman and Celtic examples, the Iberian *scutum* had a large spindle – shaped boss that could be used to punch opponents during combat. During marches, it would be hung over one's back like a backpack.

As for the cavalrymen, they would usually carry the small lightweight buckler so as to not over-encumber their mounts or limit the rider's horsemanship.[757]

Lances

Ancient Iberian warriors were heavy users of javelins. In ancient Iberia, the spear was used by all Iberians and was described by many different terms; perhaps indicating that there was a wide variety of different models. In combat, they casted this ranged weapon by volleys in order to disorganize the enemy formation before advancing into close combat with swords. The spear, which was used with deadly accuracy, was part of their armament. From modern archaeological research within the confines of the Iberian Peninsula, there seems to have been an assortment of spears which have been classified into three groups: traditional and conventional spears of wooden shafts and metal heads, the all-iron type called *soliferrum* by the Romans and lances.

Regarding the traditional spear, this first group has been divided into three subgroups according to the length of the blade: First are blades with a length of 30 cm (11inches) or more. The number of large blades that existed are considered to have been used by heavy combat infantry. The second type of blades with approximately 20 cm to 30 cm (7 to 11 inches). This suggests that they were popular and used on an everyday basis from hunting to combat. Livy called this type of Iberian spear, *phalarica.* The third type of blades measured at a length of 20 cm (7 inches) or less. This type of blade was used by the cavalry. The horsemen rode with the blade at their waists or attached to their sword

[757] Melinda, Jose, op. cit., p. 244

sheath which would not impede their movements. Near to the battlefield, the horsemen would cut a straight stem from a tree branch and put on the blade. If it was not used it was returned to its original place.

The conventional spear or javelin according to vase painting seemed to have been the weapon of choice, due to its light weight. Every individual warrior carried a bundle of javelins into battle to throw before the enemy charged their formation and at times the spears were used in hand-to-hand combat.[758] From archaeological excavations, spears heads ranged in sizes from 20 cm (7 in) to 60 cm (23 in) have been found in abundance. Longer spear heads suggest that they were used to penetrate through armor, while the shorter spear heads were probably thrown from horseback and at close range. Of all the conventional spears and javelins that the Iberians used, the *falarica* was the most dreaded. In some texts, the *falarica* is indicated as a Roman weapon, although its origin seems to be Iberian, for Livy makes a reference to it when he mentions that the *falarica* was used by the Iberians against the Carthaginians near Saguntum.[759]

The *Falarica* was a javelin with a long iron pointed rod of about 35 inches (90 cm) in length with a short wooden handle. Though the iron spearhead was a thin rod, a section of it was thick, giving the weapon weight to further improve its ability to penetrate, making the *falarica* an armor-piercing weapon. On several vase paintings, they show the use of javelin thongs, wound round the shaft to impart a stabilizing spin and an additional thrust when it was thrown.[760] This weapon was so feared that when it stuck into a shield without entering the body, it terrified the enemy.[761] Along with being a throwing spear, it was also used as a ranged incendiary device by either igniting bundles of grass or binding packs filled with a combustible substance.[762] As an incendiary device, it

758 Strabo, 10.1.12

759 Livy, 21.8

760 Martinez, Rafael T., op. cit., p.37

761 Livy, 21.8

762 Livy, 21.8; Wise, Terence, Armies of the Carthaginian Wars 265-146 BC, Osprey Publishing, Oxford, 1982, 21

was used during sieges by being thrown against wooden palisades and thatched roofs in order to start fires and cause havoc. When the Iberians were besieged, they hurled flaming *falaricas* at the besiegers' siege engines. As an incendiary device, it had an enormous psychological effect on the enemy, helping to spread fear amongst enemy troops.

The *Soliferrum,* as it was called by the Romans, was an Iberian ranged pole weapon made entirely of iron. It was forged from a single piece of iron, usually measuring between 1.5 to 2 meters in length and around one centimeter in diameter. Though slim, the central part or the *soliferrum* was usually thickened to facilitate a hand grip for the weapon. Sometimes there were moldings of about 10 centimeters wide in the middle of the weapon to further improve the grip and to prevent the weapon from slipping when hands became sweaty. The *soliferrum* was an extremely effective heavy javelin. The weight and the density of the weapon's iron shaft, its small diameter and its narrow tip granted the *soliferrum* to be an excellent armor-piercing weapon when it was thrown at close range, enabling it the ability of further penetrating heavy shields and armor. Unlike the *falarica*, the *soliferrum* remained in use in the Iberian Peninsula under Roman rule until the end of the 3rd century AD.

Another weapon that was used was the pike. Unlike spears, the pike was a long two-handed thrusting spear used extensively by the infantry as a counter-measure against cavalry assaults. The pike was extremely long, usually 10 to 14 feet (3 to 4 meters) long. It had a wooden shaft with a sharp fire hardened wooden tip. The shaft near the head of the pike was often reinforced with a wooden crosspiece to stop the horse from continuing to run itself through. This sort of pike can still be seen among the cattlemen of Andalusia, who use it to control their herd of cattle. The extreme length of such weapons required a strong piece of wood such as well-seasoned ash, which was tapered towards the point to prevent the pike from sagging at the ends. The pike's length allowed a great concentration of sharpened ends to be presented to the enemy, with their wielders at a greater distance when combating cavalry.

The collection at the Archaeological Museum of Zaragoza, there is another type of throwing weapon which is rarely found, known as a *tragula.* The tip of this barbed spear came in several different forms. Usually it had a sharpened tip with two or more small protruding spikes. This hybrid spear was something of a dart or arrow which was thrown from a long leather thong by which it was then recovered if possible.[763] As for the dart, it was a dangerous weapon in the hands of its user and deadly to its victim for the barbed dart required to be surgically removed. Some minted Roman-Iberian coins bore on the reverse side of the coin a military motif of a rider armed with a *tragula.*

Side Arms

While the sword and the spear were primary weapons, many warriors carried daggers and knives. The *gladius* was not the only weapon the Roman legionnaires used that came from Iberia. The *pugio*, a light dagger worn by Roman troops was of Iberian origin. Measuring roughly between 12 and 17 inches long (31 – 45 cm), the *pugio* was made of iron and had a sharp double-edged triangular blade. At the hilt, the blade was between two (7 cm) to 5 inches (15 cm) wide. From statues, we can see that Iberian warriors wore the *pugio* on the opposite side of the *falcata* or *espada.* In combat, it was used as a back-up weapon. A small utility knife was also used as a last-ditch weapon, a small *falcata*-style knife, a smaller version of the sword. Roughly 8 (20 cm) to 10 (25 cm) inches long, the knife had the same shaped blade as the *falcata* and was usually carried in a sheath attached to the *falcata* scabbard.

The sling was another long-ranged missile weapon to have been used on the Iberian Peninsula during Viriathus's time.[764] Many men were

[763] Martinez, Rafael T., op. cit., p.37

[764] Though the bow and arrow was used in the Peninsula arrows head finds are very rare. Due to archaeological evidence of hundreds of slingshot found thoughout the Peninsula and ancient literary description it seems that the sling was a common instrument like the sword and spear, but it was not widely used except by the masters of the sling, the Balearic warriors. The sling has had a long history on the Iberian Peninsula especially in Spain and during my research I had the opportunity to witness the shepherds of the province of Extremadura,

armed with a sling and a leather pouch of shots along with their sword and buckler. During peacetime, these men relied on its range and accuracy to keep predators such as wolves and lynxes from threatening their valuable flock. Despite using rounded rocks found in their day-to-day life, they used homemade lead shot for better performance. So ubiquitous was the sling that its ammunition remains today one of the most numerous finds at archeological sites.

The Lusitanians manufactured their slings in accordance with the height and length of their arms.[765] The best slings were generally made from the stems of the Black sedge (*Shoenus nigrican*) which was intertwined with tendons from a bull's or a horse's neck along with hair from a horse's tail.[766] Each warrior carried three slings of different lengths that were used for various distances. It has been proposed that the way these men carried the slings was that they tied the short size sling around their forehead, while the other two around the waist.[767] The idea for the length of the slings comes from the types of projectiles that have been found on excavation sites. The projectiles were small-scale, but because of the various sizes of the projectiles that were made of lead or hardened clay dictated the type of sling was made. For the heavier projectiles, smooth stones slightly larger than the lead or clay projectiles were chosen. As for the lead and clay projectiles, they are oval and approximately 5cm in length. From some archaeological excavations within the *castros* (fortified Iberian villages), it appears that these projectiles were molded in large quantities in groups of six to eight on soap stone molds.[768]

Spain use their skill. For information on ancient slingers of the Iberian Peninsula see Strabo, 3.4.15; 3.5.1; Publius Flavius Vegetius Renatus, De Re Militari, 1.16; Coronel Córdoba, José M.G., Historia del Ejercito Español: Los orígenes, Vol.1, Servicio Histórico Militar, Madrid, 1981; Cleugh, Eric, Viva Mallorca: Yesterday and Today in the Balearic Islands, Cassell, 1963; Wise, Terence, Armies of the Carthaginian Wars 265-146 BC, Osprey Publishing, Oxford, 1982, 21; Miguel Sanchez de Baêna and Paulo Alexandre Louçao, "Grandes Enigmas da História de Portugal, Vol. I, Esquilo, Lisboa, 2008, p. 72

765 Miguel Sanchez de Baêna and Paulo Alexandre Louçao, op. cit., p. 72

766 Ibid., 73

767 Ibid., 72

768 Ibid.72

Finally, there is one last weapon in their arsenal--poison. Strabo mentions that it was common for Iberian people to carry a small receptacle containing a quick-acting poison, which they did not hesitate to take, rather than being captured and sold into slavery.[769] The poison was extracted from the root of the *Ranunculus sceleratus or Ranunculus sardonia.* This poison produced a contraction of the lower jaw, giving the victim the appearance of a sinister 'sardonic' smile. This was terrifying to the Roman legionnaires, who thought that the dead man was defying them beyond the grave.[770]

Armor

Lusitanian body protection was basically similar to that of other tribes in the Peninsula but slightly different design characteristics in the way they used fabric, leather, natural material, and metal in making their armor.

The tunics and thick cloaks gave a degree of protection, which we assume were made of coarse wool or linen and dyed in earth tones allowing them to blend into their environment. Over their tunics, Lusitanian warriors wore body armor that was made from an assortment of materials from the light quilted linen-leather armor to iron breastplates. Though they wore an assortment of armor, they usually wore light armor made of leather combined with a small bronze breastplate.[771] Their light armor

[769] Strabo, 3.4.18; Martinez, Rafael, op. cit., p.8. Apparently one of the wild members of the parsley family (Apiaceae), *i.e.* fool's parsley (*Aethusa cynapsium*), poison hemlock (*Conium maculatum*), or water hemlock (*Cicuta maculata*); more likely, poison hemlock. But perhaps the herb should be identified with that deadly Sardinian herb which Pausanias (10.17) says is "like parsley," namely, celery-leaved, or marsh, crowfoot, Celery-leaved Buttercup (*Ranunculus sceleratus*; see Dioscorides, *de Mat. Med.* 2.206), and called by the Greeks "wild parsley." This Sardinian herb produced a convulsive laughter, with a drawing down of the angles of the mouth (Solinus, *Sertorius* 4.4), and ended fatally, with the proverbial "Sardonic smile" (Pausanias, *l.c.*) on the victim's face.

[770] Martinez, Rafael T., op. cit., p.8; Miguel Sanchez de Baêna and Paulo Alexandre Louçao, op. cit. p. 74

[771] This idea is based on the numerous Iberian statues of warriors that have been found throughout the Iberian Peninsula.

was made of a composite of leather and "esparto" fibers connected to metal chain links add on to absorb cutting blows. After leather tanning and drying process was complete, this light armor was sewn together and then soaked in a vinegar and salt solution to stiffen it. It was then reinforced with tightly wound padding made out of flax or esparto. Once the leather had hardened it was coated with lard or sheep tallow for waterproofing.

The second type of armor that can be seen on Iberian statues was made out of metal, which usually came in two styles: small metallic plates and chain mail. The Lusitanians inherited the Celtic technique in manufacture knitted or crocheted iron (i.e. chain mail). The chain mail shirt consisted of about five and twenty thousand metal links, all riveted and tempered by hand, which could entail approximately one year to be made.[772] The battle effectiveness of chain mail in deflecting sword blows was so amazing that many warriors made their own chain mail shirt or tunic because it was much cheaper than making armor out of metal plates and it did not require an expert blacksmith to manufacture them. Renowned for its lightness and resistance to sword blows the Romans quickly adopted Lusitanian armor into a Roman Legionnaire's protective gear lasting until the end of the 2nd century AD.[773]

As for the scaled armored seen on Iberian sculptures, it was made of small iron plates cut into 5 cm in length and 1 mm thick.[774] The scales were generally set in layered tiles and attached to a tanned leather vest that was cooked in animal intestines.[775] These metal-plated vests were fixed to the combatant's upper body via leather straps that hung from the shoulders and tied from the back.

A third type was simple metal breastplates. There breastplates varied in different shapes and sizes from round to square, and sometimes they were elaborately decorated with raised images. Generally, the *pectorales*

---

772 Miguel Sanchez de Baêna and Paulo Alexandre Louçao, op. cit., p. 58

773 Ibid., p. 58

774 Ibid

775 Ibid., 59

(chest piece) were worn using a set of three straps, one going over each shoulder and another around the man's torso. Roman *pectorale* were also used by Iberian/Lusitanian warriors, who had plundered them off Roman corpses.

The Lusitanian did not use just one type of armored but mixed armor, especially among the horsemen. The make up of the suit of armor was made of small-scaled metal plated leather that protected the chest area while the bottom part was chain mail links. The reason for this design has been suggested that it was created so as not to impede a horseman's mobility and agility.[776] This type of armor can be seen on Iberian vases found at Liria, Spain, which also corresponds to the type of armor Lusitanian horsemen might have worn.

With their upper body protected, some Lusitanians also protected their legs. They covered their legs by wearing thick wool leggings, but these were probably worn more for protection against the cold rather than from weapon blows.[777] But according to Strabo and from the few sculptures that have been discovered, it demonstrates that certain warriors actually wore metallic greaves for leg protection.[778]

The major preoccupation of a Lusitanian warrior besides protecting his body was shielding his head. We know that a majority of head gear was made of leather or of animal tendons, which unfortunately means none have survived due to the biodegradability of the material.[779] Their main headgear was a sinew hat that came in two different styles: the hoodie and skullcap. The hoodie was made out of leather or chainmail, which hung down to the soldier's shoulders protecting his head, neck and shoulders. The skullcap, on the other hand, was smaller and fitted around the man's crown, nape, and temples. Those that did not use

[776] Miguel Sanchez de Baêna and Paulo Alexandre Louçao, op. cit., p. 59

[777] Diodorus, 5.32.3

[778] Strabo, 3.3.6

[779] Miguel Sanchez de Baêna and Paulo Alexandre Louçao, op. cit., p. 59

helmets, let their hair fall free, and when on a military campaign wore a strip of leather or cloth around their head.[780]

As for the few metal helmets that have survived in the Iberian Peninsula, they seemed to have been used between the 4th century BC and 2nd century AD. Of all the helmets of that period found on Iberian Peninsula, they have been classified as *montefortino.* These helmets were mass produced and used during the First and Second Punic Wars, the Celtiberian Wars, the Lusitanian War and in the civil war between Caesar and Pompeii.

The '*montefortino*' helmets is believed to have originated in the Celtic occupied northern Italy and it soon became very common throughout the entire Western Mediterranean being that they were mass-produced and used by the Carthaginians and early Roman Republic.[781] The helmets were constructed by overlaying three 2-3 mm bronze plates at the edges and hammering down forming a fold, which was then heated up and tempered to make it stronger against sword blows.[782] This type of head

---

780 Strabo, 3.3.7

781 The **Montefortino Helmet** was a type of Roman helmet of the Roman republican era named after Montefortino. It was the first stage in the development of the galea (This helmet would become the trademark helmet of the Roman Army as seen in most Roman period movies), derived from Celtic helmet design. Similar types are to be found in Spain, Gallia, into northern Italy. Surviving examples are generally found without cheek pieces (either because they had none to begin with, or because they were only made a material which did not survive the test of time). Later Montefortino helmets are the first helmets proven to be of Roman origin, particularly through inscriptions found on them (mostly the names of the soldiers who owned them). Earlier helmets in the type are generally more decorated since, as the Roman army moved into the huge period of growth in the Marian reforms at the end of the 2nd century BC cheap, undecorated but effective helmets needed to be mass-produced for the mainly poor legionaries. Burns, Michael T., The Homogenization of Military Equipment Under the Roman Republic, Digressus, Internet Journal for the Classical World, *'Romanization'?* Digressus Supplement 1, 2003, 60-85; Miguel Sanchez de Baêna and Paulo Alexandre Louçao, op. cit., p. 59.

782 Sample of these helmets can be seen at the National Museum of Archaeology in Lisbon and at the Museu de Conimbriga (which is and entire preserved Roman

protection not only safeguarded the entire head, but the back of the neck and face for both sides of the helmets had face guards adding protection of the face against slashes. These anatomical articulated face plates were made of either metal or leather that would be clamped together under the support of the rear head guard, at the back of the helmet and by two ring on each side of the helmet in which the face plates were fastened to by hooks or rings on the helmet, then tied under the chin as a chin strap.

This conception for a helmet was so well thought out and so advanced that it has been presupposed that the Romans rapidly adopted this helmet into their army after the 2nd Punic War and maintained its design until the end of the Roman Empire. Unlike the Celt-Iberian and Roman models, the Lusitanian models only protected the cranial section of the head. Curiously, the Lusitanians seem to have not worn face guards (metal or leather) because it perhaps blocked their peripheral vision, or they just got in the way during combat. Finally, at the summit of the helmet, seats a button or mount of variable height with a hole in the middle, which soldier would place a mane of dyed horse hair of various colors on top of their helmet which was perhaps used to identify which tribe or military unit one belonged to or to signify the rank of the soldier such as a Roman centurion worn to state his status within the Roman military formation. Overall, the durability of the helmet proves that the technique and the care put into the manufacturing of these helmets was a sign of quality workmanship.

Campaign Life

According to the texts written about the Lusitanian War, the Roman campaign season took place during the spring and summer months, compared to the Lusitanians, who campaigned all-year round. During the spring and summer months, when the Romans were out of their forts either conducting training or military operations, the Lusitanian were hard at work carrying on their own military operation against the Romans, subjecting them to ambushes, raids and surprise attacks. When fall came around, the Romans usually began to wind down their

---

city); Miguel Sanchez de Baêna and Paulo Alexandre Louçao, op. cit., p. 61

campaign season and search for a place to establish a fort or secure a city or town for winter quarters. But the Lusitanians continued conducting military operations, but on a smaller scale such as harassing and raiding Roman convoys and Roman allied towns in search for provisions. By winter, the Lusitanians spend their time 'indoors' preparing for another campaign season, but at times they would attempt to sack a Roman friendly outpost or town.[783]

As for the warriors, campaign life was difficult and subject to various dangers. From the few ancient texts, we can see that the Lusitanians were constantly on the march and on the offensive, so it was necessary for Viriathus's army to survive off the land by hunting and foraging to constitute the ration of food, which they minimally ate and drank whenever possible. When these men camped at night, they slept on the ground wrapped in their wool sago.

Spoils of War

The most outstanding aspect of ancient Iberian warfare was the appropriation and distribution of spoils. Ancient warfare, just like modern warfare, was a complex mechanism that granted political prestige, social promotion and economic dividends to either a country or persons. During the Iberian wars, the great beneficiaries of this type of warfare were the warrior tribal chiefs. The territories they raided and at times conquered would bestow upon them fame and fortune followed by the control of goods and spoils once the victorious military leader emplace the tribal chief's authority.

Among the Lusitanians, it was different for instead of the tribal chief reaping the benefits, the entire tribe shared in the spoils of war and booty that was appropriated by robbing and raiding Rome's army and allies. Generally, the arrival of captured products and spoils to a community was distributed by the hierarchy from a central point. The tribal chiefs

---

[783] Dias, Jaime Lopes, Etnografia da Beira, vol.III, Centro de Tradições Populares Portuguesas da Universidade de Lisboa, Lisboa, 1929, p. 69; Octávio da Veiga Ferreira e Seomara Bastos da Veiga Ferreira, op. cit., p. 168-169.

would distribute the goods among family heads. Finally, the spoils were redistributed among the family members. This model, a modality adopted by the groups in power had their spoils distributed in the form of gifts in exchange for their support and services. This was a way to regulate social ties with other clans as well. But as in all societies, there were signs of inequality which is evident with some classical texts.[784]

Among tribal leaders, the sharing of spoils gave prestige to the tribal leader and his authority. But the way of gaining more support and obtaining more power was that these leaders not only had to win battles, but also had to maximize their booty so to offer his contingence larger gifts and offerings. E. Sanchez Morena defends his theory that a great part of Viriathus' alliances with other tribes was established not only by diplomatic negotiations, but with the exchange of gifts covered in political-religious ceremonies.[785]

On a personal level, mutual offering became an important instrument of creating social relations and personal bonds. These personal offerings were considered as a commitment among individuals and it was therefore a precious element of social bonding. The key in understanding this type of offering and gift giving created a personal *devotii,* making one man obligated to the other or each other.[786] An example of this is can be seen

---

[784] Sanchez Moreno, Eduardo, Algunas Notas Sobre la Guerra Como Estrategia de Interacción Social en la Hispania Preromana: Viriato, Jefe Redistributivo (Parte I) Habis #32, 2001, pp. 149-169 (Parte II) Habis #33, 2002, pp. 169-202; Munoz, Mauricio, op. cit., p. 74-77; Polanyi, Karl., "The economy ace instituted process", in Polanyi, K., Arensberg, C.M and Pearson, M.W., (Eds.), *Trade and Market in the Early Empires: Economies in History and Theory*, Chicago, 1957, p.250; Sahlins, M., *Stone Age Economies,* New York, 1972 (edition in Castilian: Madrid, 1977); Renfrew, C., "Trade ace action in distance", in Sabloff, J.A and Lamberg-Karlovsky, C.C., (Eds.), *Ancient Civilization and Trade*, Alburquerque, 1975, pp.8 and 11-12; Pryar, F.L., *The origins of the economy: to comparative study of distribution in primitive and peasant economies,* New York, 1977; Service, E.R., the *origins of the State and the civilization. The process of the cultural evolution,* Madrid, 1984 (2ª edition), pp.119-120.

[785] Sanchez Moreno, Eduardo, op. cit., pp. 149-169 (Parte II) Habis #33, 2002, pp. 169-202.

[786] Munoz, Mauricio, op. cit., p. 76-77

when the powerful Astolpas at Viriathus's wedding offers his guests exquisite delicacies, jewels and luxurious dresses.[787] Although the ancient sources say that Viriathus despised Astoplas for his greediness and wealth, Viriathus still recognized Astolpas' gift giving as a way to gain allies, in return for their *devotii* by his offerings and presents.[788]

Finally, there is the distribution of booty among the military. The spoils that were acquired were also used to gain the loyalty and support of the army. According to Diodorus, rewards were based on merit and loyalty. He goes on to state that Viriathus awarded men with special gifts for those that had distinguished themselves in battle, and because of this reward system along with his fair treatment, the Lusitanians followed him willingly.[789] Following the Celtic way of life and their influence upon Lusitanian society, rewarding warriors was done by giving them gifts and throwing a banquet or celebration to recognize their merit.[790] By rewarding his warriors the way he did, Portuguese and Spanish historians believe that Viriathus's actions was a deliberate attempt at destroying the social ranking that divided the aristocrats from the rest. By rewarding these simple men who possessed the true value of what men should be and not just being about someone born into privilege, he was establishing a social competitiveness among the newly established 'men of value and honor' against the old elite.

---

787 Diodorus, 33.7.1

788 Sanchez Moreno, Eduardo, op. cit., pp. 149-169 (Parte II) Habis #33, 2002, pp. 169-202.

789 Diodorus, 33.1.5

790 Tierney, J.J., "The Celtic Ethnography of Posidonius", *Proceedings of the Royal Irish Academy,* 60, C, Dublín, 1960, pp.189-275; Garcia Moreno, L.A., "Organización sociopolítica de los Celtas en la Península Ibérica", Almagro Gorbea, M. (Dir.), *Los Celtas: Hispania y Europa*, Madrid, 1993, pp.331-336; Quesada Sanz, F., "Vino, aristócratas, tumbas y guerreros en la cultura ibérica (ss.V-II a.C.)", *Verdolay*, 6, 1994, pp.99-124; *ID.*, "Vino y guerreros: banquete, valores aristocráticos y alcohol en Iberia", Celestino Pérez, S., (Ed.), *Arqueología del vino. Los orígenes del vino en Occidente,* Madrid, 1995 pp.273-296; Dominguez Monedero, A.J., "Del simposio griego a los bárbaros bebedores: el vino en Iberia y su imagen en los autores antiguos", Celestino Pérez, S., (Ed.), *Arqueología del vino. Los orígenes del vino en Occidente*, Madrid, 1995, pp.23-72.

The attitude of Viriathus in sharing the spoils of war between his people has not really been studied by historical investigation, even though it has been thoroughly referred to in classical texts that mention the division of spoils and offerings.[791] Thanks to the ancient writers from Posidonus through Diodorus, their Hellenistic and historiographic view of Viriathus as an equal and a generous man who was the prototype of "the good savage" that derived from the cynical and stoic doctrines of that time.[792] Because of this socio-economic mechanism of redistribution of goods and rewards in Lusitanian society, the classical sources portray this shepherd, thief and warrior as a proto-historic 'Robin Hood'.

---

[791] The only person who has actually studied the subject on Viriathus' policy of redistributing of wealth is Eduardo Sanchez Moreno in "Algunas Notas Sobre la Guerra Como Estrategia de Interacción Social en la Hispania Preromana: Viriato, Jefe Redistributivo"

[792] **Cynicism**: The end of life is virtue, not pleasure, and it can only be obtained by independence of all earthly possessions and pleasures.

Stoicism: Philosophy is primarily concerned with ethics. The end or purpose of life is *arete* (excellence) or virtue which is identified with "happiness." Being that the central theme is" indifference to external circumstances." Lens Tuero, J., "Viriato, héroe y rey cínico", *Estudios de Filología Griega*, 2, 1968, pp.253-272.

CHAPTER V

VIRIATHUS THE MAN

Though there is little information on the illustrious life of Viriathus, there are several classical authors that decided to touch on some aspects of this man's life due to his leadership skills and his actions that caused much terror for the soldiers of Rome, for at times he was referred to as the 'scourge of the Hispania'.

The two key sources for the study of Viriathus are Appian and Diodorus Siculus. Appian, during his life he wrote a 24-volume history on Rome in which chapter VI is dedicated to the Iberian Peninsula. One of Appian's main sources was Posidonius, a Greek polymath of his time, who wrote about the Iberian Peninsula in the middle of the 2nd century BCE. Appian also bases his work on Polybius, a contemporary Greek historian who recounts the facts about Rome's presence in Hispania. Though he wrote his history in forty books, a good part has been lost. Another key author was Diodorus, contemporary historian during Julius Caesar and Caesar Augustus' time. He wrote 'Bibliotheca' in forty volumes, many of which are now lost, but of the remaining books that have survived he collected much information on the Celtiberian and Lusitanian wars.

Both Appian's and Diodorus's descriptions rely on direct knowledge of the subject from Posidonius and Polybius', therefore; it was and has been of great value, but many other classical authors followed different routes when writing their works. Here are two major examples: The descriptions that Polybius were used in the Greek historian Strabo's writings for Polybius had detailed descriptions of the terrain, people and customs, while Posidonius's work was used by Diodorus who offers us a viewing of a more idealized view of Viriathus along with his observation and commentaries of Rome's endeavor in the Iberian Peninsula.

What is interesting about Polybius work is that he was cognizant of his opponent's military strategy, as well as the Rome's, therefore, being objective about indicating the war's bad management on part of Rome and giving credit and enormous value to Viriathus' military skills. As for Posidonius, he distorts the narrative in favor of Rome. One such example attaches the blame of Viriathus's assassination on the assassins, removing Quintus Servilius Caepio as the mastermind behind the plot.

But the official Roman version of the Lusitanian War is seen in the annals of Titus Livius's (better known as Livy) work. In his collection of 142 books, better known as 'The History of Rome', (unfortunately only 35 have been discovered) there are many extracts detailing what occurred on the Iberian Peninsula. Along with what survives of Livy's profound literary work, his work was also compiled in a 4th century AD summary called "*Periochae*" which mentions several events that occurred within the Peninsula.

We also have access to an independent version from Cassius Dio, who wrote a collection of 80 books titled "Roman History", in the middle of the 2nd century AD. Unfortunately, of the 80 books that he wrote only fragments of the first 36 books have survived, in which the Lusitanian War is mentioned in fragments in Book 22.[793]

Finally, there are some isolated mentions from other classical authors such as Florius, Orosius, Justinius, Eutropius, Veleius Paterculus,

---

[793] The books that follow to the 54th are nearly all complete. The 55th book has a considerable gap in it. The 56th to the 60th are complete. Of the next 20 books in the series, there remain only fragments. The 80th or last book covers the period from 222 to 229 (the reign of Alexander Severus).

Cicero, Aurelius Victor, Gaius Lucilius, and Frontinius. These authors show Viriathus as an extraordinary enemy of Rome.

Thus, for the study of Viriathus as a historical person, we only have Roman or Romanized Greek sources. As for the oral tradition used by the Lusitanians, Viriathus was larger than life and if any written works did exist in the Iberian language, it has been lost in time. But if an ancient history of Viriathus did exist, it would have perhaps been certainly drawn up, modified and manipulated by the Romans so as to control the Lusitanian population from making a hero and martyr out of him and to discourage any attempts at independence. As the old saying goes, "Victori spolia ire" (To the victor goes the spoils).

The Name: Viriathus

Dr. Leite de Vasconcelos writes that Viriathus is not a proper name, but a root word that stems from the Celtic word *viriola* (bracelets), while the word *viria* is the abbreviation for the Celtic word *viriola*.[794] Bracelets were used abundantly by the Iberian people and being that classical writers perhaps knew very few Celtic words, it is not surprising that they documented evidence without any proper names of certain men or peoples.

The name Viriathus, however, is more Celtic than Iberian, as demonstrated by Celtic inscriptions that emerge throughout historical Celtic lands such as the Danube region, Germania and Gaul. It has been assumed that the name, *Viria-tus* means the bearer of *viria* (bracelets).[795] Although the word has the same Celtic root, it does not have the same meaning in Latin. The Latin term for *vir* signifies the word for 'man'

---

[794] Munoz, Mauricio P., "*Viriato, A luta pela Liberdade*", Esquilo, Lisbon, 2006, p. 43, Alberto, Paulo Farmhouse, Viriato, Vultos da Antiguidade, Editorial Inquérito, 1996, p. 33; Vilatela, Luciano Perez, Lusitania: Historia y Etnología, Real Academia de la Historia, Madrid, 2000, p. 263-265; Tusculano, Victor de A Luistânia de há dois mil anos: epopeia military de Viriato, Caxias : Tip. do Reformatório Central, 1950, 61

[795] Munoz, Mauricio P., p.43

or 'rod'.[796] Though some grammarian's defend this Latin claim, there is no proof of this word usage for Viriathus's name. As for Dr. Leite de Vasconcelos's claim, historian Victor de Tusculano disagrees. He writes that Lusitanian tradition and the eloquent testimonies of Roman historians along with archeological findings demonstrate the inaccuracy of his thesis, because Viriathus is a proper name within the Lusitanian anthroponomy.[797]

Birthplace

In regard to his birthplace there has been much debate on the exact location. There have been various districts in Portugal which have contested that it was their area that is the cradle of Viriathus's birthplace – Gouveia, Linhares, Folgosinho, Valesim and Póvoa Velha. This debate began in the 1920s when Professor Adolf Schulten, a German archaeologist and historian spent a portion of his life studying the Lusitanians and Celtiberians in depth. He came to believe that Viriathus was born somewhere within the region of Serra da Estrela, the former Mons Herminius, which lies between the Tagus and Douro Rivers.[798] His justification for this claim was that Viriathus was a Lusitanian shepherd and bandit who roamed the hills and mountains of Lusitania, so why not choose the highest Sierra in Portugal as a perfect site for his birthplace!

But the basis for his argument is sketchy and perhaps incorrect, for the hills and mountains of Lusitania do not necessarily relate to just a pastoral life style and banditry, for these two elements can occur anywhere within the Iberian Peninsula from the plains of Andalusia to the Meseta Plateau, or to the coastal waters of Portugal. Furthermore,

[796] Ibid., p.43

[797] Tusculano, Victor de A Luistânia de há dois mil anos: epopeia military de Viriato, p. 61.

[798] Schulten, Adolf, "Viriatus", Neue jahrbücher für der klassiker Altertum, 39, Heidelberg, 1917, pp. 209-237. It was later translated into Spanish "Viriato", Boletín de la Biblioteca Menéndez y Pelayo, II, Santander, 1920 #3, PP. 126-149 and #4,5 and 6, pp. 272-281. In Portuguese it was put together as a book published in Porto, 1940.

he writes that Viriathus was born in the mountains of Sierra da Estrela, which lie in the western part of Lusitania, placing his birthplace near mountains or hills. But according to Diodorus, he says that Viriathus descended from the Lusitanians living along the ocean, in the occidental part of Lusitania.[799] So perhaps Diodorus's statement was either misread or misinterpreted or a mistake was done when his work was being translated from Latin. Though the Sierra da Estrela is on the eastern side of Portugal it is nowhere near the sea!

After many years of debates and discussions, there is no doubt that Viriathus's birthplace has been agreed upon. At the forefront of this new hypothesis is L. Garcia Moreno. In his work entitled *"Infância, Juventude e Primeiras Aventuras de Viriato"* (Childhood, Adolescence and First Adventures of Viriathus), he has analyzed all the data within the ancient sources on Viriathus, and he declares that there are two possible places where Viriathus may have been born.[800] The first, agrees with Diodorus's claim that he was born in Lusitania near the sea coast, while the second claims he came from the slopes of the sub-Meseta of the Betica Cordillera. The same feedback also comes from Luciano Perez Vilatela, who has dealt with the study of the Lusitanian people on a major scale.[801] Then was Professor Schulten wrong.

Both Garcia Moreno and Vilatela consider that Professor Schulten invented the Serra da Estrela theory as Viriathus's homeland because of his status within the tribe, the activities that he conducted in the area during the war and that he was of Lusitanian descent. Both these men explain why Schulten is incorrect in his theory that Viriathus was born in the wilds of the Serra da Estrela. Though both men agree with the mistake in Schulten's theory, they have their own hypothesis.

---

[799] Diodorus, 33.1.1

[800] Garcia Moreno, L., "Infância, Juventude e Primeiras Aventuras de Viriato, Caudillo Lusitano", Actas I Congreso Peninsular de Historia Antigua, Vol. II Santiago de Compostela, 1988, pp. 373-382

[801] Vilatela, Luciano Perez, Lusitania: Historia y Etnología,, p. 259-263

Garcia Moreno claims that the Roman name for the Sierra da Estrela, Mons Herminius does not appear in any of the ancient sources when referring to Viriathus. The ancient sources seem to make mention of a place called Aeminius instead, which is the name of a river and an *oppidum* (city) that was localized in the province of Lusitania or in one case a tribe called the Aeminianenses as told by Pliny.[802] This is supposedly his birthplace. While Moreno has Pliny to back his theory, Vilatela's hypothesis is backed by Diodorus and Varro. Vilatela writes that Viriathus was not exactly born in Serra da Estrela, but in another sierra that belongs to the same Central System that Serra da Estrela belongs to, but much more near to the ocean.[803] But further research into other classical works show that perhaps he was born around the area of Mons Tagrus in the area of Sintra, which is in close proximity to the Atlantic Ocean.[804] Though Viriathus' birthplace still remains a mystery, it provides a more logical connection and consistency to the classical texts than Schulten's theory.

Although all the ancient sources and some modern sources accept the origin of Viriathus as Lusitanian, some historians consider that Viriathus was born in other regions of Hispania. At the end of the 19th century and the onset of the 20th century, historians Joaquín Costa and Anselmo Arenas Lopez defended their hypothesis that Viriathus was not Lusitanian but Luso, a small tribe within the Celtiberian realm that inhabited the area around Teruel in central eastern Spain.[805] Even

---

[802] Today Aeminius is known as Coimbra, Portugal and as for the river it refers to the Minho River which makes the northern border of Portugal with Spain, so perhaps Viriathus may have been born not in Lusitania but in Galizia, which Pliny considered it to be part of Lusitania. All three can be found in Pliny, NH, 4.113, 115, 118.

[803] Diodorus, 33.1.1

[804] Varro, res Rusticae, 2.1.19; Vergilius, Georgica, 3.272; Silius Italicus, Punica, 3.378 and 16.364; Vilatela, Luciano Perez, op. cit., p. 262

[805] Costa, Joaquin, "Viriato y la Cuestión Social en España en el Siglo II Antes de Jesucristo", Tutela de Pueblos en la Historia, Madrid, 1879 and it was again published in Esitdios Ibéricos, Madrid, 1902; Arenas Lopez, Anselmo, Reivindicaciones Histórica.Viriato não era Português mas Celtibero, Guadalajara, 1900 and La Luistania Celtíbera, Madrid, 1907.

though these men covered Viriathus within the context of the Celtiberian and Luistanian wars, they emphasized that Viriathus was Celtiberian. Another author, M. Peris takes Viriathus's birthplace to the lands near Valencia in southeastern Spain, transforming Viriathus into an "Ibero-Valencian".[806] This is hard to believe for Valencia was established after the war.

In recent years, there has been a hypothesis that places Viriathus's homeland south of Lusitania and not between the Tagus and Douro Rivers but in the city of Arsa, located in Celtic Beturia (modern Andalusia). But this theory is hard to swallow, thus most historians disagree with this statement. For according to the ancient texts, they state that after the peace treaty of 140 BC was signed Q. Fabius Maximus Servilianus and Viriathus, Viriathus seems to have established a second home at Arsa.[807] This supposedly suggests that because he set up camp there it may as well been his birthplace. But many historians disagree that this was his birth place, and instead feel it was simply his second home, for it was the site where he began to establish his 'dynasty' and perhaps make Arsa the center of his power of all the land that he had taken from the Romans.

In Portugal, there have been claims that he was born in Loriga, which was actually a Lusitanian stronghold called Lobriga. During the Lusitanian War, the Romans named this fortified city, Lorica, when translated into Latin means "warlike harness". The Romans had put such a name to it, because of its strategic importance within the mountain range it was located in, and to its protagonist attitude during the war (*Lorica Lusitanorum Castrum est*). It is a name that has remained unchanged for the past two thousand years. Its significance in antiquity had played a part in the historical blazon of the village creating a theory that Viriathus was from this area. Though it is situated in the Serra da Estrela, it should be treated as mere fantasy for there is obviously no

---

[806] Peris, M., "La Lusitania Primitiva", "Campaña Luistana y Viriatense", "Fin de Viriato" and "La Patria de Viriato", Boletín de la Sociedade Castellonense de Cultura, IV, 1926.

[807] Diodorus, 23.1.6; Appian, Iber., 70

mention of this city in the classical texts when referring to Viriathus. It has been assumed that this city was picked because of its location and that in the classical text they continuously mention that Viriathus was from the mountains.[808]

But of all these theories that exist, the one that has stuck is from the late Professor Schulten who attributes Viriathus's birthplace to the hills of Mons Hermínius. His theory was taken to another level and was turned into exact history in the 1930s by fascist propaganda of the New State led by dictatorial president António de Oliveira Salazar, who spread this theory as mainstream history about the origins of Portugal. But in later state theory the 'historical' location of his birthplace was later changed to Santa Comba Dão, which in reality was the birthplace of Salazar. Though the population did not believe the second theory, they did on the first, which has lasted into the 21st century.

Of all the supposed theories that have been circling around for years, an additional theory arose around the 1990s. According to writer and journalist João Aguiar, he states that perhaps Viriathus was born in the locality of Aritius Vetium (present-day Alvega), which is a city that stands on the left bank of the river Tagus in the Serra da Estrela.[809] Unfortunately, there is no proof of this theory or detailed explanation, so it is placed as mere speculation.

Lastly, there is a theory derived by Paulo Alberto Farmhouse, who writes that according to the geographic location within the territory that Viriathus roamed, there seems to be a connection to the region of Turdetania which should not be overlooked.[810] According to his research during the war, this area of operations was much frequented; his wife was from this region; his assassins, who were his lieutenants, were from Urso, an important Turdetania city. Although there are many indicators

---

[808] Orosius, 5.4.1; Floroius, 1.33, Diodorus, 33.1.1-4; It seen that this theory cam e from Bispo-Mor do Reino, História da Lusitânia, 1580.

[809] Aguiar, João, *A Voz dos Deuses*, 13ª edição, Porto, Edições Asa, 1992

[810] Alberto, Paulo Farmhouse, op. cit., p. 37.

that point to this possibility, it does still demonstrate the difficulty of positioning with precision the provenance of his story.

Though these theories try to legitimize his birthplace, they all have a nationalistic flavor with a deep localism that seeks to claim their land to be the home of the national hero. In reality Viriathus was neither Portuguese nor Spanish, but a member of a people, called the Lusitanians that inhabited an area of the peninsula that extended from the coast of Portugal, north to the Douro River and south just past the Tagus River and towards the west to Toledo and Seville in Spain.

It seems clear that Viriathus was from Lusitania and he lived among the Lusitanians along the Atlantic Ocean as deduced from the ancient texts. It is even clearer that he resided in the southern part of Lusitania for many of the texts refer to Viriathus's campaigns as being conducted mostly in the southern region of the Iberian Peninsula with limited military operations in Central Hispania. In the end, the final outcome over the debate of whether Viriathus was born in Serra da Estrela or not will continue to be an enigma.

Besides not knowing exactly where Viriathus was born, we also do not know the exact year of his birth. One hypothesis that has been thrown around claims that he was born between 179 BCE and 170 BCE, which places Viriathus between the ages of 20 and 30 years old by the time of the Lusitanian massacre by Servius Sulpicius Galba in 150 BCE. The reason why historians pick this time frame for his birth was because 150 BCE was the year that the Viriathian war began, when Servius Sulpicius Galba; the praetor to Hispania Ulterior had massacred 9,000 Lusitanians and enslaved 20,000 in one day. Of the 1,000 that escaped, Viriathus was one. So, if we accept this historical reference and place, it places Viriathus in his 20s, which marks him as a mature young man apt at leading men into combat and conducting military operation on a major scale.

Still there are other historians that state that Viriathus was born prior to 179 BCE; some even go as far as supposing 190 BCE. This theory makes it possible that Viriathus was in his 40s at the time he started his guerrilla war. But it seems unlikely that he would have led men into battle in his 50s. So being born after the year 190 BCE may be a bit far-fetched for very few people lived that long during that time.

Personality

Though it is difficult to pinpoint the date and place of birth of Viriathus, we do know for sure that he was from a humble origin, as it has been repeatedly mentioned in the ancient sources. However, this should not be taken as absolute truth, since it deals with a traditional formula of showing a poor man rising to the top, exclusively from his personal values and morals. Ancient writers seem to treat the image of Viriathus as the ideal hero whose character would have been forged in his youth due to the environment in which he grew up in. Viriathus arises in history with a 'strong and fascinating persona, as did other barbarian military chiefs and leaders such as Vercengitorix, Clovis, Boudicca, Alaric and several others.

Viriathus is presented in ancient passages as a man whose strength and virtue came from his experience as a juvenile in the wilds of Lusitania. The ancient texts referred Viriathus as a Lusitanian from an obscure lineage, who was a man that had been labeled as a shepherd (which by the way is questionable) to an outlaw and bandit leader (latronum dux) and soon after a general and tribal chief that became famous by his achievements and deeds as a warrior. His natural attributes, agility, physical strength and skills in hand-to-hand combat are well documented.[811] It is also written that he spent most of his life living in a hostile environment, living off the land with minimum food and drink and slept in beds of whatever nature offered him, for he had contempt for all riches and luxuries of civilized life.[812] The ancient texts also document that he was a man who went straight to the point when he spoke his mind, to the Romans this as a sign of an untutored and

[811] Diodorus, 33.1.1; Cassius Dio, 78

[812] Ibid., 33.1.2

unspoiled man.[813] He was therefore, in the eyes of the Roman, a wild man that was introverted and solitary.

Viriathus was physically and spiritually a son of the mountains. His body, vigorous since birth, was strengthened each day by a rude pastoral life he led living under the open sky. Along with being a shepherd, hunter, bandit and warrior and surviving in the wilds of ancient Lusitania year after year, he was able to achieve complete domination of body and spirit. The Romans were amazed about his endurance for he was a man who never fatigued, never suffered from hunger, and knew how to take advantage of unfavorable circumstances. Cassius Dio said it best about Viriathus' physical strength and endurance:

"Starting with a natural aptitude and building on this with his training, he was swift and in flight, and he had great stamina in hand-to-hand fighting. He was happy with whatever food he could get his hands on and was satisfied to bed down in the wild. Consequently, he was above suffering from heat and cold, and was untroubled by hunger or any other hardship; as content with whatever was on hand as he was with the very best."[814]

When he became leader of the Lusitanians, Viriathus was viewed as a man who fought for liberty, justice and equality, according to some of the Roman texts. Only in rare occasions did the Iberian tribes accept or submit to the orders of one man. But because of his personality, intellect, and logic he maintained the entire time he was alive, the Romans feared, hated and respected. As a military commander, he sought loyalty and obedience. As a leader, he possessed an intelligence that was of enormous value in making important decisions during the war.[815] In short, he was not ambitious, nor power hungry, but bellicose and cognizant of the military arts and a man who was schooled in the understanding of practical affairs. Using diplomacy and strict discipline, it seems he had found the equilibrium between the authority

---

[813] Ibid., 33.7.3

[814] Cassius Dio, 78

[815] Cassius Dio, 78

that he thought was right to exercise and the extreme equality that their compatriots required, demonstrating that during his leadership there were no mutinies, rebellions, uprisings, riots nor desertions or defections which could have cause internal crises. Once again, I revert to Dio on Viriathus' mental capacity:

"He could quickly plan and execute whatever needed to be done—and he had always a clear idea of what that was. Furthermore, he knew exactly when to do it. He could pretend ignorance of the most obvious facts and just as cleverly his knowledge of the most hidden secrets. In everything he did, he was not only the general but his own second-in-command as well."[816]

With this said, Viriathus seemed to have never flaunted his power and continued to live as he done before among the Lusitanians. Even though Viriathus was superior to his fellow countrymen in his political ethos and patriotic sentiment, he made the lower social class his equal. Above all else, he led his people to believe that they possessed the gift to foresee the future with which he won the respect and confidence of his people to lead them to victory. Though he had an amazing personality and qualities, Dio delivers us an understanding about the man's greatness. But along with his personality, he possessed a great naivety because of his profound trust in others, which in the end was his demise.

Infancy and Youth

We do not completely know who the parents of Viriathus were, but according to legend his father's name was Cominio, who was chief of a small tribe situated somewhere within the realm of Lusitania.[817] At five years old, his father, before leaving for war against another Iberian tribe or the Romans, he left the family under the protection of the Igeditans, with whom the Lusitanians were allies with.[818] As legend goes, his father

---

[816] Ibid., 78

[817] Aguiar, João, *A Voz dos Deuses*, 13ª edição, Porto, Edições Asa, 1992, p.130; Munoz, Mauricio P., op. cit., p. 51.

[818] Aguiar, 130; Munoz, 51

died in combat and Viriathus grew up among the Igedium warriors and with them he learned the art of war.[819] As he grew older, according to Lusitanian customs, the first born was usually the heir of the family, and therefore Viriathus being the third child (the second being a sister and the oldest a brother) was forced, as many other young people were, to choose a different life, which usually led them to move elsewhere to make a name for themselves or live a quiet life.[820]

As the story goes by the time, he was sixteen years old, tanned by the suns rays and weathered from the wind and the free air, walking the mountains and living among the highlanders as a hunter and shepherd of sheep and goats, he had become a man. With his physical prowess at such an early age, he joined a group of bandits and soon began to stand out quickly for his qualities and amazing command capacity to lead men; in time he began to lead a life of a bandit leader of his own raiders.[821]

Though the story of his youth is based on legend not all is pure fiction. Although nothing is mentioned in the literary sources indicating his humble origins, as well as of his infancy and childhood, we do have several references about his youth as a young man from Diodorus, Florus, Dio Cassius, Orosius, and Eutropius that present him first as a shepherd and hunter, then as bandit and later a bandit chief, finally becoming a guerrilla leader and tribal chief.[822]

Marriage

The marriage of Viriathus in 141 BCE deserves some attention for it plays an important role in for what he stood for in Iberian culture. The reason for this analysis is because of A. Garcia y Bellido and H. G. Gundel, interpreted this episode as evidence of a serious class disequilibrium in Lusitanian society during this epoch of Rome's conquest of the Iberian

---

[819] Aguiar, 130; Munoz, 51

[820] Aguiar, 130; Munoz, 51

[821] Aguiar, João, *A Voz dos Deuses*, 13ª edição, Porto, Edições Asa, 1992, p. 135

[822] Diodorus, 33.1.3; Florus, 1.33.15; Dio Cassius, 73; Orosius, 5.4.1; Eutropius, 4.6

Peninsula.[823] J. Maluquer de Montes in accordance with A. Garcia y Bellido and H. G. Gundel notes that the rich nobles were proprietors of the mineral rich agricultural plains, while the poor controlled the mountain wilds by herding livestock and by reverting to banditry.[824] In this context, the marriage of Viriathus to a woman of a wealth land owner became an alliance or a union between the two social classes showing that a poor man can raise himself to the top, although there still was some animosity from the upper class.

As legend has it, Viriathus was passionately in love since a young age with Astolpas's sister or daughter whose name is believed to have been Tongina,[825] but could not marry her because he was from a lower noble class, thus Astolpas wanted to marry Tongina off to a man with greater economic means. But, when things changed for Viriathus and proposed the marriage (i.e. alliance), Astolpas accepted the marriage; even though he did not have a good relationship with Viriathus, which is evident from the attitude Viriathus had on his wedding day by rejecting the food offered to him and criticizing his host's vast wealth.[826]

---

[823] See Garcia y Bellido, Antonio, "Bandas y Guerrillas en las Luchas con Roma" Hispania, Vol. V, #trg5, p.540-550; Gundel, H.G.., "Viriato, lusitano, caudillo en las luchas contra los romanos. 147-139 a.C.", *Caesaraugusta*, 1968, pp.175-198

[824] Maluquer de Montes, Juan, "Los Pueblos de la España céltica," *Historia de España*, Tomo I, Vol. III, Pt. 1, 1976

[825] Unfortunately, we do not know the true name of his Astoplas daughter/ Viriathus' wife, although according to legend her name is Tongina, referring to her as a young and very beautiful women, with dark hair and pale radiant skin, who was modest but with great "haughtiness and firmness". We do know of certainty that she was related to the richest land owner of Betica, who is said to have been a powerful and influential man who had many connections with Rome and other Iberian tribes. As for the word daughter/sister being in quotation mark is because near the end of this section there is some controversy over the type of family relation Astoplas had with Tongina as whether he was her father or brother. Through João Aguilar book, *A Voz dos Deuses*, 13ª edição, Porto, Edições Asa, 1992 he makes several references about Tongina.

[826] Diodorus, 33.7.1-4; As for the word brother/father-in-law being in quotation mark is because near the end of this section there is some controversy over the family status of Astoplas as for was he the father or brother of Tongina.

The story of Viriathus' wedding in Diodorus book 33 deserves an in-depth look for it encompasses a discourse about his wisdom about Lusitanian social structure.[827] Looking at Diodorus's passage about Viriathus's scornfully expression about Astolpas' wealth, Diodorus stated that during the wedding celebration, great quantities of gold and silver were displayed along with many different precious stones and all sorts of embroidered robes. On seeing this vast wealth, he rose from his seat and leaned against his spear showing his contempt and disdain instead of admiration or surprise of Astolpas' wealth.[828] Diodorus goes on to say that during the wedding banquet, Viriathus in a single remark, spoke volumes of good sense and showed his ingratitude with his benefactors.[829] Diodorous states,

"...that much touted wealth of his 'father or brother-in-law' was himself subject to the man who held the spear; furthermore, that he owned him a greater debt than others, yet offered him, the true master of it all, no personal gift."[830]

Looking at this paragraph, it gives us an understanding that this statement claims that although the proud Astolpas had all the gold and silver in the world, but still bowed 'to the man who held the spear', meaning that he was still a pawn of Rome. But on the other hand, one can also interpret that instead of being under Rome's yoke of power he instead was under the power of Viriathus for he was the one who held the spear (power) for he held the people under his influence. With this statement Diodorus put words of wisdom in Viriathus' mouth about who was actually in power.

In another paragraph, Diodorus writes:

When many valuable articles were exhibited, Viriathus after lingering at these precious objects asks Astolpas, "How is it that the Romans, who

---

827 Diodorus, 33.7.1-4

828 Diodorus, 33.7.1

829 Diodorus, 33.7.2

830 Diodorus, 33.7.3

have seen all these riches at this banquet have kept their hands off these valuables despite the power to wrest from you?" Astolpas replied that no one had ever moved to seize or ask for them though many knew of the existence of his vast wealth. Viriathus then asks, "Then why in the world, if the authorities granted you immunity and the security for you to enjoy these things, did you desert them and choose to ally yourself with my nomadic life and my humble company."[831]

This was a good question. Once again Diodorus makes Viriathus out to be a wise and cultured barbarian who seems to know about politics, especially when it comes to the subject of political alliances. What kind of relation could exist between the rich Astolpas, lover of wealth and the 'miserable' Viriathus, a frugal and crude person? From the passage, we can see that Viriathus was amazed that the rich Astolpas would prefer to simultaneously hold a dangerous alliance with him and Rome instead of making a choice of one or the other, but unfortunately, it does not show any response. One can only say that the wealthy Astoplas called for a peace to be made between Viriathus and Rome, in which in the eyes of Viriathus this is a sign of submission to Rome. But for Astoplas, it was a guarantee that his tribe would survive Rome's oppression, making Astolpas in Viriathus' mind, a weak leader.

These passages also serve to confirm Viriathus' humility. J. Lens Tuero and Marco V. Garcia Quintela consider these passages as an example of Hellenic cynical and stoic doctrines, whose objectives are to paint Viriathus as the 'good savage', who was morally good and stood up for what he believed in.[832] In this sense, it is perhaps safe to say that the ancient writers, besides telling a story, were also morally edifying decadent Greek and Roman readers, while promoting that through the Iberian people were considered by the majority of the Romans as barbarians, they were somewhat civilized. The fragments about the

[831] Diodorus, 33.7.5

[832] For more information see Lens Tuero, J., "Viriato, Héroe y Rey Cínico", Estudios de Filología Griega #2, 1986, pp. 253-272 and Estudios sobre Diodoro de Sicilia, Granada, 1994, pp. 127-143; Garcia Quintela, M.V., "Viriato y la Ideología Trifuncional Indoeuropea", Polis #3, 1993, pp. 111-138

life of Viriathus that were collected by ancient historians allow the character of this historical figure to employed parables, allegory and moral examples.

Marco V. Garcia Quintela goes on to conclude that Diodorus's writing besides being historical facts on a person; it is also the base for a sort of a "capitalist ideology". This means that Astolpas' wealth is representative of the imbalances in the distribution of wealth. But there are some scholars that argue that Garcia Quintela is wrong and state that it reflects the subordination of *ploutos* (wealth) in relation to *kratós* (force, will) in a civilization that was predominantly based on a warrioristic ideology.[833]

Furthermore, according to Pastor Muñoz, he stresses that the ancient passages emphasize the physical and moral superiority of Viriathus had over Astolpas which is not surprising because it is the superiority of the warrior's values, skills and courage that in ancient times took precedence over a character that was solely distinguished by having money.[834] Finally, the presence of these two characters within these passages also represents two different social classes within Lusitanian society; the rich and the poor. From these aspects, Viriathus is the proud, self-confident and self-sufficient man who did not believe in material wealth, but in spiritual freedom and liberty.

Along with the words that transpired between both men, Diodorus goes on the say that Viriathus refused to take part in the banquet and ate a little bit of bread and meat, only after he had taken bread and meat and gave it to his men first. He then made a small sacrifice to gods and ordered one of his men to fetch his bride, where he mounted her on a horse and disappeared into the mountain wilds.[835]

Though these ancient texts give us a look at the lifestyle that these men had lived, a hard life of washing themselves in cold water and eating

[833] Garcia Quintela, M.V., "Viriato y la Ideología Trifuncional Indoeuropea", Polis #3, 1993, pp. 111-138

[834] Munoz, Mauricio P.,op. cit., p. 57-58

[835] Diodorus, 33.7.4-7

one meal a day, shows that one does not need much material wealth to be self-sustaining. On on a deeper level, each of these paragraphs exemplify his lack of social graces, but at the same time these passages also show that Viriathus was a humble man who put his soldier's before himself, a true sign of a great leader. Each of these passages about the gestures within Viriathus's personality makes part of a collection that is compared to a Hellenic motif and themes on the subject of appropriate morals and a humble life. It also illustrates that Viriathus's behavior at the banquet was perhaps a manifestation of his institutional position as a leader of warriors within Lusitanian society. As for the small sacrifice, it perhaps signifies that Viriathus was not asking for any consent from Astolpas, his only liability would be before the gods. This action on part of Viriathus was a kick in the face to tradition because a traditional Iberian marriage always required explicit consent from the family, but this was not to happen here.

Diodorus goes on to praise Viriathus's direct manner of speaking, which is derived from his lack of education. This example of Viriathus's direct wisdom is told through the accounts of how Viriathus rebuked the people of Tucca for constantly changing sides between him and the Romans. The traditional fable that Diodorus chose for his rebuke was the same that is found in the works of the Roman fabulist, Phaedrus.[836] It is precisely during the Lusitanian War that the problems of forming alliances gains complexity. During this period, the political center of power in southwest Iberian Peninsula was in Baeturia. The people and the territory that Viriathus extended his power were not just primitive tribal groupings, but more civilized than most Iberian tribes in the north and west of the peninsula for there were actual cities that had been in existence prior to most Iberian and Lusitanian towns and cities that

---

[836] It is a story of a man with two wives, one young, one older; the man goes bald because the older woman plucks out his dark hairs while the younger on plucks out his white hairs, as they both desire him to look more like them. *Fabulae Aesopiae 2.2;* According to Liv Yarrow, this illustrates how Viriathus had gained wisdom and clarity of oration without education, although Diodorus defeats his purpose by suggesting that Viriathus could 'intuit' such a common didactic illustration. Yarrow, Liv Mariah, Historiography at the end of the Republic: Provincial Perspectives on Roman Rule, Oxford University Press, 2006, p. 335

also had a social organization and a very complex political system than the rest of the tribes. With the Roman occupation of southern Spain, within these cities two parties existed, a favorable one to Romans and another to the Lusitanian war effort. Guided by the events and politics of the day, Iberian tribes had a bad habit of constantly flip-flopping on whose side they were on. With this type of behavior, Viriathus expressed a scornfully attitude towards these tribes and their leaders, such as he did with Astolpas. Astolpas's indecisive behavior of also changing sides created strong tensions between Viriathus and Astolpas and the Baeturian people. According to Professor Munoz, this tension was so intense that it may have had culminated to Astolpas's execution by Viriathus a year later.

As the reader, you ask yourself, "Was the tension between these two individuals so bad that one had the other executed?" The answer is complex. Although these two men did not like each other, as the ancient passages claim, Viriathus would not have executed Astolpas on his own just because he did not see eye to eye with Astoplas's politics for they still respected one another for both were wise and intelligent leaders of a tribe and Viriathus had married into the family.

Then why the execution? As history has it, there are three stories about Astoplas's death. The first is that sometime before Viriathus's own assassination a year later after Astoplas's death, he attempted to negotiate a peace treaty with the consul of Citerior, Marcus Popilius Laenas due to that the Lusitanians were becoming war weary. During the negotiations, Laenas demanded Viriathus to give up all Roman deserters that had joined the Lusitanian cause and some hostages which would either have been sold into slavery, imprisoned, executed or forced to commit suicide. It is believed on hearing that Astolpas was one of the men on Laenas's list which was picked to commit suicide, Viriathus, out of respect, killed Astolpas to either giving him an honorable Lusitanian death or to show that it was possible for him to be a loyal Rome ally if need be. But the plan did not work, on hearing this news of what Viriathus had done, Popilius Laenas became upset at what Viriathus did, perhaps Laenas sensed that Viriathus was not as trustworthy as he said he was, decided to cut the right hand of every Lusitanian hostage and made new demands to Viriathus for an unconditional surrender and relinquish all weapons in Lusitanian hands, if a peace settlement was to be furnished.[837]

The second story begins with the same basis that Viriathus desperately wanted peace for his war weary people but being that Viriathus had become the scourge of Rome, Laenas ordered Viriathus to execute Astolpas for the purpose of seeing how loyal Viriathus can become. To appease an exigency that was required by Laenas and to have peace, Viriathus gave in to Laenas's terms. This gesture was to show the Romans that he had submitted himself to the will of Rome.[838] Bitterly, he too had accepted the politics of his time, which in the end certainly cost him his life.

The last story is part of Portuguese legend and part factual history. The marriage of Viriathus to Tongina, Astolpas's daughter or sister, was initially seen as a good idea for it would perhaps calm down Viriathus's vengeful rage against the Romans, increase Astolpas's kingdom and bring Roman influence among the Iberians, as well as increase trade relations with the Romans and better Rome's foreign policies on Hispania. During the wedding feast, it is know that several high-ranking Roman representatives were present at the event, but on seeing that the marriage to Tongina did not curve Viriathus's hate against Rome for he spoke out against the Romans, Astolpas, to save face, committed suicide for not being able to constrain Viriathus.[839] Leanas then perhaps used Astolpas's suicide against Viriathus, by blaming that it was his fault that Astolpas committed suicide and that there would be no peace, thus turning his compatriots to assassinate Viriathus for perhaps his southern allies saw Viriathus was ambitious and power hunger and a danger to the welfare of the southern tribes in Baetica, which was home of the three assassins.

---

837 Cassius Dio 75; Munoz, Mauricio P., op. cit., p. 60.

838 Munoz, Mauricio P., op. cit., p. 60-61

839 Ibid., p. 61

This intra-family conflict, now more than in any other event, gives the reader the notion that Viriathus was, without a doubt, a leader of a nation, for he had obtained the most overwhelming victories in the history of Iberian resistance against Rome. This exchange of words between Viriathus and Astolpas shows that Viriathus saw Astolpas as a Roman pawn who had subjugated his people to the will of Rome. After the death of Astolpas, his fighters had belied the alliances with Rome and joined Viriathus's army with the idea of total liberty for their people.

But according to M. V. Garcia and B. Sergent, they believe that if we look more closely at these different moments that were composed in the reporting of the marriage, as well as Viriathus's life, there are elements of a tripartite structure. They claim that there is a tripartite ideology within the marriage text that makes a distinction between several Iberian religious and cultural particularities.[840] They claim that there are three forms of Georges Dumézil's controversial Trifunctional Hypothesis within the text about Viriathus' marriage in which the hypothesis states that Indo-European societies and religions divided everything into three. In the following section of this chapter the trifunctional theory will be analyzed.[841]

Trifunctional Hypothesis of Viriathus Life

This ideology is derived from the Indo-European theme that postulates a tripartite ideology ("idéologie tripartite") reflected in the existence of three classes or castes—priests, warriors, and commoners (farmers or tradesmen)—corresponding to the three functions of the sacral, the martial and the economic, respectively. This thesis is especially associated with the French mythographer, the late Geoges Dumézil.

---

[840] Munoz, Mauricio P., op.cit., pp. 58-62; Garcia Quintela, M.V., "Viriato y la Ideología Trifuncional Indoeuropea" Polis #3, 1993, pp. 111-138; Sergent, Bernard, "Three Notes on the Tirfunctional Indo-European Marriage", Journal of Undo-European Studies #12, 1984, pp. 179-191

[841] For more information see Dumézil, Georges. **The destiny of the warrior**, translated by Alf Hiltebeitel, Chicago and London: University of Chicago Press, 1970, 168 pages.and **Flamen-Brahman,** Paris: Paul Geuthner, 1935, 112 pages; Garcia Quintela, M.V., op. cit., pp. 111-138; Sergent, Bernard, op. cit., pp. 179-191

According to Dumézil, Proto-Indo-European society comprised three main groups corresponding to three distinct functions: the first is associated with the function of sovereignty, another with the military function, and a third with that of productivity. Sovereignty fell into two distinct and complementary sub-parts, one formal, juridical and priestly but worldly, the other powerful, unpredictable, and also priestly but rooted in the supernatural world. The second main division was connected with force, the military and war. While the role of the third, ruled by the other two, was productivity, herding, farming and crafts.[842] Its mythology was divided in the same way: each social group had its own god or family of gods to represent it and the function of the god or gods matched the function of the group. The trifunctional ideology in Lusitanian culture is present in numerous manifestations of social life, including the organization of its pantheon of gods its hierarchy, matrimony, and in the position of individuals in society.[843] It is organized around three general principles or hierarchal functions. He writes:

"The first function, which García Quintela calls (F1), groups together themes concerning the magical and cosmological aspects of the world order and the manifestations of this order among humans (agreements, pledges, etc); in social terms, it is formed by the priests and the king, who is chosen from among the warrior caste. The second function, referred to here as (F2), is organized around strength and protection and is represented socially by warriors. The third function, here designated as (F3), is connected with the reproduction of society in all of its facets, from sexual unions to the preservation and production of harvests and herds of animals, and in general to abundance and important quantities; socially, this is the activity of the producers".[844]

---

[842] Dumézil, G., Flamen-Brahman, Paris, 1929 and Mitra-Varuna, Presses Universitaires de France, 1940

[843] García Quintela, Marco V., "*The Celts in the Iberian Peninsula", e-Keltoi,* Center for Celtic Studies, University of Wisconsin-Milwaukee, Volume 6, August 10, 2005, p. 520 and "Viriato y la Ideología Trifuncional Indoeuropea" Polis #3, 1993, pp. 111-138

[844] Ibid., p.520

The theory begins by exploring the texts that present Viriathus passing through three different phases throughout his life.[845] It starts with Viriathus' youth as a shepherd and the austerity that made him physically strong (a denigrated version of motif F3). It then goes on to show how he fought against animals and wild beasts until a great crowd chose him as their chieftain, and he immediately surrounded himself with a band of thieves (F2), showing himself to be an honorable and competent military commander. Finally, he proclaimed himself the legitimate chieftain, renouncing his position as the head of the group of thieves, and set out to wage war against the Romans (F1, the transition from warrior to king).[846]

García Quintela goes on to say that there is a similar trifunctional order appearing in Cassius Dio's description of Viriathus. García Quintela states:

"The opening formula sums up the text of Diodorus mentioned above (and the same in Florus, I, 33, 15), with the sequence of a trifunctional life. An explanation is then offered of Viriathus's qualities as a warrior (F2), his austerity (F3 denigrated) and his intelligence (F1).[847] The text ends with an evocation of the 'three sins of a warrior' that Viriathus avoided.[848]

The 'three sins of a warrior' that our hero avoids, that are mentioned by Diodorus and Cassius Dio, are the desire for wealth, dynastic ambition and excess rage. One such example of these sins is from Cassius Dio, who ends one of his passages with a description of Viriathus, the warrior as "without any desire for wealth, dynastic ambition and without rage... instead with a love of fighting and combat".[849] Diodorus and Dio refer that the three failings of the Indo-European warrior had been erased

[845] García Quintela, "*The Celts in the Iberian Peninsula*", p. 520 and "Viriato y la Ideología Trifuncional Indoeuropea", pp. 111-138

[846] Ibid., p. 520

[847] Ibid., p. 520 and pp. 111-138

[848] Ibid., p. 520

[849] Cassius Dio, 22, fr. 73.4

from Viriathus's personality.[850] This is reiterated by Diodorus when he affirms that Viriathus was outstanding for his sobriety (*autarkeia*), which according to García Quintela theory makes him independent of the servitude of F3; his preference for liberty (*eleuthéria*), which was a radical affirmation of sovereignty (F1) and his bravery (*andreía*) (F2).[851] These texts situate Viriathus in a category of royalty defined according to Indo-European principles.

Furthermore, in Diodorus, Cassius Dio and Florus's texts, we find a biography that is a moral portrait of Viriathus in accordance with the rules of the theory. According to García Quintela's research, this structure coincides with the many biographies of other great leaders of Indo-European tribes and royal houses, such as the Persian king, Cyrus the Great or the Roman, Romulus, one of the founder's of Rome.[852] The text of Cassius Dio is equivalent, in the way it structures the trifunctional series, to the portrait of the "good king" or in accordance to the Romans concept of what a "noble savage" was.

On the subject of the wedding text as told by Diodorus, it is an episode narrated as a marriage rite that was purely Lusitanian and not Greek or Roman contradicting Strabo's mention of the Lusitanian wedding to a Greek one. Perhaps the reason why Strabo mentions that it is Greek in nature is because its narrative was transmitted via Hellenic language and expressions. In general terms, within the Indo-European ideology there are three types of marriage. Besides its special religious importance, it was require to have the acceptance of the guardian parents of the bride (F1); other marriages derive from the capture of the bride, or from the mutual consent of the couple to be married (F2); finally, there are marriages that occurred with a circulation of goods, or with a representation of the bride being purchased (F3).[853]

---

[850] García Quintela, "*The Celts in the Iberian Peninsula*", p. 521 and "Viriato y la Ideología Trifuncional", pp. 111-138

[851] Diodorus, 33 7.3; This is outlined in Quintela, Marco V., "*The Celts in the Iberian Peninsula*", p. 521 and at the beginning of this section.

[852] García Quintela "*The Celts in the Iberian Peninsula*", p. 521

[853] Refer to the outlined in Quintela,"*The Celts in the Iberian Peninsula*", p. 522 and at the beginning of this section.

As for the usage of the Trifunctional Hypothesis in Viriathus's wedding episode, firstly, Viriathus complains that Astolpas, had not offered him any kind of gift (F3). Secondly, tensions arise at the banquet, but the wedding continues, even though Viriathus orders his companions to bring him his wife, as if she were being captured (F2). Finally, Viriathus carries out religious ceremonies and takes his wife to share in his residence which consummates the marriage (F1).[854] Each step of the marriage defined a precise and distinct ideological focus in which G. Dumézil compares Viriathus's wedding to a similar structure between the union of young Romans and Sabine women,[855] and considers this to be an exceptional case for there are other myths that invoked the trifunctional ideology of marriage presenting a hero who married three different women according to the correct manners for each function.[856]

Trifunctionalism in Viriathus's wedding is necessary for those young Iberians who aspire to become royalty, or for the young bachelors of early Rome, for without marriage, the social order cannot be maintained. As for Viriathus, although he does well without material wealth, he needs the fecundity to establish his own royal bloodline.

Trifunctionalism brought together an explanation to the most significant episodes of Viriathus's life which were transmitted by classical sources to reflect an ideology associated with royalty that has Indo-European roots. Yet it would mean twisting the facts if we limited ourselves to this conclusion, without recognizing that the clearest, most significant and

---

[854] Ibid.

[855] The comparison to the rape of the Sabine Women will be looked into in the next section, "**Other Theories about Viriathus's Marriage**"

[856] Munoz, Mauricio P., op. cit., 58-62; Garcia Quintela, M.V., "Viriato y la Ideología Trifuncional Indoeuropea", pp. 111-138; Quintela, "*The Celts in the Iberian Peninsula",* p. 522; Sergent, Bernard, "Three Notes on the Tirfunctional Indo-European Marriage", pp. 179-191; Dumézil, Georges. **The destiny of the warrior**, translated by Alf Hiltebeitel, Chicago and London: University of Chicago Press, 1970, 168 pages.and **Flamen-Brahman,** Paris: Paul Geuthner, 1935, 112 pages.

articulated parallels come from Celtic mythology.[857] The only plausible explanation to this conclusion in reading these tales is that these tales are based on Celtic adaptations of a more general Indo-European theme, the conception of royalty as a synthesis of the three functions described above.[858] Since this theory came in the late 1970s and early 1980s there has been a mixed scholarly debated over this interpretation and many believe that it is not correct and that it tends to overstate the texts for leads to some type of objective which has no evidence, thus not making it plausible, while other disagree on certain aspect of the theory. But on the other hand, there are stern supporters of this theory.

Other Theories About Viriathus' Marriage

Some scholars think that the Trifunctional Hypothesis is not plausible but having dug deep into the ancient texts and using this hypothesis as a base to add or conjure up some new theories on the significance of Viriathus' marriage to his personality and feelings towards the Romans. Thus several new theories have been constructed such as: Viriathus not receiving any gifts or dowry from Astolpas; persisting tensions during the feast, but the marriage is still celebrated; Viriathus does not accept Astolpas' formally delivery of the bride to him, but instead orders one of his men to fetch and bring her to him, very similar to an abduction (.i.e. Rape of the Sabine Women).

Regarding the first event, Viriathus according to traditional cultural mores, Viriathus should have offered some type of gift or bride price for his bride, but he did not.[859] From a traditional bride price point of view,

---

[857] Quintela, "*The Celts in the Iberian Peninsula*", p. 254 It does not appear possible that there was a relationship between Greek ethnographers and Celtic compilers of Celtic mythology.

[858] Ibid., p.254

[859] **Bride price** also known as **bride wealth** is an amount of money or property or wealth paid by the groom or his family to the parents of a woman upon the marriage of their daughter to the groom. (*Compare* dowry, which is paid to the groom, or used by the bride to help establish the new household, and dower, which is property settled on the bride herself by the groom at the time of marriage.) In the anthropological literature bride price has often been explained in market

it was the man who endowed the woman's family with some type of gift whether it was money or material items; but from ancient texts, Iberian men did not offer gifts to a bride's family. These ancient testimonies as pointed out by J. C. Bermejo Barrera correspond to a situation in which the bride's brother endowed his sister compensation for his efforts in arranging a fiancée for her and not the parents.[860] At the same time, the newly married couple was also granted a dowry that would form part of the future hearth of the couple. But in the case of Viriathus, the text is incomplete so we must assume that he had followed traditional mores. But on the other hand, we also have to take into consideration that he did not follow Lusitanian traditions. The reason he may not have had received a dowry was perhaps Astolpas's family may have disagreed with this marriage and being that Lusitanian women were able to choose their own husband; she followed her heart. Unfortunately, we will never know the reason Viriathus did not receive a dowry, but one can only assume from his personality that he was not into wealth compared to freedom and power.

Astolpas (who represents Rome), has come to terms that this wedding is finally an amicable agreement to end the war, but in Lusitania there is a rejection since peace would have been a sign of submission on Roman terms. Viriathus in the end does not voluntarily lower himself to Rome which is signified by him taking his wife, mounting her on his horse and ride out to his secret mountain camp. In the global sense of the account both parties (Rome and Lusitania) would not give in to each other so easily.[861]

As for Viriathus's bride, she played a passive role in the scene and does not participate in any of Viriathus decisions. This is unlike Lusitanian women, as well as Celtic women in general for they played a propionate role in Celtic society, but since women played a semi-passive

---

terms, as payment made in exchange for the bride's family's loss of her labor and fertility within her kin group.

860 Bermejo Barrera, J.C. Mitologia y Mitos de La Hispania Preromana I, 2 vols., Madrid vol. 1, 1986 and vol. 2, 1994; Munoz, Mauricio P., op. cit., p. 59

861 Munoz, Mauricio P., op. cit., p. 62

or subservient role in Roman and Greek culture, it would not appear correct to show a strong leader like Viriathus dependent on a woman. Also, Viriathus' abduction of his bride falls into agreement with the ancient and modern-day practice of bride kidnapping. In the Indo-European marriage model, it seems that things were taken with force such as the autonomy of women as it is represented in mythology and history by the tribe of Benjamin in the Bible; by the Greek hero Paris stealing the beautiful Helen of Troy from her husband Menelaus, thus triggering the Trojan War; and by The Rape of the Sabine Women by Romulus, the founder of Rome, and was a common marriage practice in Sparta.[862] The presence of the three matrimonial functions (if one utilizes the trifunctional theory) this union is very similarly presented as is in the legend of the Roman abduction of the Sabine women.[863] Once again one must not forget who wrote these texts!

Finally, there is the status of Astolpas within his family comes into light. What was the family status of Astolpas? This question was first asked by Garcia Quintela who brings into light the exact interpretation of the Greek term – *synkedestés*.[864] For many years it was believed that Astolpas was the father of the bride, but through intense examination

---

[862] The Book of Judges in the Bible; Homer, *The Iliad*; Livy, *The Rape of the Sabine Women, in* Mary R. Lefkowitz & Maureen B. Fant, *Women's Life in Greece and Rome: A Source Book in Translation*, Published by JHU Press, 2005, pp. 176-178 In 326 A.D., the Emperor Constantine issued an edict prohibiting marriage by abduction. The law made kidnapping a public offense; even the kidnapped bride could be punished if she later consented to a marriage with her abductor. Judith Evans-Grubbs, "Abduction Marriage in Antiquity: A Law of Constantine (CTh IX. 24. I) and Its Social Context", *The Journal of Roman Studies*, Vol. 79, (1989), pp. 59-83, at 59, 65.

[863] Legend says that Romans abducted Sabine women to populate the newly built town of Rome, this was the first recorded example of bride kidnapping. The resulting conflict that ensued ended only by the women throwing themselves and their children between the armies of their fathers and husbands in that they decided to stay with the Romans instead of marrying Sabine men. The Rape of the Sabine Women ("rape" in this context means "kidnapping" rather than its modern meaning, see *raptio*) Munoz, Mauricio P., op. cit., p. 61-62

[864] Garcia Quintela, M.V, Chapter 3, "La leyenda de Viriato", Mitologia y Mitos de La Hispania Preromana, Madrid, 1999; Munoz, Mauricio P., op. cit., p. 60

of ancient Greek and Latin texts on the subject there has been a correction in Astolpas place within the bride's family. Thus, Astolpas was 'Viriathus' brother- in- law and not father-in-law as previously believed. Traditionally, the father gave the bride away, but as I previously mentioned, the bride was able to choose her own husband and that same sister chose a wife for her brother. So, it seems that match - making was not done by the parents, but by siblings. In the end, Astolpas was Tongina's brother.

These interpretations of Viriathus's marriage permits us as the reader, as well as scholars, to establish a relation between these episodes of Viriathus's life with an Indo-European trifunctional ideology as well as a relationship between the Lusitanian and Roman point of view and even perhaps explain specific ethnographic circumstances about the region or culture .

Viriathus's Generalship

Throughout Europe each nation has its popular barbarian hero who had squared off with Rome before and after Viriathus's claim to fame within the historical context. But of all the barbarians that fought against Rome, Viriathus is the one of the most well – known warriors, for according to Roman texts, he was more intrepid and the most tenacious that Rome ever saw to date. From studying Viriathus's military skills and leadership, he joins the ranks of other illustrious barbarian military leaders of the ancient world such as Ariovistus, Vercingetorix, Arminius, Tacfarinas and Decebalius. He has been viewed as a pragmatic man who had exceptional command skills. Like the rest of the Iberian tribes, the warlike tradition of the Lusitanians, in a pure military sense of strategy, was not a surprise to the Romans, because they had already encountered other warrior chiefs such as Punicus and Cesaros, who had given proof that they were worthy adversaries, but their fight was short lived due to the amazing strength and technology of the Roman war machine. With the appearance of Viriathus, who had some combat experience, he delivered to the Romans such an intense war that it lasted eight years and was recorded in several chapters by Roman writers. To some ancient as well as modern historians he was a political and military genius who had introduced a new military initiative: guerrilla warfare.

Though we do not exactly know what his admirable qualities were as a warrior and his exact strategy; his civic virtues and morals; nor his conception of unity and national cohesion was, he was still able to convince the chiefs of other tribes to join his cause. Elected from among other Lusitanian chiefs, Viriathus was able to bring together different Iberian tribes who had fought each other and against the Romans, in time, he managed to merge the entire western Iberia under his command. Viriathus's victories against Rome did not create jealousy, envy or rivalries from other chiefs, but great prestige as a combatant and as a leader. Besides being an amazing military commander, he was influential and a great communicator at tribal meetings and seems to have been ardently patriotic in fighting for his freedom as well as for his countrymen. Because he possessed these qualities, he established a single command and voluntary compliance that all followed blindly and because he was so respected there was neither defection nor desertion within his ranks. With this said each tribal chief acted as a subaltern deployed with a guerrilla band ordered to conduct some sort of task throughout the theater of operation.

In the aftermath of Galba's massacre of the Lusitanians in 151 BC, he was elected as a leader and organized an incredible army.[865] With more than 20,000 men, he led an amazing guerrilla campaign against the Romans which they dubbed the "Thieves War" and "Fiery War".[866] Viriathus with his vivacity, spirit, strong will, generosity and realist views, he displayed all the qualities of a skillful leader. As a military strategist, his experiences as a bandit leader during his youth enable

[865] Galba's massacre of the Luistanians resulted in 9,000 killed and 20,000 sold into slavery in Gaul and Rome while only 1,000 or so escaped Viriathus being one of them

[866] The reason why the Lusitanian War was dubbed the Thivies War was because it was being fought by thevies and not soldiers and that the Roman soldier's view the Lusitanians more as a thief than a warrior because of their prior history as raiding thieves. As for the Fiery War it was dubbed because of the ferocity that each side showed to each other.

him to form an army of guerrilla fighters and with his knowledge of all the paths, villages, caves, sources of water and terrain, he showed his talent as a military leader and tactician. Viriathus's skills and capabilities, subsequently, developed him into a master of guerrilla warfare, becoming a thorn in Rome's side. For Viriathus to have a successful leader, it seems he led his men from the front so that his soldiers would recognize him as a true leader and warrior. Furthermore, he never took more of the spoils than the share which he allotted to each of his comrades. Along with this, soldiers and people alike respected him for his striking sallies of wit, and above all else he surpassed every one of his men in temperance as well as in toil, and that he constantly slept in full armor and was always on the alert and ready for battle. It seemed as if in that thoroughly prosaic age one of the Homeric heroes had reappeared: the name of Viriathus resounded far and wide through Hispania; and the brave nation conceived that in him it had found the man who was destined to break the fetters of alien domination.[867]

It is doubtful that he was a simple shepherd who lived in the mountains of Mons Herminius, as legend has it. It is more believable that he was educated in the ways of other tribes and had access to military teachings and training that allowed him to transform his tribes of shepherds and bandits into a solid army and conduct a guerrilla war based on strategic elements and extremely sophisticated tactics. In addition, it is perhaps plausible to say that he may have had some knowledge of the Latin language, making him capable to approach diplomatic matters. From the ancient texts, it seems that he was diplomatic for they mention that the Romans had appointed Viriathus the title of, *"Amicus Populi Romani"*, which was given to tribal chiefs and kings that allied themselves or made peace with Rome. By the end of his life, Viriathus's fame reached such heights that for a long time he was the symbol of Lusitania.

---

867 Mommsen, Theodor, 'The History of Rome', Book IV: The Revolution, Chapter I: The Subject Countries Down To The Times Of The Gracchi, Translated by William Purdie Dickson, D.D., LL.D., University Of Glasgow, n.d.

CHAPTER VI

THE LUSITANIAN WAR WITH ROME BEGINS

The next series of events on the Iberian Peninsula were so substantial that literary remarks were left by several classical authors, especially Appian. The Lusitanian War, called *Purinos Polemos* (meaning *Fiery War*),[868] was a war of resistance fought between the advancing legions of the Roman Republic and the Lusitani tribes of Lusitania from 155 to 139 BCE. The efforts of the Romans in pacifying Lusitania and western part of Hispania were largely undone by the revolts of the years 155 – 133 BCE. The Lusitani revolted on two separate occasions (155 and again 146 BCE) and were then pacified. With the breakout of the Lusitanian War, in 154 BCE, another long war in Hispania Citerior began, known as the Numantine War, which was started by the Celtiberians that same year and lasted until 133 BC. The Lusitianian War and the even bloodier Celtiberian or Numantine War in Citerior marked a turning point in the history of Roman Hispania.

It is difficult to know exactly how many years the Celtiberian Wars lasted or if it was a war that strength out over years or if it was a series of small wars. Unfortunately, the data that has been available to us via the classical authors is conflicting. Appian, who collected his information from Rufus Avienus Festus and Publius Sempronius Asellius's writings, assesses that the Lusitanian War lasted seventeen years (155 – 139 BCE); Velleius Paterculus, Justinus, and Pompeius Trogus established it at ten;

---

868 This is the name given by Polybius and Appian.

Doidorus at eleven years, while Livy, Florius, Orosius and Eutropius at fourteen years.

From the work of A. Schulten and from other studies on the subject, he fixes the years at seventeen, in affirmation with Appian. However, the Lusitanian War did not last seventeen years consecutively, but was fought on two separate occasions. The first lasted 4 years: 155 to 151 BCE. It started when the Lusitanians and Vettones began to conduct large-scale raids into Roman occupied territory. The Romans reacted by sending an army to teach these two tribes a lesson, but the Romans were defeated, and an all-out war broke out. But the Lusitanian War under the leadership of Viriathus began in 147-146 BCE and ended in 139 BCE. This fearsome war was started by Roman greed which escalated into a massacre under the leadership of praetor Servius Sulpicius Galba and the proconsul Lucius Licinius Lucullus. Thus, it is impossible to explain the time frame the war lasted for it seems that each author used different figures when relating them to different starting points for the war – thus 153 or 152 might count as the outbreak point of major warfare throughout western Hispania. While 150 or 149 may be the breaking of the Luso-Roman peace treaty by Galba as a major starting point of the war.

As for the Lusitanian War one can not forget of the illustrious cavalier, sober and glorious Viriathus. In reality, he represents the true war against Rome, the ferocious fiery war, without truces, taken to effect by the Lusitanians, with a character of more defined violence that ever before. Since 219 BCE, when the first Roman troops invaded the Iberian Peninsula during the Punic Wars, it would take 200 years to Romanize the entire peninsula, and of all the tribes that inhabited the peninsula, the Lusitanians were especially hardest to conquer because of their love of freedom and independence and their love for fighting.

The Politics of Roman Imperialism in Hispania

The politics of Roman imperialism in the Iberian Peninsula began with an early trading treaty with the Carthaginians that dated from around

348 BCE.[869] The treaty forbade Roman vessels to trade beyond Mastia (present day Cartagena) in southern Spain. For a century, the Punic conquests of Hispania progressed slowly. But immediately after the First Punic War with Rome, Hamilcar Barcas, filled with bitterness at the loss of Sicily and Sardinia, set out to establish Punic power in Spain.

There is no doubt that his intention was to secure control of a sturdy population for the reemergence of a Punic army rather than revenue for the treasury and that his prime motive was to bring a war of revenge against Rome in return for the defeats he had suffered.[870] He met with striking success, for his generalship was superb and his rule was firm, but not oppressive. When he fell in battle in 229 BCE, Hasdrubal, Hamilcar's older son, succeeded and carried on the work of winning over the Iberian tribes at a more rapid pace than his father did. The Massiliots[871] as well as the Romans realized that these Carthaginian victories would soon deprive them of all their Spanish trade — for no other nation could trade where the Punic standard was planted. Again, there is little doubt that it was the affairs of trade in Hispania and Massilia that drew Rome's attention to Spain.[872]

The Massiliots had gradually lost a large part of their Iberian trade and within a year or two their flourishing colonies of Emporias and Rhodae would doubtless go under. If Rome cared little about the question of

---

[869] Polybius XXXIII, 8, 12. For an attempt at a correct understanding of this affair see *Am. Hist. Review,* XVIII.236. The war in question was undertaken by Rome wholly on Massilia's behalf and all the profits of the conquest fell to Massilia. Considering Rome's close connections with Massilia, it is not unreasonable to assume that Carthage is hereadding a clause in Rome's treaty which was devised chiefly for Massilia; Polybius. III.24 gives the treaty.

[870] Since Rome later received only half a tithe as tribute in Spain, it is probable that the Punic tribute had also been low. Frank, Tenney, Roman Imperialism, New York, Macmillan, 1914, p.73

[871] Massiliots were Greeks who founded Marseille.

[872] The Roman historians naturally forgot the important role of Massilia in the earlier proceedings, since Rome eventually assumed the whole burden of the quarrel. However, Appian, *Hann.* 2, knew that "Greeks settled in Spain" first appealed to Rome against Punic encroachment, and these were, of course, the clients of Massilia. Frank, Tenney, op. cit., p.73

open ports in Hispania, the Massiliots had other ways of arousing Rome's interest. They reported to Rome that a Punic attack upon Emporias was imminent for Carthage had supposedly declared war against Massilia, which in turn, would involve Rome because of their alliance. At the same time, representatives of Massilia began spreading rumors throughout the Roman government that the ultimate purpose of the Barcids in Hispania was to wage a war of revenge upon Rome. In the end their 'diplomacy' was effective.

Rome became thoroughly concerned about Punic advances in Hispania and sent envoys to Hasdrubal in 226 BCE with requests for a treaty defining that "the Carthaginians should not cross the river Iber (Ebro River) in arms." Rome obtained what she had desired and in pursuit of the same policy of anticipating Carthaginian military aggression, she entered into a defensive alliance with Saguntum, an independent Iberian city of considerable strength, a hundred miles south of the Iber River.[873]

Thus, matters stood when in 221 BCE, Hannibal, Hamilcar's young son, succeeded in taking command of Hispania. He at once subdued the whole peninsula as far as the Iber River, with the exception of Saguntum. Then, at the head of a splendidly trained army, in accordance with the plan and purpose that his father had taught him from youth, he made ready to bring on a war with Rome.[874] Saguntum, as it happened, offered a plausible excuse for the Carthaginians to besiege the city, for it had committed some hostile act against a Spanish tribe that was allied to Carthage. By picking up this quarrel, Hannibal perhaps hoped to force a declaration of war from Rome. If the declaration came from Rome, Carthage would be forced to support Hannibal's operation in Hispania (but not an invasion of Italy, which he did on his own initiative, for the Punic aristocracy lived by trade and not by war so they strongly favored

---

[873] The Massiliot traders may well have suggested this course to the Saguntines, since a Roman alliance would insure an "open door policy." Polybius (III, 30) places the alliance several years before 221, but apparently after the Iber treaty. The city was Spanish, as the excavations prove, not Greek, as the annalists thought. But it was strong and well governed, Polybius. III, 17.

[874] Polybius, III, 11, 12.

peace with Rome). The capture of Saguntum would wipe out the last unfriendly people in his rear, enabling him to close the harbor to the Roman navy and secure the booty with which — according to Polybius — he hoped to mollify the home government and equip his army for the long march into Italy. He accordingly attacked Saguntum in 219 BCE when the Roman consuls were busy in Illyricum.[875] After an eight-month siege, Saguntum fell. The Romans sent envoys to Carthage, demanding the punishment of Hannibal.Upon the refusal of their request, war was declared.[876]

---

[875] The Roman province of **Illyricum** replaced the formerly independent kingdom of Illyria, which stretched from the Drilon River in modern Albania to Istria (Croatia) in the west and to the Sava River (Croatia) in the north. The attack on Saguntum occurred when the Romans were involved in the **Second Illyrian War** (220 BC to 219 BC). In 219 BC the Roman Republic was at war with the Celts of Cisalpine Gaul, and the Second Punic War with Carthage was beginning. These distractions gave Demetrius the time he needed to build a new Illyrian war fleet. Leading this fleet of 90 ships, Demetrius sailed south of Lissus, violating his earlier treaty and started the war. Demetrius' fleet first attacked Pylos where he captured 50 ships after several attempts. From Pylos the fleet sailed to the Cyclades, quelling resistance they found on the way. Demetrius foolishly sent a fleet across the Adriatic, and, with the Illyrian forces divided, the Illyrian city of Dimale was captured by the Roman fleet under Lucius Aemilius Paulus. From Dimale the Roman navy went towards Pharos. The Romans routed the Illyrians and Demetrius fled to Macedon where he became a trusted councilor at the court of Philip V of Macedon and remained until his death at Messene in 214 BC.

[876] Livy and Appian, who wish to exculpate Rome, recklessly state that Hannibal broke the treaty of 226 BC by crossing the Iber to attack Saguntum, not knowing that the city lay a hundred miles south of that river. Polybius belittles Hannibal's provocation to attack Saguntum and holds that Carthage should have based her grievance upon the seizure of Sardinia twenty years before. This seems to be a very peculiar argument from a statesman of Polybius' experience, for ancient states did not assume the privilege of annulling old treaties on the ground of severity any more than modern states do. Most modern historians assert that Rome's alliance with Saguntum was an infraction of the spirit at least of the Iber treaty; for they assume that the treaty defined the Iber River as the boundary of the Punic and Roman "spheres of influence" in Spain; *E.g.,* Heitland, *The Roman Republic,* I, p. 223; Niese, *Röm. Gesch,* p. no, footnote 2; Meltzer, *Gesch. derKarthager,* II, 421; Kromayer in *Hist. Zeitschr.* 1909, p. 237; Ed. Meyer, *Kleine Schriften,* p. 269; Frank, Tenney, op. cit., p.73

Therefore, the main reason for the Roman presence in the Iberian Peninsula was to obstruct Carthaginian expansionism rather than the desire for world conquest.[877] Rome at first did not plan to conquer the

---

According to Frank, this is a grave misconception of third-century international politics. Rome had made the Saguntine alliance several years before the war, and yet not a word of protest had been raised against it. Hannibal attacked Saguntum, not on the ground that the Saguntine alliance encroached upon the Punic sphere, but on the ground of the wrongs committed by Saguntum against Spanish allies. In no ancient source is there the slightest indication that Carthage considered her rights in Spain to have been infringed by the Saguntine treaty; Frank, Tenney, Roman Imperialism, p.73; 29. Polybius (III, 29) goes so far as to claim that the Carthaginian government repudiated the Iber treaty on the ground that Hasdrubal was not authorized to make it. Polybius assumes that Rome had full power to make any alliances she chose with free states in Spain and asserts that all such allies were entitled to security by the terms of former treaties. Nor did Rome know anything of the modern doctrine of "spheres of influence," although it may have had some meaning for the ancient monarchies of the eastern Mediterranean. Rome's alliances showed in general an abhorrence of loose ends and always insisted upon clear definitions of boundaries. A penumbra of undefined influence over a hinterland of unexplored territory would have been entirely beyond Rome's understanding at that time. She had hitherto dealt with a patchwork of innumerable city-states and tribes whose petty areas in every case were precisely defined. She had signed at least a hundred alliances with such states, and the jurisdiction of each of these hundred treaties was clearly and definitely known. Not one of them assumed any kind of influence or interest beyond the precise boundaries of the signatories. Accordingly, although an affair like the Saguntine alliance would call for immediate protest during the days of Monroe Doctrines and African protectorates, there is no reason to suppose that in the third century, when it occurred, it involved any infraction of rights or that it could, in any way, have offended Hasdrubal and Hannibal, except in so far as it revealed Rome's success in gaining an ally coveted by them.

[877] When the war opened, Rome sent only a small detachment to Spain with the purpose of not conquering the peninsula, but of holding back Spanish reenforcements until the war was settled in Africa. The nations came to blows because of the Barcid family — whose war policy had met with defeat in 242 BC and 238 BC— were able to keep alive the bitter feelings aroused by former defeats and to discover a situation at the right moment whereby they could force their government to support a raid of vengeance upon Italy. If a brilliant son of Hamilcar Barcas had not survived to carry on the policy of his father till the favorable moment arrived, there is not the slightest reason for assuming that

area, but only to control the Carthaginians. During this time Rome did not see itself as imperialistic but acted on impulse of self preservation. However, the desire to take advantage of the area that later formulated an imperialistic agenda came after the Second Punic War. The Carthaginian exploitation of Iberian economy and human resources of the Peninsula offered the motivation for Rome to decide, set and explore the resources of the Peninsula for their own interests.

Though Rome came out of the struggle victorious, it suffered many losses that were irreparable, and her gains would prove a burden. The Roman oligarchy's main interested after the Second Punic War was in expansionism, and the conquest of new lands drew the Romans to the idea that it was very lucrative, even if a burden at first. For conquering this new land, it would provide Rome with a multitude of slaves, a necessary labor force, a canvass of taxes for the state, and new resources of minerals and food products, so as to ensure for the success of the Roman economic system. Thus, this all points to the economic content of Roman imperialism combined with other political, military, social and cultural factors.

The invasion of Hispania had been a political necessity during the war, since it alone could furnish the enemy with new recruits and its retention afterwards was, of course, the only conceivable course. But for the next two centuries this new province would cost the state more than it yielded.[878] Furthermore, the Spanish tribes were far from ripe for political responsibilities and they had no love for an orderly regime. Roman negotiations with each 'sovereign' tribal leader were countered with constant difficulties owing to the fact that the people were divided into innumerable tribal groups. No sooner had a Roman general sworn a treaty with a tribe, it reshaped itself into a newly formed

---

Rome and Carthage would not have found a *modus vivendi* in the same way that the neighboring powers of the eastern Mediterranean had.

878 The Barcids, in order to acquire Spain for military purposes, had imposed only a very light tribute and Rome could not expect to win it from Carthage if she increased these impositions. Consequently, the Spanish tribute was always extremely low — only half a tithe upon its poorly tilled fields. Livy, XLIII, 2, 12; Frank, Tenney, Roman Imperialism, p.75

tribe and disclaimed participation in the preceding agreement. The policing of Hispania degenerated into undignified and costly guerrilla warfare, disgraced by schemes and stratagems. Roman generals learned to deal with the trickery dealt to them. Nowhere did Roman warfare and diplomacy descend to such devious ways as in Hispania. But we shall come to this again. Suffice to say, at various times during the following century, the Roman Senate would have been relieved to hear that the whole peninsula had disappeared underwater. In the end, the Roman occupation of the Iberian Peninsula lead them to a repressive upheaval of the indigenous people.

But what we call imperialism is something very different from the European imperialism of the XIX century, for according to Theodor Mommsen, Roman imperialistic expansionism was not of an imperialistic character compared to the modern age, but a series of defensive measures adopted during a war that it considered preventive.[879]

As preventive as their policies may have been, the methods that the Romans implemented of exploiting the land and people led to the irremediable evils of the plantation system with its concomitant evils of slave labor preventing the healthy development of more productive farming at the time when Rome's population was increasing.[880] And yet, how could the government know that Rome's population would soon reach abnormal proportions in a short time making it difficult to recover the leased lands for colonization, and also that the landlord system, once firmly entrenched, would become impregnable, permanently excluded the small privately - owned farm. Perhaps the Senate did not foresee that Rome someday would govern a score of foreign lands whose armies would have to draw their strength from the Italian countryside and foreigners if the state was to survive. Rome did her best to meet the

---

[879] Mommsen, Theodor, Römische Geschichte, 8 vols., Berlin, 1903, vol. 1 and 3. Translated into Spainish Historia de Roma, Madrid 1983.

[880] It required several decades, however, before Rome became overcrowded again. During the three decadesafter the war, Rome's citizen body increased only 25 per cent, whereas the acreage of *ager Romanus* in-creased 100 per cent. See *Am. Hist. Review,* XVIII, p. 245.

situation in the light of past experience, but the problems it created by war and its hunger for expansion became too complicated and her stubbornness, along with corrupt emperors and lack of experienced leaders was inadequate to rule over such a large land mass, which it later hurt the empire.

The Punic War wrought few changes to the newly acquired province of Hispania, which had readily fallen into the form of government shaped for Sicily.[881] The federation in Italy had stood the endurance test better than it could have been anticipated, and the Senate saw no reason for introducing any innovations there. In fact, because of the general satisfaction, the Senate even grew negligent about making several well-deserved promotions towards citizenship. At the same time, the old city-state government of Rome had proved itself versatile enough to meet the exigencies of the Punic War, but the early losses on the field had been appalling, and it is usual asserted that these heavy losses were due to an oligarchical system which placed annual civil magistrates at the head of the army, causing the political situation in Hispania to be somewhat chaotic.[882]

The Politics of Roman Imperialisn upon Lusitania

One can fully endorse the idea that the Roman campaigns to conquer Lusitania were not only economical, but for political and military reasons such as for after the Second Punic War, the idea of invading Lusitania was not only a defensive measure to protect Roman gains, citizens and allies against Lusitanian incursion and raids. The Roman occupation of Hispania was a necessary operation within the Roman strategy during

---

881 The only practical difference was that the *civitates* were allowed to pay Rome specified sums of money as tribute (in this case, based upon an estimate of half a tithe on produce) instead of an annual percentage in kind. This was the usual Seleucid system, probably established in Spain by Carthage. The cities were, therefore, *slipendiariae* rather than *decumanae.* Of course there were favored cities in Spain as well as in Sicily: several *foederatae,*some *liberae,* and many which, at an early day, secured the privileges of Latin cities. See Marquardt,*Staatsverwaltung*, I, 251; Frank, Tenney, op. cit., p.76

882 Heitland, E.G., *The Roman Republic,* I, p. 227; Frank, Tenney, op. cit., p.79-80

the Second Punic War and there is no end for the practical reasons why the Romans should evacuate the immediate territory after they had gained so much and lost so much.

However, Roman intervention in the affairs of the Iberian populations disturbed the relations between the indigenous communities, which placed the Romans at a disadvantage. Roman dominion over southern and eastern Iberia was not fully ensured, for some of the communities that inhabited certain areas continual offered strong resistance. The indigenous population to get rid of Roman oppression had to make some offensive and defensive actions. The Romans reacted quickly by putting down these rebellions. As for Lusitania, this at first did not seem to have been important to the Roman initiative of extending their achievements further deep into the Iberian Peninsula for the Romans were busy in consolidating and putting down rebellions in the eastern and southern part of the peninsula. Once these areas were consolidated and under effective control it would produce excellent profits for Rome. While the Romans consolidated former Carthaginian lands, the Lusitanians took advantage of this confusing situation and began to cross over into Roman territory, devastating their newly gained territories. Because of the horror of Lusitanian incursion, the Romans reacted quickly and sent several Roman legions to patrol the territory between the Guadalquivir and Guadiana Rivers.[883] For the next several years, the Lusitanians continued their incursions into Roman- held territories which began to draw the attention of the Senate. The Lusitanian attacks did not cease until Caius Atinius, praetor of Ulterior, set out against them in 186 BCE.

After several defeats by Atinius, the Lusitanians did not launched any cross - border incursion between the years 178 and 156 BCE, besides a few skirmishes here and there along the Luso-Roman border of Baetica. But shortly afterwards, the situation changed rapidly. As we will see in the next section, the Lusitanians commanded by Punicus, attacked cities that had allied themselves to Rome. After Punicus's death the Lusitanians continued to fight under Césarus, who went onto attack one of Rome's allies, the Conii and taking their city, Conistorgis.

[883] Livy, 39.20-21

But the victory was short-lived, for after the capture of Conistorgis, Césarus was killed in battle and his army defeated by the Romans. This Lusitanian defeat led the Romans to begin the process of subduing the local population of south-west Hispania. In time, this subjugation of the populace turned violent and became the prelude to the great Lusitanian insurrection under Viriathus.

During the Lusitanian War, Roman military operations intended to prevent further Lusitanian incursions into Roman occupied territory. Even though Rome could not tolerate these incursions any longer, it had great potential at any given time to completely change the situation caused by Lusitanian incursions via peaceful means by giving them land or commercial rights. But believing in its great military prowess, the Roman Senate assumed that through continuous suppression of the Luistanians and Vetones, it would have been sufficient enough to finish these 'primitive people'. How wrong the Senate was!

However, the actions taken by the Romans against the Lusitanians and Vettones showed a weakness of Rome's strategy. The mountainous defensive castro system (walled villages) which had a vertebral column along the course of the Guadalquivir and Guardian, as well as further up towards the Douro River, left a wide zone of land with no space to restraint them. Rome was confident that its cultural movement and commercial contacts in that part of the country would produce, in the short term, the stability and pacification of the Lusitanian territory and neighboring peoples. At the same time, a strong military presence in the surrounding area was thought to instill fear in these people, but it instead agitated and aggravated many of the tribes.

In any case when the Romans reached Lusitania, they realized that they bit off more than they could chew. But until the Lusitanians were completely dominated, the Iberian Peninsula would be unstable because the Lusitanians were a strong and warlike nation. These people were so defiant that they gave hope to other tribes to continue, restart or start new rebellions against the Roman yoke of imperialism. But once the Lusitanians had been quelled, from that point on, the task of pacification would be easily facilitated. But it would take until 19 BC to completely pacify Lusitania.

With the aid of some documentary sources, the Luso-Celtiberian Wars, presented in a large part of Roman historiography as a conflict between imperialist domination and the spirit of independence of the indigenous communities, which was been seen as two positions of antagonistic ideologies. On the contrary, it seems that it was the disproportionate greedy ambition of a few individuals that made Rome's consolidation of Hispania difficult, which led to these conflicts with the indigenous population. In the end the Celtiberian Wars reached such magnitude that it forced the Roman Senate to introduce institutional changes within the province and to reorganize and strengthen the Roman army in Hispania.

The Fire is Ignited

The year 197 BCE was a year of particular significance for Hispania, with the conclusion of the division of the conquered territory; Hispania had been split into two Roman provinces: the province of Hispania Citerior and Hispania Ulterior.[884] This administrative reform of Hispania identifies a clear political process of conquest that would in the end affect the Lusitanians.

The Senate deployed qualified praetors with one or two legions along with auxiliary troops. Though these magistrates had in their hands all the administrative, judicial and military power, its management was somewhat supervised by the Senate. Representing Rome, the governors required that taxes be collected, and that each tribe should pay a tribute,

---

[884] During the first stages of Romanization, the peninsula was divided in two by the Romans for administrative purposes. The closest one to Rome was called *Citerior* and the more remote one *Ulterior*. The frontier between both was a sinuous line which ran from Cartago Nova (now Cartagena) to the Cantabrian Sea. *Hispania Ulterior* comprised what are now Andalusia, Portugal, Extremadura, León, a great portion of the former Castilla la Vieja, Galicia, Asturias, Cantabria, and the Basque Country. *Hispania Citerior* comprised the eastern part of former Castilla la Vieja, and what are now Aragon, Valencia, Catalonia, and a major part of former Castilla la Nueva.

as aid to Rome, by having their young men serve as auxiliaries in the Roman Army. Also, governors were given imperial power to issue edicts laws, and proclamations, regulate the politics of newly subjugated peoples and the right to life and death, both to the citizenry, army and the indigenous, as well as changing the status of conquered cities by having several already Romanized cities print currency and send it to the recently taken cities.

Unfortunately for the Romans strict political and military supervision, aggravated by the endless spoliation and greed of Roman magistrates who sought personal fortune rapidly caused the emergence of Iberian insurrections, strife and rebellions against them. The worst rebellions were always provoked by the excesses of Roman authorities such as was the case with the First Celtiberian War. But on the other hand, there were several tribes who were not under the Roman yoke of imperialism and pretty much did what they wanted to do, as long it did not affect the Romans, but at times these tribes went a bit too far and would raid Roman occupied towns, which the Romans did not tolerate.

The Lusitanians of all the Iberian tribes continued to be a thorn in Rome's side with their incursion and systematic raids on the Roman controlled cities and towns in territories east and south of Lusitania. Since 193 BCE, the Lusitanians had been fighting the Romans on and off. During the second half of the 2nd century BCE, they were the only people of the Iberian Peninsula that continued to resist the Roman Empire.

The first time that the Lusitanians are cited as enemies of Rome was around 194 BCE, when the Lusitanians entered Hispania Ulterior and sacked several cities in the Guadalquivir Valley.[885] Praetor P. Cornelius Scipio Nasica, cousin of Scipio Africanus and son of Gnaeus Scipio who was killed in Hispania at the Battle of Ilipa (Alcalá del Rio) during the 2nd Punic War, attacked and defeated the Lusitanians at Ilipa, who were returning to Lusitania loaded with riches. Intoxicated with loot and

---

[885] Livy, 35.1.4; Munoz, Mauricio P., *Viriato: A luta pela Liberdade*, Esquilo, Lisbon, 2000, p. 144

returning to their homeland, they were ambushed by an inferior Roman force. The battle lasted, according to Livy, for a good part of the day. The reason why the ambush was successful was because the Romans were in a close and serried formation and the Lusitanians combat effectiveness was hampered by many heads of cattle and weighted down with loot. At first the Lusitanians threw the Romans into some disorder, but soon the fighting became even. During the struggle, Nasica vowed that he would celebrate Games to Jupiter if he should rout and destroy the enemy. At length, the Roman attack became more insistent and the Lusitanians, exhausted from marching all night, began to give ground and broke off from the engagement.[886] After the battle, the Romans had supposedly killed 12,000 Lusitanians and captured 540 prisoners and only suffered 73. Having routed the enemy, the Romans returned the stolen property to their owners and kept what was unclaimed for themselves.[887] It is important to highlight the fact that after this point, the Romans saw the Lusitanians and other neighboring populations that were not under their control as uncivilized bandits and robbers of their fertile and rich lands of Baetica.

In the years 191-190 BCE, Lusitanian incursions became such a burden for Rome, that praetor Lucius Aemilius Paulus Macedonicus had to wage a harsh campaign against them.[888] The Lusitanians, according to Livy and Orosius, penetrated deep into Bastetania and defeated a Roman garrison in the vicinity of the city of Lyco.[889] The Romans are said to have suffered more than six thousand casualties. At the end of the winter of 190 BCE, Paulus hastily formed a new legion in conjunction with a collection of allied soldiers and managed to defeat the Lusitanians somewhere in Baetica. Trusting in their first victory, the Lusitanians neglected to continue on their defensive and offensive

[886] Livy, 35.1.5-11

[887] Livy, 35.1.11; The number of Lusitanian deaths is questionable for at time (just as like in modern times) the number of enemies killed was exaggerated.

[888] Livy 37.57.1; L. Aemilius Paulus Macedonicus, who with great glory had conquered king Perseus of Macedonia, was assigned to Hispania in 189. It was in Macedonia where he received the nickname Macedonicus

[889] Livy 37.46.10-12; Lyco is sometimes pronounced Llurco which is located in "Cerro de los Infantes" in Pinos Puente (Granada)

posture and instead devoted themselves to plundering. The end result of their mistake was that they were routed, and put to flight; 18,000 were killed, 3,300 captured to be sold as slaves, and their camp stormed.[890] This victory contributed much to the tranquility that followed in Hispania for the next few years. With such a large victory, Paullus returned to Rome with a multitude of gold, but for political reasons he did not obtain a triumph or the ovation. And before leaving Hispania he founded the town of Turris Lascutana which was considered as a *colonia latina libertinorum* in thanks of the local support he had against the Lusitanians.[891]

In 188 BCE, Lusitanian and Celtiberian incursions against Betica began once again.[892] These must have been so alarming that the praetors, L. Manlius Acidinus of Hispania Citerior and C. Atinius of Ulterior, sent to Rome disturbing reports about new Iberian upheavals that they requested reinforcements. Despite dispatches being sent to Rome with reports that the Celtiberians and Lusitanians were united in war and were beginning to ravage the territory of their allies, the Senate left the new magistrates to deal with the situation on their own.[893] This attitude would have dire consequences. By 186 BC, the Lusitanians crossed the Guadalquivir and took the city of Hasta (Mesas de Asta, close to Cadiz) and forced its inhabitants to declare that the Romans were hostile.

Soon after the first dispatches reached Rome. Where the original dispatches went unheeded, the Senate now listened, but it was too late. According to Livy, Atinius fought a battle with the Lusitanians in the neighborhood of Hasta. He claims that as many as 6,000 enemy were killed; the rest were routed and driven out of their camp.[894] Atinius, then led his legions to attack the fortified town of Hasta, which he captured

---

890 Livy 37.57.5; the number of Lusitanian deaths is questionable for at time (just as like in modern times) the number of enemy killed was exaggerated.

891 García Moreno, Luis A., "Sobre el decreto de Paulo Emilio y la Turris Lascutana (CIL, 12, 614)", Epigrafía hispánica de epoca romano-republicana,1986, Zaragoga, p. 195-218

892 Livy, 39.7.6

893 Livy 39.7.7-9; Munoz, Mauricio P., *Viriato: A luta pela Liberdade*, p. 136

894 Livy, 39.21.3-4

with little difficulty. But while he was approaching the walls somewhat incautiously, he was struck by a missile and in a few days later he died of his wound. When the dispatch announcing his death, the Senate was of the opinion that a courier ought to be sent to overtake the new incoming praetor C. Calpurnius at the port of Luna advising him to hasten his departure for Hispania, so that the province might not be left without an administrator.[895]

A year later, further clashes are recorded when a combined Roman force commanded by L. Quinctius Crispinus and C. Calpurnius Piso were routed by a large native force made up of Lusitanians, Celtiberians and Vaccaei close to Toletum (modern Toledo) and Dipo (locality unknown).[896] According to Livy, the Iberian victory was helped by their knowledge of the terrain and the nature of their fighting style.[897] The two Roman armies were routed and driven back to their camp. Luckily for the Romans, the Iberians did not press on their attack. This allowed the demoralized Romans to return to their camp and lick their wounds. Fearing that their camp might be stormed the next day, both commanders decided to withdraw their armies during the middle of the night.

At dawn, the Iberians formed up and marched up to the camp's rampart; surprised at finding the camp empty, they entered it and appropriated themselves to what had been left behind in the confusion of the night. They then returned to their own camp and remained inactive for several weeks. The losses of the Romans and their allies in the battle amounted to 5,000; Iberian losses unknown.[898] But, soon afterwards, somewhere near the Tagus River, the Romans ran into the Lusitanians and defeat.[899] After this campaign, Hispania was quiet throughout the winter. When

---

895 Livy, 39.21.1-5

896 Livy 39.30.2

897 Livy, 39.30.3-7

898 Livy.39.30.8

899 Livy, 39.42.1

the praetors returned to Rome, each praetor was unanimously decreed by the Senate a triumph.[900]

In 181 BCE, Livy refers to several small pitched battles between the Lusitanians and praetor P. Manlius, unfortunately he does not give information about the battles nor describe the place.[901] In 180 BC, under the praetorship of L. Postumius Albinus and T. Sempronius Gracchus, the Roman army was able to consolidate its defensive line along the Tagus River, advancing the province of Baetica's border further north.[902] Due to their continuous incursions, Albinus set out against the Lusitanians living along the southern border; managing to pacify them by force. Gracchus then worked at attempting to Romanization the area via the establishment of colonies, by the end of 179 BCE, the Romans had succeeded in pacifying the central regions of Hispania and bringing them and several Iberian tribes under their control.

On returning to Rome both men received a triumph, implying that they had conducted a successful campaign against these two tribes.[903] But these measures were not sufficient and caused a wave of new revolts, for incoming greedy praetors did not keep their word by following Gracchus policies and began violent and arbitrary campaigns against the certain Iberian tribes, leading them to address the Senate with their protests. They protested to no avail.

Livy ends his writing about the Iberian Peninsula at 181 BC with the exception of a few minor mentions of skirmishes against the Lusitanians in 163 BCE.[904] In the years of 163 and 162 BCE under the consulate of P. Cornelius Scipio Nasica Corculum and C. Marcius Figulus, the Lusitanians again rebelled, but only to be defeated, unfortunately we do not know the details.[905] After this period, there is no more news of Lusitanian incursions.

---

900 Livy, 39.42.3-4

901 Livy, 40.33.14

902 See Chapter 1 for details

903 Livy, 41.47

904 Livy, Per. 46

905 Munoz, Mauricio P., *Viriato: A luta pela Liberdade*, p. 146

Perhaps the reason Livy, as well as Appian, omits the decades of the 170s, 160s and part of the 150s, may be due to the policies and treaties that were introduced by T. Sempronius Gracchus. These policies brought relative peace between the Hispanic populations and the Romans. Another reason for little mention within the Roman historical record was because Rome had become involved in the Third Macedonian War, making Hispania a minor concern. However, this did not cease the struggle against the Romans, nor did the Lusitanians withdraw from their incursions and looting within central Hispania and the Guadalquivir Valley. The next time one reads about Roman involvement in Hispania comes from Appian's book on the Iberian Peninsula where it begins with the outbreak of the Celtiberian War in 153 BCE,[906] and the Lusitanian Wars.

The First Lusitanian War

In 155 BCE the political and military situation in the Iberian Peninsula had radically changed once again, to a point that it created an enormous concern in Rome. During this period of turmoil, the following episode came to be an important symbol of Iberian resistance for it motivated future Iberian leaders to resist Roman imperialism, at the same time it showed the Romans that the conquest of the Iberian Peninsula would be tougher than they thought.

Lusitanian incursions were systematic and well organized that one must assume that these actions must have been part of a resistance struggle for Lusitanian and Celtiberian independence against Rome rather than simple robberies. The numerous defeats suffered against the Lusitanians and Celtiberians must have deeply discouraged the Roman citizenry in

[906] The alleged reason for Roman going to war again was the action of the Celtiberian town of Segeda took to incorporate other smaller towns into its own boundaries. According to J.S. Richardson from his stern study on this affairs, writes that this seems trivival compared to the Roman respose in sending a consul with a consular army of two legions to deal with the situation, and it seems likely that at least part of the explanation lies in the need of the Senate to find somewhere for the consuls to fight in a period of relative peace. Richardson, J.S., Appian: Wars of the Romans in Iberia, Aris & Phillips Ltd., Warminster, UK, 2000, 141.

Rome for they could not understand why they were losing battle after battle against primitive tribes, as reported in the classical texts.

The first Roman episode in this new war with the Lusitanians occurred in 154 BCE. The account comes from Appian, who took his information from Polybius, who had personally participated in both Celtiberian Wars (1st Celtiberian War 181 – 179BCE and 2nd Celtiberian War 154 – 153BCE). Appian writes that the praetor of Hispania Ulterior, M. Manlius was defeated by a Vettone and Lusitanian alliance under the command of the Lusitanian warrior chief, named Punicus, who undertook to pillaging and looting of populations that had submitted themselves to Rome.[907] Punicus's forces were so determined on showing the Romans that they meant business that they even defeated praetor L. Calpurnius Piso.[908] Of the 15,000 Roman soldiers that were stationed in the area, 6,000 men were killed along with the army's commander Terencius Varro.[909] Punicus quickly took advantage of the victory and marched cross the entire Guadalquivir Plain until he reached the Mediterranean coast, where he sacked many other cities. Alarmed by Punicus's campaign many Romanized cities begged for Rome to send more troops as well as forming new Iberian auxiliary units. But this campaign was short lived for during an attack on one of these allied cities, Punicus was killed by a stone to the head.[910]

A new chief was soon chosen by the Lusitanians. Ceasarus was his name. The following year (153 BC) he led incursions as far as the city of Sexi (Almuñécar, Granada) sacking many cities along littoral Andalusia. At the same time, elections were held in Rome to elect two new praetors to Hispania. The praetors designated for Hispania Citerior was Quintus Nobilior Fulvius, while Hispania Ulterior was entrusted to Lucius Mummius. Along with these two newly elected officials, it was also decided that a strong army be sent to Hispania to remove the Celtiberian and the Lusitanian threat; the Roman Army totaled

---

907 Appian 56.234-237

908 Ibid.

909 Ibid.

910 Ibid.

approximately 30,000 men between the consular troops and Spanish auxiliary allies. On arriving in Hispania, Marcus Fulvius Nobilior quickly set out to pacify the Celtiberians. Once they were located, he managed to defeat an Iberian army made up of Celtiberians, Vettones and Vaccei near Toledo and took their leader named Hilerno prisoner.[911]

At the onset of 153 BCE the Lusitanians fought and repelled Roman soldiers from its border. Caesarus pursued them but was obliged to withdraw in the face of Mummius's large army of auxiliary legions. This major defeat, after several victories, especially at Bencatel (Vila Viçosa) phased Caesarus's confidence and he decided to take another route and attempted to continue his campaign.[912] But the Romans pursued him in a disorderly fashion, that the Lusitanians on receiving intelligence reports about their enemy turned around and ambushed Mummius's army; resulting in about 6,000 Roman deaths.[913] Ceasarus's army also recaptured the booty that had been taken from his men, as well as the Roman camp, seizing many weapons and much needed supplies. Along with this equipment and supply, they captured several Roman standards which they paraded them throughout Celtiberia in mockery of the Romans.[914] This victory rejuvenated the Lusitanian spirit to continue their fight against the invaders and encouraged the Celtiberians to reignite their fight once more.

Mummius withdrew from the campaign and took his remaining 5,000 troops and trained them at an unknown location.[915] In the meantime, he sent a dispatch to Nobilior asking for support in his campaign to annihilate Ceasarus's army. In response to Mummius's dispatch, Nobilior sent considerable reinforcements. Keeping watch to see if Ceasarus might enter or exit the province, Mummius planned to ambush

---

911 Calvert, Albert F.,Toledo: An Historical and Descriptive Account of the "City of Generations," The Spanish Series, London, J. Lane; New York, J. Lane Co., 1907, p. 4.

912 Tusculano, Victor de A Luistânia de há dois mil anos: epopeia military de Viriato, p. 28

913 Appian, 56.237

914 Ibid.

915 Appian, 57.238

these marauders, killing many in the process and take their booty as their own.[916] According to legend, during one of these Lusitanians incursions, Ceasarus was killed in an ambush where today there stands the chapel of São Tiago (Saint James) in the district of Bragança, the municipality of Vimioso, which was built on top of a Roman temple ruin that Mummius erected in compliance with a vote from his soldiers who had fought in the campaign.[917]

Soon after another Lusitanian leader rose up by the name of Caucaenus.[918] He quickly formed up an army and marched south and attacked the Conii, taking their largest city, Conistorgis.[919] The reason why the Lusitanians attacked the Conii was because they had allied themselves with the Romans. Caucaenus's troops then marched into Andalusia and crossed the Mediterranean Sea from the Strait of Gibraltar by boat. Landing somewhere between Morocco and Libya, Appian writes that Caucaenus's force was split into two and ravaged Libya, while the other part of his army laid siege to Ocilis (modern Arzila, Morocco).[920] Mummius, however, pursued them with 9,000 infantry and 500 cavalry.[921] They soon encountered one of Caucaenus's forces and a battle ensued in which the rebels suffered 15,000 casualties and the siege of Ocilis was raised.[922] Capturing the Lusitanian booty, he distributed it to his army as much loot as his men could carry and burnt the remainder in honor of the gods of war.[923]

The following year, 152 BCE, two new praetors, Marcus Attilius (Ulterior) and M. Claudius Marcellus (Citerior) were assigned to Hispania. In Rome, Mummius received the honor of a triumph for his

---

[916] Ibid.

[917] Tusculano, Victor de A Luistânia de há dois mil anos: epopeia military de Viriato, p. 28

[918] Appian, 57.239

[919] Ibid.; The Conii were a sub-group of Celts that lived in the Algarve who were Roman subject since 174 BCE

[920] Appian, 57.240

[921] Appian, 57.241

[922] Ibid; Once again 15,000 casualties seem a bit high.

[923] Appian, 57.242

victory over the Lusitanians. Because of his victory, he raised the morale of Roman citizens for many were preoccupied with the pessimistic news that was coming from Hispania. As for these two newly appointed praetors, they quickly lashed out at the troublemaking Lusitanians and Celtiberians; and luck was on the side of the Romans for Marcellus after winning several victories near Nertóbriga (which is perhaps Fregenal de la Sierra, Badajoz) made a pact with the Celtiberians, but this treaty was refused by the Roman Senate, forcing each side to continue the war.[924] But being that winter was setting in, Marcellus went into winter quarters at Cordova, where he in turn provided his auxiliary troops to Attilius in his campaign against the stubborn Lusitanians. M. Attilius with Marcellus's reinforcements penetrated Lusitania and took the city of Oxthracae (location unknown).[925] Have caused 700 causalities among the Lusitanians and taking their largest city, Attilius had so terrified all those that lived in the vicinity that the inhabitants called for peace.[926]

This peace meant nothing for the rest of the Lusitanians, because when Attilius went into winter quarters, Lusitanians from other areas went on a rampage and besieged several Romanized cities.[927] Armed Lusitanian incursion continued to blight the Betician regions and be a thorn to the Roman legions. However, shortly after, Marcellus once again approached the Roman Senate to accept his peace proposal. Under pressure from the citizenry, the Senate agreed to his proposal and terms, which set forth a brief period of tranquility in Hispania (from 151 to 143 BCE).

In 151 BCE Claudius Marcellus was replaced with Consul Lucius Licinius Lucullus with whom he shared governorship of Hispania with the now infamous praetor, Servius Sulpicius Galba – these two characters are regarded as the most despicable in the conquest of the Iberian Peninsula. The reason for this statement is because to most Iberian historian these two well established political and military men

---

924 Munoz, Mauricio P., *Viriato: A luta pela Liberdade*, p. 149

925 Appian 58.243

926 Ibid.

927 Appian, 58.244

came to Hispania to enrich themselves rather than attempt to stabilize the provinces for the benefit of the empire. In return for their greed they destabilized certain areas of the province that caused several tribes to rebel.

Galba's Massacre and the Rise of Viriathus

Praetor Servius Sulpicius Galba and Proconsul Lucius Licinius Lucullus arrived in 151 BCE. Upon reaching Hispania both men immediately began campaigning against the Iberian tribes. Lucullus was disappointed to find that the Celtiberians had made peace; so, he decided to launch his own campaign against the Vaccaei and Caucaei, massacring the second tribe after having made an agreement with them.[928] He would later be involved along with Galba in Viriathus's rise to power. As for Galba, he continued Attilius's campaign against the Lusitanians.

As mentioned in the last section, the Lusitanians from the vicinity of Oxthracae signed a peace accord with Marcus Attilius that forced the submission of several Lusitanians and Vettones tribes. But this treaty was not accepted by the Lusitanians from other areas and these tribes either broken or ignored the treaty and once again began to ransack the Roman occupied countryside.

Receiving reports that the Lusitanians were up in arms and sacking Roman settlements, Galba rapidly organized his army and marched towards Lusitania to relieve his Roman subjects who were hard pressed by the Lusitanians. Having travelled 500 *stadia* (90 km) in 24 hours, his exhausted troops were immediately formed up and sent straight into battle against a large Lusitanian force that had stationed itself

---

[928] Appian, 51.215- 53.225; The reason for his campaign against the Vaccaei and Caucaei was because Lucullus was keen for glory and needed money because of his lack of it (51.215); the undignified massacre of Cauca, a Caucaei city was located between Salamanca and Segovia. When both tribes surrendered, they signed a peace agreement, whose conditions were very harsh and were required to provide hostages, a payment of 100 talons (in what is not known), and establish a garrison of 2,000 Roman soldiers in the city (Munoz, Mauricio P., *op. cit.*, p. 148)

on the northern outskirts of Carmo (modern-day Carmona).[929] Galba succeeded in putting the enemy to flight but made the mistake of pursuing the Lusitanians. Exhausted, disorganized and scattered, his army incautiously pursued them. On seeing a weak and disorderly pursuit, the Lusitanians counter-attacked and a fierce contest ensued, in which 7,000 of the 15,000 Romans fell.[930] After this devastating defeat, Galba managed to collect the remnants of his army, and quickly took shelters in Carmo, situated a few miles away from the battlefield. Once he had assembled the remainder of his army, he marched out and took up winter-quarters at Conistorgis.[931] While wintering in Conistorgis (151-150 BC) Galba assembled about 20,000 allied troops for a new campaign when spring arrived.[932]

In Hispania Citerior, L. Licinius Lucullus who had conducted his own private campaign against Vaccaei was wintering in Turdetania. On learning that three separate Lusitanian armies were crossing into his territory, he sent his best commander against the northern group which resulted in 4,000 Lusitanian casualties.[933] While one of his trusted generals fought in the north, he organized his remaining legions and marched out of Turdetania heading south into Baetica in search of wealth and the other two groups. During his minor campaign in southern Spain, he ran into one of the groups, a medium size Lusitanian force. During the battle he killed 1,500 bandit-warriors as they were preparing to cross the Strait of Gibraltar into North Africa.[934] The rest of the rebels fled onto a hill, which Lucullus encircled and was to capture the rest of them, which were later sold into slavery.

With the arrival of Spring 150 BCE, both governors decided on a joint strategy of pillage and destruction in an attempt to put an end to the persistent raids by the Lusitanians in Roman territory. Both men set out

---

929 Appian, 58.244

930 Appian, 58.245

931 Appian, 58.246

932 Ibid.

933 Appian, 59.247

934 Appian, 59.248

in a pincer movement; Lucullus turned east towards Lusitania, while Galba left Conistorgis and marched north into Lusitania. The two forces advanced deep into Lusitania, pillaging and destroying towns. Though this strategy failed to bring to battle the bulk of the enemy's forces, it had the desired effect of forcing the Lusitanians to agree to a truce.

The Lusitanians sent an emissary, declaring that they repented for having violated the treaty which they had concluded with Atilius, and promised henceforth to observe it faithfully. Galba received the envoys and made a truce but pretended to sympathize with them; Lucullus by now had joined forces with Galba and planned that they should use the same treasonous scheme that Lucullus had used with the Caucaei.

The way in which Galba acted on this occasion is one of the most infamous and atrocious acts of treachery and cruelty that occur in Iberian history. Galba received the ambassadors kindly and lamented with sympathy of their circumstances, especially the poverty of their country that induced them to continuously indulge in banditry, break agreements and revolting against Rome. According to Appian, Galba told the envoys:

"For it is the poor quality of the soil and lack of resources that compels you to do the things you do. As an act of kindness, I will give my poor friends good land and settle them in rich country, dividing them into three sections. With this said, he proposed to the envoys that they would be resettle them on three fertile plains under the protection of Rome. To subdue them without violence, he induced them to leave their homes, and assemble into three hosts, with their women and children, and in the three different places which he had fixed upon, lands in which he would later allow each host to settle upon." [935]

While Servius Sulpicius Galba organized this false armistice, the Lusitanians celebrated this new alliance with the sacrificing of a man and a horse. Within several months, more than 30,000 Lusitanians had

[935] Appian, 59.249-250

gathered to wait for that promise to come true.[936] On an agreed date in 150 BCE the Lusitanians congregated at a place which had been arranged. He then divided them into three sections and showed each group a stretch of open land, ordering them to stay in this area until he could provide them with a town.[937] But there was to be no distribution of lands, just death and slavery.

Turning back to the first group, Galba addressed them as friends, asking them to give up their arms, for surrendering their weapons was a sign of peace and it was superfluous for an agrarian way of life. When they had done so, Galba had his men surround the Lusitanians and ordered his soldiers to kill every able-bodied man.[938] He hurried on and treated the second and third group in the same manner as the first, while each group was ignorant of what was happening to the other groups.[939]

In the aftermath of the massacre, 9,000 lay dead and as many as 20,000 were taken prisoner and either forced into slave labor or sold into slavery.[940] However, a number of Lusitanian males managed to escape from the bloody scene; one of whom was Viriathus, destined one day to be the avenger of the wrong done to his countrymen.

Appian, as well as several other authors, state that Galba, although already very wealthy, was extremely stingy and greedy.[941] Of all the loot that was produced, Appian notes that the praetor carefully allocated

---

936 30,000 is just an estimate from other sources in with many modern historians have come to agree with, but in actuality no knows for sure.

937 Appian, 60.251

938 Appian, 60.252; Orosius, 4.21.10; Many authors agree that the Romans only killed the men for out of the 30,000 Luistanians only 8,000 to 9,000 were killed.

939 Appian, 60.253

940 Once again, the number of casualties and prisoner taken is not exactly accurate for there are several sources (such as Valerius Maximus 9.6.2, Suetonius, *Galba* 3) that vary in numbers, but all modern historian agree with this count.

941 Appian, 60.255; According to J.S. Richardson's research on the war, this is the only statement about Galba's greediness in any callsical source. Richardson, J.S., Appian: Wars of the Romans in Iberia, Aris & Phillips Ltd., Warminster, UK, 2000, 154.

only a small part of this newly acquired fortune to his soldiers, another small part to his friends and as one would expect, kept the remainder for himself.[942]

After these actions, Lucullus and Galba returned to Rome in 149 BCE, richer and more powerful than before. Expecting to be honored with a triumph, these two men were accused of committing heinous acts that went against the newly instituted *Lex de rebus repetundis,* proposed by L. Calpurnius Piso in the earlier part of 149 BCE. This law basically stated that if non- Romans from the provinces complained about its magistrates and pro-magistrates who used their power wrongly to acquire personal wealth, they would be compelled to make restitutions, thus protecting all non-Roman people from violence and extortion.[943] Outraged about the incident, several Roman tribunes lead by Lucius Escribonius Libo (a plebeian) and M. Porcius Cato, instituted proceedings against Galba and Lucullus by introducing a bill *(rogation)* to release all those Lusitanians that had surrendered to him and had been sold into slavery in Gaul, also a constitutional tribunal was ordered to investigate the behavior of the praetors.[944] On hearing these declarations against Galba, several former praetors such as Q. Fulvius Nobilior who was against the *rogation,* defended Galba's actions.[945]

Lucullus who was a bit more politically cunning than Galba, bribed the senators and was freed from any charges; in return he had to build a temple to the goddess Felicitas, a forced religious act to the goddess

---

942 Appian, 60.255

943 Cicero, *Brutus*, 27.106; *Epistulae ad Atticum* (*Letters to Atticus*), 12.5(b); Livy, 98-100; Richardson, J.S., Hispaniae, Spain and the development of Roman imperialism, 218-82 BC, Cambridge Univ. Press, London, 1986, p. 137-137. On the history of leges repetundarum see Balsdon, J.P.V.D., "Thr history of the extortion court at Rome, 123-70 BC", Papers of the British School at Rome #14, 1938, pp. 98-114; Lintott, A.W., "The leges de repetundis and associate measures under the Republic" Zeitschrift der Savigny-Stiftung #98, 1981, pp. 162-212.

944 Livy, 39.40.12 and 49; Appian, 60.255; Gellius, Attic Nights, 1.12.17; Cicero, *Divinatio in Caecilium*, 20.66 and *Brutus*, 23.89; *de oratore*, 1.53.227-228; Quintilian, 2.15.8; Valerius Maximus, 8.1.2

945 Livy, per. 49

for forgiveness of his past transgressions.[946] Galba, on the other hand, decided to stand his ground and became involved in a serious judicial battle, even rejecting Cato's *rogatio*. Galba, the most celebrated orator of his generation, according to Cicero, defended himself. To achieve the compassion and pity of the senators, he appeared in front of the Senate with his children and ward, asking the Roman people to protect them if he was found guilty and sentence to death. In principle, the Senate denied absolving him of his crimes, but when he decided to deliver a large part of the booty that he had stolen in Hispania into Rome's coffers and Senator's pockets, the Senate acquitted him.[947] Money brought more compassion than words did and being that Galba was one of the richest men in Rome, he had no problem in buying compassion. It is probable that Galba was never brought before a court for had he; he would have perhaps had face condemnation. So strong was the power of money that five years later, he was elected Senate consul.

What is even more significant during this period for this story to continue was that one of the few survivors of the Galba's slaughter was a man named, Viriathus. Roman historiography relates Galba's cruel and unscrupulous episode with the ascension of Viriathus, one of Rome's newest adversaries for the next eight years. From then on, Viriathus becomes the protagonist of the Lusitanian War and his name repeatedly echoed in senatorial election speeches throughout Rome.

With the rise of Viriathus, the Lusitanians, from this point on, did not raid Baetica just for the desire of pure momentary treasures and profit, but the wanting of land for their cattle, farming and overall survival of their people due to the poor quality of soil in Lusitania.[948] In the high lands, there was much poverty and lack of vegetation, while goats

---

[946] Felicitas was unknown before the mid-2nd century BC, when a temple was dedicated to her in the Velabrum in the Campus Martius (Field of Mars) in Rome by Lucius Licinius Lucullus, who used his booty from his 151–150 BC campaign in Spain. The temple was destroyed by a fire during the reign of Claudius and was never rebuilt. Munoz, Mauricio P., *Viriato: A luta pela Liberdade*, p. 152

[947] Cicero, *Brutus*, 82 and *de oratore*, 1.58; Appian, 60.255

[948] Rodrigues, Adriano Vasco, Arqueologia da Peninsula Hispanica, Porto, 1960, p. 409

and sheep were the only thing that was able to transform into wealth and survivability.[949] In the end, the Lusitanians just want pastures of their own.

In conclusion, the 25 years of peace initiated by Sempronius Gracchus, was broken. Though Galba incited the Lusitanians, the Lusitanians were blamed for the war. Overall both sides were responsible, but in defense of the Lusitanians, the reason for initiating the war was justified for they needed land to solve their economic problems and Rome did not offer them land, but deceived them, as did Galba. Galba's failure to fulfill the peace by terror and excessive cruelty against the Lusitanians had ruined Rome's hopes and only chance at pacifying the Lusitanians and their desire of getting pastures and better farmland. Therefore, the Lusitanians were in an unbearable situation which left them no other solution than fight Rome. It is perhaps safe to say that this event caused by the Romans was the reason for the major revolts that broke out throughout the whole of Hispania between 147 and 133 BCE. As for the Lusitanian War, Galba's betrayal and massacre of the Lusitanians in 150 BCE ended the first phase of the war and began a new phase of rebellion that would spread like a wildfire throughout Hispania.

[949] Ibid.

CHAPTER VII

THE VIRIATHAN WAR (The Second Lusitanian War)

Classical authors primarily Polybius, Livy, Appian and Diodorus, highlight that the Iberian Wars which the Romans had undertaken in Hispania against the native populace were the most difficult and cruelest of all those that the Roman had engaged in so far. The Roman soldier had to face not only a dangerous enemy but also a hostile environment. It was not in vain that Polybius, an exceptional witness of the facts and friend and advisor to Publius Cornelius Scipio Aemilianus Africanus Numantinus, classified this entire period of more than 20 years of warfare as the 'fiery war'.

Slavery, murder, treason, breaches of treaties, brutal executions, massacres of both Romans and Lusitanians alike, ethnic cleansing were tactics that became part of the new style of war called 'guerrilla warfare'. The inability of Rome's military power to defeat a 'barbarous' people came to be seen by many Romans as a costly war with no end in sight, and with little in return (i.e. profits). In time, this war would begin to exhaust the patience of the Roman Senate so much that they decided to stop Iberian resistance by any means necessary. Also, Rome's praetors were urged not to look to Rome for material resources, aside from manpower, to continue the war effort. The fighting would become horribly inhumane and brutal. Death, pillaging, rape, violence, even genocide, became the practice common to all the Roman generals that were deployed to this war zone. The reason why this war became so vicious was because

Rome never wanted to accept peace with the Iberians on an equal footing; in spite of their defeats. The Romans believed that they were better than the barbaric Iberians. Therefore, the Iberians were required to surrender without conditions, something that they never would accept. In return this was the most frequent reason why the Lusitanians preferred to fight to the death rather than accept these new treaties on Roman terms. Hence, they resisted in defending their liberty to the death.

Viriathus Strikes Back

Three years (150 - 147 BCE) had passed since Galba's massacre and the Romans were beginning to become accustomed to the splendorous peaceful haven that the Peninsula had become. Of course, this was only an illusion for deep down Galba and Lucullus's massacre had left profound and bitter marks in the Lusitanian psyche, leaving a resistance movement capable to make war against the Romans. But while the Romans were enjoying their peace in Hispania, among the Lusitanians, Viriathus, a survivor of Galba's massacre, became the leader of his people with a plan to severely damage Roman rule in Lusitania and beyond. This Lusitanian leader in the words of Theodor Mommsen, "seemed as if, in that thoroughly prosaic age, one of the Homeric heroes had reappeared."[950]

Although a new hero was emerging, there is no news of any rebellious activity in Lusitania. Perhaps the reason for this was because the Lusitanians were licking their wounds and preparing themselves for a wrath of revenge. In the meantime, Rome had become involved in new commitments such as in fighting the Third Punic War (149 BC - 146 BC).[951] Also the area of the Aegean also needed Roman attention, in

---

[950] Mommsen, Theodor, 'The History of Rome', Book IV: The Revolution, Chapter I: The Subject Countries Down To The Times Of The Gracchi, Translated by William Purdie Dickson, D.D., LL.D., University Of Glasgow, n.d

[951] Third Punic War (Latin: Tertium Bellum Punicum) was the third and last of the Punic Wars fought between the former Phoenician colony of Carthage, and the Roman Republic. The war was a much smaller engagement than the two

particular the handling of insurrections in Macedonia, which had only recently come under Roman control in 148 BCE with the elimination of King Andriscus by Quintus Caecilius Metellus. With this said, whatever happened in Hispania was minor, until in 147 BCE, when the Lusitanian War began a new dimension in warfare.

Following Appian's writings, Viriathus was elected head of his tribe sometime between 150 and 147 BCE. From that moment on, it is possible that Viriathus soon began to outline his strategy and organize a small army to terrorize the Romans.[952] Unfortunately there is no record of what went on among the Lusitanians during these years, but one is sure that at the end of 147 BCE or the beginning of 146 BCE, the Lusitanians had assembled an army of 10,000 men under a nameless tribal leader and invaded the pacified area of Turdetania.[953]

Reaching the Guadalquivir Valley, the Lusitanians are intercepted near Urso (Osuna) by a Roman legion belonging to the newly elected praetor of Hispania Ulterior, Gaius Vetilius who had recently arrived from Rome with a new army, as well as commanding the army stationed in Ulterior. On receiving news that the Lusitanians were in his territory, Vetilius quickly marched against them from his winter quarters in Córdoba, with his entire army of 10,000 men.[954] He soon fell upon the Lusitanians while they were foraging for supplies, killing many of them, and forcing the rest into an unnamed place where, if they stayed, according to Appian, they were in danger of famine, and if they came out they would fall into the hands of the Romans.[955]

previous Punic Wars and primarily consisted of a single main action, the Battle of Carthage, but resulted in the complete destruction of the city of Carthage, the annexation of all remaining Carthaginian territory by Rome, and the death or enslavement of the entire Carthaginian population. The Third Punic War ended Carthage's empire.

[952] Appian, 60.254

[953] Appian, 61.256

[954] Córdoba was the capital of the Roman province of *Hispania Ulterior Baetica*. Teófilo Braga, "Viriato: A Lusitânia é a mais poderosa nação da Hispânia", Fronteira do Caos Editores, 2006 p. 32.

[955] Appian, 61.257

The Lusitanian situation with Vetilius had become despairing. Being in this unknown place, surrounded and without provision, they sent messengers to Vetilius with olive-branches (a sign of peace) asking for good land to which to settle on, and thereafter they agreed to obey the Romans in all matters.[956]

Vetilius promised to give them land if they surrendered their weapons, but when the agreement was nearly made to that effect, Viriathus, who had escaped the perfidy of Galba and who was among them as a junior chieftain, suddenly reminded them of the unreliability and the bad faith that the Romans had shown, often swearing oaths only to brake them soon after. To make matters worse, Viriathus went on to say how entire Roman legions and their leader escape from the perjuries of the Roman Senate, but the Lusitanians did not. With this said, he asked all the warriors that if they sworn an oath of obedience to him, he would show them a safe retreat from this place.[957] On this basis, negotiations with Vetilius were suspended.

Moved by his eloquent speech and excited by the new hopes with which he inspired them, the Lusitanians nominated Viriathus on the spot as their supreme commander. He quickly proposed a plan of action to break the siege that would later be quoted by Frontinus in a thesis on military strategy.[958] In Appian's report on the matter, Viriathus drew the warriors up into a battle line formation as if they were ready to fight, but gave them orders to divide themselves up into many small groups and when he gave the signal, which was his mounting of his horse, they would then scatter in all directions, break through enemy lines and make their way by different routes to the city of Tribola (a city south of Urso) and wait for him there for reassembly.[959]

While the men prepared themselves for their escape, he asked for a thousand of the best warriors - riders to stay behind with him to keep

---

956 Appian, 61.257 - 258

957 Appian, 61.258 - 259

958 Frontinus, *Stratagema*, 2.13.4

959 Appian, 62.260

Vetelius busy.[960] With these arrangements made, the Lusitanians began to flee in many different directions the moment Viriathus mounted his horse. Vetilius afraid, surprised and confused on what was happening, soon realized that it was impossible to pursue so many groups. So, instead he ordered his men to stand down against those who had scattered in different directions and turned towards Viriathus and his 1,000 warriors that were on horseback, standing on the horizon as if they were waiting for an attack. The Romans charged and a battle ensued. Having very swift horses, Viriathus and his men put their plan into effect; Viriathus allowed the Romans to attack, then retreat, again stand still and allow the Romans to attack, retreat once more.[961] This maneuver consumed the entire day and the next for he continuously had the Romans running around in circles.[962]

After two days of toying with the Romans, reckoning that his army had safely made their escape and reached Tribola, he disappeared from the battlefield like a ghost. His planned had worked! Exhausted, the Romans bivouacked for the night, while his men took advantage of the darkness and set out for Tribola via unmarked and devious paths on very agile and nimble steeds.[963] Thus Viriathus, in an unexpected way, rescue his army from a desperate situation. This feat, once known by other tribes of that vicinity, brought him fame and many reinforcements from different quarters enabling him to further wage war against the Romans for the next eight years.[964]

The Battle of Tribola

Deceived, Vetilius soon realized what had happen, and wanting to avenge his embarrassment, he slowly began searching for the Lusitanians, but the Romans were not able to follow them at an equal pace or search fast

---

[960] Appian, 62.261

[961] Appian, 62.262-263

[962] Appian, 62.262

[963] Appian, 62.263

[964] Appian, 62.264

enough due to the weight of his men's heavy armor, their ignorance of the roads and terrain, and the inferiority of their horses. On receiving intelligence that the slow-moving Romans were in the vicinity, Viriathus quickly reorganized his troops and planned and prepared his small army for a large-scale ambush.[965] Ready for war, he posted a greater part of his army in the thickets along the pass of the Sierra de Ronda, in the Barbesula River Valley (today called Guadiaro).[966]

Confident that his superiority in numbers would ensure victory, Vetilius pursued Viriathus until he came upon Tribola. Viriathus, having concealed his men in the thickets along the pass, instigated a skirmish and quickly retreated back through the pass in attempt to lure Vetilius into his trap. The Romans again underestimate their enemy. Vetilius failing to send out an effective scouting party, fell for Viriathus diversionary tactic and gave chase into the pass. When the Roman army entered the pass, Viriathus suddenly turned around and charged head on into the Roman ranks, while those laid in waiting in the wooded slope sprang the ambush. Viriathus had led Vetilius into a lethal trap. The Lusitanian swarmed the Romans like locusts from all sides, killing as many of them

---

[965] Appian, 63.266

[966] Sierra de Ronda is situated in the province of Málaga, Spain; this is also the source of the Guadiaro River. During the Roman era the Ronda pass represented the only line of communication in the Guadalquivir Valley to the ancient town Carteia (today it is a ruin which resides near the city of Algeciras and San Roque), at a distance of 60 km. The location of unknown Tribola: U. J. H Becker sought in the area of Cadis; J. F. Masdeu belong to Evora and Beja; A. Schulten follow Appian's text that refers gorge of throats profound, on the from Betis to Carteia, located in the Serra of Rhonda. In the area, there is no evidence of another road than the one that follows along the Guadiaro (Barbesula) Valley. Currently the rail line to Antequera – Rhonda runs through this area. South of Sierra da Ronda between Sierra da Ronda and Libar, a road passes through a long narrow pass in which Vetilius men had once passed through in a column formation and according to archaeological artifacts this could have been the precise place were the Lusitanians ambushed the Romans. There already existed a very ancient path that connected Acinipo (Ronda la Vieja) and Arunda (Ronda) until Carteia, this route a century later; it would turn into a major Roman road that connected Carteia to Corduba. So, to find the city of Tribola one must seek it not far from Carteia. Munoz, Mauricio P., *Viriato: A luta pela Liberdade*, p. 162-163

as they could. At the end of the battle, several hundred soldiers were surrounded, surrendered and were taken as prisoner, including Vetilius himself, while the rest ran for their lives. According to roman writers, these prisoners were treated badly, tortured and killed in revenge for Galba's action several years prior. As for Vetilius, Appian wrote that the man who captured Vetilius, not realizing who he was, but only seeing that he was old and fat, and considering him worthless, killed him.[967] But Diodorus reports a different version to which Viriathus condemns him to death. Overall, the result was disastrous for the Romans; of the 10,000 Romans soldiers over 4,000 were killed including Vetilius, as for the survivors of the massacre some 6,000 made their way with difficulty to the city of Carpessus on the Mediterranean seashore.[968] The Romans had been introduced to a new face of war; the hit and run tactic and alternating attack and retreat. After the incident, the Romans named this type of warfare, the *concursare*.[969]

Badly demoralized and incapable of counter-attacking, the Roman soldiers that escape death headed towards Carpessus, under the leadership of Vetilius's quaestor, who then stationed the men within the town's walls. Having requisitioned 5,000 allied Belli and Titthi warriors that lived in the area of the Jalón Valley, Spain, he sent them against Viriathus, who slew them all, so that there was not one soul left to tell the tale in a case to make an example of what happens to any Iberian tribe that sides with Rome. After that incident, Vetilius's quaestor remained quietly in the town waiting for assistance from Rome.

After the battle of Tribola, Appian writes with this new-found encouragement and leadership, Viriathus invaded the prosperous and

---

[967] Appian 63.267

[968] Appian, 63.267; It is often assumed that Appian meant Carteia on the Bay of Algeciras, close to Gibraltar, because other sources believed that it was formerly called by the Greeks, Tartessus, and was ruled by king Arganthonius, who is said to have lived one hundred and fifty years. Richardson, J.S., Appian: Wars of the Romans in Iberia, p.154.

[969] Martinez, Rafael T., Rome's Enemies (4): Spanish Armies, p.8; Arribas, Antonio, The Iberians, p.74.

fruitful region of Carpetania, where he plundered it freely until Gaius Plautius arrived from Rome with another army of 13,000 soldiers.[970]

In the aftermath of the battle, the Roman Senate saw Viriathus as a threat to the stability of the entire peninsula and immediately send reinforcements. But unfortunately, these reinforcements were more like replacement, thus the Romans did not have sufficient forces in Hispania to put an end to Viriathus. The reason why there were not enough forces in Hispania was because Rome was still engaged in the final struggle against Carthage (the Third Punic War) in its effort against its long-standing rival for hegemony of the western Mediterranean Sea.[971] All the Senate could do was attempt to contain Viriathus as best as they could.

On the other hand, Roman military leaders viewed him as a popular warlord among his people and an able enemy general. So, to handle this new menace, Roman generals had to change their tactics. Roman commanders stationed in Hispania came up with a strategy of dividing up their forces and attempt to surround Viriathus's small army, in an effort to surprise him at every turn in an effort to tire him out or weaken his army before the final hammer blow. According to Victor Tusculano, fresh new Roman legions were deployed to protect the southern part of Hispania, but unfortunately for them, they did not engage Viriathus in southern Lusitania, but instead in the Central Plateau and southern

---

[970] **Carpetania** was an ancient region of what is today Spain, located between the Guadarrama, the mountains of Toledo, the river Guadiana and the mountain range of Alcaraz, including approximately the present independent communities of Madrid and Castile. It was inhabited by the Carpetanians, a pre-Roman tribe. To the south dwelt the Oretanians; on the northeast were Celtiberian, to the northwest the Vacceus and Vetones. This area was easily conquered by the Romans and it was quickly integrated culturally and politically. Thus, it is practically unmentioned in the literature of the Roman conquest of Hispania. Its main urban nuclei Toletum (present-day Toledo), Complutum, present-day Alcala de Henares), Consabura, (present-day Consuegra), Segóbriga (Saelices and Laminio), soon after the conquest, it acquired municipal statutes.

[971] Allen, Stephen, Lords of Battle: The World of the Celtic Warrior, Osprey Publishing, Oxford, UK, 2007, p.150

Hispania. Though the Romans had stationed the nucleus of its army in the south, Roman military commander found it difficult to employ and engage their legions in Lusitania due to the rugged terrain. Without the conquest of the central region, Roman legions could not advance north and west without jeopardizing its overall security.[972] The way the Romans could have perhaps been able to conquer Lusitania quickly would have been by a three prong attack; one from the sea on the Atlantic coast and two from land in which the Romans could have avoid crossing the Serra da Estrela by going around it instead of through it. With this strategy the Romans would have dominated Lusitania, as well as the entire peninsula. But the lack of a sound military strategy would now result in a fight that caused major bleeding to the Romans forces.

As for Viristhus, he went on to exploit the situation by negotiating alliances with the Celtiberians and other tribes of the Meseta Central. At the same time, even though the Romans tried their best to deal with Viriathus, it was not good enough for the Romans continued losing men in large numbers.

Theater of Operations

The entire northwest of Hispania was involved, in different levels, in the Lusitanian War. But, furthermore, the war had great implications on the areas of the Meseta, Asturias, Andalusia and Cantabria. In some instances, there was a connection between Viriathus's guerrilla campaign and the Second Celtiberian War. One such example appears; Viriathus incited the Vaccaei and the Numantians against Rome, as well as the Galaician, Vaccaei, Belli, Titthi, Cantabrians, and Arevaci.

Even if the theater of operation was actually within the border of modern-day central Portugal and outskirts of Lusitania, it was in this large area called the Beiras that the Romans found it difficult to operate. Due to its thick forests and the country's high and inaccessible sierras along with the cold, rough and arid mountains of the inhospitable Meseta

[972] Tusculano, Victor de, A Luistânia de há dois mil anos: epopeia military de Viriato,p. 73-74

Central, which did not offer many possibilities for a successful Roman military campaign, this wild country caused many problems in Rome's attempt at pacification. This difficult terrain made it a safe haven for the many Lusitanian villages and fortified *castros*. However, in time the conquest of these territories was inevitability as the Romans saw the need to protect and defend their allies and their Betican possession against Lusitanians attacks.

Rome would press Lusitania with all the weight of its military power, stationing its legions near the borders of Lusitania in a show of force to maintain a policy of 'peace'. Also, during these years, Rome began to send a different type of governor to Hispania, one who was morally on the level and different from that of Galba, for Rome want to forget the cruelty of the degraded greedy that Galba and the overly ambitious Licullus had exhibited as governors. However, this Roman policy did not work for the Lusitanians who had been emotionally and spiritually scarred by so many Roman injustices that they were now blinded by rage and wanted Roman blood.

Viriathus's Guerrilla Campaign

Viriathus's victory at Tribola enabled Viriathus to roam all of Betica without opposition. The news of Viriathus's outcome reached all corners of the Hispania, vibrating patriotic enthusiasm. Furthermore, it raised the morale of the Lusitanians to the point that it served to incite widespread resistance against Rome throughout the land. With news of Viriathus's success, Viriathus had become the chief instigator of other tribal rebellions that arose throughout Hispania during an eight-year period, becoming the 'terror' of Rome. With his experience, wits and unorthodox tactics, it allowed Viriathus's army to dominate and plunder the lands of Beturia and the entire fertile Guadalquivir Valley. Though he was victorious, it did not provide large numbers of soldiers to Viriathus' cause at first. At the start of the war, only a limited number of neighboring tribal chiefs joined his cause such as Brigeu, clan chief from another Lusitanian tribe.[973] This would later change.

Brigeu's alliance (as well as with other tribal leaders) with Viriathus was the beginning of a united front against the Romans, that if successful, would ruin Rome's plans for the peninsula. Before the war, various Iberian, Celtiberian and Lusitanian tribes mutually fought against their common enemy, the Romans, with each tribe operating with complete independence from each other, until now, for somehow Viriathus's thirst for revenge had enabled him to unite many different tribes together under one commander. Viriathus's victory at Tribola had made him the uncontested general of the Lusitanians, as well as a beloved chief who was obeyed by all Lusitanians, because he had in the eyes of his countrymen embodied their aspirations of freedom and independence. But it was his hatred for Rome and his thirst for vengeance that started his glorious career.

Confident, Viriathus seemed to have come to believe that he had the power to oppose Rome, through his superior strategy, knowledge of the land and the bravery of his warriors. And though he was aware that the Roman army was concentrating its forces in Turdetania, he made the decision to turn north through the Sierra Morena and head into Carpetania, the richest and most fertile area of the Meseta. Unopposed, he continued his campaign into Carpentania towards Toletum (Toledo). According to the late Teófilo Braga, Viriathus had somehow made a defensive alliance with the Vettones and Vacceus with terms that they would have their forces meet in Toletum to plunder it.[974] With promptness, Viriathus arrived at Toletum and plunder it alongside his allies, according to Braga. He then enlarged his army by adding new allies and prepared to march through the rest of Carpetania. Viriathus marched through Carpetania, with the hope of luring out the next Roman praetor or general as he had done with Vetilius. After plundering

---

973 Tusculano, Victor de A Luistânia de há dois mil anos: epopeia military de Viriato, p. 74

974 Braga, Teófilo, "Viriato: A Lusitânia é a mais poderosa nação da Hispânia", p. 46, 50.

the countryside still unopposed, Viriathus returned to Toletum and prepared for a new phase of combat against the praetor that had just arrived from Rome with another army who was now heading towards Toletum to fight Viriathus.

Vetilius's defeat was commented on in Rome as of little importance for the Romans; as mentioned previously they were too involved in two major conflicts within their realm. But being that they had only one governor to run the entire province alone since Vetilius's death and were somewhat worried that the Lusitanian War might get out of hand, the Senate decided to elected Gaius Plautius Hypsaeus as Vetilius's successor in Ulterior.

A few months later, during the spring of 146 BCE, Plautius arrived in the province with another small army of 10,000 infantry and 1,300 cavalry. [975] Perhaps the reason that more could not be deployed was because Rome was heavily committed with its third war with Carthage. As praetor, he quickly imposed a high state of alert within his province and asked for aid from the governor of Citerior, Claudius Unimanus. At the same time, Plautius sent 4,000 - 5,000 Roman soldiers to relieve Vetilius's defeated army at Carpessus (today San Roque, Spain) and to aided Rome's allies, the Belli and Titthi. During their march, this Roman legion ran into Viriathus's army and was cut to pieces.[976] Unfortunately, there are no details of the battle. But at this point, Plautius begins his search for Viriathus with his entire army.

Plautius discovered Viriathus's whereabouts in Carpetania and attacked, but Viriathus – instead of fighting Plautius the conventional way – reverted to hit-and-run guerrilla tactics. Worried that his small army would be outnumbered, Viriathus quit Carpetania and withdrew into Lusitania. Plautius quickly instructed one of his generals named Quintus to take a legion and follow Viriathus, while he took another in an attempt to flank Viriathus's army from the south. Upon reaching a certain

[975] Appian, 64.269

[976] Appian, 63.268; Martinez, Rafael T., op. cit., p. 16; Munoz, Mauricio P., op. cit., p. 163

point both Roman armies would attack Viriathus simultaneous. During the pursuit of Viriathus's retreating army, Plautius received a dreadful report that Quintus's legion was wiped out as it reached its rendezvous point, which has been identified as Ebora (Évora).[977] Viriathus utilizing his signature 'feigned flight' tactic, turned on his pursuers and routed the Romans, killing most in the process.

With the outbreak of the Lusitanian War in 147 BCE and Viriathus's invasion into Carpetania, Plautius seems to have decided to transfer his command center of military operations against the Lusitanians to the center of the peninsula which was outside of Roman control. I believe why he left Ulterior and marched deep into Celtiberian territory was because he felt threatened by Viriathus deep incursion into Roman dominated southern lands, so perhaps, he thought that if Viriathus launched raids into southern held territory what would stop him from advancing eastward into Citerior inciting rebellion amongst the 'pacified' Iberian tribes, so it was very important to place a Roman presence in that area, which they did. By 133 BCE Carpetania had definitively become incorporated into the Roman dominion.

However victorious, Viriathus withdrew his forces into his home ground by crossing the Tagus River and setting up camp somewhere in the

---

[977] Évora has a history dating back more than two millennia. It may have been the kingdom of Astolpas (Saramago, Jose, Évora, Património da Humanidade, 1986 report to UNESCO to make Evora a World Hertiage site). It was known as Ebora by the Lusitanians, who made the town their regional capital. The Romans conquered the town in 57 B.C. and expanded it into a walled town. Vestiges from this period (city walls and ruins of Roman baths) still remain. The Romans had extensive gold mining in Portugal, and the name may be derived from that oro, aurum, gold) (Newman, Harold, R., The Mineral Industry of Portugal, 2002). Julius Caesar called it "Liberalitas Julia" (Julian generosity). The city grew in importance because it lay at the junction of several important routes. During his travels through Gaul and Lusitania, Pliny the Elder also visited this town and mentioned it in his book Naturalis Historia as Ebora Cerealis, because of its many surrounding wheat fields. In those days Évora became a flourishing city. Its high rank among municipalities in Roman Hispania is clearly shown by many inscriptions and coins. Braga, Teófilo, op. cit., p. 83 -85; Tusculano, Victor de, op. cit., p. 76 -77

hilly area, the Romans called, *Mons Veneris* (the Hill of Venus).[978] Despite his recent defeat, the determined Plautius and the rest of his forces made haste and crossed the Tagus in pursuit of the Lusitanians. Finally catching up to Viriathus and being keen to redeem his prior defeat, he attacked Viriathus. Plautius sustains another defeat with so much slaughter that he along with the survivors fled in a disorderly fashion. Plautius was so shocked about his losses that he withdrew early from the campaign season and took the rest of his army into the security of his winter quarters in Betica in the middle of the summer, refusing to venture out against Viriathus for the rest of his term as governor. According to Diodorus, Plautius was condemned upon his recall to Rome and charged with *minuta maiestas* (Little Treason) and consequently sent into exile.[979]

Viriathus's victory at the Battle of *Mons Veneris* left him with the initiative to exploit his victory in a series of attacks on Roman garrisons and towns in central Hispania which caused much damage. Now unopposed, he also went on a rampage through Central Hispania confiscating and destroying crop and pillaging town that had allied themselves with Rome, especially the Celtiberian city of Segobriga. Those towns or cities that sided and supported Viriathus were untouched and crops were paid for in booty.

---

[978] According to Professor Schulten, Mons Veneris is what is now known as Sierra de San Vicente, close to Talavera de la Reina, but according to Alarcão it may have been the Sierra de San Pedro between Cáceres and Badajoz (Alarcão, J. de, Roman Portugal, Vol. I, Aris & Phillips Ltd., Warminster, UK, 1988, p. 7 and Melena, Jose L., "Salama, Jálama y la epigrafia latina del antigo corregimiento", Symbolae Ludovico Mitxelena Septuagenario oblatae, Vitoria, 1985, p. 484-485) but Blázquez states that it was located in the well-known area the Sierra of the Serenita, in Gredos, which according to him this enclave is geographical more strategic for guerrilla operations, given its location between the valleys of Jerte and the Tormes(Blázquez, J.M., "La religiosidad de los pueblos hispanos, vista por los autores griegos y latinos", Emerita XXVI, 1958, 87); Inês Vaz, Luis João, Lusitanos no Tempo de Viriato, Esquilo, Lisboa, 2009, p. 159.

[979] Appian, 69.271-272; Diodorus 33.2; The *minuta majestas*, or simply *majestas* was based on the Roman law of treason with the original text of the law appears to have dealt with what were chiefly military offences, such as sending letters or messages to the enemy, giving up a standard or fortress, and desertion.

After defeating Plautius, Viriathus strategically based himself on *Mons Veneris,* whence he could launch raids into all the neighboring regions and continue his incursions along the Tagus River. The choice of this place as the center of his operations proves once again that Viriathus was a great strategist. Viriathus also extended his influence north to Sierra da Guadarrama, in the Sistema Central.[980] He moved hastily through this territory, forcing the habitants to respect his orders. Also around this time frame, he seems to have carried out an expedition against the Roman allied city of Segovia, which was situated in Vaccaei territory; unfortunately for the Lusitanians it was not as lucrative as Toletum.[981] His next advance occurred near the end of 146 BCE, when he made a move towards another Roman allied city, Segóbriga (actual Cabeza de Griego near Cuenca).[982] Viriathus managed to surprise its inhabitants and conquer the city by using the same tactic of ambushes, false withdrawals and surprise attack he had used against Vetilius and Plautius. The destruction of the Segobrigan army was recorded by Frontinus. He writes that Viriathus sent men to carry off their flocks of livestock. When Segobrigan soldiers saw this, they rushed out of their fortress in great numbers. The marauders pretended to flee and drew the Segobrigans into an ambush where they were cut to pieces. From a certain point of view, the defeat of these Romans cities acted as building block for Viriathus's reputation as a leader, as well as able to influence other tribes, especially the Celtiberians, to ally themselves with him.

Alarmed that Viriathus was running rampant through the Hispanic countryside and worried that he might cause trouble in Citerior, Claudius Unimanus, the governor of Citerior deployed his troops against Viriathus, presumably near the end of the campaigning season (autumn/fall) of 146 BCE. But like the previous praetors, according

---

980 The **Sierra de Guadarrama** is a mountain range forming the eastern half of the Sistema Central (a mountain range in the centre of the Iberian Peninsula), located between the Sierra de Gredos in the province of Ávila, and Sierra de Ayllón in the province of Guadalajara. The range runs southwest - northeast, extending into the province of Madrid to the south, and towards the provinces of Ávila and Segovia to the north.

981 Frontinus, 4.5.22; Orosius, 5.4.5

982 Frontinus, Stratagems, 3.10.6; 3.11.4

to Orosius and Florus, he was defeated in battle.[983] The battle was a disaster for Unimanus; he lost a legion and its standards which were taken as trophies and later publicly displayed throughout the mountain countryside on Viriathus's orders. The morale of the Roman legions fell even further after this event.

Viriathus's generalship in conducting this campaign had brought him further prestige and fame for he had showed all Iberians that it was possible to defeat Rome. With these victories, many warriors from all over the Iberian Peninsula began flocking to his standard. But with the war against Carthage finally concluded, Rome was free to solve the Iberian problem and concentrate on defeating the Lusitanians.

But before I continue with Viriathus's campaign, another individual that needs to be mentioned in this drama is Caius Nigidius, though he is only mentioned by Roman historian Sextus Aurelius Victor and several modern Portuguese and Spanish historians, Nigidius was praetor of Citerior when Unimanus was praetor of Ulterior. According to professors J.S. Richardson and E. Kornemann, they are the only two authors that try to explain and place him in the chronological sequence of the Lusitanian War. According to Richardson's research, Victor suggests that Nigidius was a praetor who was soon defeated after Unimanus.[984] But this statement is questionable for Kornemann suggests that Nigidius was the unnamed lieutenant of Fabius Aemilianus, who was left in charge when the latter went to Gades (Cadiz) in late 145 BCE (see below) and was defeated by Viriathus.[985] In this case, he was not a praetor. However, according to Richardson there may have been a chance that he was praetor of Citerior in 144 BCE for a Roman defeat is recorded, so if there was such a horrible defeat, it would have been more justifiable to have then sent Quintus Caecilius Metellus Macedonicus, the hero of the Macedonian War, after such a disaster was attributed by

---

983 Orosius, 5.4.3; Florus, 1.33.15

984 Sextus Aurelius Victor, *De Viris Illustribus Romae*, 71

985 Appian, 65.276; Kornemann, Ernst. Die neue Livius-Epitome aus Oxyrhynchus. Klio Beiheft, 2. Leipzig, 1904, p. 98 – 99; Brennan, Corey, 'Notes on the preators in Spain in the mid-second century BC' emerita 63, 1995, p. 65

Nigidius, rather than after a victory by Laelius and Aemilianus in 144 BCE.[986] But confusion arises when one looks into the classical texts for they exclude Nigidius as praetor of Citerior, placing Laelius as praetor. So, sending Metellus in 143 BCE was the result of Laelius's defeat. Thus, the lack of information about this individual and episode has caused great confusion of what occur in Citerior during 145 - 144 BCE.

Being that I mention Nigidius, I should also mention a battle that he may have been involved in as praetor, which is not well documented or known in the annals of history, but well known in Portuguese legend and folklore. This battle which has been past down from generation to generation and documented by several Portuguese authors such as Teófilo Braga and Victor de Tusculano, of which I have used as references (of these two authors, I use Braga's account of the battle, which is the better of the two), as well as the information from a stone tablet housed in the Cenáculo Museum at Évora, (discovered during the early part of the 20th century) that also mentions two names, Unimanus and C. Minicius, who was perhaps Unimanus's legion commander, at the time of the battle. According to Braga, he believes that this unknown battle was fought at Ourique in present-day Alentejo region of southern Portugal.

As the story goes, Viriathus found himself in the Alentejo region near Ebora (Évora), when the newly arrived preators to Hispania, Unimanus and Nigidius, set forth on their urgent campaign to repress the Lusitanians, to erase prior defeats. On receiving intelligence from their own spy network, both praetors combined their plan of attack into a pincer movement; Unimanus would attack from the south through the mountains of Ourique; while Nigidius who had been operating in Vaccei territory would move from the north toward Ebora, the Lusitanian capital.[987] Thus catching Viriathus between these the two legions, the Romans believed that Viriathus would certainly be defeated. And with

986 Richardson, J.S., "Hispaniae, Spain and the development of Roman imperialism, 218-82 BC", pp. 188-189

987 Braga, Teófilo, op. cit., p. 83

this complete victory, they would be then able to occupy the entire region.

On reaching Lusitania, these two generals set their plan into motion. Meanwhile, Viriathus through his vast spy network sought to smash one of the legions as quickly as possible so as not to get caught in between both, but to do that he needed to choose the battlefield and herd them in, one legion at a time. After much cat and mouse maneuvering, Viriathus decided to attack Unimanus first near Ourique for Nigidius was still days away from his position. The battle ensued, but unfortunately, there is no information about the battle beside a mention from Dio Cassius who wrote this passage, perhaps to show the tenacity of the Luistanians. Dio wrote:

In a narrow pass 300 Lusitanians faced two cohorts of 1,000 Romans. As a result of the action, the Lusitani lost 70; the Romans lost 320 men. When the victorious Lusitanians retired, one of the warriors became separated and was surrounded by a detachment of cavalry. The lone warrior quickly stabbed the horse of one of the riders with his spear, and with a blow of his sword, cut the rider's head clean off, that it caused such terror among the Romans that they prudently withdrew under the warrior's arrogant and contemptuous gaze.[988]

Besides showing the low morale of the Romans, it also details the determination of the Lusitanians. From Braga's research, it looks like perhaps this minor battle took place at Serra d'Ossa which is about 100 miles (160 km) from Ourique, but again due to the lack of information one cannot be sure if this is the exact place.[989]

Ultimately, Viriathus completely defeats Unimanus. Unimanus withdraws from the campaign to avoid greater bloodshed. But fearing

---

[988] This insert was supposedly taken from Cassius Dio's History of Rome and used in these following historical literary works, Braga, Teófilo, op cit., p. 84; Tusculano, Victor de, op. cit., p. 89-90; Martinez, Rafael T., op. cit., p. 16 and Allen, Stephen, Lords of Battle: The World of the Celtic Warrior, p.150; Munoz, Mauricio P., op. cit., p. 165.

[989] Braga, Teófilo, op. cit., p. 84; Tusculano, Victor de, op. cit., p. 89-90

persecution from Rome, he sends a messenger to ask his colleague, Nigidius to halt his march and attack the Lusitanians wherever he encounters them. Nigidius agrees and changes course, marching north where he stops in the Beira region of Portugal. Upon arrival, he sets up a camp at Viseu and conducts military operations.[990]

Viriathus, through his dedicated spy network, receives information that Nigidius had established a bivouac site at Viseu. He immediately moved into the region and attacked Nigidius. Due to Viriathus military skills, Nigidius was no match for him and is defeated. Nigidius quickly packs up and immediately withdraws to an unnamed or forgotten fortified city which Viriathus quickly besieged. Nigidius lacking provision and fearing that the city would fall to the Lusitanians, abandons the city in the dead of night. But Viriathus through his spies is informed of this movement and quietly follows Nigidius, who is obliged to fight as he flees further reducing Roman manpower and morale. Though there is little information on Nigidius's praetorship in Hispania, there is some evident from stone tablets and markers that have been discovered in that area such as the ones found in the Riba-Côa region, that this man existed.[991]

Once news of the latest developments in Hispania reached Rome, the Senate deemed the situation threatening enough that it immediately sent replacements to Plautius along with a consular army. Corresponding to the news, Consul Quintus Fabius Maximus Aemilianus, the adopted son of Lucius Aemilius Paulus, conqueror of Macedonia, was given Ulterior as his province.[992] At long last, Rome had a competent veteran general. Furthermore, Aemilianus, through connections in the Senate was able to get Gaius Laelius Sapiens, an intimate friend of Aemilianus, elected as praetor of Citerior replacing the demoralized Unimanus. The fact of the matter for why these two men were chosen as praetor was because the Scipio faction (in which he was also the adopted son of Publius Cornelius Scipio, the eldest son of the famous Publius Cornelius Scipio

---

[990] Tusculano, Victor de, op. cit., p. 88

[991] Ibid., p. 89 - 92

[992] Appian, 65.273-274

Africanus) held much power in the Senate and intended to concentrate a larger number of troops in Spain, so that they could carry out their agenda of political and administrative reforms, as well as revising their old treaties and alliances that was started by Scipio Africanus after the Second Punic War.

But because Rome was involved in other conflicts in Greece and Africa, the Romans did not have an army large enough to carry out their plan in Hispania, even though they had qualified persons to do the job. With the ending of the wars in Greece and Africa, a larger army could now be transferred to Hispania. But again, in an effort to spare the worn-out veterans of the Punic, Greek and Macedonian wars, Aemilianus had to instead levy a small field army of new recruits that consisted of 15,000 legionnaires, 2,000 cavalrymen.[993]

While Aemilianus remained in Italy organizing another army, Laelius, who was more given to peace than war, arrived in Citerior. According to Tusculano, it was perhaps a good thing he was more for peace than war for he had inherited a beaten and demoralized army. During his tenure as governor, he was more of an ambassador rather than a general, for he attempted to demonstrate that he meant to make peace with the Lusitanians by the promising that the Senate would give them land.[994]

The Lusitanians, who also wished to establish peace, were constantly reminded by those Lusitanians who had survived Galba's massacre not to trust the Romans, and so, they continued to be suspicious of all Roman praetors. The Lusitanians once again ceased to believe Rome's promises and answered with continuous fighting, for there would only be peace when the invaders abandoned their homeland.

At first Laelius did not leave the safety of his encampment until he reorganized what was left of the army, but like in all armies around the world, whether it is ancient or modern, a show of force

---

[993] Appian, 65.274

[994] Tusculano, Victor de, op. cit., p. 78 -79

was necessary, so, patrols had to be conducted. Laelius attempted to avoid full-fledge open battles, but his patrols were constantly involved in skirmishes and ambushes. Laelius became convinced that the Lusitanians would never comply or accept another peace proposal from Rome. Henceforth, his troops lived in a constant state of alert, because the guerrillas never rested and had spies everywhere. According to the Viriathus legend, there is another battle, the Battle of Carteia. This battle is not well-documented in the classical texts, but in Portuguese lore it is well known. As legend has it, Viriathus realized how cautious Laelius was and decided to take the city of Carteia.[995] Viriathus advanced towards Carteia and surprised the Romans who had set up camp in the area. The Lusitanan attack was ferocious, but the Romans responded magnificently which surprised Viriathus. After a prolong battle, Viriathus is able to thwart the Romans. Though Viriathus obtained another resounding victory, the battle obliged him to withdraw from his plans about taking Carteia, as the battle had been bloody and costly. As for the Romans, the loss of soldiers had become sensitive for their numbers were beginning to fall and not knowing when to expect reinforcements. The Romans lived in a state of anxiety, leaving Viriathus to roam around the countryside freely. And so, this status quo is maintained until Aemilianus's arrival.[996]

The Arrival of Aemilianus

Aemilianus and his army finally arrive in Beatica near the end of the summer or early fall of 145 BCE, indicating that they perhaps made their way by sea, instead of over land through Gaul; thus having had waited for the sailing season to commence.[997] On arriving in Hispania, the ships disembarked soldier after soldier in the vicinity of Cartagena.[998] The waterborne landing operation and their march east to Urso was so lengthy that Viriathus had time to prepare for another upcoming campaign. And with his network of spies, Viriathus came to

995 Ibid., p. 84 - 85

996 Ibid., p. 85

997 Munoz, Mauricio P., *op. cit.,* p. 166

998 Tusculano, Victor de, op. cit., p. 80

know the strength and weakness of this new army and began planning his campaign.

Aemilianus quickly went searching for Viriathus, marching his men east to Urso (Osuna). On receiving vital information from his spy network, Viriathus quickly moved his men into the vicinity of Urso and prepared an ambush. Arriving near Urso, the Lusitanians attacked and defeated Aemilianus's troops. There were two reasons for this disappointing Roman defeat; the army was inexperienced in combat and it did not have adequate preparation to deal with such powerful Lusitanian forces. The battle of Urso, though disappointing to the Romans, did not preoccupy Aemilianus, who kept on marching to Urso.

With the arrival of winter 145-144 BCE, Aemilianus took his army into winter quarters at Urso (Osuna) and fortified the city's square and spent the entire year (mid-145 – mid-144 BCE) training his raw recruits and securing local cooperation. He also refused to be provoked into action prematurely by the guerrilla tactics used by the Lusitanians.[999] While training his men, he was able to muster some allied forces from Urso. Not wanting to face Viriathus until his inexperienced army had been sufficiently drilled. While his army trained, he left the army in the care of his legate and went to Gades (Cadiz) to offer a sacrifice to Hercules at the famous Temple of Melqart, so that he and his army would be blessed with strength to conduct a successful campaign against Viriathus.[1000]

During Aemilianus's absence, Viriathus attacked a cohort of Roman foragers. Caught by surprise, many were killed.[1001] Using poor judgment, the legate was lured out to fight Viriathus and was swiftly

---

[999] Appian, 65.274

[1000] Appian, 65.275. Melqart, also spelled Melkart or Melkarth, was Phoenician god, chief deity of Tyre and of two of its colonies, Carthage and Gadir (Cádiz, Spain). He was also called the Tyrian Baal. Under the name Malku he was equated with the Babylonian Nergal, god of the underworld and death, and thus may have been related to the god Mot of Ras Shamra (ancient Ugarit). During the Roman occupation it was dedicated to Hercules.

[1001] Appian, 65.275

defeated, enabling Viriathus to capture standards and booty. Besides attacking Roman troops, the Lusitanians launched an attack on the town of Corduba.[1002] Although he besieged the city, he did not attack it, for it was a Roman stronghold that would have been costly to the Lusitanians. When Aemilianus returned, Viriathus consistently attempted to draw the Romans out onto the battlefield, but Aemilianus was never tempted. He continued to exercise his troops, only sending them out on patrols to come into contact with the enemy to conduct minor skirmishes in an effort to strengthen his men's resolve, test the enemy's strength and to give his soldiers much needed experience. When he sent out foraging parties, he always surrounded his light-armed forgers with heavy armed men, while he and his cavalry roamed the countryside, Aemilianus used the same maneuvers he had seen his father use in Macedonia.[1003]

At the end of winter 145 BCE, Aemilianus and Laelius were ordered by the Senate to continue their preatorships. With the onset of the campaign season (spring 144 BCE), Aemilianus deemed the army sufficiently ready to fight. Aemilianus and Laelius joined forces and attacked Viriathus. These two men miraculously were able to hide their movements that Aemilianus was able to conduct a surprise attack on the Lusitanian encampment near Beja, inflicting appreciable losses on them, forcing them to withdraw. Viriathus regained his men's composure and counter-attacked the Romans with his now famous feint retreat tactic. He attacked the Romans with such impetus that Aemilianus was forced to withdrawal, leaving the battlefield with numerous casualties and

---

[1002] Knapp, Robert, C., Roman Cordoba, Berkeley, 1983, p. 14; Tusculano, Victor de, op. cit., p. 81 The march towards Corduba, which was deep in Roman occupied territory, has been an interesting action to many military scholars and historian for that they have find Viriathus' deep southern incursion into Roman held Baetica an incredible feat of military maneuvering without ever get caught proving he was a military genius and that this action shows that the Lusitanians were conducting raids further south-east than previously thought. It is even believed that he may even have marched further east to Granada and Murcia with his eyes on Cartegena which Viriathus may have had the idea to take to port city and deny the Romans a disembarkation point.

[1003] Appian, 65.277

supply behind. After the battle, Viriathus did not stop and chased the fleeing Romans. Once again Viriathus proved to the Romans that he was the better general.

Over the course of 144 BCE, the Romans actually began to succeed in putting Viriathus's forces to flight, but this only occurred after numerous struggles. Some historians say that the reason why Viriathus began to suffer defeats is because the Roman leadership began to think and act like Viriathus. But that is not the real reason why the Romans were successful, even though it probably helped. The reason why the tables had turn was very simple, Viriathus was beginning to feel the loss of his men, as well as the lack of supply, for he had been constantly campaigning and not giving the time for his men to rest and replenish their provisions. Regardless, Viriathus was now on the run and the Romans succeeded in recapturing two of Viriathus's allied towns, of which one was plundered and the other burnt down.[1004] As for the taking of these two unnamed cities, some historians believe that the one that was plundered was Tucci (Martos, Jaén), which forced Viriathus to leave the valley of Betis, which he had dominated over a four year period. As for the second one, it still remains unknown. With Viriathus on the run, the Romans pursue the Lusitanians. Low on supplies and with the Romans close on their heels, Viriathus decides to make a pit stop at Baecula. But stopping at Baecula (Bailén) proved fatal. While his men gathered provisions and rested just outside the city, the Romans showed up at the city's front door. The Romans, who had been on the march all day, did not stop and attacked the Lusitanians, killing many more warriors. Although the Romans had finally defeated the Lusitanians, they did not destroy Viriathus's army. The reason why the Roman did not destroy Viriathus's army when they had the chance was because they quit while they were ahead, because of the incoming winter weather. According to Appian, short on supply after the battle, the Roman army went into winter quarters at Corduba.[1005] After the first phase of the campaign, it seems that Aemilianus ordered Laelius back to Citerior

---

[1004] Appian, 65.278; Tusculano, Victor de, op. cit., p. 81-82

[1005] Appian 65.278 Cicero, Brutus, 84; A. Schulten identified as Baecula (Bailén) situated on the road transducer the Guadalquivir Valley by Serra Morena until the

with his army for the classical texts do not make any further mentions of Laelius from this point on. The Romans had finally won a victory, giving them a brief respite and recovery of some key towns.

As for exactly who defeated the Lusitanians and besieged the two cities there is some confusion. Appian unfortunately does not mention the person by name but makes us assume it was Aemilianus. But Roman writer and statesman, Marcus Tullius Cicero is the only person to mention that Laelius, himself was the one that defeated Viriathus that year.[1006] Laelius's victory, although mentioned in Appain's work, fails to notice that he had omitted Laelius name in his writing, so in the end, the way it was written makes the reader think that it was Aemilianus who defeated the Lusitanians instead of Laelius.[1007]

As for Virathus, he had lost all his points of support in the Guadalquivir Valley and even all of Andalusia because Aemilianus had passed the winter in Corduba (Cordova) which had been turned into a major military base in Ulterior.

With these victories, the Romans were now prepared to occupy the entire peninsula and cease to worry of losing the entire region to a bunch of uncivilized people. Still the situation in Hispania was considered severe and Rome decided to dispatch to Ulterior, not just a praetor who only had political experience, but one with much military experience under his belt, and being that the wars that Rome was involved had recently ended, they planned to increase military presence on the peninsula and prolong the consular command to two years instead of one. This exceptional measure gives us an idea of the importance of how the Roman Senate had come to see the issue about Viriathus. Regardless of Aemilianus's successes, Viriathus's campaign against the Romans had inspired many Celtiberian tribes to follow his example. In fact, by 143

Meseta, before the Despeñaperros Pass. Schulten, A., 'Viriatus', Neue Jahrbücher 39, 1917, pp. 222.

[1006] Circero, Brutus 84 and de officiis, 2.11.40

[1007] Also see Richardson, J.S., "Hispaniae,", pp.187-189; Goukowsky, Paul, Appien. Histoire romaine II (Greek text, French translation, notes), Paris: Les Belles Léttres, 1997, p. LXVI - LXVII

BCE, Celtiberia broke out in an open insurrection that would later be known as the Numantine War[1008], which more than neutralized Rome's current good fortune against Viriathus.

But this Roman success was not of a great importance except by the fact that it was the first time that the Romans had overcome the Luistanians in ten years of fighting. Alas, these victories were temporary for after Aemilianus departed back to Rome, the Romans suffered a series of misfortunes; they were defeated battle after battle during the years of 143 - 142 BCE. Furthermore, Viriathus successful managed for the Arevaci, Belli and Titthi to break their alliance with Rome and join forces with him. During these same years, Viriathus renewed his offensive and recaptured Betican lands once again.

The next sequence of praetor, after the successful Aemilianus and Laelius, to try their mettle against Viriathus was Quintus Pompeius (Ulterior) and Q. Caecilius Metellus Macedonicus (Citerior). During 143 - 142 BCE, Pompeius lost what the former praetors had recently gained. On taking command of Ulterior, Pompeius immediately began campaigning against Viriathus. Their first encounter ended up benefiting the Luistanians. Viriathus followed his usual pattern the minute he came under attack and retreated south of the Tagus River, towards the famed Hill of Venus (*Mons Veneris*).[1009] On occupying the hill, Viriathus immediately turned upon his pursers and killed over 1,000 Romans and captured many standards and much supply. Quintus Pompeius was driven back to his camp.[1010]

After the Second Battle of *Mons Veneris*, Viriathus decided that his army's summer excursion would be to ravage the area around the Guadalquivir and retake Tucci, which had been lost to the Romans

---

[1008] Celtiberian tribes began their own war in 143 BC, the Numantine War, which would last 10 years. Appian, 66.279-280; see Appian 76.322 about the Numantine War; Simon, Helmut, Roms Kriege in Spanien, 154-133 v. Chr., Frankfurt am Main, V. Klostermann, 1962; Pérez, Antonio Alburquerque, Numancia, The Cradle of Our History, Madrid, 1984.

[1009] This is the same hill that had been the downfall of Plautius a few years before

[1010] Appian, 66.281 – 282

the previous year. Once he managed to drive out the garrison from Tucci, Viriathus occupied it and created a stronghold that supported his offensive operations and raids throughout the valley of Guadalquivir and Bastetania.[1011] While Viriathus plundered the territory, Quintus Pompeius was paralyzed, as Appian says, by his "cowardice and inexperience". Ultimately, Quintus Pompeius went into winter quarters in the middle of autumn, leaving Baetica's defense in the hands of an Iberian from the city of Italica named Gaius Marcius to fight Viriathus, which ended with negative results. The year 143 BCE had been a success that Viriathus had built himself a small 'empire' that extended from the Atlantic Ocean in the west to Meseta Central in the east, as well as Andalusia to the south.

In Citerior, Quintus Caecilius Metellus Macedonicus begins to feel the repercussions of the Lusitanian War as it had caused the Celtiberians to rebel against Rome in a new Celtiberian war, the Numantine War. The Roman Senate on receiving dispatches from Hispania becomes aware of the severity of the situation, and immediately deployed to Citerior an army of 30,000 infantry and 2,000 cavalry.[1012] Appian does not provide any news for the year 142 BCE, but Livy makes a minor note that Metellus had in some capacity fought the Lusitanians.[1013] One must conclude that the situation stayed the same with little or no military operations occurring.

By 141 BCE, the situation in Hispania had become intolerable for Rome because Viriathus's achievements and growing fame had instigated

---

[1011] Appian, 66.282; **Bastetania** derives its name from one of their cities, Basti. Apparently, it seems to have been an important establishment of a Roman foothold for the territory held the port city of Cartagena. The region is located south-east of the Iberian Peninsula, and that it was made up of the present provinces of Malaga, Granada, Almeria, and the south-east section of Jaén, the south part of Albacete and southwest of Murcia. In this region there existed ancient known cities mentioned in the classical texts such as Arkilaquis, Tutugi, Basti, Acci or Iliberri.

[1012] Munoz, Mauricio P., op. cit., p. 169

[1013] Livy, Oxyrhyncus, 167; Obsequens 22; Astin, A.E., "The Roman commander in Hispania Ulterior in 142 BC", Historia #13, 1964, pp. 254 -254

the Celtiberians to resume their war against Rome in full swing. However, his influence was not sufficient enough to achieve a union of all the Iberian people against Rome because of excessive individualism among chiefs and tribal integrity. Thus, the Iberians never managed to completely trump the Romans.

In Rome, the Iberian situation deeply disturbed the Senate and its citizens so much that the war was becoming unpopular. To rectify the problem, the Senate rapidly decided to resolve the matter by sending new legions to Hispania with the intention of putting an end to the Lusitanian and Celtiberian Wars, as well as sending two new praetors. However, the task was not easy, as several of the classical authors provide data on the following events.

During the early part of 141 BCE, Quintus Fabius Maximus Servilianus, the brother of Quintus Fabius Maximus Aemilianus succeeded the inept Quintus Pompeius. With his arrival in Hispania, he brought an army that consisted of 18,000 infantry and 1,600 cavalry. From Carthago Nova, he marched his men in two sections towards Tucci. At the same time, he sent a message to the Numidian king, Micipsa, requesting the acquisition of 10 elephants and a number of additional horsemen.[1014]

Before Servilianus's forces were joined together, Viriathus attacked one of the legions with 6,000 warriors; this was the first contest between the new Roman governor and Viriathus. During this small unnamed battle, the Romans fought well for they were able to repel the Lusitanians, but according to Appian, it seems that the battle ended in a stalemate.[1015]

When the rest of his force, which now included elephants and Numidian horsemen, had finally arrived at the outskirts of Tucci, Servilianus constructed a large base camp and advanced against Viriathus. Servilianus, after several weeks finally managed to eject the Lusitanians from the city of Tucci, which had been recaptured by Viriathus from

---

[1014] Appian, 67.283 -284 and 285

[1015] Appian, 67.284

Pompeius. The Romans' initial success in routing the Lusitanians, compelled Viriathus to withdraw back to Lusitania.

Servilianus had managed to achieve his objective of retaking Tucci, as well as liberating several other Romanized cities in Baeturia, which had fallen into Lusitanian hands.[1016] It also allowed Servilianus to plan his next conquest: the Algarve, southern Lusitania and the Tagus River Valley in Central Spain.[1017] In the course of his flight north from the Romans, Viriathus noticed that their pursuit had become disorderly and unorganized, so he took advantage of this. Rallying his men, they turned on the Romans, killing some 3,000 and driving the rest back to their camp near Tucci. During the Roman retreat, Viriathus constantly harassed the Romans by frequently conducting hit-and-run tactics at night and during the heat of the day making use of any moment at which the Romans might not expect it, thus destroying their morale. The Lusitanians continuously attacked the Roman until they reached their camp. Though they had quickly set up a perimeter defense and even put up a gallant fight, they were driven out of their camp and back towards Tucci.

After this battle, Viriathus realized he was in a desperate situation. Due to constant fighting and campaigning, his army had dwindled again in numbers and was beginning to suffer a shortage of food supplies, so, he decided to retire to the Lusitanian heartland to rebuild his army. Under the cover of night and by setting up a diversion by burning down his camp, he departed Baetica.

Failing to defeat and capture Viriathus, Servilianus decided that his army, for the rest of the year, would plunder and retake Baeturian towns that had allied themselves to Viriathus's cause. Servilianus' campaign was a success for he marched against five unnamed Baetican towns that had collaborated with Viriathus. After plundering Baeturia, he

---

[1016] Baeturia was a region in the valley of the Anas (Guadiana River Valley). Appian, 67.285 and 68.288; Iglesia, L. Garcia, 'La Beturia, un problema geografico de la Hispania Antigua', AEA 44, 1971, pp. 86-108

[1017] Appian, 68.289

turned southwest and marched against the Cunei (a group of people that inhabited southern Portugal).

But prior to Servilianus's campaign into southern Portugal, he headed south from Baeturia into Turdetania, where he captured and plundered the towns of Eiskadia, Gemmella and Obulcula, which at one point or another had been garrisoned by Viriathus's army. As for the smaller towns that were taken, Appian writes that they were pardoned.[1018] But from all the towns that were taken, Servilianus took about 10,000 prisoners that were eventually sold into slavery. But from among all these prisoners, 500 males were beheaded. Of the 500 men that were executed, they were the village and town leaders. The Iberians were not the only ones to be punished, but also Roman citizens. As for Roman subjects that had supported Viriathus's cause had their right hand cut off, while army deserters that had been captured either hiding into towns or fighting alongside the Lusitanians were executed.[1019] This was not a war waged with gentility and chivalry.

After the reoccupation of Turdetania, Servilianus marched west into the Algarve region of southern Portugal; unfortunately, Appian did not leave any information except that Servilianus conduct a military campaign against the Cunei and Conii. Appian goes on to write that Servilianus then turned north and invaded Lusitania in an attempt to bring out Viriathus from hiding.[1020] As he was on his way north, two bandit chieftains, Curius and Apuleius, attacked the Romans with a guerrilla army of 10, 000 men.[1021] The Latin names of these chieftains suggest that they may have been Iberians, who had formerly served in the Roman army as native auxiliaries and upon being discharged took

[1018] Appian, 68.290; According to A. Schulten and Munoz, these are the Celtic names for the respectively the Roman town names for Astigi (Écija), Gemellae (Guadix), Obulco (Porcuna), but according to J.S. Richardson he follows Pliny (N.H. 3.12) in that Gemella was the name give to Tucci when it became a colony in the age of Augustus. Obulcula he identifies it as La Monclova and Eiskadia is unknown except that it should be in the middle of the Guadalquivir Valley.

[1019] Appian, 68.290

[1020] Appian, 68.289

[1021] Appian, 68.289

on Roman names and citizenship or on the hand they had deserted it and kept the Latin names. No matter what this case was about their names, they attacked the Romans. But unfortunately, the classical sources give no information of the battle and whether the bandit army was Lusitanian or a mixed band of Lusitanians, Conii and Celtici, who were in league with Viriathus or not. But according to Appian, it seems that this army was more interested in plunder than in defeating Servilianus, since they had taken a considerable amount of booty from the Romans and perhaps even from the Lusitanians and other Iberian tribes.[1022] The Romans eventually rallied around their commander and were able to vanquish the guerillas and recover their booty; in the process of the fighting, Curius was killed in battle.[1023]

Appian also makes a reference to another bandit chief, named Connoba, who was set free by Servilianus after cutting off the warrior's right hand. After this humiliating act, there seems to have been increased guerrilla activity in southern Hispania and southern Lusitania.[1024] With this in mind, Viriathus may have had problems in persuading these tribes to agree to help him in his war of liberation. The absence of unity within the Iberian people compared to before, began to show a weakness in the resistance movement that may explain why Viriathus would later make peace with the Romans the following year.

On his way back from Lusitania, after the failed attempt to force Viriathus into open battle, Servilianus decided to besiege the town of Erisane (location unknown) for it had been loyal to Viriathus. Servilianus encircled the town and began to build a trench around Erisane. Viriathus rushed to its defense and successfully smuggled himself and a large contingent within the town walls under the cover of darkness. At dawn his men and the town's garrison made a successful sally against the Roman sappers working on the circumvallation trenches. Servilianus quickly marshaled the rest of his army for a fight. Shortly afterwards,

---

[1022] Appian, 68.289

[1023] Appian, 68.290

[1024] Appian, 68.291; Valerius Maximus, 2.7.11; Frontinus, Stratagem, 4.1.42; Orosius, 5.4.12

Viriathus attacked the bulk of consular army and defeated them. The Romans retreated in complete disorder, hounded by Viriathus's cavalry and infantry hot on their heels, the Lusitanians managed to herd the Romans into a precipitous place from which the Romans could not escape.[1025] Defeat of the Roman army was inevitable. The running battle came to an end when Viriathus surrounded and trapped the Romans in the narrow valley pass with high slopes. Escape was impossible and they had no choice but to surrender unconditionally.[1026]

The Peace Treaty of 140 Bc

Being that he had placed the Romans in such an unfavorable situation, Viriathus tired of so many years of war and having other tribes leaving his alliance to conduct their own campaigns, he was willing to make peace, and so, he offered Servilianus some terms for a peace agreement. The terms were of the mildest of conditions to a defeated enemy; he asked for a withdrawal of all Roman soldiers from Lusitania and that its borders should be respected and recognized as a sovereign independent nation. He also added that the Lusitanians be granted the status of "*amici populi Romani*" (Friends of the Roman people) and Viriathus would become Rome's ally. To his surprise and delight, Servilianus accepted and negotiated the peace agreement.[1027] The treaty was signed, as Livy writes, with *aequis condicionibus* (equal conditions), but some historians consider terms still favorable to Rome, for they had only to withdraw from Lusitania and not the Baetica region, which had supported Viriathus's endeavors.[1028] Once the meeting of both leaders were concluded, Viriathus presented the agreement to his people who in turned ratified it.

But in Rome, the news of the signing of the peace treaty was received in a different light, the Roman Senate had grudgingly accepted the peace agreement and granted the title *amicus populi Romani*, indicating

1025 Appian, 69.292-293
1026 Appian, 68.294-295
1027 Appian, 69.294
1028 Livy, Periochae, 54

that Rome now recognized Viriathus as a 'king'. Although Viriathus was now considered as a king, he was still dangerous that the Senate advised the incoming governors to disrupt the peace by using any means necessary, since Rome had been humiliated by a group of uncivilized barbarians, and it had also lost the rich territories in Beatica, for the tribes wanted the same thing that Viriathus had gained for Lusitania.[1029] Though it appears that the war had come to an end, resolved by an act of generosity on Viriathus part, the Lusitanians were still very problematic to Rome, in the eyes of the Senate. Unfortunately for the Lusitanians, this peace would not last long. Servilianus would remain in Hispania Ulterior as magistrate for another year (140 BCE) to oversee the peace accord.

Viriathus was at the top of his political-military career for he had achieved – after a long period of fighting – the recognition his people deserved. From this point on, Romans and Lusitanians respected their limits and boundaries established by the peace treaty.

Although Viriathus made peace with the Romans, the question arises, why, with his hated enemy at his mercy, did Viriathus let them off the hook so easily? This question has been much discussed and debated, without the historical investigation reaching a consensus, but there is a general agreement that is crucial to Viriathus's underlying motive: Realpolitik.

Realpolitik comes into play when Viriathus finally began to see that his people were tired of the war, but for him to end the war, he needed a massive victory over the Romans. And with the defeat of Servilianus, he saw an opportunity to end the war with the intention of establishing an independent territory, which Flourus would later dubbed Viriathus as the 'Romulus of Hispania'.[1030] Carried by this new-found pride of independence, the Lusitanians sought a status of alliance and delimiting borders independent of Roman authority. As already mentioned, and as far as we know, the description of the Lusitanians up to this point was

[1029] Appian,70.297

[1030] Florus 1.33

a set of tribes without a national identity. But as the Lusitanian War progressed, their tribal mindset began to change into one of nationalism. Thus, this was a chance for Viriathus to make things right. Unfortunately, the classical texts say nothing about it, but modern interpretations of the ancient texts see it in a nationalistic way.

As conditions of the treaty between Viriathus and Servilianus were simplistic, the reason for proposing the treaty was perhaps problematic. A. Schulten has pointed out best in his writing about Viriathus, "... we are facing an enigma for it is impossible that we can find in Viriathus the explanation for his clemency, because no one had never been more forewarned against the perfidy of Rome than him." With this in mind, the question is WHY was he easy on the Romans?

Nineteenth century Roman and Greek historian and author, U. J. H. Becker was the first person to study the treaty of 140 BCE, but he writes this statement with a 19th century perspective:

"He knew (Viriathus), taught by many years of experience that he was capable of shattering the impetus Roman warriors with defeats. With a defeated enemy, he expected to make old enemies into friends and for himself give his people something (land), via the generosity of a **noble** act."[1031]

Though there might seem to be a nationalistic interpretation that suggests that this historical concept from the 19th century dealt with the revolutionary cause and sympathy of Viriathus towards his people qualifying him for a 'noble and great act' and stressing the 'faith in his work and his people', it is absolutely anachronistic to think that. But the circumstances in Hispania during the 2nd century BC did not closely resemble what was seen in 19th century Europe, in other words, the Lusitanians pursued objectives that were perhaps based on self-preservation, since the subject matter of life at that time was rather harsh and complicated rather than national identity.

[1031] Becker, U.J.H., Die Kriege der Römer in Hispanien, cad. 1, Viriath un die Lusitaner, Altona, 1826, p. 10

But historians want to see Viriathus in a political sense: becoming king of an independent Lusitania, allied to Rome, rather than a crazed barbarian bent on seeking revenge until he was caught or killed. So the reasons why he may have had a change of heart and proposed a peace treaty are basically that the Lusitanians were rather tired of constantly being at war with the Romans and being that Viriathus had taken the rich lands of southern Hispania, he now wanted and sought an agreement which would give them the peace he sought, freedom from paying taxes to Rome and for his countrymen to conduct trade with Rome, since they possessed the mineral wealth of Beatica. On the other side of the spectrum, other historians make references to Viriathus's own personal agenda of beginning his own royal bloodline.[1032]

P. Bosch Gimpera and P. Aguado Bleye in R. Menéndez Pidal's book, *História de Espanha*, refer to Viriathus unusual act of signing the peace treaty as simply due to the fact that the Lusitanians were war weary and exhausted.[1033] But H.G. Gundel disagrees and defends his statement that it is not logical that this nation of warriors were fatigued from constant warfare, especially when they were ahead of the game such as when they had Servilianus's army encircled and a Lusitanian triumph was ensured.[1034]

From these two statements, many historians have come to believe that Viriathus knew the internal tensions of the Lusitanians and that his 'military' was exhausted and that, little by little, weariness from war became evident among his tribal companions. Therefore, it has been calculated that he could not maintain the war against Rome much longer as his warriors were becoming scarce and allies could not be obtained as they had become involved in their own rebellions or their tribe had come under Roman rule. Accordingly, it was concluded that the annihilation of another Roman army would not favor Viriathus's political objectives and

---

1032 Munoz, Mauricio P., op. cit., p.175

1033 Bosch Gimpera, P. and Aguado Bleye, P.,"La Conquista de España por Roma (218 a 19 a.C.)" and Chapter III, "Las guerras de Lusitanos y Celtiberos contra Roma: Prmer period (154 a 143): Viriato" in R. Menéndez Pidal's book, História de Espanha, Madrid, 1962, pp. 89-144

1034 Gundel, H.G.."Probleme der Römischen Kampfführung Gegen Viriatus", Legio VII Gemina, León, 1970, pp.111 – 130

the war would continue, and possible be even more violent than before. This concrete reflection on all that had happened to this point must have led Viriathus to engage in peace negotiations with the Romans.

These theories seem very logical in every sense for had Viriathus acted stark raving mad and had put another Roman army to the sword as he had done before, Rome would never forget, nor forgive. However long it took, it would be a war to the death and being that the Lusitanians were becoming short on manpower, provisions and being that his people were war weary, this was their best bet to end the war.

We can safely assume that both sides did not spend much time negotiating the peace terms for Viriathus saw a chance to get what he wanted, while Servilianus saw an opportunity to live another day, therefore a rapid resolution was needed. For Professor Muñoz, the treaty came about due to circumstances of time, situation and because of Viriathus's personality. Viriathus had led the war against Rome with an offensive and defensive strategy, fighting for the independence of his people and until that moment during the battle with Servilianus, he realized that this was his chance to guarantee the consolidation of his conquest through a treaty.[1035] Without a doubt the acquisition of lands, according to Muñoz, was his political objective. The desire for land had always played an essential role in all negotiations between the Romans and the Lusitanians. Knowing that the Lusitanians wanted land, the Romans used it to their own advantage, such as when Galba promised land as a way to reach peace, but then broke his pledge and slaughtered them. As we have seen, this was the principal reason for the Second Lusitanian War.

It is believed that perhaps the Viriathian War could have been prevented if it was not for Galba's deception and if Viriathus had negotiated with Vetilius, who also promise of land, but this had a different outcome for the Lusitanians bent on revenge and not want to possibly fall for the same trick twice, (if it was even a trick, for perhaps Vetilius might have been honest about his proposal) the Lusitanians declared war by completely destroying Vetilius's legion. But after eight years of war, the

---

1035 Munoz, Mauricio P., op. cit., p.177 -178

Lusitanians were becoming tired of war and wanted peace. So, when Viriathus attacked Servilianus's army with the conviction of destroying the Romans, he had a change of heart and came to the realization that he could not continue fighting forever, and if he wanted something for his people he had to, in a way, Romanize himself to gain the respect from his enemy. With respect in place, the Romans would now perhaps grant his people the land that they had already occupied in Beturia.[1036]

In addition to H. G. Gundel first statement, he tells us from his own evaluation of the 140 BCE treaty, that the treaty did not happen as a result of the previous situations that the Romans encountered in fighting Viriathus, but from other events that were occurring in that same year (i.e. the Numantine War). Furthermore, one must consider that if Rome did not accept the Lusitanian peace treaty, there might have been the possibility of a joint action with Celtiberians, who had been fighting the Romans since 143 BCE with much success.[1037] Fighting a two front war was something Rome wanted to avoid, so it was important to Rome that they sign a peace treaty with the Lusitanians.

But this peace would not last, for the Romans would break the treaty and continue the war resulting in Viriathus's death. After Viriathus's death, as we shall see in the next chapter, the remainder of his army yielded to the Romans, in that they delivered the lands back into Roman hands. This clearly shows that the possession of the fertile lands of southern Hispania

---

[1036] This theory is based on J. Costa and A. Garcia y Bellido study that have made a detailed study on the agrarian problem in Lusitania and both agree that the main objective of the Luistanians was the acquisition of lands for there existed a social problem in Lusitania, between shepards and farmers and because of the lack of good land the Lusitanians resorted to 'bandoleirismo' which had been already mentioned in chapter 3 section Land and Banditry. Also see Costa, J., "Viriato y la Cuestión Social en España en el Siglo II Antes de Jesucristo", Tutela de Pueblos en la Historia, Madrid 1879 and Estudios Ibéricos, Madrid, 1902; Garcia y Bellido, A., "Conflitos y Estructuras Sociales en la Hispania Antiga" AAVV, Madrid, 1977, pp. 13 – 60.

[1037] Gundel, H.G., "Probleme der Römischen Kampfführung Gegen Viriatus", pp.111 – 130 and "Viriato, lusitano, caudillo en las luchas contra los romanos. 147-139 a.C.", *Caesaraugusta*, 1968, pp.175-198 (translated by J.M. Blazquez).

were never fully complete in Lusitania hands for they were not able to administer, organize and maintain their gains mostly because, as many historians believe, that unlike the Romans, Lusitanians leaders had a tribal mindset, thus making a peace treaty was just a way for the Lusitanians to stop fighting and a means of making Roman pacification more effective.

As making references to Viriathus's own personal agenda, some historian believe that seeking various motives for this surprising treaty, in the first place, is based on internal difficulties within Viriathus's family affairs, such as his marriage, a year prior to the peace treaty, in which his father or brother-in-law, Astolpas, had invited the Romans to the wedding.[1038] It seems that the relationship between Viriathus and Astolpas was not on the best of terms for Viriathus despised him for his vanity in showing off his wealth and then criticizing his friendship with the Romans. This hostility would extend also to other noble Luistanians families, friends and anyone who supported Astolpas and the Romans and did not have the sense to realize what the Romans were about. These internal disagreements between the rebellious leaders and the neutral noble Lusitanian families would hinder Viriathus's military power to the point that he would be willing to make a peace agreement with the Romans. Fortunately for Viriathus, these tensions were not so serious as to reach to the extremes. Though he was forced into this unexpected political situation of making peace with Rome, Viriathus did not feel the influence nor trust the rich Lusitanian families.

With all this in mind, Viriathus must have counted with the annulment of the treaty, something that may not have happen, but something that could possibly happen, for although Servilianus had surrendered and agreed to a peace treaty, he in actuality did not represent the general opinion of the Senate. However, Viriathus seems to have been absolutely convinced that the treaty would be confirmed by Rome, granting him independence or at least, that is what he might have thought and wanted, for the following year the treaty was broken. But for now, success was total, as expected; the treaty was ratified by the Senate.

[1038] Munoz, Mauricio P., op. cit., p.175-176

Rome Attitude Towards The Treaty

Rome's attitude towards the ratification of the peace treaty with Viriathus came with two faces, the first being that they smiled and let the barbarians have their day in the sun, while deep down they had another idea. As presented by Appian, in Rome the treaty had become largely controversial for the *comitia centuriata* even though the treaty was ratified in terms that it was signed by Servilianus under duress and in a humiliating circumstance with a barbarian race on equal terms.[1039] To the Romans, as Livy states, the signing of the treaty was a 'shameful peace' technically a *foedus aequum*.[1040] This position was considered offensive to Roman dignity to have be equals to a barbarian race.

Naturally, Rome would interpose a political military action that would be totally effective in the following year. This action as we will see in the next chapter was not a sign of a broad political vision, but a risk that Rome believed would make this 'newly established small state' fold. Within the scheme of political relations with smaller states, the smaller state would always have the need to relate with a great potential powers (as in the case of Lusitania), while the larger state (i.e. Rome), in all aspects, would in the end impose its law, unless it was facing a political situation internally or externally that would totally undermined its endeavors. The small state's only possibility to break away from the power yoke of the larger state was to take whatever opportunities that arise, so as to obtain the best dividend for self sustainment and sovereignty. And that is what Viriathus thought with what would happen at the end of the war, that Rome would see Lusitania as an equal power. But that would not be the case.

1039 Ancient Roman military assembly, instituted *c.* 450 BC. It decided on war and peace, passed laws, elected consuls, praetors, and censors, and considered appeals of capital convictions. Unlike the older patrician Comitia Curiata, it included plebeians as well as patricians, assigned to classes and centuriae (centuries, or groups of 100) by wealth and the equipment they could provide for military duty. Voting started with the wealthier centuries, whose votes outweighed those of the poorer. Munoz, Mauricio P., op. cit., p.179-180; Alberto, Paulo Farmhouse, Viriato, Vultos da Antiguidade, Editorial Inquérito, Sintra, 1996, p. 45

1040 Livy, perioch. Oxy., 54

In conclusion, if Viriathus had not signed the treaty with Rome in 140 BCE after their victory over Servilianus's army, the Lusitanians perhaps would not last another year, as H. G. Gundel wrote, ".... precisely because Viriathus was not the adventurer whose only objective was to fight.., which against a large potent force.... that in time it would lead to inevitable disaster."[1041]

[1041] Gundel, H.G.., "Viriato, lusitano, caudillo en las luchas contra los romanos. 147-139 a.C.", p.175-198; Munoz, Mauricio P., op. cit., p.181

CHAPTER VIII

THE END OF THE VIRIATHAN WAR

Inevitably, the peace did not last long. The defeats and humiliation that Viriathus had inflicted on the might of Rome for so long could not be allowed to go unpunished. In 139 BCE, the Senate had elected Servilianus' brother; Q. Servilius Caepio. Though the Senate had ratified the treaty, they saw it as a 'shameful peace' (*deformem pacem*); at the same time Rome did not lack voices that spoke out against the treaty, in which they considered the peace worthless. The extent of this grudge became apparent when the next governor arrived in the province.

Servilius Caepio Breaks the Peace

The situation in Hispania change radically with the arrival of Quintus Servilius Caepio in Hispania Ulterior in 139 BCE. On analyzing the ancient texts about this time frame, it seems that Caepio was of a hawkish attitude. At the same time, he regarded this war as unfinished business for he wanted to avenge his family honor. In addition, he saw Hispania as a place for military glory, as well as a place still ripe for plundering. One example of his attitude towards the Lusitanian peace treaty was written down by Appian. Appian writes that Caepio hated the treaty so much that he constantly spoke out against it and wrote a letter claiming that the treaty was highly dishonorable and disgraceful to the Romans.[1042] One can only guess what Caepio might have written, but it seems that he may have requested authorization from the Senate to become involved in some type of action against Viriathus, for Appian writes that the Senate secretly encouraged Caepio at first to annoy Viriathus in whatever way he saw fit.[1043] With the consent of the Senate, he acted quickly in initiating hostilities against the Lusitanians. Knowing how the Roman mind worked, Viriathus refused to be provoked; and when Viriathus invoked the treaty's terms, the Senate would rein in Caepio. At the same time, despite the amity of the recent peace, it is possible that eventually some of Viriathus more hot-headed clansmen took matters into their own hands, especially now that they felt that they could defeat the Romans at will; this perhaps gave the Romans the excuse they needed to break the peace. But after Caepio's fussing over the Lusitanian matter and continually sending letters to several prominent Roman senators to support his cause, a majority of Senate decided to vote on ditching the treaty, giving Caepio the order to resume open warfare on the Lusitanians; at the same time, Marcus Popilus Lenas, governor of Citerior, was also authorized to break the peace treaty with the Numantinans, a Celtiberian tribe located in Central Hispania.[1044]

Cassius Dio writes that Caepio was an unscrupulous and harsh leader. He goes on to say that Caepio had a habit of putting his men in harm's way for he was self-centered, harsh and cruel.[1045] At first, it seemed that the bad blood between the Roman general and his men would do the Lusitanian's work of getting rid of Caepio. Unfortunately for Viriathus and his people, this was not the case. Even though the Roman army in Hispania lacked morale at this point in time, it was still large and dangerous.

[1042] Appian, 70.296; Livy, *ep. Oxy* 54 and *per.* 54; Diodorus, 33.1.4. At some point the Romans perhaps believed that Lusitanians were bound to return to their old ways

[1043] Ibid., 70.297

[1044] Ibid., 70.297

[1045] Cassius Dio History of Rome, 22.78

In 139 BCE, Caepio began a series of calculated provocations to test Viriathus's patience. Viriathus's resolve to keep the peace. But once Caepio broke it, he retaliated with his usual guerrilla tactics. Though he had reluctantly returned to arms, he still felt that a peace deal was possible.

Desperately wishing to recover certain southern region of Ulterior from Lusitanian control, Caepio from his large camp at *castra Servilia*, in the vicinity of Cáceres, began planning a series of military operations designed to provoke a reaction from the Lusitanians. Caepio would be the first Roman to march deep into Lusitania. From his base camp at *castra Servilia,* he began his march across Lusitania arriving near the Sesim, tribal capital of Cempsibriga (modern day Sesimbra, just south of Lisbon). Caepio established an encampment there, *castra Caepiana,* and began building a road (which has been recently discovered) to connect his two camps. This route would later be part of the Via da Prata (Silver Highway).[1046] According to Professor Alarcão, the base at *castra Caepiana* appears to have become a secondary operational headquarters, used to either keep the Celtici at peace or to attack Lusitania from the south.[1047]

In addition, seeing that Celiberian and Lusitanian attacks had rendered it difficult for Roman troop movements coming from the east into the western part of the country, Caepio carefully sought to facilitate troops from North Africa into western Hispania instead of marching them across the entire peninsula from Carthgo Nova on the eastern side of Hispania. Thus, the consolidation of some Atlantic ports such as *castra Caepiana* which was based near the Sado River Estuary, complied with a new policy; the establishment of *castella* in Lusitania. These *castellas* would not only protect new Roman gains in the area, but also defend the future route of the Via de Prata (Silver Highway) until *Norba Caesarina* (Cáceres).[1048] With the founding of Roman encampments

[1046] Munoz, Mauricio P., op. cit., p.184

[1047] Alarcão, J. de, Roman Portugal, Vol. II, Aris & Phillips Ltd., Warminster, UK, 1988, p.8

[1048] Munoz, Mauricio P., op. cit., p.184

and new towns along this newly established Roman road, it ensured successful movement of soldiers, persons and goods by the way of Via de Prata, as well as allowing the Romans to control the area between the Guadiana and Tagus rivers, thus blocking the Lusitanians from further incursion into Baetica.

Without means of a strong defensive position in Baeturia, within southern Hispania Ulterior, Viriathus was forced to withdraw his men and support from several cities such as Arsa and Erisane, before the superiority of the Romans, who were on the march from Carpetania recapturing and destroying Iberian property along the way. Reckoning that he did not have sufficient men to engage the Romans, Viriathus once again employed his guerrilla tactics, which had been so successful since the battle of Tribola. To successful withdraw his remaining army from Baeturia, he instructed the greater part of his army to slip away through hidden ravines and passes, while he himself drew up the remainder of his forces on an unnamed hill to give the impression that he was willing to fight. Upon receiving reports of Viriathus's location Caepio, quickly marched to the area. But Viriathus managed to get away by executing several swift surprise hit-and-run attacks. When he concluded that his army had reached their safe haven in Lusitania, he withdrew and crossed the Lusitanian border.

With the Lusitanians having escaped, Caepio followed their tracks by crossing the mountains of the Serra da Estrela. But once in Lusitania for some unknown reason he decided to turn north and penetrated the territory of the Vettones and Gallaeci, Lusitanian allies that inhabited the area between the Tagus and Douro Rivers, instead of chasing Viriathus. Lusitania had again come under attack. According to Appian, Caepio attacked the Vettones and Callaici and wasted their fields.[1049] Unfortunately, Appian once again did not write down any information on the specifics of the campaign. But this is the first mention by a classical author of Romans conducting military operations north of the

[1049] Appian, 70.300

Tagus River and close to the Atlantic coast.[1050] As for the reason why he may have pulled such a maneuver, I believe was an attempt to destroy and discourage Viriathus's allies and other tribes that may have had the notion of coming to his aid, when they were called upon. At the same time, it may have been a show of force to instill fear and dissuade rebellious fever within these tribes. In the meantime, exhausted by several years of constant war and perhaps sensing defeat in their midst, some Lusitanian tribal leaders may have demanded that Viriathus re-open negotiations with the Romans, as we shall soon see.

Exploiting a period of relative calm in his war against the Celtiberians, Popilius Laenas joins forces with Caepio and attack the Lusitanians, forming another front. According to Professor Munoz's research, Laenas seems to have invaded Lusitania by marching through the Douro River Valley.[1051] His theory is reinforced by several ruins that have been recently discovered, which suggests that for Laenas's campaign to succeed, he had to support his penetration into the heart of Lusitania by building a series of military base camps.

With the Romans breaking the peace treaty and the consequent Roman military invasion of Lusitania by two large Roman armies, Viriathus unable to continue fighting, was forced to seek peace with the governor of Citerior, Marcus Popilius Laenas. [1052] As a reader, one might ask, "Why did Viriathus chose Laenas instead of Caepio, for it was Caepio who was chasing after Viriathus the entire time and not Laenas." The answer that historians have concluded is that they assume that Viriathus contacted consul Marcus Popilius Laenas instead of Caepio because Caepio's march into Lusitania was postponed due to a mutiny among his cavalry, provoked by his harsh treatment of his men.[1053] This theory

---

[1050] Tranoy, Alain, La Galice romaine: Recherches sur le nord-Ouest de la peninsule ibérique dans l'Antiquité, Paris, 1981, p. 65-66

[1051] Munoz, Mauricio P., op. cit., p.184

[1052] Many historians believe that that Viriathus did not fight Laenas was because Appian makes no mention of any type of combat between Laenas and Viriathus.

[1053] Cassius Dio 22.78 "Caepio accomplished nothing worthy of mention against the foe, but visited many injuries upon his own men, so that he even came near being killed by them. For he treated them all, and especially the cavalry, with such

derives from a statement that Cassius Dio wrote in his book, *History of Rome*. Because of the mutiny that Caepio faced, it seems that Laenas advanced further into Lusitania than Caepio did. Thus, the reason why Viriathus may have called out to Laenas for peace.

The meeting between Viriathus and Laenas seems to have taken place in Laenas's camp. During their encounter, Laenas required as a preliminary condition to set the stage for a peace negotiation that Viriathus deliver his most influential and brave comrades in arms; this may well have included Astolpas.[1054] Viriathus agreed, and the first term of the Viriathus and Laenas meeting was satisfied. Dio Cassius wrote that Viriathus had killed a part of those he had delivered, and gave the rest to Laenas.[1055] In Strabo work, he states that among the prominent Lusitanians that were handed over to Caepio, there were Roman deserters. Once these hostages were in Roman hands, they had their right hands immediately cut off, so that they would never again

---

harshness and cruelty that a great number of unseemly jokes and stories were told about him during the nights; and the more he grew vexed at it, the more they jested in the endeavour to infuriate him. When it became known what was going on and no one could be found guilty, — though he suspected it was the doing of the cavalry,— since he could not fix the responsibility upon anybody, he turned his anger against them all, and he commanded them, six hundred in number, to cross the river beside which they were encamped, accompanied only by their grooms, and to bring wood from the mountain on which Viriathus was bivouacking. The danger was manifest to all, and the tribunes and lieutenants begged him not to destroy them. The cavalry waited for a little while, thinking he might listen to the others, and when he would not yield, they scorned to entreat him, as he was most eager for them to do, but choosing rather to perish utterly than to speak a respectful word to him, they set out on the appointed mission. And the horsemen of the allies and other volunteers accompanied them. They crossed the river, cut the wood, and piled it in all around the general's quarters, intending to burn him to death. And he would have perished in the flames, if he had fled away in time."

[1054] Cassius Dio, 22.75; According to Professor Munoz, Cassius Dio's paragragh does not mention Astolpas but it seems to suggest that many prominent Lusitanians were turned over to Laenas by Viriathus who seems to have been willing to betray the Lusitanians nobility for a peace treaty for his people. Munoz, Mauricio P.,op. cit., p.185

[1055] Cassius Dio, 22.75

strike Rome. This Roman act of cutting off hands was introduced by the Lusitanians.[1056] But of all the men that were turned in, according to Professor Munoz, one was missing, Astolpas, who is believed to have been assassinated by Viriathus's own hand, in which Cassius Dio makes the only mention by family status and not by name.[1057] Looking into this event, one could ask, why was Astolpas murdered, instead of allowing him to live? Taking into consideration all the angles, we come to the same conclusion: Though Astolpas was without any weight behind Viriathus in the Lusitanian struggle and was considered the richest land owner in the southern region and played politics with both Romans and Iberians, Viriathus, to be seen in the good graces of the Romans was in the end doing their bidding in that it would allow the Romans to control a newly acquired region. Some might interpret this as perhaps Viriathus selling himself out to the Romans for land and peace. Other may see this as he may have had his own agenda, such as establishing his own kingdom by taking over his in-law's lands once the Romans had finally recognized him as a king.

As the story continues, this was not enough for the Roman consul, and so he imposed more conditional terms upon the Lusitanians, including of deposing their weapons. The Lusitanians were ready to commit to all the Roman demands, but refused the surrendering of their weapons, which represented the largest affront that could be made to the Lusitanian people.[1058] Viriathus realizing that it was impossible for a new pact to materialize with the consul, negotiations ceased and Viriathus withdrew into the mountains. As for Laenas, he continued on his campaign across the Lusitanian province.

Pressured by his countrymen into making peace, it did not take long before Viriathus came into contact with Caepio, who had finally quelled his mutiny. Although Viriathus could have resisted a bit longer, his people were tired of war and demanded peace, so he attempt to negotiate another peace treaty. Yielding to the requests from his fellow

1056 Strabo, 3.3.6

1057 Cassius Dio, 22.75

1058 Cassius Dio, 22.75

countrymen, Viriathus sent out messengers to lure Caepio to the negotiating table. Within several weeks, contact was made and Caepio arrived near *Mons Veneris*, Viriathus's base camp.

Treason and the Death of Viriathus

The negotiation and treachery that occurred between Viriathus and Caepio is well known as reported by Appian, Diodorus, Livy and several other classical writers.[1059] Most of the sources see Caepio as the one who ended the Lusitanian War for he was the true organizer of the plot to destroy Viriathus.

History tells us that Caepio decided to attack Viriathus, who was still camped on the forested hill of *Mons Veneris* which had been utilized as Viriathus's base camp throughout the war. But given the temper of his men due to the previous mutiny, Caepio knew the risks of battle with Viriathus, both for his soldiers and especially for himself. Therefore, he tried another tactic; he attempted to negotiate with Viriathus. On the other side of the battle line, as mentioned in the previous section, Viriathus was forced into making peace with the Romans. Unfortunately, it was not documented who made the first move, but whoever it was, it resulted in an agreement that both men would meet.

According to Appian, Viriathus sent three emissaries of peace that he considered his most trusted allies, who perhaps by his standard were more intelligent and prudent than the rest of his companions. The spokesmen that were sent to Caepio's camp were three of his lieutenants: Audax, Ditalco and Minurus.[1060] In Diodorus's work he used the Hellenized forms of their names; Aulaces, Ditalkon and Nicoronte.[1061] From their supposed knowledge of the Latin language, Viriathus entrusted these men with instructions to go to Caepio's camp to negotiate and discuss

---

[1059] Appian, 74; Livy, per., 54; Diodorus, 33.1.4 and 33.21; Velleius, 2.1.3; Valerius Maximus, 9.6.4; Florus, 1.33.17; Eutropius, 4.16 and de vir. Ill., 71.3; Orosius 5.4.14

[1060] Appian, 74.311

[1061] Diodorus, 33.21

with Caepio the terms and conditions for a new peace treaty. According to Diodorus, these three men from Urso, seeing that Viriathus was eager to end the war, volunteered to meet the Romans with the promise that they would persuade Caepio to make peace, if Viriathus would send them as envoys to arrange a cessation of hostilities.[1062]

Arriving at the Roman camp, the emissaries presented to Caepio Viriathus's terms, unfortunately what the exact terms and conditions of the treaty were not written down. But what is known is that Caepio wanted to end the war on his terms and not on Viriathus's terms. Upon arrival to Caepio's camp, Viriathus's envoys were treated like royalty. Overwhelmed by the sumptuousness of Caepio's camp in the field and stupefied by what they saw, Caepio began to shower them with lavish gifts and promises of personal wealth.[1063] In the end, it was not difficult for Caepio to lead them down the road of corruption and murder.

Caepio, after several days and without difficulty, managed to finally bribe them and talked the three men into helping him end the war. Caepio assured them that this standard of living and much more could be theirs, all they needed to do was to kill Viriathus and then they would be able to obtain their rewards. After receiving personal guarantees on the promise of future wealth, as well as ensuring their personal security, the three men agreed. The three men left the camp and speedily returned back to their own encampment.

Now that you we have seen Appian's version, Diodorus writes something different. In Diodorus's version he states that these men were from Urso,[1064] which seem to play an important part in the story about Viriathus's death. Diodorus writes that these close comrades observing that Viriathus's prestige was beginning to suffer and eager to end the war themselves, they began to be apprehensive about their own necks (being that they knew what happens to Roman subjects who are caught

---

[1062] Diodorus, 33.21

[1063] Appian, 74.311

[1064] **Urso**, a town in Hispania Baetica, thus a city under Roman domination. Also, he is the only wrtier to mention where these men were from.

fighting alongside the enemy).[1065] Having showed Viriathus that they had orator skills and knowledge of Latin, they were able to convince Viriathus that they could persuade the Romans into a peace treaty.[1066]

As the story goes, Viriathus and his war council were riddle with anxiety for they expected that their three emissaries would have returned within a day or two with an answer about whether Caepio had settled on their conditions for peace. Viriathus and his council kept a constant vigil and only separated to rest when convinced that the emissaries would not arrive before the day's end. As for the emissaries, it is said that they must have returned to the vicinity of their encampment during the dead of night a few days later via impenetrable paths, only to lurk, stalk and watch for the right time to implement their heinous act of pre – planned assassination.[1067]

According to the classical authors, it seems that Viriathus was a very cautious man. Appian writes, that Viriathus slept very little due to his anxieties and worked hard in planning his next move, when he rested paranoid or perhaps always at the ready, he slept in full armor, so if woken up, he would immediately be ready for anything.[1068] Being that he was ready for anything, it can perhaps be concluded that the Lusitanians received with frequency a fair amount of night alarms and constantly receiving information from his spies, messenger and his lieutenants at all hours of the day and night. When his delegates returned to their camp in the middle of the night, they were immediately admitted to Viriathus's tent without question. Appian comments on this by saying, "…this was the reason his friends were able to come and meet him during the night." [1069] Diodorus also make a statement about the three men making their way to Viriathus tent that faithful night.[1070]

[1065] Cassius Dio, 22.75 Viriathus gave them all up to Laenas, these Roman deserters and prominent Lusitanians had their right hands immediately cut off or at times executed.

[1066] Diodorus, 33.21

[1067] Tusculano, Victor de, op. cit., p. 119.

[1068] Appian, 74.312

[1069] Ibid.

[1070] Diodorus, 33.21

The envoys returned to Viriathus's encampment and asserted to the council, according to Diodorus, that they had won the consent of the Romans to write up a new peace treaty. This aroused high hopes in Viriathus, but the reality of the situation was much different. This bit of "good news" was a way to distract Viriathus's mind as far as possible from any suspicion of the truth. After the council was dismissed, Appian goes on to write, "relying on his lack of sleep, Audax (being that he is mentioned again in Appian's text, we must assume he was the ringleader) and the other two men watched him and, just as he was about to fall asleep, taking advantage of the trust and friendship that Viriathus had in them, they entered his tent as though there was some pressing news and quickly attacked him, stabbing him in the throat, being that was the only vital area of his body that was unprotected."[1071] Viriathus had found death at the hands of his compatriots and not by that of Caepio. Because they were trusted men, nothing was noticed and they easily fled their camp into the night, and walked through trackless mountain country, crossed the Roman picket and into Caepio's camp before the murder was discovered the next morning.

As for what happened to Viriathus assassins, there are several versions. Appian's version states that the three men arrived at the Roman encampment, met with Caepio seeking their promised compensation. Caepio immediately granted them that they would soon have what they wanted and send them to Rome as heroes. Caepio let them keep what they had received in advance; but as for the rest of their rewards, he supposedly passed on his requests to Rome.[1072] Unfortunately, it ends here and what happened to the three men after, is not known.

In Eutropius's version when dealing with Viriathus's killers, Eutropius claims that when Viriathus' assassins arrived at Caepio's encampment in order to give him knowledge of the implementation of the crime and ask Q. Servilius Caepio for their payment, he answered, "*est numquam Romanis placuisse imperatores a suis militibus interfici.*" ("It was never pleasing to the Romans, that a general should be killed by his

[1071] Appian 74.313
[1072] Appian, 74.314

own soldiers.).[1073] Caepio coolly assured the assassins that they had misunderstood his meaning and that he would never have encouraged men to kill their own commander. The killers were then turned out of the Roman camp without a penny for their deed.[1074] Iberian treachery met Roman treachery.

But this treachery, was badly seen and unmoral in the eyes of Romans for Caepio was supposedly seen as a man of honor, which was far from the truth as mentioned before. But this well-known phrase "Rome does not pay traitors" is no more than an invention, but it perfectly portrays the feelings of the traditional version, which we know by Appian, Eutropius and Orosius: that the view of early Rome nobility was that it had never approved that a chief, leader or king be killed at the hands of their soldiers. It is possible that this version had been put into circulation years after this event took place, in an effort to conceal the shame that Caepio brought upon Rome of being responsible for enticing others, especially enemies of Rome to do their dirty work such as in the case of Viriathus's assassination. After this incident, Caepio was seen as a corrpt person who would later be exiled after the Battle of Arausio.[1075]

1073 Eutropius, Breviarium ab urbe condita, 4.16

1074 Valerius Maximus, Factis Dictisque Memorabilibus, 9.6.4

1075 Upon his return to Rome in 106 BCE was tried by Tribune of the Plebs, Gaius Norbanus for the loss of his entire Army (80,000 men) at the Battle of Arausio. The Battle of Arausio took place at a site between the town of Arausio (modern day Orange, Vaucluse) and the Rhône River. In the Battle of Arausio in 105 BC, Caepio along with the consul Gnaeus Mallius Maximus led two armies against the Germanic tribes (the Teutones, the Cimbri, and Tigurini/Marcomanni/Cherusci). While marching to Arausio, Caepio plundered the temples of the town of Tolosa, finding over 50,000 15 lb. bars of gold and 10,000 15 lb. bars of silver. The riches of Tolosa were shipped back to Rome, but only the silver made it; the gold was stolen by a band of marauders, who were believed to have been hired by Caepio himself. The Gold of Tolosa was never found and was said to have been passed all the way down to the last heir of the Servilii Caepiones, Marcus Junius Brutus. At the Battle of Arausio, Caepio refused to co-operate with his superior officer, consul Gnaeus Mallius Maximus, who was a New Man (was the term in ancient Rome for a man who was the first in his family to serve in the Roman Senate or, more specifically, to be elected as consul) and not a member of the Roman Elite. Caepio refused to even camp with Maximus and his troops, when it appeared

As for Servilius Caepio's deceitfulness, he was no stranger to those sorts of tactics. Its written that Gaius Servilius Structus Ahala, a descendant of Caepio's family[1076] served as his model in saving Roman interests in Hispania against the Lusitanians. As Ahala story goes, related by Livy and others, Ahala served as *magister equitum* in 439 BC, when Cincinnatus was appointed dictator on the supposition that Spurius Maelius was styling himself a king and plotting against the state. During the night on which the dictator was appointed, the capitol and all the strong posts were garrisoned by the partisans of the patricians. In the morning, when the people assembled in the forum, with Spurius Maelius among them, Ahala summoned the latter to appear before the dictator; and upon Maelius disobeying and taking refuge in the crowd, Ahala rushed into the throng and killed him. So Viriathus's death has been compared to that of the killing of Spurius Maelius, and while Ahala's act was perpetrated to please Cincinnatus and save Rome, this has also been related to that of another Servilius saving Rome by killing Viriathus, a newly established barbarian king, to please not a dictator, but the Roman Senate who saw this man as a threat to their interests in Hispania.[1077] Using underhanded means or not, Caepio seems to have release Rome from committing itself any further against a dangerous enemy.

---

that Maximus was going to reach a treaty and take the glory for the resolution, Caepio ordered his men to engage the Germans, and the battle that ensued saw the complete destruction of the Roman army. Caepio was convicted and was given the harshest sentence allowable: he was stripped of his citizenship, forbidden fire and water within eight hundred miles of Rome, nominally fined 15,000 talents (about 825,000 lb) of gold, and forbidden to see or speak to his friends or family until he had left for exile. (The huge fine—which greatly exceeded the Treasury of Rome—was never collected.). Caepio spent the rest of his life in exile in Smyrna (Today known as İzmir, Turkey) in Asia Minor.

[1076] The most famous of the early Servilii family who was famous for saving Rome from tyranny by killing Spurius Maelius in 439 BCE. Smith, Willian, "Ahala, C. Servilius Structus", in Smith, William, Dictionary of Greek and Roman Biography and Mythology, Boston: Little, Brown and Co, 1867, pp. 83; Livy, iv.13, 14, 21; Joannes Zonaras, vii. 20; Dionysius of Halicarnassus, *Exc.* Mai, i. p. 3; Cicero, *Catiline Orations* 1, *Pro Milone* 3, *Cato Maior de Senectute* 16; Valerius Maximus, v. 3. 2; Cicero, *De re publica* i. 3, *pro Dom.* 32

[1077] Tusculano, Victor de, op. cit., p. 118.

In Rome, the rumor that Caepio had a hand in Viriathus's murder was considered as an unworthy act by the Senate and the oligarchy. This unscrupulous act committed by one of its elite upper-class compatriots was seen by them as an act of moral decadence which misrepresented the fundamental ideas of the Republic. Thus in 139 BCE, when Caepio's governorship had ended and he returned to Rome, he was denied a triumph by the Senate even though he had succeeded in ending the Lusitanian War by defeating Viriathus and his successor, Tautalus.

As for Viriathus's so-called friends, these three individuals, according to Diodorus, were from Urso (Osuna), a Turdetanian city south of Cartagena which was situated in the province of Baetica. This city was once a Roman controlled city that had switched to Viriathus's side when the war began.[1078] Besides being Roman freedmen, these three individuals may have had been heads of Baetian tribesmen who had joined Viriathus's rank and file, and because of their status in Iberian society, later become to be considered close associates, placing them in a leadership position as either as his lieutenant or captain. In addition, their names were not of a Celtic origin. According to Victor Tusculano, Audax or Aulace's name is of a Phoenician or Persian origin; Ditalco/ Ditalkon, was of Greek descent or Iberian Greek, but his name also implies that he may have been of Cretan birth and Minuro is said to have been a Carthaginian name.[1079] Thus these chosen emissaries - assassins were not Lusitanian. And so, it has become an enigma as to why he chose these three individuals that were not Lusitanians and which of these two classical writers are neutral in their statement about what caused these men to betray Viriathus. In defense of these three men, given the circumstances they were involved in, it is probable that Caepio had threatened these men with the destruction of the home, if they did not cooperate with him. Thus, these men had no choice but to do what they did. I believe that anyone of Viriathus companions, whether they were Lusitanian or not, would sooner or later have done the same thing these men did if they had been threatened or bought.

1078 Diodorus, 33.21. He is the only writer to mention where these men were from

1079 Tusculano, Victor de, op. cit., p. 119

Retuning back to the Lusitanian camp, the surprising discovery of Viriathus's body by his attendants at day - break raised much commotion throughout the Lusitanian army. Overcome by grief, then fear, many of his followers felt apprehension of the coming dangers that would threatened them now that their great leader had been killed.[1080] Along with the dreadful feelings that they felt for the death of Viriathus, they were also angry for not being able to find his murderers.[1081] In the end, the death of their beloved Viriathus was devastating to their psyche, for he was the power that seems to have made the Lusitanian feel invincible. Now desolated by his death, Viriathus's countrymen must have felt doubt that they could survive much longer without him.

In conclusion, the demise of Viriathus was simply due to political and personal circumstances, from greed and self-preservation along with the politics of his people desired peace (to which Viriathus resisted). These elements had made the situation to end the war once and for all very favorable to the Romans. With Viriathus's death, the war for Lusitanian independence died with him.

The Funeral

Viriathus's funeral must have been an extraordinary sight for the classical texts state that he received more honors that the Lusitanians could afford, such as Viriathus's body being dressed in a magnificent garment and then having his body cremated on a high pyre, while many sacrifices were made to the gods on his behalf.[1082]

The entire army was present at the burial, for Appian writes that squadrons of infantry and cavalry ran around him in full armor in the "barbarian fashion" reciting praises and songs in tribute to him, while

---

[1080] Why the surprised discovery was because Viriathus had a habit of not sleeping much so according to Appian his attendants and the entire were surprised that he had changed his routine which perhaps men at that he was the last to sleep and the first to rise and walk security among his sleeping men. Appian, 74.315

[1081] Appian, 74.315-316

[1082] Appian 75.317, Diodorous, 33.22

dancing around the fire. They then sat down in silence around his burning body, until the pyre burnt out. Once the flames were out, immersed in deep emotional pain for the loss of their leader, the Lusitanians watched as his ashes were collected into an urn. Once the funeral rites had ended, 200 pairs of gladiators conducted mock gladiatorial games of combat in front of his grave, in dedication to his courage and warrior spirit.[1083]

As for the location of Viriathus's camp and grave, no Roman historian indicates the place where the crime was perpetrated or where his grave is located. In addition, the Lusitanians seem to not have made any type of pilgrimages to his grave site, for many of his followers and supporters were forced to hide from persecution for several years after Viriathus's death, thus the location of his grave had been forgotten.

Since the 1500s AD or perhaps even earlier, many historians and later 19th century archaeologists have attempted to locate his grave but to no avail.[1084] The earliest recorded so-called discovery of Viriathus's grave was by João de Barros, who has been called the *Portuguese Livy*, for he is one of the first great Portuguese historians, famous for his *Décadas da Ásia* ("Decades of Asia"), a history of the Portuguese in India and Asia. According to Barros, he supposedly found the grave on a farmstead by discovering a gravestone or funerary marker with a Latin inscription about Viriathus. While Brás Garcia de Mascarenhas, poet, historian

---

1083 Appian, 75.317; Diodorus 33.2; Gladiatorial games used in funerary rites was first recorded by Livy, who dates the earliest Roman gladiator games to 264 BC, in the early stages of Rome's First Punic War against Carthage. According to Livy, Decimus Iunius Brutus Scaeva had three gladiator pairs fight to the death in Rome's 'cattle market' Forum (Forum Boarium) to honor his dead father, Brutus Pera (Livy, per., 16; Valerius Maximus, 2.4.6). This is described as munus (plural munera): a commemorative duty owed a dead ancestor by his aristocratic descendants. But as for the gladiatorial games, in general, in the late 1st century BC Nicolaus of Damascus believed that these games were of Etruscan origin. But at the same time, Nicolaus cites Posidonius' support for a Celtic origin, while Hermippus' for a Mantinean (therefore Greek) origin (Welch, Katherine E. The Roman Amphitheatre: From Its Origins to the Colosseum. Cambridge, U.K.: Cambridge University Press, 2007, p. 16-17)

1084 These are just a few of the many references that I found which have been around for some time

and military hero of the Portuguese War of Restoration (1640- 1668) and author of the epic poem "*Viriato Trágico*", believes that Viriathus's final resting place was in the ancient city of Saguntum, located near Valencia, Spain. According to legend it is believed that when Caepio relocated many of Viriathus's warriors and their families they took his remains with them and reburied them there. Nineteeth century historian, Augusto Soares de Azevedo Barbosa Pinho Leal wrote that Viriathus is perhaps buried in Numão, a town that was erected by the survivors of the siege of Numancia in 133 BCE; but most writers since then have come to an speculative agreement that perhaps Viriathus's ashes are buried somewhere around *Cava de Viriato*, in Viseu Portugal.[1085] But these are speculations for no hard evidence has been found to date.

As for the popular belief that he may be buried at *Cava de Viriato,* it is unsound for it was a Roman military camp created after Viriathus death. According to Jorge Alarcão, the encampment has been traditionally considered a Roman army base built by Sextus Iunius Brutus during his governorship (137-136 BCE) and was used throughout the entire Roman occupation of Lusitania. After the Romans left the Iberian Peninsula, it fell to the Islamic occupation of the peninsula, for there is evidence that shows that the Arabs had modified the military base during the wars against the peninsula's Christian kingdoms in the 990s AD.[1086] As for the Lusitanians occupying the area, it is only speculative as mentioned before, for to date no Lusitanian artifacts have been discovered in the area.

Tautalus and the End of the Lusitanian War

The death of Viriathus signified the end of Lusitanian resistance against Roman expansion in western Hispania. Though the Lusitanians were devastated by Viriathus's death and the Lusitanian army had become increasingly smaller, the Lusitanians still had the desire to continue the fight against the Romans. As soon as Viriathus was buried, a successor

[1085] Tusculano, Victor de, op. cit., p. 121.

[1086] Mantas, Vasco Gil, "Indícios de um Campo Romano na Cava de Viriato?". Al-Madan. IIª Série. 12: 2003, p. 40-42.

was quickly elected. Viriathus's successor was a man named Tautalus (by Appian) or Tautamus (by Diodorus) and according the ancient texts was, "not of the same quality as Viriathus."[1087]

Tautalus wanted to finish what Viriathus had started, so he reorganized the army and launched a 'military' expedition to the east towards Saguntum on the eastern seacoast of Spain, in an attempt to retake southern Hispania. The campaign began with incursions into the fertile lands of Beatica in Hispania Ulterior, continuing on until he reached the mineral rich land of Bastetania, near Cartago Nova (Cartagena). Instead of advancing towards Saguntum, he decides to attack Cartago Nova. Far away from their homeland and fatigued from being constantly on the move, Tautalus's army was defeated and driven away. Realizing that he would not be able to complete Viriathus's dream of defeating the Romans and establish a free Lusitanian, he turned back.[1088] Without Viriathus's skills and tactical leadership in war, they were unable to resist for much longer.

While Tautalus ran rampant across Ulterior, Caepio prepared his army to move against Tautalus. At the Betis River (Guadalquivir), Caepio met Tautalus for the first and only time. As Tautalus's army crossed the river, Caepio spotted the Lusitanians and quickly ordered his men to attack them, unfortunately not one classical writer wrote about the battle, except that it happened, and that the final outcome of the battle was a Lusitanian defeat and Tautalus's surrender.[1089] Although they had elected a new leader, who was committed to continue the war, the heart of it had gone out with Viriathus's death. Thus, the Lusitanian War had come to an end.[1090]

Caepio had easily obtained the victory that had evaded his predecessors for so long and the Lusitanians were now obliged to sue for peace

---

[1087] Diodorus, 33.1.4

[1088] Appian, 75.321

[1089] Appian, 75.321

[1090] After the death of Viriathus, many Lusitanians and their allies split, especially in the north of Portugal and Spain, and continued the war on their own as we shall see in the next chapter.

without conditions. Fortunately for the Lusitanians, they did not suffer the cruelties that Galba or Laenas had previously perpetrated. With great benevolence, Caepio did just as Galba had promised before massacring them in 150 BCE; he allocated land and even threw in a city. Although a decade of war had depopulated much of the country, Caepio promise to settle the Lusitanians on lands fertile enough to support them without them resorting to brigandage.[1091] Luckily for the Lusitanians, because of the respect that the Romans had for their fighting prowess, the Lusitanians compared to other Iberian tribes were subsequently treated with greater leniency. With the war at its end, the Romans would now be able to extend its empire further west and north-west. Although the war had ended and their empire enlarged, it would take another century for the Romans to feel secure in Lusitania, after that we hear no more of victorious Lusitanian campaigns or of charismatic native chiefs.

What honorable generals had failed to do in years of open warfare, a duplicitous bully had accomplished it by treachery in a short single campaign. Overall, Viriathus's death began the integration of the Lusitanian territory into the Roman Empire. Nevertheless, total pacification of Lusitania was only achieved under Caesar Augustus. J. J. Sayas puts it best when he wrote, "The betrayal of Viriathus accelerated the end of the Lusitanian resistance, but if he had lived, he would have prolonged the war, but he would still not have been able to impede Roman military expansion into Lusitania."[1092] Although Rome had won the war, the Romans had learned several valuable lessons that would late help them to further expand their empire against barbarian tribe in Gaul and Germania as well as in the east.

[1091] Appian, 75.321

[1092] Sayas, J.J., "Algunas Consideraciones sobre Cuestiones Relacionadas con la Conquista y Romanización de las Tierras Extremeñas", El Proceso Histórico de la Luistania Oriental en Época Preromana y Romana, Mérida, 1993, p. 189 and "El bandolerismo lusitano y la falta de tierras", Homenaje al Prof. Antonio de Bethencourt y Massieu, Espacio, Tiempo y Forma #4, 1989, pp. 708-710.

CHAPTER IX

CAMPAIGNS OF LUSITANIAN PACIFICATION

After Viriathus's death, the unconditional surrender of Tautalus, and the start of Decimus Iunius Brutus's Lusitanian campaign, the situation in that region changed radically. The Lusitanians in time, would become Romanized by acquiring Roman culture, language, laws, technology and even through marriage. As the years passed, the Lusitanian way of life and language, ingrained with Latin, would evolve into what would become the Portuguese people and language. By the time Lusitania was pacified, there would be neither need for pacts nor peace treaties for the Romanized Lusitanians had the same advantages as Roman citizens did. The absolute truth is that the Romans sought to improve the conditions of places they occupied, but at the same time they had a tendency to exploit and confiscate everything that produced wealth, while forcing its new subjects to pay taxes, whereas rebellious locals were sold into slavery. What could be seen as Roman pacification could also be perceived as Roman exploitation.

After the war, as well as the end of the Celtiberian War, many of the local inhabitants became subjugated and some became slaves forced work for rich land proprietors throughout the empire. By the 2nd century BCE, the number of slaves was well beyond that of free men. Historians, I believe, nourish a particular admiration for the Roman Empire. There is a natural seduction about how a primitive tribe became an advanced empire, but sometimes we, as historians, are forgetful of how bloody the creation of the Empire was, through its many armed conflict and the displacement, enslavement and even annihilation of many native and foreign tribes and peoples.

Though Viriathus's Lusitanian War had end, there was still much campaigning to be done against the last strongholds of Viriathus's army that consisted of the northern Lusitanian tribes and Viriathus's former allies. If the Romans want to control the entire western section of the peninsula, they first had to pacify Lusitania and Galica. To do this, they had to set out on a campaign of punishment and persecution.

Brutus's Campaign of Pacification

In 138 BCE, following Caepio, the next governor of Ulterior was Decimus Iunius Brutus, who was an illustrious speaker, man of great culture and literary patron of his friend, the poet Lucius Accius. Upon taking office, he immediately set out to quell the remaining Lusitanians and other northern Iberian tribes that had monopolized on the fighting against Rome during this time period, and although some tribes collaborated between themselves, we can say that this war was never jointly organized, thus ended quickly.

His first action prior to his campaign was the fortification of Olisipo (Lisbon) and building a base of operations close to Moron (location unknown), a Lusitanian city on the banks of the Tagus River.[1093] This military base was 500 *stades* (92.5Km or 57miles) from the sea. The exact location of the military base camp is uncertain, but Iberian archaeologist believe it may be around the vicinity of Santarém or Alpiarça. But according to Professor Alarcão, the site is perhaps somewhere north of Santarém, according to artifacts found in the area of Chões de Alpompé in Vale de Figueira.[1094] But other archaeologists believe that Brutus's camp is at Alto de Castilla in Alpiarça.[1095]

[1093] Strabo, 3.3.1

[1094] Alarcão, J. de, Roman Portugal, Vol. II, Aris & Phillips Ltd., Warminster, UK, 1988, p.8; Alberto, Paulo Farmhouse, Viriato, Vultos da Antiguidade, Editorial Inquérito, 1996, p. 53

[1095] Curchin, Leonard, A., Roman Spain, Barnes & Noble Inc, NY, 1995, p. 38

The reason why Brutus may have fortified Olisipo was because of the rise of Iberian guerrilla activity in and around Lusitania, so it was necessary for the Romans to launch a military campaign against the central and northern tribes, for if they had not conducted military operations the flame of rebellion would have reignited and spread across the country like wildfire and Rome would have lost everything it had accomplished up to this point. On a personal level, it was also necessary for Brutus to lead a campaign as a means of promoting his military and political career, as well as for the simple covetousness of instilling new lands into the Roman dominion. With the unexpected defeats that the Roman army suffered in central Hispania during the Iberian wars and Lusitanian War, D. Iunius Brutus decided to arrive by ship onto Olisipo's shores instead of marching across southern Hispania into Lusitania. At Olisipo, he quickly ordered his army to fortify the city and built a port. This was to ensure that the Romans had a foothold in the western part of the Iberian Peninsula that would enable them to navigation into the interior of the country via its rivers and deliver food and supply to a western port, instead of the long journey across the Peninsula from an eastern Spanish port.[1096] Sailing through the Strait of Gibraltar and right into Olisipo was much easier than marching across an area than was unknown and dangerous. As for having conducted military operation in the vicinity of the Tagus River Valley prior to his march north, we can only assume that Brutus may have conducted some sort of minor military operations during this campaign, but unfortunately Roman historians did not provide us details.

During 138 – 137 BCE, from his Olisipo base camp, Brutus advanced north along an existing Atlantic coastal road from Olisipo (Lisbon) to a fortified Callaici and Bracarii city which would later be renamed Bracara (Braga).[1097] Brutus conducted his campaign much different from

---

[1096] Strabo. 3.3.1

[1097] The **Gallaeci**, **Callaeci**, or **Callaici** were a Pre- Roman Celtic single or various tribe living in the northwest of the Iberian Peninsula, north of the Douro River in Northern Portugal and Galicia (Spain). The other tribe known as the Bracarenses, a tribe who occupied what is now Galicia and northern Portugal. The Romans began their conquest of the region around 136 BC, and during the

previous praetors. Though he was sent out to deal with the Lusitanians and their allies, he gave up the idea of chasing them throughout the entire territory that bordered along the following rivers: the Tagus, the Durius (Douro R.), the Lethes (Lima R.), and the Baenis (Minho River), all of which were navigable rivers that would later be used to transport supply and provisions. Thinking it difficult to catch up with these warriors, who knew how to move around the countryside rapidly, he decided to turn against their towns and *castros.* According to Appian, Brutus's idea of turning on the *castros* and towns to punish the Iberian population for rebelling against Roman authority would further disintegrate the Lusitanian army in that the warriors would desert and return to their home so as to protect their loved ones from the incoming onslaught of Roman soldiers, thus disbanding the troublesome rebel army.[1098] At the same time, he and his army would make a profit by taking these towns of their booty, returning to Rome as rich men.

Brutus covered the journey from Olisipo to Cales (Oporto), until he reached the mouth of the Douro River. Up to this point in the history of the Roman invasion of the Iberian Peninsula, he was the only Roman to have led any type of expeditionary army this far north, but it did not stop here. From several classical texts that mention his campaign, it seems he was determined to cross the famous River Lima, which was believed to be the River of Forgetfulness, further north of Cales, then penetrate deep into the unknown and towards the point of the land known as *terrae finis*, 'end of the earth'. Faithful to his strategy he stuck close to the seashore and lowlands, disregarding the highlands, so as not to get himself surrounded or trap by a guerrilla army and for him to have easy accessibility to Iberian town from the coast, whose villages, towns

---

times of Emperor Caesar Augustus (around the year 20 BC) the city of **Bracara Augusta** was founded in the context of the administrative needs of the new Roman territory. Bracara was dedicated to the Emperor, hence its name Augusta. The city of Bracara Augusta developed greatly during the 1st century AD and reached its maximum extension in the 2nd century. Towards the end of the 3rd century, Emperor Diocletianus promoted the city to the status of capital city of the newly-founded province of Gallaecia.

[1098] Appian, 71.302

and cities could be taken easily without too many Roman casualties. But though this was a great strategy on part of Brutus, his army on the other hand, would suffer a setback on a spiritual level for the Roman soldier was religious and superstitious. Believing in the spirit world and underworld, an entire imaginary realm of myths and legends and the dangers that laid ahead within the confines of these unknown lands, fearful rumors and stories began to spread throughout the Roman rank and file about evil Celtic deities.

Following his strategy, he continued to march north killing and destroying everything they encountered when the natives did not surrender. On crossing the Douro, Brutus penetrated further into an unknown world that was somewhat different from what most of his soldiers were used to. From Velleius Peterculus, we have information that this unknown hostile land was humid, rainy, oceanic, and difficult terrain.[1099] During the campaign many Iberians, who had fought alongside Viriathus, spread the word about how the Romans conducted business and fled to the mountains laden with all they could carry. Some tribes decided to resist, not only did the men fight, but their women fought and died alongside their men, resulting in massive loss of life on both sides. But for those tribes, villages or towns that quietly surrendered, Brutus pardoned them, but divided up their wealth among his army.[1100]

Having crossed the Douro River, Brutus continues to march north until he arrived at the Lusitanian city of Citânia de Briteiros.[1101] Knowing that the inhabitants were ready to put up an obstinate and ferocious resistance, Brutus decided he did not want to fight, but rather take

---

[1099] Rufus Festus Avienus, 5.1; Velleius Peterculus, II5; Vilatela, L.P., Lusitania: Historia y etnologia< Royal Academia de la Historia, 2000, p21

[1100] Appian, 71.303

[1101] The site is situated on a small promontory called Monte de São Romão near the Ave River, in the Northern region of Portugal, between the *freguesias* (parish or county) of Salvador de Briteiros and Donim, about 15 kilometers north-west of Guimarães. The location provides an extensive view over the navigable Ave River and its valley, and over an early north-south trade and communication path between the Douro and Minho river valleys. Cividade Hill (153 metres is one of the two hills next to the city of Póvoa de Varzim in Portugal.

the city peaceable. He sent emissaries with a peace proposal. The Lusitanians responded arrogantly. Brutus answered back that if they did not surrender, he would burn the city to the ground; still the Lusitanian response was negative. The general ordered the city to be assaulted. The Romans suffer high losses, but Brutus took the city, many Lusitanians died with their weapons in hand. Upholding to his promise, Brutus devastates the city, and left not one stone standing. Today the ruins of the old city still stand and on visiting it one can still see Brutus's devastation.[1102]

From this point on the historical record is fragmented for several classical authors mention Brutus's campaign in a non-chronological order. From what I could put together, Brutus continued to advance north, makes a move on to the city of Talabriga (Cabeço do Vouga and Marnel near Aveiro)[1103] Brutus besieged the city and demanded from them that they return all Roman deserters, release all Roman prisoners and that they lay down their weapons and no harm would come to them. In addition to these terms, he ordered that all its inhabitants leave the city. The city's population peaceful accepted the terms and left the city, when suddenly his army surrounded them. Having encircled the city's inhabitants, he made a speech recounting how many times they had revolted and waged war against the Romans and because of this he would not be wrong in massacring all of them. Having had instilled fear and the belief that he was about to inflict something terrible on the city's population, he suddenly emancipated them with a warning, but took away their horses,

---

1102 Tusculano, Victor de op. cit., p. 131; Alarcão, J. de, Roman Portugal, p. 9; Coelho da Silva, Armando, "A cultura castreja no Noroeste de Portugal: habitat e cronologias", *Portugalia*, 4/5, 1983-84, 128; Flores Gomes, José Manuel & Carneiro, Deolinda: *Subtus Montis Terroso* CMPV (2005), "Origens do Povoamento" pp.74-76.

1103 The site of Talabriga is unknown, but it has been suggested that it stood on the banks of the Vouga River, which spills into the Atlantic Ocean at Aveiro, about 50 km south of Oporto. Alarcão, J. de, op. cit., p.9; Osland, Daniel K., Early Roman Cities of Lusitania, Master of Arts Thesis, University of Cincinnati, 2005, p. 112 - 114

grain, money and precious goods and chattels, allowing them to return to their city.[1104] His action was quite contrary to what they had expected.

Brutus then for some unknown reason decides to turn slightly east in the direction of the Lusitanian city of Araduca (Guimarães) and Sabroso (São Martinho de Sande), finding the same resistance as in Citânia de Briteiros. Sabroso was completely demolished stone by stone.[1105] As for Araduca, though the ancient texts do not mention this city during Brutus campaign, it was supposedly also destroyed, according to Tusculano.[1106] While some cities were let off easy because they had surrendered to Brutus army, others were not so lucky. The ones that had put up stiff resistance suffered horribly under his hand. These towns were basically burned to the ground, just as he had done to Citânia de Briteiros and Sabroso.[1107] According to archaeological evidence, this hill-top fort was completely covered by a thick layer of ash, signifying that during Brutus's campaign, fire was set to these castros to make them an example of, so that others *castros* would surrender to him rather than be annihilated.[1108]

In Valerius Maximus's writings, he mentions a Lusitanian city by the name of Cinginna (Covilhã) to which Brutus came upon. Arriving at the city's gate, he demanded that if they wanted to remain free, they had

---

[1104] Appian, 73.308-30

[1105] Florus, 1.33.12; Orosius, 5.5.12; Plutrach; Quaest. Rom., 34; Curchin, Leonard, A., Roman Spain, p. 38; Sabroso Castro is the ruins of a former Castro that was totally destroyed during Decimus Brutus campaign.

[1106] Tusculano, Victor de op. cit., p. 132

[1107] Hawkes, C.F.C., "North-western castros: Excavation, archaeology and history", Actas do II Congreso nacional de arqueologia, Coimbra, 1971, pp. 283-286; Flores Gomes, José Manuel & Carneiro, Deolinda, Subtus Montis Terroso CMPV, "Origens do Povoamento", 2005, pp.74-76; Coelho da Silva, Armando, "A cultura castreja no Noroeste de Portugal: habitat e cronologias", Portugalia, 4/5, 1983-84, 128; Troncoso, Víctor Alonso, Primeras etapas en la conquista romana de Gallaecia, MIIITARIA. Reaismc, de Cultura Militar n. 8. servicio de Publicaciunes, 13CM. Madrid, 1996, p. 61

[1108] Flores Gomes, José Manuel & Carneiro, Deolinda, Subtus Montis Terroso CMPV, "Origens do Povoamento", pp.74-76; Coelho da Silva, Armando, "A cultura castreja no Noroeste de Portugal, p. 128.

to surrender all their precious metals. The inhabitants answered back that they did not have gold to buy their freedom, but instead they had iron weapons to defend their freedom.[1109] From the historical record, the *castro* (fortified town) was destroyed; unfortunately, Maximus did not leave us details of what happened. But from the words of Valerius Maximus, it is clear what Brutus sought was gold.

Since ancient times, the north-west was an area that was known to hold large quantities of gold as confirmed by the studies on *castro* jewelry incurred by Monteagudo and Cuevillas.[1110] During the time of Posidonius, it was well known that the northwestern region of the Iberian Peninsula was rich in silver, tin and gold.[1111] The old Tartestian road, which would later become known as the 'Via de la Plata', was in reality the main route of retrieving gold from the northwest. Knowing that this was an untapped region full of mineral wealth. It was perhaps the reason for his campaign in northern Lusitania. By the end of the campaign, both he and his soldiers had plundered and looted so many towns along the Atlantic coast that Brutus had amassed such a fortune that it permitted him to construct, besides other things, on his arrival back in Rome, a temple dedicated to Mars. Besides booty, Roman legionnaires also took clothing used to protect themselves from the harsh climate and animals that were deemed useful, such as cattle and horses.

During his campaign against the northern Lusitanians, Orosius mentions that Brutus routed an army of 60,000 Gallaeci and Callaici

---

[1109] Valerius Maximus 6.4 ext 1; Marco Simón, Francisco, Intimidación y terror en la época de las guerras Celtibéricas in *Terror et pavor. Violenza, intimidazione, clandestinità nel mondo antico*, Atti del convegno internazionale, Cividale del Friuli, 22-24 settembre 2005, Pisa, Edizioni ETS, 2006, pp. 197-213; Mera, Josefa Martinez, Expedicións Militares a Gallaecia na Época Republicana, Universidade Santiago de Compostela, n.d., p. 311

[1110] Monteagudo, L., Neuves joyas preromanoas del Norte de Portugal, *AEArq.* 18, 1945 ; Lopez Cuevillas, F., Las joyas castreñas, Madrid, 1958

[1111] Strabo 3.2.9

near the Douro River that had come to the aid of the Lusitanians.[1112] From this point on, the classical texts seems to indicate that the defeat was so demoralizing that Lusitanian and Gallaeci resistance against the Romans ended there. Though a classical text makes mention of such a large tribal army, it seems unlikely that the Gallaeci, themselves, could have gathered such a large army. But if such an army did exist, it was perhaps made up of other surrounding tribes. As for the Gallaeci coming to the rescue of the Lusitanians, ancient Iberian historian, N. Santos, writes that it is not surprising that the Gallaeci came to the aid of their Lusitanian ally, even though they were not part of any Lusitanian tribal confederation. Perhaps the main reason the entire tribe united for this action was not only in order to support the neighboring populations in their struggle against Rome, but also to prevent the Romans from invading their territory.[1113] In the end, this battle shows an exertion of a great psychological impact that the Roman invasion had among the *castro* tribes that lived around the Douro River. It is therefore safe to say, according to Lopez Cuevillas, that the year 139 BCE was the entry date of the Gallaeci in the annals of ancient history, the first mention of these people in the Roman historiography.[1114]

Unfortunately, history has not given us a place were the battle occurred nor has it produced the chronologically time frame that made Brutus a name. For C. Torres Rodriguez and Alain Tranoy, this major battle took place during the early part of the campaign season. From their research based on Ovid's work, the battle may have taken place on 9 June 137 BCE, for it was commemorated in Rome a year later, during the inauguration of the construction of Brutus's temple dedicated to

---

[1112] Orosius, 5.5.12; Lombardero, Alfonso Carbonell, The Gaels in Gallaecia, 2000 http://www.galeon.com/lombardero/Lombardero1.htm

[1113] Santos Yanguas, N., El ejército y la romanización de Gallaecia, Oviedo, 1988, p. 29

[1114] Troncoso, Víctor Alonso, *Primeras etapas en la conquista romana de Gallaecia, MIIITARIA. Reaismc, de Cultura Militar* n. 8. servicio de Publicaciunes, 13CM. Madrid, 1996, p. 56; Lopez Cuevillas, F., *Cómo Galicia, entró en la historia.* Boletín de la Real Academia Gallega, 25, 1955, p. 19-30

Mars.[1115] In addition, this documented victory was the icing on the cake for Brutus for on his return to Rome, he was received as a hero's welcome with the *cognomen* (surname) of Gallaicus.[1116]

During his rampageous campaign he decided to turn back to a northwesterly direction and advanced across another river, the Nimis. From here, Brutus marched against the Bracari, for they had attacked and plundered Brutus's supply trains.[1117] Appian wrote that they were the most warlike people of all the Gallaecian tribes. They were so warlike that according to Appian, their women (who were now the majority) fought alongside their men in full armor and died bravely.[1118] Of the women that were taken as prisoners, some of them killed themselves, while others murdered their children before killing themselves, preferring death with honor to slavery.[1119] From Tusculano's study on the subject, this heroic resistance occurred in the town that would become modern – day Braga, Portugal.[1120]

[1115] Ovid, Fastrum Libre VI, 461; Torres Rodríguez, C. La Galicia romana, Coruña, 1982; Tranoy, Alain, La Galice romaine Recherches sur le nord-ouest de la péninsule ibérique ´dans L'antiquité. Paris, 1981, p. 198

[1116] Ovid, Fastrum Libre, VI, 461-462

[1117] Appian, 72.304; According to J.S. Richardson, Schweighäuser and Goukowsky, three individual who have studied Appian's work in detail state that this river is unknown. However, this river is named by Strabo as the Baenis which what Appian is mentioned in paragragh 71.301. Unless this is another of Appian's geographical confusions, this maybe the river Nebis as it is documented by Pomponius Mela, 3.10. But his description of it as 'another river' suggests that this is a river that he had not mentioned before. Richardson, J.S., Appian: Wars of the Romans in Iberia, Aris & Phillips Ltd., Warminster, UK, 2000, 141; Schweihäuser, J., Appiani Historiae Romanae, 3 vols., Leipzig 1785, vol.3, pp. 297-298; Goukowsky, Paul, ed., *Appien. Histoire Romaine* Livre VI. L'Iberique, Paris: Les Belles Léttres, 1997, p.66, n. 405. * The **Bracari** were an ancient Celtic tribe of Gallaecia, akin to the Calaicians or Gallaeci, living in the northwest of modern Portugal, in the province of Minho, between the Tâmega and Cávado

[1118] Appian, 72.302

[1119] Ibid., 72.306

[1120] Tusculano, Victor de, op. cit., p. 121.

Having subjugated a large portion of the northern Lusitanian tribes, Brutus's campaign was in full swing, until his army arrived at the banks of the Lethes (Lima) River, which was known as the River of Forgetfulness.[1121] At the bank of the Lima River, Decimus Junius Brutus sought to dispose of the myths and superstitions of the river, for it was impeding his military campaign into the area further north. According to several classical texts, his soldiers refused to cross in fear of the River of Forgetfulness; as the story goes, Brutus grabbed the standard from its bearer and crossed over with it by himself, persuading them to follow. Having crossed the river, he called out to his soldiers on the other side, one by one, by name. The soldiers, astonished that their general remembered their names, they crossed the river without fear.[1122] This act proved that the Lima was not as dangerous as the local myths described.

Florus mention of an incident that occurred after the "attempted mutiny" on crossing the Lima River had been put down. Brutus continued his advance north, but his progress was halted when his army arrived at the banks of the Minho River estuary. Brutus could not go any further because his men's fears intensified with the image that they were treading at the ends of the world and the beginning of the underworld. This idea had been ingrained into the soldiers' psyche when they had watched in horror the sun set into the sea, setting its waters ablaze and growing in size, causing panic among many of them, who had never seen a sunset. From this point on, it seems that many of Brutus's men had had enough and began to either planning to desert or mutiny, leading Brutus to decide to end the campaign at the banks of the Minho River and return homewards.[1123]

[1121] Amongst a number of authors from Antiquity, the tiny Lima River near Xinzo de Limia in the province of Ourense in Galicia (Spain) was said to have the same properties of memory loss as the legendary mythical Lethe River.

[1122] Orosius, *Adv px.,* V, 5, 12; Livy, *per.* 55 and *ep. Oxy* 55; Florus, 1.33.12; Plutarch, *Quaest. Rom.*, 34; A. M. Romero Masió, X. M. Pose Mesura, *Gal/cia nos textos clásicos,* Coruña, 1988, passim; García Quintela, M., *El rio del Olvido,* en J. C. Bermejo Barrera, *Mitología y mitos de la Hispan/a prerromana IL* Madrid, 1986, pp. 75-86.

[1123] Florus, 1.33.12

In fact, much more than just the sunset stirred up the men, for deep in their hearts these acts of nature was perhaps interpreted as an evil omen. Along with this superstitious fear was the fact that in the rear of Brutus's army, the Lusitanians and the Gallacci were threatening his lines of communication to his bases on the Tagus River, these were the two true deciding factors to Brutus ending the campaign. Though he had gone deep into northern Portugal and Spain, and his supply line was under threat, and a majority of the north-western Iberian tribes had been defeated, Brutus was still able to consolidate his conquests during his march north and reconsolidate on his way back to Olisipo. But as life has it, all good things come to an end. Even though he was able to consolidate a good portion of what he conquered and had further plans to continue north, his campaign had come to an abrupt halt because some cities that had previously surrendered to Brutus began to revolt and so Brutus had to subdue them before another large-scale rebellion broke out or got out of hand. Brutus had, therefore, to confront this threat and return south to fight the rebels and reconsolidate this newly gain territory.

Unfortunately, we do not have information about Brutus's southward march back toward his base at Olisipo or about his quelling of the rebellious tribesmen or the consolidation of the newly conquered territory. But one thing is certain, with the destruction of Lusitanian and Gallaeci towns and cities, their will to continue on fighting quickly melted away as soon as Brutus's army was in the vicinity. Perhaps this may be the reason there is a lack of information. With the consolidation of these lands, the northern tribes were forced to accept a peace treaty, whose terms were seen as lenient for the Romans had only given them land to cultivate and a town, just as Caepio had done in the south after Viriathus's death.

The Senate, after this long and difficult war had finally understood that if they wanted to pacify this 'wild country of savages', it was necessary to resolve the social and economic problems that existed in this region. For this reason, it offered new lands to the Lusitanians, but this time they held to their word and delivered on their promise of handing over some land and a town, especially those who desisted from fighting against Rome and volunteered to fight for Rome.

But instead of giving the Lusitanians land within their border, Brutus relocated many of the warriors and their families eastward into Spain and established a city named, Valentia, which meant "strength" and "valour" in Latin.[1124] The city was named for the Roman practice of recognizing the valor of former Roman soldiers after a war, but this time the Romans were showing respect to an incredible former adversary. The location of the city mentioned by Diodorus and Livy has caused some arguments among many scholars.

The first site has been identified by some scholars as Valencia de Alcántara in Spain.[1125] Some critics cannot accept this identification and suggest that many of the Lusitanians may have been settled somewhere northeast of the Alentejo, Portugal instead of Valencia de Alcántara in eastern Spain.[1126] While other scholars argue that the other scholars are completely wrong with the locations and that the foundation of Valentia in the 2nd century BC was in the east coast of Spain at the site where modern-day Valencia exists today. The reason why the Lusitanians were resettled so far from their homeland was because many of the warriors who had fought against Rome were former rebels who had been in Viriathus's army, as well as in the campaign against Brutus. To allow them to stay in Lusitania was very risky, so it was a wise decision on part of Brutus to relocate these people as far as possible, to not allow them to regroup and instigate another rebellion. Thus, it was important that the Romans invest their time into founding Lusitanian towns with *jus Latinum* (Latin rights) and citizenship. The newly signed peace

[1124] Diodorus, 33.1.3; Livy, *periochae*, 55.4

[1125] Le Roux, Patrick, L'armée romaine et l'organisation des provinces ibériques d'Auguste á l'invasion de 409, Paris, 1982, p. 36-37; Ventura Canejero, Augustin, "qui sub Viriatho militaverunt" Archivo de Prehistoria Levantina #16, 1981, pp. 539-551. **Valencia de Alcántara** today is a Spanish town near the Portuguese border (District of Portalegre) located in Cáceres province.

[1126] Alarcão, Jorge de, "Sobre a romanização do Alentejo e do Algarve: A propósito de uma obra de José d'Encarnação", Arqueologia #11, 1985, p.100.

treaty had finally brought the Lusitanian War to an end; no doubt it brought much relief to both sides.

Along with the relocation of the Lusitanians, Brutus also founded a city in his name. At the end of Brutus's campaign, Stephanus Byzantinus mentions that he founded a city named on his behalf, Brutobriga.[1127] Besides bearing the name "Bruto", it also implies that the city was established in a Celtic area because of the use of the suffix -briga. As for the location, it has not been discovered as of yet, except minted coins bearing the city's name have been found.[1128] But since the 1900s there has been arguments between Portuguese and Spanish scholars and archaeologists about the location of Brutobriga. On the Spanish side, they claim that it is situated somewhere in the district of Viana del Bollo, while the Portuguese claim it was built somewhere along the banks of the Lima River. But according to Professor Jorge de Alarcão, minted coins found around the river's vicinity imply that it may have been a maritime city, thus it was established somewhere near the river.[1129] Unfortunately, due to the lack of private and governmental funding, excavations are not possible at the moment. Another point about Brutobriga is that we do not know if the town was intended to be as a new settlement for Roman soldiers that had participated in his campaign or whether it was a native town that simply took the Roman commander's name to honor him.

Brutus's victorious expedition against northern Lusitania and Gallaecia was a hard pill to swallow for all the western tribes that had lived on the coast of the Algarve in southern Portugal to the Minho River in northern Portugal, for they had finally become fully aware of the type of military power Rome was and that they were going to stay. From this

[1127] Fear, A.T., Rome and Baetica: Urbanization in Southern Spain c.50 BC-AD 150, Oxford University Press, 1996, 38

[1128] Stephanus Byzantinus work can be seen in Fontes Hispaniae Antiquae, IV, 140 and VII, 427; Alarcão, J. de, Roman Portugal, p. 9; Fear, A.T., Rome and Baetica: Urbanization in Southern Spain c.50 BC-AD 150, Oxford University Press, 1996, 38

[1129] José Leite Vasconcellos and L. Figueiredo da Guerra, "Limia e Brutobriga", O Arqueólogo português, Museu Nacional de Arqueologia (Portugal), Museu Ethnologico Português (Lisbon, Portugal), vol. V, 1900, p. 4-6.

point on, the tribes had now or would become nominal subjects under the authority of the governors of Hispania Ulterior. Though this land had fallen under Roman rule, the emergence of industry, such as the amphorae trade in the area of Viana do Castelo (a district located in the northwest of Portugal, bordered by Spain) illustrates the progressive opening of the indigenous world to the outside Roman world.[1130] Along with commercial industry, the Roman military with the experience it had gain fighting the Lusitanians, give us an understanding about the progression of its military weaponry and strategy, which would become useful in the next century against other non-tactical barbarian tribes that the Roman army would encounter.[1131]

Brutus's advance through this theater of operation was the second largest military conquest of Hispania since Scipio Africanus.[1132] The final defeat of the Lusitanians was welcomed in Rome and, above all, Baetica, and for the rest of the 2nd century BCE and the entire 1st century BCE, the Romans consolidated Lusitania through the establishment of military posts and large-scale urbanization project under Caesar Augustus, some of which would later become *civitates.* But before Roman could consolidate and reorganize it into administrative centers within the realm of the growing Roman Empire, Lusitania to completely submit itself to Rome, the Celtiberians of Numancia in Celtiberia needed to be defeated.[1133] Only then would Western and Central Iberia finally be at peace.

1130 Naveiro López, L., *El comercio antiguo en el noroeste peninsular,* Coruña, 1991, pp 175-6.

1131 Santos Yanguas, N., El ejército y la romanización de Gallaecia, Oviedo, 1988

1132 Vilatela, L.P., Lusitania: Historia y etnología, R. Acad. de la Hist., 2000, p. 218

1133 (*Numancia* in Spanish) is the name of an ancient Celtiberian settlement, whose remains are located 7 km north of the city of Soria, on a hill known as Cerro de la Muela in the municipality of Garray. As for the war, the **Numantine War** was the last conflict of the Celtiberian Wars. The war was fought contemporaneously with the Lusitanian War in Hispania Ulterior. It was a twenty-year long conflict between the Celtiberian tribes of Hispania Citerior and the Roman government. During Viriathus's Lusitanian War had spilled over into Citerior, open warfare had reinvigorated in 143 BC, Rome sent a series of generals to the Iberian Peninsula to deal with the Numantines. In that year, Quintus Caecilius Metellus Macedonicus

In a nutshell, Lusitania was only conquered because Viriathus was assassinated. If Viriathus had lived or had the Lusitanians elected or found a military leader near equal to Viriathus, it is possible that the Romans would have been stopped at its borders or not have had the chance to disembark it soldiers on the Lusitanian coast. Although the Lusitanian War may have lasted several more years, eventually Rome would have conquered it sooner or later.

Campaigns After Brutus

At the end of Brutus's campaign, the Romans believed that they had conquered the barbarians and would now begin to incorporate them into Rome's expanding empire. But for that to happen they needed to emplace a control element over the hostile insubordinate people. With the local under control, Rome would also initiate in incorporating into its growing empire the territory between the Douro and Minho rivers plus the area extending east along the Douro River further into the country's interior in to central Spain. As for the unoccupied areas of Celtiberia in central Spain, the Basque country in northeastern Spain,

---

tried and failed to take their main city Numancia by siege but subjugated all the other tribes of the Arevaci instead. His successor, Quintus Pompeius, was inept and suffered severe defeats at their hands, so he secretly negotiated a peace with the city abiding by the previous treaty. Yet in 138 BC a new general arrived, Marcus Pompillius Laenas, and when the Numantine envoys came to finish their obligations of the peace treaty, Pompeius disavowed negotiating any such peace. The matter was referred to the Senate for a judgment. Rome decided to ignore Pompeius' peace and sent Gaius Hostilius Mancinus to continue the war in 136 BC, who assaulted Numancia and was repulsed several times before being routed and encircled, and so forced to accept a treaty. The Senate did not ratify his treaty either. His successors Lucius Furius Philus and Gaius Calpurnius Piso avoided any type of conflict with the Numantines. In 134 BC, the Consul Scipio Aemilianus was sent to Hispania Citerior to end the war. He recruited 20,000 men and 40,000 allies, including Numidian cavalry under Jugurtha, the Berber king of Numidia. Scipio built a ring of seven fortresses around Numantia itself before beginning the siege. After suffering pestilence and famine, most of the surviving Numantines committed suicide rather than surrender to Rome. The great Roman victory over Numantia ushered in an era of lasting peace in Hispania until the Sertorian War over half a century later.

Asturias, Galicia and Cantabria in northwestern Spain, these areas would not be occupied until the end of the 1st century BCE. To many Romans, those who were ambitious, considered the new territory a field fertile for political and military promotions and a place ripe for entrepreneurialism. Thus, the fall of Lusitania produced a chain reaction that led to a mass migration of Roman citizens, which would expand deeper into the rest of the territory, even if it was of little economic interest to Rome. But from a military and political point of view, it was important for any individual who had personal ambition to move up the ranks in the military or gain fame as a politician to be elected to the Senate later on. Thus, the Lusitanian territory constituted one of these areas for someone to become somebody in Roman society, the individual would have to serve his time overseas.

But now that Lusitania was in Roman hands, the Romans began feeding money to Romanize Lusitania. This should have been an effective and reasonable way to put an end to the Lusitanian way of life, but it did not always work out for the Romans, because they still treated these 'Romanized Iberians' as second – class citizens. Thus, the lack of sensitivity on part of Rome made the situation worse. Even after Lusitania had been conquered, the Lusitanians did not conform or agree with the tiny distribution of land that was given to them and although without an organized army, they at times continued to rise up against Rome during the following years.

Though many Lusitanian rebellions are mentioned, there is not enough information about these insurrections, except excerpts. Perhaps the reason why that is, was because after the fall of Numantia in 133 BCE, there was little interest in what was happening in Hispania to peek our ancient authors to write about for the next half a century, plus Rome was involved in other major conflicts that were more interesting than minor rebellions. The wars that followed within the Roman Republic were a type of warfare that was essentially of not Romans fighting for glory and wealth against indigenous inhabitants, but wars against Roman and Roman for these civil wars had become an extension of the political struggles that racked the capital itself. But when warfare of a substantial importance did arise in Hispania it was written about. Hispania at first was spared such scenes until the arrival of Quintus Sertorius in Hispania Citerior in 83 BCE, who started the Sertonian War (80 – 72 BCE).[1134] Hispania would again be mention in the civil war between Julius Caesar and Pompey.[1135]

But prior to Sertorius, the Romans continued to fight the rebellious Lusitanians off and on. During the praetorships of Caius Marius (114 BCE) and L. Calpurnius Piso (112 BCE). Ulterior was on fire once again when the Lusitanians rose up in rebellion. These new Lusitanian incursions into Baetica occurred because the Lusitanians seemed to not have been satisfied with the distribution of lands that had been given to them by the Romans. Beside the land issue, the rebellion was also based on their treatment by the Romans. At first, the Lusitanians were well treated after the Lusitanian War. But after several years, they were oppressed again.[1136] During this campaign, the Romans scored several victories against the Lusitanian under the command of Praetor Gaius Marius and later by Decimus Junius Brutus (who replaced Marius in 113 BCE) and Piso. The Lusitanians were eventually defeated by M. Iunius Silanus the following year. Unfortunately, once again history has dealt us a blow for we do not have any information about the campaigns.

The years later, we hear once again of more Lusitanian rebellions, met by the Romans with varying degrees of success. In 109 BCE, preator to Ulterior, Quintius Servilius Caepio's son, Quintius Servilius Caepio the Younger, like his father faced the Lusitanians and achieved such a

---

1134 The **Sertorian War** was a conflict of the Roman civil wars in which a coalition of Iberians and Romans fought against the representatives of the regime established by Sulla. It takes its name from Quintus Sertorius, the main leader of the opposition to Sulla. The war lasted from 80 BC to 72 BC. The war is notable for Sertorius' successful use of guerrilla warfare. The war ended after Sertorius was assassinated by Marcus Preperna, who was then promptly defeated by Pompey.

1135 Richardson, J.S., The Period of the Civil Wars, 133-44BC, *The Romans in Spain*, Blackwell, 1996, p. **83**-126

1136 Fontes Hispaniae Antiquae, IV, 144 and 145; Guadan, A.M., Numismática ibérica e ibero-romana, Madrid, 1969, p. 128 and 216

great victory that on his arrival back in Rome in 107 BCE a triumph was celebrated in Rome.[1137] In 105 BCE, another Lusitanian rebellion broke out that resulting in a Lusitanian victory, stated by Julius Obsequens.[1138] In 102 BCE, the Roman defeated the Lusitanians under preator Marcus Marius, brother of Caius Marius and governor of Hispania Citerior.[1139] In 101 or100 BCE, under the governorship of Lucius Cornelius Dolabella until the preatorship of C. Coelius Caldus in 99 or 98 BCE, war broke out once more proving that the Lusitanians were in a state of agitation, which the Romans had a difficult time in quelling the Lusitanians.[1140] In 93 BC, Consul P.Licinius Crassus fought the Lusitanians and won, returning to Rome in triumph.[1141] These bits of data prove that relations between the Romans and the Lusitanians still remained imbalanced.

Even with the lack of information that the sources provide, a clear picture of the last 50 - year period shows that the Roman preators that governed Lusitania continued to treat the Lusitanians as second – class citizens and at time had done little the change the situation. This period of warfare exhibits that the state of affairs had changed little since the early and middle second century BCE. Warfare was still the main preoccupation of the praetors and consuls who governed the two provinces, even though the Romans did what they could to make life better in Lusitania. In spite of all these Roman military victories and economic and administrative support, the social and political organization of the Lusitanians and their way of life did not disappear completely with the Roman conquest of Lusitania. After a long series of costly and hostile armed conflicts with the Lusitanians, the Romans by the middle of the 1st century would finally managed to place the indigenous population of Lusitania within the Roman orbit of its

---

1137 Eutropius, Historiae Romanae Breviarium, 4.27; Sources on these triumphs are given by Degrassi, Attilio in Inscr. Ital., 13 vols, vol. 1, Rome, 1947, pp. 85 and 561-2.

1138 Julius Obsequens, Iulii Obsequentis ab anno urbis conditae dv prodigiorum liber, 42

1139 Appian, 100.433

1140 Degrassi, Attilio in Inscr. Ital., 13 vols, vol. 1, Rome, 1947, pp. 85 and 561-562.

1141 Ibid., 85 and 562-563

cultural and political policies, forcing most of them to descent from the mountains onto the plains to improve their situation.[1142]

Some modern historians question why did it take the Romans so long to stop the Lusitanians? The answer is that at first they were ineffective for this was the first time that they had encountered a people who did not have a standing army or political agendas compared to the Carthaginians during the 1st and 2nd Punic Wars. Also historians do not take into consideration the natural conditions of the terrain where there were wide areas that were not easily accessible to control or get to, which would have not allow the Romans to fully commit themselves to a military campaign so rapidly and so large, thus give the Lusitanians room to operate freely. But as in every war the powers that confront an unknown enemy will eventually adapt and overcome it shortcoming and defeat them in time.

Once these areas had come under Roman control and the people treated somewhat fairly, the warlike Lusitanians, rather than fight the Romans, fought for them as auxiliary soldiers of Rome. Many Lusitani participated during the civil war between the factions of Lucius Cornelius Sulla and Gaius Marius which had spilled into the Iberian Peninsula in 83 BCE, which was known as the Sertorian War.[1143] During the civil war, Sertorius, who was a supporter of Marius, led a mixed army of Romans, Libyans, Celtiberians, Cilician pirates from Turkey, Lusitanians and several other Iberian tribesmen against Sulla's incoming army. Like Viriathus, he was murdered by two of his most trusted officers in 72 BCE, thus ending this war.

Up to this point, starting with Decimus Iunius Brutus's campaign, it did not support an effective occupation of Lusitania nor did Sertorius's War lead to a real Roman domination of the region, especially since his campaign was fought as a civil war, instead of a war of liberation or

[1142] Dio Cassius, 37.52-53

[1143] See Plutarch's lives of Sertorius and Pompey; Appian, *Bell. civ.* and *Hispanica*; the fragments of Sallust; Dio Cassius xxxvi; P. O. Spann, Quintus Sertorius and the Legacy of Sulla (1987)

conquest in hopes that Lusitanian could still have a chance to become independent from the Rome. But after so many years of fighting the Lusitanian military power had declined and that many of their youths had one way or another become Romanized that it would not be until Julius Caesar's governship that Lusitania began to truly become Romanized.

The classical sources are silent about what happened in Lusitania during the years between Sertorius's death and the governorship of Julius Caesar, whose stay in Lusitania does not have seem to have been as memorable as that of Gaul and Egypt. Memorable or not, he in 61 BCE broke the peace and attacked the Lusitani and Callaici by ordering the inhabitants to leave behind their way of life and their hilltop forts and move onto the plains.[1144] Knowing that they would refuse this request, gave Caesar the reason to attack them.

Caesar who was still in debt when he was appointed to govern Hispania, needing to satisfy his creditors before he could leave for his praetorship in Hispania Ulterior, he turned to Marcus Licinius Crassus, one of Rome's richest men, for help. In return for political support in his opposition to the interests of Gnaeus Pompeius Magnus also known as Pompey, Crassus paid some of Caesar's debts and acted as guarantor for others. To avoid becoming a private citizen and open himself up to prosecution for his debts, Caesar left for his province before Crassus's praetorship had ended. In Hispania his indebtedness caused him to attack the Callaici and Lusitani, being hailed as *imperator* by his troops.[1145]

Besides campaigning against the Iberians to pay off his debt with the booty he took from the natives, Professor Alarcão suggests that Caesar's campaign of 61 BCE was perhaps conducted to subdue the native inhabitants even further. He also suggests that Caesar attempted to guarantee peace for several more years, rather than colonize the land with permanent military outposts with the exception of Scallabis (Santarém) which was established by Caesar as a base to conduct his

[1144] Dio Cassius, 37.53-53

[1145] Plutarch, "*The life of Julius Caesar*", Parallel Lives, 11–12; Suetonius, *Julius Caesar,* The Lives of the Caesars, 18.1

campaign.[1146] Still after 61 BCE, Roman settlements became a reality throughout Lusitania and its legions were frequently moved around between the Tagus and Douro Rivers as the case would be when any foreign force occupying another country.

After Sertorius's War and somewhat between Caesar's praetorship, little was written about the events in Hispania, until the outbreak of Julius Caesar's Civil War (49 – 44 BCE), where several large-scale battles were fought, to which the Lusitanians fought as auxiliary troops on both sides. Even though they did this, the majority of them, from classical accounts mention that the majority of the Lusitanians, sided with Pompey instead with Caesar for many remembered his campaign against them in 61 BCE.

Another mention of the Lusitanians comes after Caesar's victory at Ilerda in 49 BCE. Caesar's newly appointed governor of Ulterior, Quintus Cassius Longinus took over the province. Longinus, who had been left behind in Spain as pro-praetor of Ulterior, and either through his natural disposition or hatred he had contracted among his peers during the civil war in Spain due to a wound he had treacherously received as quaestor, he decided to start his own campaign against the Iberians. Whether it was based on revenge, greed or both we do not know, but one thing is certain; he displayed his temper upon the natives.[1147] It is also stated that Longinus was conscious of the discontent around him.[1148] To secure himself against disaffection from his own men, he endeavored

---

[1146] Alarcão, J. de, Roman Portugal, Vol. II, p. 9

[1147] Aulus Hirtius, De Bello Alexandrino (The Alexandrian War), 48.1-2 Being greatly in debt, he resolved to pay it by laying heavy burdens upon the province and made his liberalities a pretense to justify the most exorbitant demands. He taxed the rich at his discretion and compelled them to pay, without the least regard to their remonstrances; frequently making light and trifling offenses of all manner of extortions. All methods of gain were pursued, whether great and reputable or mean and sordid. None that had any thing to lose could escape accusation; insomuch, that the plunder of their private fortunes was aggravated by the dangers they were exposed to from pretended crimes. It is for this reason that the provincials and even his own dependents formed conspiracies against his life.

[1148] Ibid., 48.2

to gain their love and respect by assembling them and promising them a hundred sesterces each.[1149] It is from here that Longinus set off and attacked the Lusitanian town of Medobriga.[1150] Soon after, having made himself master of Medobriga, he charged up Mount Herminius, where the Medobrigians had retired. Once Mount Herminus was taken, he was saluted by the army as *imperator*, where he gave them another hundred sesterces each.[1151] Soon after this campaign (48 BCE) Longinus received orders from Caesar to deploy to Africa with his legions from Lusitania and a local auxiliary army.[1152] But Longinus would never see Africa, for his quaestor Marcellus mutinied against him.[1153] Unfortunately, the mutiny came to late for his tyrannical government in Hispania had greatly injured Caesar's progress for another civil war broke out.

After Longinus's disgraceful exit from Hispania in 47 BCE, Caius Trebonius (a Caesar supporter) was named praetor of Ulterior. Soon after he took office, civil war broke out again between Caesar and Pompey's sons, Sextus Pompeius Magnus Pius and Gnaeus Pompeius, along with Caesar's former praetorian legate, Titus Labienus. Once again during the civil war, it seems that the majority of the Lusitanians joined Pompey's forces for there is an account that at the battle of Ategua (Espejo, Spain), Munatius Flaccus, one of Pompey's commanders, seeing the inhabitants deserting their city, sent the Lusitanians to punish its inhabitants: the men were beheaded and the women and children were impaled.[1154]

[1149] Ibid., 48.3

[1150] Ibid., 48.4

[1151] Ibid., 48.5

[1152] Ibid., 51.1 and 3

[1153] Some of his troops revolted under the quaestor Marcellus, who was proclaimed governor of the province. Cassius was surrounded by Marcellus in Ulia. Bogud, king of Mauretania, and Marcellus Lepidus, proconsul of *Hispania Citerior*, to whom Cassius had applied for assistance, negotiated an arrangement with Marcellus whereby Cassius was to be allowed to go free with the legions that remained loyal to him. Cassius sent his troops into winter quarters, hastened on board ship at Malaca with his ill-gotten gains, but was wrecked in a storm at the mouth of the Iberus (Ebro).

[1154] Valerius Maxmius, 9.2.4 Today the city is an ancient ruin north of Espejo, Spain

Iberian cities, such as Ategua, were caught in the middle of the civil wars, whether they had taken sides or not during these civil wars is not very clear in the classical accounts, except that in several occasions they seem to have wanted to be left alone or not get involved. Unfortunately, they were forced into a serious predicament because the majority of the cities or towns did not want to get involved, but they always did for there was in every village, town and city a small minority of Romanized Iberians that either supported Caesar or Pompey. Thus, in the end they suffered the consequences of being besieged or plundered, such as was the case of Ategua and soon to be Hispalis (Seville).

Caesar marched onto Hispalis and sent several of his deputies to sue for a defensive alliance, which the leaders of Hispalis turned down. Though the citizens assured him that they were able to defend their town for Pompey's forces, Caesar still sent one of his lieutenants named Caninius, along with some troops to encamp near the city. In town, a strong party of Pompeian supporters, displeased to see Caesar's troops well received within the city's walls, secretly deputed a zealous partisan of Pompey by the name of Philo to reach Pompey's sons and report Caesar's activities in the area. On his way to report to Pompey's, he encounters a well - known Lusitanian leader, Cecilius Niger who was encamped near the town of Lennio, with a strong Lusitanian army. Knowing that the Lusitanians had sided with the Pompeys, Philo begged for his assistance. Niger broke camp and headed out. The Lusitanians arrive at Hispalis by nightfall and surprises the town's sentinels and the populace. Well received by the townsfolk, they immediately shut the gates and set up defensive positions.[1155]

Several hours later, instead of defending the town against Caesar's legion of a future attack, the Lusitanians suddenly began plundering Hispalis. Through military intelligence, Caesar was told what was happening within the city's wall, determined to beat Pompey, he made a plan. Not wanting to press the Lusitanians into a fight just yet, he laid out a plan to his war council to allow the Lusitanians to escape in the night and then later attack their disorganized withdrawal. For this plan

---

[1155] Aulus Hirtius, Bellum Hispaniense (The Spanish War), 35

to succeed, it had to work in this manner for Caesar did not want to lose anymore men over some barbarians that controlled the defensive position. Plus, he believed that a larger battle was soon to come against the Pompey brothers, so this surprise ambush against the Lusitanians had to work so to future stop the loss of Roman soldiers and cause losses to the other side instead.

Unbeknownst to Caesar, the Lusitanians had a plan of their own that just about ruined Caesar's planned ambush. Before they escaped, several Lusitanians snuck past the Roman camp and set fire to their ships that were docked on the Guadalquivir River. While the Romans were surprised and completely distracted with extinguishing the flames, the Lusitanians began to escape. But Caesar being quick on his feet, recovered. While the Roman infantry was busy putting out the fires, the Lusitanians were overtaken by his cavalry. A majority of the Lusitanians, according to Hirtius, were cut to pieces.[1156]

As mentioned before during the Roman civil war, many Lusitanians had fought for both sided. What is interesting to note is that from this point on the Romans would enlist a massive number of Iberians as auxiliary troops into the Roman legions, especially the Lusitanians, Callaecians and Celtiberians. It has been calculated that of the total of Roman auxiliary troops within its western European army, Iberian soldier made up 30% of the total force.[1157]

Following the incident at Hispalis, Ceasar defeated Pompey's sons at the battle of Munda.[1158] Near the end of the battle, Pompey's army was defeated; the Pompey brothers fled in disorder. Caesar sent troops in pursuit. Hirtius writes that during the pursuit, a Lusitanian warrior (one who had joined Caesar) discovered the place where one of the Pompey brothers, Gnaeus Pompeius hid; he was quickly surrounded by Caesar

---

[1156] Ibid., 36

[1157] Lombardero, Alfonso Carbonell, The Gaels in Gallaecia,2000 http://www.galeon.com/lombardero/Lombardero1.htm

[1158] For a decent reading about the battle of Munda see the Wikipedia article at http://en.wikipedia.org/wiki/Battle_of_Munda; Munda is the name of a plain in southern Spain

cavalry and infantry. Seeing himself betrayed, he took refuge in a post fortified by its natural surroundings. Several attempted to storm it were repulsed, so the general in charge of this operation decided to besiege the 'fort' instead. Surrounded and his resources cut off, many of Gnaeus' men began to surrender, while others loyal to him fought on to the death. After several days, Gnaeus was captured and beheaded.[1159]

After Gnaeus Pompeius death and Sextus Pompey's escape from Hispania, Caesar was still not able to gain total possession of the Iberian Peninsula. The Lusitanians and other native warriors that had supported the Pompey faction continued on fighting Caesar. These remaining natives rallied into an army and advanced against Gaius Didius, Caesar loyal naval commander whose ships were docked somewhere near Gades (Cadiz).[1160]

Though the preservation of the fleet was principally his main concern, he became engaged with the troublesome Lusitanians. Therefore, he was obliged to leave his fort in order to restrain the frequent enemy attacks. These daily skirmishes gave them an opportunity of projecting an ambuscade; for which purpose the Lusitanians divided their troops into three bodies. Some were prepared to set fire to the fleet, while the other two were to come to their relief. Their plan of attack was so well arranged that they could advance into battle formations without anyone seeing them. As the story goes, Didius sallied out according to Roman military custom; when upon a signal being given by the Lusitanian commander, one of the parties advanced to set fire to the fleet; and another, counterfeiting a retreat, drew in Didius into an ambush, where he was surrounded and slain along with most of his men, although they had fought valiantly. But some of his men managed to escape in boats, which they found further down the coast; others endeavored to reach the galleys that had not caught fire by swimming towards them; once on broad they weighed anchor and sailed out to sea.[1161] This was a devastating defeat for the Romans and an incredible victory for the

[1159] Aulus Hirtius, Bellum Hispaniense (The Spanish War), 38 and 39
[1160] Aulus Hirtius, Bellum Hispaniense (The Spanish War), 40
[1161] Aulus Hirtius, Bellum Hispaniense (The Spanish War), 40 and 41

Lusitanians since Viriathus's campaign against the Romans; as booty, the Lusitanians had captured a mass quantity of provisions. And yet, this is the last we hear of the Lusitanians as a rebellious lot.

The period of the civil war between Julius Caesar and the Pompey family, despite the insecurity of the time and the several battles, seems to have led to the eventual Romanization of Lusitania. The need for fresh troops led to the incorporation of Lusitanian men into the ranks of the Roman army, especially the legions of Pompey.[1162] The recruitment of Lusitanians into a professional army led them to being granted Roman citizenship and rights. This was also a useful channel for their warlike qualities and traditions. Professor Alarcão says it best when he wrote, "The war between the Lusitanians and Romans became to a certain extend a war between Lusitanians associated with Romans, against other Romans."[1163] From this unexpected and surprising alliance a strong friendship was forged which led to the extinction of their ancient hatred for one another. This companionship would become so strong that several emperors, starting with Julius Caesar, used Lusitanians, Celtiberians and other Iberian warriors as bodyguards because of their loyalty to their leader.[1164]

[1162] Le Roux, Patrick, L'armée romaine et l'organisation des provinces....., p. 46-47; Alarcão, J. de, Roman Portugal, Vol. II, p. 12

[1163] Alarcão, J. de, Roman Portugal, Vol. II, p. 12

[1164] Appian, Bellum Civile, 109, Suetonius, Augustus, 49 Saddington Dennis Bain, The development of the Roman auxiliary forces from Caesar to Vespasian: 49 B.C.-A.D. 79, University of Zimbabwe, 1982, p. 26; Martinez, Rafael T., op. cit., p.6

CHAPTER X

THE ROMANIZATION OF LUSITANIA

At the end of the 1st century BC -- two hundred years after the conquest of Hispania had begun -- Gaius Octavius Julius Caesar Augustus finally pacified Lusitania, Callaecia, Asturia and Cantabria bringing them all under Roman control.[1165] With Augustus's military campaigns in the northwest successfully concluded, he began to remold Lusitania, which was still mostly pastoral. With Hispania's pacification complete, Augustus instilled many political and administrative structure and policies, which some are still in use today such as the welfare system and taxes. As for the later history of Lusitania from Augustus onwards, it is practically unknown besides a few literary mentions. Though much has been written about Rome's purpose and development, Roman daily life, Roman religion, art and architecture of the Roman world, inadequate attention has been paid to Romanization of its satellite states.

Romanization of the Iberian Peninsula, as well as other future Roman provinces, was a gradual process of cultural assimilation, in which the conquered "barbarians" (non-Greco-Romans) gradually adopted and

---

[1165] Le Roux, Patrick, L'armée romaine et l'organisation des provinces ibériques d'Auguste á l'invasion de 409, Paris, 1982, p. 52-69; Tranoy, Alain, La Galice romaine: Recherches sur le nord-Ouest de la peninsule ibérique dans l'Antiquité, Paris, 1981, p. 132-144; Syme, Ronald, 'The Spanish War of Augustus (26-25 BC)', American Journal of Philology #55 1934, p.293-317; Rodriguez Colmenero, A., Augusto e Hispania: Conquista y organización del Norte peninsular, Bilboa, 1979, p. 24-130

largely replaced their own native culture (which in many cases were quite developed) with the culture of their conquerors - the Romans, as in this case. The acculturation proceeded from the top down, with the upper classes adopting Roman culture first, and though the old ways lingered longest in outlying districts among peasants; they too would become assimilated into the Roman culture.

The Creation of Lusitania: Its Boundaries, Districts and Roads

During the onset of the Romanization of Lusitania, some tribes continued to rebel until 19 BCE. In other cases, small groups broke away from the tribe and formed 'guerrilla gangs' as a means of self-defense against the further expansion of the newly acquired Roman state. These 'gangs' were small and mobile but lacked leadership such as the like of Viriathus. Though these two group were a minor nuisance to Rome, Rome continued its progress in Romanizing Lusitania by first encouraging (or requiring) its people (i.e. the upper class) within the state's border to form centralized policies to start producing some type of tax, and placing responsibility on local leaders to instill a relationship with other neighboring states and tribes. But tribal leaders in lieu of forming their own borders centralizing Roman administrative policies and political and social institutions within the guidelines given to them by Rome, they instead began to misuse the money and power that was handed to them. Instead of rebuilding their lands, they used the money to support a stable army that could fight other states or tribes in an attempt to gain more land and power. This caused a problem to Roman administrators as it incited various tribes, especially the Lusitanians, to fight and defend their land against other tribes.

To prevent these territorial issues between tribes, Augustus instituted a new administrative reorganization. Dio Cassius writes that in 27 BCE, Augustus divided Hispania into three provinces: Baetica which was given to the Senate and Lusitania and Tarraconensis which he kept for himself.[1166] It seems that the formation of Lusitania as a separate autonomous province may have taken place immediately after the campaigns of 26 -25 BCE which led to the annexation of Callaecia, Asturia and Cantabria; it is also believed that this event may have even taken place a few years later in 22 BCE under the consulship of L Sestius Quirinalis Albinianus.[1167] In addition to these likely dates, Professors Alarcão, Tranoy and Solana Sainz suggest that the formation of Lusitania may have occurred later between the years 16 and 13 BCE.[1168] The third possible date of 19 BCE was the year Augustus sent Agrippa to the north of the Peninsula to quell the Cantabri tribe.[1169] With the formation of Lusitania, it removed all Lusitanian territorial ambitions. It is evident that before the administrative division was carried out by the Romans, the concept of Lusitania was a vague one, since it defined a people, the Lusitanians, and not a territorial constituency which was strictly delimited.

As for why Augustus assigned the apportionment of the provinces in this way was to lead the Roman people away from the idea that he was all monarchical in his way of ruling the fledgling empire. Augustus Caesar's decision to undertake this route was because in his youth he had seen through his uncle, Julius Caesar, what was happening in Hispania. So to control and pacify the area, he promise that for the next ten years he would help the Senate by taking over two of the provinces and build and run the government of these provinces (along with several other province through out the empire), to which he had promised to

---

1166 Dio Cassius 53.12.4-5

1167 Tranoy, Alain, La Galice romaine: Recherches sur le nord-Ouest de la peninsule ibérique dans l'Antiquité, Paris, 1981, p. 149 and 326-327; Alarcão, J. de, Roman Portugal, Vol. II, Aris & Phillips Ltd., Warminster, UK, 1988, p. 15

1168 Dio Cassius, 54.11.2-5; Pliny, 4.118; Tranoy, La Galice romaine, p. 146-147; Alarcão, Roman Portugal, 15-16; Solana Sainz, Jose Maria, Los Canatabros y la ciudad de Iuliobriga, Santander, 1981, 116-119

1169 Dio Cassius, 54.11.2-5; Solana Sainz, Los Canatabros y la ciudad de Iuliobriga, 1981, p. 116-119. Although we know that there was an uprising by the Cantabri and that Agrippa waged war against yhem in 19BC, this revolt may not have been the only reason for the journey for Augustus's son-in-law. Agrippa could have also come to reorganize the administration and to found the province of Lusitania.

reduce his power over them in time, and boastfully added, if they should be pacified sooner, he would sooner restore them back to the Senate's control.[1170]

Under Augustus' reign the province of Lusitania was created. He first began to organize the colonial regime by first creating the name Lusitania after it people and establishing its borders. Secondly, he founded several Luso-Roman cities and towns and began an urban development program of existing Lusitanian cities in to *oppida* (Latin word meaning enclosed space; referring to the main settlement in any administrative area of ancient Rome) and lastly, the marking boundaries of the *civitates* (districts).[1171]

But before all this could happen, a border needed to be established, which posed a problem. Strabo's account says that Lusitania extended from Baetica up to the Douro River.[1172] According to Professor Alarcão, he believes that Strabo was referring to an earlier administrative union

---

[1170] Dio Cassius., 53.13.1

[1171] Romanised urban settlements of native tribes were also called *civitates* and were usually re-founded close to the site of an old, pre-Roman capital. The term was applied not only to friendly native tribes and their towns but also to local government divisions in peaceful provinces that carried out civil administration. Land destined to become a civitas was officially divided up, some being granted to the locals and some being owned by the civil government. A basic street grid would be surveyed in but the development of the civitas from there was left to the inhabitants although occasional imperial grants for new public buildings would be made. The civitates were regional market towns complete with a basilica and forum complex providing an administrative and economic focus. Civitates had a primary purpose of stimulating the local economy in order to raise taxes and produce raw materials. All this activity was administered by an *ordo* or *curia*, a civitas council consisting of men of sufficient social rank to be able to stand for public office. As for defensive measures, they were limited at the civitates, rarely more than palisaded earthworks in times of trouble, if even that. Towards the end of the empire, the civitates' use local militias, led by a decurion (A cavalry officer in command of a troop or *turma* of thirty soldiers in the army of the Roman Empire), which served as the only defensive force in outlying Romanised areas threatened by barbarians.

[1172] Strabo, 3.4.20

prior to a Callaecia division from Lusitania, which may have been altered by Augustus when he placed the northern boundary of Lusitania at the Douro River after 4 BC.[1173] With Lusitanian in his hands, Emperor Augustus makes a new administrative division, creating the province of Hispania Ulterior Lusitania, whose capital was to be *Emerita Augusta* (currently Mérida). Originally Lusitania included the territories of Asturias and Gallaecia, but these were later ceded to the jurisdiction of *Provincia Tarraconensis* and the former remained as *Provincia Lusitania*. In the south, the boundaries were the same as that of modern Portugal's boundaries.[1174] Overall, we are not sure exactly how far into Spain the province extended, but it is believed that it may have stretched as far as Toledo and Salamanca.

When Lusitania was organized as a separate province, Augustus divided it into *civitates*. This extended and formalized mapping of the territory defining where the new towns were to be established, but before this could occur, the territory had to be surveyed and marked out.[1175] When new Roman colonies were founded within newly conquered territories, their new colonies were centuriated, to facilitate the assignation of plots of land to the new settlers.[1176] Thus centuriation gave a visible sense of

---

[1173] Alarcão, J. de, op. cit., p. 16; Alföldy, Geza, Fasti Hispanienses: Senatorische Reichsbeamte und Offiziere in den Spanischen Provinzen der Römisches von Augustus bis Diokletian, Wiesbaden, 1969, pp. 9-10

[1174] Pliny, 3.1.6 and 4.22.115, Pomponiua Mela, 2,87

[1175] The Romans were the first to use boundary markers (termini Augustales) to set up the limits of the new territories to physically mark the landscape of the new Roman world. Besides being referred to as boundary markers, in Hispania, some of the boundary markers were actually used as altars for cultic activity. It seems that the gods were called upon to sanction this new organization of the newly established rural space. Frontinus, De Agrorum Qualitate, 4; Aggenus Urbicus, Commentum de Agrorum Qualitate., 4; Hyginus, Constit Limit 162; Jean Gérard Gorges, and Manuel Salines de Frías, eds., article by J.C. Edmondson, "Creating a Provincial Landscape: Roman Imperialism and Rural Change in Lusitania", Les campagnes de Lusitanie romaine, Casa de Velázquez, Madrid, p.27-28; Stylow, A.U., 'Apuntes sobre epigrafia de época flavia en Hispania', Gerión #4, 1986, pp. 285-311

[1176] The Romans practiced of formally dividing up the countryside (*territorium*) around newly established *coloniae* into square blocks as allotments for the

order to the rural landscape.[1177] Once these projects were completed, it is believed that every provincial community received a copy of a *forma* (map) of its rural territory, which was supposedly kept in the city's archives while another copy was sometimes inscribed on bronze and displayed in public, making the world around the inhabitants visually comprehensible, giving them a greater sense of place.[1178]

The Roman genius for administrative organization is well illustrated in Portugal, like many other Roman provinces, Lusitania was divided into *civitates*, which were usually modeled on the boundaries of pre-Roman tribes or *populi.* Every *civitas* had its own administrative capital that was often an ancient settlement that was rebuilt on the Roman urban model with the necessary grid-iron street patterns along with its public monuments and services such as running water and sewage. In the case of Lusitania, the *civitates* seem to have been established by Julius Caesar or Augustus Caesar. The capitals of the *civitates* were called *oppida.* They had local assemblies and two to four magistrates, who were regularly elected and in charge of the city administration.[1179] The *oppidum* would have had a *territorium* and magistrates to administer its affairs. According to Professor Alarcão, it was quite possible that the administration was controlled at a local level by native representatives from different *populi.*[1180] Adopting Augustus's policies to the local social

---

occupants of the colony. The blocks were typically 776 yards along each side, the boundaries being formed by roads or substantial fences/hedges. Once established the regular grid pattern usually survives into much later times even though the land tenure system changes. Jean Gérard Gorges, and Manuel Salines de Frías, eds, op. cit., p. 27-28

[1177] **Centuriation** was a system of marking out the land in squares or rectangles, by means of *limites*, boundaries, normally prior to distribution in a colonial foundation. (The units of *centuria* are explained by Varro, *De re rustica* 1. 10.)

[1178] Jean Gérard Gorges, and Manuel Salines de Frías, eds., op. cit., p.27-28; Fernandez, P. Sáez, "Estudio sobre una inscripción catastral colindante com Lacimurga", Habis #21, 1990, 205-227; Nicolet, C., L'inventaire du monde: Géographie et politique aux origins de l'Empire romain, Paris, 1988, chap. 7.

[1179] Alarcão, J. de, Roman Portugal, Vol. I, p. 15

[1180] Alarcão, Roman Portugal, p. 30- 31, Tranoy, Alain, La Galice romaine: Recherches sur le nord-Ouest de la peninsule ibérique dans l'Antiquité, Paris, 1981, p. 60-74

conditions of his various subjects, Augustus would have established chieftains in some places and magistrates in others, who may have been appointed by the regional administration or elected by councils of elders.[1181] After a while the *populi* would have become part of the *civitates* and the tribal princes or elected local officials would have been either replaced by or promoted to municipal administrators with an assembly and elected *duumvirate* (an alliance between two equally powerful political or military leaders).

Once an *oppidum* had become well established it could aspire to become a *municipium* which was basically a self-governing community with several grades of importance and legal rights. Many Luso-Roman towns achieved this status under the reigns of Julius Caesar and Augustus Ceasar. When the *oppidum* was promoted to a *municipium*, the *civitas* was assigned to a Roman voting tribe, the unit into which the citizens were enrolled.[1182] The Lusitanians fell into the Galeria and Quiria tribes. Towns that received the status of *municipia* under Caesar and Augustus

---

[1181] Alarcão, p. 31

[1182] Alarcão, p.15; Tsirkin, Ju. B., "Romanisation of Spain: Socio-Political Aspects: Part III Romanisation during the Early Empire", Gerión #12, 1994, pp. 217-253; M. L. Genderson, "Julius Caesar and Latium inSpain", *VDI4(1946),* 58, 63, 65, n. 8; F. Vittinghoff, *op. dL,* 105; E. Ritterling, «Legio", *RE* Hbd. 23(1924), Sp. 1631; The citizens of Rome were divided into voting groups or tribes. Originally there were three Romulean tribes but they were likely replaced or reorganized under Servius Tullius with four urban tribes and later increased to 16 rustic tribes, in the *ager Romanus*. Tribes were added a few at a time over the years as new Italian territory was incorporated into the Romans ever expanding empire, but with the addition of two more tribes in Picenum between 242 BC and 241 BC the number of tribes was set at 35. Each tribe had its own officials, and many important activities were organized on a tribal basis including the *census*, collection of taxes, and voting in the Comitia Populi Tributa and the Comitia Plebis Tributa. They were so important that a Roman's full name included the name of his tribe along with the name of his father and grandfather. Of the 35 tribes, four of the tribes (Collina, Esquilina, Palatina, and Suburana) were urban tribes; the rest are rural tribes. In ancient times citizens who owned land outside the city of Rome were enrolled in rural tribes, while those who lived exclusively in the city belonged to urban tribes. The result was that the urban tribes had much less power in the voting assemblies than the rural tribes had.

appeared to have had their citizens enrolled in the Galeria tribe; those elevated later on by the Flavians were enrolled into the Quirina tribe and given municipal rights.[1183]

The highest ranking of the town could achieve was the status of *colonia*, which were settlements of veteran soldiers that were granted citizenship after they had served out their time in the army. Sometimes the *colonia* was established with citizens brought in to help 'civilize' the natives in the newly conquered territories. In Portugal, Pax Julia (Beja) and Scallabis (Santarém) were given this status.[1184]

With the *colonia* being the highest rank, a city could achieve, there were also two other city classifications used by the Romans; *vicus* and *castellum.* The usage of the word *vicus* was designated to a town or city of less importance than an *oppidum* or a *civitas,* though it could have been bigger, richer, more populous, more industrious or commercial. In addition, for one of these towns to become a *vicus*, a military base was usually attached to it. While the word *castellum,* was used to identify Iberian hilltop forts.

Prior to the classification and city rankings, between the conflicts that occurred, the Lusitanian War until the Sertorius War in the 1st century

---

[1183] Alarcão, p.15; The gens Galeria was a very ancient patrician family, which already existed at the time of Romulus, and probably included in the original hundred gentes remembered by the historian Titus Livius. According to Theodor Mommsen the antiquity of this family can be deduced from the fact that it gave its name to one of ancient rural tribes, the homonymous Tribe Galeria. The origin of Gens Galeria was probably Sabin, apparently due to a family group from the area of *Rio Galera*, river flowing east of Lake Bracciano, which took its name. http://www.novaroma.org/nr/Category:Gens_Galeria_(Nova_Roma). Quirina tribe was pre-eminent of the Flavian emperors but proir to that it was one of the last tribes to be added to the final count of 35 tribes that was created in 241 BC on territory confiscated from the Sabini. The tribe was original filled with the Sabini that were granted incomplete citizenship at the beginning of the 3rd century but were later made full citizen. Williamson, Callie, The Laws of the Roman People: Public Law in the Expansion and Decline of the Roman Republic, University of Michigan, 2005, p.225

[1184] Alarcão, Roman Portugal, p.15

BCE, the Romans created a series of military villages whose names revealed an aspect of military character: *castra* or *castrum* (military camp), *praesidium* (military outpost of fort), *praetorium* (Commanding officer's residence in a fort). Within the Lusitanian territory, towns were explicitly mentioned with the term *castra*, supplemented by an adjective derived from the name of the founder of the site (such as Castra Caepiona, Castra Caeciliana, Castra Liciana and Castra Servilia), which at the time of Roman occupation of Lusitania these sites were all basically military camps.[1185] Thus the military forts in occupied territory later turned into towns and cities promoting the integration of Lusitanian territory into a Roman one, due to the heavy Roman presence and influences.

Along with these administrative creations, beginning with Augustus Caesar and ending with Vespasian, a new type of administrative district was "created", the *conventus* (diocese). This was primarily a legal term since the capital of the *conventus* was the place where the governor and his delegates passed judgment on issues that were beyond the capability of the local officials of the *civitates;* moreover, it had an assembly of representatives of component cities to advise, consult and report to the governor.[1186] Though the *conventus* was created as an administrative district, its origins can be trace back to the Republican period perhaps beginning Julius Caesar or even earlier.[1187] Originally the *conventus* was known as a *conventus civium Romanorum*, which was an unofficial association of Roman citizens in distant lands, who joined together for matter such as trade and defense.[1188] These *conventus* were naturally located in major towns and cities where Romans citizens congregated on a regular basis to conduct business, exchange ideas and discuss news about the area. Since these locations acted as a central meeting place, it became convenient for the provincial governor or his delegates to visit and dispense their authority during their annual circuit of visits to each town or city.

[1185] Munoz, Mauricio P., op. cit., p.199

[1186] Alarcão, Roman Portugal, p.33

[1187] Suetonius, *Julius*, 7; Caesar, *Bellum Civile*, 2.19.3

[1188] Curchin, Leonard, A., Roman Spain, Barnes & Noble Inc, NY, 1995, p. 57

Under Augustus, the *conventus* transformed. The *conventus* was instilled as a governmental body that primarily dealt with judicial matters. While still centered in a major town or city, it referred not to an association, but to a geographic region comprised of many lesser towns, whose inhabitants would have to travel the central towns to engage in lawsuits.[1189] In addition to this judicial function, the capital of the *conventus* not only retained its status as a commercial center, but also as an administrative center with its own *concilium* (parliament). Besides being the administrative center of the *conventus,* it also became an important religious center to the imperial religious cult within that district, so altars, shrines and temples were built to the protector god or gods of the *conventus* or *flamines* of the imperial cult.[1190] Of the twelve *conventus* that were formed in Hispania, three were in Lusitania: Emeritensis, Pacensis and Scalabitanus.[1191] Unfortunately there is no written record on the boundaries of the three *conventus*, but it seems reasonable that they including a large number of *civitates*. It is believed that Conventus Scalabitanus incorporated the land between the Douro and the Tagus River and the Conventus Pacensis was made up of all of southern Portugal, while Conventus Emeritensis the smallest of the three-lay west of Scalabitanus and held the region between Serra de Gardunha and Serra de Estrela.

Urbanization

The grounds that I previously mentioned in the last section may apply in particular to the Lusitanian territory conquered by Rome. From a geographical point of view, Lusitania was an agglomeration of various regions with different levels of wealth. But from an ethnic point of view, Lusitania comprised of tribes with various degrees of cultural development, boasting an incipient vertex of urbanism at the time of

---

1189 Curchin, Roman Spain, p.58

1190 Étienne, Robert, Le culte impérial dans la péninsule Ibérique, d'Auguste à Dioclétien, Paris, 1974, pp. 177-185; Curchin, Roman Spain, p.58. A **flamen** was a name given to a priest assigned to a state-supported god or goddess in Roman religion

1191 Pliny, NH, 4.117; Alarcão, Roman Portugal, p.32

Rome's conquest of Hispania. These people had suffered Celtic, and now Roman cultural changes and transformations. They also integrated influences from neighboring peoples, and although progressive and variable, these influences together with other cultural and environmental elements, marked a process that more than ruptured their continuity and development. It is very likely that all these elements and cultural developments shaped the Lusitanians and the various peoples that the classical texts mention as habitants of Roman Lusitania.

Cities were the focal point of Roman assimilation, thanks to the leadership of the local elite. Most cities in Hispania originated as pre-Roman towns, but with the coming of the Romans, local leaders seized the initiative to upgrade their community and status by allowing the Romans to instill their colonial model upon the city's residents. By the end of the age of the Republic, these towns were effectively Romanized and the towns within the peninsula's interior and to the west were making an effort to catch up. By the end of Augustus's reign, the entire peninsula began to enjoy, under peaceful conditions, the benefits of urban life. Moreover, all Roman citizens and Romanized native were allowed to participate in local government through popular assembly in electing magistrates. Life in Hispania became so good that even ex-slave that became freedmen though ineligible for magistracies could become government employees or officials of the imperial religious cult, if they were able to afford the entrance fee.[1192]

By the beginning of the first century A.D., Romanization was well underway in southern Portugal. A Senate was established at Ebora (present-day Évora); schools of Greek and Latin were opened; industries such as brick making, tile making, and iron smelting were developed. Gradually, Roman civilization was extended to northern Portugal, as well. The Lusitanians were forced out of their hilltop fortifications and settled in bottom lands in Roman towns (*citânias*). The *citânias* were one of the most important institutions imposed on Lusitania during the Roman occupation. It was in the *citânias* that the Lusitanians acquired

[1192] Curchin, Leonard, A., Roman Spain, p.85 and 105

Roman civilization in which they learned Latin and were introduced to Roman culture, administration and religion. All in all, the Roman occupation left a profound cultural, economic, and administrative imprint on the entire Iberian Peninsula that remains to the present day.

Once the invasion and conquest of Hispania was complete, the colonization of the region was comprehensive and permanent. Large numbers of colonists arrived from Italy, which an infrastructure of roads and towns was built, and Roman citizenship became universal to all Lusitanian by 73 AD. Iberian and other native languages by this time gradually began to disappear. It seems that the whole of Lusitania, as well as other regions throughout Hispania, were completely Romanized by the beginning of the 1st century AD. Though we see and understand that Romanization transformed the social and economic structures of pre-Roman populations, we also see that Romanization had produced no profound effect upon Lusitania until the upbringing of the next generation of Lusitanians known as Luso-Romans.

As for the history of the capital cities of the *conventus* and other major towns of importance there is little written data on the historical evolution and physical development of each one. But one thing is certain that the Romans did very little to actually build an entire town from scratch and that the Romanization of Lusitanian towns and cities began with Julius and Augustus Caesar, as the archaeological record shows. Romans would usually build on or improved pre-Roman settlements that were already developed, especially in the Algarve and on the Atlantic coastline. But at times, they would establish a town for the reason of resettling rebellious tribesmen, as we saw with the Lusitanian in the founding of Valencia in the previous chapter, or settling Roman veterans as in Beja known by the Romans as Pax Julia, where Julius Caesar mixed native Iberians with Roman army veterans and colonists.

It is clear, through archaeological and epigraphical evidence that the rebellious Roman praetor, Sertorius and one-time praetor of Hispania, Julius Caesar began to develop Lusitania prior to Augustus. But it was not until Augustus Caesar that significant contributions to the urban development of Lusitania were made. Although it was a difficult task, he accomplished it with amazing ambition. Even after the Julio-Claudian dynasty, the Flavian dynasty continued to bring many improvements to Lusitanian urban life. From Augustus's reign to the beginning of the 2nd century AD there was much building and rebuilding within the Lusitania's borders. Thereafter, through archaeological and epigraphical evidence, construction stagnated for various reasons. By the end of the 3rd century and the onset of the 4th century AD, Lusitania, as well as much of the Western Roman Empire began to surround their cities with walls and change or destroy many Roman edifices an architectural occurrence came with the coming of the barbarian hordes into Roman territory.

The walls not only changed the look of the cities, but also changed the type of construction and quality of city life, making them more crowded. The consequences of a wall were that only a small part of the city was enclosed, thus leaving other homes, amphitheater, temples, baths and other structures outside the city's defense. Being that many of these beautiful structures were left out in the open and abandoned, many of the buildings were demolished and used to build the city's wall. Adding to the threat of invasion and the destruction of many Roman architectural wonders was the decline in paganism and the adoption of Christianity as the official state religion. This led to many temples being destroyed or configured into churches which are still in use today. One last example of this large-scale change was that many Roman towns and cities were dependent on a water supply brought in by an aqueduct, but the barbarian dangers led newly walled cities to construct large cisterns inside the city wall, to guarantee, if only for some time, their survival in case the city was besieged.

One must remember that the founding of a new city or the rebuilding of a pre-Roman town or city, just like today in constructing a building, required immense public investment of money and human resources such as laborers and craftsmen. Such simple task as the squaring and fitting of stone blocks, construction of arch ways, making concrete, plastering walls and other specialized skills were unknown to the local inhabitants, so it was important to bring in colonists to these areas with special incentives. Besides requiring cash and technical expertise to build a Romanesque style city, it was important to Rome to Romanize the natives with social and cultural norms and mores of the Roman way of life. To civilize the local inhabitants would have required Roman immigrants, whose daily life and customs was the best way to assimilate the natives. Without educating the locals on the Roman ways or the teaching of required skills would have left all of Augustus's endeavors useless.

Besides spending large amounts of money and time, improving Lusitanian cities and towns, the Romans also spent a large amount of effort, expanding the road network of its new province by cutting and paving roadways, constructing bridges and emplacing milestones along the roads. Peripheral regions of the provinces no longer seemed remote and cut off from the rest. Roads would now connect many cities and towns such as the one connecting Olisipo (Lisbon) to Bracara Augustus (Braga), and Bracara Augustus to Ebora (Évora) which became major commercial roads.[1193] Not only did these roads interconnect Lusitanian cities, but several of these 'highways' connected roads that led into Spain, to this day many of the roads are still in use. Along these major roads, *miliarium* (milestones) were provided to help guide the traveler, no longer were people in doubt where they were going or how far they had to go.[1194] In this context it did not matter if people travelled far on these roads. The milestones helped to make people aware that they were now linked to a wider and very Roman world.

[1193] Alarcão, J. de, op. cit., p. 49-61; Saa, Mario, As grandes vias da Lusitania, 6 vols., Lisboa, 1956; Jean Gérard Gorges, and Manuel Salines de Frías, eds., op. cit., p.27-28.

[1194] A milestone, or miliarium, was a circular column on a solid rectangular base, set for more than 2 feet (60 cm) into the ground, standing 5 feet (1.50 m) high, 20 inches (50 cm) in diameter, and weighing more than 2 tons. At the base was inscribed the number of the mile relative to the road it was on and the distance to the nearest major city center. Siliéres, P., les voies de communication de l'Hispanie méridionale, Paris, 1990, pp. 53-57 and 791-794; Jean Gérard Gorges, and Manuel Salines de Frías, eds., op. cit., p.27-28.

Though cultural, social and architectural changes were many throughout the Roman occupation, Lusitania had escaped the realities of the barbarian invasions of the 3rd and 4th century AD, but like the rest of the Western Roman Empire during its decline, it suffered from inflation, economic recession and social unrest. It would not be until the 5th century AD that the barbarian invasion had reached the Iberian Peninsula's borders that change was put into effect by the invading Alans, Vandals, Visigoths and Suebis. One has only to read the Chronicle of Hydacius, who was the Bishop of Chaves, who wrote a horrid account of these invasions.

Social Classes

The Upper Class

The Roman Empire was characterized by a social inequality and imbalance of wealth; even Roman upper class was not homogeneous.[1195] In Hispania, the 'Hispano-Roman' upper class was composed of a combination of Roman settlers and Romanized indigenes. The first group, the settlers, became an elite class the minute they set foot in Hispania for they were basically Roman by birth or veterans that had completed their military service and decided to settle in Hispania establishing Roman colonies. The second group was made up of local nobility that become local magistrates and abandoned their ancestral nomenclature and adopted Roman names.[1196] As Hispania became more Romanized, there is some evidence of the *decurial* class that included wealth freedmen and their sons, showing that it was possible for local citizens to gain admission into the ranks of the elite, providing that they had proved their merit through financial success and had built up a network of supporters in the local Senate through business dealings, marital ties, or patron-client relationships.[1197] Despite such opportunities for advancement, the *decurions* were not elected to a governmental

[1195] Within Roman society its upper class comprised of three classes: senatorial, equities and decurions (local aristocrats) that were based on wealth and free birth.
[1196] Curchin, Leonard, A., Roman Spain, p.78; Etienne, Robert, "Sénateurs originaries de la province de Lusitanie", Tituli, vol. 5, 1982, pp.521-529
[1197] Curchin, Roman Spain, p. 82-83

position like the magistrates, but remained as an exclusive club for 'socially accepted families'.[1198]

Freemen

All freeborn Roman citizens that belonged to the lower classes were called *plebs* (commoners). These Roman citizens had *conubium*, the right to contract a legal marriage with another Roman citizen and beget legitimate children who were themselves Roman citizens. But those who were freeborn men and women that lived within Roman territories were called *peregrine* (foreigner). Noncitizens, or *peregrini*, generally remained subject to whatever legal system was in effect when their provincial communities were annexed by Rome. Beginning with the reign of the emperor Augustus (27 BCE–14 AD), institutionalized practices permitted provincials to become citizens, generally by serving either in the Roman army or on a city council.[1199] And because citizen rights were inherited, the number of Roman citizens quickly increased. The group received what was called the Latin Right, which was a form of citizenship with fewer rights than full Roman citizenship that was granted Italy, especially Latium (modern region of Lazio, Italy were Italy's capital Rome is situated). Gradually, Roman citizenship extended to communities throughout the empire.[1200] These citizens had rights under Roman law, but could not vote, although their leading magistrates could become full citizens because they worked for the Roman government. Free-born foreign subjects, the *peregrini*, followed laws that existed to govern their conduct and disputes. This would change in 212 AD, when Marcus Aurelius Antoninus and Marcus Aurelius Severus Antoninus, also known as Caracalla, extended full

[1198] Curchin, Leonard, A., The Local Magistrates of Roman Spain, University of Toronto Press, Toronto, 1990, pp. 21-27

[1199] Mathisen, Ralph W., "*Peregrini*, *Barbari*, and *Cives Romani*: Concepts of Citizenship and the Legal Identity of Barbarians in the Later Roman Empire" The American Historical Review vol.111, no.4, Oct. 2006, pp.1011-1040

[1200] **Latium**, the cradle of Rome, consisted originally of the coastal plain from the mouth of the Tiber to the Circeian promontory, and its adjacent foothills. M. Cary and H.H. Scullard, A History of Rome, Basingstoke, Hampshire: Palgrave, 3rd ed. 1979, p.31

Roman citizenship to all freeborn people living within the Roman Empire.[1201]

The next class within the *plebs* was the Freedmen (*liberti*), who were freed slaves that had a form of Latin Right. Besides the slave class, freedmen made up the bulk of the Iberian population. Many Iberian freedmen engaged in commerce, amassing vast fortunes that often rivaled those of the wealthiest patricians. The majority of freedmen, however, joined the plebeian classes, and often worked as farmers or tradesman. Social mobility beyond the leap from slavery to freedom was limited. Wealthy freedmen could purchase a position of *servi Augustalis*, an official of the imperial religious cult but could not hold political office.[1202] However, local prominent freedmen were sometimes made honorary magistrates which would allow their sons to enter into the world of Roman politics.[1203] They could also improve their status through marriage with someone from a higher rank, such as a freedwoman of a local magistrate, though freedmen could not marry their patronesses.[1204] But there were some who enjoyed their freedom and became wealthy men, such as the group belong to *liberti Augusti,* individuals freed by the emperor. These men played a major role in the imperial civil service. Although freedmen were not allowed to vote during the Republic and the early Empire, children of freedmen were

---

[1201] Mathisen, Ralph W., "*Peregrini, Barbari,* and *Cives Romani,* p. 1118; Sasse, Christoph, *Die Constitutio Antoniniana: Eine Untersuchung über den Umfang der Bürgerrechtsverleihung auf Grund von Papyrus Gissensis 40 I,* Wiesbaden, 1958; Adam Lukaszewicz, "Zum Papyrus Gissensis 40 I 9 ('Constitutio Antoniniana')," *The Journal of Juristic Papyrology* 20, 1990: 93–101; and Garnsey, "Roman Citizenship and Roman Law," an expanded version of a section on "Citizens and Aliens," in Peter Garnsey and Caroline Humfress, eds., *The Evolution of the Late Antique World,* Cambridge, 2001, pp. 88–91.

[1202] Curchin, Leonard, A., Roman Spain, p. 84

[1203] Mangas, J.., Esclavos y libertos en la España romana, Salamanca, 1971, pp. 388-485; Curchin, L.A., "Social relations in Central Spain: Patrons, freedmen and slaves in the life of a Roman provincial hinterland", Ancient Society, vol. 18, 1987 and Roman Spain, New York, 1991, p.84

[1204] Paulus, *Sententiae,* 2.19.9; Corpus Inscriptionnum Latinarum II, 4524 and 6014 translated by A. Hübner, Berlin, 1869: Curchin, Roman Spain, p. 84

automatically granted the status of Roman citizen. Overall their status varied from generation to generation throughout the Republic.

It is quite ironic that of all the people that made up the bulk of the *liberti* class, the *plebs rustica* (the rural class) are the ones we know least about. Their sole purpose in life was to produce enough to pay taxes and rents and provide for their families. In Hispania, as elsewhere throughout the empire, poverty was king, as the classical sources indicate.[1205] To further insult this class, they were labeled and scorned by city dwellers as uncultured bumpkins.[1206] Though they were seen as lower class they played an important role within Roman society as their main purpose was food production.[1207] Peasant family life on a farm was harsh for they lived in cramped conditions in rude cottages along with their livestock and had a diet that consisted of milk, beer, cheese, vegetables, goat's meat and acorn bread.[1208]

Slaves

Little is known of slaves (*servi*) in Hispania, apart from that they were used as servants, miners, factory workers, construction and farmers on large estates. Unlike in modern times, Roman slavery was not based on race, but on conquest of territory. Slaves in Hispania originally were for the most part 'prisoners of war' and conquered people captured during sieges and other military campaigns throughout the Roman Empire. At first, they had no rights whatsoever and could be disposed of by their owners at any time. As time went on, however, the Senate and later Emperors enacted legislation meant to protect the lives and health

---

1205 Livy, 21.43.8; Appian, 59.249 – 250; Strabo, 3.3.5

1206 Curchin, Roman Spain, p. 84

1207 MacMullen, R., Roman social relations 50 BC to AD 284, Yale Univ. Press, New Haven, 1974, pp. 28-32; Curchin, L.A., Non-Slave Labour in Roman Spain, Gerión vol.4, 1986, pp. 178-181

1208 Strabo (3.3.7 and 3.3.5) and Columella (7.2.1) makes mention about how this class lived. As for living with livestock in certain rural areas of the Iberian Peninsula this is still practiced but the change is that the animals do not co-habitant within the same living quarter as people but are instead placed in the basement of a farmstead.

of slaves. However, until slavery was abolished, Romans habitually used their slaves for manual labor, as gladiators, for servitude and sexual purposes.[1209] Though they had no rights, they still received a *peculium* (allowance) and were permitted to take a slave partner known as *contubernalius*, and raise a family, thus providing their master with a new generation of slaves, although many *testators* (person who makes a will) freed the slaves whom they believed to be their natural children.[1210]

Another difference between Roman slavery and its modern variety was manumission – the ability of slaves to be freed. Roman owners freed their slaves in considerable numbers: some freed them outright, while others allowed them to buy their own freedom. The prospect of possible freedom through manumission encouraged most slaves to be obedient and hard-working. Formal manumission was performed by a magistrate and gave freed men full Roman citizenship.[1211] The one exception was that they were not allowed to hold office. However, the law gave any children born to freedmen, after formal manumission, full rights of citizenship, including the right to hold office. Slaves freed informally did not become citizens and any property or wealth they accumulated reverted to their former owners when they died. However, Rome's rigid society attached importance to social status and even successful freedmen usually found the stigma of slavery hard to overcome – the degradation lasted well beyond the slavery itself.

Women and Marriage

Iberian women in the eye of the Romans were seen as tough and unfeminine, weighing against unflattering stereotypes. But tombstone

---

[1209] Sheldon, Natasha, Roman Slavery in Urban and Rural Pompeii, Archaeological Evidence for the Lives of Roman Slaves, Archaeology, Apr. 2009 **http://archaeology.suite101.com/article.cfm/roman_slavery_in_urban_and_rural_pompeii#ixzz0Qo8r7h2g**

[1210] Mangas, J.., Esclavos y libertos en la España romana, Salamanca, 1971, pp. 130-131

[1211] Palmer, Bonnie, 'The Cultural Significance of Roman Manumission', Ex Post Facto: Journal of the History Students of San Francisco State University, vol. 5, 1996, p.23-41

relief sculptures and vase paintings portrayed another side to Iberian women. These women were depicted as tough but sensitive and skillful people. Though the Romans saw these women as uncultured with their barbaric customs, these women under Roman occupation, continued to have many rights and hold employment compared to their Roman counterpart.[1212]

With regards to intermarriage, barbarians and Romans were perfectly free to marry each other so long as the marriages were "between persons of equal social status, with no law impeding them."[1213] This notion of marital exclusivity was current in other spheres of contemporary Roman thought. The late 4th century Spanish poet Prudentius, for example, stated:

"A common law makes us equal ... the native city embraces in its unifying walls fellow citizens (*cives congenitos*) ... Foreign peoples now congregate with the right of marriage (*ius conubii*): for with mixed blood, one family is created from different peoples."[1214]

Roman Military Service

Although there was no profession army, the Lusitanians, as well as the rest of the Iberians had a long history of serving in foreign armies as mercenaries and auxiliary soldiers. Tacitus observed that their physical strength and excellent fighting abilities made an impact upon the Roman army.[1215] Through Roman military indoctrination, it helped to Romanize the recruits, qualifying them for Roman citizenship upon discharge from the military.[1216] The large number of Iberian men that served in the Roman army illustrates the continuing and integral role that the

1212 Albertos, M.L., 'La Mujer hispano-romana a través de la epigrafía', Revista de la Universidad de Madrid #109, 1977, pp.179-198

1213 Mathisen, Ralph W., "*Peregrini*, *Barbari*, and *Cives Romani*, p.1133

1214 Prudentius *Contra Symmachum* 2.598–614

1215 Tacitus, Annals, 3.40; Diodorus, 5.33.2; Vegetius, Epitoma rei militaris, 1.1; also see Chapter 5 on Lusitanian influences on the Roman military

1216 This comes from a example of a bronze tablet from 89 BC that records the granting of Roman citizenship to an entire Iberian troop of cavalrymen who

Iberians played within the Roman war machine; even some Iberian served in the emperor's Praetorian Guard and urban cohorts in Rome.[1217] The majority of Iberians that lived in the northern part of the Peninsula served in the frontier especially in Britain and Germania because they were accustomed to cold and damp climates, while those that came from the south served in Gaul or in the eastern frontier. It has been assumed that by an unspecified process, some barbarians after completing their long military service were granted some type of citizenship, but many scholars believed that perhaps only military officers became Roman citizens and not the soldiers.[1218] Emilienne Demougeot, for example, conjectured that barbarians, who became members of the field army, held Roman military or civilian office and were allowed to marry Roman women once they became citizens.[1219] Barbarian soldiers were also eligible for veterans' benefits such as land grants and tax breaks.[1220]

---

fought with distinction during the Social War (91-88 BC) under Pompey's father, Gnaeus Pompeius Strabo, Curchin, Leonard, A., Roman Spain, p.101

[1217] Cagnat, René, L'année Epigraphique, Collège de France, Paris, 1930, 57 and René Cagnat and Maurice Besnier 1933, 95

[1218] Sherwin-White, Adrian N., *The Roman Citizenship*, 2nd ed., Oxford, 1979, 380ff.; Rosario Soraci, *Richerche sui conubia tra Romani e Germani nei secoli I–VI*, Catania, 1965; rev. ed. 1974; Roger C. Blockley, "Roman-Barbarian Marriages in the Later Empire," *Florilegium* 4, 1982, pp. 63–79; Demougeot, Emilienne, "Restrictions, à l'expansion du droit de cité dans la seconde moitié du IVe siècle," *Ktema* 6, 1981, pp.381–393, p 387; Peter Heather, *Goths and Romans, 332–489*,Oxford, 1991, pp.164–165; Liebeschuetz, Wolf, "Citizen Status and Law, in the Roman Empire and the Visigothic Kingdom," in Pohl and Reimitz, *Strategies of Distinction*, 131–152, 134–137; Sirks, A. J. Boudewijn, "Shifting Frontiers in the Law: Romans, Provincials, and Barbarians," in Ralph Mathisen and Hagith Sivan, eds., *Shifting Frontiers in Late Antiquity* (Aldershot, 1996), 146–157, 150 ("Roman and indigenous law still coexisted")," 149, states simply, "they did not become Roman citizens."

[1219] Mathisen, Ralph W., op. cit., p.1124; Demougeot, op. cit., pp.384–387.

[1220] Mathisen, Ralph W., op. cit., p.1129; Theodosian Code for a better understanding og this code see Teodor Mommsen, Paul M. Meyer, and Paul Krüger, eds., *Theodosiani libri XVI*, Berlin, 1902, 5.11.7 (365) 7.20.3 (p.320), 7.20.4 (325), 7.20.8 (364), 7.20.11 (373), 7.20.12 (400).

While military service was a prominent way of many Iberians to leaving the Iberian Peninsula, others left and became merchants selling Iberian goods and leaving their cultural footprint behind.

While there were other Iberian individuals that left their mark on history such as the famous Lusitanian charioteer, Appuleius Diocles, rhetorician and poet, Seneca, writer, Columella, grammarian, Quintilius, poet, Martial and even emperors such as Trajan thus showing that Roman influence had a large impact in defining Hispania.

Roman Law

In the world of Roman officialdom during the Roman Republic (509–27 BCE) and the first few centuries of the Roman Empire, citizenship denoted an elite legal status to which certain rights, privileges, and obligations were accrued under the law.[1221] For example, in private life, citizens could marry, make wills, and carry on business under the protection of Roman law and impose lawsuit against other Roman citizens. Noncitizens generally remained subject to whatever legal system was in effect when their provincial communities were annexed by Rome. Thus, the laws which applied a judgment to the Iberian population were not Roman laws, but tribal laws because the Iberians at the time of Roman conquest of Hispania were not Roman citizenship and it was only to Roman citizens that Roman law applied. But beginning with the reign of Emperor Augustus (27 BC–14 AD), institutionalized practices permitted provincials to become citizens, by serving either in the Roman army or on a city council. And because citizen rights were inherited,

[1221] Mathisen, Ralph W., op. cit., p. 1115; For Roman citizenship, see Adrian N. Sherwin-White, *The Roman Citizenship*, 2nd ed., Oxford, 1979; Claude Nicolet, *The World of the Citizen in Republican Rome*, trans. Paul S. Falla, London, 1980; Claude Nicolet, *Le métier de citoyen dans la Rome républicaine*, 2nd ed., Paris, 1989; Paulo Donati Giacomini and Gabrielle Poma, eds., *Cittadini e non cittadini nel Mondo Romano: Guida ai testi e ai documenti,* Bologna, 1996; Jane F. Gardner, *Being a Roman Citizen,* London, 1993; David Noy, *Foreigners at Rome: Citizens and Strangers*, London, 2000; Geoffrey E. M. de Ste-Croix, *Class Struggle in the Ancient Greek World*, Ithaca, N.Y., 1981, pp. 453–461

the number of Roman citizens quickly increased.[1222] Recognition of the legitimacy of such legal foreign systems must have taken place during the formal organization of the province. As the province was being organized, jurisdictional boundaries were established; at the same time a commission oversaw that process and drew the boundaries for assize districts, revenue collection, and myriad other purposes.[1223]

Though the Iberian tribes still followed their own laws during the early part of the Roman occupation, in time they began to follow Roman laws as the Romans pacified the western half of the peninsula by forcing certain Roman laws upon the indigenous people such as a ban on Roman-barbarian marriages, this law was another example of the Roman fondness for prohibiting or regulating marriages between persons from different social, legal, or even religious backgrounds.[1224]

Luso-Roman Economy

Lusitania had resources that were very important to the economy of the Roman Empire, thus the Romans quickly took charge of its economical resource,s which were primarily based on agricultural along with two other important industries; mining and fishing. Roman Lusitania had developed a large industry of 'tinned fish' and sauce making called *garum* that was widely exported throughout the empire. The other major industry was mining, giving them access to natural resources to fashion such items as weapons. Though the Lusitanians were agriculturalists, the Romans taught them to grow olives for oil and grape for wine.

[1222] Mathisen, Ralph W., op. cit., p. 1115

[1223] Ando, Clifford, Citizens and Aliens in Roman Law, University of Southern California, 2006, p. 18

[1224] Gaudemet, Jean,, "L'étranger au bas-empire", *L'étranger, I, Recueils de la Société Jean Bodin* 9, Brussels, 1958, 99209-235, 223; Demougeot, Emilienne, "Le 'conubium' et la citoyenneté conféré aux soldats barbares du Bas-Empire", *Sodalitas: Scritti in onore di Antonio Guarino*, 5 vols., Naples, 1984, vol. 4: pp.1633–1643; Bianchini, Maria, "Ancora in tema di unioni, fra barbari e Romani," *Atti dell' Accademia romanistica constantiana* 7, 1988: 225–249

Agriculture

Agriculture played a significant part in the development of Roman Lusitania, especially in the south and along the coastal strip. With the occupation of Lusitania, the Romans put in to effect a deep structural reform by consolidating the deprived land into properties and infusing into the Lusitanians the ideology of the profit making. But first, the Romans had to instill in the minds of the Lusitanians the idea of setting up farms, which the Romans began by taking up as much rural space one could handle and establishing a large estate. In the north, compared to the south, farmable land was maintained as free pastures, while fallowed farmland was to be used in the spring and summer to grow seasonal vegetables. In the south, especially in the Alentejo region, where the Roman occupation was slower, Luso-Roman farming took place in large estates or villas called *latifundia*, which many are still standing today; unfortunately a large number of them have not yet been excavated. These *latifundias* were characteristic of the Roman Empire which would reach its highest development in Sicily, Spain, and North Africa. The establishment of these *latifundias* destroyed many ancient forests and dried up swamp areas, changing these areas into hospitable valleys, where settlements were built along with conditions that were made to grow edible food products. In Lusitania, this agricultural system would produce cereals, grains, olives, grapes, legumes, fruits and livestock.

The Alentejo region provided a setting for the *latifundias* to be erected, for its rolling hills and flat gentle plains were and still are suited for growing cereals, grains, olive trees and grapes, while in the north the land was (and still is) arable for agriculture. With varying degrees of soil conditions in the Alentejo, the type of land usage that was used was a system of crop rotation; even though at times the profit margin may have been low, it was necessary for it to confer various benefits to the soil. To make up for the losses, pigs were allowed to forage in the surrounding plains of ilex and cork oak, while shepherds herded sheep and goats within the fallow acres of the *latifunda* so that they would be fertilized and be able to produce during the following season. Along with this system of crop and land rotation, olive trees were planted among wheat fields to help in olive oil production. This was the only way a living could be hatched out in this area.

In José María Blázquez Martínez's work on the impacts of the Roman conquest of the Peninsula, he writes that Hispania after it had been pacified made up five percent of the grain harvest that was used by the Roman Empire, and also could now collect their value in money by instilling taxes on the populace.[1225] Thus bring in to Rome a large profit margin than they had before. But in 124 BCE, Gaius Sempronius Gracchus prompted the Senate to sell the wheat sent to Rome by the praetors from Spain, then sending the money back to the Iberian cities to be used to build public project.[1226] This return would and was at some point beneficial to the province, but the entire wheat profit was not sent to Hispania, but distributed within Rome. Wheat shipments to Rome had become important resource in this stage of the empire's development to desperately feed its growing population.

On the Atlantic coast, the land was blasted by gale winds and rain, making the soil a bit more hospitable for food production. In addition, the land was particularly excellent for olives for they thrive well in limestone type soils that are found around Elvas, Moura, Cano and Pavia. Along with the production of olive oil, viticulture was very lucrative for Lusitania. Before the famous Douro wines became well

---

[1225] Livy, 43.2; Cicero, Verr. 3.6; Valerius Maximus 8.7.1; Blázquez Martinez, José María, "El impacto de la conquista de Hispania por Roma (154-83 a.C.)", Klio 41, 1963, p.178 and Antigua: Historia y Arqueología de las civilizaciones: (http://descargas.cervantesvirtual.com/servlet/SirveObras/01305020888359846423802/014615.pdf?incr=1)
At this point the Romans in the provinces of Sardinia and Sicily continued with the Carthaginian tax as well in Hispania, which was to charge the tenth of cereals. The principle contributions were set by the praetors, but Roman authorities did not set fix prices on wheat and did not place tax collectors in the cities (G. Bloch y J. Carcopino, Des Gracques a Sulla, Paris 1952, p.126; M. ROSTOVTZEFF, Historia social y económica del Mundo Romano, Madrid 1937, p.51; L. Pareti, Storia di Roma 3 vols., Turin 1953, vol. 2, p.794).

[1226] Plutarch, quaest. Graec. 6

known, the Romans concentrated their viticulture in the valleys of the Sado and Guadiana Rivers (Both rivers systems are in the Alentejo region) and along the main road from Olisipo (Lisbon) to Emerita (Mérida) via Ebora (Évora).[1227]

Unfortunately we know very little about life in these *latifundias* or about agriculture in Roman Portugal, but one thing is certain, life in the country villa was based on raising cattle, horses, pigs, goats and sheep as well as growing cereals, grains, vines, fruits, olives, vegetables according to the suitability of the soil, and the proximity of towns and cities that provided an income for the landowner. In the end the development of horticulture, viticulture, cerealiculture (as the French say), was primarily developed to supply the cities food and the objective of exporting a new food supply to Rome.

One can only imagine that the Roman settlers at the end of the Republic and the beginning of the Imperial periods brought with them new technology and management techniques and methods for agricultural improvements, along with the introduction of new seeds and animal breeds. Sadly, there had been very little written about Roman innovations and technology that were introduced into Lusitania such as agricultural implements, field cultivation and fertilization, irrigation, pruning, fruit production, wine making, olive oil production and animal husbandry. But all is not lost; since the late 1980s there have been several in depth studies about the Roman 'agricultural revolution' in Lusitania such as Roman hydrology and about surviving agriculture tools.

Other Roman Economies

Garum and Salted Fish

However, not all villas were limited to agriculture. Along the coast and river outlets that drained into the sea, these villas were involved in the production of *garum* and drying and salting fish. They found this industry to be more lucrative than agriculture. Thus many smaller

[1227] Alarcão, Roman Portugal, Vol. I, p. 63

latifundia, especially those on the coast and those built along the estuaries of the Tagus, Sado Rivers and the Algarve coast became engaged in the fishing industry as well as preserving fish in fish-salting tanks and producing *garum* sauce making.[1228]

During the Roman period, Lusitania led the way in establishing the Iberian Peninsula as a major exporter of salted commercial products that supplied salted fish to the Empire. According to Leonard Curchin, the making of dry-salted fish began by gutting and cutting the fish into cubes or triangular chucks, with slits in the flesh to aid the penetration of the salt; the pieces were then thrown into large rectangular vats with an equal quantity of salt. The fish was then left in these vats for 20 days so that the salt would seep into the flesh for flavor. The fish was then removed and packed into amphorae and sealed with wood or cork.[1229] This process may have been also used to cure meats. The salt used in this process was undoubtedly obtained by evaporating sea water in huge salt pans called *salinae* and any surplus salt was sold as a food preservative.[1230]

Lusitania's productivity was evident not only in their salted meats and fish, but also with the making of *garum* sauce, which was more profitable than salted fish.[1231] *Garum* was prepared from the viscera, innards and blood of various fish such as mackerel, tuna, eel, and other small fish. Before the process was started it may have been a common practice for fishermen to lay out their catch according to the type of fish. This allowed *garum* makers to pick the exact ingredients they needed.[1232] The

---

1228 Alarcão, Roman Portugal, p. 87; Edmondson, J., Two Industries in Roman Lusitania; Mining and Garum Production, British Archaeological Reports, Oxford, 1987, p. 114-115

1229 Curchin, Leonard, A., Roman Spain, Barnes & Noble Inc, NY, 1995, p. 143

1230 Eupolis, 186; Curchin, Leonard, A., Roman Spain, p. 143; Edmondson, J., Two Industries in Roman Lusitania; Mining and Garum Production, British Archaeological Reports, Oxford, 1987, p. 114-115

1231 Curtis, Robert I., "In Defense of Garum" The Classical Journal #78 (February-March 1983, pp. 232-240

1232 Curtis, Robert I., The Garum Shop of Pompeii. Cronache Pompeiane, XXXI. 94, 1979, p.5-23

fish was first macerated in salt, and days later it was crushed and placed in a bath of brine to allow fermentation. The fish and brine would cure in the sun for one to three months, where the mixture fermented and liquefied in the dry warm air, the salt inhibiting the common agents of decay. In some cases, for quicker fermentation it was stored in a heated room. Concentrated decoctions of aromatic herbs, varying according to the locale, were then added. The end product was a very nutritious thick liquid that retained a high amount of protein and amino acids, along with a good deal of minerals omega oil, DHA and B and D vitamins.[1233] After several decantations, a black sauce emerged which added great zest to bland dishes. A fine strainer would be inserted into the fermenting vessel and the thick liquid was ladled out into amphorae for exportation.

This industry was not only for domestic consumption, but for overseas exportation. This was another way for smaller landowners to make an income. Lusitania *garum* known as *garum hispanicum*, was so popular that *garum* amphorae from Lusitania have been found as far as Palestine. Thus, in times before the discovery of the Spices Isles and India, Portugal and coastal Spain were one of the main producers of *garum*; this product was one of the few seasoning available at the time and highly prized. So highly prized, Pliny writes that it cost 1,000 sesterces (about $1,500) for about two congii (about 1.5 gallons).[1234]

Wine

One of the lasting legacies of the Roman Empire was the establishment of a wine culture in lands that would become world renowned wine regions. Under the Romans, Portugal's wine production started in earnest. Portuguese wines were apparently so popular in Rome that its demand outstripped the province's small supply, making it a rare commodity. Strabo mentions that vines were grown around the mouth

---

[1233] Curtis, Robert I., *Salted Fish Products in Ancient Medicine*, Journal of the History of Medicine and Allied Sciences, XXXIX. 4, 1984, pp. 430-445

[1234] Pliny, 31.43

of the Tagus.[1235] As for the interior of Lusitania, such as the well-known Douro region, the heartland of today's port wine industry, during the Roman era it was just beginning to grow vines, so a wine industry was non-existent.[1236] The Roman influence of new techniques and the development of road networks brought new economic opportunities to Lusitania, elevating winemaking from a private agricultural crop for personal consumption to a viable commercial enterprise. Still unlike the rest of Hispania, Lusitania did not develop into a wine-producing region under the Romans, until Portugal began to import its wine to England at the beginning of the 18th century AD when a cut in the duty tax on Portuguese wines happily coincided with a ban on the importation of French wines to Britain.[1237]

Manufactured Goods

Some landowners made their income in other ways by making pottery, tiles, bricks, glass making and so on, while others turned their land into smelting plants and stone quarry sites. Some went on the engage in the textile industry by dying and weaving cloth. As for mining, the State owned the mines but citizens were still able to rent the land and buy mining rights.

Amphora Production[1238]

The production of *garum* and wine complemented each other with another important export of the Iberian Peninsula, the amphora. Hundreds of amphorae have been found in Portugal signifying that there existed a major amphora industry in Lusitania. The amphora was a type of ceramic vase with two handles and a long neck narrower

---

[1235] Strabo, 3.3.1

[1236] Russell Cortez, F., 'As escavações arqueológicas do "castellum" de Fonte do Milho', Anais do Instituto do Vinho do Porto, Vol. 12, 1951, pp. 17-88

[1237] Robert Joseph, Sophie Blacksell, Sarah Sørensen, The wine Travel Guide to the World, Footprint Handbooks, 2006, p. 108

[1238] For more information on amphorae in Lusitania see Martín, Julián de Francisco, Conquista y romanización de Lusitania, 2nd ed., Salamanca, 1996, p. 348; in Hispania see Beltran, M., Las ánforas romanas de España, Zaragoza, 1970

than the body, which in this case were used to package and transport *garum* and wine. Because of conserved remains of *garum* found in vases throughout the Spanish peninsula and outside the province such as in Italy, Britain and Gaul, archaeologists have been able to better understand the history of this Iberian industry and economy during the period of Roman occupation. In Lusitania, most of the amphora workshops discovered up to this point are on the left bank of the Tagus River and on the right bank of the Sado; both on the lower reaches of these rivers.[1239] Though these two areas were the provinces' major producer of amphorae, there were other sites such as at Salacia (Alcácer do Sal). According to Professor Alarcão, the geographical locations, and the types of clay used to make amphorae and kilns found in these workshops must have been associated with the preparation of *garum* and salt-fish products which was important in those areas. In the Algarve there are several amphorae 'factories' which were not far from *garum* producers and fish preserving factories.

Mining

Of these industries that I have just mentioned, mining was entirely state ran and it was the second most profitable industry in Lusitania, but only after the metal ores had been reached. In Roman Lusitania the minerals that were mined were gold and silver of course, along with copper, lead, tin iron and semi-precious stones.[1240] The majority of the mines in Lusitania were state owned but there were a few like Aljustrel, where the state allowed private citizen to have mining rights.[1241] But other mines such as at Vipasca, the mines were leased by the state to individuals who organized themselves into a mining company.[1242] As for those mines that dug up gold, the State had a greater interest in having direct control over it.

1239 Alarcão, J. de, Roman Portugal, Vol. I, p. 86-87 and Appendix 3

1240 Encarnação, José, Inscrições romanas do conventus pacensis: Subsídios para o estudo da romanização, Coimbra, 1984, pp. 257-259 and 262-264; Azevedo, Pedro de, "As pedras preciosas de Lisboa (Belas) na História", O Archeologo Português #23, 1918, p. 158-202

1241 Alarcão, Roman Portugal, p. 73

1242 Ibid., 73

"Mining companies" were allowed to control up to five working mines although we do not know whether the law permitted this as a minimum or maximum for each company. On being rewarded these concessions, the 'tenants' would have to pay a tax called a *pittaciarium* and had to start working within 25 days of getting its lease. Along with this tax there were other stipulations within the contract that the mining company had signed with the State.[1243] Though the mines were State property, the concessionaries were still responsible for its upkeep; for one example from the tablet of Aljustrel, concessionaries were forbidden to make holes that would put safety of the miners, the mine and operation of the its drainage at risk.[1244]

Being that mining was only profitable once the ore had been reached, the mining company was made to pay a second tax on what they found such as 4,000 *sestertii* for silver.[1245] Along with these taxes, the concessionary (mining company) had to pay to the State half the value of the minerals that were extracted and being there were no State run smelting plants, the ore was weighed at the pithead and then the tax was assessed; only when this was paid was the concessionary allowed to transport the ore to the foundry.[1246] To perhaps avoid in paying this tax, it is probably that much smuggling took place, but this was at the cost of the miners for if caught these individuals were severely punished. The policing of the mines fell upon the military. This small garrison was responsible for seeing that no smuggling took place and collecting taxes and overseeing that the regulations about time limits, transport, pit props, distance between the pits and drainage were observed. Besides forcing these private mining companies to pay several types of taxes, the State also held a monopoly of the service industry such as shoemakers, tailors, barbers and anyone else who helped serve the miners had to pay rent for

---

[1243] A copy of this contract is a bronze tablet seen at the Instituto Nacional de Engenharia, Tecnologia e Inovação, I.P. Centro de Informação Científica e Técnica in Amadora

[1244] Ibid.

[1245] Alarcão, Roman Portugal, p. 74

[1246] Ibid., 74

their concessions.[1247] With gold mines such as Três Minas, the military had more direct control in running the mine for it would administer and discipline the workers and act as skilled mining engineers. At the same time, unlike the mines at Vipasca, the Romans used slaves in the gold mines instead of private citizens.

Pottery

Besides using clay to make roofing tiles and amphorae, pottery was another commodity. The production of pottery, especially in northern Lusitania, was of a low grade quality named *terra sigillata hispanica* compared to the better quality *terra sigillata* (stamped earth) which was intended for domestic use.[1248] Spanish *sigillata* has been found outside the Iberian Peninsula in Morocco, Algeria, France, Germany and Britain and even Italy, this shows that even though it was a cheap quality, it was largely exported due perhaps for its low prices at the market.[1249]

Prior to the pottery industry in Lusitania, pottery was first imported from Italy and then southern Gaul during the onset of the 1st century AD. During Brutus' campaign, potters followed the army and the *figlinarius* (potter) who were attached to the legions were perhaps producing their own pottery by using 'Spanish' clay. As for the Lusitanian pottery industry, it may have begun before 50 AD, but it was not until the second half of the 1st century AD that the Lusitanian pottery industry reached its high point in being mass produced, only to dwindle and in some areas even ceased production at the beginning of the 2nd century AD.[1250] In the Alentejo there seems to have been factories that produced imitations

1247 Ibid., 74

1248 Alarcão, Roman Portugal, p. 75; Mezquiriz de Catalán, M.A., Terra sigillata hispánica, 2 vols., Valencia, 1961; Mayet, F., Les céramiques à parois fines dans la Péninsule Ibérique, Paris, 1975 and Les céramiques sigillées hispaniques, Paris, 1984.

1249 Ibid.

1250 Adília M. Alarcão and Alina M. Martins, "Uma cerâmica aparentada com as paredes finas de Merida", Conimbriga #15, 1976, pp. 91-109

of a higher quality ceramic pottery from other areas such as the higher quality Southern Gaulish or Spanish Merida styled *sigillata*.[1251]

Apart from the domestic decorative pottery that was produced in certain areas, coarse ware was made all over the country. Pottery for the kitchens, as opposed to the tables of the better-off, and for all types of poor people, "coarse ware" was more likely to be made locally. Unfortunately, the study of Lusitanian coarse ware is lacking, although attempts have been conducted to give a push into classifying these artifacts and material. Besides making pottery, oil lamps were mass produced, as well as amphorae for the transportation of liquid goods as mentioned before.

Glass ware

According to Alarcão's study on Roman Lusitania no major glasswork industry has yet been found in Portugal, but glass waste at Braga and the ruins of Conimbriga near Coimbra suggest that there may have workshops that produced the common green glass for everyday glassware such as bottles, jars of all sizes and other popular products.[1252]

Jewelry

Jewelry to the Lusitanian as well as to the Romans was extremely ornamental.[1253] Lusitanian jewelers made everything from simple to

---

[1251] Alarcão, J. de, Roman Portugal, Vol. I, p. p. 83-84 and 86; *Terra sigillata hispanica* ranged from a color of rosy beige to bright red to light brown with a variety of shapes and designs.

[1252] Alarcão, Roman Portugal, p. 87; Alarcão, Adília M., Colecções do Museo Monográfico de Conimbriga, Conimbriga, 1984, p. 23; J.J. Rigaud de Sousa and Eduardo Alberto Pires de Oliveira, "Subsídios para o estudo das olarias de Bracara Augusta", Trabalhos de Antropologia e Etnologia #24 (2), 1982, pp. 360-370

[1253] For a detailed history about Lusitanian jewelry see Cardozo, Mario, Joalharia Lusitana, Universidade de Coimbra, 1959; Ferreira de Silva, Armando Coelho, "Ourivesaria proto-histórica em território português", in De Ulisses a Viriato: O primeiro milénio a.C., Jorge de Alarcão (ed.), Museu Nacional de Arqueologia, Lisboa, 1996, p. 139-146

intricate necklaces, bracelets, armlets, brooches, rings and earrings. The Roman hunger for jewelry made the Lusitanians make jewelry from any raw material they thought was precious such as gold, silver, copper, bronze, precious stones such as quartz, turquoise and opals, or other material such amber and even bones. From archeological artifacts found near Monte de São Félix, Portugal in 1904, it seems that men enjoyed wearing torque or smooth rounded necklaces and armlets and round or flat bracelets, while women wore a much larger variety, but it seems that they had a desire for the more intricate type of jewelry.[1254] Lusitanian jewelry reveals a developed technique, very similar to what was done throughout the Mediterranean, namely with the use of plates and solders, filigree and granulated techniques. Though everyone wore jewelry it played a part in class distinction.[1255]

Construction and Architecture

During the pre-Roman era, building methods in Lusitania were fundamentally simple; rough stone walls put together with or without mortar. Another method that was use was mud bricks (adobes) and lath-and-plaster. As for roofing, it was made of straw and wood. But with the coming of the Romans all that changed, building technical innovations were introduced such as squared blocks of stone mortar, *Opus caementicium* and *opus signinum* (types of concrete), tiles, small clay bricks stucco and vaulted ceilings. These material novelties lead to the erection of better structures. In addition, this also gave rise to the use of new raw material such as clay, limestone and quicklime.

[1254] In 1904, a bricklayer while it built a mill in the top of São Félix's Monte, close to small Castro of Laundos, he/she finds a púcaro there inside with jewels, these jewels were bought by Rocha Peixoto that took them to the Museum of As for the torque type necklace worn by the men it did not signify one's social class, but one's power and authority within the tribe Porto. Silva, Armando Coelho Ferreira da, "A Cultura Castreja no Noroeste de Portugal"", Museu Arqueológico da Citânia de Sanfins, Paços de Ferreira, 1986; Octávio da Veiga Ferreira e Seomara Bastos da Veiga Ferreira, A Vida dos Lusitanos no Tempo de Viriato, Polis, Lisboa, 1969, p.86.

[1255] Octávio da Veiga Ferreira e Seomara Bastos da Veiga Ferreira, op. cit., p.86.

Architectural forms depended both on the materials used and the construction techniques employed, as well as the social purposes for which the buildings were intended for. Take temples for example, its shape varied according to the liturgy celebrated in them; theaters arose out of the requirements of drama and its architecture evolved to the demands of what type of plays would be staged there; baths were designed for the needs of Roman bathers and the amphitheater's shape determined what type of gladiatorial games would take place within. It is therefore logical to say that because of the Roman conquest of Lusitania and the transformation of its society, it brought about a real architectural revolution.[1256] In the end, advances in architecture on the Iberian Peninsula, began with the Romans.

Of the Romans techniques that were utilized during the occupation of Lusitania were the lath-and-plaster technique and the use of cement and bricks. Modeled stucco was employed throughout the Roman Empire. The Romans used mixtures of lime and sand to build up preparatory layers over which finer applications of gypsum, lime, sand and marble dust were made; pozzolanic materials were sometimes added to produce a more rapid set. The method of using lath and plaster was a durable and not a very expensive technique for the process began with wood laths. These narrow strips of wood were nailed horizontally across the wall studs. Next, temporary lath guides were placed vertically to the wall, usually vertically at the studs. Stucco was then applied, typically using a wooden board as the application tool. The applier then dragged the board upward over the wall, forcing the stucco into the gaps between the lath and leaving a layer on the front of the temporary guides. A helper would then feed new stucco onto the board in quantity. When the wall is fully covered, the vertical lath "guides" are removed, and their "slots" were filled in, leaving a fairly uniform undercoat.

The Romans made use of fired bricks, and the Roman legions, which operated mobile kilns, introduced bricks to many parts of the empire. Upon occupying new lands, the Romans would introduce the craft of

[1256] Alarcão, J. de, Roman Portugal, Vol. I, p. 109

brick – making to the local populations.[1257] Roman bricks were often stamped with the mark of the legion that supervised their production. Roman brick was almost invariably of a lesser height and longer than modern brick, but was made in a variety of different shapes and sizes.[1258] Shapes included square, rectangular, triangular and round, and the largest bricks found have measured over three feet in length.[1259] The utilization of bricks allowed Luso-Romans to build an assortment of houses and buildings. For public buildings, ashlar stone blocks and dressed stone work were the rule; and even when the walls were generally made of mud or clay bricks, they required stone for their foundation, thresholds and door and window frames.[1260]

Stone was also used for many purposes such as to pave roads, make querns for funerary and honorary stelae, baths, etc., but to construction such magnificent works, stone quarries were needed. Traces of Roman quarrying in Portugal are practically non-existent today and the study of the origins of stone use is very rare. There is however, some evidence that stone was quarried in the Alentejo, the Beiras, and modern-day province of Estremadura and in the Algarve. From Professor Alarcão's in depth study on Roman Portugal, these quarries produced local stone that was normally used such as schist, granite, limestone and marble.[1261]

Clay was used in a variety of building material such as *tegulae* and *imbrices*, both were a type of tiles for coving and roofs; also bricks of various sizes and shapes were used in construction of buildings and roads, and *suspensurae* for hypocausts and columns; terracotta pipes, *tegulae mamatae* for insulation of bath houses and many other. Though these clay materials were manufactured in Lusitania, many of the tile and brick factories have not been discovered; the ones that have been

---

1257 Walters, Henry Beauchamp and Birch, Samuel, History of Ancient Pottery: Greek, Etruscan, and Roman, J. Murray, 1905, p. 330–40

1258 Juracek, Jack, Surfaces: Visual Research for Artists, Architects, and Designers, W. W. Norton & Company, 1996, p. 310

1259 Peet, Stephen Denison, The American Antiquarian and Oriental Journal, Jameson & Morse, 1911, pp. 35–36

1260 Alarcão, J. de, op. cit., p. 80

1261 Alarcão, J de, op. cit., p. 80-81

found and excavated represents a tiny portion of what must have existed during the Roman occupation.[1262]

As for the other building material that were used was quicklime and *opus signinum*, unfortunately there is very little information on these two materials. The making of quicklime may have become an industry in areas of Portugal where there existed limestone deposits. Concrete (*Opus caementicium*) during the Roman Empire was made from quicklime, pozzolanic ash or pozzolana, and an aggregate of pumice. Its widespread use in many Roman structures, a key event in the history of architecture termed the Concrete Revolution, freed Roman construction from the restrictions of stone and brick material and allowed for revolutionarily new designs both in terms of structural complexity and dimension.[1263] In Roman times, gypsum and lime were used as binders, but volcanic dusts such as pozzolana were favored, when it could be obtained. But the type of material that was used in Roman Italy was different from what was found in the other provinces. In Lusitania, the lack of pozzolanic ash for *opus caementicium* was replaced with other materials. According to Professor Alarcão, it seems that the Luso-Romans made their own concrete.[1264] The crushing of tiles to prepare *opus signinum* was mixed with lime, sand, and powered clay bricks, at times crushed stones were added into the mixture. Any builder's yard would yield enough broke tile and bricks along with the sandy terrain of the country to develop into a major industry in its own right. But besides using *opus signinum* which may have been a bit expensive, the Luso-Romans were able to make a low-quality cement of sand, water, and artificial pozzolans (broken stones and baked clay).

But for the Romans to build such wonderful building, they first had to set up a city plan. Much has been written about the purpose, development, daily life and architecture of Roman cities, but inadequate attention has been paid to about its role in Romanizing conquered territories. Cities

---

[1262] Alarcão, J de, op. cit., p. 81-82

[1263] Lancaster, Lynne, *Concrete Vaulted Construction in Imperial Rome. Innovations in Context*, Cambridge University Press, 2005

[1264] Alarcão, op. cit., p. 83

were the focal point of assimilation that helped to form the cultural and social structure of Roman civilization: commerce was centralized, conquered lands were 'civilized", and the population was usually under control. It has also been claimed that urbanization was a deliberate attempt by Rome to re-channel the efforts of the Iberian elite from a rebellious lot into a sable community.[1265] Somewhat cynical, this statement assumes that the Romans had premeditated intentions to impose cities on the conquered, but apart from a handful of colonies that Rome had established throughout the empire, Rome could claim little credit in founding cities. Most Romanized cities as those in Hispania, as well as elsewhere, began as pre-Roman towns, thus by the end of the Republican era these towns, although not founded by Romans, were effectively Romanized.

Under the peaceful conditions of Augustus's reign and onwards, Iberian cities became satiated with monumental building, temples and statues.[1266] Not only could the elite enjoy the benefits of urban life, but the lower classes also could. Moreover, all Iberians that became Roman citizens were now entitled to participate in local government through a popular assembly, by which magistrates were elected. Even ex-slaves, though ineligible for magistracies, could become officials if they were able to afford an entrance fee.

As for Roman architecture, it declared a functional and pragmatic spirit that spread out from Rome and conquered the whole known world. It is clear that the Romans adopted Etruscan and Greek influences, but it was the Romans that developed its own highly distinctive architectural style by introducing the previously little-use of arches, vaults and domes. In Hispania, urban design of Roman cities followed clear laws of development for public and military services. The Roman city was basically composed by a number of identical components, disposed in a special way - parallel and equal distant - separated by streets. The

---

[1265] Roldán Hervás, J.M., 'Las guerras de Lusitania (155-138 BC) y Celtiberia (153-133 BC)' in R. Menéndez Pidal (ed.) Historia de España, 2nd ed., 2 vols., Madrid, 1982, vol. I, p. 115.

[1266] Curchin, Leonard, A., Roman Spain, p.105

whole, forms a unit of rectangular designs surrounded by a parametric wall with watchtowers. All the streets were equal except for two: The North-South one -*kardo maximus*- and the East-West one -*decumanus*. Both areas were wider for they were the ends at which the doors of the city walls were placed.

The center of the city was where the very important social and cultural systems called forums and markets were placed. These components were necessary for the design of public buildings: amphitheatre, theater, temples, market, forum and so on. There were also other great communitarian buildings throughout the city such as *basilicae, termae*, gyms and bathhouses. In addition, housing could be divided into *house*, *domus, insula* and *villa*. There were also *casae* or housing for lower classes and ex-slaves. Unfortunately, because of modern urbanization many of these building structures have all disappeared in our time.

Textiles

The textile industry in Hispania was praised by the Romans for its Iberian linen, which was popular amongst men and women, especially for the men for when women wore Iberian linen, 'it was so sheer that they were reproached for wearing "woven wind."[1267] It is also believed that the Romans used linen as an undergarment. The majority of the linen industry throughout the entire country was home – spun as proven by the discovery of thousand of loom weights and spindle whorls. Although linen was home spun, it is difficult to say whether there were linen factories, which was possible, but unfortunately it is hard to tell for a study on the subject has not been conducted. Wool is also made. The most famous woolen cloth, according to the Romans, was woven at Salacia (Alcácer do Sal) in Lusitania; its beautiful smooth fleece produced attractive checkered patterns of black and white.[1268] Along with the making of linen and wool, dying also played a part in the textile industry, but unfortunately there is little information that tells us

[1267] Gaius Petronius Arbiter, The Satyricon of Petronius Arbiter, Chapter 55

[1268] Strabo, 3.2.6; Martín, Julián de Francisco, Conquista y romanización de Lusitania, 2nd ed., Salamanca, 1996, p. 348

whether it was a major factory size industry or if there were workshops spread throughout the province that exported their product to Rome.

Religion

Luso-Roman Religion

It is said that Rome had more gods than citizens, but Hispania had more gods than Rome. Their profusion is attributed to several factors: the plurality of indigenous tribes each with its own pantheon, the implantation of successive foreign cults, and the polytheistic nature of ancient religions which allowed all these gods to co-exist without inherent contradiction.[1269] Since the Romans were usually tolerant of other people's belief systems, they allowed their religion as well as the indigenous gods to flourish throughout the province. None the less, there was a tendency to adopt Roman gods or to modify the indigenous cults to conform with a Roman one and at time mix together a native god with a Roman god forming somewhat a new god.

Lusitania which was among the last region of Hispania to come under Roman control can be divided into two religious' spheres. The first is the south – the Algarve, the Alentejo and the coastal zones between the Tagus and Vouga Rivers; the second comprises the inland area between the Tagus and the Douro Rivers and north of the Douro.[1270] This religious division into two contrasting regions, though an over simplification, will be useful for tracing the spread of the Roman classical religion.

Roman civilization first penetrated the south as we can see from the ruins of buildings, numerous villas, their mosaics and the large number of artifacts that have been found. By the time of Augustus, the north was still predominantly indigenous as demonstrated by the lack of artifacts and mosaics, which are rare. Also, very few villas have been found and town are few in the north compared to the south. It may be correct that in the north the social structure was different, more rural with a less

---

[1269] Curchin, Leonard, A., Roman Spain, 1995, p.154.

[1270] Alarcão, J. de, Roman Portugal, Vol. I, p. 98

developed social system and economy. This division is also discussed by Pliny, who describes Lusitania from the north to south, in which he gives the name of *populi* (tribes) until he reaches the Vouga River; thereafter he gives the names of *oppida* (towns). It appears that the Vouga was some kind of cultural divide between the Romanized section of Lusitania and the indigenous cultures. Finally, the two regions are marked by ethnic division. In the north, the native Indo-European pre-Celtic people dominated, in the south, tribes of other origins influenced by more advanced outside civilizations inhabited the area. Thus, this is the separation of the two regions by the time the Romans had completed their conquest of Lusitania.

When it comes to religion, it seems that the worship of Roman gods was strongest in the more Romanized south, though it is not clear how this came about. But, given Roman tolerance to foreign religions, why was the widespread conversion of Roman deities in Lusitania so strong? We can only image that it was in the cities that the Luso-Roman origins began with the coming of Roman colonists, settlers, craftsmen, soldiers, and merchants. To some extent there may have been a perception that the gods of the conqueror were more potent or had stronger powers than those of the vanquished.[1271] But more importantly the worship of Roman gods was an integral component of Romanization, a *sine qua non* of being accepted as a Roman. Though this is a possible theory, what is reality is that there is not much of a wholesale abandonment of the native gods, but reconciliation with the Roman pantheon through the process of conflation which Tacitus termed *interpretatio Romana*.[1272] In time, these Roman religious beliefs moved into the rural areas when country folk would come into contact with Roman gods when they went to the cities. Although rural regions were becoming Romanized, they likely clung to their traditional gods long after the Roman gods had been supplanted into Lusitanian towns. Religion in the end was

[1271] Vasconcelos, J.L de, *Religiões da Lusitânia*, vol. III, 1913, Imprensa Nacional--- Casa da Moeda, Lisboa, 1897-1913, p 193; Curchin, Leonard, A., Roman Spain, p. 155

[1272] Tacitus, Germania, 43

and still is among the most conservative institution that is usually the last to surrender.

If the less Romanized parts of the peninsula tend to contain the lion's share of indigenous gods, the majority of Roman gods were worshipped along the vastly Romanized Mediterranean coast. But one must also not forget that this was made possible by the Phoenician and Greeks, who instilled their culture on the Iberians, particularly in the south of Spain, thus driving out the native gods.[1273] So it was easy for the introduction of Roman gods into the Iberian pantheon. Of all the Roman gods that came to be in Lusitania, it seem that at least 40 played an important part in Lusitanian religion,[1274] while there were a small number *of nymphae, lares* and *genius* who also had a role in the Luso-Roman religion, but they were used more frequently in the backwoods area of Roman Lusitania.[1275] Still the lack of epigraphic material and sculptures are a serious drawback to our understanding of the exact number of gods that existed in Lusitania, as well as how these gods and their cults functioned in the province.

Eastern Cults

With the Roman conquest of Hispania, there came other foreigners from the east, such as the Egyptians; besides bring in material goods, they brought new ideas, technology and religion into Lusitania's major urban areas. As these towns became cities and capitals of a *conventus* and commercial centers, they began to attract many freemen and foreigners, thus Luso-Roman society was fertile ground for Eastern and African religions. Of the eastern religions or cults (*sacra peregrini*) there is evidence of several eastern cults that made a home in Lusitania, according

1273 Curchin, Leonard, A., Roman Spain, p.160

1274 Vasconcelos, J.L de, *Religiões da Lusitânia*, vol III, p. 220-312. Here are some of the gods that played a role in Luso-Roman religion was Jupiter, Juno, Apollo, Diana, Luna, Soli, Proserpina, Poemana, Ceres, Tellus, Dionysus, Neptune, Mars, Aesculapius, Hygia, Salus, Victoria, Venus, Cupid, Mercury, Minerva, Hercules, Volcanus, Concordia, Pietas, Iuventus, Pax, Fortuna, Eventus, Phoebus, Successa and Fata.

1275 Ibid., pp. 254-261 and 291-298

to the inscriptions that have been discovered throughout the years. Of these inscriptions there seems to have been seven Eastern mystery cults that had a foothold in Lusitania: Cybele and Attis of Phrygia, Isis and Serapis of Egypt, Mithras of Persia, Caelestis of Carthage and Astarte of Mesopotamian origin.[1276] As Lusitania became more Roman with each passing decade, public officials, especially during the Antonines and Severines dynasty, were keen to syncretize religions thus making a strong impact on Hispania.

Imperial Cult

The Imperial cult was based on the supposed divinity of the emperor, which had essentially a political purpose of strengthening the loyalty of the provinces to the current ruler. In Hispania, the imperial cult was easily reconcilable with Iberian traditions of the *devotio Iberica* which strengthened the belief in the imperial cult to the point that individuals would die for their leader. Once the indigenous people accepted Roman leadership, it became natural for them to treat an outstanding Roman official -- especially a general -- as a god. Though Spain was in the forefront of emperor worship in the Roman west, in Lusitania it did not occur until Caesar Augustus became *Imperatori*. Augustus was staying in Tarraco in 26-25 BCE, when a delegation arrived from Mytilene, Greece to bestow divine honors upon him. Not to be outdone, the people of Tarraco built an altar to him and on one occasion they enthusiastically informed him that a palm tree had miraculously sprung out of it. Sarcastically, Augustus replied that they did not light sacrificial fires on the altar.[1277] From this point on, all incoming emperors were paid homage. In Lusitania, the imperial cult may have appeared around 19 BCE after Augustus's death via its military governor, L. Sestius Quirinalis Albinianus.[1278] Along

---

[1276] Ibid., p. 328 – 358

[1277] Inscriptiones Graecae IV, 39; Quintilian, 6.33.77

[1278] Pliny the Elder, Historia Naturalis, 4.111; Ptolemy, Geographia, 2.6.3; Pomponeus Mela, 3.13; Fishwick, Duncan, *The Imperial Cult in the Latin West: Studies in the Ruler Cult of the Western Provinces of the Roman Empire*, volume 3, Brill, 2002. vol 3, p.1-7

with this information the oldest inscription that shows that Lusitania followed the imperial cult is from 5 or 4 BCE, proving the existence of the cult.[1279]

The Imperial cult came to Lusitania in two phases. The first phase was based on tributes to Emperor Augustus in that altars and statues were consecrated to him and several other emperors that followed. But by the time of Tiberius, the imperial cult in Lusitania had entered its second phase in that temples and colleges for priests were beginning to sprout up in several municipalities.[1280] But still the Lusitanians used their traditional priests who were not elected from the local elite, unlike their Roman and Iberian counterparts, but were skilled tradesmen.

These imperial cults not only deified emperors, but also the emperor's protective spirit and household gods. This tendency expanded until a large number of gods and goddesses were inducted into the Augustan pantheon, becoming in effect the emperor's own gods.[1281] Bearing on the evidence that is available, it seems that the worship of the imperial cult flourished during the 1st and 2nd AD, but declined at the beginning of the 3rd century AD with the coming of Christianity.

Language

Assimilation of Latin came later to Gallaecia and Lusitania than to the other administrative regions, and further variations in Latin were

---

[1279] Encarnação, Jose, Inscrições romanas do conventus pacensis: Subsidios para o estudo da romanização, Coimbra, 1984, 256-257; This inscription was consecrated in Salacia to Emperor Augustus by Vicanus, son of Boutius.

[1280] Fishwick, Duncan, "An early provincial priest of Lusitania, Historia #31, Wiesbaden, 1982, pp. 249-252; Pierre and Monique Lévêque, 'Sculptures", in J. Alarcão and R. Etienne, Fouilles de Conimbriga II, Épigraphie et Sculpture, Paris, 1976, pp. 235-247; Etienne, Robert, Le culte imperial dans la Péninsule Ibérique d'Auguste à Dioclétien, Ecole Française de Rome, Paris, 1974, p. 199-200,238-239, 252-254; Alarcão, J. de, Roman Portugal, Vol. I, p. 105-107

[1281] Etienne, Robert, Le culte imperial dans la Péninsule Ibérique, pp. 346-349; Curchin, Leonard, Roman Spain, p. 162

caused by differing tribal migration patterns and regional dialects.[1282] Moreover, Lusitania was essentially rural in nature and more isolated compared to the rest of Hispania. This explains in part the differences between modern Portuguese and Spanish.

During the long process of colonization and assimilation, the dialect of the Roman Empire, known as **Vulgar Latin**, diffused throughout the Iberian Peninsula. Vulgar Latin, or *Lingua Romana* – "vulgar" in the sense of "common, or "of the people" differed in grammar and syntax from classical Latin, the written and literary language of the Roman Empire, which had been developed in its standard form by Roman writers and grammarians of the first century BCE. Vulgar Latin had spread throughout the western provinces of the Roman Empire by soldiers, merchants, travellers and, later by Christian preachers. Latin in time became a highly varied, mobile and fluid form of spoken discourse. Through the influence of local or pre-Roman languages, Latinized regional variations developed that Rome became dependent on the extent of communications via interpreters or officials that had learned these newly Latinized dialect.[1283] With the decline and fall of the Roman Empire, communication in Latin became more erratic that these regional dialects began to form into local languages, later becoming Portuguese and Spanish.

Although some of the pre-Roman Iberian languages became Latinized, many others succumbed and disappeared from human history due to the pressure and prestige of Latin. But of all the dialect that had existed in the Iberian Peninsula, the Basque language is believed to be still used in its original form. Overall, it has been estimated that from around 600 AD, local dialects of Vulgar Latin were no longer mutually intelligible, and, thereafter, many regions began a process of the crystallization of these dialects into the early forms of Romance languages, such as Portuguese, Spanish, French, Romanian and several other European languages.

[1282] Mattoso Camara, Joaquim, The Portuguese Language, translated by Anthony J. Naro, University of Chicago Press, 1972, p.8-9

[1283] Mattoso Camara, Joaquim, The Portuguese Language, p. 172

Though Rome had Romanized a major part of the Iberian Peninsula, there still existed issues in dealing with Romanization and resistance to it. Strabo boasted that by the early 1st century AD the inhabitants of Hispania Ulterior was completely pacified, but one must remember that Ulterior by this time was a Roman province for about 200 years. Though this was applicable to the cities, this was probably not true for the countryside. It is generally believed that the conquest of the entire peninsula was considered complete by 19 BCE, although it had taken two centuries compared to Julius Caesar conquering Gaul in less than a decade. Therefore, we can see that Romanization was resisted, becoming a slow and gradual process. Though Romanization took hold in political, social and economic spheres; in religion language and art, the old ways died hard. In regions isolated by natural topographical structure like mountains, and distances and of lower cultural levels, Romanization fought an uphill battle.

According to Leonard Curchin, Rome was not committed to imposing her culture on the provinces in any thorough or systematic manner.[1284] Official policy was chiefly aimed at pacification, justice and tax collection.[1285] In religion, he writes that the polytheistic Romans were tolerant of other religions except those that posed a political threat, while in material culture, Roman goods were introduced not by official policy but by free enterprise; Roman imports found new markets.[1286] On a social level, Iberian took Roman names and attempted to further their careers via advancements or family prestige. As a community, the Iberians took strides to gain Rome's grants of *ius Latii* to provincial communities, which were handed as a favor rather than an imposition.[1287] With this said complete Romanization still failed to take over the entire peninsula.

Curchin writes that Romanization failed in three essential areas: dispersion, depth and durability. In dispersion of the Roman culture, despite the high grade of Romanization in the south and east, the western

1284 Curchin, Roman Spain, p. 191

1285 Ibid., p. 191

1286 Ibid., p. 191

1287 Ibid., p. 191

and north-western region were only partly assimilated, but other such as the Cantabrians and the Basques, were never Romanized.[1288] Secondly, in depth, although much of the peninsula was Romanized, it was but a superficial veneer, barely masking the indigenous subculture.[1289] Thirdly, in durability, by the Late Empire, the north, central and western regions became de-Romanized and pre-Roman cultures re-emerged.[1290] In short, Romanization was not homogeneous, but a process that varied from region to region and from tribe to tribe.

1288 Ibid., p. 191-192

1289 Ibid., p. 192

1290 Ibid., 192

CHAPTER XI

VIRIATHUS THE KING AND THE LEGEND

Viriathus's Leadership in Hispania Ulterior

What position did occupy Viriathus in the Lusitanian army? His position appears in the ancient sources in different forms. The classical sources habitually use the term '*dux*' (Latin for chief or commander) such as in Frontinus's work referring him as '*dux Lusitanorum*', and in another passage he also calls him '*dux Celtiberorum*'.[1291] This title reference was given to Viriathus by Frontinus only when Viriathus in 143 BC was already a Lusitanian chieftain and general.

Other Latin authors, like Veleius Paterculus, Eutropius, Diodorus and several others use the title '*dux latronum*' (chief of thieves). He has also been called '*Lusitanus latro*' (Lusitanian thief) in a testimony by Seneca, who mentions how frustrated he was by Viriathus's attack on Cordova.[1292] This title according to Professor Muñoz, given by Seneca is without a doubt a reference to the type military strategy (i.e. guerrilla tactics) that Viriathus used to fight the Romans and how it was despised by them, calling the Lusitanian War a *latrocinium* (thief's war) and not *bellum iustum* (just war).

[1291] Frontinus, Strategemata, Book 2

[1292] Meyer, Heinrich, Anthologia veterum latinorum epigrammatum et poematum, Volume 1, Lipsiae, apud Gerhardum Fleischerum, 1835, p. 46, paragraph 128.

Of course, the first Latin author that considered him a tribal chief or general was Livy who wrote, "*mox iusti quoque exercitus dux factus*" (was quickly nominated the general of the army). Justinus shares the same consideration when he wrote: *in tanta saeculorum series mullus illis hominibus Hispaniae dux magnus praeter Viriathum fuit* (in so many centuries there was not one man in Hispania that was a great general, except for Viriathus).

Besides the term *dux,* some Latin author also used the word *imperator* (commander in chief, general, emperor). Florus writes of him as, "*ex latrone subito dux atque imperator"* (of a thief he passed on to be chief and quickly to General of the Army); also, Eutropius expressed the same, while Dio Cassius and Appian use the Greek term *strategós*. Of all the terms used, the word *rex* is rarely mentioned besides by Diodorus and Strabo, but it does not correspond to the terminology that recognizes the denomination of the applied word for king. Though several different words have identified Viriathus's leadership position during his eight – year war, the terminology that sticks in the mind of most historians on this subject is that Viriathus had been considered as a general or chief of the Lusitanian army, instead of a king of the Lusitanian people.

The acceptance of his leadership is addressed explicitly by Appian, but with his death, his army undid itself and the power of his successor was not the same to that of Viriathus. Viriathus possessed excellent qualities as tribal chief and military leader. Because of these leadership qualities, he has been considered to be the "savior' or "liberator" of Hispania, but in reality he never was able to become these two things.

Besides holding a leadership position, after Galba's massacre in 147 BCE, Viriathus came to the forefront of history as a military genius and the creator of guerrilla warfare by defeating several Roman praetors and their numerous legions. Following these defeats, Rome attempted to make a pact with the rebels, and although Viriathus at first was opposed to it, in time Viriathus became merciful, turning him into a wise general and chief, who was recognized as not only as a tribal leader of Lusitania, but of Turdetania also. Starting from this point on, Viriathus was considered by many historians to be "a chief of the Lusitanians" as well as a leader of various tribes due to his amazing leadership skills and use of military tactics.

But the power that Viriathus had over western Hispania did not last very long. With his brother or father-in-law's death ordained by Viriathus, the degradation of his authority began. But before his downfall and at the peak of his power, Viriathus celebrated his marriage outside Lusitania either in Turdetania or in Bastetania, to show the Romans that were invited to the ceremony that he was in control of the reconquered territory.

Though Viriathus showed the Romans his power, could he have been a friend of Rome? This was unthinkable in a man like him, who had an internal hatred for Rome. However, in 140 BCE, at the peak of his political and military career, we see a change in his attitude in that he sought to make peace with Rome, wanting to put an end to the war.

The signing of the peace treaty of 140 BCE was not the result of the Lusitanians tried of war, but of his military advantage that he had over Servilianus, enabling Viriathus to negotiate, at that moment, his conditions for a peace treaty. It was the first time that he had the Romans totally cornered, forcing their hand to sign a peace treaty or else.

Viriathus's treaty with the defeated Servilianus in 140 BCE has a tendency to favor him as a peacemaker for he began negotiations with the Roman, bring peace to the Lusitanians and instilling on the Romans a treaty of equal conditions (aequis conditionibus), but unfortunately this treaty was taken by Rome as a disgrace.

But in reality, Viriathus knew that by destroying this Roman army, the war would continue, and that Rome would send more legions than before to either annihilate his army or wipe out the entire tribe. At the same time, he began to detect that his army was fatigue and weary after their first encounter with Servilianus, for the Lusitanians were forced to retreat back across the border into Lusitania in search of provisions and reinforcements. A third reason is perhaps reinforced by his people's lack of enthusiasm to continue to fight and realizing that if he pushed his people a bit further to continue their fight, it could have ended in mutiny, and he would have lost the power that he fought so hard to achieve. Within these three scenarios, perhaps lies the reason why Viriathus decided to conduct peace negotiation instead of continue fighting.

The peace treaty reveals that the causes of the problems that the Lusitanians faced were poverty and the poor land conditions for cultivation. Thus, the treaty provided conditions that the Lusitanians needed to have better lives and to have landholdings in Baeturia, south of the Tagus River. Had the Romans not broken the treaty and allowed the Lusitanians to control this area, this would have overcome the chronic lack of good lands for farming, and the lack of pastures for their herds, and the war would have ended.

Within the Roman Senate though, the story was different in that there existed two parties, a hawkish party and one that favored the peace treaty. The hawk party considered the treaty signed with these conditions was an offense to the Roman State and so it did not accept the Lusitanian peace treaty. As for the "dove" party, it seems they felt that they were winners because their members were more interested in the commercial and economic value of the Iberian coast and in exploration by penetrating into the rest the peninsula's interior. In the eye of these Romans, the land was inhabited by savages who only lived for war, but with the right influences and time these people would become 'Roman subjects' that could be exploited. Unfortunately, the following year the Romans broke the peace.

It is indubitable that the peace of 140 BCE meant for Viriathus the abandonment of further campaigning against Rome. Thus, it is believed by some historians that he may have been or had lost some of his power. Although a peace treaty was signed, the Romans had the upper hand, Consul Roman Popilius Lenas, an expert of indigenous idiosyncrasy, imposed hard conditions upon the Lusitanians: first, hostages and delivery of Roman deserters; then, taxes; and finally, the surrendering of their weapons, as well as ordering Viriathus to betray and execute many of his companions, among them his brother-in-law, Astolpas. With these deaths, Viriathus had practically dug his own grave. It is perhaps a reality that many of his former allies and Lusitanian noble family members did forget this betrayal. Thus, it may be true that some of them may have had a hand in his murder. But unfortunately, this theory is lost to us.

Though Viriathus seemed to have constantly tried to maintain his conquered lands, supported by an anti-Roman population, Viriathus's absolute power over Lusitania and the territories he captured did not remain absolute. His shameful act, in the eyes of his tribesmen broke oaths that Viriathus and his allies had made to each other. It is without a doubt that his murder, committed by Audax, Ditalco, and Minuro may have had something to do with Viriathus's betrayal of his allies. Viriathus's attempt to make peace with Rome by sacrificing some of his allies seems to have backfired as evidenced by his assassination.

But prior to his death, Viriathus did not abandon the idea of trying to get a Lusitanian influence on Celtiberian towns such as Tucci and Arsa. He never got them to come over to his side though; instead they went on to fight their own war of independence. On the other hand, he fought for the Lusitanians who sought out agricultural lands to cultivate. Though the Romans had offered land several times; the Lusitanian had always been lured to make peace as promised. But the results were always the same, false. The tendency for Viriathus to become a 'king' of a State was inevitable, but only if he succeeded in defeating the Romans, and build an effective and very organized tribal governmental structure. Unfortunately, for the Lusitanians, it never reached that point because of two reasons; he clearly never established a border between his newly acquired territory and his unexpected death.

Viriathus's tragic death created the total dismemberment of the Lusitani tribe, which ended the Lusitanian struggle. His successor, Tautalus, elected in a tribal assembly did not have the personal attributes Viriathus had and soon after having been elected, he yielded unconditional to the Romans.

Besides his leadership, Viriathus appears to have been fair in sharing booty as we had seen in Diodorus's work. For all his qualities, it was admired by Cícero, who introduced him as an example of justice, austerity and incorruptibility in various paragraphs within his work, *De Officiis.*

The data on Viriathus's sharing of wealth with others, conveys Sanchez Moreno's ideas that the Lusitanians had a complex social and political system that bestowed military prestige, social promotion and wealth upon its leaders. The majority of these benefits of the taking of booty usually went to the tribal chiefs. The spoils were then distributed among their upper – class

subjects or among those who participated in the campaign. In the case of Viriathus, the distribution of wealth was equal among his men that according to the classical writers, they characterized him as just, fair and equal, which were signs of a good leader. As for the form of wealth redistribution, it has been identified as the proper way that primitive organizations adopted a socio-economic system of partnerships that was based on interactions through bartering. In this sense, it is necessary to understand the function of Viriathus's division of spoils.

Viriathus' attitude about the division is explained in the classical texts by mentioning that he shared his booty among his men. Compared to the rest of the tribal leaders, whose primacy in the division and distribution of their spoils was usually shared among the warriors and allies. Sanchez Moreno characterizes Viriathus as a moralistic warrior, who was known for his generosity and fairness more than other chiefs.

Though he was a warrior's warrior, to gain the fidelity and adhesion of his troops it was important to manipulate the men by concession of gifts or rewards, as deduced by the ancient texts. In this sense, the offerings worked as a commitment of loyalty among individuals and as an element to engage a social relationship between warriors and their people to consolidated prestige and authority. Besides gaining the confidence of his people, Viriathus also established with other tribal chiefs' diplomatic ties, reiterated with the exchange of offerings in political and religious ceremonies. This way, the redistribution of wealth was a reflex of the establishment of personal ties.

Viriathus, The Lusitanian King

Let us think of Viriathus as king of the Lusitanians. Several historical passages within the classical texts about Viriathus express an ideology of royalty, as it is considered by M.V. Garcia Quintela and Maricio Pastor Muñoz.

To establish Viriathus's mark on Iberian history, he was considered a 'king' by his people. Therefore, it is necessary to analyze, thoroughly, testimonies that defined Viriathus's personality trait that were considered by the classical authors 'kingly'.

In this analysis of kingship, Viriathus is represented first as a bandit chief; followed by his transformation into a military leader with an end result that shifted him, if not directly, into a king, at least in a close atmosphere of royalty. Most of these ancient testimonies refer to Viriathus not as a *latrone,* but as *dynastés*, a term that designated chiefs of smaller political groups (i.e. chief of a group of bandits). With this in mind, as a leader of such a group, Viriathus would have to exercise great responsibility in leading such a group.

Much of the texts structure, as well as the vocabulary used, were utilized in relation to the kings of the Hellenistic monarchies. Thus Viriathus is described as if he acceded into a type of royalty granted by a consensus among his partisans.[1293] According to Professor Muñoz, Viriathus has been compared to kings that were sovereigns of their homeland, but though they were kings their status was rejected by the Romans for in

[1293] Muñoz, Mauricio Pastor, Viriato, O herói lusitano que lutou pela iberdade do seu povo, p. 233

the eyes of the Romans only they were the rulers, while all other were uncivilized barbarians.[1294]

According to Professor Muñoz and M.V. Garcia Quintela, this royal political system was very similar to the one of the Celts pursued, where the king came from the warrior class and his position was elective and revocable: though the king was in power, his power was still controlled by his subjects. A king did not get to pass on their throne to a relative or son when they died, as in other civilizations in history.[1295]

Though Viriathus did not inherit his chieftain and was instead elected, it marked the institutional change of bandit chief to tribal chief, granting him a 'kingship' over all Lusitanians. M.V. Garcia Quintela concluded by saying that the royalty of the Lusitanians was very similar to that of the Celts, and not of the Hellenistic monarchies as some historians have stated.[1296]

He also points out that these classical authors knew how to capture in detail the legend of Viriathus by interpreting the indigenous ideology in agreement with traditional Greek ethnography. The stories and anecdotes, as well as the structure of Lusitanian sacrificial rites, were the vehicles of transmission of the legend of Viriathus.

Overall, these classical stories about Viriathus seem to be an attempt to explain that Lusitanian ideologies went through in a mythology process that presented Viriathus as leader of men who fought for a cause he believed in, to being adapted for a larger glory as a leader in a critical situation belonging to an entire community. The Romans and Greeks that heard of and collected these stories about Viriathus, had captured the last shades of those stories and adapted them to their ideologies and norms of traditional ethnography; therefore, the fragments that we read

[1294] Ibid. 234

[1295] Muñoz, Mauricio Pastor, op. cit., p. 235; Garcia Quintela, M.V., 'Viriato y la Ideología Trifuncional Indoeuropea" Polis #3, 1993, pp.111-138

[1296] Ibid.

today written by the classical authors are fragmented tracks of those final adaptations.

Was Viriathus, Romulus of Hispania?

Of the classical texts, Florus deduced that Viriathus was a historical personage of Romulus, the creator and father of Rome. With Viriathus as king, these classical authors seem to illustrate through their works, Viriathus had played such an important part in the history of Hispania that Florus compared Viriathus to Romulus.[1297]

A suggestive and interesting analytical work comes from Raquel Lopez Melero, who writes if Viriathus has been considered to be called the Romulus of Hispania, this title was political rhetoric exaggerated by Florus. This controversial work had caused waves among Iberian historians that has caused Lopez Melero to defend her thesis by stating:

"...the consideration of Viriathus as someone that almost had consolidated a regnum does not seem to be absurd, or an exaggeration. …for if he had consolidated a strong indigenous power, Rome would have had unavoidably be obligated to recognize this new king and establish a independent Iberian state within the Roman realm." [1298]

It seems evident that this idea was not unanimously accepted, since it was believed that the Romans would totally have Lusitania under their submission and quickly Romanize it. This of course did not happen for Viriathus became Rome's opposition to their conquest. For Rome to control the entire Iberian Peninsula would mean great economical profits and increase its power against Carthage, but instead of gaining the economical advantage, the Romans began losing their war against Viriathus (including the Celtiberian War), for these wars became a large military expense that was surpassing their earnings.

[1297] Florus, 1.33.15

[1298] Lopez Melero, Raquel, "Viriatus Hispaniae Romulus" Espacio, Tiempo y Forma, Serie II, Historia Antigua, I, 1988, pp. 247-262, p. 247

Perhaps had the Roman Senate been a bit more favorable to the ratification of Servilianus peace treaty of 140 BCE, the war would have ended that moment instead of lasting another year or two. This of course would have changed Viriathus's fate and the outcome of Luso-Roman relations would have been drastically different from what history recorded, but instead the Senate quickly revoked the treaty by allowing the new governor, Servilianus Scipio to break the treaty and continue on fighting which resulted in Viriathus's death. Unfortunately, this moment in time effectively was a blow to Viriathus's destiny that caused him to become known as 'Romulus of Hispania'.

According to Rachel Lopez Melero's work on the subject of Viriathus, as "Romulus of Hispania", there are various key points for her possible hypothesis. Prior to the Lusitanian War, there was no Roman initiative for territorial expansion, and, although it appears that Rome was in total control of the entire territory on the left bank of the Baetis River (Guadalquivir River), the apparent lack of military positions north of the river points to a stabilization of their conquests.

But the large-scale 'offensive' raids of the Lusitanians, which started in mid 2nd century BCE, revealed the vulnerability of the Baetis defensive line, based on R. Knapp work, *Aspects of the Roman Experience in Iberia, 206 – 100 BC.* Knapp writes that "the determining factor of rethinking of the southern border translated into a clear initiative of Roman expansion toward the north."[1299] However, in the early stages of this expansionist process, Rome, occupied by the military needs of other fronts, appeared to have maintained a defensive attitude on the peninsula, believing that the problem was minor and could be resolved by a base of military operations that was ordered to punish cities and tribes that turn hostile against Rome, or the annihilation the indigenous troops that opposed them or bandit raiders.[1300] Because of Lusitanian

[1299] Knapp, Robert C., Aspects of the Roman Experience in Iberia, 206 – 100 BC, Vol. 9 of Anejos de Hispania antique, Colegio Universitario de Alava, p. 29-30

[1300] Lopez Melero, Raquel, "Viriatus Hispaniae Romulus" Espacio, Tiempo y Forma, Serie II, Historia Antigua, I, 1988, pp. 247-262, p. 251

incursion into Roman territory, the Romans had to react. Therefore, the start of the Lusitanian War.

Although this is what the Roman historiography states, Lopez Melero believes that the Roman conquest of Lusitania went deeper than what the Romans claimed. The ability of Rome to overcome any indigenous resistance on the Peninsula when given a favorable combination of sufficient availability of troops and a general to effectively command them, the Romans were undefeatable. From a military view point, Viriathus and his eventual successors were doomed, for the behavior that Rome portrayed towards the Iberians indicated that territorial expansion was the main motive to economically exploit annexed areas and safeguard Roman citizens.[1301]

The background information of Viriathus' involvement with a number of major urban centers outside Lusitania suggests, according to Lopez Melero, that there was a connection between the Lusitanians and cities in southern Hispania that wanted to join in with Viriathus, on the basis of a united action to achieve independence from Rome. This confederation, if successful, would have been beneficial for both parties: the Lusitanian would have gained the lands that they wanted and the rest of Hispania would be free of the Roman economic yoke that oppressed them. Had Viriathus won, making him the 'Romulus of Hispania', we must admit that his cause would potentially cause harm to Rome's image across barbarian Europe, the Greeks and their enemy the Carthaginians in North Africa. To prevent Viriathus' coalition from spreading to other Iberian regions, giving him a reasonable chance for ultimate victory against Rome; southern Iberian cities that sided with Viriathus would suffer the punishment from the Romans, therefore, many Iberian chieftains would have to reach a peace on *ex aequo,* (on equal footing) weakening their strong support for Viriathus' cause, which would identify them as the losers in the conflict. Hence in the eyes of the Romans, Viriathus was seen directly as a threat.

[1301] Ibid., p. 248

The turning point between this attitude and the decision to extend the territory further north from the Baetis River after the Servilianus peace treaty of 140 BCE, was done to pacify the troublesome Lusitanian tribes once and for all, but more importantly, it was to deny Viriathus from owning fertile farm land that was hard fought and taken away from the Carthaginians. So, giving it away to a barbarian was a disgrace.

Another important factor that Lopez Melero points out that may have prevented Viriathus to becoming "Romulus of Hispania" was the ethnic identification, social and geographical spread of integrated elements that sided with Viriathus. Unfortunately, there is a serious documentary deficiency on the subject, not only because of lack of data, but because some of which exists are not reliable. But overall Roman sources show that Viriathus became a character of legend, and, moreover, there is a natural tendency of national historiography to rehabilitate the image of the provincial governors, as the enemy who often used foul play in the defense of their interests, to build up there opponent to a status of hero. All these deviations and adhesions have been adulterated to constitute the shortfalls in the information and the inability to geographically identify many of the cities that are mentioned in the classical sources that were involved directly or indirectly with Viriathus's campaigns. It is also sad that there is no information to determine who were the chieftains that were under his command, what areas were they from, what were their social extraction or what political relationship they had with Viriathus, apart from the military. And, of course, the question is further complicated, when we come to the consideration of the population centers that were not Lusitanian, who join Viriathus's cause.

Another factor is the connections between Viriathus with indigenous areas that were not Lusitanian. This indigenous involvement in Viriathus's cause suggests that there was a combination of interests between the Lusitanian and cities from the south, on the basis that a unified action was necessary to achieve independence from Rome in which would be beneficial for both parties: the Lusitanians could establish their own state, and the others would be free from the power that oppressed these tribes, thus the presence of those cities that rallied to Viriathus's cause helped to strengthen those ties. This coalition, which began to extend to other Iberian regions, conferred viability to Viriathus's cause, giving him some reasonable chance for a final victory against Rome; however, it did not last long for though the cities were united to his cause, it was the cities and not Viriathus's army which truly suffered the punishment that the Romans instilled upon them, weakening these strong supporters, who would identify themselves as the losers of the conflict. However, if Viriathus had, in effect doubled his army, his cause perhaps may have had the potential to shift the tide of the war to his side, but being that Viriathus did not expand his army, it instead debilitated his war effort, shifting the tide towards the Romans. That is why the balance of Viriathus's rise to power was constantly threatened.[1302]

The final assessment of Lopez Melero's statements leads me to draw three fundamental factors that stopped Viriathus from becoming Romulus of Hispania: 1) the capacity of Viriathus's resistance and subversion was limited due to disagreements on who was leader; 2) his capacity of stirring up trouble was affected by the internal factors of instability which allowed Rome at times to capitalize on; 3) Viriathus's death was unquestionable the element that presented the Romans the decisive key for completely ending Lusitanian resistance, so it was imperative that the Roman neutralize him as quickly as possible.

Therefore, it would not be wrong to say that Viriathus decided to end the war as he did with the defeat of Servilianus's army instead of continuing to fight on. Though some historians state that the end of the war was due to an impulse of generosity, others argue it was luck that found Viriathus in a favorable situation to accomplish his personal ambition: to become absolute ruler of an independent Lusitania. Hence, Viriathus took a risk on the hope that the Senate would ratify the treaty. But it was not ratified, making his dream of perhaps becoming Romulus of Hispania, just a dream instead of a reality.

1302 Bermejo Barrera, J.C., Mitología y mitos de la Hispania prerromana 2, Madrid, 1986, p. 45

Regrettably, the terms of the treaty are very ambiguous. But within the treaty, it is probable that it considered Viriathus becoming *'amicu populi Romani'* and allowed that his partisans establish themselves in their own little kingdom as Roman subjects within Roman territory. In some sense, it would have been understandable if the Senate had ratified the peace treaty, because it would have been advantageous to the Romans. As a 'friend of the Romans", Viriathus would not be able to restart his war against Rome, or support any of Rome's enemy, instead he would have to provide support to fight alongside Rome against her enemies. If the Lusitanians were not uprooted they would draw some advantage from the armistice, for the cities involved in Viriathus's cause would gain some beneficial outcomes from the treaty; it would have virtually dashed any possibility of the Iberians returning to lead any future hostilities against the Romans. Though he may have had curved any possible Roman intervention of Lusitania, the bellicose Lusitanians, who were the destabilizing agents, at least in the south, would have now become Roman subjects, generators of profits for Rome.

However, interpretation of the peace treaty of 140 BCE to some historians does not seem to be a convincing one. They state that it is not easy to believe that Viriathus was lucky to be placed in an excellent position to give the Romans a definitive blow by forcing them into a treaty. Secondly, it is hard to believe that Servilianus after suffering a major defeat, convinced the Senate to revoke Viriathus's treaty.

Viriathus's peace terms, as stated by Appian, referred to land concessions to be given to his people.[1303] This non-Roman treaty placed demands on Rome, which made them think that they were being forced to recognize the independence of former Roman controlled cities and territories that were now in Viriathus's hands; the Romans refused to ratify the peace treaty which was *'pax in aequibus condicionibus facta'* ('done in conditions of equality'); seen by the Roman Senate as *'deformis'* ('of a shameful peace'), Livy attributes.[1304] The Romans at that time felt that the relinquishing of these lands was not very important, compared to

[1303] Appian, 69.294

[1304] Livy, Perioche 54 and Epit.Oxy, 185

the neutralization of Viriathus which was most important above all else because the Romans to continue their conquest of the Iberian Peninsula had to first defeat Viriathus and then the Celtiberians before they could continue their territorial expansion north of the Guadalquivir River. So, the Senate considered him a threat to Rome for they were being forced to recognize this new independent state in their 'sphere of influence'. Therefore, it was necessary for the Senate to not ratify the peace treaty.

Several members of the Senate, as well as Caepio, understood that Viriathus could further increase his domain further deep into Iberian areas that had not submit themselves to Rome's control, subsequently increasing Viriathus's power at Rome's expense. It was imperative, therefore, that Rome continue conducting military campaigns to quell Viriathus and reduce the nucleus of Iberian independence that was causing financial difficulties to Rome's other enterprises. With this in mind, perhaps Caepio and several Senate members saw the dangers of Viriathus becoming known as the Romulus of Hispania. According to Appian, the Senate resisted to commence hostilities against the Lusitanians in an open fashion, so it secretly authorized Scipio to irritate Viriathus into action to the point where he would be blamed for restarting the war, thus giving Rome a reason to conquer Lusitania and putting an end to Viriathus. In the eyes of the Romans, Viriathus would have been seen as the instigator for breaking his own treaty.

Although I have mentioned why he may have instigated the war to continue, unfortunately, we cannot establish the exact reasons which prompted Servilianus Caepio, to seek the necessary authorization of the Senate. Though it is possible that he may have been motivated by simple personal ambition or the aspiration to loot and seek glory and triumph. It is possible that perhaps he saw from a political standpoint that Viriathus was still a threat to Rome by allowing Rome to recognize Lusitania as an independent nation.

This political situation of breaking the peace treaty may have enhanced Viriathus's power, which could have resulted in further enhancing his scope of his domain throughout the rest of Hispania that was still not subject to Roman control. Therefore, Viriathus's growing power would multiply into a major military force to be reckoned with and perhaps cost Rome dearly, so the decision of 141 BCE was of great significance to Rome's expansion of its Iberian empire.

But for us to test this theory, we would have of know the type of political bonds that linked Viriathus to the populations or cities that depended on him. But in reality, there is very little that we know in that respect. The only thing that seems clear is that both the Romans and the Iberians had recognized him as a military leader. It is also probable that Rome foresaw an embryo of a *regnum*, justifying the Senate's concern in destroying the rebellion. The urgency in which the Senate intervened by breaking the peace with Viriathus indicates that his power made him appear very charismatic with a strong following.

As for the title of *amicus populi Romani*, given from the constitutional Roman point of view, it was granted on certain occasion to foreign kings and princes who had befriended Rome. It was also at times granted to certain prestigious foreign individual that had presented themselves in good light in the eyes of the Senate. Besides this tidbit of information, the Latin and Greek sources lack terms that truly expressed Viriathus's royal status as king, preventing scholars from thinking he had reached something more than just being a tribal chief and rebel general.

The terms that are used in the sources, superficially mention his position as 'king'. Diodorus uses the term *dynastés*. But the particular word, *dynastés*, is ambiguous, which could classify as a *regulus* (a petty king of a small state). The image Diodorus uses is too conventional and does not determine Viriathus's political status. On the other hand, according to Roman writers, he was a 'barbarian king' who had outstanding ethical and individual qualities that socially functioned in a simplistic and uncomplicated manner. Besides being married to a princess, Viriathus was never pronounced as king nor did he descend from a long line of a royal household. Thus, the term dynasty is a deceiving word that does not strictly denote a royal origin.

Concerning Viriathus's death, Caepio, according to most classical authors, bribed the three ambassadors that were sent by Viriathus to negotiate the peace treaty. On the contrary, Diodorus in defense of the Romans, saying they were the correspondents that proposed the murder of Viriathus to Caepio in exchange for their personal safety and riches. Though there are two versions, the responsibility of Viriathus's death still falls upon the Romans and the three assassins. It is possible that the assassins had decided to kill Viriathus not just to guarantee their personal safety or to get rich, but to provide to their city favorable conditions once they returned to their homes.

Diodorus writes that Viriathus's three traitors were citizens from Urso, who according to Appian, appeared before Caepio with a peace proposal, but instead of making peace, they were bribed. Though Viriathus continued to hold on to his power in Lusitania, he had definitely lost the accession of the southern cities, which were at this point at the mercy of Rome and began to suffer the costs of repression. It is credible that these three individuals of Urso, which was a southern city, decided to assassinate Viriathus not for their personal safety, which was not at the time especially threatened, or to get rich quick, but to provide their cities favorable conditions from the Romans. This could have been the context that alluded Diodorus, to blame the three men for assassinating Viriathus. In the end Viriathus's death because of an error in his judgment in choosing his compatriots has left open the question of whether Viriathus was truly the Romulus of Hispania.

Viriathus, Warrior King

Viriathus congregated a series of virtues held by warriors that were admired by populations that lived a warrior's lifestyle. Viriathus was, according to the ancient texts, a warrior that sought a warrior's way of life and the only thing that he wanted was the prestige and esteem that was measured by the honors that his people had rendered to other warriors before him who were full of wisdom and courage. Valor and fighting prowess were fundamentally part of a warrior's life, but to be a king, fighting skill and bravery had to accompany oratory skills, as well as generosity to his people. These values in the end transformed him into hero. Upon his death, his followers consecrated him at his funeral as a hero. As a hero, he was exalted to a cult status for it was a substantial element in Iberian culture to honor the life of a warrior who had given so much to his people.

From an Indo-European ideological point of view, Viriathus's status as a warrior basically described him as the bearer of the lance and behaving like a warrior (uncivilized).[1305] Various examples exist to support this idea. The first point comes in the form of how he recruited his warriors which were loyal to their leader until death.[1306] The second example is that Viriathus is presented as a warrior chief to a group of war like people, whose members were personally linked to him through a warrior culture.[1307] This shows that his true vocation was not banditry, as most historians claim, but military, making him fall in Dumézil's Indo-European trifunctional category of the warrior class. This can be vaguely seen in the classical texts, placing a value on his military virtue in a positive way.

Throughout the classical texts, they make references on his capacities that made him a great leader. To become such a leader, the texts give a few examples of him undergoing a life of hard self-discipline and living an austere and private life away from the luxury, making him a true warrior. But on the other hand, there is also a negative side that a warrior hero should not follow. In Cassius Dio's work, he formulates the theme "the three sins of the warrior", things that a hero and king should avoid while manifesting the qualities specific to a warrior king's

---

[1305] Garcia Quintela, M.V., "Viriato y la Ideología Trifuncional Indoeuropea", Polis #3, 1993, pp. 111-138. The Trifunctional hypothesis, forwarded by French mythographer Georges Dumézil from 1929, postulates an idéolgie tripartite ("tripartite ideology") in prehistoric Proto-Indo-European society, reflected in the existence of classes or castes, those of priests, warriors, and commoners (farmers or pastoralists), corresponding to the three functions of the sacral, the martial and the economic, respectively. For an idea about this theory see: http://en.wikipedia.org/wiki/Trifunctional_hypothesis; Muñoz, Mauricio Pastor, Viriato, p. 231

[1306] Ibid, p. 231

[1307] Ibid., p. 232

character.[1308] Although these sins were loosely mentioned before, Viriathus's personality seemed to have avoided them, making him an incorruptible hero. For his qualities, he was admired by Cicero, who presented him as an example of justice, austerity and incorruptibility as seen in various passages of his writing, such as in Book II of *De Officiis*.

Though Viriathus was from the start a barbaric hero, he came to be considered at the end of his life, a king, so to speak. The classical texts characterize him with an 'internal beauty', as Professor Muñoz puts it.[1309] This beauty is the "beauty of spirit of the superior man" that not only correlations with his physical aspect, but with his internal spirit. However, from these internal values that characterizes this man, the informed leader and responsible military mind, there were negative values present as well.

In the final analysis, J. Alvar believes that although the classical texts viewed this ancient Roman enemy as a bandit for many years after his death, the destiny of this adversary was determined by virtues, measured largely on the scale of a warrior's value system, to becoming a national hero. Viriathus, in this aspect, was a popular military leader and effective enough to successful have faced the Roman army, giving him the attributes to be called a hero; at the same time, his success had not been so pernicious that it provokes bitterness, as well as admiration among his enemies and admirers.

[1308] Dumézil analyzes the three "sins" of the warrior in the Indo-European tradition: against the king, against the priest, against the laws originating in the State. The triple sins in this theory are against the three offices of kingship/ priesthood, warrior, and state. The hero commits sacrilege of some kind against his sovereign lord, his king, and comes under the ban of heaven and the gods. Then he has to fail as a warrior - fleeing from battle, showing cowardice when faced by a challenger - and loses his strength of arms. Then sin against the state. This "sinning against the state" means, sinning against the people, the home, family, and even marriage.

[1309] Muñoz, Mauricio Pastor, Viriato, O herói lusitano que lutou pela iberdade do seu povo, p. 245

His condition as leader of a 'primitive people' allowed the attributes and all the characteristics of a hero convert and transform his story into a man's model that lives in righteous agreement with the nature and himself. In the end, Diodorus sought in Viriathus the representation of moral good, a mirror in which reflected the lost qualities of Rome and through Viriathus, Diodorus attempted to recover or make Romans see, if they wanted to read between the lines, Rome needed to get back on track and become righteous once more to assure its political domain and territorial gains throughout the known world.

So, the question remains, was Viriathus a warrior hero or a warrior king? One cannot give an exact response, because this man lived in a Celtic world different from the Roman one. Unlike Roman leaders, who usually reigned for their entire lives, Celtic kings were usually elected from among the warrior class; the king would have been the best of the warriors and one who did not commit the sins of man or lack faults of his own. This can be the case for Viriathus. Viriathus was an excellent warrior, who was according to the classical texts, 'the best of all', and held the values and virtues needed to be elected as king. But was he truly king of the Lusitanians? That is for you the reader to decide.

Viriathus's Legacy: The Creation of a Legend

Viriathus is not just a historical character who was first a shepherd that became a warrior and later a leader of a nation, but a hero. Viriathus's life and exploits, of what we know about him, were transformed by his people and even his enemy, into legend. During his lifetime, whenever his people saw themselves forced to gather strength to defend their homeland from invasion, or suffered misfortunes, stories about Viriathus increased the mythical character. This interesting use of myth turned this simple man into a living legend, which has become an essential part of the Iberian Peninsula's history.

The Iberian Renaissance brought in the birth of Classical Archaeology and the rebirth of the study of ancient classical literature. With this resurgence, the illustration of Viriathus and his legend became linked to the Portuguese and Spanish spirit to the point that his name has attributed to the cohesion of nationalistic fervor, even when both cultures faced internal and external political problems, as well as governmental repressions brought on by fascist dictatorships during the last century. But in what moment did Viriathus become legend? Or, when was his legend created and the myth of Viriathus elaborated? To answer this question, it is necessary to revert back to the ancient texts.

Thanks to Diodorus and Appian, we have an idea about the military campaigns and politics of the Lusitanian War, as well as about the character and virtues of Viriathus. The classical texts offer two images of the Lusitanian War: one that presents the exaltation of the virtues of Rome in which neither an exceptional and virtuous barbarian chieftain nor people could resist; on the other hand, the second version offers the image of a man of exceptional character who was able to and had the willpower to defeat Rome, but because of greed and jealously he was betrayed by his own people showing that though this man was a hero, corruption still roamed wild. Though many of these ancient authors demonstrate to readers the power that Rome was, they still had a special sympathy for the Lusitanians and their leader to the point that they considered him as a model of moral values.

There is no doubt that most of the information about Viriathus's life and character are exemplary representations of a historical figure as a model of virtue. They are also ideas that projected the simple happiness within primitive people that were born in the fields and in contact with nature along: a frugal character and austere, disciplined, capable of resisting the asperities of the time and of controlling their desire.[1310]

All of the aspects referenced in the classical sources presuppose that the first step in the elaboration of the myth of Viriathus rested on local lore that grew into a full-blown legend within the Iberian Peninsula. Within Portuguese and Spanish history, his story was tentatively

---

1310 Muñoz, Mauricio Pastor, Viriato, O herói lusitano que lutou pela iberdade do seu povo, p. 213-214

repeated without end in every regional locality, that in time he became a national symbol.

Though he has been made into a hero, this idea of a 'national hero' during Viriathus lifetime was not the case for Portugal, for Portugal nor Spain did not exist yet. The only thing that is evident is that Viriathus was not Portuguese or Spanish but Lusitanian. But as the centuries passed these local tribes united, thanks to Romanization, and began to form a national identity and brought with it the story of Viriathus and the peninsula's history.

The process of Portuguese appropriation of Viriathus or the connection of his character to the geographical space known as Portugal began with André de Resende and Father Bernardo de Brito during the late 15th century.[1311] And continued into the 20th century by A. Guerra and C. Fabião that considered ancient Lusitania as a pre-configuration of today's modern Portugal.

In the late 19th century Dr. Augusto Ferreira do Amaral writes that Viriathus was the voice of the Portuguese Renaissance for he was the embryo of the Portuguese homeland, the first symbol of identity and of differentiation in relation to the remaining peninsular people.[1312] While Sergio Franklin de Sousa Rodrigues claims that the Portuguese oral tradition attributed to Viriathus becoming the mythical hero, who founded the Portuguese nation out of the ashes of Lusitania.[1313] Further inspiring the Portuguese claim on Viriathus.

However, the Spaniards also began to claim Viriathus as their own. The first text to exaltation Viriathus and the Lusitanians came from Afonso X in his work on the history of Spain, *Crónica Geral de Espanha* (1344), which he represents Viriathus as a herculean hero without a country that fought the Romans to establish a Hispanic nation for his people.

1311 Guerra, A. and Fabião, C., 'Viriato: Genealogia de um Mito", Penélope, Fazer e Desfazer a História #8, 1992, pp. 9-23

1312 Chamorro, Victor, "Viriato, historia compartida, mito desputado" Agora Academia, Cáceres 2002, p.65

1313 Ibid., p. 65

With the onset of the Renaissance, the classics were rediscovered in Portugal that many historian of that age began to identify and recognize ancient Lusitania as Portugal's namesake such as in a1532 work entitled *Auto da Lusitania* by Gil Vicente. From these early writings come two epic poems that made Viriathus into a Portuguese hero. The first is the famous *Os Lusíadas* (1572) from Luis Vaz de Camões, in the mid-15th century, and the second is entitled *Viriato Trágico* (1699) written by Brás Garcia of Mascarenhas at the end of the 16th century. This author was an enthusiastic defender to restore the Portuguese monarchy of D. João IV from the Spanish, thus making his poem an authentic nationalistic manifestation that claimed Viriathus, like the king, came from a long line of Portuguese heroes that had defended their homeland from foreign invaders.[1314]

Historical study of Viriathus did not start until 1593 with André de Resende's book titled, *Antiguidades da Lusitania.* Resende's work marks the beginning of archaeology and anthropology in Portugal for his studied stated that the Portuguese were descended from the Lusitanians, and Portugal was historical Lusitania. This was followed by Father Bernardo de Brito in 1597 with *Monarquia Lusitania.* In his work, he tries to justify the idea of the history of a Portuguese homeland starting from one of Noah's son from antiquity to his time. In volume one of this two volume book, it identified the Portuguese and the Lusitanians as one in the same. Though it was 'historical' the main objective of the book was to glorify the Lusitanians and the hero that had opposed the Roman Empire, and like them, the Portuguese should follow their example and free themselves of the Spanish yoke that had been occupying Portuguese territory since 1580, helping in giving patriotic fire to begin the Restoration War (1640-1668).[1315]

[1314] Inês Vaz,, J.L., Lusitanos no Tempo de Viriato, p. 196

[1315] The 1580 Portuguese succession crisis came about as a result of the 1578 death of young King Sebastian I of Portugal in the Battle of Alcácer Quibir. As Sebastian had no immediate heirs, this event prompted a dynastic crisis, with internal and external battles between several pretenders to the Portuguese throne; in addition, because Sebastian's body was never found, several impostors emerged over the next several years claiming to be the young king, further confusing the situation. Ultimately, after a three year war known as the War of the Portuguese

During the 18th century, Spanish historian J.F. Masdeus contributed and reinforced the Portuguese appropriation of Viriathus's legend in a detailed description that stated that Viriathus's character was Portuguese and not Lusitanian. This work enforced the idea that the Portuguese were the true descendants of the Lustianians.[1316]

The 19th century saw the emergence of major historical studies and of archeological science. This was the beginning for many scholars, historians, archaeologists and researchers who began to distance themselves more and more from the imaginative antiquarian. The reformulation and revision of Portugal's history began to change or debunk many of the myths that had been created in its history; one of these men that led the revision was Alexandre Herculano, who was one of the most lucid individuals in that respect.

But the literary attempts of making Viriathus Portuguese saw in the middle of the 19th century a downturn as a national hero, for Alexandre Herculano, the creator of scientific historiography in Portugal, was the biggest advocate in rejecting any relation of continuity between the Lusitanian and the Portuguese– a theory that was systematically repeated in all the manuals and school programs in Portugal at the end of the 19th century until the early mid-20th century. This refers to the Lusitanian resistance and the episode of Viriathus as a man

---

Succession, Phillip II of Spain gained control of the country, uniting Portugal and Spain in the Iberian Union, a personal union that would last for 60 years, during which time the Portuguese Empire declined. The revolution of 1640 ended the sixty-year period of dual monarchy in Portugal and Spain under the Spanish Habsburgs. The period from 1640 to 1668 was marked by periodic skirmishes between Portugal and Spain, as well as short episodes of more serious warfare, much of it occasioned by Spanish and Portuguese entanglements with non-Iberian powers. In 1662, Spain had committed itself to a major effort to end the Portuguese rebellion. Portugal, with the intercession of its English ally, had sought a truce, but after the Portuguese victory at the Battle of Montes Claros and with the signing of a Franco-Portuguese treaty in 1667, Spain finally agreed to recognize Portugal's independence on 13 February 1668 with the Treaty of Lisbon.

[1316] Masdeu, J.F., Historia Crítica de España y de la Cultura Española, Madrid, 1783

born from the Lusitanian tribe and not Portuguese.[1317] However, A. Herculano's theory was largely rejected by J. Leite de Vasconcelos, who continued to proclaim Resende's theory that the Portuguese were related to the Lusitanians.[1318] Though he was the first to try a systemization of Iberian tribes that inhabited Lusitania, his investigative work had a fundamental objective to prove that there was a direct relation between the Lusitanians and the Portuguese. Leite de Vasconcelos's claim was reinforced by Portugal's renowned archaeologists Francisco Martins Sarmento's archaeological excavations of *castros* in northern Portugal. Still today there are scholars that continue to affirm this identification.

Just as in Portugal, in Spain the Viriathus legend also thrived throughout the ages. At the start of the 1600s, Viriathus was recognized by both the Portuguese and Spanish as the first Iberian hero who had become a legend thanks to Miguel de Cervantes Saavedra in two of his works, *Novelas Exemplares* (1613), and his play, *O Cerco de Numância* (1585) in which he uses a character with the name Viriathus. Also, in *Engenhoso Fidalgo Dom Quixote de la Mancha* (1605- vol.1 and 1615- vol.2), where Dom Quixote advises the *cónego* to stop reading books of cavaliers and that instead read accounts of the great heroes from antiquity, among them Viriathus. Another author first to mention Viriathus was Félix Lope de Vega y Carpio who wrote *La Arcadia* (1598). In his work, he compared Viriathus to Hannibal and Julius Caesar. This was followed by González Bustos, in 1668, in a comedy entitled *O Espanhol Viriato*. During this same time, Jose Zorrilla dedicated several poems to this ancient hero. While Bustos wrote a comedy, a tragedy was written a century and half later by Hernando de Pizarro, titled *Viriato* (1843). All of these begin with Viriathus being from Spain. With these early works, various Spanish authors between the 1600s to the 20th century began to exalt Viriathus. Like the Portuguese, these authors added a Spanish character. But the first historical work on the subject came from Father Juan de Mariana. In his 1623 work of the history of Spain known as

---

1317 Herculano, Alexandre., História de Portugal Desde o Começo da Monarquia até ao Fim do Reinado de Afonso III, 3rd ed. Lisboa, 1868; Inês Vaz,, J.L., Lusitanos no Tempo de Viriato, p. 197

1318 Inês Vaz, J.L., op. cit., p. 193

História Geral de Espanha, he pointed out Viriathus as 'the liberator of all Spain.'

From Father Mariana's work, by the 18th and 19th century, many Spanish scholars began to refer Viriathus as a Spanish hero who was a Celtiberian and not Lusitanian. Other referred to him as more regional, such as Valencian in southeastern Spain. By the end of the 19th century and the start of the 20th century, Spanish authors and artists represented Viriathus as a Celtiberian. So strong was the belief that Viriathus was Celtiberian and not Lusitanian, that the Spanish sculptor Eduardo Barrón González in 1884 was the first person to sculpt a statue of Viriathus and instead of giving it to the Portuguese, he placed it in the city of Zamora, which is near the Portuguese border at a site which is known today as Plaza de Viriato.

The Legacy Continues

At the onset of the 20th century, Portuguese and Spanish scholar and historians began to debate about what tribe or region Viriathus was from. From this early time period several significant works were written. Starting with 1900, Spanish historian A. Arenas Lopez was the first that I found, which was not lost or destroyed, since Father Mariana wrote an entire biography on Viriathus that debates his regional and national identity. In Arenas Lopez's book, '*Reivindicaciones históicas: Viriato no fué portugués si no celtibero: su biografia*', he indicates that Viriathus was a Celtiberian tribal chief. This was followed by another of his works entitled, '*La Lusitania Celtíbera*', in 1907, claiming that Lusitania was part of the Celtiberian realm, thus reinforcing Viriathus's origin. Beginning in 1920, Spanish historian, M. Peris came to the forefront with four research papers in 1926, stating that Viriathus was from the region of Valencia, but this theory as well as other Spanish and Portuguese regional theories that continued throughout the 20th century were not taken serious for they mostly dealt with local lore and myth rather than scientific evidence. On the Portuguese side, Teófilo Braga in 1904 wrote, '*Viriatho*', this historical novel described in vivid and colorful details the war years until his death. At the same time, though fictionalized, Braga made strong suggestions throughout the book that Viriathus was a Lusitanian.

Surprisingly, the person that contributed to the appropriation of Viriathus into Portuguese history and psyche and the rest of the western world during the early part of the 20th century was German historian and Iberian archeologist Adolf Schulten with his work entitled, *'Viriato'* (1917), translated into Spanish in 1920 and Portuguese in 1927. His work on Viriathus and his three-volume masterpiece on pre-Roman Hispania made a large impact on Iberian Peninsula's anthropological, archaeological and historical community.

Schulten's work on ancient Hispania to this day has had a profound effect on all those who came after him. In his work, he wrote that the Lusitanians were of Celtic origin, but though they were Celts they had their own identity and culture unlike the Celtiberians. But opposite of Schulten's Celtic hypothesis, some Iberian scholars, historians, archaeologists and researchers argued that the Lusitanians were of a native Iberian origin, not Celtic. Even though they may have been Iberian in origin, they were influenced by the Celtic immigration into the Iberian Peninsula from Central Europe. From these two theories, the question of origin still remains open to this day. As for Schulten, his work still remains the basis for historical research on the subject and is the most cited work on the history of pre-Roman Hispania.

The rise of Fascism on the Iberian Peninsula had a major influence on the dictators of Portugal and Spain in their "struggle for the independence of their people, threatened by foreign domination." This influence is evident during the Spanish Civil War when a unit of 10,000 Portuguese volunteers chose the name of Viriathus (*Os Viriatos*) to fight on the nationalist side during the Spanish Civil War in the 1930s as well as in World War Two when Spain and Portugal sent an army division known as the "Blue Division" against Communist Russia.

The exaltation of Viriathus as a 'Portuguese hero and leader' and commemorations of the foundation of the new Portuguese Republic in

1932 gave a new impulse to the profile of its charismatic leader of the State New, Antonio de Oliveira Salazar. It is in this sense that one should understand the work of A. Athayde, translator of the Schulten's work, *'Viriathus'*, who defends the Portuguese origin of the hero. Meanwhile, J. Lopes Dias, in the speech that announced the inauguration of Viriathus's statue at Viseu by sculptor Mariano Benlliure, he exalted Viriathus as Portugal's first national hero, which related with the coming of the New State, while proclaiming that the region of Beira Alta was Viriathus's homeland; also Victor de Tusculano, further instilled into the Portuguese psyche the hero as the precursor to Portuguese history.[1319] Though all of these individuals follow A. Schulten work as historical proof, their theories are more based on nationalistic or regionalistic ideology rather than historical rigidity. But in 1943, Damião Peres published a book titled "*Como Nasceu Portugal*" (How Portugal was Born), which caused some turmoil with the newly established fascist scholarly regime. His work devastated the theory of the umbilical connection between the Portuguese with Lusitanians and that the idea of the formation of Portugal did not start with Viriathus, but with the political will of Portugal's first king, D. Afonso Henrique. Peres statement angered Portugal's top scholar Antonio Augusto Mendes Correia and the fascist regime, of which they had revised Portugal history by contesting A. Herculano work and reclaiming that the Portuguese were the true descendants of the Lusitanians and that the Portuguese nation began with Viriathus.

As for the fascist regime, known as the *Estado Novo* (the New State) (1932-1976) besides taking control of the country's military, administration, press, religion, and the people's will, it also attempted to revise the country's entire history. Ignoring past theories on the Celtic origin of the Lusitanians, the Fascist revision of the country's history began with the Lusitanians belonging to an early race of hominids different from the other known races such as the Neanderthal. This theory was based on a 'newly discovered' race of men, as claimed by the fascist government

[1319] Muñoz, Mauricio Pastor, op. cit., p. 213-214; Athayde, A., "Viriato na Realidade Histórica e na Ficção Literária", Prisma, Porto, 1937; Tusculano, Victor de, A Lusitânia de há Dois Mil Anos. Epopeia Militar de Viriato, Caxias, 1950

called '*homo taganus'* who had lived on the banks of Riberia de Muge, a tributary of the Tagus River in the district of Santarém.[1320]

During the regime of António de Oliveira Salazar's *Estado Novo,* the government made the question of race a fundamental idea of national pride within its colonial empire and for that it was important to maintain and propagandized the most possible idea of the umbilical relationship with the Lusitanians. Therefore, history was taught in primary schools and high schools transmitted the idea that the purity of the Portuguese bloodline began with the *homo taganus* and that the formation of the Portuguese homeland started with Viriathus's Lusitania, exalting Lusitanian bravery and Viriathus's dedication to his homeland, which all Portuguese citizen should mimic.

The Portuguese State had, and still does, claim the honor of being the homeland of Viriathus. Though most Portuguese believe that he was from the region of Beira Alta, where the Serra de Estrela is situated,

1320 The existence of a Neolithic/Mesolithic people in the lower valley of the Tagus River was first discovered in 1863 by Carlos Ribeiro. Under the auspices of the Geological Survey in Lisbon research and occasional excavations of these people continued on until 1954. During the fascist regime, Antonio Augusto Mendes Correia, the promoter of the Portuguese/Lusitanian ancestry believed that this African prehistoric race had migrated from North Africa onto the Iberian Peninsula. But there was some disagreement between want the government wanted to promote and his idea of what the Portuguese family tree was. While the government quickly promoted the people from the Muge, Mendes Correia believed that these people contributed little to the ethnogenesis of the Portuguese nation whose roots should have been sought in the dolmen builder of the later Neolithic period. Inês Vaz, J.L., Lusitanos no Tempo de Viriato, Esquilo Ltd., Lisboa, 2009, p. 200; Correia, Antonio Augusto Mendes Correia, 'Origiins of the Portuguese', American Jounral of Physical Anthropology 2, #2, 1919, p. 117-145; Ferembach, Denise, 'Le gisement mésolithique de Miota do Sebastião, Muge, Portugal II', Anthropologie, Direcção-Geral dos Assuntos Culturais, Lisbon, 1974; Roche, Jean, 'Le gisement mésolithique de Miota do Sebastião, Muge, Portugal, Instituto para a Alta Cultura, Lisbon, 1960 and L'industrie préhistorique de Cabeço da Amoreira (Muge), Instituto para a Alta Cultura, Porto, 1951; Zilhão, João, 'Muge Shell Middens' P. Bogucki and P.J. Crabtree (eds.), Ancient Europe 8,000 BC – AD 1000, Encyclopedia of the Barbarian World, vol. 1, New York, 2004, pp. 164-166

other towns within Portugal debate this belief and cited that they own the right to claim their town as his birthplace such as, Póvoa Velha, Seia, Gouveia, Loriga, Folgosinho Valenzim, Videmonte, Sena Covilhã Termo de Lumiar and even Viseu, a city that has been made famous for its ancient military encampment dubbed Cava de Viriato, which according to local tradition is where Viriathus supposedly took refuge during his later campaign against the Romans.[1321]

Though Viriathus has been seen as a Portuguese hero, there were some historians and scholars that refused to follow these nationalistic theories and instead studied the Lusitanian realm by its historical content. On one side, Portugal is integral part of the occidental civilization, heirs of the Roman legacy and of Romanization; on the other hand, Viriathus represented the opposition to Rome, the resistance to Romanization. With this in mind the question arose on how can we possibly reconcile both elements into Portuguese history? The solution came by placing Viriathus and Romanization in two different chapters. At the beginning of the 20th century, the story of Viriathus and of his resistance to the Roman conquest was only taught in the Portuguese school system. It was not until the end of the fascist regime in 1975 that Romanization and its effect on the country began to be taught, instilling on the population not only the Viriathus story, but the formation of a Roman colony that would later become Portugal.

Near the end of the Portuguese dictatorship of Salazar's regime, the nationalistic theories of the aforementioned authors became so contradictory it was difficult to understand or make sense of their theories. When the Portuguese became involved in their African colonial wars of the 1960s and 1970s, they faced African rebels who through Portuguese indoctrination had come to identify themselves with Viriathus, thus making Viriathus not just a Portuguese hero but also an African one causing many Portuguese to think about how unjust

---

[1321] From archaeological excavations conducted in the mid-20th century shows that this site was more of a Roman military base founded by Decius Brutus in his campaign against the Lusitanians and Galaicians in 138 BC rather than a Lusitanian encampment.

the colonies were. Little by little, patriotic exaltation about Viriathus began to dissipate, that it almost disappeared from being taught in school by 1968.[1322]

With the end of the dictatorship in 1976 did a revision about the Viriathus legend emerged with a new generation of historians such as J. Alarcão, Rui Centeno, M. Cardoza, H.G. Gundel and J.L. Inês Vaz, who used historical and factual aspects and research about the subject for scholarly purposes, instead of a means of propaganda or using myth and legend as factual data.

It is not until the beginning of the 20th century that the exaltation of the Viriathus legend acquired a new meaning and would be used in the defense of nationalism and regionalism within Spain. A. Arenas Lopez is the first to state and defend the theory that Viriathus was not Portuguese or Spanish but Celtiberian.[1323] J. Costa, is of the same opinion that Viriathus was of Celtiberian origin rather than a Lusitanian and that these 'facts', he insisted, are based on the ideas already expressed in the works from J. de Mariana and A. Schulten, although Costa's work was more based on social and economic aspects of Hispania, which were later further developed by J. Caro Baroja and A. Garcia y Bellido in the 1980s.[1324] A. Gonzalez del Campo and Vitor Chamorro considered Viriathus a Lusitanian from the Spanish province of Estremadura and like these two men, many poets and writers from this area proclaimed him to be of this region.[1325]

[1322] Muñoz, Mauricio Pastor, op. cit., p. 218

[1323] Arenas López, A., Reivindicaciones Históricas, Viriato no Fue Portugués, Sino Celtíbero, Guadalajara, 1900

[1324] Costa, J., "Viriato y la Cuestión Social en España en el Siglo II Antes de Jesucristo", Tutela de Pueblos en la Historia, Madrid, 1879; Caro Baroja, J., Regímenes Sociales y Económicos de la España Preromana", Revista Internacional de Sociología #1, 1943, pp. 149-152; Garcia Bellido, A., Conflictos y Estructuras Sociales en la Hispania Antigua, Madrid, 1977.

[1325] Muñoz, Mauricio Pastor, op. cit., p. 218

Though these historians believed that Viriathus was from Central Spain, M. Peris turned Viriathus into an Iberian from the region of Valencia.[1326] Like the Portuguese, Spanish revisionist historians began to theorize that perhaps Viriathus was not from Lusitania, but from other regions within Spain. According to J. Osório de Castro, there are more than seventy towns across Spain that claims that they are Viriathus's birthplace or place of death.[1327]

These nationalist and regionalist ideas concerning the Viriathus legend was also used by painters and authors that were inspired by this historical time period that they contributed to the spread of idolizing Viriathus. The same nationalist ideas about this Lusitanian leader were, as in Portugal, placed in Spanish school books in the 1930s, so that the young generation could learn how Viriathus the poor shepherd became a great commander and fought against Rome for ten years. As with the Portuguese, the revision of the Viriathus story in Franco's Spain was also made to instill patriotism and confidence within a generation that had been treated badly for so many years by its former government and to show that any man could rise above his status.

The nationalistic Spanish version of Viriathus appears as the precursor as the precursor of Francico Franco during post-war 1945 in which A. Garcia y Bellido published "*Bandos y Guerrilhas en las Luchas con Roma*", showing Viriathus as a warrior who fought for the independence of his people; but the main subject of the work was that guerrilla warfare was something genuinely Hispanic, which has been followed by other cultures throughout the centuries.[1328]

School text of that time transmitted the image of Viriathus, by referring him as hero of a war for the independence of his 'Spanish Homeland', pointing out that even the Romans ended up recognizing Viriathus as

---

[1326] Peris, M., "La Lusitania Primitiva", Boletín de la Sociedad Castellonense de Cultura, 1920; Campaña Lusitania y Viriatense, 1926; Fin de Viriato y la Patria de Viriato, 1926

[1327] Muñoz, Mauricio Pastor, op. cit., p. 218

[1328] Garcia y Bellido, A., "Bandos y Guerrilhas en las Luchas con Roma", Hispania vol. V, no. 21, 1945

the leader of the Lusitanian resistance and that only by betrayal would the Romans succeed in putting down this 'rebellion'. Thus, the theme of Viriathus and Franco's dictatorship during the mid-20th century of Spanish history, compare both men as being builders of the Spanish nation. In the eyes of these Portuguese and Spanish fascist governments, they had the trust of their people and to assure their fidelity, these governments transformed the myth of Viriathus into a nationalistic hero. Since the end of Franco's regime, this ideological propaganda has disappeared. From that point on, the myth of Viriathus in Spain, just as it happened in Portugal, faded away.

But this nationalistic interpretation should be not relate with historical works in which Portuguese and Spanish scholars attempted to develop their theories based on fact, which were seen as anti-Salazar and anti-Franco at the end of the Second World War. It was these educated scholarly men that began to downplay the mythical status of Viriathus and place him as a historical personage of him as a bandit, warrior, general, and ruler of the Lusitanians and not of the Spanish or Portuguese.

With Franco's death and the end of his fascist regime, new and revised literature about Viriathus began to reappear in the late 1970s that by the mid-1980s all nationalistic and regionalistic propaganda literature had disappeared. The myth of Viriathus which began with the classical authors of ancient Rome, and that continued throughout the ages, is of a man from an ancient society, whose values, they differentiate substantially from the Romans, had fought until the end against the inevitable submission to the might of a much more powerful enemy. Though the Portuguese and Spanish dictatorships ended in the mid-1970s, one can still point out the capacity by which the fascist interpretation of history had their influence over the Iberian population that for the last 34 years both countries still see Viriathus as a national hero.

It was not until 2000 that the first true biography about Viriathus was published in Spain by professor and Spanish historian Maurício Pastor Muñoz. His work published in Portuguese and Spanish was the culmination of other studies done by past Iberian historians on more specific aspects about the life and times of Viriathus and the Lusitanians.

As for the overall analysis, the literary works on Viriathus and the Lusitanians can be distinguished in three clear phases. From the classical authors to the onset of the Renaissance, Viriathus was represented as the ideal Iberian hero who seemed to have believed in no borders. But that soon changed when Portugal and Spain began to compete against one other over land and sea power that Viriathus was portrayed as a national or regional hero who fought an unjust enemy. The idea of him being a national hero lasted until the demise of the fascist governments of both countries at the end of 20th century. The nationalistic ideal has begun to fade away as a new archeology evidence countered nationalistic tradition, ushering in a clearer picture of Viriathus as a product of an ancient people from the Iberian Peninsula; the Lusitanians.

Not only was Viriathus part of the world of history and literature, but also of art. In paintings, sculpture and music, artists were sensitive to Lusitanian culture, but the one problem they did face in the myth of Viriathus was his physiognomy: how to create an image of a character that is only known through literary texts, where no references to his physical appearance are made. Still artists came up with their own rendition of what he may have looked like and what the Lusitanians wore, of which there several varied representations of Viriathus from shepherd to warrior.

The oldest artistic representation of Viriathus can be seen in an edition of Brás Garcia de Mascarenhas. In de Mascarenhas' book illustration, Viriathus has his left hand raised, as in taking an oath of revenge, for he is surrounded by the bodies of his compatriots who had just been slaughtered by Galba. Viewing this representation, the Lusitanians' and Viriathus's dress is out of place for they are in Roman clothing and not in traditional Lusitanian grab. Perhaps the reason the Lusitanians were drawn wearing Roman clothing and not presented as barbarian and savage people as the classical texts claim was because Renaissance Iberian painters and scholars may have refused to dress them in barbarian clothing for, they may have not wanted to give a bad image of their ancestors.

As time passed it became disgraceful that this Lusitanian hero was portrayed wearing Roman attire even after the way he was is treated by the Romans for being their enemy. In later subsequent drawings the correct clothing type, of more primitive style, corresponded to the people of Lusitania instead of Hellenic apparel, was portrayed. From this historical accuracy the first of this type of primitive dress figuration is shown by the Portuguese painter Augusto Roquemont's "*Juramento dos Lusitanos*" displayed at the National Museum of Soares of the Reis in Oporto, where Viriathus is portrayed in a tunic, a leather belt, beard and long hair, barefoot, and armed with a lance, giving him a character composition of a warrior.

Though over a dozen paintings of Viriathus were created by the end of the 18th century, a sculpture of him was not made until 1884 by Spanish sculptor Eduardo Barrón. Viriathus is represented in a form of a Greco-Roman athlete who stands bare-chested with his right arm extended as if he was promising an oath, while holding in his left hand a king's scepter and his tunic, suspended over his forearm. The statue is raised on a granite unfinished jagged pedestal which is said to represents the hills where Viriathus walked and at his feet is the symbol of the beginnings of his life, a sheep. At the base of the statue the inscription reads: *Terror Romanorum*. Of the statues that were made since 1884, this is the only one in which Viriathus holds a scepter identifying him as a king. This statue according to Professor Muñoz became an important work for other sculptors to follow, for the sculpture possesses very concrete iconographic elements that truly characterize the hero – our protagonist. [1329]

Another well-known statue of Viriathus stands in Viseu near the famous *Cava de Viriato*, where the vestige of a former Roman army camp still stands. Sponsored and funded by Ourivesaria Artisticas Aliança in Oporto, it commissioned the Spanish sculptor Mariano Benliure to

[1329] Muñoz, Mauricio Pastor, op. cit., p. 268

create a beautiful piece of work to commemorate 300th anniversary of Portuguese independence from Spain. The dioramic statue is set around a large piece of granite along with small boulders surrounding it, emphasizing that the Portuguese nation is strong and immortal; the high rock also stands for the Serra da Estrela, where he had situated his army against countless Roman legions. As for the statue, a breaded and long-haired Viriathus stands at the top of the rock's ledge in the middle of the 'wild mountains' in an attack position dressed in a tunic and a fur cloak with his shield and *falcata* at the ready, signifying his invincibility; a man who would have obtained complete victory over Hispania had he not been treacherously assassinated. On the side of the rocky crag that serves as a pedestal, some companions waiting for his signal to attack, while next to the warriors, a wolf has a threatening snarl before the approaching enemy. At the base of the pedestal there is an inscription and a dedication to the *Mocidade Portuguesa* (The Portuguese Youth Movement).[1330] This entire beautifully crafted work of art shows how nature, man and animal, have the burning of a warrior's passion to sacrifices themselves for the defense of their sacred native land, bring into the Portuguese psyche courage, energy, and the untamable feeling of independence.

Of these two statues, the statue at Zamora, Spain presents Viriathus as a king and in the artistic classical stance of a warrior.[1331] In Viseu. Portugal, the statue appears as an austere representation of the barbaric

---

[1330] The Mocidade Portuguesa (Portuguese Youth) was a Portuguese youth organization under the right-wing regime of the Estado Novo. Membership was compulsory between the ages of 7 and 14 and voluntary until the age of 25. Founded in 1936, it was originally inspired upon the model of the Italian Fascist Opera Nazionale Balilla and the Nazi Hitler Youth. However, in 1940 the Germanophile National Secretary Francisco Nobre Guedes was replaced by the Anglophile Marcelo Caetano, who gave the organization a different orientation, withdrawing from the Hitler Youth and abandoning its paramilitary feature, and approached it via the Catholic Church and other youth organizations as the Boy Scout Movement. It was dissolved in 1974, after the fall of the dictatorship in a democratic military coup called the Carnation Revolution, for it was considered as a Fascist organization.

[1331] Vaz, J.L., Lusitanos no Tempo de Viriato, p. 208; For information on the Classic Stance see http://www.ludus.org.uk/r/essayclassicstance.html

highlander in contact with nature, with a face well roasted by the times and of bad weather.[1332] According to Carlos Fabião and Amílcar Guerra, "It is the most interesting for it corresponds well to the stoic archetype that is found in the Hellenistic historiography."[1333] Comparing the two statues, both do not stop being interesting for the one in Zamora is of a perfectly nude classic and in Viseu is of a stoic nature.

Since 1940 several other statues have been sculpted, the last being in 1998, erected in town of Cabanas de Viriato, Portugal. In Spain, in 2005 the post office commissioned a .20 cent euro stamp with the illustration of Viriathus that shows its continuous remembrance of their hero. Since the publishing of Mauricio Pastor's book in 2004 and a 2nd edition in 2006, there has been a popular resurgence in the story of Viriathus that several other books about Viriathus and the Lusitanian culture have been published. In 2009 a documentary (the first of its kind) was made followed a television docudrama series in 2010 on Spanish television Channel, Antenna3, which can today be watched online at http://www.antena3.com/videos/hispania/temporada-2/capitulo-1.html. In 2016, the History Channel featured a documentary titled 'Barbarians Rising", which the first episode was about Viriathus.

In short, all of these representations show the permanence of Viriathus attributed values throughout the last few centuries. Historical recognition of Viriathus placed him among similar heroes from Antiquity with Romanized sceneries and Greco-Roman decorations and the allusion that he was a 'good savage'. The nationalistic conceptions of the 19th century united the vitalization of a Lusitanian man who by the time of his death had acquired an iconography exclusively from the literary knowledge that made artists capable of painting and sculpting him.

1332 Vaz, J.L., op. cit., p. 208

1333 Carlos Fabião and Amílcar Guerra, 'Viriato: em torno da iconografia de um mito', Actas dos IV Cursos Internacionais de Verão de Cascais (7 – 12 July 1997), Cascais, 1998, vol. 3, p. 33 – 79 and Viriato: Genealogia de um Mito, Penélope, Fazer e Desfazer a Historia, 8, 1992, p. 9-23.

Overall, thanks to Roman historians and writers, who honored Viriathus's memory in their writings, they enhanced his fame by eulogizing his strategy and military tactics, while at the same time supplying this historical figure with personality and morals. The fame of Viriathus is not lost to us. The Romans recognized his greatness and from their experience in dealing with a man such as him, they improved their military effectiveness as well as their foreign policies when they would later deal with other tribes throughout their growing empire.

According to J. Alvar, it does not seem logical to think that the classical authors transmitted the acquired information on their heroic enemies without subjective interpretations.[1334] Instead he finds it necessary to discover the motives that led to the creation, adaptation, assimilation, usurpation or rejection of the alienated hero with Roman historiography. After his death, he was then transformed into *exemplum* (moral) to be written down by ancient or modern historian as an example of what a warrior should be. The simple reading of the texts demonstrates that the creation of a historiography of this type was aesthetic. On the other hand, it would be unthinkable to write so much historical information without producing in the narration the facts. But this also creates a large problem of profiling for it causes many writers in the past a degree of literary manipulation of the historical facts.

In the history of military warfare, Viriathus occupies a place of honor on the subject of guerrilla warfare. He was a master of guerrilla tactics and he can be considered as a man who knew how to choose and plan this type of war and fought it with amazing aptitude and a dedicated force of warriors that impeded the Roman army's effectiveness. The spirit of freedom of the Lusitanians and Iberians in general can be seen in all their success during those difficult centuries.

The final analysis about Viriathus, is that though he was either Portuguese nor Spanish but Lusitanian, he was, is, and will always be known as the 'Iberian' who fought Rome for the independence of not only the Lusitanians, but for all the tribes that inhabited the entire Iberian Peninsula.

[1334] Alvar, J., Heróis e Anti-heróis na Antiguidade Clássica, Madrid, 1997, pp. 137-153

ABOUT THE AUTHOR

Luis Silva was born in Portugal. Emigrated to New Jersey with his family after the fall of the Salazar regime. After high school he joined the US Army and became a paratrooper in the famed 82d Airborne and went on to serve in Operation Just Cause and Desert Shield/Storm. After five years of service, he decided to get out and travel, before settling down in Portugal. But on his arrival to Portugal, he was told that he had to complete his compulsory military service in the Portuguese Army, which he did. He subsequently joined the French Foreign Legion before eventually returning to the USA with a wife and rejoined the US Army, after some struggling in trying to adapt to civilian life. Amidst all this soldiering he found the time to gain a degree in History and Political Science. After having served 29 years in the military, today he works in real estate and lives and works between New Jersey, Virginia, Portugal and France.